*A March of Liberty*

# A March of Liberty

## A CONSTITUTIONAL HISTORY
## OF THE UNITED STATES

VOLUME I: FROM THE FOUNDING TO 1890

*Second Edition*

### MELVIN I. UROFSKY
*Virginia Commonwealth University*

### PAUL FINKELMAN
*University of Tulsa College of Law*

New York   Oxford
OXFORD UNIVERSITY PRESS
2002

Oxford University Press

Oxford   New York
Athens   Auckland   Bangkok   Bogotá   Buenos Aires   Calcutta
Cape Town   Chennai   Dar es Salaam   Delhi   Florence   Hong Kong   Istanbul
Karachi   Kuala Lumpur   Madrid   Melbourne   Mexico City   Mumbai
Nairobi   Paris   São Paulo   Shanghai   Singapore   Taipei   Tokyo   Toronto   Warsaw

and associated companies in
Berlin   Ibadan

Published by Oxford University Press, Inc.
198 Madison Avenue, New York, New York, 10016
http://www.oup-usa.org

Oxford is a registered trademark of Oxford University Press

**Library of Congress Cataloging-in-Publication Data**

Urofsky, Melvin I.
    A march of liberty : a constitutional history of the United States / Melvin I. Urofsky,
Paul Finkelman.—2nd ed.
        p. cm.
    Includes bibliographical references and index.
    Contents: v. 1. From the founding to 1890—v. 2. From 1877 to the present.
    ISBN 0-19-512634-3 (v. 1 : cloth)—ISBN 0-19-512635-1 (v. 1 : pbk.)—ISBN
0-19-512636-X (v. 2 : cloth)—ISBN 0-19-512637-8 (v. 2 : pbk)
    1. Constitutional history—United States.   I. Finkelman, Paul, 1949-II. Title.

KF4541.U76 2002
342.73'029—dc21                                                              2001037041

Printing number: 9 8 7 6 5 4 3 2 1

Printed in the United States of America
on acid-free paper

Let me not to the marriage of true minds
Admit impediments. Love is not love
Which alters when it alteration finds,
Or bends with the remover to remove:
O no! it is an ever-fixed mark,
That looks on tempests and is never shaken;
It is the star to every wandering bark,
Whose worth's unknown, although his height be taken.
Love's not Time's fool, though rosy lips and cheeks
Within his bending sickle's compass come;
Love alters not with his brief hours and weeks,
But bears it out even to the edge of doom.
    If this be error, and upon me prov'd,
    I never writ, nor no man ever lov'd.

SHAKESPEARE, SONNET CXVI

# Contents

## 5.  THE CRISIS OF CONFEDERATION                                    80

## 6.  A MORE PERFECT UNION                                            93

## 7.  LAUNCHING THE GREAT EXPERIMENT                                  120

## 8.  THE SUPREME COURT: THE FIRST DECADE                             147

## 9.  THE CHANGING FACE OF THE LAW                                    165

# CONTENTS

# *Preface*

The transformation of American constitutional and legal history over the past few decades has been remarkable. What was once little more than an examination of the "great cases" has now expanded to include the economic, social, and political as well as the legal circumstances surrounding those controversies. Although great constitutional scholars such as E. S. Corwin and J. Willard Hurst had always understood the interconnection between law and history, in far too many universities a wide and often uncrossed street separated history and government departments from law schools. Today, more and more law schools are offering courses in legal and constitutional history and hiring nonlawyers who can bring the insights of other disciplines to bear on the law. Historians, on the other hand, are demonstrating that they can explicate the legal rulings in a case and place them in a developmental context.

The first edition of *A March of Liberty* attempted to blend the so-called new legal history with the usual emphasis on great cases. Large sections were devoted to topics that did not appear in the traditional constitutional history texts: common law developments, the relationship of commercial growth to legal change, the rise of the legal profession, changes in legal education, and the handling of certain key issues at the state level. These section grew out of a belief that the Supreme Court does not act in a vacuum, and that the great powers of the federal government to regulate interstate commerce, for example, is closely related to commercial law and economic developments in the states. In some instances, the high court reflects trends already apparent at the state level; in other cases, its decisions determine what happens in state law.

The generous reception accorded to that first edition made it clear that many teachers who have been trained in the new legal and constitutional history found its premises welcome, and they reported that their classes found it "student friendly" as well. When it came time to revise the text, the large growth that had taken place in legal and constitutional studies pointed to the clear need of a coauthor. Both of us share the premises that underlay the first edition of *A March of Liberty*, and hope that this edition will carry on that view.

As in the first edition, no claims are made for total inclusion; even a work many times longer than this would be hard-pressed to cover everything. It is, as are all books, reflective of the authors' priorities—namely, what we teach in our own courses. But we have had the good fortune to have consulted with many colleagues who teach constitutional history, and to learn what they consider important; the feedback we have received from the first edition led us to leave certain things alone, revise others in the light of new scholarship, and to add some issues that had not been treated. As with the first edition, we wish to point out to readers that this is a survey of a large and growing field, and the bibliographic notes at the end of each chapter are but a small indication of the wealth of materials awaiting their perusal.

We have also benefited from having the manuscript read by people who are not only our colleagues, but who have a discerning eye. This edition is better for having been read by Richard Polenberg of Cornell University, Judith Schafer of Tulane University, Rebecca Shoemaker of Indiana State University, and William M. Wiecek of Syracuse University Law School. We are grateful to them but, needless to say, any errors or defects in the book remain our responsibility.

We would also like to thank everyone at Oxford University Press who worked on this project: Peter Coveney, Linda Jarkesy, Robert Tempio, Christine D'Antonio, and Natalie Goldstein.

Finally, the book is dedicated to our wives, who when they promised to take us "for better or for worse," were not told that they would also have to take our books and the writing of them as well. To them this edition is but a small token of love and expiation.

Melvin I. Urofsky
Paul Finkelman

*A March of Liberty*

# 1

# *From the Old World to the New*

*Magna Carta and the Rule of Law • The Common Law Enthroned • Organizing for Settlement • The Merchant Colonies: Virginia and Massachusetts • The Compact Colonies • The Proprietary Colonies • Growth of Legislative Dominance • The English Revolutions and the Dominion of New England • For Further Reading*

THE ENGLISH SETTLERS who came to Virginia and Massachusetts early in the seventeenth century—and others who followed to populate the Eastern seaboard of North America—brought with them a rich legal and constitutional heritage. Although conditions in the New World eventually transformed English law into new forms, basic principles remained intact. When the colonists declared their independence from the mother country, in 1776, they claimed to do so as Englishmen, asserting rights that they said belonged to all Englishmen. To understand the bases of the American constitutional and legal system, we must therefore begin with a brief look at the English legal traditions and philosophy on the eve of colonization.

## Magna Carta and the Rule of Law

"The British Constitution," Prime Minister William Gladstone once said, "is the most subtle organism which has proceeded from progressive history." There is, in fact, no British Constitution in the sense of a single document enunciating the fundamental law of the land. Rather, it is a complex tapestry of acts, charters, pronouncements, and judicial decisions. Many people start with Magna Carta (the "Great Charter") that King John I (1199–1216), also known as John Lackland, reluctantly signed at Runnymede on June 15, 1215. Most importantly, Magna Carta embodied the principle that no person, not even the king, is above the law. The Magna Carta, however, only continued promises made in Henry I's Coronation Charter in the twelfth century, in which the king promised not to abuse his powers and assured his barons that their privileges would be safe.

Henry I (1100–1135), as well as his successors, usually made these promises to secure the throne, in a time when the crown often went to whomever could seize and hold it rather than to a hereditary heir. To secure the support of the leading nobles, a would-be king pledged not to misuse the royal prerogatives.

Equally important to the development of English law and eventually American constitutionalism, were the innovations made by King Henry II (1154–1189). In the last decade and half of his reign, Henry II began to replace the trial by ordeal with the precursor of the modern jury trial. He also instituted what became the grand jury, as he sent his judges around the country and established a centralized system of courts and laws. These changes were not made to bring liberty to the average Briton, but rather to regularize the administration of law and justice. Nevertheless, they were the first steps in creating the English and then the American system of law.

Henry II's youngest son became King John I in 1199. John's reign was marked by one failure after another, and he became increasingly tyrannical. Ultimately, his vices exceeded the tolerance of his barons, and they forced him, if he wished to remain on the throne, to make a new set of concessions. Unlike earlier unilateral charters, the Magna Carta viewed the king and nobles as equal partners to a bargain for the good governance of the realm. Its sixty-three chapters resemble a feudal conveyance, setting out the rights and obligations of the king and his tenants-in-chief.

The greatest importance of the Magna Carta is not its detailed list of grievances that the barons had about John's rule, but the broad assertions of immutable principles that later generations have read into them. The Great Charter's deliberate vagueness could be interpreted in the most far-reaching terms, and not surprisingly, ever since it has been printed as the first law in the collected statutes of the realm. Although he probably did not intend to, John bequeathed to his people the root principle of both the English and American constitutional schemes—that a fundamental law exists beyond which no one, not even the king, may trespass.

The *rule of law*, as it came to be known, had to be fleshed out beyond the vague promises of a reluctant king, and in the following centuries several developments marked this maturation. John and his son, Henry III (1216–1272), both viewed the Runnymede document as something to be regretted and, if possible, renounced. Henry's misrule, as well as his need for money to finance irresponsible schemes, led to the next major clash between the king and nobles. In 1258, the Great Council of the Magnates, already being called a "Parliament" (derived from the French word *parler*, meaning "to talk"), forced Henry to accept the Provisions of Oxford, which fundamentally reorganized the machinery of the state. The Provisions established a permanent council of fifteen to sit with the king, advise him on policy, and, if need be, veto his acts. The desperate Henry accepted them but soon reneged.

In 1264, Civil War broke out between Henry and most of the nobles. Led by Simon de Montfort, Earl of Leicester, who was also the king's brother-in-law, the nobles defeated and captured Henry at the Battle of Lewes. With Henry in prison, de Montfort called a Great Council, or Parliament in 1265. Delegates to this Parliament included, in addition to the nobility, representatives from shires, cities, and boroughs; knights and commoners; as well as bishops and barons. De Montfort was killed at the Battle of Evesham later that year, and after the battle Henry III regained the throne.

In 1346 and 1354, Parliament altered the Magna Carta with two significant changes. Originally Magna Carta had said that no "freeman" could be "captured, or imprisoned or disseised or outlawed or exiled or in any way destroyed . . . except by lawful judgment of his peers or by the law of the land." In 1346, Parliament provided that "every Man may be free to sue for and defend his Right in our Courts and elsewhere, according to the Law." This expanded Magna Carta to protect "every Man" in England and no longer limited its provisions to the nobility. In 1354, Parliament confirmed this expansion of the protections of the Magna Carta, and also used, for the first time in England, the phrase "due process of law." The new law declared: "no Man of what Estate or Condition that he be, shall be put out of Land or Tenement, nor taken, nor imprisoned, nor put to Death, without being brought to answer by due Process of Law." This phrase, dating from 1354, would be reiterated in the Fifth and Fourteenth Amendments to the United States Constitution and become a key concept in the expansion of individual liberty and the fair administration of justice in the twenty-first century.

In 1485, Henry Tudor became the last English monarch to gain the crown on the battlefield, when he defeated King Richard III at the Battle of Bosworth Field. Crowned as King Henry VII (1485–1509), the new king faced a whole series of checks upon the royal authority. The two most important checks prevented the king from levying any tax without the assent of Parliament and further provided that no law, either of a general or temporary nature, had any authority unless approved by Parliament as well.

Parliament signified a body assembled to discuss matters. The right to talk freely is the foundation on which the idea of parliamentary government rests. (It is worth noting that the U.S. Constitution explicitly protects that right of members of Congress to speak freely in debate without fear of lawsuit or prosecution for anything they say.) In Parliament, as in Congress, the talk, of course, is about what the government should or should not do, which in the fifteenth century meant what the king could or could not do. Eventually the original gathering split into two chambers, a House of Lords—comprising the hereditary nobility and the princes of the Church—and the House of Commons—representing the gentry and the growing commercial classes. The growth of a deliberative body, without whose assent the king could not act, proved crucial in the development of the rule of law, for it divided the government into different branches, each wary of the other's powers, yet forced to cooperate since neither could act alone. If in former times kings claimed to rule by divine grant of authority, Parliament, especially the Commons, owed its mandate to popular support. Thus a second pillar of constitutional government developed—the right of the people, through their representatives, to participate as equal partners in the government.

A third aspect of the rule of law involved the administration of law and justice. In feudal times, justice in any land had been whatever the king and the nobles had said it was, with either the monarch or specified designees mediating disputes and punishing criminals. (A separate and independent ecclesiastical court system administered canon law, the religious regulations of the church.) During Norman times, the king dispensed justice through the Curia Regis, or king's courts, which served as courts of last resort for appeals from local magistrates, heard complaints from the king's tenants-in-chief, and tried cases in which the Crown had a special interest, primarily enforcement of criminal statutes. The Curia Regis would not be considered independent by today's standards, since they handled legislative, executive, and administrative, as well as judicial matters; reported directly to the king; and served as an agency of the royal government. As the realm grew, however, the work load expanded and additional courts had to be created.

First came the Exchequer, which handled government finances and heard cases relating to the royal revenue. Next came the Court of Common Pleas, which developed in response to complaints about the poor quality of itinerant magistrates, called the Justices in Eyre, whom the king sent around the country to hear local disputes. Created in 1178 by Henry II (1154–1189), Common Pleas dealt with essentially private law cases, disputes between subjects. Originally this court followed the person of the king, who frequently moved from one of his castles or residences to another in order to govern affairs in different parts of the country. From the beginning, however, this proved burdensome to litigants, because Henry II and his immediate successor, Richard I (1189–1199) spent long periods entirely out of the country, thus preventing these courts from meeting at all. By the time of John (1199–1216), the bench had been permanently located in Westminster. Chapter 17 of the Magna Carta confirmed this, as well as the understanding that the king himself would no longer judge private lawsuits elsewhere.

About a century later, the final dissolution of the Curia Regis occurred with the creation of the King's Bench. This court handled criminal cases, in addition to certain civil cases where the Crown had an interest, such as trespass, in which the defendant had been charged with breaking the king's peace. Now only one step remained to create the basic framework of the English court system—the development of the court of Chancery in the fourteenth century. Because the law could often be so rigid as to deny justice in particular cases, appeals would be taken to the chancellor, who in the beginning was also a clergyman. The chancellor was not bound by the technical rules of law, procedure, or even evidence. His role was to provide fairness, or equity. The chancellor was said to function as the king's conscience, which in part explains why the early chancellors were priests, such as Thomas à Becket. In the law courts, like the Court of King's Bench, judgments were always in the form of money, the loser paid the winner; but the Chancery, or Equity Courts as they were also called, could direct persons to do or cease doing certain acts. With these courts in place, the older feudal law of the lord and vassal gave way to an elaborate system of the king's justice.

## The Common Law Enthroned

With the creation of the court system also came the common law, the rules and procedures devised by judges, that was common throughout the land. In contrast to the relatively inflexible Roman codes on the continent, English common law proved a remarkably resilient system, able to adapt basic principles to changing conditions. There have been times when the law and its procedures appeared too rigid, but in the long run one could hardly wish for a better law system to meet new social and economic developments.

Originally, the king's courts depended on a variety of royal writs to effect their goals, and the abuses of the writ-making power led to a clause in the Oxford Provisions that no new forms of writs should be created without the consent of both the king and Parliament. As a result, new causes of action had to fit into existing writs, a job that became the province of specialists, the small cadre of the king's judges and the attorneys who appeared before them. By the end of the thirteenth century, there existed the basic outlines of the legal profession in England, a profession already marked by insularity and inbreeding. The tradition soon rose that judges would only be appointed from the practitioners before the courts, and, by royal order, they also controlled legal education. The Inns of Court, sometimes called the "third university" (Oxford and Cambridge were the other two), became the center of English law. Would-be lawyers came there to read the law, serve a form of apprenticeship, and learn from specialists such as Serjeant of the Law found in Geoffrey Chaucer's *Canterbury Tales* (late fourteenth Century):

> In termes hadde he caas and doomes alle,
> That from the tyme of kyng William were falle . . .
> And every statut could he pleyn by rote.

Henceforth the common lawyers, according to one scholar, "more than any other class, molded and preserved both Parliamentary government and the rule of law as the essential elements of the English Constitution." In the two centuries before American colonization, these two institutions, the Parliament and the common law, developed those principles and traditions to which Thomas Jefferson and others appealed in 1776.

Magna Carta had tentatively set out the principle that the king is not above the law. Parliament validated this notion in 1399, when that body forced the tyrannical King Richard II (1377–1399) to abdicate. No longer would a king, as Richard had been accused, have "the laws in his mouth," that is, the law would no longer be whatever he said it was. The basic charge against Richard, in fact, had been that he had broken the law. To ensure this would not happen again, Parliament slowly strengthened its power over the purse, by requiring its assent to any new levies and through supervision of expended funds. In addition to making audits, the Parliament of 1376 for the first time used the power of impeachment to remove and punish royal ministers who overstepped the bounds of their office or abused their trust.

In his classic study of English law *De Laudibus Legum Anglie,* written in 1469, Sir John Fortescue asserted that "the king makes not the laws, nor imposes subsidies, without the consent of the three estates [the House of Lords, the House of Commons, and the Clergy] of the realm." The strong rule of the Tudors in the sixteenth century often masked the fact that parliamentary power reached new heights under Henry VIII (1509–1547) and Elizabeth I (1558–1603). Although Parliament often did their will, the two monarchs also recognized more and more authority as residing in the legislative rather than in the executive arm of government. The Tudor Parliaments granted so much to their sovereigns because they received so much in return. The unfortunate Stuarts, who succeeded them in the seventeenth century, failed to recognize this and believed they could govern as they wished. To their sorrow, they soon learned that Parliament jealously guarded its prerogatives; moreover, the common law set up additional barriers to autocracy.

Sir Edward Coke (1552–1634), the leading common lawyer of his day, labored throughout his life to maintain the supremacy of law and of the Parliament. To him, the common law represented "the perfection of reason," and in its antiquities he found the great strength England needed. He treasured above all else Henry de Bracton's celebrated aphorism that the king himself was under the law. Coke dramatically asserted this on November 13, 1608, when James I (1603–1625), the first of the Stuart kings, told all his judges that since they acted as his surrogates, he could at will remove cases from their jurisdictions and decide them by himself.

Coke replied that cases had to be judged by the law of England. The king replied that since the law rested upon reason, he had as much of that quality as did his judges. Coke responded, respectfully but forcefully, that the law was not simple, and His Majesty not being learned in it, should leave legal matters to his judges and lawyers.

"That means," declared an outraged James, "that I shall be under the law, which it is treason to affirm."

Coke courageously stood his ground and quoted from Bracton, "The king should not be under man, but under God and law," which sent the absolutist Stuart monarch into a fit.

Not only did Coke assert that the law bound the king, but in *Dr. Bonham's Case* (1610), he declared Parliament to be similarly bound. "The common law," he ruled, "will control Acts of Parliament, and sometimes adjudge them to be utterly void; for when an Act of Parliament is against common right and reason or repugnant, or impossible to perform, the common law will control it, and adjudge such act to be void." Some scholars have found in this case the origins of judicial review, the power of courts to invalidate legislation; the argument is there, but it would be more than two centuries before the judiciary actively used such a power.

James I managed to dismiss Coke as Chief Justice of the King's Bench, but the ideas of proper government and the rule of law that Coke espoused could not be put down. He soon emerged as a leader of Parliament, guiding that body in its continuing struggle with the Stuarts and earning a seven-month stay in the Tower for his opposition to royal absolutism. In the twilight of his life, he set down his ideas on the rule of law and government in *The Institutes of the Laws of England*, which became a landmark in English law and cast a powerful influence over America as well. While Parliament fought the Stuarts, other Englishmen crossed the Atlantic, carrying with them the belief in the rule of law.

## Organizing for Settlement

Whether the rights of Englishmen would reach the New World remained far from certain at the beginning of the seventeenth century, since England had made no major claims in the Western hemisphere. The papal bull of 1493 had divided the newly discovered lands across the sea between Spain and Portugal. In 1533, King Henry VIII broke with Rome and established the Anglican Church within his realm. Thereafter, Catholic Europe was determined to prevent heretical England from sharing in the riches of America. But, as a Protestant nation Britain had no reason to heed the Pope or any of Europe's Catholic monarchs.

Britain's claim to land in the New World, based primarily on the superficial explorations of John Cabot at the end of the fifteenth century, could hardly be described as substantial. But when England turned its eyes west at the end of the sixteenth century, these weak claims were strong enough for Queen Elizabeth I. When the Spanish ambassador protested Sir Francis Drake's expedition of 1577 to 1580, the Queen responded that Spain had no claim to the new lands, "except they have established a few settlements and named rivers and capes. . . . Prescription without possession is not valid."

Determined to extend English influence across the ocean, Elizabeth authorized Sir Walter Raleigh in 1584 to seek out American lands "not actually possessed by any Christian Prince, nor inhabited by Christian People." She had earlier issued letters patent to the English navigator Sir Humphrey Gilbert in 1578 much to the same effect, which contained two crucial clauses that appeared in varying form in most future grants. One clause declared that the settlers would retain all privileges enjoyed by persons who were natives of England, "as if they were borne and personally residaunte [in] our saide realme." Here lay the basis for the claim (accepted on both sides of the Atlantic) that the colonists and their children would remain Englishmen and that the rights of Englishmen crossed the seas with them. When a bill later appeared in the House of Lords in 1648 to affirm the settlers' status, the Lords considered it unnecessary to restate the obvious.

The second clause in Gilbert's patent recognized that some laws would be necessary for the governance of Her Majesty's overseas domain, and these should be "as neare as conveniently . . . agreable to the forme of the lawes and pollicies of England." The "lawes and pollicies" of England, however, were far from straightforward. Common law, statutes, ecclesiastical dicta, admiralty, equity, and feudal restraints still jostled together unceremoniously in the legal marketplace. The skeleton of the rule of law may have had some flesh on it, but its growth remained far from complete. What exactly did "convenient" mean? Who would decide if the colonists acted conveniently or inconveniently? What would be agreeable to the Crown?

Elizabeth and her advisers recognized that law, in one form or another, would play an important role in settlement and early colonial life. By the sixteenth century, law had become a central feature of English society and provided an anchor in a world beset by change. The Englishmen of Elizabeth's time cherished order. "Observe degree, priority and place," wrote Shakespeare in *Troilus and Cressida*. "Take but degree away, and hark what discord follows." It is one of the great ironies of history that a people so devoted to order and stability could challenge the unknown frontiers of a new world and sink roots where few of the old principles and rules made any sense. But at least in the beginning, the settlers tried to emulate the familiar system they had left behind. The pattern of settlement encouraged, as much as it could, the transfer of custom and culture from Old England to the New World.

## The Merchant Colonies: Virginia and Massachusetts

The initial impetus for colonization came from companies of merchants and investors, who believed that the riches of America could best be exploited through establishing permanent colonies. These companies had grown out of the medieval guilds, and by Elizabeth's time, various groups of traders had secured royal licenses and monopolies, raising their venture capital by selling shares of stock. The Muscovy Company (1555) opened Russia and central Asia to English trade, as did the Eastland (1579) and the Levant (1592) companies in the Baltic and eastern Mediterranean. The most famous and powerful, the East India Company (1600), became the instrument of English expansion in the Indian subcontinent, wresting control of that rich market from the Dutch, Portuguese, and French.

The charter typically gave the company certain recognized legal rights and specified the terms of organizational governance. Customarily, a council of some six to twenty men, named in the document, held full control of the operations. The charter spelled out the purposes, trade privileges, grants of land, and monopolies, as well as authority to set up the necessary instruments of governance. In 1606, two groups of merchant secured grants from the Crown in a single charter. The Virginia Company of London received the right to establish colonies between the 34th and 41st parallels on the new continent, whereas the Virginia Company of Plymouth secured a similar grant between the 38th and 45th lines of latitude, with competing colonies to be located at least a hundred miles from one another. Separate stock subscriptions would be issued for each new voyage.

The London Company, by its charter, would have a governor and advisory council of thirteen to direct its affairs, and the stockholders were to assemble from time to time in a "general court." One indication of Stuart interest can be gleaned from the unusual step of including in the charter a Royal Council in London to oversee activities that might affect the Crown's interests, such as trade. Under this charter, the London Company established Jamestown in 1607.

For the first ten years of its existence, government in Jamestown fluctuated between anarchy and despotism. Petty wrangling, refusal to work, disease, starvation, trouble with the Indians, incompetent leadership, and a host of other problems repeatedly brought the colony near to extinction. Charter revisions in 1609 and 1612 strengthened the firm's management, turned it into a regular joint stock company with more than seven hundred shareholders, and extended its boundaries to include Bermuda. The company resorted to semi-autocracy in 1610, replacing the local governor and council with a governor and captain general with the power to promulgate laws. However, the settlement still failed to attract new colonists.

To encourage greater immigration, the London Company reorganized the local government. In 1619, it ordered the establishment of a local representative assembly, called the House of Burgesses, which was modeled after the general court or stockholders' meeting in London. The local council, which initially met with the general court, was the counterpart of the company's London council. With this reorganization, the Virginia Company bestowed a colonial government upon its settlement—governor, council, and assembly. The reorganization failed to save the faltering company, however, and in 1624, it lost its charter. James I named a royal governor, and the following year confirmed Virginia as a royal colony. The House of Burgesses, which did not meet from 1623 to 1628, resumed its annual sessions, and in 1639, Charles I recognized its right to a permanent existence. By then Virginia's economic success, based on the profitable cultivation of tobacco, had been assured.

Ultimately the Virginia form of government became the model for all the American colonies, but the early seventeenth century saw other experiments as well. Although few of them succeeded, all in one way or another contributed to the experience upon which the American constitutional and legal system would grow. Each colony had its own imperative, affecting both form and substance.

The other Virginia Company, that of Plymouth, failed in its effort to establish the Sagadahoc colony in Maine, and the next group to seek a charter had somewhat different motives from those that had animated the earlier adventurers. The middle-class Puritans who founded the Massachusetts Bay Company were less concerned with making a profit than their Virginia counterparts. Their main goal was to create a "Zion in the wilderness," a place where coreligionists would be free to worship God in their own manner. In June 1630, aboard the ship *The Arbella* John Winthrop told his fellow settlers in his famous sermon, "A Model of Christian Charity":

> For we must Consider that we shall be as a City upon a Hill, the eyes of all people are upon us; so that if we shall deal falsely with our God in this work we have undertaken and so cause him to withdraw his present help from us, we shall be made a story and a by-word through the world.

When a number of influential members of the company decided to emigrate themselves, they proposed using the charter as the colony's governance document and moving the governing council to Massachusetts. In the Cambridge Agreement of 1629, the stockholders wishing to stay in England consented to the proposal, provided they were given exclusive trading concessions with the colony. Several months later, the government and the charter of the company moved to Massachusetts Bay.

From its first settlement, Massachusetts provided the seed for truly representative government and also linked the original venture colonies to the compact theory developed more thoroughly in the smaller New England settlements. Puritan theology rested on the idea of a covenant, a contract between God and the people, in which the people promised unquestioning faith and obedience in return for divine grace. The covenant spurred the Puritans to build a holy society and also informed the nature of government in the Bay colony. The temporal leaders believed they ruled by God's dispensation, and therefore assumed the people would defer to them in secular affairs with the same diffidence they showed in religious matters.

As a result, Governor John Winthrop and his associates initially tried to run Massachusetts as a Calvinist oligarchy, although it turned out to be an oligarchy that provided a far more popular government than in England. In order to preserve the religious nature of the colony, they limited freeman status only to members of the church, but, at least when the colony began this included virtually all adult males. The freeholders elected the lowest government officials, called magistrates, who in turn chose the governor and deputy governor. The governor and magistrates together passed all laws, levied all taxes, and ran the colony.

By 1634, however, the freeholders had become dissatisfied with this arrangement and demanded to see the charter to determine whether Winthrop had the power he claimed or if the people could assert greater influence in government. Winthrop reluctantly produced the document, and the freeholders quickly ascertained that lawmaking power resided not with the governor or his council, but with the general court. They forced Winthrop to begin calling regular sessions, and from that time on, the supremacy of the general court, which, despite its name, was actually a legislature, could not be denied. Although there would be some structural changes, such as the introduction of a second legislative chamber in 1644, the development of a powerful legislative tradition, akin to that of Parliament, had taken root in the New World.

## The Compact Colonies

Although Virginia and Massachusetts dominated the early colonial scheme, a number of smaller settlements that sprang up in New England introduced another strand into the constitutional tapestry, that of a compact. Emigres from the Bay area settled in Plymouth, Providence Plantation, New Haven, and several of the Connecticut River towns on the basis of an agreement among the people to establish a polity. John Calvin, as well as Richard Hooker, an Anglican theologian and the author of *The Laws of Ecclesiastical Polity*, had both argued that the church came into being by common consent and, by extension, so did society and government. Those who wished to establish a new world based on Scriptures viewed the creation of church, society, and state as one and the same.

The most extreme English Protestants were the Separatists. Theologically, they differed little from the Puritans. But unlike the Puritans who thought they could "purify" the Church of England, the Separatists despaired of ever cleansing the established Anglican Church of what they perceived as a lingering popery, and they wanted to separate themselves from its corruption in order to begin anew. Under James I, their protests soon led to their persecution, and after a brief exile in Holland, they secured permission from the Virginia Company of London to found a settlement in America. In 1620, the first group of Separatists, traveling on *The Mayflower*, landed at Plymouth on Cape Cod Bay. Aware of the troubles that had plagued Jamestown, they recognized the need for a viable and effective government. But since they had sailed without royal charter, and landed far from their authorized destination, they felt free to apply the compact theory of church to the body politic. With Miles Standish and his soldiers looking on to ensure agreement, the adult males signed the Mayflower Compact (1620), declaring that they "solemnly and mutually in the presence of God and one another, covenant and combine ourselves together into a civil body politick." Although the Plymouth colony eventually merged into Massachusetts Bay, the Mayflower Compact worked and provided the only formal governance document of the colony in its seventy-one years of existence. More importantly, it stood as the earliest example of the English in America creating a constitution for their own self-government. It would be a precedent that the Revolutionaries of 1775 and the Founders of 1787 would remember.

The Plymouth settlers also developed a sophisticated set of laws that provided greater liberty in America than England. In 1623, the colony established a jury trial for all crimes. Other laws followed and were compiled in what is known as the Plymouth Code of 1636, which is usually considered the first legal code in the colonies. By adopting written laws on such matters as marriage, inheritance, trials, and land ownership, the code gave settlers a certainty about what the law allowed and did not allow. In some ways the code simply reflected contemporary English practice, but in others, such as creating civil marriage, enhanced protections and economic rights for women in general and widows in particular, and a civil system for recording wills or deeds, the code broke new and important ground that would eventually influence the nation after Independence.

More immediately, the Mayflower Compact and then the Plymouth Code served as models for other small colonies as well. Roger Williams and his followers, after fleeing Massachusetts in l636, founded Providence on the basis of a mutually executed compact.

Three years later the Connecticut River towns of Hartford, Windsor, and Wethersfield joined together to create a government patterned after that of Massachusetts. The Fundamental Orders of Connecticut provided for a governor, deputy governor, and magistrates to meet with a general court; the latter possessed not only all lawmaking authority, but had power over the governor as well. By far the most ambitious of all the compacts, the Fundamental Orders resemble in many ways a modern constitution, setting out a particular scheme of government and defining the powers and authority of its components. Whereas the American Constitution of 1787 is superior to the agencies it establishes and can be amended only by the people, the Connecticut General Court could amend the Fundamental Orders on its own. Not until the eighteenth century would American colonists distinguish between a supreme organic law and legislative enactments.

None of the compact colonies, including New Haven, which drew up an agreement in 1643, had any of the contractual guarantees provided in the royal charters of Virginia and Massachusetts. With the English Civil War and the Cromwell Protectorate, the compact colonies, all Puritan, had little to fear. With the Stuart Restoration in 1660, however, they all hastened to recognize Charles II, seeking in turn royal confirmation of their status. Charles granted charters to all but Plymouth (which continued with only its compact until 1691), and although minor modifications made the charters more like that of Massachusetts, for the most part the compact colonies continued to enjoy virtual autonomy. Although the charters required Connecticut and Rhode Island to send their laws to the Privy Council in London for review, the colonists never did so and, almost alone among the colonies, elected their own governors. The original compacts had now become royal charters, but in thought and practice this made little difference. New England, and later the rest of the country, persisted in viewing government as a compact among the governed and as legitimate only insofar as it enjoyed the support of those under its authority.

## The Proprietary Colonies

The compact colonies, in terms of constitutional theory, certainly essayed the most radical experiments, although the idea of compact had been present in political and religious writings before the seventeenth century. Virginia and Massachusetts represented the use of a relatively new legal instrument, the joint stock company, for an innovative purpose. But under the Stuarts, several colonies began as versions of that ancient feudal device, the conveyance of a fiefdom from a lord to his vassal.

In 1632, Charles I presented George Calvert, Lord Baltimore, with a proprietary grant for Maryland, and the warrant gave Baltimore all the rights, privileges, and immunities enjoyed then or in the past by the Bishop of Durham. In the fourteenth and fifteenth centuries, the Palatinate of Durham had been practically independent, and thus Baltimore would now be virtually an autonomous feudal lord, owing minimal fealty to the Crown. Further provisions endorsed Baltimore's powers. All writs ran in his name; he could but did not have to convene an assembly; he had the power of subinfeudation, and his vassals owed their allegiance to him, not to the king.

A similar charter made thirty years later by Charles II granted Carolina to eight nobles for their loyalty during his exile and their help in the Restoration. Like Baltimore, they too enjoyed the status of Durham, and aside from the standard proviso that local laws conform as much as possible to those of England, they had few limits on their autonomy.

In 1664, Charles granted his brother, the Duke of York (later James II), proprietorship over the Dutch colony of Nieuw Nederlant (New Netherlands), which York immediately annexed. Although this grant included no reference to Durham, the Duke nonetheless enjoyed full sovereignty. He exercised his authority within a few months by ceding a separate proprietary grant over the Jerseys to Carolina proprietors John Berkeley and George Carteret. Even though York's action violated his own patent, no one challenged it, and New Jersey came into being, although from the 1690s until the 1730s the royal governor of New York would also serve as the governor of New Jersey.

By now, however, some English political leaders had begun to question the autonomy granted to the proprietary colonies. Although still a wilderness compared to England, the American colonies showed much promise of wealth, and each year thousands of new settlers left the mother country to seek their fortunes across the Atlantic. Rule of the colonies had to be brought within the purview of the Crown and Parliament, not only to protect the settlers, but also to ensure conformity with England's laws and its developing mercantile system. The 1681 grant to Quaker William Penn, the founder of Pennsylvania, unlike the earlier proprietary grants, had a number of restrictions on his authority. He had to call an assembly, obey the Navigation Acts, submit all laws for approval to the Privy Council, permit appeals from the colony's courts to the Crown, admit the king's customs officers, and recognize the king's right to levy taxes. The last proprietary grant, that of Georgia to General James Oglethorpe in 1732, had similar restrictions and also included a specific understanding that it would expire in twenty years.

## Growth of Legislative Dominance

Despite the autocratic powers granted in these charters, within a few years the proprietors or their surrogates gave up any pretense to feudal rule. Sooner or later, all of them convened popular assemblies and promulgated new rules guaranteeing rights. Like the joint stock ventures, proprietary colonies did not turn profits; almost all who came to live there sought only to build new homes for themselves, not to turn quick profits for speculators or overlords. In these new homes, they demanded, and usually gained, the rights they had enjoyed in the mother country. By the end of the seventeenth century, they not only had transported much of the English legal heritage to the New World, but they had expanded upon it.

The basic framework of local colonial government—governor, council, and assembly—reflected the fight for parliamentary ascendancy, but the colonial legislatures from the start had greater influence on local matters than did Westminster. No House of Lords contended with Commons; the colonial assemblies more nearly reflected the social structure of the settlements and had correspondingly higher support from the people. No matter how strong the governor was, except in Rhode Island and Connecticut, he remained the company's or the king's surrogate, since he owed his office not to God or heredity, but to his employer's pleasure, and through either success or failure, would probably be gone within a few years. Stability and power naturally gravitated to the assemblies, which eventually came to dominate colonial government.

## The English Revolutions and the Dominion of New England

Even the great political disturbances in the mother country did not seriously retard this trend, nor did early efforts to impose some form of imperial organization on the North American colonies. Charles I, who succeeded his father, James I, in 1625, proved even more stubborn about the royal prerogatives. He ruled without Parliament from 1628 to 1640, even levying taxes by royal decree. His Archbishop of Canterbury, William Laud, systematically persecuted the Puritans (thus encouraging greater emigration to New England) but went too far when he tried to impose Anglican worship on Presbyterian Scotland. The Scots rose in revolt in 1638, and two years later Charles, in dire need of money and support, had to summon Parliament into session. This would be called the Long Parliament, because it stayed in session from 1640 to 1653, and it would not be formally dissolved until 1660. Instead of giving the king new revenues, the Long Parliament ultimately impeached Laud, condemned to death the king's chief minister, the Earl of Strafford, and abolished the prerogative courts established by Charles. In 1642, when the king tried to arrest five members of Parliament, civil war broke out. The royal forces collapsed in 1646, and the rebels tried Charles for treason and executed him in 1649. The Puritans eventually installed Oliver Cromwell as Lord Protector in 1653, a post he held until his death five years later. His son proved too weak to continue the Protectorate, of which the people had already grown weary, and in 1660, Charles II accepted the crown in a restoration agreement that provided that the king ruled the country jointly with Parliament.

Because of their distance from the upheaval, the American colonies felt little of the disturbances at home. The Restoration did lead to some charter revisions, but for the most part, the colonies merely continued their steady growth and expansion. Charles II, however, was determined to bring some administrative order out of the chaos of colonial management. He designated the Lords of Trade and Plantations as privy councilors and charged them to force the colonies to abide by the growing number of mercantile regulations designed to bring more profit to England. The councilors soon had the power, through their access to the king, to name governors, send instructions, and handle all correspondence dealing with colonial affairs. Customs inspectors now appeared for the first time in the colonies, and royal officials pressured the settlements to bring their local practices more in line with those of England.

Massachusetts, still a bulwark of Puritanism, refused to do so. It delayed adopting the new oath of allegiance, failed to repeal laws that ran contrary to those of the mother country, insisted on using membership in the Puritan Church instead of property along with membership in the Anglican Church as the basis for voting, and adamantly opposed the adoption of the Anglican Book of Common Prayer. The colony's officials told Edward Randolph, the surveyor-general of customs, "that the legislative power is and abides in them solely to act and make laws" by virtue of their charter. The Lords of Trade then instituted a court suit, and in 1684, they secured the annulment of the Massachusetts charter. When James II succeeded to the throne the following year, he tried to reimpose royal authority not only at home, but over his recalcitrant overseas domains as well. He quickly approved a proposal to create a Dominion of New England, covering all the territory from Maine to New Jersey.

The accession of James turned his proprietorship of New York into a royal colony. James, however, viewed all the English settlements in the New World as existing by royal favor, outside the restraints that Parliament imposed on royal authority in the home islands. He decided to abolish all vestiges of local self-government and to institute a simple, autocratic system in which the settlers worked, obeyed the laws handed down from London, paid their taxes, and caused no trouble by pretensions to self-government. The Dominion of New England would implement this scheme, as well as bolster England's strategic position against both the French and the Indians.

The new governor, Sir Edmund Andros, arrived in Boston in 1686, and within two years had secured royal rule throughout the Dominion. He appointed a new council in Massachusetts loyal to the king and opposed to the Puritan hierarchy, and forced Plymouth, New Hampshire, Rhode Island, Connecticut, and Maine to submit to his rule. In effect, Andros, acting for James II, dismissed the elected legislatures in eight colonies and overthrew nearly a half-century of constitutional development. In Massachusetts, the Puritans detested Andros not only for interfering with their government, but for subverting their religious dominance as well by insisting on religious toleration for some non-Puritans. In these and numerous other ways, such as limiting town meetings to once a year, Andros tried to shift the basis for governmental legitimacy from the consent of the governed to royal sufferance. All of this might well have led to an armed rebellion in the colonies had not James II, by his open avowal of Catholicism and his autocratic rule, triggered the Glorious Revolution at home. This successful revolution sent James into exile and brought to the throne his properly Anglican daughter, Mary, and her Dutch husband, Prince William of Orange.

News of the Glorious Revolution brought joy to the colonies, and mimicking the home country, Boston placed Andros and his advisers under arrest. The new Monarchs, William and Mary, quickly agreed to dismantle the Dominion, and all the colonies reverted to their former status, with the exception of Plymouth, which joined with Massachusetts Bay. The proprietary colonies became royal colonies, although Pennsylvania reverted to proprietary status in 1694, as did Maryland in 1715, when the new Lord Baltimore converted to the Anglican faith.

The Glorious Revolution of 1688 did have significant constitutional effects upon American development through the passage in England of the English Bill of Rights (1689) and the Toleration Act of 1689. Passed to pacify contentious factions in the mother country, it set a tone for the Americans to follow. Moreover, the overthrow of James II set an example to the colonies that they would recall in 1776. Also significant for the later constitutional developments in the United States was the "Act for regulating Tryals in Cases of Treason and Misprison of Treason," passed by Parliament in 1695. This law required, for the first time, that treason be proved by two witnesses, thus preventing treason convictions in secret trials or by allegation and innuendo. This language would be adopted by the Constitutional Convention in 1787, appropriately banning from the United States the type of unfair and outrageous treason trials that had plagued England in the sixteenth and seventeenth centuries.

Perhaps the most significant legacy of the Glorious Revolution was not a particular statute, but rather a philosophical notion that kings should not rule by divine right, and that the people of a nation had natural rights that no government could take from them. The most important articulation of these ideas came in John Locke's *Two Treatises on Government* (1690), published to justify the revolution. In careful and clear prose Locke not only denied the divine authority of kings, but set forth a contract theory of government that bound monarchs as well as subjects. Locke argued that all people enjoyed certain "natural" rights, including life, liberty, and the enjoyment of property. Men came together and contracted the form of government they deemed best able to protect these rights. When kings, as partners to the contract, violated the rights of the people, they in turn could, if necessary, overthrow the king and change the form of government in order to reclaim their liberties.

Whatever historical problems may be found in Locke's theory of the origins of government, it fit in perfectly with the American experience of the seventeenth century. Whether as a company charter, compact, or royal grant, all the colonies had been founded through some form of contractual agreement. Locke's theories imbued these contracts with qualities that had not, with the exception of the compacts, ever been intended. Eventually his views of the contractual nature of government, of reciprocal obligations between sovereign and subject, became accepted even more on this side of the Atlantic than in England, and figured prominently in the development of American ideas on the nature of government.

By the time of the American Revolution many Americans had internalized Locke's notions of a social contract based on natural rights, the rule of law, and government holding power with the consent of the governed. The writings of the English libertarian philosophers, such as are found in *Cato's Letters*, written by John Trenchard and Thomas Gordon, drew on Locke and made his philosophy accessible to general readers. American newspapers, like John Peter Zenger's *New York Weekly Journal*, published and republished *Cato's Letters* throughout the eighteenth century. During the American Revolution the most popular tract, Thomas Paine's *Common Sense* (1776), also reflected Lockean ideas, especially about the dangers and illegitimacy of a hereditary monarchy. Much of the theory of the Declaration of Independence seems to come directly from Locke. Jefferson's famous assertion that people were entitled to "life, liberty, and the pursuit of happiness" seemed to be a paraphrase of Locke's trinity of "life, liberty, and property." Jefferson claimed not to have consulted the philosopher, but rather asserted, with some truth, that Locke was "in the air."

## For Further Reading

The English roots of American constitutionalism can be explored in J. W. Gough, *Fundamental Law in English Constitutional History* (1955), and E. S. Corwin, *The "Higher Law" Background of Constitutional Law* (1955). More popular treatments are A. E. Dick Howard, *The Road from Runnymede: Magna Carta and Constitutionalism in America* (1968), and William F. Swindler, *Magna Carta: Legend and Legacy* (1967). See also R. C. Van Caenegem, *Birth of the English Common Law* (1973). Also useful are Peter Charles Hoffer, *Law and People in Colonial America* (rev. ed., 1999), and Leonard W. Levy, *Origins of the Bill of Rights* (1999).

Wallace Notestein, *The English People on the Eve of Colonization* (1954), remains a valuable portrait of early Stuart England, whereas Bernard Bailyn, *The Peopling of British North*

*America: An Introduction* (1986), is a brilliant discussion of the forces leading to migration. Among the best books on this period is Catherine Drinker Bowen, *The Lion and the Throne: The Life and Times of Sir Edward Coke* (1956). Lawrence Henry Gipson's magisterial *The British Empire Before the American Revolution,* 15 vols. (1936–1970), provides the fullest portrait of the American colonies and their interaction with the mother country; a shorter survey is Clarence L. Ver Steeg, *The Formative Years, 1607–1763* (1964).

A good collection of early statutes and laws is found in W. Keith Kavenagh, *Foundations of Colonial America: A Documentary History*, 7 vols. (reprint, 1983). Also useful is Jacob E. Cooke, ed., *Encyclopedia of the North American Colonies*, 3 vols. (1993).

There are many studies of each of the original thirteen colonies, and nearly all of them devote significant space to governmental structure. In particular, however, see David S. Lovejoy, *The Glorious Revolution in America* (1972), which sees the political and constitutional turmoil as strengthening rather than weakening the bonds of the empire; Mary J. J. Jones, *Congregational Commonwealth: Connecticut, 1636–1662* (1968), a good study of the interlocking nature of church and state in New England; Michael Kammen, *Deputyes and Libertyes: The Origins of Representative Government in Colonial America* (1969), which points up the early acquisition of power by the colonial assemblies; and Richard P. Gildrie, *Salem, Massachusetts, 1626–1683* (1972), an exploration of a covenant community. On Locke and his importance for the development of American thought, see Joyce Appleby, *Capitalism and the New Social Order: The Republican Vision of the 1790s* (1984) and Edward J. Harpham, ed., *John Locke's Two Treatises on Government: New Interpretations* (1992), but for a different view, which rejects the importance of Locke, see J. G. A. Pocock, *The Machiavellian Moment: Florentine Political Thought and the Atlantic Republican Tradition* (1975).

# 2

# Law in Colonial America

*Settler and Indian Views of Land • Simplifying Property Law • Personal Status: Women • Laborers • Slaves • Religion • Criminal Law • Lawyers and Practice • The Privy Council and Imperial Courts • Witchcraft and Press Freedom • For Further Reading*

THE THEME OF American law in the colonial period is change, as the needs of a rapidly growing frontier society adapted the English heritage to meet new conditions. Changes took place in all areas, ranging from property to personal status, reflecting the social, economic, and political transformation of the colonies. By the eve of the American Revolution, the legal systems of the thirteen colonies, although reflecting their common English origin, had evolved along distinctly American lines.

The colonies also laid the groundwork for the creation of constitutional government in the late eighteenth century. Struggles between colonial governors and popularly elected assemblies led to an almost innate sense among Americans of the need for separation of powers. The arbitrary removal of judges by high-handed royal governors helped lay the groundwork for a constitution that made judges immune from political pressures. The excesses of the Salem witch trials in the 1690s were sometimes mentioned in the debates over the Constitution in the late 1780s, when Americans demanded a bill of rights that protected fundamental due process in criminal trials. The Antifederalists who demanded a bill of rights, and the Federalists in Congress like James Madison who wrote the Bill of Rights, drew on many more immediate sources in creating a system of due process. But, at least some of the participants in this debate recalled the witch trials, using them to illustrate an extreme example of the dangers of law and order without due process. Similarly, the attempt of the royal governor of New York to suppress the colonial newspaperman John Peter Zenger was remembered during the Revolution and during the debate over the Constitution, as Americans argued for explicit protections for a free press. The evolution of religious diversity in the colonies, which was deliberate in some places—like Rhode Island, Pennsylvania, and South Carolina—and accidental in others—like New York—set the stage for a constitution that prohibited religious tests for office holding and for a bill of rights that prevented the establishment of a national church, while promising the free exercise of religion for everyone.

More tragically, the colonial period also witnessed the creation of racially based slavery, which would ultimately undermine the Constitution and lead to a civil war. By the end of the seventeenth century, American courts and legislatures had created the basis of an independent American law of slavery that departed sharply from the common law traditions of the English colonists.

## Settler and Indian Views of Land

The early settlers, with a few exceptions, paid little thought to the rights or customs of the natives already in the New World, an attitude that would mark colonial and later national policies toward the Indians. The colonists brought their own notions of property with them, ideas sharply at odds with how Indians viewed land.

Free land had long since disappeared in England; title to nearly every acre was held by designated owners, and English law spelled out who could own, convey, or lease land. Except in unusual situations, land usually passed from a father to the eldest son through a legal rule known as primogeniture; similarly, landowners often placed legal restrictions on land, known as entails, which prevented future owners from dividing or selling it. Thus, in England, land passed from generation to generation, which preserved the large estates of the wealthy. By the time of the settlement of the New World, England had a highly developed law of real property, which was predicated on the private ownership of land and reaffirmed and supported the relationship between land ownership and social status.

In feudal times, most estates had included "common" lands, where tenants could graze their animals apart from the designated plots they farmed. However, changes in land ownership and land use began with the English Reformation under King Henry VIII (1509–1547).

Henry confiscated church-owned manors, and many properties soon passed into the hands of the newly prosperous city merchants. These merchants viewed their new estates as investments to be used to turn a profit as efficaciously as did their commercial properties. If a tenant could not pay his rent, he would have to make way for a new tenant. When land could be more profitably used to raise sheep for the burgeoning woolens industry, farmers would be evicted and the pastures enclosed. Throughout, the sense of property as a personal possession gained footing in English culture and law.

The emerging new sense of property undermined the traditional rights of peasants to live on and farm church and manorial lands. Such notions of property also ran counter to Indian views of land, in which there might be some recognized hunting or farming rights for the tribe, but no sense of personal ownership remotely comparable to that of the English. Indians did not "buy" or "sell" land, because as neither individuals nor tribes did Native Americans view themselves as "owning" the land. If one tribe, for whatever reason, transferred the use of land to another tribe, it did so as a free gift, with nominal presents given in return to complete the ceremony. The idea that an individual exchanged land for an equivalent value, and then took sole possession of it, had no meaning among the Native Americans, and this led to continuous misunder-

standing between them and the settlers. The colonists, with their trinkets and other merchandise, believed they had bought permanent title; the Indians, on the other hand,
viewed these transactions as merely allowing another tribe—the English or the Dutch—
access to the land that belonged in common to all members of their tribe.

Even had the settlers understood this cultural discrepancy, it would have made little difference. From the start, most Europeans saw the Indians as savages and barbar-
ians, whose lands could be taken by conquest in a "just war." The primal right of self-
preservation justified the taking of land; in addition, some colonists invoked religion.
A complacent John Winthrop affirmed if "Our God" chose "to give" the land "to us
. . . who shall control Him or His terms?" If one preferred to be legalistic, the Indians
did not mark or fence off their property as "civilized" men did; as little more than no-
mads, they had no valid claim to any particular property. Thus the land belonged not
to them, but to those who could take it and establish the proper indicia of ownership.

A few settlers did appreciate the Indian view. Roger Williams, the founder of
Rhode Island, recognized that the agricultural basis of tribal economy indicated a real
claim to the land, even if it did not take the more familiar forms of European title. But
Williams remained almost alone in believing that Englishmen had no rights to the land
except those given to them by the Indians. Even William Penn, who tried sincerely and
often successfully to establish good relationships with the Indians, nonetheless relied
on his royal patent. In the end, bloodshed and disease solved the problem, as the Indians succumbed to either the white man's superior arms or more commonly to the fatal viruses imported from the Old World. Weakened by diseases, Indians moved off
the Eastern seaboard. As the settlers displaced the Indians, they attempted to imitate
the familiar land laws they had known in England.

## Simplifying Property Law

Although one talks of owning land, what is really meant is that a person owns the rights
to certain uses of that land. For example, a landlord leases property to tenants; both
have certain rights in the same land. The owner is entitled to the rents and to assurances that at the end of the lease, the property will be returned in substantially the condition in which it was rented. The tenant, during the period of his leasehold, is free to
farm the land or otherwise use it. The state collects taxes and can seize land for non-
payment of taxes, and if the owner has borrowed money, the lender also has a security interest in the property.

In England, all ownership of land theoretically lay with the Crown. Through a
complex system known as subinfeudation, the king assigned rights to his chief vassals,
who in turn could assign smaller portions to their own underlings. The feudal structure had nearly withered away by the time the colonists set out for the New World,
but the legal devices, developed over centuries, to identify and protect rights to usage,
traveled across the ocean and provided a starting point for the colonists in their effort
to tame the frontier. The social and economic basis of English land law, however,
proved inapplicable in America.

By 1600, tenants in England were no longer required to give personal or military
service to lords. In lieu of these and other obligations, tenants paid an annual fee, called

a *quitrent*, to the owner. The colonial charters called for the colonists to pay a similar fee to either the proprietor or the Crown. But whereas the absence of unclaimed land made the quitrent system enforceable in England, the dominating fact of the New World—the seemingly endless supply of free and open land—made collections difficult, especially from small holders. Eviction did not work, since newer settlers usually wanted to stake out their own homesteads, and those evicted could usually find unsettled land elsewhere. The proprietor or Crown tried to collect the fees out of a desire for cash that, unlike land, remained in short supply in the colonies. Attempts to enforce quitrents caused much strife and probably yielded less in revenue than the costs of collection.

In New England, the early settlers tried to manage the land in a common manner, akin to the model of the early feudal manor. Common lands and fields abounded, with families living in towns and farming scattered plots nearby. But assignment of land reflected another English heritage, the relation of property to status. In England, the major property holders had been the great lords, and the rising middle class in Tudor times had attempted to buy land to acquire the status and prestige that accompanied property. A person's station in New England determined his allotment of land, whether large or small, and how desirably it was located. Strangers received no land, and if a man left the town, he forfeited his holding. But this system also made no sense, since it rested on the false assumption of limited land. Dissatisfaction with one's assignment need not be suppressed; relief lay, as it did from quitrents, in picking up and finding new, unclaimed lands.

Throughout the colonies efforts to re-create familiar usages consistently failed. Georgia vainly attempted a system of grants in *tale male,* in which the entire estate had to pass to a male heir; failing sons, a man's property reverted to the proprietor. Feudal manor courts in Maryland also died a quick death. Only in the great holdings along the Hudson River were the Dutch patroons and their English successors able to impose a semifeudal system, one that survived until the New York "rent wars" of the nineteenth century.

Its abundance did not make land any less important in the New World than in the old; ownership still conveyed rights and privileges to freeholders that were denied to others. But whereas land related closely to status in England, in America it eventually attached to contractual relations in an open market. One secured property not so much through inheritance as through settling and purchasing. A number of colonies promised land in order to attract settlers. William Penn offered fifty acres to a master for each servant he brought over, and the servant received a similar grant when his term of indenture ended. Virginia and the Carolinas also gave "head rights" to new settlers as well as to colonists bringing servants and slaves into the colony. After 1705, male indentured servants in Virginia received land when they completed their servitude. This had been the policy in New England since the earliest settlement of that region.

The bountiful supply of land, the thousands of Englishmen eager to become freeholders, and the absence of lawyers skilled in the antique complexities of conveyance, in addition to the rapid turnover of property as families moved from one place to another, necessarily led to a much simplified law. Although the symbolic *livery of seisin*, by which a grantor conveyed land literally through handing over "turf and twig," remained a custom in the Southern colonies, most Americans utilized a modification of the English deed based on "bargain and sale." In many areas, a simple piece of paper or an endorsement on the back of the original patent sufficed. Eventually a system of registration developed, with the recording of the transfer in a public office serving as proof of title. The various complicated actions that tied up ownership and use in England also gave way to simpler forms. By the middle of the eighteenth century, a single action, often called a "plea of land," could be heard in the civil courts to determine contested ownership, reclaim forfeited leases, or eject unlawful users.

English law on succession at death also failed to survive the Atlantic voyage. In England, the common law governed disposition of the deceased's land, whereas church law controlled his personal property. Primogeniture directed that land succeed to the eldest son; originally a device to ensure the continuation of a vassal's military fealty to his overlord, this rule nonetheless survived in many parts of England into the twentieth century. In the Southern colonies, with their larger estates and conservative traditions, primogeniture remained a feature of the law until the Revolution. The other colonies either never adopted or soon abandoned it. Massachusetts did provide for a double portion for the eldest son, but that appears to have been more a reflection of biblical rather than English law. The idea of a partible inheritance, in which land as well as personal property could be apportioned among several heirs, became the rule in New England, and eventually in the rest of the country, too.

The lack of extensive common law courts and the complete absence of church courts also broke down much of the legal distinction between real and personal property. Last wills and testaments, already widely adopted among the English middle class, fit in nicely with colonial needs and greatly simplified the complexities of the English probate process. American wills varied from simple directions—such as "I leave all to my beloved wife Sally"—to detailed inventories with complicated divisions. Colonial courts tended to be equally flexible, applying common sense rather than legalistic formulas to ensure orderly transfer. If "upon just cause alleged" the magistrate found the testator's instructions to be confusing, unwise, or unfair, he could change the terms. Similarly, American courts tried to determine, in the absence of a will, what the deceased would have wanted. This flexibility remained a feature of American law so long as the country consisted of small communities marked by extensive personal ties. Eventually, urban growth and the volume of probated wills led to more formal, and more rigid, rules.

## Personal Status: Women

In Tudor England, women had few legal rights, and married women even fewer. Samuel Richardson's novel *Pamela* (1740) described marriage as "a state of humiliation for women," a fair estimate of their legal condition at the time. Married women had no power to contract or possess property in their own right and were totally excluded from the political process. The common law viewed the husband as the unqualified lord of his household, with full power and control over his wife and children. Even if he beat her, she rarely had recourse in law. Widows and some women who engaged in business did enjoy the status of *feme sole* (a woman alone) for commercial transactions. But despite the accomplishments of "Good Queen Bess," England remained a man's world, with women considered, in fact and in law, as inferiors with few legal rights or protections.

In the colonies, women acquired expanded legal rights as a result of economic, social, and religious forces. The Reformation viewed marriage as a civil contract based on mutual consent, which could, like other contracts, be dissolved. The idea of mutuality provided the theoretical justification for improving women's status, and colonial courts, especially in New England, took several steps to turn this into reality. All the colonies accepted prenuptial contracts, which gave American women an advantage denied to most of their English sisters. Laws required husbands to provide adequate support for their families and protected married women from personal abuse and cruelty.

Many gains, however, appeared more in the abstract than in practice. Only a minority of women signed prenuptial agreements; few families had enough property to settle on a daughter to necessitate protecting it from her husband's control. Wealthy widows seemed to have been the greatest users of the device. Even when the legal rights of women changed, the New World provided little machinery for enforcement. Women could secure divorces in New England, although in practice the courts granted very few petitions, and then more to men than to women. Other colonies provided for divorce through individual legislative acts, but the Privy Council tended to disallow them as "improper and unconstitutional." In unsatisfactory marriages, men could—and did—walk away, disappearing to the West, an avenue unavailable to most colonial women. The deserted wife, although freed from the tyranny of a husband, discovered that the courts or the legislature replaced the husband as the final arbiter of her rights.

Women made greater legal gains in areas outside marriage. Unlike England, the colonies, especially in the seventeenth century, had an acute shortage of women. This scarcity made those who were here more valued and led to their better treatment. The general labor shortage meant that women participated more in the economic life of the colonies, and this added to their stature. Although it did not win them political rights, or make married women capable of acting as independent legal entities, in economic matters women gained significantly.

In 1718, Pennsylvania enacted a *feme sole* trader act to cover the many cases of women taking over businesses upon the death or desertion of their spouses. This law reflected the reality of conditions in the New World and the need for new laws and new legal structures to accommodate these new conditions. Many male merchants returned to England on business. But a trip back to England might take months or even years, and under traditional English law the wife who remained in Pennsylvania would not have had the rights to run the family business or buy and sell property. In the absence of the husband, the local courts could, if necessary, assume control of his property and provide a support allowance for the family. Such static legal rules were counterproductive in the dynamic world of colonial America. Thus, Pennsylvania's *feme sole* trader act enabled women to engage in trade, support themselves, take care of their children, and assume liability for their husband's debts. The law indicates that the legislators saw expanding the rights of women as necessary to economic stability and growth.

Even without such laws, colonial records indicate that women ran commercial establishments, owned and conveyed land, and frequently represented their husbands in legal matters, suing on contract or tort claims and defending against suits. Mistress Margaret Brent of Maryland provides the most celebrated seventeenth-century instance of a woman acting as an attorney. She, two brothers, and a sister brought several servants with them to Maryland and received in turn large tracts of land. She ran her plantation so well that her brothers turned over management of their affairs to her when they were absent. As executrix of Governor Leonard Calvert's estate, she settled his affairs, paid off the militia, and averted a mutiny. But when, as "his Lordship's Attorney," she demanded a vote in the Assembly to look after his interests better, the governor, although acknowledging her talents, firmly denied her request.

## Personal Status: Laborers

Because the colonies suffered chronic labor shortages, laws regulating labor soon departed from the English model. The colonies had to attract new workers while attempting to control labor costs that were pushed up by scarcity. As early as 1633, Governor Winthrop complained that workmen had raised their wages "to an excessive rate, so as a carpenter would have three shillings the day, a laborer two shillings and sixpence." Commodities soon cost double what they did in England, leading the General Court to fix by law maximum prices and wages. Although such laws remained on the books throughout the seventeenth century, they proved largely ineffectual. The more powerful economic laws of supply and demand and the continued shortage of labor frustrated enforcement. Beyond that, if workers found local laws too restrictive, they could always pick up their tools and move to an area with less control and greater opportunity.

In the long run, the solution called for increasing the labor supply. Some skilled labor freely migrated to America, eager to take advantage of economic opportunities that were unavailable in England. Tens of thousands of Englishmen who lacked special skills came to the colonies as indentured servants; some estimates suggest that as many as half of all white settlers either came as "redemptioners" or indentured themselves upon arrival. Quite a few had been tricked or coerced into passage; settlement companies emptied English almshouses and jails in their search for workers. These men, women, and children signed contracts that bound them for a period of two to seven years—or for children until they reached age 21—in return for their passage, room, board, and maintenance. At the end of their service, they received their freedom dues, which variously consisted of food, money, tobacco, clothing, and tools. Sometimes they received a grant of land. Indenture bore much resemblance to apprenticeship, a system to regulate labor and ensure that all persons in society contributed their labor for the commonweal. Indentures also allowed impoverished Europeans to have their passage to America paid by someone else in return for their labor for a set term of years.

Especially in the seventeenth century, and more so in the South than the North, indentured servants were often treated little better than slaves. They could not leave their residence or workplace, or marry, without their master's permission; moreover, their service could, without their consent, be sold to others. Servants who ran away or broke other rules were often severely whipped and then required to serve their masters, or the colony, for additional years. But once their indenture ended, they retained no disabilities and could make their way up the social and economic ladder if they had the necessary talent, energy, and luck. Some, but not all, did quite well. Daniel Dulany, for example, came to Maryland in 1703 as an indentured servant. A lawyer who needed a clerk bought his service, and at the end of his term Dulany himself became a lawyer and then a prosperous landowner. Similarly, Matthew Lyon came to as a redemptioner before the Revolution and went on to serve six terms in Congress. Few ever rose as high as Dulany or Lyon, but a goodly number became members of the "middling" class, solid farmers and tradesmen who constituted the backbone of society.

## Personal Status: Slaves

Africans, America's unwilling immigrants, were less fortunate than the white indentured servants. The first group of "twenty and odd Negars" arrived in Virginia in 1619. Initially, they were treated as indentured servants. At what point the *legal* status of blacks changed is nearly impossible to determine. By mid-seventeenth century, some areas of the Chesapeake saw Africans serving for life and their children similarly condemned; other blacks went free at the end of a fixed term; still others purchased their liberty. The records of the Virginia colony illustrate how slavery developed in that jurisdiction. Where Virginia led, the rest of the colonies followed.

Indicative of the legal evolution of slavery was the case of John Punch. In 1640, Punch and two white men, all characterized as "servants," ran away from their Virginia master. The two whites were whipped and sentenced to serve their master for an extra year, and then to serve the colony for three more years. Of the black servant, the court declared: "the third being a negro named John Punch shall serve his said master or his assigns for the time of his natural Life here or elsewhere." No white ever received such a punishment in Virginia or any of the other colonies. Clearly, the Virginia court felt it was permissible—even proper—to sentence a black to lifetime servitude for running away.

That same year, the court sentenced five white servants to various punishments for running away, but did not add any time to the service of the lone black, which leads to the strong presumption that he was already considered a slave. By this time, white masters were treating their black servants as slaves. In the 1640s and 1650s, we find records of blacks being sold or bequeathed as servants for life, with a similar interest in their children. However, the status of blacks was not yet settled. In 1672 and again in 1673, a Virginia court ruled that black servants imported from Africa were entitled to their freedom once they had served their indentures. However, these may have been among the last Africans to be brought to Virginia and treated as indentured servants.

In 1659, a Virginia law mentioned "negro slaves" brought by Dutch traders. An act of 1661–62 required that white servants who absconded with "negroes who are incapable of making satisfaction of addition of a time" would have to serve the owners of the blacks for any time lost while the runaways were out of the custody of their masters. Clearly, only a slave was "incapable" of having time added to his indenture.

Three acts passed in the 1660s further fastened the chains of slavery on Africans in Virginia. A 1662 law declared that the children of black women would follow the status of their mother rather than their father. This was a complete rejection of English common law, and illustrates how slavery was creating a new "American" law. An act of 1667 declared "that baptisme of slaves doth not exampt them from bondage." This too ran counter to the notion that members of the Church of England were inherently free people. Finally, a 1669 act "about the casuall killing of slaves," modified the common law by exempting masters from any criminal sanctions if they killed their slaves while punishing them or subduing them if they resisted their bondage.

By the early eighteenth century, slave codes governed nearly every aspect of slave life. These codes were, for the most part, designed to prevent slaves from escaping or revolting. Harsh punishments awaited slaves, and sometimes free blacks, who challenged the emerging system of bondage in the American colonies. Virginia's law of 1723, for example, provided the death penalty for slaves conspiring to revolt. The same law also declared that slaves who were "found notoriously guilty of going abroad in the night or running away, and lying out," would be punished "by dismembering, or any other way." Slaves or free blacks who gave false testimony at the trial of another black were to "have an ear nailed to the pillory, and there to stand for the space of one hour, and then the said ear to be cut off; and thereafter, the other ear nailed in like manner, and cut off," and then the guilty party was to receive "thirty-nine lashes, well laid on, on his or her bare back, at the common whipping post."

By 1700, laws prohibited sexual relations between blacks and whites as well as interracial marriage. After 1650, there is no evidence that white men or black women were punished for nonmarital interracial sex. However, anyone involved in an interracial marriage after about 1690 was likely to be punished. As early as 1664, a Maryland statute provided that any white woman marrying a slave or bearing a child by a black man would become a slave herself and continue in that condition so long as her mate lived; their children would be bound for life as well. Other Southern colonies adopted similar laws.

Masters had complete control over their slaves and could act as judge and jury in cases of wrongdoing. Serious crimes committed by slaves—such as murder, battery on a white, rape of a white, and arson—were dealt with by civil courts, in which slaves faced often unfair trials and cruel punishments. Because slaves soon became regarded, in law and fact, as chattels, their punishment for crime normally took the form of whipping or mutilation, since execution deprived the owner of valuable property. When a black murdered a white, however, the death sentence would be imposed, and in some colonies the owner was compensated from the public purse.

Slave codes existed in all the colonies but were most restrictive in the South, which had the bulk of black slaves. All the Northern colonies had some slaves, and slavery was particularly important in New York City and southern New Jersey. Northern whites appeared to fear blacks and slaves almost as much as Southern planters. Boston, for example, passed emergency regulations in 1723, punishing any black caught near a fire, and New York passed stringent limits on how far slaves could travel away from their homes, with death as the penalty for violation. In 1741, the New York Supreme Court ordered the execution of nearly thirty slaves, many of them by burning, as a punishment for a conspiracy to revolt.

Horrible punishments like those inflicted by New York were not uncommon. Harsh punishments served to warn other slaves of the penalty for rebellion. After the Stono Rebellion in 1739, in South Carolina scores of slave rebels were hanged. The officials then placed the heads of the dead slaves on the top of the mileposts along the colony's roads to serve as a gruesome warning of the power of the legal system to punish would-be rebels.

The slave codes degraded all blacks, free Negroes as well as those in bondage. The codes—and the horrific punishments meted out under them—reflected the prejudices and fears of white colonists toward persons who had never desired to settle in the New World and whose future would be marred by centuries of involuntary servitude and persecution.

# Religion

Since ancient times, religion and the state had been closely intertwined. With the rise of the Catholic Church, most people accepted the idea that there could or should be only one religion, just as it made sense to have only one king. Both church and state persecuted dissenters because their beliefs threatened to undermine social stability as well as the common religion. The Reformation in the sixteenth century led to bloody warfare between Catholics and Protestants, tearing apart the religious unity of Europe. In those countries where the dissenters prevailed, they quickly established the new faith and proceeded to persecute Catholics as they themselves had earlier been persecuted. The Jews presented a unique religious problem that most countries solved by isolating them legally, socially, and economically, or, as in the case of England in the thirteenth century and Spain in the fifteenth century, expelling them.

Henry VIII and Parliament, in disestablishing the Catholic Church in England, never intended to raise up religious toleration in its stead. The Church of England, with relatively minor doctrinal and ritual changes but with significant institutional changes, became the official state religion, and dissenters were persecuted as vigorously as before. Mary I (1553–1558) tried to bring back Catholicism and earned her nickname "Bloody Mary" for ordering the execution, usually by burning at the stake, of scores of Protestant leaders. Only her timely death, five years into her reign, prevented religious bloodshed from erupting into civil war.

Probably more than any monarch of her time, Elizabeth I (1558–1603) did not care about the private beliefs of her subjects. She said she did not seek "windows into men's souls" and insisted only on outward conformity to preserve social order and peace. Her successor, James I (1603–1625), was somewhat less tolerant, and his antagonism toward Protestant dissenters would eventually lead to the Pilgrim settlement at Plymouth. Charles I's (1625–1649) equally dim view of religious pluralism led to the persecution of Puritans, which in turn stimulated the massive Puritan migration to Massachusetts in the 1630s and the English Civil War of the 1640s.

The English who came in the first half of the seventeenth century—even those who fled religious persecution—did not carry in their cultural baggage any belief in religious pluralism or toleration. Like their monarchs, they too believed in only one approach to faith. Thus, once here, they set about establishing religion as a bulwark of both state and society. The only important exception to this general observation was Roger Williams, the Puritan minister who established the Rhode Island colony and founded the Baptist Faith.

The laws of every colony implemented the moral and religious precepts of the prevailing church, be it Puritanism in New England or the Anglican faith in the Southern colonies. The first General Assembly of Virginia passed a law in 1619 penalizing those who engaged in "idleness, gaming, drunkenness & excesse in apparel." Massachusetts passed similar laws against "Idle persons." Connecticut fined people for dancing and singing in bars, Plymouth prohibited the use of tobacco, and Massachusetts prohibited the inns and taverns from allowing patrons to play shuffleboard. In general, New England especially tried to legislate morality, and sprinkled its statute books liberally with scriptural citations. Justice in Massachusetts would be dispensed "according to the word of God." The other colonies failed to emulate this neobiblical approach, but they nonetheless agreed that the law should embody prevailing morality and enforce religious conformity. Most of the colonial statute books provided fines for people who failed to attend church regularly, although in many places, especially the South and the West, enforcement was lax.

Such laws succeeded, at least initially, far better in New England than in the South. The abundance of ministers, the close ties between religious and lay leaders, and the organization of society in compact towns allowed religion to permeate all aspects of life. Deviation from the norm led to prosecution and, in a few cases, death. In the 1659, Massachusetts executed four Quakers who persisted in entering the colony, disturbing the peace, and challenging the legal authority of those in power. "Experience will teach Churches and Christians," declared Nathaniel Ward in 1645, "that it is farre better to live in a State united, though somewhat Corrupt, than in a State, whereof some Part is Incorrupt, and all the rest divided." Not for him the "laxe Tolerations" he saw in other colonies. By later standards, this "laxe Toleration" hardly approached religious freedom for either individuals or dissident groups. True, the founders of Pennsylvania, Rhode Island, and to some extent South Carolina favored tolerance, but they were the exceptions. As late as 1742, Connecticut, in the maelstrom of the Great Awakening, passed the so-called Intolerant Acts against Separatists, regulating their preachers and disallowing their marriages and baptisms.

In the South, ties between the Church of England and the state started strongly, but soon broke down. The scarcity of clergymen and the large size of parishes, some fifty miles across, made it impossible to police morality as might be done in small towns. Moreover, local vestrymen, like their Northern neighbors, insisted on local control of churches as against colonial officials. Without bishops to establish the hierarchical ties that bound church and state together in England, Anglican priests in the colonies found themselves at the mercy of local planters who, although not notably tolerant, had no great desire to impose religious rigor on their neighbors. By the time of the Great Awakening in the early eighteenth century, itinerant spokesmen from dissenting sects were preaching openly in Virginia in defiance of regulations, although often they faced fines, jail terms, and sometimes savage treatment.

Because so many dissenters lived in New York, New Jersey, South Carolina, and Maryland, the officially established Anglican church remained weak. Even in New England, the growth of dissenting groups could not be retarded, and the new royal charter in 1691 forced Massachusetts to repeal some of its more intolerant laws. The Salem witchcraft trials of the following year indicated that, although zealots still held to the old ways, the religious uniformity of the early settlers had fractured badly.

More and more arguments were heard calling for religious freedom that only a short time earlier would have been branded as heresy. The Maryland Toleration Act of 1649 granted freedom of worship to "any person whatsoever within this Province professing to believe in Jesus Christ." However, another portion of that act limited this liberty to trinitarians and further provided a death penalty for anyone who should "blaspheme God . . . or shall deny our Saviour Jesus Christ to bee the sonne of God, or shall deny the holy Trinity the father sonne and holy Ghost. . . ." This was clearly a step toward religious liberty, but only a halting one. Jews and nontrinitarian Christians, as well as religious skeptics, could face the death penalty under this law. By the end of the century Rhode Island, Pennsylvania, and South Carolina all offered more substantial religious liberty. New York had no formal religious freedom, but in practice allowed all worshipers.

Despite intolerance, especially in New England, and the establishment of official churches in all colonies, there was more religious diversity, and greater religious toleration, in the American colonies than anywhere else in the Western world, except perhaps Holland. Rhode Island and Pennsylvania explicitly opened their doors to all religious groups in the seventeenth century, while South Carolina's Fundamental Constitution of 1669 declared that "No person whatsoever shall disturb, molest, or persecute another, for his speculative opinions in religion, or his way of worship." In 1654, Jews found refuge in Dutch New Amsterdam, which became New York in 1664. Other Jews settled in Rhode Island, Pennsylvania, South and North Carolina, and Georgia. Twenty years after the British had taken over New York, Governor Thomas Dongan reported: "Here bee not many of the Church of England; [a] few Roman Catholicks; abundance of Quakers preachers men and women especially; Singing Quakers, Ranting Quakers; Sabbatarians; Antisabbatarians; some Anabaptists; some Independents; some Jews; in short of all opinions there are some, and the most part none at all."

In many ways the Dutch model, which New York incorporated, would become the pattern of all America. While the colony was under Dutch control the Governor-General, Peter Stuyvesant, attempted to expel various religious minorities, including Lutherans, Quakers, and Jews. Each time, the leaders of the Dutch West Indies Company, who resided in Holland and had invested in the colony, overruled him. Their point was always the same: the colony's prosperity depended on settlers, and while members of the Dutch Reform Church were most desirable, *any* settler would do. Thus, when Stuyvesant tried to expel a group of Quakers, who were disruptive and antagonistic to his authority, the directors of the Dutch West Indies Company told him: "we doubt very much, whether we can proceed against them rigorously without diminishing the population and stopping immigration, which must be favored at a so tender stage of the country's existence." The Dutch investors in the colony understood that a frontier society in need of labor had little time to devote to enforcing conformity or prying into individual conscience. Most of the other colonies, especially outside New England, soon learned this lesson. Thus, after the early years, no one religious sect, even the established churches, ever enjoyed the monopoly of the faith that was common in Europe, and necessity eventually turned despised tolerance into a virtue. Pluralism soon became not only accepted, but praised.

By the middle of the eighteenth century, even Massachusetts and Connecticut, bastions of religious orthodoxy, were beginning to hear arguments in favor of religious liberty. The "Right of private Judgement and worshipping GOD according to the Conscience," argued Elisha Williams of Connecticut, constituted a "natural and unalienable Right." The social contract theory of English philosopher John Locke, even before the Revolution, came to include freedom of religion. John Cleaveland, a minister in Ipswich, Massachusetts, argued in 1747 that when a church failed to meet the spiritual needs of its members, the covenant by which it had been established could be dissolved, be it for doctrinal reasons or for failure of the clergy. Although established churches in the colonies still drew support from public taxes, by 1776 this too had become an article of grievance among Americans, who disestablished many of the colonial churches during or soon after the Revolution.

## Criminal Law

The fact that many colonists eventually objected to religious conformity did not mean they did not take moral laws seriously. The codes of all the colonies had a strong moral flavor and provided severe punishment for deviant behavior. Although many crimes called for the death penalty, the colonies had far fewer capital offenses on the books than did the mother country. During the seventeenth and eighteenth centuries, the number of capital crimes in England increased from 50 to more than 200. In contrast, the first Pennsylvania criminal code (1676) had only eleven capital crimes, and the other colonies had roughly the same number. Similarly, the Massachusetts Body of Liberties (1641) had twelve capital offenses, eleven of which, including idolatry, blasphemy, bestiality, homosexual acts, and adultery, were based on the Old Testament. Even for those who violated these laws, all but the most heinous offenders escaped execution. The criminal codes of the colonies existed less to protect life and property than to control the social order.

Thus public humiliation constituted an important feature of colonial justice, with public whippings and occasional executions serving as a warning to the populace. In 1639, the Plymouth colony provided that persons living "idly and loosely" be brought before the governor to be punished. For minor offenses, a few hours in the stocks might suffice. In East Jersey, drunkards were to "be put in stocks, until they are sober, or during the pleasure of the officer in chief." Perhaps the most famous example of public humiliation is Nathaniel Hawthorne's fictional account, *The Scarlet Letter* (1850), in which Hester Prynne had to wear the scarlet "A" as a mark of her adultery. Much more than in our era, society intended punishment to identify and shame the offender. The community banished repeat offenders, having judged them, in effect, as unworthy to remain in the society. When the wrongdoing involved property, courts often ordered restitution and could impose fines for nearly all crimes.

Aside from slave codes, nothing so systematic as a "criminal justice system" existed in colonial society. There were neither police nor prisons, just local jails operated by the county courts. Only toward the end of the colonial period did some of the urban areas establish more formal institutions. The county sheriff, in addition to enforcing the law, also carried out many executive functions of local government, such as collecting taxes and supervising elections. As for enforcing the law, the sheriff reacted to complaints lodged by either the local courts or the grand juries; he did not attempt to prevent crime as do modern police officials. And because he was paid according to a system of fees, corruption often marked the office. A similar problem arose with other law enforcement officials. In New York and other colonies, prosecutors were paid for each case they argued. In the early 1720s, the popularly elected New York assembly censured Attorney General Bradley because he was in the habit of filing charges through informations on his own motion, in order "to squeeze money" rather "than from any just cause." Throughout the colonial era, some royal officials as well as the assemblies tried to clean up this system, but others, like Attorney General Bradley, resisted such reforms.

Criminal law not only regulated moral life, but controlled social behavior as well. Servant and slave codes, for example, kept the lower strata of society in line. Refusal of indentured servants to fulfill their contracts or illegitimate pregnancies by servant girls led not to fines (which they had no money to pay) or imprisonment, but to whipping, sometimes branding in the early years, and added years of service. Slaves, like indentured servants lost value if they could not work, so punishment took such forms as whipping, or in cases of rape, castration—painful and degrading punishments to be sure, but ones that did not permanently impair slaves' ability to labor.

Criminal statutes in all the colonies not only punished offenders, but also warned others not to engage in similar behavior. Punishment shamed the wrongdoer and branded him or her, sometimes literally, as a sinner. When necessary, the law could be severe, and executions did take place. The goal of the criminal law, however, seemed directed more toward rehabilitation than toward mere retribution. As American society developed and grew more open and flexible, so too did its criminal law.

## Lawyers and Practice

It is not only in retrospect that one can see how English law, based on a certain set of assumptions and facts, did not meet the needs of colonial American society. Eighteenth-century contemporary observers, even as they valued much of their heritage, recognized that conditions on this side of the Atlantic required change.

In 1712, for example, the South Carolina legislature, upon the recommendation of Chief Justice Nicholas Trott, then reenacted 167 specific English statutes and declared the rest "impracticable in this Province." Three years later, North Carolina made a sim-

---

COLONIAL RECOGNITION OF THE INAPPLICABILITY OF ENGLISH LAW TO AMERICAN CIRCUMSTANCES

The preamble to an act by the South Carolina Provincial Assembly in 1712 noted that:

> many of the statute laws of the Kingdom of England or South Britain, by reason of the different ways of agriculture and the differing productions of the earth of this Province from that of England, are altogether useless, and many others (which otherwise are very good) either by reason of their limitation to particular places, or because in themselves they are only executive by such nominal officers as are not in or suitable for the Constitution of this Government, are thereby become impracticable here.

ilar declaration as to which English laws remained operative there. Other colonies, in a less precise manner, also indicated they did not consider large sections of English law applicable to them.

English law, it should be recalled, included numerous branches, such as common and statutory law, equity, and admiralty, with an intricate system of pleadings and writs, which, as Lord Coke had told James I in 1608, only lawyers could understand. But what if there were no lawyers? As a class, lawyers had already bred much mistrust at home.

Many American colonists also mistrusted lawyers. Massachusetts Bay prohibited pleading for hire in 1641, but in 1673 backed away from this position. By 1702, the Massachusetts government not only recognized the reality of lawyers, but passed legislation limiting their fees to no more than twelve shillings in any case. In 1643, Virginia required that all lawyers be licensed and also limited their fees to a maximum of twenty pounds of tobacco for any case. The 1669 Fundamental Constitutions of the Carolinas termed it "a base and vile thing to plead for money or reward." Thomas Morton, who arrived in Plymouth around 1624, may have been the first American lawyer; he soon wound up in jail, and his outrageous behavior (he danced around a Maypole, among other things) led to his expulsion from the colony. The Quakers opposed adversary pleadings in principle, and of Pennsylvania one said: "They have no lawyers. Everyone is to tell his own case, or some friend for him. . . . ' Tis a happy country." Colonial documents are full of denunciations of lawyers as social parasites.

Certainly the informality that marked early American law made it possible for colonial courts in large measure to dispense with attorneys. Judges often helped litigants frame their petitions in the proper form and attempted to keep judicial proceedings as simple as possible. Some colonies, such as Massachusetts, evidently managed to survive quite well throughout much of the seventeenth century without practicing lawyers. Although after 1673, Massachusetts permitted lawyers to accept money, the General Court strictly regulated fees. Men who took up this work could rarely earn a living at it and most practiced law in addition to another calling, such as operating a tavern or farming.

The absence of professionally trained lawyers did not deprive the colonies of legal knowledge. A number of settlers had had some legal training or education in England, and even if they did not practice the profession in the New World, they provided the modicum of expertise that the simple seaboard societies needed. John Winthrop, Thomas Dudley, and the Reverend Nathaniel Ward all brought knowledge of English law with them. Winthrop had studied at the Inns of Court, served as a justice of the peace, and thus presided over all manner of civil and criminal cases. He had also practiced law in London and later as an attorney in His Majesty's Court of Wards and Liveries. Such experiences helped him prepare to govern Massachusetts. Similarly, Nathaniel Ward's legal experience led him to propose a code of laws that found its way into the Massachusetts Bay Colony's Laws and Liberties of 1648.

Despite the desire to keep lawyers out of the colonies, as the society and economy grew so too did the need for men trained in the intricacies of the law. Merchants in litigation, landowners contesting title, faulty conveyances of property, the complexities of inheritance as wealth accumulated, all called for more than a passing acquaintance with the law. As much as the settlers might have preferred simple resolution of disputes, the disputes themselves were often far from simple. Slowly, more and more attorneys, either trained formally at the Inns of Court or less formally as clerks or apprentices, found society requiring their services.

The development of a more extensive court system tied in to the imperial government also required trained lawyers. Early colonial courts, although adhering in general to English practice, resembled the smaller, informal county courts of the mother country rather than the great courts in London. They not only handled civil and criminal cases, but in many areas constituted the legislative and judicial branches of county government as well. People looked forward to the monthly "Court Days" in Virginia, for example, as major events; the citizenry from the surrounding countryside trooped into town to conduct business, talk politics, and socialize. Whatever business one had with the local government—tax assessment, apprenticeship contracts, or litigation—it would all be handled before the same tribunal.

The justice of the peace, an office that had developed far back in English history, provided the base of the judicial system. An individual did not have to be a lawyer, or even have any legal training, to fill this office, and in most places, politics determined who received the commission. Justices of the peace could try even capital crimes involving slaves in some colonies, but in general, they tried only minor cases individually. More serious or complicated matters would be held over to be heard by a panel of several justices. These "session courts" met periodically; in New York, they convened quarterly in the more populated areas and semiannually in the rural regions. In Virginia, by the time of the Revolution, county courts met monthly.

A major departure from English practice soon arose in the trying of criminal cases. In Great Britain, private counsel prosecuted all but the most important cases, and the defendant could do little more than challenge narrow points of law. In the colonies, public prosecutors, known as district or county attorneys, represented the government in all criminal cases. Originally appointed by the governor, in some places the prosecutor became an elected official who carried considerable political influence. Initially few defendants had access to counsel, but as the legal profession grew, persons accused of a crime came to employ counsel if they could afford it. American practice also gave defense attorneys wide latitude in arguing their clients' innocence. Certainly by the time of the Revolution, the notion that a fair trial required counsel for the accused enjoyed wide acceptance.

## The Privy Council and Imperial Courts

County courts remained the heart of the colonial system throughout the seventeenth century, but major changes occurred beginning around the turn of the century. Following the Glorious Revolution, English officials sought to bring the colonies within a tighter imperial control. The Massachusetts charter of 1691, for example, provided for both a right of appeal in cases involving more than £300 and Crown review of colonial legislation. But the Privy Council never developed any systematic controls that might have guided either colonial courts or assemblies. It decided matters on an *ad hoc* basis and issued no written reports. Although a few decisions, such as *Winthrop v. Lechmere* in the 1720s, nullifying Connecticut's intestacy laws, touched upon major issues, the Privy Council and its committees for the most part functioned in an almost haphazard manner, with frequent delays. But because the council recognized that American conditions differed from English ones, it never tried to impose a strict conformity of American law to English law, so that the two deviated more and more as the years passed.

The Crown eventually introduced new courts that had previously not existed in the colonies. Admiralty, for example, had earlier been handled mostly by the royal governors, but by 1763, nine separate vice-admiralty courts had been established. Violation of trade laws, questions of seamen's wages, and all matters dealing with maritime commerce came before these courts, which, following British procedure, tried them without a jury. Because the colonies engaged in extensive ocean commerce, they needed a vice-admiralty system, but because the courts attempted to enforce the unpopular trade and navigation acts, and because they had no juries, the colonists distrusted them. Imperial efforts to strengthen these courts became one of the major grievances leading to the Revolution.

The chancery courts also aroused popular opposition, because these courts, using equity jurisprudence, often sided with elite landowners in disputes with poorer settlers. The Carolinas, Maryland, New York, and New Jersey had separate courts of equity, whereas in other colonies, such as Delaware, the common law courts sat in special sessions as courts of equity. In some colonies, the governor handled the duties of chancellor. Since the courts or chancellors often utilized the system to collect taxes or perform other executive functions, and, like admiralty, tried cases without a jury, they too gave rise to numerous complaints. Although the system had originally begun in England as an effort to correct inequities in the law, it eventually developed its own problems, especially frequent delays that consumed large amounts of money in lawyer and court fees, as well as caused hardship. Yet equity, like admiralty, filled an important need in the law system, and despite their complaints as colonists, after independence the Americans not only kept both types of courts but also incorporated them into the state constitutions and, in 1787, the national Constitution.

Other specialized courts could be found throughout the colonies. Many of the colonies established traveling courts of oyer and terminer to hear criminal cases in small towns, while Southern colonies set up summary courts to deal with slave crimes. Larger communities had borough courts, and Georgia created a strangers' court. In all these tribunals, lawyers found more and more business, because as the legal system grew, it shed its earlier informality and adopted the more stringent and technical procedures of English law. Precedent, by which judges relied upon earlier cases to decide new controversies, restricted innovation. Massachusetts, for example, by the eve of the Revolution had forsaken its earlier experimentation and had become judicially quite conservative. In 1762, Chief Justice Thomas Hutchinson ordered that judges and lawyers in the Bay colony wear appropriate English gowns and wigs, and two years later New York required similar costuming. Technicalities, ancient writs, reliance on precedent, and the growing use of defense counsel in criminal cases required men who had more than a passing knowledge of Coke or Littleton. The colonies now needed lawyers, and well before the Revolution, a self-consciously elite profession had emerged in America that enjoyed considerable popular esteem and influence.

# Witchcraft and Press Freedom

Two legal events of the colonial period—the Salem witch trials and the libel prosecution of John Peter Zenger—helped shape the way Americans would later think about fundamental liberties and constitutional government.

## *The Salem Witch Trials*

In 1691, a group of teenage and preteen girls in Salem, Massachusetts were caught practicing "white magic" with the help of a West Indian slave named Tituba. The girls were trying to tell the future by examining a makeshift crystal ball. Once caught, some became hysterical, at least in part because their actions were both illegal and sinful in Puritan Massachusetts. When doctors could not cure the hysteria, they concluded that the afflicted girls were in fact bewitched.

Suspicion immediately fell on Tituba and a few known malcontents and others with reputations as witches or nonconformists. Within weeks, however, the accusations spread to more prominent people, including members of the local Puritan church. The colony's new royal governor, Sir William Phips, appointed his lieutenant governor, William Staughton, to act as a judge for those accused. Phips then went on a fruitless military expedition against the French and their Indian allies in Canada.

When Phips returned in late summer of 1692, he expected to find the witchcraft problem over. Instead, he found that nineteen people had been hanged as witches, along with two dogs, one man had been pressed to death with heavy weights for refusing to testify, a few others had died in jail, and hundreds were in jails, awaiting trials. Phips quickly put an end to the trials and, within months, all those in jail were released.

The trials undermined Puritanism in Massachusetts and forever after made Americans aware of the dangers when religious orthodoxy dominates government. The trials also taught Americans lessons about government, law, and fair trials that would shape later constitutional developments. In the late eighteenth century, some arguments for separation of church and state were influenced by the events in Salem.

So too were arguments for the separation of powers. Lieutenant Governor Staughton served as both judge and executioner, because after he presided over the trials as a temporary judge, he then signed death warrants in his role as acting governor. Furthermore, as acting governor he in effect also represented the prosecution in these cases. His role underscored the importance of separation of powers, which Americans took to heart when they wrote and adopted the national Constitution in 1787–88.

Finally, the Salem trials have become a model for the denial of due process. The accused were often convicted on unsubstantiated testimony, including claims by the afflicted girls that they had been harmed by the image or "specter" of the accused witch. Only the afflicted girls could see these specters, but nevertheless, this testimony sent nearly two dozen people to their death.

The Salem defendants were also denied protection against self-incrimination, the right to an attorney, or even the right to call witnesses on their own behalf. Rebecca Nurse, a saintly old woman and longtime member of the Salem church, was convicted, and executed, after a jury initially found her innocent. The judge simply directed the jury to reconsider its verdict. The trials were held in an atmosphere of total chaos, where it was sometimes difficult for the defendants to even hear the questions asked of them.

The Constitution, the Bill of Rights, and modern decisions interpreting both, reflect the understanding that trials must be fair, open, and conducted with dignity. Modern law also understands that defendants have rights that must be protected by the court. In other words, the Salem trials have served, for more than three centuries, as a model of how not to conduct the business of the government.

## Zenger's Case

The trial of John Peter Zenger also pointed the way toward constitutional government, an independent judiciary, and the Bill of Rights. The controversy in New York began when a new royal governor, Col. William Cosby, arbitrarily removed Chief Justice Lewis Morris from office because he did not like Morris's ruling in a case involving Cosby's own salary. Cosby then appointed a crony, James DeLancey to be the new chief justice. Morris and his political allies soon hired Zenger to publish a newspaper, *The New York Weekly Journal*, which vigorously attacked Governor Cosby and his administration. After a series of futile attempts to have a grand jury indict Zenger, Governor Cosby's attorney general, Richard Bradley, brought an information charging the printer with seditious libel. At a preliminary hearing Zenger's attorney, James Alexander, challenged the legality of the removal of Chief Justice Morris and the subsequent appointment of Chief Justice James DeLancey. Cosby had appointed DeLancey to serve at "the pleasure" of the governor, rather than "during good behavior," which meant as long as he did his job properly and was not corrupt. But, because he served at the "pleasure" of the governor, Zenger's attorneys believed DeLancey would be neither impartial nor fair. DeLancey proved Alexander was in fact correct in his suspicions, by disbarring Alexander and his co-counsel, William Smith. In doing this, DeLancey and Cosby hoped to deprive Zenger of meaningful counsel. In a subsequent preliminary hearing the sheriff, also a Cosby appointee, tried to stack the jury with friends of the governor.

Alexander, however, found a new attorney to take over the case, Andrew Hamilton of Philadelphia, who was the most famous lawyer in the colonies. Hamilton worked with an outline of the case developed by James Alexander. Defying the rules of libel law at the time, Hamilton argued that his client should be acquitted because what he had published about the governor was in fact true. Although apparently guilty under the accepted understanding of libel law, the jury acquitted Zenger.

Andrew Hamilton won his case because a jury of New Yorkers asserted the right to decide the entire case—both the facts and the law—and accepted the argument that a truthful statement could not be a libel. Zenger's case did not, however, become a precedent for a new common law rule on the law of libel. "Truth as a defense" did not become the new standard for libel cases according to the accepted reading of Anglo-American law. This is not really surprising; the case did not come from a great colonial jurist who wrote a carefully thought out and learned opinion. On the contrary, it was the product of a single-minded jury, determined to acquit a man whose only crime was exposing the venality of the governor.

If this case did not set a new legal precedent, it did set an important political precedent. Andrew Hamilton had discussed the law as it ought to be, under the conditions of colonial America, rather than the law as it was in England. His argument made sense to Americans. Things were simply different in America. A static, unchanging law was inappropriate for the colonies. It was the political argument that carried the day in Zenger's case and a political precedent that emerged from it. By the end of the century, the legal theory would also gain acceptance, as both England and the newly independent United States passed laws in the 1790s allowing "truth as a defense" in a seditious libel case. However, in prosecutions under the Sedition Act of 1798, federalist judges would ignore this rule.

One measure of the significance of this proceeding is the controversy it caused in the Anglo-American world. Judging from the volume of printed material concerning it, we must conclude that Zenger's case was important to eighteenth-century English and American lawyers and political thinkers. In 1736, James Alexander published an account of the case, entitled *A Brief Narrative of the Case and Tryal of John Peter Zenger, Printer of the New York Weekly Journal*. This book contained the substance of Andrew Hamilton's argument and was probably in many places a word-for-word rendition of the trial. It contained a summary of the arguments of Attorney General Bradley and the statements and rulings of Chief Justice DeLancey.

Government officials in Barbados soon attacked the arguments of Zenger's attorney, and James Alexander replied with essays in defense of the verdict and the theory that truth should be a defense to a libel. This was in defiance of existing libel law, and with good reason, because Alexander was in effect arguing for a new, American law.

Zenger's *Brief Narrative* would be reprinted throughout the eighteenth century in England and America. New American editions appeared during the crisis with Great Britain in 1770, when the American printer Alexander McDougall was indicted by British authorities. It reappeared during the sedition act controversy in 1799. During the debate over the Constitution, some antifederalists cited Zenger's case as a reason for demanding a bill of rights. Zenger's case led "A Democratic Federalist" to argue that "there is no knowing what corrupt and wicked judges may do in process of time, when they are not restrained by express law."

For Americans at the time of the adoption of the Constitution, and even today, Zenger's case has stood for a number of fundamental principles of constitutionalism. The right to a fair jury, an impartial judge, and a grand jury indictment are all tied to the Zenger case. When the framers made federal judges lifetime appointees they may well have remembered how Governor Cosby had fired Chief Justice Lewis Morris because he did not like his rulings, and then replaced him with DeLancey. It is significant, perhaps, that Chief Justice Morris's grandson, Gouverneur Morris, was one of the most active members of the Constitutional Convention.

In recent years, the Supreme Court has cited Zenger as an early example of the importance of the right to an attorney. Most importantly, of course, Zenger stands for the idea of a free press. While not immediately adopted as a common law precedent, it radically altered the way Americans thought about law and freedom. In that sense, it was a vital precedent for the Revolution, the Constitution, and the Bill of Rights.

# For Further Reading

The pioneering study by Richard B. Morris, *Studies in the History of American Law, With Special Reference to the Seventeenth and Eighteenth Centuries* (1930), is receiving renewed appreciation; many of its insights into colonial American law have held up well. Stephen Botein's brief book, *Early Law in American Society* (1983) is good on the few themes it addresses, but the standard general work is undoubtedly Lawrence M. Friedman's *A History of American Law* (2nd ed., 1985), Part I. Friedman argues convincingly that law mirrors social demands and needs; it has no life of its own, but always interacts with society and is subject to shifts in power. Also useful as a survey is Kermit L. Hall, *The Magic Mirror* (1989). On lawyers in the colonies, see A. G. Roeber, *Faithful Magistrates and Republican Lawyers: Creators of Virginia Legal Culture, 1680–1810* (1981). Also useful is Peter Charles Hoffer, *Law and People in Colonial America* (rev. ed., 1999). A good collection of early statutes and laws is found in W. Keith Kavenagh, *Foundations of Colonial America: A Documentary History*, 7 vols. (reprint, 1983). Also useful is Jacob E. Cooke, ed., *Encyclopedia of the North American Colonies*, 3 vols. (1993).

Good general surveys on the English background of early American law are Alan Harding, *A Social History of English Law* (1966) and J. H. Baker, *An Introduction to English Legal History* (3rd ed., 1990). See also George L. Haskins, *Law and Authority in Early Massachusetts* (1960), which claims that the different conditions within each colony led to thirteen separate law systems, and the various essays in David H. Flaherty, ed., *Essays in the History of Early American Law* (1969). For a good case study of colonial law see Bruce H. Mann, *Neighbors and Strangers: Law and Community in Early Connecticut* (1987).

An introduction to Indian views on land is Imre Sutton, *Indian Land Tenure: Bibliographic Essays and a Guide to the Literature* (1975), especially the piece on "Aboriginal Occupancy and Territoriality." See also Anthony F. C. Wallace, "Political Organization and Land Tenure Among the Northern Indians, 1600–1830," 13 *Southwest Journal of Anthropology* 301 (1957). For the relation between land and social structure, see Sumner C. Powell, *Puritan Village* (1965). Beverly W. Bond, Jr., *The Quit-Rent System in the American Colonies* (1919), is one of the few monographs on land law; Morris, *Studies*, has good material on land law in general and on primogeniture and entail.

The best survey on women and law in this period is Sandra F. VanBurkleo *"Belonging to the World": Women's Rights and American Constitutional Culture* (2001). Both VanBurkleo and Roger Thompson, *Women in Stuart England and America: A Comparative Study* (1974), find evidence for more "freeing" of women in the colonies. A useful overview is Carol Ruth Berkin, "Within the Conjuror's Circle: Women in Colonial America," in Thomas R. Frazier, ed., *The Underside of American History* (3rd ed., 1978). See also Nancy F. Cott, "Divorce and the Changing Status of Women in Eighteenth Century Massachusetts," 415 *William and Mary Quarterly* 29 (1972); Marylynn Salmon, "Equality or Submersion? *Feme Couvert* Status in Early Pennsylvania," in Carol Berkin and Mary Beth Norton, eds., *Women of America: A History* (1979), which examines women's legal disabilities; and Joan R. Gunderson and Gwen V. Gampel, "Married Women's Legal Status in Eighteenth-Century New York and Virginia," 39 *William and Mary Quarterly* 114 (1982), which stresses practices benefiting women that were different from those in England. Excellent studies of the changing nature of women's legal rights and the economy are Cornelia Hughes Dayton, *Women Before the Bar: Gender, Law and Society in Connecticut, 1639–1789* (1995), and Mary Beth Norton, *Founding Mothers and Fathers: Gendered Power and the Forming of American Society* (1996).

The standard survey on labor law remains Richard B. Morris, *Government and Labor in Early America* (1945). For indentured servants, see Abbott E. Smith, *Colonists in Bondage: White Servitude and Convict Labor in America. 1607–1776* (1947). Work on the law of slavery has become a small industry. Among other works, see William M. Wiececk, "The Statutory Law of

Slavery and Race in the Thirteen Mainland Colonies of British America," 34 *William and Mary Quarterly* 258 (1977); Paul Finkelman, *The Law of Freedom and Bondage* (1986); Paul Finkelman, "The Crime of Color," 67 *Tulane Law Review* 2063 (1993); A. Leon Higginbotham, *In the Matter of Color* (1977); Philip Schwarz, *Twice Condemned: Slaves and the Criminal Laws of Virginia, 1705–1865* (1988); and Thomas D. Morris, *Southern Slavery and the Law, 1619–1869* (1996).

David H. Flaherty provides a good overview of the interaction of the state and religion in "Law and the Enforcement of Morals in Early America," 5 *Perspectives in American History* 20 (1971). Other useful studies include Carl Bridenbaugh, *Mitre and Sceptre* (1962), on the Anglicans, and Frederick B. Tolles, *Meeting House and Counting House* (1948), on the Quakers. The literature on the Puritan view is enormous, but see especially Emil Oberholzer, Jr., "The Church in New England Society," in James Smith, ed., *Seventeenth-Century America* (1959). David T. Konig, *Law and Society in Puritan Massachusetts: Essex County, 1629–1692* (1979), attacks the myth that early colonists sought to avoid legal controversy; Konig sees the Puritans as an extremely litigious people, but this helped to make the courts, and not the churches, the chief instruments of social control.

Criminal law also served to enforce moral standards, and there have been some interesting recent studies. Douglas Greenberg, *Crime and Law Enforcement in the Colony of New York, 1691–1776* (1976), focuses on the social history of law and shows how the pattern of criminal prosecutions mirrored social antagonisms. The older book by Julius Goebel, Jr. and T. Raymond Naughton, *Law Enforcement in Colonial New York* (1944), is still valuable on the law. Bradley Chapin's *Criminal Justice in Colonial America* (1983), posits a far more humane justice system than probably existed. An interesting comparative study is Michael S. Hindus, *Prison and Plantation: Crime, Justice, and Authority in Massachusetts and South Carolina, 1767–1878* (1980), while mostly focused on the the period after the Revolution, offers some insights into the colonial period.

Joseph H. Smith, *Appeals to the Privy Council from the American Plantations* (1950), is the standard work; see also his essay on "Administrative Control of the Courts of the American Plantations," in Flaherty, *Essays,* and Carl W. Ubbelohde, *The Vice-Admiralty Courts and the American Revolution* (1960).

On the roots of the Bill of Rights in the colonial period, see Leonard W. Levy, *Origins of the Bill of Rights* (1999). On Zenger, see Paul Finkelman, ed., *A Brief Narrative of the Tryal of John Peter Zenger* (1997); on Salem, see Paul Boyer and Stephen Nissenbaum, *Salem Possessed: The Social Origins of Witchcraft* (1974).

# 3

# The Road to Independence

*The Mercantile System • Colonial Governments • Writs of Assistance • The Parsons Cause and the Two Penny Act • Colonial Constitutional Thought • Republican Ideology • The British View • The Stamp Act and the Colonial Response • The Townshend Duties • Tea and the Coercive Acts • The First Continental Congress • Parting of the Ways • The Declaration of Independence • Conclusion • For Further Reading*

WHATEVER INTERPRETATION ONE wishes to put on the American Revolution—economic, social, or political—the growing rift between Great Britain and her American colonies following the wars against the French and the Indians in the mid-eighteenth century involved fundamental constitutional issues. Both sides appealed to the same traditions, cited the same sources, and claimed the same doctrines, but the century and a half of experience in the New World led the colonists to different conclusions. Beyond this, the decade prior to the rebellion also witnessed a breakdown in imperial government. As radical as the final step of revolt may have been, declaring their independence appeared to the colonists as the logical and inevitable culmination of events.

## The Mercantile System

In the latter seventeenth and first half of the eighteenth centuries, Great Britain slowly developed a system of imperial government designed primarily to enhance its economy. The theory of mercantilism viewed the colonies, many of which had originally begun as commercial ventures, as economically subservient to the needs of England, providing raw materials for home industry and a market for finished goods. Mercantilism also benefited the colonies, and much of the colonial prosperity derived from this imperial policy.

Imperial policy, however, lacked a grand design, so that on the eve of the American Revolution the English politician Edmund Burke, who sympathized with the revolutionary cause, wrote: "The settlement of our colonies was never pursued upon any regular plan; but they were formed, grew, and flourished, as accidents, the nature of the climate, or the dispositions of private men happened to operate." The tension between Parliament and the Stuarts precluded much attention to the colonies in the seventeenth century, but as time went on, the royal government slowly evolved some semblance of a policy that managed to function until 1765.

The mercantile system originated during the Protectorate with the Navigation Act of 1651, which excluded nearly all foreign shipping from English and colonial trade. Goods imported into England or the colonies had to be carried on British ships, and the majority of their crews had to be English. This definition included ships owned by colonists and deemed colonial sailors English citizens.

After the restoration of the Stuart monarchy in 1660, the government extended Cromwell's policy. The Navigation Act of 1660 enlarged the English crew requirement to three-fourths rather than a bare majority and also enumerated certain goods that could be shipped only to Great Britain or to another colony. The government of King Charles II (1660–1685) soon sought to make England the funnel for all items from the continent destined for the colonies. To enforce this policy, the Navigation Act of 1673 required every captain loading enumerated goods either to post bond that he would land in England, or if destined to another colony, to pay the duty that would have been collected in London.

Although the policy appears straightforward enough—to give English (and colonial) ships and crews a monopoly of imperial trade—enforcement proved another story. Charles II attempted some bureaucratic control through the Lords of Trade and Plantations, as well as through the establishment of customs officials, responsible directly to the Crown, in all the colonies. The continuing conflict between New England merchants, intent on ignoring these rules, and Stuart customs officers led in part to the revocation of the Massachusetts charter in 1684 and the brief tenure of the Dominion of New England.

The accession of William III (1689–1702) and Mary II (1689–1694) following the Glorious Revolution in 1689 saw a continued expansion of the mercantile policy. The Navigation Act of 1696 recapitulated the previous laws and attempted to tighten administration through a number of provisions. Colonial governors had to take a special oath to enforce the Navigation Acts; customs officials could use writs of assistance, general search warrants that did not specify the place to be searched; and violators could be tried, not before sympathetic local juries, but in vice-admiralty courts that sat without a jury. That same year, William III created the Board of Trade to replace the Lords of Trade and Plantations. For the rest of the colonial period, the board oversaw and helped to determine imperial economic policy.

The range of this policy ran from fixing bounties for the production of certain raw materials, such as naval stores and indigo, to restricting colonial products that might compete with English manufactures. The Woolen Act (1699) prohibited colonial export of raw wool, woolen yarn, and cloth; the Hat Act (1732) forbade export of beaver hats out of the colony in which they had been made and limited colonial hatters to no more than two apprentices. The Iron Act (1750) curtailed iron manufacture, and the Currency Act (1751) rigidly regulated the issuance of colonial credit by restricting the circulation of paper money. The mercantile system had as its ultimate goal not only the binding of the mother country and colonies together through economic ties, but making the empire as economically self-sufficient as possible. Because the British government recognized that mercantilism, even if designed primarily to benefit the mother country, could not be a one-way street, many of these laws protected and encouraged colonial commerce and in no small measure accounted for the enormous prosperity enjoyed on the Atlantic seaboard.

The colonists widely ignored these laws. Extensive smuggling occurred, especially in New England, and frontier conditions made it difficult to police many of the regulations. At least until the Seven Years War (1756–1763) the British government seemed content with nominal enforcement, since violations, although depriving the Exchequer of some revenue, neither seriously undermined the system nor threatened British security. Edmund Burke characterized this period as one of "wise and salutary neglect," as evidenced, for example, by how rarely the Board of Trade disallowed colonial laws. Of the 8,563 statutes examined, the board vetoed only 469—about 5 percent—even though far more could have been held inconsistent with the laws of England.

All this began to change with the great war for empire between France and Great Britain from 1756 to 1763. At the end of the fighting, England claimed, with the exception of New Orleans, all the land in North America east of the Mississippi River, as well as present-day Canada and much of the West Indies. The colonists enjoyed a new sense of security, freed from threats from the French and their Indian allies. Nearly two million colonists now lived in settlements stretching from Maine to northern Florida, and despite their heterogeneous backgrounds, they were rapidly developing a common attitude, an American outlook, that differed significantly from the view in London.

Prosperity contributed to this new sense of self-confidence. Despite the Iron Act (1750), the colonial iron trade was threatening to drive British products out of the imperial market; by 1775, the colonies had more furnaces and forges than England and Wales combined, and the colonial output of pig and bar iron exceeded that of the mother country. The plentiful supply of lumber gave the colonies a decided advantage in shipbuilding: it cost less than half as much to lay down a keel in Massachusetts as in Great Britain. Wherever one went there were prosperous farms, growing towns and cities, and well-to-do plantations.

## Colonial Governments

The prosperity of the eighteenth century provided the stability in which the colonists could develop local governmental institutions. The "salutary neglect" of the mother country from about 1720 to 1763 tolerated local autonomy so long as it did not hinder economic growth. Moreover, the Stuart idea of centralized control declined, and although several royal agencies shared nominal authority for directing colonial affairs, in practice none of them exercised effective power. As a result, Americans essentially governed themselves within a loose imperial framework.

Their governance, however, utilized English law, English-style institutions, and English ideas of government. Chief among these was the idea of balance, not the separated powers and checks embodied in the 1787 Constitution, but a balance among the different elements of society. In England, the king and the two houses of Parliament represented different strata of society and shared the tasks of governing. The monarch still exercised great authority, and the division among the executive, legislative, and judicial functions remained blurred. A similar pattern emerged in the colonies.

The typical colonial government had a governor (named either by the Crown or the proprietor), an appointed council, and an elected assembly. Together they took care of the business of government. Although the governor was primarily an executive, he sat with the council and shared in the legislative work; the council (the least powerful part of the government) often served as the colony's high court; and members of the lower chamber frequently acted as magistrates. Visitors in the early eighteenth century would have noticed minor differences between the mother country and the colonies, but they would have been far more impressed with the similarities in thought and practice.

Between 1720 and 1770, however, a major change took place in the colonies, as the lower house—the elected assembly—amassed a greater share of the governing power, until it finally became the dominant branch. In hindsight, the Revolutionary generation would explain the growth of assembly power as the result of colonial struggles to exercise the rights of Englishmen against governors attempting to wield arbitrary power. In fact, the story is far less dramatic. The everyday business of governance, such as the building and maintenance of roads, defense against Indian raids, land policy, and other such matters required legislative decisions.

Gradually, and with no clearly defined plan, the assemblies began exercising a variety of prerogatives. They chose their own officers, sat without the governor present, and initiated legislation. More consciously, they sought and achieved many of the privileges enjoyed by Parliament—freedom of speech, immunity from arrest, and power over their proceedings. Just as Parliament had gained control over taxation and finance, so did the colonial assemblies. Having gained the power to initiate revenue measures, they realized how potent a weapon it could be. A continuing struggle between the royal authorities and the colonial legislatures revolved around the Crown's demands for a permanent revenue and the assemblies' refusal to vote other than an annual appropriation.

In acting for the king, the governors theoretically exercised his authority. They could call the assemblies into session, veto legislation, control expenditures, enforce the laws, make appointments, and do everything else the king could do if he were present. In practice, the governor had far less power and occupied an unenviable position between the London government demanding him to do more and the assemblies forcing him to do less. Instructions from England often ignored political reality and failed to spell out how much discretionary power the governor could exercise. The assemblies quickly learned that they could prevent governors from carrying out unpopular policies by refusing to vote the necessary funds to implement the policies or pay the salaries. Until the eve of the Revolution, the salaries of royal officials in the colonies depended on assembly appropriations.

The governor did have enough power, however, to prevent the assembly from taking full control of the government. He could veto legislation, prorogue (dismiss) the assembly, appoint officials without its approval, and prevent the legislature from meeting on its own initiative. But the power of the purse gave the assemblies an advantage, one reinforced by the fact that an expanding electorate provided the legislatures with a popular mandate. By the 1760s, the assemblies represented the colonists far more responsively than Parliament spoke for the English people.

## Writs of Assistance

Although the assemblies paid for local needs, the mother country paid the lion's share of colonial expenditures. In 1700, the Crown paid out £3,750,000 annually for the administration and defense of the North American colonies; by 1755, the figure had risen to £6,500,000. Yet the colonists seemingly took it all for granted, and during the war between Britain and France, they paid scant attention to imperial needs. Smuggling continued unabated, and when the powerful French fleet of Admiral de Beaufremont lay at anchor at Cap François in the French West Indies, New England merchantmen provisioned it so well that in the spring of 1757 it could sail all the way to Cape Breton to check the British attack on the island. In late 1759, Vice Admiral Thomas Cotes declared from his station in the West Indies that the "vile Illicit Trade that has been carried on here ever since the commencement of the present War is really and still remains infamous and barefaced."

Planning to launch a full-scale attack on the illegal trade, the customs officers at Salem petitioned the Massachusetts Superior Court for writs of assistance in November 1760. Such writs would give royal officials virtually unlimited power to search wherever they wished, to look for whatever they wanted. The officials needed court approval because King George II had died the preceding month, and all previous writs in his name expired with him. Chief Justice Stephen Sewall questioned the legality of the writs and ordered a full hearing at the February 1761 term of the court. But before the arguments took place, Sewall died, and Thomas Hutchinson, a staunch defender of royal government, took his place. Massachusetts merchants predictably opposed the writs, but the court had ample precedent to issue them. Apparently first authorized in the days of Charles II, their use had been extended to the colonies under William and Mary, and the Massachusetts courts had issued writs to various customs officials in 1755, 1758, 1759, and 1760. James Otis led the fight against them and was like "a flame on fire" according to John Adams. More than a half century after the event, Adams recalled the speech as "the first scene of the first act of opposition to the arbitrary claims of Great Britain. Then and there, the child Independence was born."

Otis denounced the open-ended nature of the writs, arguing that they went "against the fundamental principles of law." He did not deny the power of the government to search a person's house looking for a particular item under the authority of a search warrant; but the writ of assistance allowed authorities to look for anything in anyone's home at any time. Such power invited abuse and violated the spirit of the laws. Any such abuse, Otis claimed, "against the Constitution is void; an act against natural equity is void; and if an act of Parliament should be made, in the very words of this petition, it would be void. The executive Courts must pass it into disuse." Although arguments of this sort had been heard before in England, such as Coke's dictum in Dr. Bonham's Case and in the writings of some of the radical theorists, never before had it been heard so openly in the colonies. The idea of a fundamental law that limited government would become perhaps the most powerful and pervasive of all arguments in the decade before the Revolution.

At the time, Otis appeared unwilling to follow his thesis to its logical conclusion—namely, laws and governments that violated natural rights should be resisted—and his ambivalence on this subject marked all his writings. In theory, he continued to uphold the power of Parliament, but in practice, he expressed numerous reservations about its use. In his attack on the writs, though, he denied to Parliament the competence to place all people owing fealty to the Crown under equal obligations and thus raised the fundamental issue of which sovereign power Parliament could in fact exercise over the colonies.

Chief Justice Hutchinson decided to seek further guidance on this issue, and after consulting with London, the court issued the writs. In 1767, the Townshend Revenue Act specifically affirmed the power of the colonial courts to grant the writs, but in practice, officials could never again use them in Massachusetts. In most colonies, the courts declared the provisions of the Townshend Act unconstitutional. At the time, few people paid much attention to the Otis argument or to a similar speech by Patrick Henry two years later in Virginia, in which the fiery orator questioned the constitutional right of the Privy Council to disallow colonial laws. Nonetheless, these arguments marked the opening salvos in the constitutional debate over the nature of imperial relations and powers. Not by coincidence, though, the debate grew in intensity as the administration of the imperial government collapsed.

The controversy over the writs of assistance must also be understood as a key event leading to the adoption of the Bill of Rights in 1791. As legal historian Leonard W. Levy has written in *The Origins of the Bill of Rights*: "a straight line of progression runs from Otis's argument in 1761 . . . to Madison's introduction of the proposal that became the Fourth Amendment."

## The Parsons Cause and the Two Penny Act

While the colonists in Massachusetts were struggling against the writs of assistants, those in Virginia faced a different, but equally significant struggle with British power. The Anglican Church was the established church in Virginia. Thus, the colony was responsible for the salaries of Anglican priests. Since the 1620s Virginians had been using tobacco—or more precisely receipts for tobacco stored in public warehouses—as currency. In 1748, the colony fixed the salaries for the Anglican clergy at 17,200 pounds of tobacco a year. However, crop failures and a rise in the price of tobacco inflated the value of this payment scheme. In 1755, the colony passed a law declaring that all contracts for payment in tobacco could be paid off in cash, at two pence per pound. At the time, tobacco had reached the almost unheard of price of six pence a pound. The law expired after ten months, but was reenacted in anticipation (which proved correct) of another crop failure in 1758.

While most Virginians accepted this reasonable economic regulation, most of the Anglican clergy complained. More concerned about their own pocketbooks than the souls of their parishioners, the Anglican clergy complained to authorities in London, and in 1759, the royal government vetoed these laws. In 1762, Rev. James Maury sued in Hanover County to recover the difference between his two penny a pound payment and the actual per-pound value of tobacco. At a trial in 1763, a jury ruled in favor of Rev. Maury, but gave him damages of only one penny. The issued died down after a Virginia court upheld the Two Penny Act in 1764, and the Privy Council in London refused to overturn that result in 1767.

The controversy raised one immediate issue of constitutional importance and pointed the way to a second one. This first issue concerned the right of the people of Virginia, through their elected legislature, to regulate the local economy. In defending the law, Patrick Henry argued that the king had violated his own charter with Virginia in disallowing the law. In effect, Henry was arguing that the royal veto of the Two Penny Act was unconstitutional.

In the long run, this incident undermined the idea of an established church in Virginia and other colonies. By this time, many Virginians followed other faiths. The Baptists, Methodists, Presbyterians, Quakers, and other nonconforming Protestants resented being taxed to support the Anglican clergy. The logical step, which Virginia adopted after the Revolution, was to remove religion from politics by disestablishing the state church.

## Colonial Constitutional Thought

Looking at the events between 1765 and 1776, one can see the pattern of imperial failure. But the events by themselves do not explain why in so short a time a prosperous and secure people, proud to claim the title of Englishmen, rebelled against the mother country and their lawful king, to whom most of them pledged their fealty and affection. At least part of the answer can be found in the ideological debates that preceded independence. The colonists believed themselves never truer to their English heritage than in rebeling against the government of George III.

The best sources for understanding the colonists' fears and hopes during this period are the more than 400 pamphlets they penned in the years leading up to the break with England. These documents presented the common sources and beliefs they saw as inherited from the mother country, but that were now jeopardized, as historian Bernard Bailyn put it in *The Ideological Origins of the American Revolution*, "by a comprehensive conspiracy against liberty throughout the English-speaking world," of which the "oppression in America was only the most immediately visible part." In defeating what they perceived as an attack upon their liberties, they appealed to tradition for their justification.

First, colonists cited ancient Rome, and pointed out how corruption similar to that now at work in England had destroyed the republic. Second, they relied on the rationalist writers of the Enlightenment, especially the natural rights theory developed in John Locke's *Second Treatise on Government*, together with seventeenth-century continental writers such as Hugo Grotius and Samuel Pufendorf on the laws of nature and of nations. Third, the colonists held as particularly important the common law, and like Coke, saw it as the repository of the good and noble in human history. The common law, considered as authority, as principle incarnate, as the framework of social relations, justified their arguments. A fourth, and equally important source, the covenant theology of New England, expressed in practice the social contract theory of the Enlightenment. Together, these ideas of natural rights, of a contractual basis for society, and of a law that protected liberty, formed the foundations of revolutionary ideology.

Not surprisingly, colonial writers found much to applaud in the works of those English radicals who similarly feared corruption and the effects they saw it had on their own liberty. The polemical writings of such men as John Trenchard, Thomas Gordon, Bishop Benjamin Hoadley, and Viscount Bolingbroke, which were eagerly read, quoted, reprinted, and plagiarized on this side of the Atlantic, fueled colonial fears. English radicals saw government—any government—as by nature hostile to liberty, and they argued therefore that it should survive only on the tolerance of those whom it governed. If government became too oppressive, if it exceeded its prescribed limits, it should be overthrown. Liberty, they declared, could be maintained only by constant vigilance against government.

The idea that governmental power naturally subverted liberty and law would be a constant throughout this period, and later would account for the deliberately weak governments created for the states and the nation following the Revolution. Government preyed upon the governed, who acquiesced by their weakness. In pamphlet after pamphlet, writers hammered at the incapacity of human beings to withstand the temptations of power. To prevent enslavement, people had to watch their government constantly and control its excesses. Thus, for example, the colonists feared standing armies, which could enforce a malignant government's designs against the people. "No worse state of thralldom" existed, declared the Anglican minister Samuel Seabury, "than a military power in any government, unchecked and uncontrolled by the civil power." He and other colonial writers frequently pointed to the unhappy case of Denmark, where the army had been used to snuff out parliamentary liberties.

The colonists saw as their chief bulwark against tyranny the English constitution, which John Adams, summarizing common sentiment, described as "the most perfect combination of human powers in society which finite human wisdom has yet contrived and reduced to practice for the preservation of liberty and the production of happiness." The constitution embodied not only traditions, laws, and institutions, but the principles that animated them, leading, in Adams's words, toward "a frame, a scheme, a system, a combination of powers for a certain end, namely—the good of the whole community."

The success of the English constitution lay in its balancing of forces and sharing of powers, so that no one element in the society could gain the upper hand against the others. Executive power, normally the province of royalty, had been diluted through the institution of trial by jury, so that the people themselves could form a bulwark against executive perversion of justice. The law, in all its manifestations, expressed the protections free people had erected to preserve their natural rights, which, John Dickinson wrote in 1766, "are created in us by the decrees of Providence, which established the laws of our nature. They are born in us; exist with us; and cannot be taken away from us by any human power without taking our lives." The common law, according to James Otis, in its essence did no more and no less than articulate the "natural absolute personal rights of individuals."

Yet in the decade preceding the rebellion, many colonists saw this wonderful edifice of protection under attack by venal, would-be despots. "The august and once revered fortress of English freedom," lamented the Boston Town Meeting in 1770, "the admirable work of ages, the BRITISH CONSTITUTION, seems fast tottering into fatal and inevitable ruin." Efforts by the Church of England, for example, to crush dissenting sects and establish a bishopric in America could be seen as the ages-old stratagem of tyrants seeking to use a compliant church to crush liberty. The disallowance of colonial laws granting judges life tenure—a status they had enjoyed in the mother country since 1701—could be read as nothing less than a deliberate effort to pervert justice, similar to the extension of the vice-admiralty courts, which preyed upon people denied the protection of jury trials. Although "single acts of tyranny may be ascribed to the accidental opinions of a day," Thomas Jefferson warned, "a series of oppressions, begun at a distinguished period and pursued unalterably through every change of ministries, too plainly prove a deliberate and systematical plan of reducing us to slavery." Jefferson, like many of the colonists, often used slavery as a metaphor for British oppression. Supporters of the Empire found this language exceedingly ironic, especially from men like Jefferson, who owned about 150 slaves at this time.

## Republican Ideology

Although the colonists did not realize it at the time, they had already begun to move away from the British ideal of mixed government, in which the various elements of society were balanced, and toward what later writers have called the "republican ideology." Instead of concentrating on how the mechanics of government prevented one part of society from dominating another, the Americans started to explore the sources of political authority. Even though the English government had long contained a democratic element, this had been relatively minor; the consent of the governed counted less than ensuring that most parts of society had their proper influence, with the upper classes wielding the greatest power. Ever since the downfall of the ancient Greek republics, popularly controlled government had been derided as too weak to rule effectively.

American writers, relying on some of the radical English theorists, now began talking about government as a public matter, as a concern for all the people and not just for a ruling elite. The people had not only a right but an obligation to participate in governance, since government existed to protect the rights and well-being of the entire population, not just a small part. Republican government derived its authority from the people, and no matter what particular form it took, the government existed and could be justified only so long as it served the needs of the people. In turn, the people had to take part in governing, if not as actual officials, then by participating in the choosing of those officials and by voicing their concerns.

Today, it is difficult to realize how radical a proposition republican ideology appeared at the time. In one stroke, it eliminated the need for the monarchy and the aristocracy—the two groups that had dominated government for centuries—and cut the ground out from under the British concept of government as being balanced among the dominant groups. Although it expressed greater concern for individual rights than did the British model, republican ideology did not exalt the individual. It still placed the interests of the group as a whole at the apex of governmental concerns. This "commonwealth" spirit, as the seventeenth-century English writer James Harrington and others had expressed it, required the individual to suppress some personal desires for the good of the whole, on the assumption that if the whole society prospered and enjoyed liberty, so would its individual members.

This commonwealth or "corporatist" strain derived less from Lockean liberalism than from the writings of another seventeenth-century Englishman, Thomas Hobbes, but it is difficult to ascribe consistency to the republican ideology. Although emphasizing group welfare and responsibilities, it did not deny individualism, which at all times played a strong role in American thought. In fact, we can see a basic tension between the individual and the society marking much of American history. Depending on circumstances, one or the other strand temporarily gained ascendancy. The needs of society dominated in the years immediately preceding and during the Revolution, while the state constitutions and the Articles of Confederation expressed the individualistic or at least a localist ideal. At no time, however, did Americans view the individual as having a right to pursue his or her own happiness at the expense of the public good. Jefferson's famous phrase, "the pursuit of happiness," is properly interpreted as public happiness.

Because of what they perceived as the tyrannical excesses of royal government, the Americans developed the notion of limited government as part of their republican ideology. Some writers have called this "negative" liberty, in the sense that barriers are erected to prevent government from acting in certain ways, in contrast to "positive" liberty, which requires government to protect particular rights. To limit government, Americans relied on a variety of legal traditions, including common law notions of property, as well as rights and privileges vested in the ancient but ill-defined notions of due process of law and fundamental law.

The republican ideology blended these concepts of liberty, requiring that all the people participate in the public business of government, that government be limited in its powers so that it could not erode the people's liberty, and that the powers it did have be used to advance the commonweal and protect the people's liberties.

## The British View

Although some colonists saw a dark conspiracy behind every British act, officials in London had a quite different interpretation of their policies. First, most Englishmen believed that they had more liberty than any other people on Earth, and the Americans shared in this liberty. As the Prince of Wales, who would become King George III, asserted, "The pride, the glory of Britain and the direct end of its Constitution" was "political liberty." As Gordon Wood noted in *The Radicalism of the American Revolution*, "No unruly American provincial could have put it better." Thus, leaders in Britain were often simply astounded that the Americans should complain about English "tyranny," when in fact everyone on both sides of the Atlantic conceded that the people in England, as well as Englishmen in the American colonies, had more liberty than any other people on Earth. Ironically, at the very time the Americans were beginning to complain about English "tyranny," American courts were aping English customs and traditions. Courts in New York required robes for jurists and wigs for attorneys, in order expected the storm that broke in the colonies upon news of the Stamp Act. There had, after all, been stamp taxes in England since 1694, and later American governments would use them extensively. But crowds now gathered in every colony beneath "Liberty trees" or around "Liberty poles" to protest. In Boston, a mob destroyed the stamp office and so frightened the local agent, Andrew Oliver, that he resigned his commission, an example agents in other colonies soon emulated. By November 1, the date of implementation, the Stamp Act was a dead letter. The colonists refused to use the stamps, and newspapers appeared with a skull and crossbones in the corner where the stamp belonged. Never before had there been such open defiance of the mother country; and, most alarming, this defiance had been organized.

In May 1765, the Virginia House of Burgesses passed the Virginia Resolves, a series of resolutions inspired by Patrick Henry's "torrents of sublime eloquence." Virginians claimed all the rights of Englishmen and argued that they could therefore be taxed only by their own representatives and only with their own consent. Other colonies followed the Virginia lead, and in June, Massachusetts issued a circular letter inviting the other assemblies to join in planning how to secure relief from the tax. The Stamp Act Congress, as it came to be called, met in New York in October, with twenty-seven delegates from nine colonies. (Three other colonies probably would have attended, but their assemblies had adjourned before the invitation arrived.) The Congress issued a Declaration of the Rights and Grievances of the Colonies, a petition to the king for relief, and another petition to the Parliament calling for repeal of the Stamp Act.

The arguments heard during the furor over the Stamp Act echoed repeatedly over the next ten years: Great Britain had no right to tax the colonies without their consent; no taxation could be imposed except by the people's representatives; and any effort by Parliament in this direction violated the colonists' rights as Englishmen. The colonists denied Parliament any authority to tax them. "The people of these colonies," the Stamp Act Congress resolved, "are not and, from their local circumstances, cannot be represented in the House of Commons in Great Britain." If there could be no representation, and no taxation was legitimate without representation, then there could be no taxes at all other than those the colonists, through their elected assemblies, imposed on themselves.

The Stamp Act died a quick death. The government could not enforce it without colonial cooperation; attempts to impose it on ships sailing for England led to a severe drop in trade, which raised loud protests from British merchants and manufacturers. At the same time, the king dismissed Grenville (over matters not related to the Stamp Act) and installed the Marquis of Rockingham, whose political faction included Edmund Burke and others sympathetic to the colonists. Rockingham wanted to repeal the act, while avoiding the impression that Parliament had surrendered to colonial pressure. He seized on a minor distinction between "external" taxes on trade and "internal" taxes within the colonies and, with the help of Benjamin Franklin, led Parliament to acquiesce in the totally false view that the colonies were objecting only to the imposition of internal taxes. In addition, Parliament passed the Declaratory Act, which asserted its full power to make laws binding on the colonies "in all cases whatsoever." Shortly after, the government reduced the widely evaded molasses tax from three pence to one—less than the cost of bribing customs officials—in the hope of securing some revenue from the colonies.

to promote the "Dignity Authority Solemnity and Decorum of the Cour
colonies adopted similar accoutrements of British courts to give greater resp
to the colonial legal system, which, after all, protected American liberty in the
just as similar courts protected liberty in the mother country.

Thus, the English government believed it was only reasonable for the pr
American colonies to pay a fair share of the costs of administering and protect
and their liberty. When George Grenville became prime minister in 1763, F
England triumphant after its war with France, but staggering under a war deb
million. An able man, Grenville saw the obvious; he had to raise revenue,
colonies were not contributing their share of the defense costs. In fact, the colon
paid nothing toward the various wars with the French and the Indians in the eig
century, since Parliament had reimbursed the colonial assemblies for all exper
curred on behalf of the royal forces. Beyond that, tariffs went practically unco
because of the lax administration of the trade laws.

The major tariff at the time called for a payment of six pence per gallon
ported molasses. Originally enacted in 1733, the measure had been designed l
revenue than to prevent trade with the French sugar islands. New England im
vast quantities of molasses to make rum, an essential part of its trade, and to avo
tax colonial merchantmen smuggled in most of their cargoes. Grenville propo
compromise between the British West Indies planters, who wanted protection, a
New England merchants; he halved the duty to three pence, but added more cu
officials to ensure its collection. If properly enforced, the duty should have yi
£45,000 annually, a substantial increase over previous revenues, but still only a
tion of the colonial costs.

In England, most observers thought the Sugar Act of 1764 was a fair measure
colonial merchants, who were used to paying nothing, protested. In the Massachu
House of Representatives, James Otis attacked laws that had "a tendency to dep
the Colonies of some of their essential rights as British Subjects and . . . particul
the Right of assessing their own Taxes." Otis and others noted that for the first ti
Parliament had adopted duties for the specific purpose of raising revenue, and
merely to regulate trade.

## The Stamp Act and the Colonial Response

The following year, Grenville took another step in his plan to get the colonies to p
the costs related to them, including the maintenance of 10,000 troops stationed the
In February 1765, he proposed creating revenue stamps, ranging in cost from thr
pence to £6, and required their use on all legal documents and printed matter, eve
college diplomas and playing cards. Although colonial agents in London proteste
they had no alternative to offer, and the bill itself passed Parliament almost unnotice
At the same time, Grenville secured approval of the Quartering Act, in effect also
tax measure, requiring the colonies to supply British troops with provisions and barracks, or submit to their use of inns and vacant buildings. Although applying to all the
colonies, it affected mainly New York, headquarters of the British forces.

No one in Great Britain, not even American agents such as Benjamin Franklin,

The Stamp Act and its repeal set the pattern that followed. England would attempt to secure revenue from the colonies, revenue aimed only at supporting the costs of administering and protecting them; the colonists would denounce such taxes as a threat to their liberties, and protest; Parliament would then back down, even as it continued to claim powers to govern the colonies as it wished. With each incident, the colonists grew bolder in their defiance, and the royal government became more desperate. Throughout it all, the Americans were developing powerful constitutional arguments that would not only justify their rebellion, but would prepare the groundwork for their later experiments in creating government.

## The Townshend Duties

After the repeal of the Stamp Act, the Crown had to extend domestic taxes—including a tariff on every window of every house in Britain—in order to raise needed revenue. Higher land taxes also led to riots over the jump in bread prices, which a new government, headed by the elderly Earl of Chatham, William Pitt, could not ignore. The guiding hand in the new administration soon proved to be that of Charles Townshend, the Chancellor of the Exchequer. For Townshend, the inequity between the overtaxed mother country and her prosperous, practically untaxed colonies had to be remedied. His first step was to reduce the British land tax by one shilling, a popular relief measure, but one that cost the government a half million pounds annually.

Then, in February 1766, Townshend announced to Parliament: "I do not know any distinctions between internal and external taxes; it is a distinction without a difference, it is perfect nonsense. If we have a right to impose one, we have the other." Looking up at the colonial agents sitting in the gallery, he declared: "I speak this aloud that you may hear me." A few weeks later, he proposed new revenue measures. Although he reiterated that he himself saw no difference between internal and external taxes, he conceded that the colonists had made the distinction. Thus, the government would confine itself to regulation of trade. The Revenue Act of 1767 levied tariffs on colonial imports of glass, lead, paints, paper, and tea. In addition, a Board of Customs Commissioners would now sit in Boston, the acknowledged center of smuggling, and vice-admiralty courts would henceforth hold sessions in Halifax, Boston, Philadelphia, and Charleston. The fourth of the Townshend Acts suspended all of the New York Assembly's acts until the colony complied with the Quartering Act of 1765.

The revenue measure called for only a small increase in colonial tariffs and at best would yield £35,000 to £40,000 a year, less than one-tenth of the deficit caused by the loss of the land tax. The only criticism of the bill in the Commons was that the tariffs were not high enough. The Townshend duties brought in £31,000 the first year at a cost of £13,000, for a net return of £18,000. Nevertheless, the laws precipitated an enormous outcry, partly because of the suppression of the New York Assembly and partly as a response to any tax increase at all. From the viewpoint of those who always saw a British conspiracy, however, the greatest danger came from the proposed use of the revenue. Townshend intended to use the money to pay the salaries of governors and other officials, thus freeing them from dependence on colonial legislatures.

This time American resistance came not only from hotheads like James Otis and

Patrick Henry, but from moderates as well. In one of the most influential pamphlets published before the Revolution, *Letters from a Pennsylvania Farmer*, John Dickinson, a conservative lawyer, denied the authority of Parliament to levy internal or external taxes. "If the Parliament succeeds in this attempt," he warned, "other statutes will impose other duties . . . and thus Parliament will levy upon us such sums of money as they choose to take, without any other LIMITATION than their PLEASURE." Although he conceded the right of the Crown to regulate trade, he argued that this power could not be used to raise revenue. As for the great debt of the mother country, the cause of all these taxes, Dickinson's attitude reflected that of most colonists—the war for empire had been for England's benefit, so England should pay for it.

Nearly everything connected with the Townshend duties appeared to confirm colonial fears. The revenue would be used for salaries of colonial governors, judges and other royal officials in order to destroy the assemblies, the bulwarks of colonial liberty. No longer would the popularly elected colonial assemblies be able to exercise the power of the purse over colonial officials. Meanwhile, the attack on New York only presaged worse things to come. To enforce the acts and preserve order after a series of protests, the government ordered more troops to the colonies, some of whom wound up camping on the Boston Common. The creation of new customs offices and vice-admiralty courts not only indicated an evil design on freedom, but also manifested the corruption endemic in Britain. The people named to these posts, charged Benjamin Franklin, "came only to make money as fast as they can; are sometimes men of vicious character and broken fortunes, sent by a minister merely to get them out of the way."

The colonial response, in addition to riots and increased smuggling, included another circular letter from the Massachusetts assembly, restating the illegality of parliamentary taxation and urging the other colonies to resist. Lord Hillsborough, the newly appointed secretary of state for the colonies, ordered the letter withdrawn; when the assembly, by a vote of 92 to 17, refused, Governor Francis Bernard dissolved it, which was interpreted as yet another sign of royal intent to crush colonial liberty. Soon the number "92" came to have a symbolic meaning, and as such might be seen as an early example of the real world use of symbolic speech in the era before the Revolution. Thus, it is possible to see in the revolutionary era precursors of constitutional values and rights that would fully come into their own over the next two centuries and beyond.

At the same time in Virginia the House of Burgesses defiantly reasserted its exclusive right to tax Virginians, and the other colonies passed similar resolutions. A nonimportation agreement soon led to a drastic reduction in trade with the mother country, so that by 1769, the Townshend duties brought in only £3,500, less than one-tenth of the original estimate and far less than the cost of collection.

Once again the scenario repeated itself. Hurt by the loss of trade, British merchants clamored for Parliament to act, and in 1770, the new prime minister, Lord Frederick North, repealed all the duties save that on tea, which was to remain as a symbol of British authority. The repeal came just in time, for an unfortunate confrontation between a colonial mob and British troops in Boston on March 5 left five Bostonians dead and eight wounded. This confrontation, known as the Boston Massacre, stood as an example of the dangers of standing armies. Meanwhile, effective royal government rapidly deteriorated, and following the repeal of the Townshend duties, the assemblies provided the only real government in the colonies.

## Tea and the Coercive Acts

The lifting of taxes and withdrawal of troops led to a two-year detente of sorts, in which a surface calm masked the continuing constitutional debate over the nature of imperial relations. By now, Committees of Correspondence existed in all the colonies, ready to alert one another to any real or imagined British wrongdoing, while pamphleteers kept up their barrage attacking corruption and tyranny in the mother country. Throughout all this, the colonists continued to pledge fealty to George III, blaming the detested policies on his advisers.

The passage in 1773 of the Tea Act shattered the peace. Designed by Lord North to help save the financially troubled East India Company, the measure provided for refunding the export duty of twelve pence on all tea shipped to the colonies and collecting only the three pence duty payable at the colonial port. By this arrangement, the colonists would get tea far more cheaply than could people in England, cheaper even than black market Dutch tea brought in by smugglers, but the East India Company would have a monopoly not only on the wholesale, but on the retail trade as well, thus harming numerous colonial merchants. Lord North hoped that cheap tea would secure colonial compliance with the revenue collectors and the new tea monopoly, but the Committees of Correspondence immediately protested and forced many of the company's agents to resign. On December 16, the Sons of Liberty, thinly disguised as Mohawk Indians, boarded three ships in Boston harbor; cheered on by a large crowd on shore, they broke open the tea chests and dumped the contents into the water.

By itself the Tea Act could not have sparked such a stormy renewal of protest. It involved a minimal amount of money, and from a strictly economic viewpoint, the colonists would have benefited by securing the most popular drink in the country at a greatly reduced price. Although some merchants, now excluded from selling tea, resented the act and participated in the protest, by themselves they could not have aroused the populace. But the implications of the act—namely, that the Crown could manipulate the colonial economy and colonial rights at will—seemed to bear out what the pamphleteers had been claiming for nearly a decade. The London government, in John Adams's words, "threw off the mask," and was about to implement its evil plan.

In the spring of 1774, Parliament passed a series of laws known as Coercive Acts to punish Boston for its resistance to the tea act. These laws made rebellion in America inevitable. The government closed the port of Boston until compensation was made for the destroyed tea; the Administration of Justice Act permitted trials to be held in England for certain offenses committed in Massachusetts, bypassing local courts; the Massachusetts Government Act placed all powers, including those previously exercised by town meetings and juries, into the hands of executive officials responsible to the Crown; and the Quartering Act permitted the seizure of unoccupied buildings to house troops solely on the order of the governors, even if barracks space remained available.

The Quebec Act, passed at the same time, extended the boundaries of that Catholic province, one governed solely by executive prerogatives, into lands claimed by Virginia, Massachusetts, and Connecticut, and closed them to further American settlement. Even though all the acts were strongly criticized in Parliament by members either opposed to the government or sympathetic to the colonists, Lord North had his way. After a decade of caving in to colonial opposition, His Majesty's government intended to exert its sovereignty.

To colonial leaders, the Coercive or "Intolerable" Acts confirmed their worst fears about the existence of "a settled, fixed plan for enslaving the colonies." Even moderates like John Dickinson, although hoping that ties between the mother country and the colonies could be maintained by fealty to a common monarch, believed that "a plan had been deliberately framed and pertinaciously adhered to . . . to sacrifice to a passion for arbitrary dominion the universal property, liberty, safety, honor, happiness and prosperity of us unoffending yet devoted Americans." George Washington, who in collaboration with his northern Virginia neighbor George Mason wrote the Fairfax Resolves of 1774, found evidence of a "regular, systematic plan" of oppression. Yet even this late, most writers still put the blame on George III's ministers, rather than on the monarch himself. In Farmington, Connecticut, a thousand inhabitants resolved that "the present ministry being instigated by the devil and led by their wicked and corrupt hearts, have a design to take away our liberties and properties, and to enslave us forever." This desire somehow to preserve the king's innocence reflected the colonists' fear of a total break and their recognition that only the monarchy could serve as a continuing bridge to the mother country. But something had to be done and soon, before the corruption of England destroyed American liberty.

## The First Continental Congress

The impetus for the next step came from Virginia. In Williamsburg, young Thomas Jefferson proposed to the House of Burgesses that June 1, the effective date of the Boston Port Act, be set aside as a day of fasting and prayer. The governor immediately dissolved the assembly, but the members went down the street to the Raleigh Tavern, where they drew up a resolution calling for a "Continental Congress." Similar appeals were soon issued by other colonies, and Massachusetts suggested a meeting in Philadelphia in September. George Washington, on his way to represent Virginia, wrote: "The crisis is arrived when we must assert our rights, or submit to every imposition that can be heaped upon us, till custom and use shall make us as tame and abject slaves."

Legally, the fifty-five delegates who gathered at Carpenter's Hall on September 5, 1774, had no authority at all. True, they had been named by their respective assemblies or, where the legislature could not meet, by irregular conventions. All the North American colonies sent delegates except Georgia, the Floridas, Quebec, Nova Scotia, and Newfoundland. They agreed to vote by colonies—although Patrick Henry urged them to vote as individuals, on the grounds that they had not come there as Virginians or New Yorkers, but as Americans. In fact, just the opposite was true. Colonial writers had developed a constitutional theory that viewed elected delegates not as independent legislators charged with taking a broad overview, but as tightly bound spokesmen for their particular constituencies. New England, for example, had a long tradition in which town meetings issued specific instructions to their assemblymen on how to vote on various matters.

Just the reverse of this theory prevailed in the mother country. At a time when several large cities had no seats in Parliament, Englishmen espoused the notion of "virtual representation," which viewed Parliament as the assembly of all Englishmen; each member looked after the general welfare, not so much for his particular district, but for the nation as a whole. As constitutional theory, this idea had grown alongside England's transformation from a loose confederation of fiefdoms into a unified nation. By this view, the Americans, even without representation in the Commons, had virtual representation there, because its members looked after the interests of all parts of the empire. During the debates over the Stamp Act and the Townshend duties, the colonial cry of "No taxation without representation" had been met by a somewhat puzzled response in England.

Most colonists, however, now shared little sense of common interest with residents of the British Isles; but they had not yet come to see themselves as "Americans" either. Their loyalties were to their respective colonies, and representatives to the assemblies functioned primarily as attorneys for their constituencies, much as had members of the early Parliaments. The experience of the last decade convinced many to agree with Daniel Dulany of Maryland that a representative's primary duty was to protect the people who had elected him from any encroachments by the government. The proper view, James Wilson of Pennsylvania wrote, is for representatives to be the "creatures" of their constituents and to be held fully "accountable for the use of that power which is delegated unto them." But what power had been delegated to the First Continental Congress? Its members had no specific mandate and knew that their proposals would have to be approved by the individual colonies.

The delegates to the Continental Congress hoped, although many feared it was already too late, to develop some plan that would maintain formal ties to England, while removing direct parliamentary authority over the colonies. Joseph Galloway of Pennsylvania proposed a plan of union, similar to Benjamin Franklin's suggestion at the Albany Congress twenty years earlier, in which an American council chosen by the assemblies would have joint authority alongside Parliament. This proposal received support from only five colonies. Instead, the Continental Congress adopted the more radical Suffolk Resolves, which termed the Intolerable Acts null and void and called for economic sanctions against Great Britain.

Congress then approved a Declaration of American Rights, which recognized Parliament's right to regulate trade and those matters directly related to imperial affairs, but denied it any authority in colonial government. In addition, Congress sent the king a petition for relief and issued addresses to the people of Great Britain explaining how the Americans were merely defending their rights as English citizens. Aware that Parliament would hardly agree to their demands, Congress also called on the colonies to boycott British goods and urged the formation of committees in every town to enforce nonimportation.

Had the Crown been willing to grant the colonies internal autonomy, there might not have been a revolution, for the Americans still retained enormous affection and respect for their English heritage. Self-government, but nothing less, would have satisfied them, since that would have put an end to what they perceived as Parliament's efforts to encroach on colonial liberties. Some in Britain recognized the force of the colonial arguments and concerns, at least in part. Pitt urged acceptance of the American view on taxation and suggested a compromise by which the colonies would vote a revenue to the Crown. Edmund Burke agreed, and in an eloquent plea for conciliation, he declared the American actions to be fully consonant with English principles.

But the majority in both Lords and Commons had no patience for further colonial impudence and declared Massachusetts to be in a state of rebellion. Lord North did offer a conciliatory resolution in February 1775, by which Parliament offered to refrain from imposing any taxes on the colonies save those regulating trade, if the colonies would "voluntarily" contribute set quotas for defense of the empire. But as Burke noted, North's formula would only lead to new quarrels.

## Parting of the Ways

Too many quarrels already existed. The Massachusetts House of Representatives met in October 1774, in defiance of Governor Thomas Gage, and ordered preparations to resist royal authority; the following April, Redcoats and Minutemen exchanged shots at Lexington and Concord. By the time the Second Continental Congress met in Philadelphia on May 10, 1775, royal troops in Boston were under siege by the Massachusetts militia, and Fort Ticonderoga had fallen to Ethan Allen and his Green Mountain Boys. Lacking any specific legal authority, Congress nonetheless "adopted" the ragtag army surrounding Boston as its own, and on June 15, it named George Washington commander-in-chief. To support this venture, it voted to issue $2 million in paper money, which the colonies would pledge to redeem in proportion to their population.

Although the chances for compromise with the mother country appeared dim, in July 1775, Congress issued two documents written by John Dickinson. One, known as the Olive Branch Petition, restated colonial loyalty to George III and begged him to put an end to the hostilities. Realizing that such a plea had little hope of success, the following day Congress published a "Declaration of the Causes and Necessity of Taking Up Arms," which rehearsed all the grievances that had been building for more than a decade. When the Olive Branch petition reached London, the king would not even look at it, and on August 23, he issued a proclamation declaring the colonies to be in a state of rebellion.

The colonies stood poised to declare their independence, a step greatly hastened by the publication of Thomas Paine's *Common Sense*. Although the pamphlet did not appear until January 1776, its ideas had already received wide circulation in the form of serialized newspaper articles. Paine attacked the last tenuous link binding the colonies to the mother country, allegiance to the king. In brilliant fashion, he demolished the argument that George III had had nothing to do with the attacks upon American freedom; rather, the king and his friends shared responsibility with

Parliament for all that had happened. Americans must look to their own interests, and once having done so, they would recognize the obvious: "TIS TIME TO PART!" Within three months, more than 100,000 copies of the most radical pamphlet of the time were circulating among the colonists. One by one, the assemblies instructed their delegates to support independence, and on July 2, 1776, Congress adopted Richard Henry Lee's resolution "that these United Colonies are, and of right ought to be, free and independent states." A few days later, it adopted the Declaration of Independence.

Years later, John Adams, reflecting on these events, declared that "the Revolution was effected before the war commenced. The Revolution was in the minds of the people." Certainly, the debate over the constitutional issues—that is, the powers of the imperial government as opposed to the rights of the colonies—appears to have been all but concluded before Galloway introduced his plan for union or Richard Henry Lee declared that the colonies should be independent states.

Independent state governments had by now appeared in every colony. Popularly elected assemblies had either replaced or coopted the colonial legislatures, while royal officials had vacated their offices or, in the case of the governors, had found themselves powerless. Americans—that is, men who were self-consciously loyal not to Great Britain but to their own colonies—had taken over most of the executive and judicial offices. The new state governments had authorized the delegates to the Second Continental Congress to cut the remaining ties to the empire, although there was little agreement on how far or how fast this should happen. Massachusetts, the Carolinas, Georgia, and Virginia all voted for complete and immediate separation, but the middle colonies, from New York to Maryland, initially held back. During June 1776, however, events in those colonies spurred them down the road toward independence, even as a committee composed of Thomas Jefferson (who did most of the writing), John Adams, Benjamin Franklin, Roger Sherman, and Robert R. Livingston labored on the document that would formalize the separation.

## The Declaration of Independence

The Declaration of Independence, said John Adams, had not a single new idea in it, and it certainly shows the influence of John Locke and other English writers, as well as the notions of government that had been discussed intensively in the colonies for nearly fifteen years in hundreds of pamphlets. The Declaration is, in fact, a propaganda document designed to justify radical, unprecedented, and unlawful action, by shifting blame to a wicked king and Parliament while maintaining that the colonists had done no more than protect their God-given rights. By putting aside for the moment Jefferson's magnificent generalizations about human liberty, and examining the document on its own terms, we find the ablest of all the revolutionary documents.

Like all good propagandists, Jefferson distorted history to serve his purpose. Drawing heavily on Locke's compact theory of government, he charged the British king with having violated that unwritten agreement. The Crown had claimed prerogatives it had never been granted, while a perverse Parliament had attempted to legislate in areas over which it had never enjoyed sovereignty. He termed Parliament "foreign to our constitution, and unacknowledged by our laws," a statement that most colonists prior to 1756 would have had difficulty endorsing. Certainly for the larger part of the colonial period, Parliament had determined policy for America, and the right of the Crown to disallow colonial statutes had gone unchallenged for decades. But now the colonies claimed those rights that King George III allegedly had subverted. He had withdrawn his protection; he was seeking an "absolute Despotism"; he had, in short, breached the contract.

The long list of grievances Jefferson marshaled to support this charge is hardly convincing to an objective observer. George III may not have been a good king, but he was far from the tyrannical ogre portrayed in the Declaration. Nonetheless, such accusations seemed necessary to justify the colonists' radical step of dissolving "the Political Bands which have connected them with another, and to assume the Powers of the Earth, the separate and equal Station to which the Laws of Nature and of Nature's God entitle them." Politically, the Declaration provided Americans with a convincing apologia for separation, and because they succeeded in their revolution, later generations have tended to take the bill of indictment at face value. Certainly, in pledging their lives, their fortunes, and their sacred honor, the fifty-six men who signed the document indicated that they saw no way to preserve their liberties other than through rebellion.

## Conclusion

Constitutionally, the Declaration of Independence served several purposes. It enshrined the compact theory as the heart of American philosophy on government, not only for the revolutionary generation, but for all succeeding ones as well. Long after the particular grievances against George III had been forgotten, the belief that government existed to preserve the rights of the people—and could be dissolved if it failed to do so—remained a prime article of faith for Americans. Moreover, Jefferson's noble statement of the rights of man became a beacon for future generations, not only in the United States, but throughout the world.

Not a few Englishmen read the Declaration and wondered, as did Samuel Johnson, "How is it that we hear the loudest *yelps* for liberty among the drivers of negroes?" Certainly this was true of Jefferson, who owned about 150 human beings when he wrote the Declaration. But, despite the obvious contradiction between the practices of the primary author of the Declaration, the path of American constitutional development would eventually be directed toward the implementation of Jefferson's premises that certain truths are self-evident, that all men are created equal, that they are endowed with certain unalienable rights, and that governments derive their power from the consent of the governed. Such sentiments have not lost their power to inspire men and women to this day.

# For Further Reading

The literature on American colonial life and the coming of independence is immense. Some older works, such as Charles M. Andrews, *The Colonial Period of American History*, Vol. 4 (1938) and Leonard W. Labaree, *Royal Government in America* (1930), are still rewarding for an overview of imperial policy, as are the relevant volumes of Lawrence Henry Gipson's *The British Empire Before the American Revolution*, 15 vols. (1936–1970). More recent works that shed light on this period include Peter Onuf, ed., *Jeffersonian Legacies* (1993); Donald L. Robinson, *Slavery in the Structure of American Politics, 1765–1820* (1971); William M. Wiecek, *The Sources of Antislavery Constitutionalism in America, 1760–1848* (1977); J. R. Pole, *The Pursuit of Equality in American History* (1978); and Paul Finkelman, *Slavery and the Founders: Race and Liberty in the Age of Jefferson* (2nd ed., 2001).

The theory of mercantilism is explained in Eli Heckscher, *Mercantilism,* 2 vols. (1935); for its practice, see, among others, Thomas C. Barrows, *Trade and Empire* (1967) and O. M. Dickerson, *The Navigation Acts and the American Revolution* (1951). The tensions resulting from imperial policy are explored in Ian K. Steele, *The Politics of Colonial Policy: The Board of Trade in Colonial Administration, 1696–1720* (1968).

There are a number of works on government in the different colonies, such as Lucille Griffith, *The Virginia House of Burgesses, 1750–1774* (1963); George E. Frakes, *Laboratory for Liberty: The South Carolina Legislative Committee System, 1719–1776* (1970); and Jack P. Greene, *The Quest for Power: The Lower Houses of Assembly in the Southern Royal Colonies, 1689–1776* (1963). More general works include Lawrence Leder, *Liberty and Authority: Early American Political Ideology, 1689–1763* (1968).

The debate over the sources of American constitutional thought has been vigorous and gives no indication of fading away. Among works that find the source in Lockean liberalism are Benjamin F. Wright, Jr., *American Interpretations of Natural Law* (1931) and Clinton Rossiter, *Seedtime of the Republic* (1953). Chester J. Antieau, *Rights of Our Fathers* (1968), reasserts the claim that the natural rights doctrine was the most popular political philosophy in eighteenth-century America. George Mace, on the other hand, in *Locke, Hobbes, and "The Federalist Papers"* (1979), argues that Hobbes and not Locke is the real intellectual and political forebear of constitutional thought because of his views on the need for the balancing of factions.

One of the most influential works of our time is Bernard Bailyn, *The Ideological Origins of the American Revolution* (1967), an expansion of his introduction to the four-volume *Pamphlets of the American Revolution* (1965– ). There, and in *The Origin of American Politics* (1968), Bailyn argues that American constitutional thought derived from the republican thought of the British "commonwealthmen" such as John Trenchard and Thomas Gordon. He also makes a very strong statement summing up the theory that the American Revolution was, above all else, a constitutional struggle. Other works that emphasize republican ideology include Gordon Wood, *The Creation of the American Republic, 1776–1787* (1969); Gordon Wood, *The Radicalism of the American Revolution* (1992); Garry Wills, *Inventing America: Jefferson's Declaration of Independence* (1978); and Morton White, *The Philosophy of the American Revolution* (1978). For a fascinating study in intellectual influence, see J. G. A. Pocock, *The Machiavellian Moment: Florentine Political Thought and the Atlantic Republican Tradition* (1975).

How these views affected the course of events is described in Pauline Maier, *From Resistance to Revolution: Colonial Radicals and the Development of American Opposition to Great Britain, 1765–1776* (1972). How the ideas matured and affected particular individuals is examined in Peter Shaw, *The Character of John Adams* (1976) and Dumas Malone, *Jefferson, the Virginian* (1948).

The English perspective is elegantly explored by Sir Lewis Namier in *England in the Age of the American Revolution* (1961); see also Bernard Donoughue, *British Politics and the American Revolution: The Path to War* (1964). Edmund S. Morgan and Helen Morgan, *Prologue to Revolution: The Stamp Act Crisis* (1953), remains the best work on that subject for the colonial view; the imperial side is examined in P. D. G. Thomas, *British Politics and the Stamp Act Crisis* (1975). See also Benjamin Larabee, *The Boston Tea Party* (1964) for a discussion of the last stages of mercantilism. Carl Becker, *The Declaration of Independence* (1922), is a classic still worth reading, although some of his arguments are no longer accepted. Other interpretations of the events in Philadelphia that spring of 1776 are in Wills, *Inventing America,* and the relevant chapters of Merrill Jensen, *The Founding of a Nation* (1968).

# 4

# *The Revolutionary Era*

*Congress Governs • The Articles of Confederation • New State Governments • Conservatives and Radicals • State Constitutions • Religious Freedom • Slavery • Judicial Review and the Success and Failure of State Constitutions in the Revolutionary Era • The Common Law Survives • Blackstone's Influence • Conclusion • For Further Reading*

W ITH INDEPENDENCE PROCLAIMED, a new chapter in American history began. People who for more than a century and a half had considered themselves primarily English citizens in imperial outposts now proudly declared themselves "Americans." However, although they continued to treasure much of their English heritage, they were also determined to discard those aspects they believed detrimental to their liberty. Even while fighting the Revolution, Americans began their first experiments in molding new governments, both in state constitutions and in the Articles of Confederation. They did not, however, write on an empty slate, and these initial forays clearly reflected the ideas of the Enlightenment as well as the American's experience with partial self-government in the colonial period. The founders of the new state governments, as well as of the new national government, also drew on their English heritage, especially the tumultuous events of the seventeenth century that led to the English Civil War, the beheading of King Charles I, and the Glorious Revolution.

Before creating a new constitutional order, the Americans first had to secure their independence and provide legitimacy to their government.

## Congress Governs

Although residents of the thirteen rebelling colonies called themselves Americans, there were nearly as many factors dividing as uniting them. The New England farmer had little in common with the Tidewater planter or the Philadelphia merchant. Different religious, economic, and social systems, as well as intellectual patterns, could easily have sent the colonies along divergent paths. But the external crisis provided a common danger, and the appointment of George Washington as commander-in-chief created a rallying point for the militia and Continental troops. With the exception of declaring independence, no other act of the Second Continental Congress proved so decisive to the ultimate victory. But while Washington fought the British, Congress and the states had to govern the new country.

Until 1781, the Second Continental Congress, with its committees and administrative officials, served as the central government of the United States. No written constitution legitimized its acts; no courts approved its legislation. Yet, drawing on the theory that all sovereign governments enjoyed inherent powers to rule, Congress went about its business, and its achievements reinforced its legitimacy. Its record, by any criterion, is impressive: Congress declared independence; appointed officers to conduct the war; established a navy and marine corps; formed a small but effective diplomatic service; negotiated treaties with European countries and with various Indian tribes; issued currency and borrowed money; set up a postal service; and drew up the nation's first written constitution, the Articles of Confederation and Perpetual Union. It also offered guidance to the states, as they wrote their own constitutions. Had the war been lost, all these acts would, of course, have been nullified (as the work of the Confederate Congress would be after the Civil War). But military victory not only legitimated congressional policies; it also established the basis for an ongoing central government.

What constitutional form the new nation would take remained far from clear during the Revolution. From the start, tensions existed between the states and Congress. Some states asserted their own independence and acted as if they were sovereign powers. A few sent diplomatic representatives to Europe, where they attempted to borrow money. Nearly all kept close tabs on their representatives to the Congress, and a number of important measures, including the Declaration of Independence, could not be approved until delegates received instructions from the state legislatures.

Some historians have argued that during the Revolutionary period the real power lay with the states, with Congress little more than "the central office of a continental political signal system." It is true that after 1776, Congress lost many of its most brilliant figures. George Washington, John Adams, Thomas Jefferson, and Benjamin Franklin, all departed for the military or to take up different state or national offices. Other key members, like John Dickinson, were in and out of Congress, serving in the military as well as in state government. Congress often seemed immobilized by conflicting personal and ideological interests as well as by regional antagonisms, and critics point to indecision, chronic absenteeism (which sometimes prevented any business being transacted), and petty self-seeking. The failures of the Congress have been well catalogued, including the inability to establish a stable currency, interference in military matters, and naivete in foreign affairs. Nonetheless, given the extremely difficult conditions under which it labored, it is clear that the Second Continental Congress accomplished much in the face of enormous obstacles, including of course a war against the world's strongest military power.

# The Articles of Confederation

In 1775, more than a year before it declared independence, the Second Continental Congress had begun to discuss the idea of a formal union. Benjamin Franklin had put forward a plan entitled "Articles of Confederation and Perpetual Union," which most delegates immediately realized entailed independence from Great Britain. So long as they remained unwilling to take the one step (union), they would not move on the other (independence). The New Jersey and North Carolina legislatures explicitly rejected Franklin's plan; the latter declared that "a further confederacy ought only to be adopted in case of the last extremity." When Richard Henry Lee finally offered his resolution for independence on June 7, 1776, he too called for the establishment of a confederation. Although it would take five years to work out the details, nearly all the delegates assumed that the colonies had to unite constitutionally in order to secure and preserve their independence from Great Britain. They further agreed that Congress should be the agency to draft the document and should submit it to the states for ratification.

A constitution defines the nature of a government, but there was little agreement among either the delegates to the Congress or the states as to what form the new union should take. Nonetheless, on June 12, Congress appointed a committee, consisting of one representative from each state, to come up with a plan; within a month the committee presented its draft to Congress. Although derived in part from Franklin's plan and in part from the experience of the Congress, the proposal, drafted primarily by John Dickinson, who had returned from military service as a delegate from Delaware, went much further toward creating a powerful and effective central government than most delegates or states wanted to consider at the time.

The Dickinson draft provided for a one-house, or unicameral, legislature with members chosen annually by the states. Following the existing pattern of the Congress, votes would be cast by states rather than by individual delegates, and all states would have an equal vote. Both explicitly and implicitly, the legislature would enjoy large powers, lacking only the very important ability to levy taxes; revenue would continue to be raised and controlled by the states. Congress, if the states consented, could name commissions to settle boundary disputes; Congress could also set limits to claims on western lands and form new states when necessary. In theory, with the exception of the taxing power, the lack of a national court system, and the lack of a national executive, the government proposed by Dickinson and his committee might have been nearly as strong as that created under the Constitution of 1787. Although the committee hoped for quick approval, the proposal touched off a bitter controversy and lengthy debate.

Delegates from the more populous states objected to the provision for equal voting; they wanted some form of proportional representation reflecting their larger populations and the greater sums they would be contributing to the government. The smaller states rejected this view, believing that any proportional system would lead to domination by Virginia, Pennsylvania, and Massachusetts. How the financial levies would be assessed proved another sticking point.

The issue of financing the government also led to the first of many heated debates over the place of slavery in the new republic. Southerners argued that the population basis proposed by the committee would be acceptable only if slaves were excluded from the count, while Northerners insisted that it include slaves. Southerners responded that slaves were "property" and warned that if there was to be a debate over the status of slavery, then there could be no national government. Thomas Lynch of South Carolina argued that since slaves were "property, why should they be taxed more than the land, sheep, cattle, [or] horses" of the North. Benjamin Franklin wryly answered because slaves were different than these other kinds of property. Franklin reminded the Congress that "sheep will never make any insurrections." The issue of slavery did not break the confederation apart at this time, but its corrosive potential was clearly present at the founding. In the vote over taxing slaves, seven northern states voted one way, while Virginia, Maryland, Delaware, and the Carolinas voted against them.

Since more than half the states claimed western lands on the basis of their original patents, they objected to the provision giving Congress the authority to set western boundaries. The six small states lacking even shadowy claims to western territory supported the Dickinson proposal as the only fair basis to ensure equal opportunity to all Americans to settle and exploit the area. They also feared that if the larger states retained these western lands, they would become even more powerful and thus gain permanent control over the government.

Throughout the following year, Congress wrestled with revisions that it hoped would secure prompt acceptance by the states. Several times work had to be stopped as Congress fled to Baltimore or to York, Pennsylvania, to escape approaching English troops. The low ebb of American military fortunes did impel Congress to greater efforts at compromise, since the delegates believed that only an effective union would assure independence and gain foreign support. Congress approved a new draft that retained voting by states, set no western boundaries for the "landed" states, and assessed financial contributions according to the value of improved lands rather than population. Congress submitted the Articles to the states in November 1777; it acknowledged that the instrument would not be satisfactory to everyone, but begged that local interests be set aside for the good of the patriot cause. Rather naively, the delegates hoped that the new union could be proclaimed by the second anniversary of the Declaration of Independence.

Such would not be the case. The states acted slowly and attached numerous conditions and amendments to the Articles, all of which Congress rejected in June. By the end of the summer of 1778, ten states had ratified, but Maryland, New Jersey, and Delaware continued to insist that Congress have the power to set western boundaries for the landed states. Once again Congress appealed to the patriotism of the dissidents, and New Jersey and Delaware signed the following winter; Maryland, however, held out. Since implementation of the Articles required unanimous consent, Virginia, which claimed more western land than any other state, proposed, in the spring of 1779, that a new union be formed without Maryland. Fearing that an incomplete union would be as dangerous as no union at all, the larger states, starting with New York, indicated a willingness to abandon their western claims. Despite the objections of speculators who stood to lose large interests, all the landed states ceded their western claims to Congress by early 1781. In February, the Maryland legislature finally instructed its delegates to sign the instrument, and on March 1, 1781, Congress, amidst much public rejoicing, proclaimed the creation of a perpetual union.

In practical terms, the Articles did not greatly alter how Congress had governed since 1775. The new Congress had roughly the same powers as the previous one. Each state had between two and seven delegates, but only one vote. Among the new provisions, one required the assent of nine states for important decisions such as ratifying treaties, making war, or borrowing money. When Congress recessed, a "Committee of States," with one representative from each state, would serve as an interim government with all powers to act except in those areas requiring the approval of nine states. Congress also received the power to create executive departments, and it ultimately established five—foreign affairs, finance, admiralty, war, and a post office. In general, the Articles left no doubt that in the federal system its Framers envisioned, the sovereignty of the states stood higher than that of the national government.

As experience would soon show, the Articles of Confederation failed to cement an enduring union; its deficiencies, especially when compared with the Constitution of 1787, have led many observers to discount its importance. Even in 1781, some contemporaries doubted whether government under the Articles would work efficiently. But the Framers of this first national constitution never claimed perfection for it; and while the Union was to be "perpetual," the Framers of the Articles did not expect their handiwork to exist in perpetuity. Rather, they expected changes to be made and built an amendment process into the document. Indeed, with some amendments, the Articles might well have served the new nation as a usable scheme of government for many years.

Despite their problems, the Articles did mark a major step in forging a permanent union out of thirteen disparate states. In ratifying the Articles, the states indicated their willingness to join in the nation-making process; despite their fears of powerful government, they understood the necessity of some centralized authority. The government after 1781 had powers exceeding those of the Second Continental Congress; more important, those powers derived from a written document that had been solemnly ratified by the states.

## New State Governments

While Congress wrestled with the problem of a national constitution, the thirteen new states attempted to put their own governments in order. Many people thought that with independence the colonies would dissolve, leaving only the new nation. For example, Patrick Henry told his fellow delegates to the Congress: "Where are your landmarks, your boundaries of Colonies? . . . The distinctions between Virginians, Pennsylvanians, New Yorkers and New Englanders are no more. I am not a Virginian; I am an American . . . All distinctions are thrown down; all America is one mass." Henry would later oppose a strong national government and work hard to defeat ratification of the Constitution of 1787. But, in the heat of the revolutionary moment, he articulated the notion of a true, unified nation.

However, with no experience other than as individual colonies, and with Congress neither seeking nor advocating a single government, the states drew upon the traditions they knew best: their own charters as well as the great documents of English liberties. Although several states requested advice from the Congress as to the form their future governments should take, in the main they built on the foundations of their colonial structures.

As the royal governors fled the continent or retreated to British lines, the newly formed states elected their own governors and other officials, usually granting them fewer powers than their royal predecessors; the legislatures remained practically unchanged; the major alteration in the court systems involved simply the mode of appointing judges. Connecticut and Rhode Island adopted their colonial charters, with minor adjustments, keeping them well into the nineteenth century.

The New England states believed that their written charters had made them more secure in their liberties, and all the states assumed that some sort of fundamental law, embodied in a written document, would be required to guarantee their independence and liberties. Constitutions also provided another rallying point in the struggle for independence. The drafters of the New Jersey constitution of 1776 wrote in the document that it was "absolutely necessary, not only for the preservation of good order, but also the more effectually to unite the people and enable them to exert their whole force in their own necessary defense."

Most state constitutions emphasized a distribution and balance of powers, ideas derived not from the parliamentary model, but from the writings of English and continental writers, especially John Locke and the Baron de Montesquieu, as well as the political experience the Americans had learned during the Colonial period. The papers of the leading American political thinkers, such as John Adams and Thomas Jefferson, are full of references to such ideas, and a number of Americans blamed English tyranny on the failure to keep executive, legislative, and judicial functions separate. The pamphlets of the revolutionary era, above all the "Novanglus" papers of John Adams, all called for separation of functions in order to carry out the great goal of government— the preservation of individual liberties. The idea of checks and balances, formalized in a written fundamental document, had become well known by the time the states set about writing their constitutions.

One pamphlet that received wide circulation at this time summarized much of this thought. At the request of Richard Henry Lee, John Adams composed his "Thoughts on Government" to serve as a model for the states. Adams proposed a popularly elected House of Commons, which in turn would elect an upper legislative chamber; together they would choose the governor and other executive officers. The governor would have fairly extensive powers, including a veto on legislation, command of the militia, and, with the consent of the upper house, the appointment of inferior officials and judges. As soon as independence had been secured and more tranquil times arrived, the election of the governor could be transferred to the people. With this proposal in mind, on May 10, 1776, Congress passed Adams's resolution that all states not yet provided with a permanent constitution should quickly adopt one.

Constitution-making varied from state to state. New Hampshire and South Carolina, where Tory opposition to independence ran strong, hastily drew up documents designed to last only until the emergency ended and an accommodation could be made with the mother country. Both documents had to be rewritten within a few years. In the other two states that adopted constitutions before July 1776, Virginia and New Jersey, stronger revolutionary sentiment meant that more care and thought went into the drafting. Both constitutions, although written in the midst of political turmoil, lasted well into the nineteenth century. Rhode Island and Connecticut decided to retain their colonial charters, modifying them to remove any references to England and the Crown. Massachusetts, acting as if it had always been an independent state, simply continued self-government under its 1691 charter, but without a royal governor. In 1780, the Bay State adopted a Constitution written largely by John Adams and then ratified by the state's voters.

None of the states initially convened a specially elected convention for the task of drafting a constitution. Many states treated their constitution as a piece of legislation; Virginia, for example, designated its constitution as Chapters I and II of the Commonwealth's statutes. Many Americans did not consider designing a constitution as either a rigorous or a unique task; they simply wanted their basic rights protected by a written instrument. Until 1778, none of the states submitted its work to a popular vote. The Congress did urge upon the states the need for "full and free representation of the people" in such an undertaking, a direct reflection of Locke's compact theory of government.

Initially, the legislatures saw no need for special conventions, since elections for new assemblies took place in nearly all the states. In seven states there were special legislative elections because drafting a constitution would be among the tasks of the body. In September 1776, the general court of Massachusetts asked the towns whether they would permit it to draft a new constitution. Concord, along with the other towns, vigorously opposed the idea. In a strongly worded resolution to the general court, the Concord town meeting described the purpose of the new constitution as being "to secure the subject in the possession and enjoyment of their rights and privileges, against any encroachment of the governing part." If one assembly of the general court could enact a fundamental law, then another could just as easily retract it. Only the people, in special convocation, had the power to create a fundamental law. In Pittsfield, the town meeting demanded that any constitution be validated by popular approval. Nonetheless, the legislature drafted a constitution, which the people overwhelmingly defeated through votes in the state's town meetings in 1778. Among their many complaints, the people of Massachusetts objected to the constitution because it did not end slavery in the new state and because it did not allow blacks and Indians to vote. In 1780, the people of Massachusetts approved a constitution written at a state constitutional convention. This new document had a powerful declaration of rights written by John Adams.

Similarly, in New Hampshire in 1779, the towns disapproved the first constitution proposed by a convention; in 1783, a second convention drafted a document that finally received public approbation in 1784. Like the Massachusetts constitution, New Hampshire's began with a universal call for equality and liberty, declaring that "all men are born equally free and independent."

Although unusual at the time, the procedure used by Massachusetts and New Hampshire marked the beginning of the now familiar devices of constitutional conventions and public ratification. Moreover, the need for popular approval confirmed the idea that constitutions were superior to regular legislation, setting up a hierarchy of values that would later become the basis for judicial review.

In most states, however, popular involvement centered on elections to the legislatures. The hotly fought contests pitted conservatives desiring to maintain elite control of state government against radicals committed to introducing greater democracy. Yet, despite manifest inequities in many states in apportioning delegates, nearly every legislature or convention included that state's ablest political thinkers. Virginia boasted George Mason, James Madison, and Edmund Pendleton; South Carolina, John Rutledge and Henry Laurens; John Jay, Robert R. Livingston, and Gouverneur Morris participated in New York. John Adams drafted much of the Massachusetts constitution adopted in 1780. Considering that many of them had to attend to the daily press of business relating to the war, the fact that some constitutions proved ill founded and short-lived is less striking than the high quality and significant political advances and innovations that characterized the majority.

## Conservatives and Radicals

There is a continuing historical debate over how much republican reform actually occurred during the Revolution, and whether the American people merely substituted a local elite to rule in place of the royally sponsored aristocracy. The debates over the state constitutions provide evidence of both trends. Although no clear alignment of specific socioeconomic factions developed, two major groupings did emerge.

Conservatives throughout the nation argued for a balance in the powers of government, with fairly strong executive and judicial branches to check the excesses of a popularly elected legislature. They wanted proper deference paid to wealth, so they proposed property qualifications for both voting and officeholding. Most of these men had been influential in the colonies, and they wanted, as much as possible, to perpetuate the old economic and political relationships—minus the Crown. Instead of the king and his surrogates, they wanted the propertied, the educated, and the socially eminent to govern. They feared majority rule because they believed the lower classes to be not only incapable of government, but depraved as well. Although the conservatives had not hesitated to encourage "mob rule" in the earlier protests against Great Britain, they now predicted anarchy or tyranny should the mob gain control. Given their way, some would have imposed an American aristocracy, with society ruled by the better classes; they read Locke as the landed aristocracy and British merchants had done following the Glorious Revolution. In this view of the compact theory of government, the lower classes had little to say and did not deserve to be full partners. For the conservatives, government existed to maintain social order and to preserve wealth.

The second group, the radicals, did not view independence as the sole aim of the Revolution; they wanted to secure what they considered basic human rights. They saw the question less as whether British or American governors would rule, but as how to limit government of any sort in order to preserve their liberties. They read their Locke to emphasize the social contract in which all the governed participated equally. Suffrage, therefore, should be available to all free men, regardless of wealth, and legislatures should be fairly apportioned so that no one faction could control the state. They wanted to concentrate power in popularly elected assemblies, since such bodies had proven receptive to the popular will during the colonial era. The radicals thought of government as a necessary institution, but one which had to be continuously watched lest it erode their liberties. Many wanted legislators to be elected annually, to keep them constantly under the direct influence of the voters. Governors and judges would be kept in check by severely limiting their powers and restricting their terms in office.

In the struggle between conservatives and radicals, the latter enjoyed important advantages. The Tories, most of whom would have allied with the conservatives, took little part in the deliberations, while many men who would not have been permitted to vote under colonial rules had helped to choose revolutionary conventions and legislatures; they now clung to the ballot, considering it their right, and sided with the radicals. Moreover, in the struggle against Britain, most revolutionaries utilized the rhetoric of natural rights, and the conservatives found it awkward to deny demands made by their fellow patriots in the name of those rights. Fortunately for the future of the country, class lines were still fluid, and many men who by birth or property would have been conservative in a more stratified society shared the views of the radicals. Some of the most eloquent defenses of individual liberties came from well-to-do planters, property owners, and merchants such as Thomas Jefferson, George Wythe, Benjamin Franklin, and Elbridge Gerry. As a result, in many places victory went to the faction that won over the large group of uncommitted moderates.

## State Constitutions

In those states where either the conservatives or the radicals gained the upper hand, the resulting constitutions often proved ill suited to the needs of government—although the documents in some cases remained in force for decades. In North Carolina, for example, where the radicals controlled the drafting committee, they created a nearly powerless executive. The governor had only a one-year term and could not serve more than three terms in any six-year period; his executive council had to keep a journal, which the assembly could examine on demand; and he could neither appoint any of the important state officers nor veto any legislation. He could grant pardons and reprieves and, in unusual circumstances, command the militia. As one satisfied radical put it, the governor had "power" to sign a receipt for his salary. The excesses royal governors inflicted upon North Carolina before the Revolution would not be repeated.

In Virginia, moderates gained control, and by correcting the most glaring abuses of the colonial government, they forestalled more radical measures. By 1775, the Tidewater and the Piedmont regions, normally political enemies, stood united in condemning the royal government. Inequities in taxation, representation, economic regulations, as well as the established status of the Church of England "urgently required reformation," as Jefferson noted, but many of these issues were in fact glossed over as moderates pushed for a government that would immediately meet the needs of the state. Although the Old Dominion had its share of more extreme radicals and conservatives, the moderates managed to secure a document that worked fairly well for more than fifty years. Clearly democratic in nature, its well-defined functions balanced the governmental departments; although imperfect in some areas, it represented a significant improvement over the colonial scheme.

The Virginia constitution's crowning glory, the Declaration of Rights, came from the hand of the learned George Mason. In few other documents of the time can one see so clearly how Americans cherished and expanded on their English heritage while incorporating many of the lessons of the colonial experience. Mason asserted that all authority is derived from the people, who, when government becomes evil, have the power to change it. The declaration guaranteed a trial by jury, prohibited cruel and unusual punishments and abuses of search warrants, and affirmed freedom of the press and the subordination of the military to the civil power. Although it served as a model for similar enactments in other states, as well as for the later federal Bill of Rights, it was hardly complete. It did not guarantee the right of habeas corpus freedom of speech, assembly, or petition; and it failed to prohibit double jeopardy or ban bills of attainder, which Governor Thomas Jefferson, among others, used to arrest Tories during the Revolution. James Madison was particularly disappointed that the Virginia Declaration of Rights did not disestablish the Episcopal Church, which had replaced the Anglican Church as the official religion of the state. Most importantly, the Virginia aristocrats who so eloquently advocated liberty for themselves, did not consider the liberty of their enslaved black neighbors. This was also true for the constitution-makers in the other southern states.

Conservative thought dominated constitution-making in Maryland and New York, where local aristocracies retained control for another generation. Maryland, although limiting the governor's power, provided for a bicameral legislature, with the upper house chosen indirectly through an electoral college, an idea proposed unsuccessfully by Mason in Virginia. Officeholders and legislators had to meet substantial property qualifications, especially in the senate, where each member had to own at least £1,000 in property. The governor had to be worth at least £5,000, including a £1,000 freehold estate. He also had to be a Christian.

In New York, the drafters operated under considerable difficulty, since much of the early fighting in the war took place there, and the British occupied New York City throughout the war. John Jay, credited as the constitution's chief author, left his seat in Congress to do the work, with a copy of Adams's "Thoughts on Government" in his pocket. His labors produced a document that most contemporaries believed the best of the early state constitutions. It provided for clearly defined responsibilities among the branches, a popularly elected governor with adequate powers, and a judiciary whose duties were spelled out far better than in most states. The bicameral legislature had a lower house fairly apportioned by population, and periodic adjustments were required according to a mandated septennial census. Property qualifications continued for most voters, although at the insistence of Gouverneur Morris, freemen in Albany and New York City retained their colonial privilege of suffrage. The constitution's chief defects lay in two innovative agencies, the council for appointments and the council for revision, which were designed as conservative checks on the legislature and the governor. Both councils ultimately proved unworkable, something impossible to determine in 1777. Unlike every other state, New York provided full religious freedom for all people and had no religious qualifications for officeholding. New York's constitution contrasted sharply, for example, with Maryland's, which limited "religious liberty" only to people "professing the Christian religion."

Whatever their individual differences, the various state constitutions shared many common features. In general, they all provided for an elected assembly; every state but Pennsylvania had a bicameral legislature; all had a governor, although in some states the people elected the chief executive and in others the legislature made the choice; and all had some property requirements for both officeholding, the ballot, or both although these varied considerably and had significant exceptions. Moreover, with land so cheap, in most states a large majority of the free males could meet the property qualifications, at least for the ballot, and the voting population of the new states greatly exceeded that of the colonies. Nevertheless, the property requirements tended to diminish the political voice of urban dwellers, sailors, and free blacks, even in places like New York, Pennsylvania, and North Carolina, where there were no racial restrictions on voting at this time. All the state constitutions tried, with varying degrees of success, to provide for separation of powers, and most contained some form of bill of rights. Many of the inequities in apportionment disappeared; in Virginia, for example, the Piedmont and Shenandoah regions for the first time had representation reflecting their populations.

For the most part, the bulk of governmental power resided in the assemblies. A few states gave their governor ample powers, but only Massachusetts allowed him an effective veto over legislation. In colonial times the governor had represented the oppressive hand of the Crown, and the revolutionaries now sought to limit the danger they believed inherent in the executive. The Maryland constitution of 1776 condemned "a long continuance" in "executive departments" as "dangerous to liberty," and rotation, therefore, "one of the best securities of personal freedom." The framers limited the governor to a one-year term, with a maximum of three successive terms. There would then be a four-year hiatus before that person would be eligible for reelection.

## Religious Freedom

One measure of the limited radicalism of the American Revolution can been seen in the various states' provisions for religious freedom. Before the Revolutionary War, despite established churches in nine colonies, religious toleration had been fairly extensive, the result of a frontier society peopled by numerous religious groups. Only Rhode Island, however, provided for complete religious freedom, and even there Catholics and Jews faced some limits on officeholding and the franchise. In the other colonies, restrictions varied from mild in New York, Delaware, and Pennsylvania to onerous in New England, Maryland, and Virginia. Connecticut law still required church attendance, while Maryland allowed the prosecution of people who openly rejected the divinity of Christ. In Virginia, taxes supported the Church of England; dissenters needed a permit from the government to build churches, and their ministers needed a license to preach. Baptist preachers were often fined, whipped, or imprisoned, in what James Madison called the "diabolical Hell . . . of persecution."

The move to disestablish the Church of England, which enjoyed official status in parts of New York and all the colonies from Maryland to Georgia, became part of the revolutionary demand—No English rule, no English church! Because the Anglicans did not constitute a majority in any of these states, it proved relatively easy to reduce the Church of England to the level of other denominations. However, even this "disestablishment" was not complete. In 1776, the best that James Madison and other advocates of religious freedom could win was a promise of a right to the "free exercise of religion." Those exercising that freedom of choice still had to pay taxes to support the Episcopal Church. The same Virginia legislature that adopted the Declaration of

Rights for the state also reestablished the Anglican Church under an Americanized name as the Episcopal Church. The legislature removed references to the king and his family, and instead had the new church pray for the well-being of the elected officials of Virginia. But, the church itself remained the official religion of the state. In 1779, Thomas Jefferson proposed a Statute of Religious Freedom, but the state legislature rejected it.

In New England, with the exception of Rhode Island, the Congregational churches remained even more secure. Under the new state constitutions they lost a few privileges, but remained state sponsored into the nineteenth century. New Hampshire continued to provide public support for "public Protestant teachers" until 1968, nearly two centuries after the Revolution. Other states, like New Jersey and North Carolina, disestablished their official churches and also promised freedom of worship to all, but they did not adopt full religious freedom. A number of states guaranteed civil rights only to Protestants or Christians.

Given the views of the founders on organized religion and traditional theology, it seems surprising that more was not done to create full religious freedom. "At the time of the Revolution most of the founding fathers had not put much emotional stock in religion," historian Gordon Wood writes in *The Radicalism of the American Revolution* and "at best, most of the revolutionary gentry only passively believed in organized Christianity and, at worst, privately scorned and ridiculed it." Even John Adams, who had once contemplated training for the ministry, "thought that the argument for Christ's divinity was an 'awful blasphemy.'"

Yet, despite the secularism of the leadership, every revolutionary state but New York and Virginia had a religious test for officeholding in its first constitution. New Jersey and the Carolinas insisted that officeholders be Protestant; Massachusetts required that they declare themselves to be Christian; and Delaware demanded that legislators and other officials affirm their belief in the Trinity. These tests were surprisingly long-lived. New Jersey would not allow non-Protestants to hold public office until 1874, nearly a full century after the Revolution began, while North Carolina kept its religious test until 1868. New Hampshire waited until 1877 to remove its religious test. Maryland barred Jews from holding office until 1826, but retained some religious tests for officeholding until the Supreme Court struck down that provision of the Maryland constitution in *Torasco v. Watkins* in 1961. A number of states, including New York (which otherwise had no religious tests for officeholding), prohibited members of the clergy from holding office. The Supreme Court finally struck such provisions down in *McDaniel v. Paty*, in 1978.

Equally significant, most of the states retained some official tax support for various churches. Some, like Virginia and Massachusetts, tenaciously held on to an established church throughout the Revolution.

Despite the survival of religious establishments and religious tests for officeholding during the Revolution, there was also a trend toward religious liberty. The Virginia Declaration of Rights of 1776 included the principle of religious toleration, but not full religious freedom. After the Revolution, in what is one of the great landmarks of American liberty, Virginia adopted Thomas Jefferson's Statute of Religious Freedom in 1786. The act, one of the three accomplishments Jefferson wanted inscribed on his tombstone, condemned all efforts to use the power of government for the benefit of any religion. "Truth is great," the act declared, "and will prevail if left to herself." This act disestablished the church in Virginia, but still left the government with the power to regulate all churches, to license preachers, and decide if a new church could be incorporated. While the law led to fairly open free exercise for Virginia's white population, it did not create full separation of church and state.

## Slavery

For all the rhetoric of individual liberties, nearly one in five Americans was bound to perpetual slavery at the beginning of the Revolution. The Revolution altered American conceptions of slavery and, for some slaves, led to freedom. At the beginning of the Revolution, Lord Dunmore offered liberty to slaves who would fight against the American cause, and thousands of slaves joined him. Other slaves fought for the patriot side and gained their freedom that way. Still other slaves took advantage of the dislocations and chaos of the war to find freedom in a new place.

During the Revolution, the English Tory Samuel Johnson caustically asked, "How is it that we hear the loudest *yelps* for liberty among the drivers of negroes?" Most of the revolutionaries in Virginia or elsewhere in the South had no plausible answer to Johnson's question. Thomas Jefferson offered a typical Southern response to the Revolution. As a legislator he refused to propose any law that undermined the strength of slavery in Virginia. In fact, he proposed new criminal laws to strengthen punishments for black criminals. As governor, Jefferson did not suggest enlisting slaves, even when his state was under assault by Lord Cornwallis's army. Moreover, Jefferson never contemplated either enlisting his own slaves in the patriot army or emancipating them during the Revolution. Some patriots in the North and the South wanted to make the great sentiments of the Declaration of Independence real for all persons. In 1782, with Jefferson temporarily out of government service, Virginia passed legislation allowing masters to voluntarily free their slaves. In the next quarter century, some 30,000 slaves would gain their liberty under this law. Similarly, in Maryland and the Carolinas, individual masters manumitted numerous slaves during this period. Some Southerners enlisted their own slaves, and two prominent South Carolinians, John and Henry Laurens, argued for wholesale enlistment of slaves, but their proposal went nowhere.

A combination of revolutionary ideology and religious sentiment led to more radical changes in the northern states. In 1775, the first antislavery society was founded in Philadelphia, and many patriots, conservative as well as radical, supported emancipation. During the war hundreds of Northern blacks, many of whom had been recently manumitted, served in the militia and Continental Army. In 1780, Pennsylvania enacted a statute requiring gradual emancipation, and that same year the Massachusetts bill of rights included the statement that "All men are created free and equal." Three years later, the state's highest court interpreted this to mean that slavery would no longer be allowed in the Commonwealth. All of the other Northern states followed these examples between 1783 and 1804, when New Jersey became the last state to adopt a gradual emancipation act.

In the South, however, where the vast majority of slaves resided, a variety of social and economic factors easily defeated any antislavery sentiment found there; by the 1780s, in fact, Southerners sought to protect rather than destroy their "peculiar institution." The country would be torn apart by decades of civil discord and then war it-self before the concept of human equality and freedom for all persons, black and white, would be accepted as the law of the land.

## Judicial Review and the Success and Failure of State Constitutions in the Revolutionary Era

None of the early state constitutions gave state courts specific power to nullify legislation. The general radical trend toward concentrating power in the assemblies implied that they would judge the constitutionality of their own acts. New York did vest some review authority in the Council of Revision, as did Pennsylvania and Vermont in their Councils of Censors. Massachusetts required advisory opinions from its Supreme Judicial Court before a bill could be passed but did not provide for any postenactment review. All other state constitutions were silent on the issue. The first hesitant step toward judicial review appeared in *Holmes v. Walton,* a New Jersey case of 1780, but there is considerable debate over the extent to which state courts exercised this power in the 1780s, or how much the people assumed that courts inherently held this authority, a controversy for which the documentary evidence is sparse.

All told, considering the haste and the difficult circumstances in which the drafters worked, one is amazed at the longevity of what they wrought. North Carolina's constitution lasted 75 years; that of New Jersey, 68; Maryland, 65; and Virginia, 54. Connecticut's colonial charter functioned as its constitution for 42 years, Rhode Island's for 64. Even the New York document, despite growing problems with sections such as the councils of revision and appointment, remained substantially unaltered for 45 years. Massachusetts's constitution of 1780, although amended a number of times, remains in force to this day.

Others had briefer careers, their inherent defects and excesses soon corrected by experience. Whatever their deficiencies, however, all proved invaluable as experiments in government-making, guides that would be carefully scrutinized by those who drew up the federal Constitution of 1787. Most important, Americans, now freed from British authority, learned to exercise that most precious of all the rights they claimed—to be ruled by a form of government they themselves had chosen.

## The Common Law Survives

As in most wars, the daily life of the people continued during the Revolution, although they now had to contend with shortages, the absence of men from farms and shops, and other problems attendant on the conflict. Since at no time during the Revolution did the British army occupy more than a small portion of the United States, the life of the citizenry in many areas appeared, on the surface at least, little different from what it had been before. In law, for example, people still sued one another, conveyed property, made contracts, and wrote wills. But now a new question intruded into the law, namely, what law applied? Until 1776, English common and statutory law, modified by some local adjustments, had governed legal affairs. With allegiance to the Crown ended, how much, if any, English law would remain in control in American courts, and how would that determination be made?

Although some patriots wanted to establish American law on a new basis, the English common law comprised the only law most American lawyers and judges knew. While denouncing British legislative policy, Americans for the most part defended the common law, wanting only to purify it from George III's "corruption." They revered the common law as expounded in the constitutionalism of Sir Edward Coke, of whom Jefferson said: "a sounder Whig never wrote, nor of profounder learning in the orthodox doctrines of British liberties." When the First Continental Congress adopted a Declaration of Rights in 1776, it declared the colonies "entitled to the common law of England" as well as to the benefit of those English statutes that "existed at the time of colonization; and which they have, by experience, respectively found to be applicable to their several local and other circumstances."

One state after another adopted this view. In 1776, the Virginia legislature ruled that the "common law of England, all statutes or acts of Parliament made in aid of the common law to the fourth year of the reign of King James the first [1607] and which are of a general nature, not local to that kingdom . . . shall be considered in full force." The Delaware constitution of that year included a similar provision, while New York on several occasions pronounced that the common law, although not all of the king's statutes, would remain in effect. These various "reception" statutes, by which American law received and incorporated the English common law, provided a crucial link of continuity between colonial law and postrevolutionary development. Many of them are still found in state codes, with occasional cases turning on whether and when certain English doctrines became American as well.

## Blackstone's Influence

The states not only clung to the common law, but in the cities as well as on the frontier, lawyers and judges began to rely more and more on Sir William Blackstone's four-volume *Commentaries on the Laws of England* (1765–1769) as their guide to the law. Blackstone's treatise originated in a series of lectures he had given at Oxford University to educate the sons of landed gentry in the basic principles of the law, so that they could carry out their future duties as magistrates wisely and well. He had organized his lectures into four broad divisions: rights of individuals (constitutional protections), wrongs to individuals (torts), rights to things (property and contract), and wrongs to the state (criminal law). Although never intended as a definitive compendium, and despite its many generalities and omissions (there is only one paragraph on bailments, for example), the commentaries soon became the standard reference on English law in America as well as in Great Britain. An American edition, printed in 1771–1772 on a subscription basis for $16 a set, sold an astonishing 1,557 sets. Countless lawyers and judges traveled the circuits with their four volumes of Blackstone, two in each saddlebag. For some Americans, such as Jefferson, Blackstone proved not only too English but too Tory in his views. Yet none of the signers of the Declaration of Independence, thirty of whom were lawyers or judges, could have quarreled with Blackstone's interpretation of the common law as the font of the liberties of the

English people, which, he wrote, "may be reduced to three principle or primary articles: the right of personal security, the right of personal liberty, and the right of private property."

Blackstone's interpretations profoundly influenced American law for generations, and while a slavish adherence to some of his statements produced curious anomalies of law on the frontier, his basic philosophy fit in perfectly with American needs. Among other things, he separated the complex writ procedure (which would finally be abolished in England in 1836) from the rules of law, the underlying principles of which he described as moral responsibility and accountability. Moralism constituted the greatest characteristic of eighteenth- and nineteenth-century law, and Blackstone summed this up best when he declared: "Law is that which commands what is right and prohibits that which is wrong." In a famous essay in 1900, James Barr Ames saw the whole development of modern law as a movement toward the moral, and American judges often appeared very concerned, some might say preoccupied, with imposing moral values in law.

For most people in the eighteenth century, morality related to God, and Blackstone placed God's law at the apex of all legal systems. Next came the law of nature, those ethical precepts that are universal in character, followed by the law of nations, including treaties between sovereigns. At the base, and inferior to the others, stood municipal law, the most mutable of the four, comprising the local laws of each country. The authority of each of the three lower levels derived from its compatibility with higher law; no law of a parliament, for example, could be valid if it conflicted with either God's law or the law of nature; it was not simply "bad" law—it had no force whatsoever. In the Declaration of Independence, Jefferson used this notion to condemn English legislation and royal acts because they ran against "the Laws of Nature and of Nature's God." Rebellion could thus be justified, following Blackstone, that most Tory of English law writers, as adherence in the strictest sense to the rule of law itself.

Blackstone introduced another element that became extremely important in American law—the doctrine of *stare decisis,* according to which the rulings in earlier cases would determine decisions in later conflicts. At the time he wrote, no more than fifteen to eighteen judges sat on the four major English courts, and although they knew and discussed earlier cases and hoped to square their decisions with the great previous holdings, they did not consider them binding. Blackstone, seeking to create easy-to-follow rules for his students (who would be magistrates, not lawyers), suggested in a single paragraph the notion of binding precedents, which American lawyers and judges soon erected into a central tenet of their jurisprudence.

This development benefited from the concurrent movement to report cases. By 1750, about 150 volumes of early English cases had been gathered, which varied greatly in quality and accuracy according to the reporter. There were no official American reports in colonial times, and a practicing lawyer in Boston or Philadelphia had to rely on English reports or secondhand descriptions that had been picked out of English treatises. Evidently, some manuscript volumes circulated, and this trend accelerated during the early national period, but they could not satisfy the needs of the bar. In 1789, Ephraim Kirby published a volume of *Connecticut Reports,* and the following year Alexander Dallas issued a volume of Pennsylvania decisions, some of which dated back to 1754. Within a short time, case reports appeared for almost every state and became an essential feature of American law.

A final aspect of Blackstonian thought that greatly affected American legal and constitutional development derived from his vesting in the judiciary the power to interpret law that was superior to that of other branches of government. Since judges could be expected to know not only the principles of law but the binding precedents as well, they could definitively say which statutes did or did not conform to higher law. Placing such power in the hands of the most conservative group in society no doubt appealed to the Tory writer; judges would then be, as Coke described them, "the Lions under the Throne," preserving the law against king, Parliament, or the mob. Jefferson and other democrats understandably opposed this idea, which they saw as negating the will of the people, and no state constitution adopted following the Revolution gave judges the power of judicial review. Nonetheless, Blackstone's idea soon gained currency in the United States, and a clear line runs from the *Commentaries* to Chief Justice Marshall's dictum in *Marbury v. Madison* (see Chapter 10).

The common law, however, had to be Americanized, a process that by its nature would be evolutionary and take several decades. Much as lawyers and judges in the new republic relied on Blackstone, frontier conditions, as well as patriotic fervor and the development of written constitutions, necessitated changes to meet new circumstances. Few of these changes would be seen immediately; closing the royal courts and their replacement within a few years by state courts constituted the most visible difference between prerevolutionary and postrevolutionary law.

But change did take place, and it is a theme we will return to again. One example of how this change would occur is the publication, in 1803, of an Americanized edition of Blackstone, written by St. George Tucker, a keen supporter of Jefferson and a professor of law at the College of William and Mary. Tucker's five-volume treatise, known as *Tucker's Blackstone*, modified the Englishman's four-volume work by incorporating the ideology and constitutional change of the revolutionary ear. As its long subtitle declared, this set modified the work of the Tory Blackstone by examining his work "With Notes of Reference to The Constitution and Laws of the United States; and of the Commonwealth of Virginia."

# Conclusion

The work of the Second Continental Congress in drafting and securing adoption of the Articles of Confederation set the stage for the development of national sovereignty, while state constitutions launched a parallel effort in setting the former colonies onto a path that diverged sharply from English practice. Both the Articles and many of the early state constitutions had serious defects that would soon have to be corrected. But a foundation now existed for the great changes that would take place in the next half century.

# For Further Reading

Congress's role during the war and some of the nonmilitary problems it faced are examined in Jack M. Rakove, *The Beginnings of National Politics: An Interpretive History of the Continental Congress* (1979), and H. James Henderson, *Party Politics in the Continental Congress* (1973).

Among older works, Jennings B. Sanders, *Evolution of the Executive Departments of the Continental Congress, 1774–1789* (1935), is still useful. Harry M. Ward, *"Unite or Die": Intercolony Relations, 1690–1763* (1971), traces the various factors that both hindered and facilitated union. See also Max Savelle, "Nationalism and Other Loyalties in the American Revolution," 67 *American Historical Review* 90 (1962). On the ideology of the Revolution itself, see Gordon Wood, *The Radicalism of the American Revolution* (1992).

The "critical period" view of the Confederation is best articulated in the classic work by Andrew C. McLaughlin, *The Confederation and the Constitution, 1781–1789* (1905). The leading champion of the Articles, Merrill Jensen, argued that they expressed the "democratic spirit" of the Revolution. See his *The Articles of Confederation: An Interpretation of the Societal-Constitutional History of the American Revolution, 1774–1781* (1940). More recent and more balanced accounts include Edmund S. Morgan, *The Birth of the Republic, 1763–1789* (1956), and Forrest McDonald, *E Pluribus Unum: The Formation of the American Republic, 1776–1790* (1965).

The classic work on the states remains Allan Nevins, *The American States During and After the Revolution, 1775–1789* (1924), but it should be used with Jackson Turner Main, *The Sovereign States, 1775–1783* (1973), which argues that the war neither destroyed the old order nor created a new one, but accelerated trends already present. See also Ronald Hoffman and Peter J. Albert, eds., *Sovereign States in an Age of Uncertainty* (1981), and Peter S. Onuf, *The Origin of the Federal Republic: Jurisdictional Controversies in the United States, 1775–1787* (1983). Onuf examines how states first exercised their sovereignty and the problems that arose when they could not confirm their boundary lines.

The first state constitutions have been examined in a number of works. Willi Paul Adams, *The First American Constitutions: Republican Ideology and the Making of the State Constitutions in the Revolutionary Era* (1980), is a near encyclopedic survey of political thought and constitution-making. Also useful for the state constitutions is Mark W. Kruman, *Between Authority & Liberty: State Constitution Making in Revolutionary America* (1997). See also Donald S. Lutz, *Popular Consent and Popular Control: Whig Political Theory in the Early State Constitutions* (1980), and Donald Lutz, *The Origins of American Constitutionalism* (1988). Studies focusing on particular states include Robert P. Sutton, *Revolution to Secession: Constitution Making in the Old Dominion* (1989); Jere N. Daniel, *Experiment in Republicanism: New Hampshire Politics and the American Revolution, 1741–1794* (1970); and Ronald M. Peters, Jr., *The Massachusetts Constitution of 1780: A Social Compact* (1978). See also the materials collected in Oscar Handlin and Mary Handlin, eds., *The Popular Sources of Political Authority: Documents on the Massachusetts Constitution of 1780* (1966). For the Southern states, see the relevant chapters of Fletcher M. Green, *Constitutional Development of the South Atlantic States, 1776–1860* (1930).

J. Franklin Jameson's *The American Revolution Considered as a Social Movement* (1925) first put forward the idea of social democracy accompanying political independence. The "democratic" nature of the Revolution continues to generate heat and some light. See, among others, Merrill Jensen, *The Founding of a Nation* (1968) and *The American Revolution Within America* (1974); Elisha P. Douglass, *Rebels and Democrats: The Struggle for Equal Political Rights and Majority Rule During the American Revolution* (1955); and Jackson Turner Main, *The Social Structure of Revolutionary America* (1965). State studies include Robert Brown, *Middle Class Democracy and the Revolution in Massachusetts, 1691–1780* (1955), and Rhys Isaac, *The Transformation of Virginia, 1740–1790* (1982).

Disestablishment and religious freedom are explored in Thomas E. Buckley, S.J., *Church and State in Revolutionary Virginia, 1776–1787* (1977); Morton Borden, *Jews, Turks, and Infidels* (1984); Sidney Mead, *The Lively Experiment* (1963); and William Miller, *The First Freedom* (1985). Slavery and emancipation during the revolutionary era are addressed in Paul Finkelman, *Slavery and the Founders: Race and Liberty in the Age of Jefferson* (1995), Donald L. Robinson, *Slavery in the Structure of American Politics, 1765–1820* (1971), and Arthur Zilversmit, *The First Emancipation* (1965). For the common law see Lawrence Friedman, *A History of American Law* (1972), Part II, *passim;* John Phillip Reid, *In a Defiant Stance: The Condition of Law in Massachusetts Bay, the Irish Comparison, and the Coming of the American Revolution* (1977); and William E. Nelson, *The Americanization of the Common Law: The Impact of Legal Change on Massachusetts Society, 1760–1830* (1975). The first American edition of Blackstone has been recently reprinted and is thus more easily available to students and scholars: St. George Tucker, *Blackstone's Commentaries: With Notes of Reference to The Constitution and Laws of the United States; and of the Commonwealth of Virginia, in Five Volumes*, edited by Paul Finkelman and David Cobin (1997).

# 5

# The Crisis of Confederation

*Defects of the Articles • A Government Without Energy • Western Land Policy • Northwest Ordinance • Shays's Rebellion • Madison and the Annapolis Convention • Toward the Philadelphia Convention • For Further Reading*

THE ARTICLES OF Confederation provided a government that was able to develop an alliance with France, successfully wage war with Great Britain, and ultimately conclude a peace treaty that secured the independence of the former colonies. These were significant accomplishments.

Despite these successes, the government created by the Articles was deeply flawed. Under different circumstances and with some major revisions, the Articles of Confederation might have served as the fundamental law of the new republic for decades to come. But, these revisions were next to impossible to achieve because the Articles could not be amended without the unanimous consent of all the states.

With the end of the Revolution's economic difficulties, tensions in foreign affairs, social disorder, and the stubbornness of some states revealed the fundamental weakness of the Articles. This in turn led to demands for a new constitution that would empower the central government to run the nation's affairs, and to do so more effectively.

The result, the Constitution of 1787, has been called the greatest scheme of government ever devised. At some levels it has certainly served the United States well for 200 years. The political structure created in 1787 remains intact. From election to election, the transition from one Congress to another, or one president to another, has been remarkably smooth. With the addition of the Bill of Rights in 1791, and the Thirteenth, Fourteenth, and Fifteenth amendments between 1865 and 1870, the Constitution has been critical in developing and protecting enormous personal liberty. The stability of government produced by the Constitution has also led to unparalleled economic prosperity for most Americans.

However, the document created in 1787 and immediately amended by the Bill of Rights in 1791, was not perfect. Most obviously, the Constitution created a governmental system that was unable to cope with slavery. This defect nearly destroyed the nation and led to a Civil War that cost the lives of more than 600,000 Americans. The full promise of the Constitution could not be achieved until there was a fundamental restructuring of the relationship between the states and the national government. The Civil War Amendments (Thirteenth, Fourteenth, and Fifteenth) radically changed the system of government created in 1787. Even then, the promise of equality in those amendments would not be achieved for more than a century.

Despite its many changes over more than two centuries, the political theories of the Founders remain critical to modern constitutional law. The shaping of the Constitution in 1787, and the debates that attended its ratification, shed much light on those theories. And those theories continue to influence the constitutional development of the nation. To understand the creation of this Constitution, we must first turn to the situation in America on the eve of the Philadelphia Convention of 1787.

## Defects of the Articles

At the Harvard commencement in the spring of 1787, John Quincy Adams told his fellow graduates that the United States was then in a "critical period." A century later, the historian John Fiske used the same phrase as the title for his study of the nation under the Articles of Confederation. Ever since, most historians have adopted the concept of a "critical period" to describe conditions between 1781 and 1787.

A minority of scholars, such as Merrill Jensen and Staughton Lynd, have argued that the Articles operated more successfully than is commonly believed and that the Articles implemented the democratic vision of the wartime radicals as expressed in the Declaration of Independence. These scholars see the adoption of the Constitution as a counterrevolution of the conservatives. A close examination, however, demonstrates how the structural defects of the unamended Articles would have prevented effective government for the new nation. Moreover, such an examination illuminates the fundamentally undemocratic nature of the Articles.

Under the Articles the Congress could ask for money from the states, but could not levy taxes; it could negotiate treaties, but could not compel the states to abide by them; it could borrow money, but could not provide for repayment. Indeed, Congress was practically powerless to respond to the problems of the postwar depression or to manage the nation's foreign affairs.

The committee that drafted the Articles, chaired by John Dickinson of Delaware, had anticipated that the Articles would need to be changed. The committee members understood that a document written to create a government during a revolution might not work after independence had been achieved and peace had returned to the land. Unfortunately, the drafters chose an amendment process that doomed the Articles and at the same time virtually prevented any change in them. The committee required the unanimous approval of all the states to amend the Articles. This effectively made change impossible.

The fear of domination by the larger states had led to the provisions requiring unanimity, but this provision made it impossible to secure a change in the Articles even on relatively minor issues. Throughout the life of the Articles a single state could veto any amendment, no matter how popular it was in the rest of the country. It is no wonder that despite almost universal agreement that the Articles were defective, they were never amended.

Under the Articles, even the passage of simple legislation was cumbersome. The Articles provided that each state have one vote, but that each state delegation consist of at least two, and no more than seven, members. No state could vote on the floor of Congress unless at least two of its delegates were present. These provisions set the stage for legislative paralysis. Illness, inclement weather, the difficulties of travel, and the complications of the war and its aftermath often kept delegates away from the Congress, leaving states unable to vote because only one delegate was present. State delegations that were evenly divided also could not vote, because the delegates on one side canceled those on the other.

Even when most states were represented, the legislative process was cumbersome. For most legislation, a simple majority of the states present was necessary. But, for a number of important issues, including those involving war, peace, and the expenditure of funds to support the army, the Articles required the agreement of nine states. Often, the Congress found it impossible to pass anything on these matters because only eight state delegations were even present with at least two members.

The constitutional defects of the government under the Articles provide one key to understanding the workings of the Philadelphia Convention. In essence, the Articles created a government that was incapable of making decisions or operating in a complex world. The revolutionaries who wrote the Articles were so concerned about preventing tyranny and not replacing King George with an American monarch that they created a government that was incapable of action. To use a favorite phrase of the Founders—the government under the Articles "lacked energy." This lack of "energy" motivated the delegates at the Philadelphia Convention, who were determined to create a new structure for a government with energy.

---

## THE "SUPERMAJORITY" CLAUSE OF THE ARTICLES OF CONFEDERATION

The Articles of Confederation required a "supermajority" of nine states to conduct the most important business of the government. Article IX, Paragraph 6 of the Articles provided:

> The United States Congress assembled shall never engage in a war, nor grant letters of marque and reprisal in time of peace, nor enter into any treaties or alliances, nor coin money, nor regulate the defence and welfare of the United States, or any of them, nor emit bills, nor borrow money on the credit of the United States, nor appropriate money, nor agree upon the number of vessels of war, to be built or purchased, or the number of land or sea forces to be raised, nor appoint a commander in chief of the army or navy, unless nine States assent to the same: nor shall a question on any other point, except for adjourning from day to day be determined, unless by the majority of a vote of the United States in Congress assembled.

# A Government Without Energy

The national government under the Articles of Confederation, to put it bluntly, lacked the minimal structure and powers needed to govern. Most importantly of all, the Articles were so cautiously created that they were virtually unamendable. The stubbornness of a single state could block needed changes. Even in the unlikely event that all the states did agree to a change, the poor transportation and communication systems of the new nation made ratification of a change by all thirteen states slow, cumbersome, and in fact, all but impossible.

Any attempt to change the Articles was also hampered by the fact that the system of government did not provide for a national executive. There was no American president, governor, or king. There was no one to lead the nation, organize the government, or even cajole the legislature into action. There was not even an officeholder to serve as a figurehead, to represent the very sovereignty of this new nation. This was particularly odd, since every one of the new American states had an elected governor, who served as an independent chief executive. Even the states most fearful of executive power recognized the need for someone to serve as chief executive in the state government. Americans understood, as their state governments reveal, that successful government required a "head" of the government. But, America remained "headless" under the Articles, with no one to lead; thus, the delegates to the Congress, usually with only limited vision of local needs, could never agree on a national agenda.

Without an executive branch, all power resided in a single body—the Congress. This might have been fine if the Congress had had a speaker or prime minister with power and authority, as the British Parliament did. But, the Congress lacked such an office. The presiding officer of the body—ironically called "the president" of the Congress—had little power or authority. Nor, for that matter, did the Congress itself have much power.

The legislature was also weak because of the cumbersome concept of state equality. The states could send as many as seven delegates to Congress, but each state had only one vote. This meant that for every vote, the delegates had to huddle and decide how their state would vote. More importantly, this equality undermined national unity and strengthened localism. Delegates from the states with the largest populations—like Pennsylvania, Virginia, and Massachusetts—wondered why their states had the same political power as small New Jersey, tiny Delaware, and truly minuscule Rhode Island.

The Articles also failed to create a national court system, and thus disputes between states or citizens of different states could not be settled by a single, national judicial tribunal. Under the Articles one state court might order a judgment in favor of one side of a dispute, and a court in a different state could rule for the other side in the same lawsuit. Just as there was no national executive to lead, there was no national court system to resolve conflicting legal decisions. The Articles did allow Congress to settle some disputes between states, and Congress used this power on a few occasions, including one involving the western boundary of Pennsylvania. But, Congress could not be expected to resolve private disputes between citizens of different states. Nor could Congress constantly monitor the rulings of state courts, even on issues involving the national government. And, if Congress had monitored the state courts, the lack of a national judiciary would still have undermined the government under the Articles.

Although the Articles provided no separate executive for the government, the document did authorize Congress to establish some executive departments. Ultimately, Congress created five, but the distrust of a powerful executive during the latter colonial era led Congress to keep power in its own hands as much as possible. To do so, it set up committee after committee to deal with each problem it faced. During his career in the Congress, John Adams served on more than eighty different committees.

Of the five departments, the most effective proved to be finance, headed by the Philadelphia merchant Robert Morris. An extremely capable man, Morris managed, although often through sleight of hand, to keep the government financially afloat, and even imposed some order on the chaotic national accounts. But lacking any reliable income, he could do nothing to reduce or even halt the growing national debt. The other departments fared less well; when the first head of foreign affairs, Robert R. Livingston, resigned in May 1783, the office remained vacant for many months until John Jay could be induced to accept the post. Conceivably, had the times been more stable and problems less pressing, the combination of Congress and departments might ultimately have developed into a parliamentary cabinet system akin to that of Great Britain. But, without a single executive, it is unlikely that such a system could have evolved until the Articles were amended, which was almost impossible, given the requirement of unanimity and the uncooperative nature of some of the state governments.

In the absence of a constitutionally designated president or prime minister, Robert Morris emerged as the strongest single figure in the Confederation government, and his aims, to provide for sound currency and effective government, anticipated those of Alexander Hamilton a decade later. But the Articles gave Congress no independent taxing power, and throughout the period the government could do little more than ask the states to pay their assessments. Several states recognized the gravity of the problem, and in 1781, Morris nearly secured for Congress the power to impose a 5 percent impost duty payable directly to the national government. But this involved amending the Articles, a process requiring unanimous consent by all thirteen states. Twelve agreed, but Rhode Island refused, and its veto defeated any hope Morris or the Congress might have had for achieving fiscal stability for the government. Two years later, a proposal to give Congress power to collect import fees for twenty-five years met a similar fate. As a result, the national debt grew from $11 million to $28 million, while the currency and notes issued by Congress declined in value. Only timely loans from Dutch bankers enabled the government to avoid bankruptcy.

Another significant defect was Congress's lack of power to regulate either interstate or international commerce. Each state, therefore, not only controlled its internal commercial affairs but could also erect barriers against goods coming in from overseas or from other states. Although foreign trade revived considerably after the Treaty of Paris, British imperial policy now excluded American shipping from many of its former channels of trade. In retaliation, a number of states laid tonnage fees on British ships and special tariffs on British goods. For a while, Massachusetts closed the port of Boston to all British ships. British captains, however, thwarted this policy by unloading their cargoes in adjacent states; local merchants then shipped the goods overland or on coastal packets. Some states charged tariffs on goods coming in from neighboring states, giving the impression of interstate commercial warfare.

To rectify this situation, Congress in 1784 urged an amendment to the Articles to permit it to impose uniform navigation acts; despite widespread support throughout the country, the proposal failed to win ratification because two states, Rhode Island and North Carolina, vetoed it. Once again the requirement of unanimity allowed a tiny minority to frustrate the will of the majority. The inability of Congress either to secure an adequate revenue or to impose a uniform trade policy underscored what remained one of the greatest weakness of the Articles—the need for unanimity in order to amend the document.

The Confederation also faced numerous problems in foreign affairs, and in its relations with Great Britain, for example, some of these difficulties can be traced directly to defects in the Articles. Despite the 1783 Paris Treaty, the British had refused to vacate a string of forts stretching from Lake Champlain to Michilimackinac. From these forts they exercised considerable influence over the Indian tribes and were suspected of inciting them to make periodic raids on American settlements. The British claimed that they need not abandon the forts since the Americans had failed to pay their debts, although the treaty only called for the Congress to urge the states not to place impediments in the way of British creditors seeking collection. Similarly, the treaty required Congress to recommend that the states restore any confiscated Loyalist estates.

Congress had made these "earnest recommendations," but the states had refused to comply. Pennsylvania did pay the Penn Family $650,000 in compensation for seized lands, but that proved the exception. For the most part, Tories who had left the country rarely regained their property, and Congress had no power to compel the states to make restitution. The states not only ignored the treaty provisions regarding the Tories; they actively opposed the sections calling on them to open state courts to British creditors. Virginia, where planters had incurred the heaviest debts, passed laws hampering recovery. "If we are now to pay the debts due to the British merchants," the Virginia planter George Mason asked, "what have we been fighting for all this while?" Other Virginians, like Patrick Henry, agreed. Again, Congress could do absolutely nothing to force the states to act in this matter. Significantly, many of those who later opposed the Constitution, like Mason and Henry, were deeply concerned about being forced to pay their debts to their British creditors if a stronger national government came into being.

Had there been a functioning court system under the Articles, the national government might have sued the states to compel them to fulfill their obligations under the treaty. But, the Articles also failed to create a national court system.

---

## COLONIAL CURRENCY

During this period Congress and the states used a variety of currencies, with some areas retaining the British pound and others adopting the dollar. Spanish silver coins, which could be easily broken into eight pieces (pieces of eight) freely circulated, and later became the standard for the silver dollar. The dollar itself became the standard measure of money after the adoption of the Constitution.

# Western Land Policy

It is all too easy in the light of these handicaps to overlook the significant achievements of the government under the Articles. The Confederation negotiated a peace treaty; it carried on diplomatic relations with foreign countries; it held the new country together; it settled land disputes with the Indian tribes; and in two brilliant pieces of legislation, it established a farsighted policy for the settlement and incorporation of western lands. In this last area, at least, Congress had constitutional authority to deal with the matter, and its success buttresses the argument that the failure of government in the "critical period" derived from the defects of the Articles and not from political incompetence.

Once the states had ceded their claims to western lands to the national government, Congress had to develop plans for their future disposal. Between 1784 and 1787, this policy emerged in three ordinances, implementing an earlier resolution in 1779 that the lands ceded by the states "shall be . . . formed into distinct Republican states" equal to the existing states.

The Ordinance of 1784, drafted by Thomas Jefferson, called for creating new states in the western territories and admitting them into the Union as equals with the original states. This set a policy that would be applied throughout the continental United States, that the territories would not become "colonies" of the older states, but instead would be developed with eventual statehood in mind. A territory would be adopted as a state as soon as its population equaled that of the smallest existing state. Although this act set the goal, the specific details remained vague. Moreover, the Ordinance would go into effect only when the western land was put up for sale. As a result, this law never was implemented, and was officially repealed by the Northwest Ordinance of 1787.

In the Land Ordinance of 1785, Congress provided for a rectangular survey of the western territories into townships six-miles square. Each township would be subdivided into 36 sections one-mile square, or 640 acres. Land offices would sell the land at public auction at no less than $1 an acre, with a 640-acre minimum and no provisions for credit. The Congress reserved four sections of each township for its own use and set aside one section for the support of education. Jefferson, whose committee drafted the ordinance, saw this huge public domain as a source of revenue for the money-starved Confederation. But the lack of credit excluded many small farmers, and land speculation companies did most of the business in the territory for the next fifty years. The companies did, however, subdivide sections and sell smaller parcels on credit, so the act achieved one of its goals—bringing in settlers.

# Northwest Ordinance

Two years later, Congress passed the Northwest Ordinance—the most important piece of legislation in the Confederation period—which provided for territorial government and the method by which territories would become states. Unlike other regulations of the western territories, this Ordinance was limited to the land "northwest of the Ohio River."

Initially, governors and judges appointed by Congress would rule the area. When the territory contained five thousand free adult male inhabitants, the voters could elect a territorial legislature, with the status of a subordinate colonial assembly, which in turn would send a nonvoting delegate to Congress. No more than five or fewer than three states were to be carved out of the Northwest Territory; whenever any of these parts had 60,000 free inhabitants, it could be admitted to the Union on an equal basis with the existing states.

The Ordinance included a bill of rights that guaranteed religious freedom, representation proportional to population, trial by jury, habeas corpus and the application of the common law, protected private property, and the prohibition of cruel or unusual punishments. One article, a direct reflection of Jeffersonian thought, held that "Religion, morality and knowledge, being necessary to good government and the happiness of mankind, schools and the means of education shall be forever encouraged."

The Ordinance is perhaps most remembered for its provision on slavery. Between May 1786 and May 1787, Congress intermittently discussed what became the Northwest Ordinance. On July 11 and July 12, 1787 the Congress voted on the text and scheduled it for a third, and final reading in July 13. At the last possible moment, Congressman Nathan Dane offered an amendment that became Article VI of the Ordinance. This stated:

> There shall be neither slavery nor involuntary servitude in the said territory, otherwise than in the punishment of crimes, whereof the party shall have been duly convicted: provided always, that any person escaping into the same, from whom labour or service is lawfully claimed in any one of the original states, such fugitive may be lawfully reclaimed, and conveyed to the person claiming his or her labour or service as aforesaid.

In the nineteenth century, Americans, especially in the North, would look back on this eleventh-hour addition as a great antislavery achievement. However, it is unclear exactly what the article was intended to accomplish. Slaves were already in the territory, and the rest of the Ordinance referred to "free" people and the "free" population, which assumed an unfree, or slave population.

At the time of its passage, the Ordinance did not threaten slavery in the South. It may even have strengthened slavery there. Nor did the Ordinance immediately or directly affect slavery in the territory north of the Ohio River. Indeed, slavery continued in the region for decades. The early territorial governors, first under the Articles of Confederation and then under the Constitution, ignored the antislavery provisions. Hundreds of slaves were take into what became Indiana and Illinois, and as late as the 1840s, some blacks were held in slavery in Illinois. Nevertheless, this provision would be a central part of the debates over slavery in the territories that would dominate the constitutional politics of the 1840s and 1850s.

A different pattern developed south of the Ohio River, which marked the lower boundary of the Northwest Territory. For the time being, Virginia, North Carolina, and Georgia retained title to the western lands. Settlement proceeded there at a rapid pace, and slaveholders believed that these southwestern lands (which permitted slavery) would ultimately swing the balance of political power to the South. The abolition of slavery in the Northwest Territory had been purchased at the cost of its continued existence south of the Ohio.

Southerners in Congress in fact supported the slavery prohibition in the northwest because they saw it as protecting slavery south of the Ohio. They also believed that this would prevent the northwest from competing economically with the South. In addition, the fugitive slave provision in Article VI of the ordinance, the first of its kind in the nation, protected the property interest of Southern slaveowners.

The Northwest Ordinance turned out to be a precursor to what became a central issue in the decades before the Civil War: the problem of slavery in territories. With the Louisiana Purchase (1803), the United States would acquire new territories west of the Mississippi. In 1820, when Missouri sought entrance into the Union, Northerners in Congress tried to extend the Northwest Ordinance line, to prohibit slavery in most of the lands acquired from France. The debate over slavery in the Louisiana Territory and other new territories would eventually reach the Supreme Court, in *Dred Scott v. Sandford* (1857). However, the issue would not be finally resolved until the Civil War led to the end of slavery throughout the nation.

The Ordinances of 1785 and 1787 marked the high point of the Confederation government and set the policy for the nation's westward expansion. In determining that new states would be equal in every way to the original members of the Union, it prevented any division in the country between old and new states, with the latter consigned to a perpetually inferior status. The wisdom of the acts can be gauged from the fact that, with minor alterations, the 1785 Ordinance remained the national policy for the sale and distribution of western lands until the Homestead Act of 1862, while the Northwest Ordinance of 1787 set the pattern for the government and incorporation of all succeeding new states. Yet at the same time that Congress enacted this far-reaching legislation, it proved utterly incapable of dealing with a serious crisis, which resulted in the rapid crumbling of public confidence in the government under the Articles.

## Shays's Rebellion

The issue of a sound currency grew to crisis proportion in 1786. The value of paper money issued by the Continental Congress practically evaporated, while the bonds issued during the Revolution and Confederation depreciated sharply, dropping to little more than 15 cents on the dollar. The shortage of cash led to the popular demand for the states to issue paper currency and for the postponement of tax and debt payments. Farmers especially found themselves squeezed by the depression, with little money coming in and creditors and tax collectors demanding payment in hard currency. In 1785 and 1786, seven states responded to the problem by issuing paper currency. Five states—Pennsylvania, New York, New Jersey, South Carolina, and Rhode Island—used the unbacked money to provide credit to farmers through state loans, taking mortgages on their farms as security. In North Carolina and in particular Rhode Island, the debtor factions pushed through one scheme after another to relieve the pressure on borrowers.

In 1786, Rhode Island issued over £100,000 in paper money and declared it legal tender for the payment of all debts. Creditors fled the state to avoid having to accept the worthless paper, while merchants closed their doors rather than exchange goods for it. Rioting mobs led the state legislature to pass a "forcing act," which levied fines to persons refusing to take the currency at face value. The law provided that defendants would be tried "without trial by jury, according to the laws of the land." The statute reached the state's highest court, the Superior Court of Judicature, in *Trevett v. Weeden* (1786). Weeden's lawyer argued that the legislature could not pass a law "repugnant to the Constitution," and invited the high court to strike down the law. The court avoided this issue by refusing to hear a case under this act, arguing that it lacked jurisdiction. However, some of the judges indicated they believed the law was "unconstitutional," and at least one also argued it was "internally repugnant" because it was not possible to be tried by "the law of the land" while being denied a jury trial.

*Trevett v. Weeden* has sometimes seen as one of the earliest examples of judicial review. It did not quite create a precedent for judicial review, since the judges did not actually declare the law unconstitutional, but rather declared they did not have jurisdiction. Nevertheless, the case illustrates that even before the adoption of the U.S. Constitution, lawyers and judges were using the language and the theories of judicial review. The legislature considered impeaching the judges, but in the end it left them in office and instead repealed the forcing act; two years later, it also revoked the legal tender law.

To conservatives, this mob action raised the specter of their most dreaded fear—anarchy—a specter that seemed to materialize in western Massachusetts in 1787. The Bay State had been under the control of conservatives since 1780, and the General Court, responding to pressure from wealthy Boston creditors, moved to pay off the state debt through large court fees and poll and land taxes. The levies fell most heavily on farmers and the urban poor, who had no money to pay and whose petitions for redress fell on deaf ears in the legislature. When the assembly adjourned in late 1786, without providing relief, three western counties erupted in revolt.

Armed bands roamed the countryside, closing the courts and preventing foreclosures. A ragtag "army" under Daniel Shays marched on an arsenal at Springfield in January 1787, where the militia easily dispersed it with a single volley, leaving four dead. Soon after, General Benjamin Lincoln routed the remainder of the Shaysites at Petersham. The courts sentenced fourteen of the leaders to hang, but the governor pardoned or released all fourteen ringleaders after a short jail term, and the General Court quickly passed legislation suspending direct taxes for a year, lowering court fees, and exempting household goods, clothing, and tools from debt liens.

The pitiful revolt had been put down quickly. So too had a smaller revolt in New Hampshire. But these revolts served as a climax to growing conservative worries over the viability of the Confederation government. Before the full extent of Shays's Rebellion become known, Massachusetts had appealed to Congress for help in putting down the insurrection, but Congress was unable to help. George Washington wrote: "I am mortified beyond expression that in the moment of our acknowledged independence we should by our conduct verify the predictions of our transatlantic foe, and render ourselves ridiculous and contemptible in the eyes of all Europe." Great Britain, despite accusations that it had secretly fomented the uprising, actually had had nothing to do with it; nonetheless, Tories in London took hope that the new nation would soon collapse. Only Thomas Jefferson, the American ambassador to France, insulated from events in Paris and, as a planter sympathetic to the debtor cause, viewed Shays's Rebellion with equanimity. Failing to understand the danger posed by armed rebellion, and separated by an ocean from the American scene, Jefferson wrote Madison:

> I hold it, that a little rebellion, now and then, is a good thing, and as necessary in the political world as the storms in the physical. Unsuccessful rebellions, indeed, generally establish the encroachments on the rights of people which have produced them. An observation of this truth should render honest republican governments so mild in their punishment of rebellion so as not to discourage them too much.

However, most American leaders, viewed the revolt with horror. They were determined to remake the national government into one with energy, organization, and military power sufficient to resist enemies, both foreign and domestic.

## Madison and the Annapolis Convention

Because the names of Thomas Jefferson and James Madison have been closely linked as the "great collaborators," one tends to ignore the significant areas in which they disagreed. In regard to Shays's Rebellion, Madison definitely parted company with his friend, and like John Adams, viewed with horror the attack on law and order in Massachusetts. Where Jefferson saw the greatest danger to democracy as the tyranny of centralized authority, Madison feared the undisciplined power of mobs to trample on both individual and property rights. Jefferson envisioned a natural harmony between the different elements of society; Madison recognized the inherent conflict between factions that could rupture the body politic. Jefferson's thought reflected his experience in Europe, where he saw firsthand how ruthless governments preyed on the people, with society split between the powerful and the powerless, between the "wolves and sheep." Madison, living in the United States throughout the critical years of the Confederation, witnessed the inflationary moves of state legislatures attempting to appease an unruly populace and saw the need for a stable central authority.

Such concerns had led Madison and others to begin discussions on strengthening the national government even before the rebellion. Unable to convince his colleagues in the Virginia assembly that the Articles of Confederation needed revision, Madison sought other avenues to pursue this goal. In March 1785, he helped arrange a meeting of commissioners from Virginia and Maryland at Mount Vernon to settle outstanding problems in the Potomac River and Chesapeake Bay. Until 1776, the British had managed to hold down friction between the two colonies, but following independence, tensions flared up over problems of navigation, fishing, lighthouses, and customs duties. In 1777, Virginia had proposed a meeting with Maryland to settle the disputes, and the instructions to the Maryland commissioners indicate that Virginia threatened to impose taxes on all Maryland ships passing through the Bay if Virginians could not sail and fish freely in the Potomac and those parts of the Bay claimed by Maryland. Nothing came of this meeting, but in 1785, the commissioners agreed on the necessity for interstate cooperation, and the Maryland delegates suggested that Pennsylvania and Delaware, which also had interests in these waters, be brought into the talks. The Virginia legislature endorsed the findings and at Madison's suggestion issued an invitation to all thirteen states to attend a meeting to discuss general commercial problems.

Only five states attended the Annapolis Convention in September 1786—New York, New Jersey, Pennsylvania, Delaware, and Virginia. The commissioners elected John Dickinson of Delaware as chairman, but they could agree on little else. With so few states present, the delegates had little choice but to return home. Apparent failure, however, turned into success when Alexander Hamilton of New York proposed that they issue a report calling for a national convention to secure a more powerful central government that was capable of meeting the crisis before them. Madison urged Hamilton to tone down his draft, since as it stood it would certainly fail to win approval of the Virginia assembly. In a brilliant revision, Hamilton subtly linked a call for a general commercial convention into one pointing to a total constitutional overhaul, and in words adopted by the gathering, on September 14, 1786, he announced

> that the power of regulating trade is of such comprehensive extent, and will enter so far into the general System of the federal government, that to give it efficacy, and to obviate questions and doubts concerning its precise nature and limits, may require a correspondent adjustment of other parts of the Federal System.

## Toward the Philadelphia Convention

The failure of the Annapolis Convention was much like the failure of the Congress under the Articles. Too often, the Congress could not function because too few states were represented, and the state delegates that did show up came too late. This was what happened in Annapolis. Only a few states sent delegates and some arrived after the Convention had already adjourned in failure. Even the host state, Maryland, failed to appoint delegates.

But, ironically, the failure of the Annapolis meeting provided the impetus for change. Finally some politicians with a national vision—like Hamilton and Madison—realized that individuals with energy and imagination had to overcome the inertia of what many were beginning to call the imbecility of the Articles. Those delegates who had come to Annapolis left with a sense of determination. They returned to their respective states and began working for truly national convention to revise the Articles. The failure at Annapolis might yet be salvaged and even turned to an advantage. The nation seemed in crisis, and something dramatic was needed to save the Revolution and the republic.

## For Further Reading

Merrill Jensen, *The New Nation: A History of the United States During the Confederation, 1781–1789* (1950), paints government under the Articles in its most positive light. Also useful is Staughton Lynd, *Class Conflict, Slavery and the United States Constitution* (1967). The extent of particular problems is explored in Frederick W. Marks III, *Independence on Trial* (1973), which sees the inability of the states to control foreign trade as a crucial factor leading to the

Constitution, and E. James Ferguson, *The Power of the Purse: A History of American Public Finance, 1776–1790* (1961), which analyzes the Confederation's enormous credit problems. Clarence L. Ver Steeg's biography of *Robert Morris: Revolutionary Financier* (1954) examines the central figure of the Confederation government. Some of the essays in John Porter Bloom, ed., *The American Territorial System* (1974), deal with the Northwest Ordinance and evolving national land policy.

On the Northwest Ordinance, see Peter Onuf, *Statehood and Union: A History of the Northwest Ordinance* (1987), and Paul Finkelman, *Slavery and the Founders: Race and Liberty in the Age of Jefferson* (1995).

Problems faced by the states are examined in Ronald J. Hoffman and Peter J. Albert, *Sovereign States in an Age of Uncertainty* (1981); Richard P. McCormick, *Experiment in Independence: New Jersey in the Critical Period 1781–1789* (1950); and Florence Parker Simister, *The Fire's Center: Rhode Island in the Revolutionary Era, 1763–1790* (1978). On Shays's Rebellion, see David P. Szatmary, *Shays's Rebellion: The Making of an Agrarian Insurrection* (1980), and Robert A. Gross, *In Debt to Shays: The Bicentennial of an Agrarian Rebellion* (1993).

# 6

# A More Perfect Union

*The Philadelphia Convention • Representation and the Structure of Government • Slavery and Representation • The Executive Branch • The Judicial Branch • The Powers of the New Government • Regulating Commerce • Concluding the Convention • The Constitution and Federalism • Checks and Balances • The Debate over Ratification • Federalists and Antifederalists • Ratification • Conclusion: The Constitution and Democracy • For Further Reading*

AFTER THE FAILED Annapolis Convention, James Madison returned to Virginia and immediately drafted a resolution by which the state appointed representatives to a federal convention. As the biggest state, Virginia had to take the lead. The Virginia act authorizing the appointment of delegates reflected the sense of urgency felt by many Americans. The General Assembly declared it could

> no longer doubt that the crisis is arrived at which the good people of America are to decide the solemn question, whether they will be wise and magnanimous [in their] efforts to reap the just fruits of that independence, which they have so gloriously acquired, and of that union which they have cemented with so much of their common blood; or whether by giving way to unmanly jealousies and prejudices, or to partial and transitory interests, they will renounce the auspicious blessings prepared for them by the revolution, and furnish its enemies an eventual triumph over those by whose virtue and valor it has been accomplished.

As the Virginia legislature saw it, to work for a stronger union was an act of the highest patriotism; opposition reflected selfish prejudices or worse.

By early February 1787, New Jersey, Pennsylvania, North Carolina, New Hampshire, Delaware, and Georgia had joined in the call. Although Congress initially stalled on the issue, once seven states had indicated their willingness to participate, Congress agreed, and on February 21, 1787, declared it "expedient" to convene a convention "for the sole and express purpose of revising the Articles of Confederation." With the news that George Washington had agreed to attend as a delegate from Virginia, the support for the convention increased.

While Congress talked about "revising the Articles of Confederation," political leaders throughout the nation had grander plans. The Virginia act calling for the appointment of delegates explicitly said it was "for the purpose of revising the federal constitution." Similarly, after the Annapolis Convention, Alexander Hamilton had called for a meeting in Philadelphia "to render the Constitution of the federal government adequate to the exigencies of the Union."

All Americans, however, were not happy with the idea of a convention. Rhode Island would remain aloof from the proceedings throughout and never send delegates to Philadelphia. A quorum of the New York delegation would leave in early July, disgusted with the idea of a stronger union. Moreover, not all the named delegates ever arrived. The twelve states that did send delegates chose a total of seventy-three men, but ultimately only fifty-five showed up. Patrick Henry of Virginia was chosen but refused to attend, later claiming "I smelt a rat." In fact, what he "smelt" was a stronger national government, and he wanted no part of it. Neither did Richard Henry Lee of Virginia nor Willie Jones of North Carolina, who also opposed a stronger government and declined to serve.

Henry, Lee, Jones, and other opponents of a stronger government generally chose a strategy of nonparticipation. In the end, this strengthened the cause of the supporters of a new constitution. With a few notable exceptions, those who eventually came to the Philadelphia convention wanted a stronger national government. Luckily, they could attend to the business of writing a constitution without men like Henry, Lee, Jones, or after early July the anti-nationalists from New York hampering their project.

Fifty-five delegates from twelve states ultimately attended the convention in Philadelphia at one point or another. None were there all at the same time. After four months of labor, thirty-nine signed their names to the Constitution they had drafted. Most of the nonsigners had left the Convention early. Some, like George Wythe of Virginia, supported the Constitution, but left for personal reasons. A number of opponents of the whole process, including Luther Martin and John Francis Mercer, both of Maryland, and Robert Yates and John Lansing, Jr. of New York, had left in disgust. On the last day of the Convention, three remaining delegates—Elbridge Gerry of Massachusetts and George Mason and Edmund Randolph of Virginia—all significant participants in the Convention, refused to sign the final document.

## The Philadelphia Convention

The delegates to the Constitutional Convention in Philadelphia, despite their average age of forty-two, were fully conversant with the political theories of the Enlightenment. More importantly, they all had extensive experience in government. Among them were state governors, state supreme court justices, numerous former congressmen, state attorneys general, former diplomats, former army officers and other military heroes, and of course most prominently, General George Washington. Their backgrounds served them well. As John Dickinson warned, "Experience must be our only guide; reason may mislead us."

Although the document they drafted reflected many of the ideas of eighteenth-century British and Continental writers, the problems faced by the Confederation remained uppermost in their minds. Section after section of the Constitution is a direct response to the defects of the Articles. Other sections reflected the colonists' long struggle with Great Britain, and even the history of Britain's stuggles against the Stuart monarchs in the seventeenth century. But the Constitution is far more than merely a reaction to the difficulties of previous years. Many parts of the Constitution reflect the ideas of a generation of men who had fought for, and achieved, self-government, and did not want to lose that precious victory.

Few gatherings in history could boast such a concentration of talent. Although John Adams and Thomas Jefferson were conspicuous by their absence (one serving as ambassador to England, the other to France), many of the great figures of the revolutionary era participated in this crowning work of establishing the new nation. George Washington, the victorious commander-in-chief of the war, and Benjamin Franklin, who had been urging a union of the colonies since 1754, brought their prestige, talents, and enormous experience to the Convention. Indeed, many scholars believe that without the presence of Washington, who inspired confidence among all his contemporaries, the Convention would have failed.

Joining Washington and Franklin were a host of other experienced, talented, and energetic leaders from all over the young nation, including: George Mason, author of the Virgina Bill of Rights; Virginia's governor, Edmund Randolph; James Wilson of Pennsylvania, possibly the ablest lawyer in the country; Alexander Hamilton of New York, the brilliant rising star of the New York Bar, who had been Washington's aide-de-camp throughout much of the war; Roger Sherman of Connecticut, one of the most experienced politicians in the nation; Elbridge Gerry of Massachusetts, a wealthy investor and shrewd politican; and Charles Cotesworth Pinckney, a wealthy planter from South Carolina, who had long urged a more powerful national government. After seeing the list of delegates from his office in Paris, Jefferson declared, with his characteristic exaggeration, that the convention was populated by "demi-gods."

The most important of these "demi-gods" was James Madison, only thirty-six years old at the time, who contributed his encyclopedic knowledge of political history and thought as well as his indefatigable energy. Madison is frequently acknowledged as "the father of the Constitution," in recognition of the key role he played at Philadelphia, but as he modestly told one admirer nearly fifty years later: "You give me a credit to which I have no claim. . . . This was not, like the fabled Goddess of Wisdom, the offspring of a single brain. It ought to be regarded as the work of many heads & many hands."

On May 14, the appointed day for the convention to begin, only the Virginia and Pennsylvania delegations had arrived. Some of the delegates wondered if this meeting would end in failure, like the Annapolis Convention had a year before. But, transportation was difficult in the young country. The Pennsylvanians and Virginians spent the next ten days getting to know each other better, and greeting new delegates as they filtered into the city. By May 25, twenty-nine representatives from nine states had arrived, and the Convention began. They unanimously elected George Washington as president of the Convention, and his calming influence contributed enormously to the relatively smooth and effective proceedings.

The delegates immediately voted to meet behind closed doors, in order to block untoward pressure and prevent speechmaking to the galleries. Although some news leaked out from time to time, the Convention preserved a remarkable degree of secrecy throughout the hot summer of 1787. Fortunately for history, James Madison kept a detailed set of notes, which were posthumously published in 1840. These have been supplemented by notes and diaries of a number of other delegates, and provide Americans with a general picture of what happened at the Convention. However, the combined notes of all the delegates do not produce a full record of what happened at the Convention. Often, these records contain only a summary of a speech or a debate. This is especially important to consider when we try to get at what the "intentions of the framers" might have been. Many conservative scholars and jurists, including Chief Justice William Rehnquist, have argued for a "jurisprudence of original intent." However, the incomplete record of the debates in 1787 illustrates the difficulty—perhaps the impossibility—of determining that intent.

## Representation and the Structure of Government

On May 29, Governor Edmund Randolph of Virginia submitted to the Convention a series of resolutions known as the Virginia Plan, or the Randolph Plan, although Madison had drafted most of it with advice from Washington. In introducing these resolutions, Randolph spoke of the "crisis" of the nation "and the necessity of preventing the fulfillment of the prophecies of the American downfall." This plan would create an entirely new form of government in the United States. The power of the central government would be vastly enhanced at the expense of the states. The new Congress would have greater powers to tax, to secure the nation "against foreign invasion," to settle disagreements between states, and to regulate commerce.

In presenting the Virginia Plan, Governor Randolph openly called on the Convention to ignore its instructions to limit its work to revising the Articles and instead, to draft and submit a wholly new proposal to the states. The Virginia Plan proposed separate executive, legislative, and judicial branches with a strong national government that could enact laws binding on the states as well as on individual citizens. Under Randolph's plan the legislative power would be lodged in a bicameral Congress, with a lower house chosen by popular vote and an upper chamber elected by the lower house from nominations submitted by the state legislatures. The Congress would have the power to disallow state laws, and it could define the limits of the national government's authority as well as that of the states. In introducing the plan, Randolph told the delegates what most of them already knew or believed, that "the prospect of anarchy from the laxity of government" was everywhere. He urged his colleagues not to miss this "opportunity of establishing general peace, harmony, happiness and liberty" in the nation.

The Virginia Plan called for a radical restructuring of American politics, with a shift of power from the states to the national government. It also called for a powerful Congress in which representation would be based on population.

Some delegates, like Lansing and Yates of New York, instinctively opposed the first of these changes. The overwhelming majority of the delegates, however, favored creating a much stronger national government. That was why the Convention had been called in the first place; that is why they had journeyed to Philadelphia. However, most of the delegates from the smaller states feared that congressional representation based on population would lead to domination of the nation by the largest states, especially Virginia. Debates over representation and the powers of Congress would take up about two-thirds of the delegates' time.

The proposal to base representation on population also raised a more enduring problem: the place of slavery in the new nation. Randolph's plan tried to hedge the issue, declaring "that the rights of suffrage in the National Legislature ought to be proportioned to the Quotas of contribution, or to the number of free inhabitants, as the one or the other rule may seem best in different cases." This evasive language fooled no one. Almost immediately, delegates ceased to consider the merits of population-based representation and instead began to debate whether to count "inhabitants" or "free inhabitants" for purposes of representation. At this early stage in the proceedings the Convention managed to defer this issue for a time, but it would come back, again and again. From the end of May until the middle of June, the delegates debated the merits of the Virginia Plan. Most agreed on the need for a stronger national government, but the issue of population-based representation clouded all discussions. Until that was settled, it would cloud every discussion of the powers of the government. The small states were opposed to population-based representation and thus did not want to grant too many powers to the new government under such a system of representation. The large states favored population-based representation, but were reluctant to support vast powers for the new national government until this issue was settled in their favor.

With Rhode Island not represented, and the New Hampshire delegation not yet at the Convengtion, the larger states had the votes to push through population-based representation if they all voted together. But, a close vote over such an important matter would not bode well for the Constitution, and might prevent its adoption by the states.

The size of states did not always determine how they might vote. Two of the three members of the New York delegation, while representating a large state, were opposed to a stronger national government. Georgia, on the other hand, was a small state, but voted like a large state because its delegates expected the state to become a major center of population in the near future.

On June 15, William Paterson responded to the Virginia Plan with the New Jersey Plan, which kept the existing structure of Congress, in which each state had only one vote. This plan, however, did give Congress the power to impose taxes, regulate commerce, and name a plural executive and a federal supreme court. Since the New Jersey Plan hewed to the instructions that the Convention limit itself to revising the Articles, the delegates now had to choose what course they would follow. On June 19, they decided to work toward a national government, as Randolph had suggested. At this point, the delegates agreed that the central government should have broad powers, especially in the areas of taxation and regulation of trade; state powers had to be curtailed correspondingly.

From the very beginning of the Convention until early July, the issue of representation threatened to tear the Convention apart. The larger states generally supported the Virginia Plan, with population-based representation, while the smaller states opposed the scheme. On June 11, Roger Sherman proposed a plan that would eventually break the impasse. Known as the Connecticut Compromise, frequently called the "Great Compromise," Sherman proposed that the House of Representatives would be apportioned according to population, while each state would have two votes in the Senate. However, it would take more than a month of debate before the Convention would adopt Sherman's proposal, and even then a number of delegates, including James Madison and James Wilson, would be unhappy with the result.

By early July, the delegates had settled on the general outline of a new system of government that would be nationalist in scope and undermine the powers of the states. This prompted two of the three New York delegates, who were adamantly opposed to weakening the states, to head home. Alexander Hamilton remained as the lone New Yorker at the Convention, but the Convention rules required that votes be by states, not by individuals, and that at least two delegates had to be present for a state to vote. Thus, Hamilton could speak, but not vote.

The issue of representation continued to fester. Madison and James Wilson of Pennsylvania were adamantly opposed to the idea of equal state representation in the Senate because it was fundamentally undemocratic. But, the small states continued to fight for equality in the Senate, and on July 16, a few members of the large state delegations, including Benjamin Franklin and George Mason, joined them. On July 16, the Convention decided, by a one state majority, to accepted the idea of equality in the Senate. This led to an odd shift in the Convention. The delegates from the small states now favored a stronger federal government, while some of the nationalists, including Madison, were less enthusiastic about centralizing power because the national government would not be representative of the population of the country.

## Slavery and Representation

While the allocation of power in the national legislature had been the central issue in the creation of a new government, settling the composition of Congress did not solve all the problems of the Convention. Indeed, during the debates over representation, James Madison argued that the large state/small state issue was a false one, and that the real division was between the slave and free states. The day before, June 29, Alexan-

---

### REPRESENTATION AND SLAVERY

Trying to get the Convention to focus on the political realities of representation, rather than the fears of the small states, Madison noted:

that the States were divided into different interests not by their difference of size, but by other circumstances; the most material of which resulted partly from climate, but principally from their having or not having slaves. These two causes concurred in forming the great division of interests in the U. States. It did not lie between the large and small States: it lay between the Northern and Southern, and if any defensive power were necessary, it ought to be mutually given to these two interests.

der Hamilton had made a similar observation. Hamilton, not surprisingly perhaps, saw the issue solely in economic terms. "The only considerable distinction of interests, lay between the carrying and non-carrying States, which divide instead of uniting the largest States." Other delegates from the North and the South made the same point.

Indeed, throughout the debates slavery threatened to tear the Convention apart. Southerners wanted slaves counted equally with free people for purposes of representation. Northerners objected on both political and moral grounds. The political argument was simply that since slaves were not considered to be "persons," but were property, they ought not be counted for purposes of representation. Early in the Convention, Elbridge Gerry of Massachusetts sarcastically asked: "Blacks are property, and are used to the southward as horses and cattle to the northward; and why should their representation be increased to the southward on account of the number of slaves, than horses or oxen to the north?"

On July 9, after the Convention had agreed to the Connecticut Compromise, the delegates spent four days debating the relationship between slavery and representation. William Paterson of New Jersey regarded

> slaves in no light but as property. They are no free agents, have no personal liberty, no faculty of acquiring property, but on the contrary are themselves property, and like other property entirely at the will of the Master.

Paterson pointedly asked, "Has a man in Virga. a number of votes in proportion to the number of his slaves?" He asked, "Why should they be represented in the Genl. Gov't.[?]" Finally, Paterson argued that counting slaves for purposes of representation encouraged the slave trade.

Southerners responded that slaves produced great wealth, which had to be represented in Congress. General Charles Cotesworth Pinckney, of South Carolina, argued that the South did not require "a majority of representatives, but [he] wished them to have something like an equality." Otherwise, Congress would pass laws favorable to the North, and the southern states would "be nothing more than overseers for the Northern States." Even some Northerners agreed that slaves had to be counted in some way. Rufus King of Massachusetts warned that the South would not unite with the rest of the country "unless some respect were paid to their superior wealth."

---

## A RESPONSE TO THE SOUTH

Gouverneur Morris was one of the wealthiest delegates to the Convention, with vast landholdings in New York and New Jersey. His family had been leaders of New York and New Jersey politics for three generations. Reflecting the moral problems posed by slavery, he argued that allowing the counting of slaves for representation:

> when fairly explained comes to this: that the inhabitant of Georgia and South Carolina who goes to the Coast of Africa, and in defiance of the most sacred laws of humanity tears away his fellow creatures from their dearest connections and damns them to the most cruel bondages, shall have more votes in a Government instituted for protection of the rights of mankind, than the Citizen of Pennsylvania or New Jersey who views with a laudable horror, so nefarious a practice.

Debate over counting slaves for representation came up again and again. Two or three times the Convention seemed to have settled the issue, but it would reemerge and have to be reconsidered. Passions ran high. In early August, Gouverneur Morris declared that "domestic slavery," was "the curse of heaven on the States where it prevailed."

By the middle of August, however, the northern states had agreed to the "three-fifths compromise," in which five slaves would count as three free people for purposes of representation. This was not a compromise about race, because free blacks would count as any other free person for representation. Nor was this a compromise over taxation. The initial agreement over representation came long before any discussion of population-based taxation. Southerners were willing to be taxed fully for their slaves, *if* they could count slaves fully for representation. Moreover, many delegates doubted that the new government would ever be able to implement a direct tax based on population. Gouverneur Morris protested it was "idle to suppose that the General Government can stretch its hand directly into the pockets of the people scattered over so vast a Country." In the end, the three-fifths clause was a compromise over political power. The South demanded, and won, extra representation for its slaves, even though the people filling the seats in Congress created by counting slaves would always vote against the interests of the slaves.

## The Executive Branch

Initially the delegates were deeply divided over the nature of the executive. Some feared any single executive. Even Governor Edmund Randolph, who had proposed the Virginia Plan with its single excutive, feared that if implemented, it would lead to a monarchy. Some, like Alexander Hamilton, favored an executive who could serve for life, like a king. At various points in the Convention, delegates proposed a single seven-year term, and a life term, before finally settling on four-year terms, with no term limit. At one point, Benjamin Franklin suggested that the president get no salary, so that only those truly devoted to national service would seek the job. The Convention listened politely to the proposal, because of the prestige of its author, and then completely ignored it.

Some delegates wanted the executive to have an absolute veto over acts of Congress, while others feared any veto. The system adopted, with a veto that could be overturned by a two-thirds majority, satisfied almost everyone at the Convention.

The method of choosing a chief executive was equally troubling. On July 17, for example, the Convention considered, and rejected by wide margins, election of the president by the Congress, direct election by the people, and election by the state legislatures. Ultimately, the delegates chose an odd system of election. Each state would get a number of presidential electors equal to its seats in the House of Representatives plus its two senators. The states could decide for themselves how to choose these electors. The electors would make up something called the electoral college, which then elects the president.

The system was highly undemocratic, since the people were removed from the election of the president. Some delegates pushed for the direct election of the president, but this was voted down, with overwhelming opposition from the South. The reason was clear. If the people directly elected the president then those states with the most voters would have the most influence over the election. Some southern states, like South Carolina, had severely restrictive rules for who could vote. Thus, in a popular election those states would have less of a voice. More importantly, the issue of slavery doomed the direct election of the president.

Having already given the South extra representation for its slaves in the Congress, the South now saw that it needed the same sort of extra power in the election of the president. James Madison instinctively favored election of the president by the people. He told the Convention that "the people at large" were "the fittest" to choose the president. But "one difficulty . . . of a serious nature" made election by the people impossible. Madison noted that in a direct election of the president the South "could have no influence in the election on the score of the Negroes." In order to guarantee that the nonvoting slaves could nevertheless influence the presidential election, Madison favored the creation of the electoral college. Under this system each state was given a number of electors equal to its total congressional and senatorial representation. This meant that the three-fifths clause would help determine the outcome of presidential elections. Thus, the fundamentally antidemocratic electoral college developed, at least in part, to protect the interests of slavery.

## The Judicial Branch

The structure of the new government also included a federal court system, although the powers of these courts were not fully debated. The delegates spent a great deal of energy deciding how the judges should be chosen before settling on presidential appointment with Senate confirmation. Similarly, they debated the terms of office and the proper standard for removal by impeachment.

To the frustration of many modern scholars, the delegates did not explicitly discuss the idea of judicial review. However, the language of the Constitution, combined with the very lack of debate over the powers of the courts suggests that the delegates expected the national courts to enforce the Constitution. Thus, Article III began by noting that "The judicial Power of the United States, shall be vested in one supreme Court, and in such inferior Courts as the Congress may from time to time ordain and establish." Given such language, there could be no doubt where the final judicial authority

---

JAMES MADISON AND THE ELECTORAL COLLEGE

Madison's support for the electorial college ultimately paid off well for him. In the very close election of 1800, the slaveholder Thomas Jefferson was elected president by the electoral votes based on counting slaves, thus defeating the nonslaveowner John Adams. Jefferson's choice for secretary of state was Madison, who used that office as a stepping stone to the presidency.

in the nation lay. The Court's jurisdiction was set out in equally sweeping language: "The judicial Power shall extend to all Cases" which might arise "under this Constitution, the Laws of the United States, and Treaties made, under their authority."

In addition to these provisions in Article III, the Framers also made sure that state judicial officers understood the superior position of the federal Constitution and the judiciary it created. Thus, Article VI contained the Supremacy Clause, which declared: "This Constitution, and the Laws of the United States which shall be made in Pursuance thereof; and all Treaties made, or which shall be made, under the Authority of the United States, shall be the supreme Law of the Land; and the Judges in every State shall be bound thereby, any Thing in the Constitution or Laws of any State to the Contrary notwithstanding." Furthermore, all "Members of the several State Legislatures and all executive and judicial Officers" of "the several States, shall be bound by Oath or Affirmation, to support this Constitution." Clearly, the Framers intended the Constitution, treaties, and federal laws to be superior to all state laws, and for all state officeholders to accept and acknowledge this federal supremacy. The federal courts were just as certainly empowered to enforce these schemes, and it would be hard to imagine how that could be done without federal judges having the authority to strike down, or at least declare unenforceable, any laws, state or federal, that violated the Constitution.

## The Powers of the New Government

The goal of most of the delegates in Philadelphia was to create a government that would have "energy" and be able to deal successfully with the problems the nation faced. Power had to lie somewhere. The Articles of Confederation either left power in the hands of thirteen separate states, to act as they wished, or created a power vacuum in which nothing could be accomplished. The Framers in Philadelphia were determined to avoid both problems.

Many of the debates in Philadelphia directly addressed the perceived weaknesses of the Articles of Confederation. Most of the delegates agreed that Congress should have the power to collect taxes independently, regulate the currency, raise an army, and most important of all, conduct foreign affairs without having to rely on the states for enforcement of its treaties and agreements. The delegates had little disagreement over the need for a separate federal court system to prevent states from obstructing justice or impeding implementation of treaties that called for judicial settlement of disputes.

The power to declare war, make peace, and control the army was more complicated. Some delegates thought it should be in the hands of the chief executive, others in the hands of Congress. In the end, the Convention compromised. The president was the commander-in-chief of the army and could negotiate treaties. Only Congress could declare war, and treaties could not be concluded without a supermajority of the Senate. The delegates feared a professional, or standing army, but knew one was necessary. They compromised again, by limiting military appropriations to two years and empowering Congress to pass rules for the army and navy, thus putting the military under the control of the civilian government.

Meanwhile, under the new Constitution the states lost considerable power. They could no longer issue money, abrogate contracts, make treaties with foreign countries, or levy tariffs on export duties. Simple majorities in Congress, as well as a modified amendment process, prevented any one state from obstructing the will of the majority. On the other hand, the Convention defeated Madison's proposal to allow Congress to overrule state laws directly. Equally important, the structure of the government made it difficult, or even impossible, for Congress to regulate the actions of individuals directly. Even in the modern era, with the benefit of various amendments and hundreds of precedents expanding the power of Congress, there are still many areas of life that Congress has no power to control.

In the end, many of the powers of Congress were listed in Article I, Section 8, known as the enumerated powers clause. Article I, Section 9 listed limitations on congressional power. The delegates virogorously debated these provisions, and in the end denied the Congress several explicit powers that some delegates wanted. One example of this was the power to grant charters of incorporation. James Madison, Charles Pinckney, Benjamin Franklin, James Wilson, and Edmund Randolph thought Congress should have the power "to grant charters of incorporation in cases where the Public good may require them." They believed such a power was important because at the time no state had general incorporation laws. They envisioned federally chartered corporations that would operate in more than one state. But protests from Rufus King of Massachusetts, George Mason, and others defeated this proposal.

During the ratification debates defenders of the Constitution argued that it created a government of limited and enumerated powers. The federalists argued that Congress could legislate only where it had specific powers. However, opponents of the Constitution were worried about the vagueness of congressional power. Specifically, they feared two provisions of Article I, Sec. 8: the commerce clause—granting Congress power "To regulate Commerce with foreign Nations, and among the several States, and with the Indian Tribes"; the "necessary and proper clause," also known as the "elastic clause"—which provides that Congress shall have the power: "To make all Laws which shall be necessary and proper for carrying into Execution the foregoing Power, and all other Powers vested by this Constitution in the Government of the United States, or in any Department or Officer thereof."

As we will see later, these two clauses would make the Constitution flexible and give Congress the power to deal with problems unanticipated by the Framers. They are probably the most important clauses in the document produced in Philadelphia for the development of American constitutinal law.

## Regulating Commerce

The main impetus for the Convention came from the need to have some standard regulations of domestic and international commerce. The Annapolis Convention had been called to discuss general commercial problems. That meeting failed, but it led to the calling of the Philadelphia Convention. Not surprisingly perhaps, given this background, the most important, and divisive, debate over the powers of Congress concerned economic regulation. The strongest nationalists at the Convention wanted to give the national government power to regulate most commerce. However, there was a sectional spin on this debate. Southerners generally opposed national regulation of commerce because their region was a net exporter of agricultural products (mostly to-bacco and rice) and an importer of manufactured products. Most of the imports came through northern ports on either British ships or those sailing from New England or the middle states. Southerners saw themselves as at the mercy of these distant forces. They feared that if Congress could regulate commerce, Northerners would protect their own economic interest at the expense of the South. Southerners also feared that Con-gress would levy taxes on exports, which would adversely affect their economic in-terests. In one debate, George Mason "professed his jealousy for the productions" of the Southern or as he called them, "the staple States." On the other side of the issue, Gouverneur Morris, a wealthy landowner, with property in New York and New Jer-sey, but representing Pennsylvania at the Convention, declared that a prohibition on taxing exports was "radically objectionable."

Slavery also complicated the debate over commercial regulation. On July 23, when the Convention agreed to send the draft of the Constitution to a Committee of Detail, General Charles Cotesworth Pinckney "reminded the Convention that if the Commit-tee should fail to insert some security to the Southern States against an emancipation of slaves, and taxes on exports, he should be bound by duty to his State to vote against their Report." He seemed to fear that a national commercial power would allow the Congress to end the African slave trade, or perhaps even strike at slavery in the exist-ing states.

The report of the Committee of Detail, delivered on August 6, appeared to have taken to heart Pinckney's demand for "some security to the Southern States." The re-port prohibited taxation of both exports and imported slaves. Moreover, the clause pro-hibited Congress from ever banning the African slave trade. The draft document al-lowed Congress to regulate commerce by a simple majority, but required a two-thirds majority for the passage of "navigation acts." This led to a floor fight on the issues of commerce, navigation, and the slave trave.

During the Revolution, all of the states had banned or suspended the importation of new slaves from Africa. The motivations for these bans were complex, and included economic concerns, fear of newly imported slaves revolting, and humanitarian revul-sion at the horrors of the African trade. Even many slaveowners reasoned it was one thing to own people who were born and raised as slaves in this country; it was another to kidnap people on the coast of Africa and drag them to America in chains. Thus in the Convention there was strong sentiment to end the African trade, not only from northern colonies like Pennsylvania and New Jersey, but also from Virginia and Delaware. The deep South, led by South Carolina, argued that the slave trade was es-sential for its particapation in the Union.

What followed was a strange alliance between New England and the deep South, against Virginia and the middle states. Roger Sherman of Connecticut argued that there should be "as few objections as possible" to the new Constitution, and thus South Car-olina should be allowed to continue the slave trade if it wished. Oliver Ellsworth, also of Connecticut, refused to debate the "morality or wisdom of slavery" and simply as-serted that "what enriches a part enriches the whole." George Mason of Virginia, who owned over 100 slaves of his own, nevertheless called the African trade an "infernal" and "nefarious traffic." Ellsworth responded that to ban the African trade would be "unjust towards S. Carolina and Georgia." The Convention had now witnessed the unusual phenomenon of a New Englander defending the slave trade against the attacks of a Virginian.

The South Carolinians then joined in. Charles Pinckney, citing ancient Rome and Greece, declared that slavery was "justified by the example of all the world." He warned that any prohibition of the slave trade would "produce serious objections to the Constitution which he wished to see adopted." His cousin, Charles Cotesworth Pinckney, declared that "S. Carolina and Georgia cannot do without slaves" and thus a prohibition of the slave trade would be "an exclusion of S. Carolina from the Union." Delegates from Georgia and North Carolina echoed these positions.

On a series of votes involving commerce and slavery an alliance between New England and the deep South emerged. This might be called the "dirty compromise" of the Convention. The South Carolina delegation would support the commerce clause if New England would support a prohibition on export taxes and a protection for the slave trade. Over the objections of James Madison, George Washington, and the delegates from the middle states, the Convention banned all taxes on exports. Had Connecticut and Massachusetts voted with the North, the result would have been reversed.

The Convention then turned to the slave trade. The highly respected John Dickinson argued that allowing the trade was "inadmissible on every principle of honor and safety." He doubted that the deep South would refuse to join the Union over the slave trade, especially since at the time no state was actually importing slaves. Other delegates made the same point, but to no avail. The Convention voted to prohibit Congress from banning the slave trade for at least twenty years, but during that time Congress would have the power to impose a nominal tax on every imported slave. Madison complained that this provision was "dishonorable to the National character" and to the Constitution, and the "twenty years will produce all the mischief that can be apprehended from the liberty to import slaves." He was correct; before 1808, South Carolina and Georgia would import about 100,000 enslaved Africans.

The next day, August 29, the Convention adopted the commerce clause. In the debate, General Charles Cotesworth Pinckney claimed "it was the true interest of the S. States to have no regulation of commerce." But, in one of the most revealing statements of the Convention, Pinckney explained that he would support a clause requiring only a simple majority for passage of commercial legislation, because of the New England delegates' "liberal conduct towards the views of South Carolina." Similarly, Pierce Butler of South Carolina declared that the interests of the southern and eastern states were "as different as the interests of Russia and Turkey." Nevertheless, he was "desirous of conciliating the affections of the East," and so he also supported the commerce clause. Immediately after this vote, Butler introduced the Fugitive Slave Clause, which was passed without any debate or formal vote.

## Concluding the Convention

With the vote on the Fugitive Slave Clause, which obligated the Northern states to return escaped slaves "on claim" of their owners, the "dirty compromise" was complete and the last major issue of the Convention had been settled. Fine points had to be worked out, but a spirit of sectional harmony prevailed, and the rivalries between the large and small states were all but forgotten. Finally, after four months, the task came to an end, and on September 17, 1787, the remaining delegates signed what William Gladstone would later describe as "the most wonderful work ever struck off at a given time by the brain and purpose of man." On the last day Elbridge Gerry, George Mason, and Edmund Randolph refused to sign the document. All three noted the lack of a Bill of Rights, which Mason pleaded with the Convention to add. Gerry also opposed the compromise over the African slave trade. Randolph was simply uncertain of his true feelings, although he would later support the Constitution in the Virginia ratification debates, and then serve in George Washington's cabinet. Gerry supported the Constitution after ratification, and in 1813, he would take the oath as vice president of the United States under the Constitution.

Trying to show a united front to the nation, the delegates carefully declared that the Constitution was "done in Convention by the Unanimous Consent of the States present . . ." This was true but misleading. New York State could not actually vote on the document, because it lacked a quorum of at least two delegates. Nevertheless, the Convention allowed New York's single delegate, Alexander Hamilton, to sign the Constitution as though New York had signed on to the Constitution. Similarly, this phrasing ignored the fact that three of the delegates at the Convention refused to sign the Constitution.

The signing by "unanimous consent" was possible only because most of the opponents of the Constitution had either never shown up, like Patrick Henry and Richard Henry Lee, or had gone home, like Yates and Lansing of New York and Luther Martin and John Francis Mercer of Maryland. Had all the opponents of the Constitution come to the Convention and remained to the end, the unanimity would doubtless have been shattered.

## The Constitution and Federalism

Despite the many differences that distinguished the government under the Constitution from that under the Articles, both were federalist in nature. The Founders believed that governmental powers had to be distributed between the national and the state governments and that this division would not only serve a balancing function, but would also protect individual liberties. As Madison wrote in *Federalist 51*:

> In a free government the security for civil rights must be the same as that for religious rights . . . security in both cases will depend on the number of interests and sects. . . . This view on the subject must particularly recommend a proper federal system to all the sincere and considerate friends of republican government.

The philosophical roots of federalism derived not only from European writers, but from the American experience as well. The early Puritans took the Reformation view of a religious convenant and applied it to social and political affairs. John Winthrop, the first governor of Massachusetts, wrote of the "liberty I call civil or federal; it may

## THE CONSTITUTION AND THE ARTICLES OF CONFEDERATION

The Constitution differed from the Articles of Confederation in a variety of ways, as this chart illustrates.

| *Articles of Confederation (1781)* | *The Constitution (1787)* |
| --- | --- |
| No executive branch | Independent president with extensive powers |
| No federal judiciary | A Supreme Court and inferior federal courts |
| Unanimous consent of states | Simpler amending process requiring 2/3 of Congress and 3/4 of states |
| All states have an equal vote in the Congress | All states have 2 votes in Senate; proportional vote according to population in House of Representatives |
| States superior to central government | National government in federal scheme superior to states |
| Sovereignty located in the states | Sovereignty located in the people |
| Congress lacked powers to<br>• regulate interstate and foreign commerce<br>• raise taxes<br>• control currency<br>• enforce its laws<br>• enforce treaty provisions | Congress had power to<br>• regulate interstate and foreign commerce<br>• raise taxes<br>• control currency<br>• enforce its laws<br>• enforce treaty provisions |
| No provisions for checks and balances or separation of powers | Clear system of checks and balances through separation of powers |

also be termed moral, with reference to the covenant between God and man, in the moral law, and the political covenants and constitutions, amongst men themselves."

The federalism embodied in the Constitution is uniquely American. For the first three-quarters of the twentieth century, there was a major shift in power from the states to the national government. But, in the last two decades of the century, there was a significant shift of power back to states, stimulated by concepts such as "new federalism," and embraced by politicians and Supreme Court Justices. The idea of a partnership remains a central tenet of constitutional thought. If the Union is no longer "a regular marriage," as Lincoln phrased it, it still remains, in the words of Chief Justice Salmon P. Chase in *Texas v. White* (1869): "an indestructible Union of indestructible States." The Framers saw both state and national governments as active participants in the political process, and the Supreme Court has devoted a great deal of effort over the last 200 years to defining the nature and limits of this partnership.

While the states and the federal government shared powers, the Constitution clearly put the sovereignty of the nation over that of the states, although it would take a civil war to finally confirm this view. The very first words of the preamble, "We the People of the United States," indicated that the Constitution, and the government it created, derived its authority and legitimacy directly from the people and not, as under the Articles, from the states. Article VI reinforced this point, declaring the Constitution and laws and treaties made by the national government the supreme law of the land, with the judges in every state bound by them, and with state constitutions and laws giving way to those of the United States.

## Checks and Balances

Perhaps the most striking feature of the Constitution was how extensively it implemented the prevailing notions of separation of powers. Unlike the Articles and most state constitutions, clear lines divided the executive, legislative, and judicial functions. In a sharp departure from recent experience, the Framers placed enormous executive power in the hands of the president, a complete turnabout from the state models with their weak executives. The president as chief executive officer had a veto power, served as commander-in-chief of the armed forces, and appointed all executive and judicial officers, although with Senate confirmation. Hamilton and Wilson wanted to make the president even more independent by having him elected directly by the people, but in the end the Convention adopted indirect election through the electoral college. The Convention left the method of choosing electors to the states, and by the 1830s nearly all the states had electors chosen by popular vote. Similarly, Article III gave federal courts more extensive power than most state courts then enjoyed. Although judicial review is not explicitly mentioned, the Framers assumed that the courts would exercise this power, since they inserted the Supremacy Clause in Article VI and specifically rejected a proposal that Congress settle any conflicts between state and federal authority.

At the same time, the Constitution's scheme of government provided a series of checks to prevent any one branch from overpowering the others. Although some parallels may be found in the British government, the Senate did not equate to the House of Lords, nor the president, to the king. Representatives, directly elected, had only two-year terms, so the people would have frequent opportunities to determine if their services had been satisfactory. Senators, indirectly elected, would have longer terms; the Framers originally intended members of the upper house to be somewhat akin to the colonial councillors, men of substance who, insulated from frequent elections, would take a more deliberative view. The president could veto bills, but Congress could override him. Judges received life tenure, but they could be removed for misbehavior. The president and Congress each had extensive powers, but most of these powers had to be exercised in cooperation with each other.

Finally, the Framers realized that their handiwork would have to be adjusted from time to time, and although they did not want to make the amendment process too easy, neither did they want to re-create the impasse experienced under the Articles, by which any one state could block revision. Amendments to the Constitution could be proposed by a two-thirds vote in both houses of Congress, or by a convention specially called by two-thirds of the states. Ratification was accomplished by three-fourths of the states acting either through their legislatures or in special conventions. This high threshhold for ratification of amendments gave ample protection to every section of the nation. Southerners were particularly pleased about this because it meant that the national government could never abolish slavery as long as the South voted as a block to prevent a constitutional amendment on the subject. Indeed, only secession and civil war would allow for this constitutional change.

Recognizing that the Constitution would not stand any chance of approval if subjected to the rule of unanimity required by the Articles, the Convention provided in Article VII that confirmation by nine states would be sufficient to put the Constitution into effect. Moreover, the states were required to call ratification conventions, since the Framers feared that the state legislatures would be reluctant to support the new Constitution, which would diminish their influence. Considering that a constitution already existed, with a designated amendment procedure, this approach constituted a revolution in itself. By this time, however, the Confederation Congress itself had agreed to the need for a new scheme of government. After defeating motions to censure the Convention for exceeding its instruction, Congress submitted the Constitution to the states on September 28, 1787, less than two weeks after the Philadelphia Convention had completed its work.

## The Debate over Ratification

The debates over the Constitution provide the best illustrations we have of the conflicting political theories of the revolutionary era. The writings of both supporters and opponents of ratification indicate the values, fears, and ideals they held for the new nation. Some of the writings, especially *The Federalist*, rank among history's most important statements about the nature of government, and they are still helpful today in determining the goals and intentions of the Framers. But the statements of those who opposed ratification also remain useful. At the same time, whenever we read the arguments surrounding ratification, it is important to remember that they were part of a political debate, designed to sway voters. Thus, writers on both sides exaggerated the virtues and drawbacks of the Constitution. *The Federalist Papers*, for example, were written by Hamilton, Madison, and John Jay for the purpose of convincing the voters of New York to support the Constitution. Thus, these essays do not discuss some issues—like the Fugitive Slave Clause of Article IV—because any analysis of such issues would only have undermined support for the Constitution in that state.

The advocates of the new document quickly organized and adopted the name "federalists," although they might more properly be called "nationalists." Their opponents—who actually favored a truer federalist system, with more responsibility and authority in the states—became known as the "antifederalists."

From the start, the initiative resided with the federalists. Their leaders, fresh from the Philadelphia Convention, already knew both the document and the arguments surrounding the major points; they were better organized and often represented the more articulate elements in the community. Most important, they advocated a well-reasoned solution to the problems of the Confederation, problems that by this time the whole country recognized. The antifederalists had difficulty defending the Articles and had no coherent counterproposal to make in lieu of the Constitution.

Tactically, the antifederalists were their own worst enemies. In the fall of 1787, antifederalists controlled the governments in three major states: Virginia, North Carolina, and New York. Had the opponents of the Constitution acted quickly and decisively, they might have ended the ratification struggle before it got off the ground. They could have called an immediate convention in each state, and quickly defeated the document. Instead, the antifederalists delayed and procrastinated, in the hope that the whole issue might just fade away. Meanwhile, where the Constitution had great support the Federalists moved quickly, piling one ratification on top of another. By the time the Virginia convention actually met, eight states had ratified or were about to do so.

Even when they did call conventions in those states where they held the balance of power, the antifederalists squandered their political capital by dragging out the process and endlessly debating every word of the Constitution. These tactics of delay gave the federalists time to lobby wavering delegates and to gather support for their cause.

These debates also convinced some moderate antifederalists to change their minds, as the full discussion of the Constitution revealed that it was not nearly as dangerous as the extreme antifederalists claimed. Samuel Adams, for example, came to the Massachusetts convention opposed to the Constitution, but after listening to all the debates he changed his mind and voted for ratification. The New York convention was thoroughly dominated by antifederalists, but by the time the vote took place, ten states, including Virginia, had ratified the Constitution. This forced some antifederalists to "betray" their constituents, and vote for ratification. The federalists approached the ratification fight aggressively and with an almost modern sense of politics. The antifederalists believed they could defeat the Constitution by delay. In the end, this tactic backfired.

The debates over ratification took place in every state, and for several months much of the country's attention focused on the crucial question of what form of government the new nation should adopt. The press carried many of the arguments, writers on both sides utilizing the familiar technique of publishing essays under classical pseudonyms. Head and shoulders above the rest stood the eighty-five essays that appeared in the New York press between October 1787 and May 1788 over the name "Publius," which are known collectively as *The Federalist Papers*. Of them, John Jay of New York wrote five before illness forced his withdrawal from the project, James Madison of Virginia wrote thirty, and Alexander Hamilton of New York wrote a majority of the balance; the authorship of several remains in doubt.

Hamilton and Madison worked at near fever pitch for six months, but aside from a division of topics, they cannot be said to have been full collaborators. As Madison told Jefferson: "Though carried on in concert, the writers are not mutually answerable for all the ideas of each other, there being seldom time for even a perusal of the pieces by any but the writer before they were wanted at the press, sometimes hardly by the writer himself." Thus, the work lacks philosophical uniformity. Instead, two distinct strands of political thought can be discerned. Hamilton's views have been characterized as an early system of economic nationalism, with the government an active agent to promote the "general interests" of the people, as interpreted through the "sounder" judgment of the commercial elite. Hamilton appealed directly to those groups that had suffered most from the ineffectiveness of the Confederation, holding out the prospect of stability and prosperity under the Constitution.

Madison argued for a limited and balanced government, devoted primarily to securing individual justice and equality, with popular sovereignty as its only defensible source. In perhaps the most famous single essay, No. 10, Madison asserted that the size and diversity of the country, and the interplay among competing factions, would make it impossible for any single interest to create a majority and seize control of the government. At the time, conventional wisdom held that republics could succeed only in small, homogeneous countries like Switzerland or the Netherlands; larger countries would inevitably deteriorate into anarchy, followed by a tyranny of the strongest faction. In *Federalist 10*, Madison insisted on just the contrary: Given a system of strong checks and balances, size and diversity could only strengthen the polity. "Extend the sphere," he argued, "and you take in a greater variety of parties and interests; you make it less probable that a majority of the whole will have a common motive to invade the rights of other citizens."

By enlarging the scope of government, Madison went on to explain, the Constitution provided the ideal republican solution for the problem of competing interests. The different factions would have a larger area in which to compete and iron out their differences. Republicanism recognized the heterogeneous nature of a free society and took these differences (which traditionally had been seen as destructive of both liberty and effective government) and turned them into assets. The open competition, the need to adjust and compromise, would force the majority to heed the rights of minorities in order to gain their support.

For the federalists, the proposed Constitution not only remedied the many defects they perceived in the Articles of Confederation, but it held out promise for an effective government that could guide the United States to security and prosperity. To achieve these ends, they believed it necessary to shift power away from the states into a central administration, one strong enough not only to weather external attack but also to compel the states to accept treaties and national laws. Many antifederalists, aware of the problems besetting the country, agreed in principle with the need for a national government. But they feared and opposed the new balance of powers, believing that strong state governments provided the only sure defense of their liberties against a potentially tyrannical central authority.

Other antifederalists, however, argued that the nation was only just recovering from the war against England. The peace, after all, was only four years old. The postwar depression was ending and the new government was just beginning to have a chance to prove its worth. Give the government under the Articles time to work, they said, before replacing it with a strong central government that would threaten individual liberty everywhere.

The antifederalists also tried to downplay the supposed crisis facing the nation, maintaining that the Confederation could solve existing problems. The anonymous author of the "Letters of the Federal Farmer," argued that "It is natural for men, who wish to hasten the adoption of a measure, to tell us, now is the crisis—now is the crucial moment which must be seized, or all will be lost." Similarly, Patrick Henry, recalling the Revolution, noted that "It was but yesterday when our enemies marched in triumph through our country." He asked Virginians, "Where is the peril now, compared to that?" Without such a peril, why rush into a new government?

These antifederalists argued that there is a constant struggle between individuals seeking to retain their natural rights and governments attempting to take away their liberty. Because the people kept state governments under close control, they posed little threat to individual rights. But to shift power to a central authority beyond the immediate control of the people would tilt the balance away from freedom. Comments such as those by George Washington, in his letter transmitting the Constitution to the Continental Congress, that "individuals entering into society must give up a share of liberty to preserve the rest," struck terror into men who saw danger to personal rights from every quarter.

The fear for individual liberties, and especially the absence of a bill of rights, alarmed people who otherwise favored the new document. Hamilton, in *Federalist 84* insisted that a separate bill of rights was unnecessary, because "the constitution is itself . . . A BILL OF RIGHTS." But Jefferson, after receiving a copy of the proposed Constitution, disagreed. He told Madison that he liked very much the new scheme of government and thought it had many praiseworthy features. But where were the guarantees of freedom of religion and of the press, protection against standing armies, and the other assurances that by now existed in every state constitution? "A bill of rights," he concluded, "is what the people are entitled to against every government on earth, general or particular, and what no just government should refuse, or rest upon inferences." The absence of a bill of rights became one of the chief arguments against the Constitution. Several states proposed amendments, in the form of a bill of rights, after they ratified the Constitution. The antifederalists in many states tried to make ratification contingent on the adoption of a bill of rights, but everywhere the federalists defeated this move.

Most of the proposed amendments by the antifederalists, were not, however about civil liberties. They called for structural changes, to weaken the national government. Antifederalsts were far more concerned with a national army under the control of the president, for example, than with freedom of speech or religion. In fact, some antifederalists were actively hostile to religious liberty, complaining that the Constitution banned religious tests for office holding and would thus allow Catholics, Jews, and Muslims to hold office.

Many antifederalists believed the new Constitution would create a tyranny. A strong president looked suspiciously like a king to some Americans. The Senate, with its six-year terms, looked too much like the House of Lords. The House of Representatives would be elected every two years, instead of annually, as many state legislatures were. The standing army would support these aristocratic officeholders. Even the seat of government seemed to threaten the republic. It would be remote, distant from the people, and under the control of no one.

Finally, some antifederalists were shocked at the compromises over the slave trade and slavery. A New Yorker complained that the Constitution condoned "drenching the bowels of Africa in gore, for the sake of enslaving its free-born innocent inhabitants." In New Hampshire, Joshua Atherton opposed ratification because it would make all Americans "consenters to, and partakers in, the sin and guilt of this abominable traffic." A Virginian thought the slave trade provision was an "excellent clause" for "an Algerian constitution: but not so well calculated (I hope) for the latitude of America."

The antifederalists tried to pick apart the scheme of government by attacking specific features: the judiciary would be oppressive, the president would be a worse despot than the king, the government existed for the benefit of the merchants. But in the end, they most feared the shift of power. As Elbridge Gerry wrote: "The constitution proposed has few if any federal features; but is rather a system of national government."

The antifederalists generally fell into two camps. Some, like Patrick Henry of Virginia, opposed any change in the governmental system and were willing to use *any* argument to defeat ratification, because the national Constitution would undermine their political power. Henry, for example, argued in the Virginia ratifying convention that the Constitution immorally protected slavery, but also that under the Constitution the government would be able to free all the slaves. Other hardcore antifederalists complained that the lack of a religious test for officeholding would lead, as one opponent of the Constitution put it, to the situation where "a Turk, a Jew, a Roman Catholic, and what is worse than all, a Universalist, may be President of the United States," while another complained that "pagans of every kind" would come to the country and "at some future period this might endanger the character of the United States." Federalists pointed out how absurd such fears were in the overwhelmingly Protestant nation. Other antifederalists argued that the senators serving six years, in cahoots with the president, would use the standing army to create a dictatorship. Madison and other federalists scoffed at such nonsense, pointing out that the voters of America would never choose such people for public office.

Some of the more moderate antifederalists, on the other hand, actually favored a stronger national government but were not pleased with some sections of the Constitution, or were deeply concerned about the lack of a bill of rights to protect the fundamental liberties of the people. Madison consistently denied that the Constitution threatened liberty or that a bill of rights would protect liberty. But, he acknowledged that their fears were honestly held, and not based on selfish and narrow political goals.

In general, the antifederalists feared the Constitution, believing it would lead to tyranny. They equally feared the supporters of the Constitution, who they accused of being monarchists and aristocrats. "A Turk," sarcastically praised the Constitution, declaring "Your President general will greatly resemble in his power the mighty, Ahdul Ahmed, our august Sultan—the senate will be his divan—your standing army will come in the place of our janizaires—your judges, unchecked by vile juries may with great propriety be styled cadis. . . ." The federalists, on the other hand, had little appreciation for their opponents, referring to them as "Demagogues and vicious characters," "wicked," "malignant, ignorant, and short-sighted triflers." A federalist in North Carolina referred to the antifederalists as "a blind stupid set, that wish Damnation to their Country," who were "fools and knaves" opposed to "any man of abilities and virtue." A New Hampshire federalist thought opponents of the Constitution were "*fools, blockheads*, and *mad men*."

## Federalists and Antifederalists

Historians have spent much time attempting to discern some pattern that dictated which groups or individuals supported the Constitution, and which opposed it. The issue received little attention in the nineteenth century, as one writer after another heaped praise on the generation, often echoing Jefferson's description of the Philadelphia Convention as "an assembly of demigods." But in 1913, historian Charles A. Beard advanced the thesis in *An Economic Interpretation of the Constitution* that the Framers had had strong pecuniary interests in securing a stronger government. Beard described the federalists as men of "personalty," merchants and lawyers who held government bonds, speculators in western lands, and creditors in general whose wealth was in paper. Creditors and speculators stood to gain from such features as the prohibitions against states issuing currency or abrogating contracts. Their opponents consisted of holders of "realty," small farmers and planters whose wealth consisted of land and slaves. Beard's book in part reflected the frustrations of Americans who had seen the Supreme Court strike down Progressive Era reforms, such as the graduated income tax, regulations to protect workers from long hours and dangerous working conditions, and attempts to destroy monopolies and trusts. In essence, Beard's book questioned the legitimacy of the Constitution, and by extension, the Supreme Court decisions striking down reformist legislation.

Beard's book touched off an ongoing debate. Historians have thoroughly demolished Beard's distinction between personalty as a factor in determining who supported or opposed the Constitution. James Madison, the "father of the Constitution," had no personalty, while some antifederalists, such as Elbridge Gerry, held large amounts of notes. After doing extensive research into the actual holdings of the Framers, using material unavailable to Beard, Forrest McDonald concluded that Beard's "economic interpretation of the Constitution does not work." However, if Beard's thesis does not explain why some people supported the Constitution and others opposed it, his book has forced scholars to see the Convention for what it was: a gathering of men whose interests, both enlightened and selfish, affected the drafting of the Constitution. Northerners used the Convention to protect their interests in giving Congress the power to regulate interstate and international commerce; Southerners likewise protected slavery and their status as a sectional minority.

But, knowing that economic considerations played a part in the drafting and ratification of the Constitution does not explain why some Americans supported it and others did not. In his study of the antifederalists and the ratifying conventions, Jackson Turner Main drew a distinction between "cosmopolitan" and "localist" elements, whose contrasting experiences led them to opposing views on the Constitution. The localists had little knowledge of or interest in events beyond their town or state, while the cosmopolitans had a broader outlook, were often better educated and more widely traveled, and viewed politics in national rather than parochial terms. Although Main's thesis is useful, it tends to ignore the real philosophical differences between the federalists and their support of a strong central government and the antifederalists who feared that individual rights would be sacrificed for the sake of government efficiency. Background, education, and experience surely played important roles, but so did ideas concerning the nature of government, and these ideas seemed to be distributed among all groups in American society.

Similar to Main's thesis is the analysis put forward by Eric McKitrick and Stanley Elkins, who labeled the Founding Fathers as the "young men of the Revolution." As noted earlier, the average age of the men at the Philadelphia Convention was forty-two. They had, for the most part, come to political maturity at the time of the War for Independence; they held important offices, many of them for the first time, under the

Continental Congress and not in state governments. They learned to see the world around them in terms of the nation's needs and problems, as opposed to the more parochial viewpoints of the states. The success of the United States headed their agenda, and the Constitution represented a distinct improvement in the odds of the young nation actually surviving. The antifederalists, on the other hand, had made their reputations primarily in the states, before the Revolution, and their political thinking reflected their adherence to the state as the primary locus of government. Most of them had never held national office and never learned to take the larger, national view, of the new nation. The shift of power proposed in the new Constitution threatened their political base, and they naturally resisted. This was true even for those opponents of the Constitution who had national experience, such as Patrick Henry and Richard Henry Lee of Virginia, George Clinton of New York, and Samuel Chase of Maryland.

Dovetailing with this analysis is that of Pauline Maier: that many of the opponents of the Constitution were not selfish and narrow politicians, but rather, they were older men, shaped by the oppressive British government of the colonial period. For the "Old Revolutionaries," as she called them, a centralized government was inherently a threat to liberty. "I meet with a National Government," Samuel Adams said after reading the Constitution, "instead of a Federal Union of Sovereign States." Although Adams ultimately voted for ratification, he initially opposed the Constitution. As Maier wrote, these Old Revolutionaries believed "if ratified, the constitution would accomplish what the British had attempted without success; it would destroy the powers of the separate states." Patrick Henry failed to see any "beautiful features" when he looked at the Constitution. Instead, he saw something "horribly frightful. Among other deformities, it has an awful squinting; it squints toward monarchy."

Just as the "Old Revolutionaries" opposed the Constitution, the children of the Revolution supported it. They were more focused on the new nation than on the old struggles with Britain. They were younger and perhaps more willing to take risks. But, of course, there are contradictions here too. John Adams fully supported the Constitution, and in the end even his older cousin, Sam, voted for ratification. In Virginia the older revolutionary George Washington was as staunch a federalists as one could find.

Finally, it is possible to see some geographic patterns in support of ratification. In Massachusetts, for example, the eastern delegates, especially those from places tied to trade and commerce, were overwhelmingly federalists. At the Massachusetts ratifying convention, Suffolk County, which included Boston, voted 34 to 5 for ratification, and Essex County, with the port cities of Salem and Newburyport, voted 38 to 6 for ratification. But in the west, only 6 of 22 delegates from Berkshire County supported the Constitution. Other westerners also opposed the Constitution. The same pattern could be found in Virginia, with support coming from the eastern planters. But even this theory falls apart when we consider Georgia, which was almost entirely frontier, and where support was strong everywhere.

# Ratification

Undoubtedly all these theories contain kernels of truth, some more than others. In the end, however, the states, one by one, and for a variety of reasons, came over to the federalist position. Delaware, Pennsylvania, and New Jersey ratified before the end of 1787, Georgia and Connecticut followed early in January 1788. Massachusetts saw the first close fight, but the state convention approved the Constitution on February 6 by a vote of 187 to 168. By June 21, Maryland, South Carolina, and New Hampshire had ratified, providing the necessary nine states to put the Constitution into effect. But Virginia and New York had still not acted, and without their participation the Union could not succeed. Both states had strong antifederalist elements. But the same stratagem employed in Massachusetts, the recommendation of adding a bill of rights in the near future, won over sufficient votes in Virginia to secure ratification on June 25, by a vote of 89 to 79. In New York, Alexander Hamilton and John Jay engineered one delay after another in the hope that the antifederalists' opposition would weaken as they saw other states ratify. Foolishly, the Antifederalists, who had the votes to defeat the Constitution, went along with this strategy by insisting on a line-by-line discussion of it. Thus, by mid-July, the New York antifederalists found themselves forced to concede defeat, not in their state, but in the nation. With Virginia's ratification, New York faced the possibility of being out of the new government, which would be formed with ten states. On July 26, 1788, antifederalists from the New York City area swallowed hard and voted to ratify. The narrow margin of 30 to 27 was enough to make New York the eleventh pillar of the federal Union. North Carolina held out until an actual bill of rights had been submitted by Congress, and finally ratified on November 21, 1789. Rhode Island, stubborn to the last, did not ratify until May 29, 1790. By then, however, the new ship of state had already been launched. After adopting an ordinance fixing the seat of the new government in New York City and arranging for the election of the president and the convening of the next Congress on March 4, 1789, the Confederation Congress adjourned permanently on October 10, 1788.

## Conclusion: The Constitution and Democracy

In retrospect, we now know how successfully the Framers wrought their work; if not an "assembly of demi-gods," they nonetheless created a brilliant scheme of government that has survived, with some major changes, for over 200 years. Although it is possible that amendments to the Articles might have enabled the Confederation to function more effectively for a number of years, eventually some radical surgery would have been necessary. The weaknesses of the Articles may actually have been their greatest contribution to constitutional development. Theoretically, the Articles should have worked, but they did not. This led the Framers to rely, not on abstract theory, but on concrete experience. It may well have been impossible to have secured the strong government established in the Constitution without the experience of the Confederation.

This does not mean, however, that the Constitution represented a conservative counterrevolution overthrowing the democratically inspired Articles of Confederation, as Beard and others have suggested. The fact that revolutionary leaders in the states and Congress attempted to prevent the abuses they suffered under British rule is understandable; all the early state constitutions as well as the Articles reacted to the causes of rebellion listed in the Declaration of Independence. In doing so, they swung the pendulum from government that was too centralized and too powerful to government that was too weak to be effective. Thus, sooner or later—in most cases sooner—they had to redress this imbalance. The fact that in all cases these changes strengthened the national government does not mean that it lessened democracy.

To portray the Confederation, or the Revolution itself, as democratic is to lift the lid on a box full of contradictions. Why did the allegedly democratic states retain property qualifications for voters and often impose far higher standards for officeholders than the federal Constitution? One of the great accomplishments of the Philadelphia Convention was to ban religious tests for officeholding at the federal level. But such requirements remained in place in all but two of the allegedly more "democratic" state constitutions. If, on the other hand, one views the state legislatures as firmly in the control of the people, then how can one say that the people did not participate in adopting the Constitution? How could state legislatures that passed controversial debtor relief laws and issued worthless paper money have elected delegates solely committed to creditor interests to draw up a constitution that would prevent such actions in the future? Either the American Revolution was a social movement that brought power to the common man, who in turn controlled the legislatures that elected delegates to the conventions, or it was not a great social movement, in which case there is no way to maintain that a higher level of democracy existed under the Articles than under the Constitution.

In the debates over the Constitution, many of the charges and countercharges can be dismissed as little more than inflamed rhetoric. Beyond these, however, both sides did discuss significant ideas seriously, and one is struck less by the discord than by how much they agreed on goals. Both sides recognized the need for a national government, both sides conceded the inability of the Articles as they then stood to meet the demands of a growing country, and both sides understood the necessity of preserving individual rights. Perhaps more than anything else, their essential agreement can be seen in how, once the Constitution had been ratified, most antifederalists joined wholeheartedly with the federalists in the effort to make the new government work.

Only 5,000 words long, the Constitution of 1787, with its relatively few amendments (see the appendix), has provided an effective framework for governing the United States through more than 200 tumultuous years. Its various clauses and articles have been interpreted and reinterpreted to meet the changing needs of a developing nation. What those words have meant at different times in our history will be the primary focus of the rest of this book.

## For Further Reading

Merrill Jensen, *The New Nation: A History of the United States During the Confederation, 1781–1789* (1950), paints government under the Articles in its most positive light. The extent of particular problems are explored in Frederick W. Marks III, *Independence on Trial* (1973), which sees the inability of the states to control foreign trade as a crucial factor leading to the Constitution, and E. James Ferguson, *The Power of the Purse: A History of American Public Finance, 1776–1790* (1961), which analyzes the Confederation's enormous credit problems. Clarence L. Ver Steeg's biography of *Robert Morris: Revolutionary Financier* (1954), examines the central figure of the Confederation government. Some of the essays in John Porter Bloom, ed., *The American Territorial System* (1974), deal with the Northwest Ordinance and evolving federal land policy.

Problems faced by the states are examined in Richard P. McCormick, *Experiment in Independence: New Jersey in the Critical Period 1781–1789* (1950), and Florence Parker Simister, *The Fire's Center: Rhode Island in the Revolutionary Era, 1763–1790* (1978). For the Shays episode, see Marion L. Starkey, *A Little Rebellion* (1955).

For the Philadelphia Convention, Max Farrand, ed., *The Records of the Federal Convention of 1787,* 4 vols. (1911–1937), constitutes the documentary foundation based on Madison's notes. Single-volume narratives include Max Farrand, *The Framing of the Constitution* (1913), Charles Warren, *The Making of the Constitution* (1929), David G. Smith, *The Convention and the Constitution* (1965), and Clinton L. Rossiter, 1787: *The Grand Convention* (1966). On Madison himself, see Ralph Ketcham, *James Madison: A Biography* (1971). On the nature of the men who opposed the new Constitution, see Pauline Maier, *The Old Revolutionaries* (1980). On problems of original intent, see Paul Finkelman, "The Constitution and the Intentions of the Framers: The Limits of Historical Analysis," 50 *University of Pittsburgh Law Review* 349 (1989).

The problem of slavery at the convention is the subject of Paul Finkelman, *Slavery and the Founders: Race and Liberty in the Age of Jefferson* (1995), especially chapter 1, "Making a Covenant with Death: Slavery and the Constitutional Convention." See also Staughton Lynd, *Class Conflict, Slavery and the United States Constitution* (1967), and the relevant chapters in Donald L. Robinson, *Slavery in the Structure of American Politics, 1765–1820* (1982), and William M. Wiecek, *The Sources of Antislavery Constitutionalism in America, 1760–1848* (1977).

The struggle for ratification is the subject of the multi-volume collection edited by Merrill Jensen, *The Documentary History of the Ratification of the Constitution* (1976– ), which is nearing completion. On the debates in the state ratifying conventions, see Jonathan Elliot, ed., *The Debates in the Several State Conventions on the Adoption of the Federal Constitution,* 5 vols. (1936). The best introduction to the federalists remains *The Federalist,* available in several editions. Garry Wills, *Explaining America: The Federalist* (1981), is a perceptive interpretation. See also Douglass Adair's classic article, "The Tenth Federalist Revisited," 8 *William and Mary Quarterly* 3rd ser, 48 (1951), and the fascinating nonideological approach taken by Stanley Elkins and Eric McKitrick in "The Founding Fathers: Young Men of the Revolution," 67 *Political Science Quarterly* 181 (1961).

Robert Rutland, *The Ordeal of the Constitution: The Antifederalists and the Ratification Struggle of 1787–1788* (1966), accepts the need for a new government structure, and charges the antifederalists with exploiting regional jealousies to preserve the status quo. Alpheus T. Mason, *The States Rights Debate: Antifederalism and the Constitution* (1964), also sees the Constitution's opponents as primarily interested in maintaining parochial vested interests. Cecilia Kenyon, "Men of Little Faith: The Anti-Federalists on the Nature of Republican Government," 12 *William and Mary Quarterly,* 3rd ser. 3 (1955), accuses them of not really having faith in the people. Jackson Turner Main, *The AntiFederalists: Critics of the Constitution, 1781–1788* (1961), takes a longer view.

Recently, the antifederalists have been undergoing something of a historiographical rehabilitation. Herbert J. Storing and Murray Dry have edited *The Complete Anti-Federalist,* 7 vols. (1981), a collection of writings opposing the Constitution. Volume I is a very sympathetic work by Storing, *What the Anti-Federalists Were For,* and emphasizes their commitment to the preservation of liberty and individual rights. The best work on the antifederalists is Saul Cornell, *The Other Founders: Anti-Federalism & The Dissenting Tradition in America, 1788–1828* (1999). Stephen R. Boyd, *The Politics of Opposition: Antifederalists and the Acceptance of the Constitution* (1979), and Linda G. DePauw, *The Eleventh Pillar: New York State and the Federal Con-*

*stitution* (1966), see the federalists and antifederalists as having far more in common than previously supposed. For a recent critique of the antifederalists and those who defend them, see Paul Finkelman, "Turning Losers into Winners: What Can We Learn from the Antifederalists, if Anything?," 79 *Texas Law Review* 849 (2001).

No single study of the Constitution has caused more debate than Charles A. Beard's *An Economic Interpretation of the Constitution* (1913). Attacks on it include Robert E. Brown, *Charles Beard and the Constitution* (1956); Forrest McDonald, *We the People: The Economic Origins of the Constitution* (1958); and Benjamin F. Wright, *Consensus and Continuity, 1776–1787* (1958). At present, most scholars concede that economic considerations played some role in the drafting and adoption of the Constitution but that political and ideological matters proved far more important.

There are innumerable studies analyzing the Constitution from particular ideological or philosophical viewpoints. George Dargo, *Roots of the Republic: A New Perspective on Early American Constitutionalism* (1974) reminds us that the Framers did not start from scratch, but that Americans had already developed mature political ideas by 1787. See also S. Rufus Davis, *The Federal Principle: A Journey Through Time in Quest of Meaning* (1978); Rozanne Rothman, *Acts and Enactments: The Constitutional Convention of 1787* (1974); and Robert A. Rossum and Gary L. McDowell, eds., *The American Founding: Politics, Statesmanship, and the Constitution* (1981). Forrest McDonald, *Novus Ordo Seclorum: The Intellectual Origins of the Constitution* (1985), takes some issue with the prevailing republican ideology interpretation.

# 7

# *Launching the Great Experiment*

*Washington Takes Office • The Bill of Rights • The Government Takes Shape • Raising a Revenue • Hamilton's Financial Program • The Bank of the United States • The Hamilton–Jefferson Debate • The Whiskey Rebellion • The Slave Trade and the Fugitive Slave Law of 1793 • Defining Presidential Power • Presidential Conduct of Foreign Affairs • The Neutrality Proclamation • Jay's Treaty • Conclusion: Washington's Achievements • For Further Reading*

WHEN GEORGE WASHINGTON took the oath as president of the United States in New York on April 30, 1789, he faced numerous problems. The Confederation, for example, had left him little more than a few clerks, an empty treasury, and millions in foreign debt. His greatest challenge—and his greatest opportunity—lay in creating a viable and effective governmental structure out of the framework sketched by the Constitution. He proceeded, cautiously but firmly, to establish that government. The next eight years saw the nature and powers of the presidency fleshed out, the cabinet system founded, a federal judiciary created, a financial system implemented, American credit secured, and American territory cleared of British and Spanish forces. And although Washington, like many of his contemporaries, failed to understand its importance in a republic, a political party system also began to evolve.

## Washington Takes Office

By late 1788, the Confederation had practically ceased to function. Congress lacked a quorum after October, and although John Jay continued to serve as secretary of foreign affairs, he could not conduct any business and even lacked authority to permit Jefferson to return home from his post as ambassador to France. Nonetheless, Washington had high hopes for the future. The postwar recession ended, commerce prospered, and American ships plied the oceans, even to China and the East Indies. A series of poor harvests in Europe created a demand for American agricultural products, and farmers enjoyed greater prosperity than at any time since before the Revolution. All across the country Americans were building bridges, turnpikes, and canals.

The returning prosperity led many states to repeal their paper money and debtor relief laws. Several states had passed into the control of the federalists, who now proceeded to bring state constitutions into line with the federal document. Pennsylvania replaced its unicameral assembly with two legislative houses, and a number of states greatly increased the powers of their governors and granted the judiciary life tenure during good behavior. Even if people still distrusted too strong an authority, they at least seemed prepared to give state governments sufficient power to function effectively.

The 1788 elections also placed control of the new government in the hands of its friends. The election of Washington had been a foregone conclusion and, in fact, had played a significant role in the ratification debates. John Adams received the vice presidency, and federalists held the overwhelming majority of seats in both the Senate and House of Representatives. Only Virginia chose antifederalists for the Senate. The federalist Fisher Ames described the eight antifederalists in the House as "so lukewarm as scarcely to deserve the appellation." Fully half the members of the Constitutional Convention served the new government as legislators, administrative officers, or judges.

Despite the many pressing problems facing the country, practically the first issue Congress turned to involved how the president and other high officials of the government should be addressed. At the 1787 Convention, Alexander Hamilton had put forward a proposal that would have made the chief executive a monarch for life. His proposal went nowhere in a convention of dedicated republicans. Nevertheless, both in the Convention and in the new government a number of federalists wanted to fashion the government after the British model. The Senate particularly seemed dedicated to the trappings of royalty. Although the House of Representatives immediately opened its proceedings to the public, the Senate initially followed the example of the House of Lords (as well as that of the Continental Congress) by meeting in closed session. The upper chamber also wanted the president addressed as "His Excellency" or "His Elective Highness," and a committee recommended "His Highness the President of the United States and Protector of the Rights of the Same."

Much as they revered Washington, who personally neither wanted nor gave any encouragement to those pushing for such exalted titles, many members of Congress feared that such trappings would be the first step, as Patrick Henry warned, in a "bold push for the American throne." Henry and other extreme Antifederalists worried that some future president, would become a Caesar, "a NERO, CALIGULA," or some other tyrant. A joint committee of the two houses failed to reach agreement on a title, and the Senate finally gave up, but not before it put itself on record as favoring a title for the chief magistrate "from a decent respect for the opinion and practice of civilized nations."

Looking back nearly two centuries, we are liable to dismiss the debate over titles (which consumed nearly all the Senate's time from April 23 to May 14) as a tempest in a teapot, but it had a larger significance. Americans, through much of the 180 years following Jamestown, had lived under a monarch. The approximately fourteen years that the United States had been a republic had been rocky, and much doubt still existed as to whether a republican form of government would be successful. By opting for the appellation "the President of the United States," the First Congress indicated its faith that simplicity in title best suited a republican nation. The debate did not align federalist against antifederalist. The Constitution, as in so many other areas, was silent on this point; how the early administrations filled in such blanks significantly affected the future form and nature of the government.

Washington, relieved not to be weighted down with pretentious titles, nonetheless understood the symbolic importance of the presidency, and he intended to dignify the office by action and demeanor. A man respected rather than loved by contemporaries, he eschewed familiarity and had no intention of making himself a "man of the people." Gouverneur Morris—on a bet, according to one story—once slapped Washington on the back at a social event when the Constitutional Convention was in recess. Washington responded to this familiarity with an icy stare that put a chill on the entire gathering. Washington brought to the presidency this sense of dignity that helped make the office of the president, rather than the officeholder, the embodiment of the nation's sovereignty. To use a modern term, from the beginning Washington appeared and acted "presidential." While in office Washington sought advice from Adams, Madison, Hamilton, and Jay on proper presidential etiquette, and made it clear that he intended to establish dignity in his office.

He formulated a set of rules that, among other things, provided for periodic levees, no display of extravagance, the entertaining of "official persons" only, and no return of visits. When he toured New England in the fall of 1789, Governor John Hancock of Massachusetts, irritated by his failure to be elected vice president, refused to pay the first call upon Washington after his arrival in Boston. Washington stayed in his room until Hancock, realizing that the populace would not countenance such an insult to the chief magistrate, finally gave in, and, feigning illness, had himself carried in a litter to Washington's room. We might dismiss this as a petty social tiff, but it demonstrated that just as the Constitution now reigned supreme over state law, so the chief executive of the United States took precedence over state officials.

Washington had little to rely on in shaping the presidency other than the familiar British precedents, the often vague mandate of the Constitution, and his own common sense. After delivering his inaugural address in person, both houses of Congress made replies, and then Washington responded formally, much as the king and the two houses of Parliament did in opening sessions. The first year or so of his administration saw many social events in which guests behaved toward the president much as Englishmen did toward the king in similar situations, and Washington himself rode around New York in a carriage drawn by six horses and escorted by uniformed outriders. Starting with Jefferson, presidents would develop a more informal style, but Washington did not believe that ceremony by itself was incompatible with a republican government. After the drift of the Confederation, people no doubt welcomed the sense of dignity with which he sought to endow the office. Washington himself, as he so often said, would have been happier back in his beloved Mount Vernon, freed from the responsibilities of office.

# The Bill of Rights

Of all the accomplishments of that First Congress, in the long run none proved more important to the preservation of American liberties than the Bill of Rights. The evolution of these amendments illustrates the complexity surrounding the creation of the new government under the Constitution. James Madison is generally accepted as the "father" of the Bill of Rights. He introduced the measures in the House of Representatives and pushed for the Congress to approve them and send them on to the states. Yet, Madison's paternity was clearly reluctant. At the Constitutional Convention and during the ratification struggle, Madison opposed a bill of rights as both dangerous and unnecessary. Even when he introduced them in Congress, he did so with little enthusiasm. He told the Congress that "that in a certain form and to a certain extent" a bill of rights "was neither improper nor altogether useless." Equally odd, the leading antifederalists who demanded a bill of rights before the ratification of the Constitution generally opposed their adoption after the new government was in place. Indeed, Virginia, where antifederalist sentiment was strongest, and where the demand for a bill of rights was greatest, was the *last* state to ratify the Bill of Rights.

During the ratification struggle, the antifederalists argued strenuously for a bill of rights. Several state ratifying conventions had proposed amendments, and by the time the Constitution was in place the states had sent to Congress a grand total of 210 proposed amendments. These amendments touched on more than eighty different subjects, and many state conventions proposed the same amendments.

The amendments can be divided into two categories: those proposing structural changes, to in effect rewrite the Constitution, and those designed to form a bill of rights designed to protect individual liberty in the new nation. Hardcore antifederalists, such as Patrick Henry of Virginia, were far more interested in the first group than the second. They wanted to cripple the new government with amendments that would sap its "energy" and make it subservient to the states. At the same time, Henry and his allies were demanding a second convention. They claimed they wanted this convention to add a bill of rights and correct other "defects" in the Constitution, but what they most wanted was to go back, as much as possible, to the old Confederation.

While the antifederalists demanded a bill of rights during the ratification struggle, the federalists were almost unanimous in their belief that a bill of rights was unnecessary, useless, and probably dangerous. Most federalists believed that the call for a bill of rights was simply a tactic by narrow-minded politicians who wanted to defeat the Constitution. In New York, the anonymous "Caesar" thought that the demands for a bill of rights were made by "designing croakers" in order "to frighten the people with ideal bugbears." Madison believed Patrick Henry and his allies sought amendments that would "strike at the essence of the System." He believed Henry's group had "disunion assuredly for its object" and that disunion was the "real tendency" of all antifederalists. Thus Madison felt that there could be "no middle ground" between supporters and opponents of the Constitution.

During and after the Convention, federalists argued that the Constitution created a government of limited and enumerated powers, and thus a bill of rights was unnecessary. In the Convention, Roger Sherman opposed an explicit protection for a free

## WHY A BILL OF RIGHTS WAS UNNECESSARY:
## THE FEDERALIST POSITION

During the ratification struggle, Alexander Hamilton argued in *Federalist 84* that a bill of rights was simply unnecessary: "why declare that things shall not be done which there is no power to do? Why, for instance, should it be said that the liberty of the press shall not be restrained, when no power is given by which restrictions may be imposed?" He further argued that a bill of rights was "not only unnecessary in the proposed Constitution, but would even be dangerous. They would contain various exceptions to powers not granted; and, on this very account, would afford a colorable pretext to claim more than were granted."

press because "The power of Congress does not extend to the Press." In other debates, the nationalists at the Convention argued that the states, not the national government, could protect individual rights. Pennsylvania's James Wilson asserted that one purpose of the states was "to preserve the rights of individuals." Oliver Ellsworth of Connecticut explained that he looked to the state governments "for the preservation of his rights." After ratification, James Madison would assert that "the rights in question are reserved by the manner in which the federal powers are granted."

North Carolina's James Iredell argued that in England a bill of rights was necessary because of the Crown's "usurpations" of the people's liberties. But, under the new Constitution the people delegated power to the national government," and thus Iredell argued, that such usurpations by the national government were impossible. Iredell asserted that under the Constitution the government could no more "impose a King upon America" than "go one step in any other respect beyond the terms of their institution."

The Federalists also argued that a bill of rights would be useless. At the Convention, Daniel Carroll of Maryland and James Wilson argued that "these prohibitions in the State Constitutions have no effect," and thus it was "useless to insert them" in the national Constitution. In *Federalist 48* Madison also argued that bills of rights were useless, and that people should not put their faith in "parchment barriers against the encroaching spirit of power." In a letter to Jefferson more than a year after the Convention, Madison elaborated: "experience proves the inefficacy of a bill of rights on those occasions when its control is most needed. Repeated violations of these parchment barriers have been committed by overbearing majorities in every state." He noted that in Virginia he had "seen the bill of rights violated in every instance where it has been opposed to a popular current." He warned that "restrictions however strongly marked on paper will never be regarded when opposed to the decided sense of the public; and after repeated violations in extraordinary cases, they will lose even their ordinary efficacy."

Federalists also argued that a bill of rights might actually be dangerous. This was based on the legal theory that any rights not enumerated in a bill of rights would have been given up. This argument assumed that a complete enumeration of all rights would be impossible. In the Pennsylvania ratifying convention, James Wilson asked who would "be bold enough to undertake to enumerate all the rights of the people?" He thought no one could, but warned that "if the enumeration is not complete, everything not expressly mentioned will be presumed to be purposely omitted." Madison agreed, telling Jefferson if a bill of rights was added to the Constitution it had to "be so framed as not to imply powers not meant to be included in the enumeration."

Madison further worried that a bill of rights might be dangerous because it would not fully secure all rights. He feared that New Englanders would weaken any attempt to constitutionalize a separation of church and state and that the "rights of Conscience" would be "narrowed much more" by a bill of rights than any government would dare do on its own. An incomplete or limited protection of conscience was, in Madison's mind, worse than none at all.

While campaigning for ratification, and later for Congress, Madison encountered what he considered honest, well-meaning citizens who feared the national government would trample their liberties. He denied that such fears were justified and tried to dispel their "absurd and groundless prejudices against" the Constitution. He was far more worried about the oppressive nature of local and state governments. Nevertheless, Madison began to understand that some supporters of a bill of rights were not unscrupulous opponents of the Constitution.

After ratification of the Constitution was successful, Madison promised his constituents that if elected to Congress he would propose a bill of rights. He still did not believe one was necessary, but he acknowledged that "political truths declared" in a "solemn manner" would "acquire by degrees the character of fundamental maxims of free Government, and as they become incorporated with the national sentiment, counteract the impulses of interest and passion." He also thought that although the majority would still ignore the bill of rights when convenient, those oppressed by the majority might find "a bill of rights will be a good ground for an appeal to the sense of the community." Finally, he conceded a small point to the opposition, noting that perhaps "a succession of artful and ambitious rulers, may by gradual & well-timed advances, finally erect an independent Government on the subversion of liberty," and a bill of rights would be "prudent," "especially when the precaution can do no injury."

Thus, early in the first Congress, James Madison introduced some of these amendments. He unequivocally opposed "a re-consideration of the whole structure of the government," but he would accept some amendments, even though he had "never considered this provision so essential to the federal constitution." But, with the Constitution ratified, Madison was willing to concede that some amendments might not be "altogether useless."

Originally, Madison intended that amendments would be worked into the text of the Constitution, since, he feared, if set apart at the end they might be treated as secondary and different. Although he failed in this, his worries proved unfounded; amendments to the Constitution have been treated by the people and their government as equal and integral parts of the Constitution.

The confusion in the First Congress over exactly what the Bill of Rights should include worked against Madison's proposal; the legislators wanted to avoid general philosophical statements in favor of specifics, and Madison's proposed first amendment died in committee. So too did his proposal that conscientious objectors be excused from military service.

In late April 1789, the House approved seventeen amendments and forwarded them to the Senate for its concurrence. The upper chamber, however, rejected some of Madison's wording and condensed several sections into shorter, more succinct form. The Senate dropped a general statement, which Madison said he prized above all the others, that prohibited the states from infringing on personal rights. After the Senate completed its revisions, twelve amendments remained. A joint committee of the House and Senate ironed out the remaining differences, and on September 24, 1789, the House gave its approval, followed a day later by the Senate.

Of the twelve amendments submitted to the states, the first two, concerning adjustments in congressional representation and limits on compensation for members of Congress, failed to win approval. The remaining ten went into effect when Virginia, the eleventh state, ratified in December 1791. Virginia delayed so long because the antifederalists there, led by Patrick Henry, understood that once ratified, a bill of rights would undermine or destroy opposition to the Constitution by most rank-and-file antifederalists. This would forever prevent the calling of a second convention or of the adoption of new amendments to restructure the government.

The ten amendments that were ratified comprised an essential catalogue of the rights Americans held dear from both their English heritage and their own experience. Some of the amendments limited the government from infringing on citizens' personal freedom and liberty, others placed restraints on the way government operated. Not all the amendments were aimed at individuals. The Second and Tenth amendments provided protections for the states against the national government. The Establishment Clause of the First Amendment may have been intended to prevent the national government from interfering with existing state establishments of religion, as well as banning any national establishment.

The language of the Bill of Rights has a curious ring to modern ears, because many of the protections are actually framed as negative rights. Thus, the First Amendment begins "Congress shall make no law. . . ." The First Amendment in effect, does not give someone freedom of speech, but rather prevents Congress from passing a law preventing freedom of speech. As written and adopted, the amendments did not limit the actions of the states. Madison had hoped for a provision that would have required the states to grant "equal right of conscience . . . freedom of speech or the press, . . . [and] the right of trial by jury in criminal cases." Madison thought this was "the most valuable amendment in the whole list." Although the House approved this clause, the Sen-

---

## HOW LONG THE STATES HAVE TO RATIFY AN AMENDMENT

Unlike modern practice, there was no time limit on when these amendments could be approved. Over the years, numerous state legislatures have ratified the proposed Second Amendment, limiting when Congress can raise its own salary. In 1992, more than two centuries after it had been first sent to the states, the secretary of state declared that a sufficient number of states had ratified this amendment, which is now officially part of the Constitution as Amendment 27 (see Chapter 44).

ate did not, and thus these rights would not become applicable to the states until after the adoption of the Fourteenth Amendment (1868) and its modern development, starting with *Gitlow v. New York* (1925).

Many of the provisions of the amendments seemed to be direct responses to American colonial history. The requirement of warrants (Fourth Amendment) for searches came out of the struggle over general warrants and the writs of assistance; the Sixth Amendment requirements that a trial be by jury in the district where the alleged crime took place had its origin in the attempt by Britain to try colonists in admiralty courts. Other provisions—the Eighth Amendment ban on cruel and unusual punishments— came out of the history of England and America in the fifteenth and sixteenth centuries. Still, other aspects of the Bill of Rights were really quite new and creative. Only a few states had a protection for freedom of speech (found in the First Amendment), for example, and there is little history of that right before this time. Similarly, a right to counsel in criminal cases was distinctly not part of the common law, but Madison and his colleagues understood its value, and put it in the document. Finally, some rights, like the Fifth Amendment guarantee that no one would "be deprived of life, liberty or property without due process of law," were rooted in Magna Carta itself. On the other end of the scale, the Tenth Amendment's origins were but a few years old; it was derived almost word for word from the Articles of Confederation, but with the term "expressly" deliberately omitted to indicate that the Framers did not want to hamper the national government. The Amendment held that "the powers not delegated to the United States by the Constitution, nor prohibited by it to the States, are reserved to the States respectively, or to the people." It became the focus of sectional animosities in the nineteenth century and of states' rights debates in the twentieth. In recent years, the courts have found new meaning for this provision, which was designed to protect the states from too much encroachment by the national government.

The Ninth Amendment was Madison's most creative. Throughout the debate over amendments Madison had been troubled by the notion that any rights not explicitly protected under a bill of rights would be constructively given up. To get around this, he drafted what became the Ninth Amendment, which provides that the "enunciation in the Constitution, of certain rights, shall not be construed to deny or disparage others retained by the people." It has had a limited history of adjudication, in part because jurists, politicians, and many citizens have became more formalistic in their understanding of the Constitution than Madison was.

Even before the Bill of Rights received final approval by the states, one of its goals had been achieved. North Carolina pronounced itself satisfied that the defects in the Constitution had been remedied, and joined the Union late in 1789. Six months later, Rhode Island finally ratified the Constitution, thus completing the roster of the original thirteen colonies.

By itself, no scrap of paper can guarantee civil liberties, and the history of the Bill of Rights has consisted of resistance to its limitations on the one hand and expansion of its coverage on the other. Perhaps most important for the future, courts would have constitutional authority to intercede when fundamental liberties stood endangered. But, in the end, as twentieth-century jurist Learned Hand reminded us, only the people, through their own efforts, can preserve their liberties. Nonetheless, over the years, James Madison's prediction has been confirmed: "The political truths declared in that solemn manner acquire by degrees the character of fundamental maxims of free Government, and as they become incorporated with the national sentiment, counteract the impulse of interest and passion." There would be continuous threats to these liberties, and occasionally, the forces of political passion or bigotry would prevail; but in the past two centuries, the Bill of Rights, which some contemporaries dismissed as a restatement of the obvious, has acquired a life of its own, and its fundamental rights have expanded far beyond their original meaning.

## The Government Takes Shape

In domestic affairs as in foreign policy, the Washington administration had to translate the constitutional outline into a working model, and its decisions would determine the nature of American government for decades to come. From the Confederation the new administration inherited little: a foreign office with John Jay and two clerks; a treasury board with no money; a secretary of war with an army of 672 officers and men; no navy; no revenue, and no means of collecting any; and a heavy foreign and domestic debt. When Washington pledged his "last drop of blood" to ensure that the new government under the Constitution should have a fair trial, he voiced the hopes and apprehensions of all Americans.

During its first session, Congress created several departments, and Washington chose to treat the heads of these departments as a cabinet, a term unknown to the Constitution. All succeeding presidents have followed this practice. Washington appointed Thomas Jefferson, only recently returned from France, as secretary of state; his former aide, Alexander Hamilton, took command of the treasury; General Henry Knox, the only holdover from the Confederation, continued as secretary of war. After 1792, the attorney general, former Virginia governor Edmund Randolph, also met regularly with the cabinet, but unlike the other three, he headed no department. At the time, the attorney general served only as the legal adviser to the government—and at a meager salary—since Congress expected him to maintain a private law practice on the side.

The Constitution, aside from expressly mandating a Supreme Court, left the structure of the federal court system to the Congress. In the Judiciary Act of 1789, Congress established a Supreme Court with six judges and thirteen federal district courts. From these courts, appeals could be taken to three circuit courts, composed of two Supreme Court justices and the district judge, with circuit courts meeting twice a year in each district. The work and duties of these courts will be examined in the next chapter.

## Raising a Revenue

Of all the problems facing the government, none proved more critical than revenue. The Constitution had at last provided the federal government with an independent means to raise funds. Congress had the authority to "lay and collect Taxes, Duties, Imposts and Excises," and as practically its first order of business, it proceeded to exercise that power. Nearly everyone agreed that the main source of revenue should be tariff and tonnage duties; Americans imported nearly all their manufactured goods, as well as important raw materials such as molasses. But although tariff and tonnage fees would certainly provide sufficient income to pay the government's operating expenses plus principal and interest on the debt, they also impinged directly on vested local interests. Northern manufacturers wanted a high protective tariff; Southern planters wanted a low one. New England rum producers opposed more than a nominal fee on molasses, while Southerners called for a heavy tax on this "luxury." Congress faced the same regional and economic antagonisms that had paralyzed the Confederation; its ability to act effectively would be the first test of the viability of the new Constitution.

James Madison, who quickly emerged as a leader of Congress just as he had done at the Constitutional Convention, was the key figure in the passage of the Tariff Act of 1789. In its final form, the tariff reflected Madison's skill as a negotiator in carving out an acceptable compromise among all factions. The measure taxed most articles at an *ad valorem* rate of 5 percent, with duties as high as 50 percent on some manufactured goods. The Senate reduced the molasses tax from 6 cents a gallon to $2^1/_2$ cents, and Madison accurately noted that the high-duty articles "were pretty generally taxed for the benefit of the manufacturing part of the northern community." Although he recognized that a larger burden fell on the South, Madison acted as a nationalist, and like Hamilton, believed that a commercial North and an agricultural South complemented each other. A "perfect accordance of interests" between the two sections would operate, he suggested, for the greater welfare of the society.

Madison ran into greater difficulty when he attempted to utilize tonnage duties as an instrument of national policy. In effect, he proposed an American navigation system that would benefit Americans and their foreign allies and punish those unfriendly to the nation. The coastal trade would be reserved for American ships, and goods imported on American vessels would pay a lower fee than those coming in on foreign bottoms. The opposition arose when he proposed a third, far higher rate for countries that had no commercial treaty with the United States. No one doubted Madison meant to punish Great Britain, which had steadfastly refused even to discuss a commercial agreement since 1783.

Madison intended to use the new powers of the federal government to endear it to the people by striking out at their enemies. He failed to appreciate, however, that the proposal, which only a few years earlier would have been warmly applauded by American merchants, now raised fears that the new government would cripple commerce. Even without a treaty, trade between Great Britain and the United States had revived to its prewar level. America relied on British ships to carry its produce to European markets, and without British imports, where would the tariff revenues come from to pay off the debt? So the final form of the tonnage legislation assessed American ships only 6 cents a ton and foreign vessels 50 cents, but made no distinction between British and other foreign ships. Thus Congress, even while rejecting Madison's more extreme proposal, indicated that it intended to use its new powers in a nationalistic manner.

Congress proceeded with full speed that first session to flesh out the governmental outline. In creating the executive departments, Congress grappled with several questions of form and responsibility for which the Constitution provided no guidance. The great power that financier Robert Morris had wielded as head of finances during the

latter part of the Confederation led some legislators to insist that a board directly responsible to Congress be established, so no one individual could control what everyone expected to be the most important department. Here again Madison's arguments
proved persuasive. "Inconsistent, unproductive, and expensive schemes," he warned,
"will be more injurious to our constituents than the entire influence which the well-di-
gested plans of a well-informed officer can have." A board would certainly diffuse
power, but it would also lessen efficiency and effectiveness. Instead of a board, Congress created a Department of the Treasury headed by a single secretary, appointed by
and responsible to the president.

Congress, however, had no intention of giving up the power of the purse to the
president. To ensure some congressional control, the treasury secretary, unlike other
department heads, would make his reports directly to Congress rather than through the
president. Congress also retained the right to examine all the department's records and
required the secretary to provide information directly to the legislature whenever requested.

## Hamilton's Financial Program

The search for financial stability during the Washington administration led to the most
important constitutional debate of the era, the resolution of which, more than any other
event, determined the future course of constitutional and governmental development
in the United States. It focused on the fiscal plan Secretary of the Treasury Alexander
Hamilton presented in 1790, especially the proposed Bank of the United States. The
arguments presaged not only the political division between Hamiltonian Federalists
and Jeffersonian Republicans, but also the two major schools of constitutional interpretation in the early decades of the Republic: a strict, even literal, construction (Jefferson) as opposed to a pragmatic and broad reading of the document (Hamilton).

Shortly before Congress adjourned at the end of September 1789, it requested the
new treasury secretary to report a plan at its next session for the "support of public
credit as a matter of high importance to the national honor and prosperity." Hamilton
worked assiduously over the next few months, and had his "Report on the Public Credit"
ready when Congress reassembled in January 1790. He asked for the privilege of presenting it orally in the House of Representatives, although aware that the lower chamber had already, over Madison's objections, rejected department heads speaking in Congress as "indelicate" and "dictatorial." The House rebuffed Hamilton's request, and in
doing so strengthened, even if only marginally, the principle of separation of powers.

Next to revenue, the new government needed credit, and to convince both foreign
and domestic lenders to buy the securities of the United States, it had to assure the
lenders that their investment would be safe, with both principal and interest paid. The
spectacle of the last years of the Confederation, with the government living hand to
mouth and begging loans from Dutch bankers, remained fresh in the minds of congressmen, and everyone recognized that the new government would not survive unless
it could establish firm credit. Before new borrowing capacity could be secured, the
government had to arrange to pay or refinance the existing debt, a staggering $50 mil-
lion. Of this, the governments of Spain and France, as well as private bankers in the

Netherlands, held $11,700,000, while American citizens claimed the balance. Few members of Congress wanted to repeat the wholesale repudiation of 1780, when the Continental Congress had arbitrarily set an official value against its currency of $40 paper to $1 specie, thus magically reducing the debt from $400 million to $10 million.

Nonetheless, many congressmen advocated paying that part of the debt owed to American citizens at less than face value. The foreign debt would have to be paid in full as a matter of both principle and expediency. But why, the argument ran, should the same formula apply to the domestic debt? After all, many of the original purchasers had long since sold their securities for as little as 15 cents on the dollar; to pay the current holders at par would only reward speculators. Further, the debt had been incurred during a highly inflationary period; now that more stable times had arrived, why should the government pay in dear money what it had borrowed in cheap money?

To the wealthy, many of whom had indeed speculated in the bonds, the notion of repudiating the debt, even in part, smacked of the worst excesses of the Confederation. Hamilton, who believed that the government would never endure without the support of this group, agreed. A petition from Pennsylvania creditors made far better sense to him: "A debt originating in the patriotism that achieved the independence may thus be converted into a cement that shall strengthen and perpetuate the Union of America." This Hamilton proposed to do.

Rejecting all notions that the debt, either in whole or in part, be scaled down, he insisted that the government's obligations be paid in full. "A government which does not rest on the laws of justice," he warned in his report, "rests on that of force. There is no middle ground." The government had contracted with parties who had purchased the securities in good faith; the bargain now had to be kept. He proposed to convert $13 million of interest in arrears into principal, and then fund the entire debt at par, pledging a certain portion of the government's revenues to regular payment of both principal and future interest.

Hamilton's nationalist views emerged not only in the proposal to fund the nation's debt, but in his more controversial plan to have the federal government assume the state debts resulting from their expenditures during the Revolution. During the Confederation, some states had assumed part of the federal debt, and, as early as 1783, Madison had suggested that a strong national government could legitimately take over state obligations. If it had been constitutionally possible under the Articles, then no one could claim—and Madison, despite his objections to the plan, never did—that the government under the Constitution could not do so as well. The plan, if executed, would bring the creditors of both the states and the nation into closer ties and greater support of the new government. Moreover, although it would have been foolhardy to say so, the plan would also tie the states more closely—and in a secondary role—to the Union.

Hamilton's report immediately raised cries of unconstitutionality in the South; the Virginia assembly adopted a resolution condemning the proposal as repugnant to the Constitution. The real objection, however, could be found in the fact that citizens living north of the Mason-Dixon line held 80 percent of the national debt and nearly all the outstanding state debts as well. The debate in Congress revolved around sectional interests, although opponents often took the higher ground that Hamilton's plan would reward speculators and penalize those states that, at great sacrifice, had paid off all or part of their debts.

In July 1790, the deadlock broke, not from force of argument, but by a simple political deal. Jefferson and Madison agreed to support assumption in return for Hamilton's using his influence to move the capital from New York, first to Philadelphia for ten years, and then to a permanent site on the Potomac River. An additional suggestion by Representative Roger Sherman of Connecticut that states with small debts be compensated by grants from the federal government sweetened the deal, making it more palatable to the southern states. In August, by a narrow margin, Congress accepted the essential features of Hamilton's report.

As a result, the national debt swelled to over $80 million and required nearly four-fifths of the government's annual expenditures. But, as Hamilton had predicted, the credit of the United States, practically nonexistent in early 1789, soon achieved a sound, even enviable position, with American bonds selling at or above par in the Amsterdam market. As conditions in Europe deteriorated because of the French Revolution and ensuing war, foreign investors sheltered their funds in American securities. In the United States, the bonds themselves circulated as a medium of exchange in a country that was short of specie, helping to stimulate commercial prosperity.

Resentment, however, continued in the South. In the debate over ratification in Virginia, Patrick Henry had predicted that the northern states, "not satisfied with a majority in the legislative councils must have all our property," and many of his fellow Southerners now lamented that they had taken his warnings too lightly. George Mason complained that Hamilton "had done us more injury than Great Britain & all her fleets & armies." Sectional opposition increased in January 1791, when Hamilton, in response to a congressional request for further recommendations to sustain the public credit, submitted a proposal to establish a Bank of the United States.

## The Bank of the United States

The tariff provided revenue and the funding and assumption measures brought order out of the government's financial chaos, but the nation still lacked an adequate circulating currency and a central bank. Hamilton had as his model the Bank of England, which served as the main depository of government funds, the issuer of currency, and the regulator of smaller banks. The Bank of the United States would do all this and more; it would be the fiscal agent of the government, facilitate tax collection, and stimulate the flow of capital into and around the country. The Bank, as the treasury secretary affirmed, would be "a political machine of the greatest importance to the State."

In his report, Hamilton made only passing mention of the Constitution, praising it for the "additional security to property" that it "happily gives." On the floor of the House, however, Madison argued that the Constitution endowed the federal government with only limited powers, those specifically enumerated, and no others. To incorporate a bank, he contended, required a substantive power not granted by the Constitution, and it could not be deduced by implication as a mere accessory "evidently and necessarily involved in an express power." The broad phrases of the "necessary and proper" clause or the words "common defense and general welfare" should not be construed to expand the government's powers beyond those that the Constitutional Convention had so carefully enumerated. Although Madison had earlier espoused a broader construction, he had always doubted Congress's authority to charter a bank. In 1781, he had acquiesced in the Confederation Congress's charter of the Bank of North America, and at the 1787 Convention, he had proposed, in order to clarify matters, that Congress be expressly permitted to charter corporations, including banks. The other delegates, however, chose not to list this power, some because they feared it would be used to charter banks, and others because they assumed that it was inherent in a sovereign government.

In a second speech a few days later, Madison vented his sectional antagonism to banks, which he labeled as "powerful machines" operating beyond and indifferent to the will of the people. Another Southerner declared that he would no more be seen entering a bank than a house of ill repute, while others warned that Hamilton's proposed alliance between bank and government openly invited corruption. The bank bill, however, passed the House 37 to 20, and the Senate by a vote of 16 to 6. All 6 negative votes in the upper chamber came from the South, as did 15 of the dissents in the House.

## The Hamilton–Jefferson Debate

Although Washington favored the bill, Madison's objections troubled him, and so, as was his custom, he sought advice. Washington asked Madison to prepare a possible veto message should he decide against the measure. Madison's memorandum reiterated the constitutional objections he had raised on the floor of the House, but it also suggested that the president could veto the bill on grounds of unsuitability. Washington also sought opinions from Jefferson and Attorney General Edmund Randolph; both considered the bill unconstitutional. Jefferson agreed fully with Madison that if one used the "general welfare" clause to sanction the bank, then nothing limited what the government could do.

Jefferson explained the proper construction of the Constitution as "where a phrase will bear either of two meanings, to give it that which will allow some meaning to the other parts of the instrument, and not that which would render all the others useless." Neither the taxing power nor the necessary and proper clause supported justification for a bank charter. The Constitutional Convention had not intended to give Congress a free hand, but to "lace them up straightly within the enumerated powers." The necessary and proper clause meant no more than that Congress could enact measures *indispensable* to carrying the enumerated powers into effect in a narrowly defined manner. Jefferson claimed that the Convention had rejected giving Congress the authority to grant charters, because it had feared that Congress might do just what Hamilton now proposed—charter a bank.

Washington now turned to his treasury head, showed him these objections, and invited a reply. Working at top speed, Hamilton prepared a 15,000-word "Opinion on the Constitutionality of the Bank of February 23, 1791," perhaps the most influential constitutional document of the Washington administration, and generally considered to be one of the most forceful arguments ever written in support of the idea that the words of the Constitution "ought to be construed liberally in advancement of the public good." According to Hamilton's reading of the necessary and proper clause, the word "necessary" meant "needful, requisite, incidental, useful, or conducive to." If

Congress truly intended to legislate for the nation, then like all sovereigns, it had to have the authority to pursue the general goals of the Constitution, such as common defense and general welfare, by all the means fairly applicable to the attainment of those ends.

Instead of viewing the enumerated powers as the sole authority of the government, Hamilton argued that the Convention had expressly indicated the most important functions, and then had provided, through the necessary and proper clause and elsewhere, *implied* powers as well. The delegates had not wanted to legislate for the nation, but to provide a framework of government, leaving particular means to future congresses to enact as circumstances and wisdom decreed. Congress had the express power to lay and collect taxes, regulate trade, and coin money, so it must also have the implied power to provide an appropriate mechanism by which to exercise these functions. The only limit on sovereignty existed in the specific prohibitions of the Constitution.

The debate between Hamilton and Jefferson, which Hamilton easily won (Washington signed the bank bill), represented far more than differing modes of textual interpretation. Jefferson and Madison feared a strong national government, and although they recognized the need for some central authority, they wanted it to do no more than was absolutely necessary. They desired to preserve authority for the states, believing that the states, being closer to the people, would be more likely to safeguard their rights. At the same time, they disliked Hamilton's economic programs, and believed that the bank in particular would harm the Southern whites.

Hamilton did not want to restrict individual rights; indeed the strong national government he envisioned would ultimately prove to be a more effective protector of civil liberties than the states. But he had seen the chaos of the Confederation, and he believed that only a powerful central agency could ensure the economic stability on which the nation's future prosperity and happiness depended. A government, by its nature, had to be able to govern, and while Hamilton recognized constitutional limits—which he had helped to draft—he claimed for that government all other powers inherent in sovereignty. Instead of constraining the government, its enumerated powers marked the starting point of what it could and should do. Just as Jefferson spoke for an agrarian view of the future, Hamilton spoke for commerce, and in the end his constitutional view not only prevailed, but also enabled the nation to achieve the economic strength that would make it a world power.

---

## CHIEF JUSTICE JOHN MARSHALL ON THE CONSTITUTIONALITY OF THE BANK

In *McCulloch v. Maryland* (1819) Chief Justice John Marshall would sustain the Second Bank of the United States. Drawing from Hamilton's arguments in 1791, Marshall wrote:

> Let the end be legitimate, let it be within the scope of the Constitution, and all means which are appropriate, which are plainly adapted to that end, which are not prohibited, but consistent with the letter and spirit of the Constitution, are constitutional.

# The Whiskey Rebellion

By 1792, largely as a result of Hamilton's program, the debt resulting from the Revolution had been consolidated and the government had begun making regular payments on principal and interest. Much of the government's income came from tariffs and tonnage fees, but the assumption of state debts required additional revenue, and at Hamilton's urging, Congress in 1791, authorized an excise tax on distilled whiskey. Despite the unpopularity of the measure, both Federalists and Republicans had voted for it, since they saw no alternative way to meet the government's obligations. Hamilton knew the excise tax would be disliked by western farmers, who objected not only to the high rate (about 25 percent of the net price per gallon), but also to the assumption of state debts that had necessitated the tax. The rural areas saw little of either bank notes or specie, and whiskey served as a medium of exchange in most of the trans-Allegheny area. Moreover, since at the time the Mississippi River remained closed to Americans, conversion of grain into whiskey provided farmers the only feasible means of marketing their crops.

The tax seemed reasonable to Hamilton since it allowed western farmers to help support the national government. These farmers purchased few imported goods, and thus did not contribute to the tax coffers through tariffs. But, they produced enormous quantities of whiskey. Much was consumed locally, but much was sent east, where the demand for whiskey was strong. Indeed, at this time, annual consumption of whiskey and other spirits was about three gallons per capita. In this "alcoholic republic," the Whiskey Tax made sense.

From the beginning the tax was a failure. Many distillers evaded the law altogether, while others under-reported their production. In 1792, Congress exempted "personal stills," which led to further evasions and fraud. The tax yielded less than two-thirds of the anticipated revenue. Although rumblings of discontent had been heard from the start, the crisis broke in the summer of 1794. In four western counties of Pennsylvania, rebellious farmers terrorized tax collectors, robbed the mail, disrupted judicial proceedings, and even threatened to attack Pittsburgh. Washington issued a proclamation calling on the insurgents to disperse and appointed a commission to offer amnesty to those who pledged obedience to the law, but neither measure seemed effective. Disaffection in Maryland, Georgia, and the Carolinas increased fears that the whole West might rise in revolt. For the Federalists, the so-called Whiskey Rebellion brought back nightmares of Shays's uprising. Hamilton put the matter bluntly: "Shall the majority govern or be governed? shall the nation rule or be ruled? shall the general will prevail, or the will of a faction? shall there be government or no government?"

The answer came quickly. On August 4, 1794, Associate Justice James Wilson of the Supreme Court certified that the situation in western Pennsylvania had gone beyond the control of either U.S. marshals or ordinary judicial proceedings. This gave Washington, under a 1792 statute, the authority to call out the state militias, and he asked for nearly 13,000 troops to put down the rebellion. So many men answered the president's call that the army threatened to become unmanageable because of its great size.

The insurgents, who had boasted they would march unhindered on the government at Philadelphia, suddenly faced an army larger than the one Washington had commanded during the Revolution. The rebels melted away; government forces, led by Alexander Hamilton, took a handful of prisoners, and the two ringleaders, David Bradford and James Marshel, fled west across the Ohio. Courts found only two of the prisoners guilty of high treason, and Washington pardoned them both, terming one a simpleton and the other insane. The crisis thus ended, and although it could not be said that the government gained in popularity because of its actions, the firmness Washington had displayed convincingly demonstrated the ability of the government under the Constitution, unlike that of the Confederation, to meet internal crises.

## The Slave Trade and the Fugitive Slave Law of 1793

Just as slavery complicated the Constitutional Convention, so too did it affect the creation of the new government under the Constitution. In 1789 and 1790, Congress considered bills and petitions on the African slave trade, and between 1791 and 1793, Congress and the executive branch grappled with the meaning of the Constitution's Fugitive Slave Clause. The debates over both issues provided hints of the fundamental threat slavery posed to the nation. In the discussion of the slave trade, Southerners challenged the right of Northerners even to question the institution of slavery. In the adoption of the Fugitive Slave Law of 1793, Southerners demanded protection for their interests while the governor and attorney general of Virginia adamantly refused to cooperate with either the national government or the state of Pennsylvania to return whites accused of kidnaping and enslaving a free black.

The Constitutional Convention had prohibited Congress from ending the African slave trade until at least 1808, but allowed for a ten dollar tax on all imported slaves. In 1789, Congressman Josiah Parker of Virginia proposed such a tax. He was greeted by a chorus of opposition from Georgia and South Carolina. Shifting the debate, Congressman James Jackson of Georgia attacked the idea of freeing slaves, as if a tax on imported slaves was equivalent to a general emancipation. Reviving the coalition that had brought about the compromise over the slave trade and commerce at the Convention, New Englanders also attacked the idea of a tax on imported slaves. Parker withdrew his proposal at this time, but later introduced it as a separate measure. The House immediately tabled the tax, and it died. There would be no reconsideration of a tax on imported slaves until 1804.

In 1790, Benjamin Franklin, acting in his role as president of the Pennsylvania Abolition Society, petitioned Congress to "step the very verge of the power vested in you" to discourage "every species of traffic in the persons of our fellow men." Nothing in this petition urged unconstitutional acts by Congress. The slave trade provision left Congress with enormous latitude, which Congress might have used to prohibit American ships from participating in it, to regulate conditions on ships bringing slaves to the United States, or in other ways to discourage the trade. Nevertheless, Southerners attacked Franklin with a fury unknown in the young Republic. They warned he would start a civil war with such petitions, and equated any regulation of the slave trade with emancipation.

In response, some Northerners suggested that Congress use money from the sale of land to buy all slaves in the country. Madison, attempting to avoid a debate on this dangerous subject, managed to get the petition sent to a committee, which ultimately reported that Congress did indeed have enormous powers to regulate the trade, although not to end it. This led to a floor debate, in which South Carolina's congressmen defended slavery on biblical, economic, social, and racial grounds, arguing that slavery was a positive good and that blacks were unfit for freedom.

In the end, after much debate indicating the depth of disagreement over this issue, the House did nothing. Meanwhile, in March 1790, Benjamin Franklin published a biting satirical attack on slavery, which stung the slaveowners in Congress while reminding Northerners of the fundamental flaw in the national Union. It was a fitting farewell, from the most senior of the Constitution's signers, who died in April.

In July 1791, a new test of the Constitution began to emerge. Earlier that year, Governor Thomas Mifflin of Pennsylvania had asked the governor of Virginia to extradite three Virginians who were accused of kidnaping a free black in Pennsylvania and enslaving him in Virginia. Article IV, Section 2 of the Constitution provided that a fugitive from justice "shall on Demand of the executive Authority of the State from which he fled, be delivered up" and returned. Despite this obligation, Governor Beverley Randolph of Virginia refused to order the arrest of the men. Virginia took the position that kidnaping a free black was not a felony in Virginia, and thus no extradition was necessary. After months of fruitless negotiations, Governor Mifflin sent copies of his correspondence to President Washington, who in turn handed the matter over to his attorney general, Edmund Randolph. Attorney General Randolph tried to mediate the issue, but the Virginians were adamant in their refusal to cooperate. In October 1791, President Washington sent all his correspondence on the matter to Congress, which in February 1793, came back with a law dealing with extradition and fugitive slaves.

The Constitution dealt with both extradition and fugitive slaves in Article IV. Neither provision indicates that the Congress has a role to play in the process. Rather, the Constitution implies that the return of fugitive criminals and fugitive slaves would be left to the states to work out. Nevertheless, in the sixteen months that Congress considered this issue no one raised a constitutional question. The law ultimately empowered the federal courts and all state courts to participate in the return of fugitive slaves. It was a highly nationalistic bill, the first federal statute creating law enforcement at the local level. By empowering state judges and magistrates to enforce the law, it in effect made state officials an arm of the national government. At first glance, it seems logical that the emerging southern strict constructionists—those who fought against the Bank of the United States, for example—would have vigorously opposed a bill on any other subject that imposed such a sweeping national power. But, the strict constructionists from the South were nowhere to be seen in these debates. On the final vote in the House, two southern antifederalists voted against the bill, perhaps because they did not like the nationalistic nature of the law. But, otherwise, the South was unwavering in its support of the bill. Madison's arguments against the Bank of the United States might easily have been applied to this law, which authorized state officials to act as judges and policemen for the federal government, based on a constitutional clause that on its face gave Congress no jurisdiction at all. But in the House, Madison was silent, as was Jefferson in the cabinet. One explanation for this may be that where slavery was concerned, strange constitutional doctrine and peculiar political alliances could be expected to emerge.

## Defining Presidential Power

Washington followed what he perceived as the Constitution's general rules, although not always successfully. Initially, he appeared willing to grant the Senate more authority than that body wanted. The Constitution directs the president, in regard to treaties, to act with "the advice and consent" of the Senate. In August 1789, Washington went to the Senate, took the vice president's chair, and requested advice and consent from the senators regarding negotiations with the southern Indians. He had prepared a list of seven questions, which Vice President John Adams read aloud, asking at the end of each one, "Do you advise and consent?" The uneasy senators remained silent until Robert Morris suggested that the president's questions required study, and he moved that they be referred to a committee of five. William Maclay, a senator from Pennsylvania, reported that Washington then "started up in a violent fit," exclaiming "This defeats every purpose of my coming here." The Senate, to conciliate the president, agreed to give its answer within three days, and Washington left the chamber in "sullen dignity."

Despite Maclay's waspish comments that the president wanted to overawe the Senate and thus gain acceptance of his proposals, Washington had no such intentions. He had tried to follow, too literally, the constitutional command, and he immediately recognized his mistake. Subsequently, he communicated with the Senate solely in writing, which in fact better suited his temperament. Moreover, he did not always seek that body's advice from the start; the negotiations that led to Jay's Treaty began without consultation between the president and the Senate. Here, as in other areas, Washington established the precedent and thus the meaning of a particular constitutional direction. The advice and consent of the Senate came to mean a *post hoc* approval or denial of a treaty, although presidents, depending on circumstances, have often sought informal advice during negotiations.

Washington, however, was never a narrow constitutional literalist. He understood from experience that governmental affairs required flexibility on the part of those entrusted with their direction, and this in turn meant that the Constitution had to be interpreted in a flexible manner. Although the Constitution requires that the president seek the Senate's advice and consent when appointing "Ambassadors [and] other public Ministers and Consuls," Washington did not interpret this to mean that all diplomatic appointments had to be cleared with the upper house. In October 1789, he sent Gouverneur Morris as a special agent to determine Great Britain's willingness to conclude a commercial treaty. Later on, in a similar manner, he directed John Jay to negotiate outstanding differences between the two countries. In neither case did Washington seek Senate approval of the person or the mission.

Congress recognized the president's control over appointments in the debate over creation of the State Department, when the House considered an amendment that would have prevented the president from removing the secretary without the advice and consent of the Senate. A large majority believed the president should have the power of removal, but members differed on whether the Constitution already implied such authority, or if this power required an express grant by Congress. Madison, who would within a few months argue vehemently against Hamilton's theory of implied powers, at this time upheld the proposition that Article II's general grant of executive author-

## THE CONSTITUTIONALITY OF PRESIDENTIAL APPOINTMENT AND REMOVAL

The power of the president to remove appointees reemerged during Reconstruction, when Congress passed the Tenure of Office Act to prevent President Andrew Johnson from removing federal officials appointed by Lincoln. When Johnson ignored this law, the House of Representatives impeached him. In *Myers v. United States* (1926) the Supreme Court implicitly held the Tenure of Office Act unconstitutional, but then backed away from this conclusion in *Humphrey's Executor v. United States* (1935). Constitutional theorists differ on the constitutionality of Congress prohibiting the president from removing appointees.

ity did not permit Congress to modify or diminish presidential power, be it expressed or implied, and that the removal of executive officials clearly inhered in the executive function. The final bill explicitly authorized the president to remove appointees without Senate approval, and then implied that he had this right under the Constitution, even though it was not stated anywhere in that document.

## Presidential Conduct of Foreign Affairs

In foreign affairs generally, Washington directed policy personally, a precedent that would be followed by every succeeding chief executive. Although the secretary of state handled normal communications between the United States and foreign countries, that officer clearly obeyed the president, in whose hands final decisions rested. The Constitution, however, is unclear on the foreign powers of the president. Article II directs that the president nominate ambassadors and consuls, make treaties, receive foreign emissaries, and serve as commander-in-chief of the armed forces, all of which relate to foreign policy. But at least some of this power is shared with Congress. The Senate must confirm appointments and ratify treaties, while the authority to declare and finance war, as well as to regulate foreign trade, rests with the entire Congress. Article I, Section 8, also grants Congress the power to define and punish piracy, other felonies on the high seas, and offenses against the law of nations, as well as the power to grant letters of marque and reprisal and to determine the rules of capture of ships in international waters.

Nonetheless, many of the Founders referred to the president, in John Marshall's words, as "the sole organ of the nation in its external relations, and its sole representative with foreign nations." In *Federalist 75,* Hamilton, in discussing the treaty-making role, spoke of "the constitutional agency of the President in the conduct of foreign negotiations." Similarly, while secretary of state, Thomas Jefferson asserted that the president

> being the only channel of communication between this country and foreign nations, it
> is from him alone that foreign nations or their agents are to learn what is or has been

the will of the nation; and whatever he communicates as such, they have a right, and are bound to consider as the expression of the nation, and no foreign agent can be allowed to question it.

Congress confirmed presidential authority in this area when it established a secretary and department for foreign affairs. It left the duties in large measure to the discretion of the president, and "the said principal officer shall conduct the business of the said department in such manner as the President of the United States shall from time to time order or instruct."

Although twentieth-century Congresses, especially since World War II and Vietnam, have clashed with presidents in efforts to assert a more coordinate role in setting foreign policy, the tendency throughout most of our history has been for the president to control this area. Washington forcefully set an example in the neutrality crisis of 1793, which raised the most important constitutional questions relating to the direction of foreign policy during his administration.

## The Neutrality Proclamation

In 1778, the Continental Congress had signed a treaty of alliance with France, then under the rule of King Louis XVI. In 1792, following the Revolution of 1789, France proclaimed itself a republic, declared war on Great Britain, and dispatched a special emissary to the United States, "Citizen" Edmond Genêt, to secure American support under the Franco-American treaty of 1778. Washington recognized the new French government and received Genêt, but strenuously avoided involvement in the European war. The ensuing political debate over the power to issue a declaration of American neutrality, was complicated by the fact that the Constitution stood silent on this issue.

As usual, Washington sought advice from many people, including his cabinet officers. Just as Jefferson had been consulted on domestic matters unrelated to his duties as secretary of state, so now Hamilton contributed to this debate on foreign affairs; he also prevailed in this matter.

Jefferson, committed to a literal reading of the Constitution, argued that since only Congress could declare war, it alone had the power to affirm neutrality. Hamilton, on the other hand, believed that the president could issue a proclamation of neutrality on his own constitutional authority. Washington listened to his advisors debate the issue in several intense cabinet meetings. Since Congress had just adjourned and it would

---

### THE PRESIDENT, THE COURT, AND FOREIGN POLICY

In *U.S. v. Curtiss-Wright Export Corp.* (1936) the Supreme Court spoke of "the very delicate, plenary and exclusive power of the President as the sole organ of the federal government in the field of international relations." Perhaps no one put it more bluntly than President Harry S. Truman, when he said: "I make American foreign policy."

take several weeks before to convene a special session—and since fighting had already begun between France and Great Britain—he finally adopted Hamilton's view. Washington's proclamation of April 22, 1793, declared America's intention to be rigorously neutral in the conflict, although, as a sop to Jefferson, the word "neutrality" never appeared in the text.

Aside from the political differences between the pro-British Federalists and the pro-French followers of Jefferson, many Americans objected to this exercise of presidential authority, which exceeded even that possessed by the king of England. The press was soon filled with charges that Washington had acted unconstitutionally. Madison, for example, believed the proclamation violated the Constitution "by making the Executive Magistrate the organ of the disposition, the duty and the interest of the nation in relation to war and peace." The brash Genêt further exacerbated the controversy by mistakenly assuming that Washington's decision to remain neutral did not reflect the sentiments of the country, and he appealed to the American people to support France.

Hamilton responded with seven letters, which he signed "Pacificus," and published in the *Gazette of the United States*. In these letters he defended both the administration's policy and its constitutionality. Hamilton denied that Washington had "stepped beyond the bounds of his constitutional authority and duty," because the president was "the organ of intercourse between the nation and foreign nations" and thus the "interpreter of the national treaties." In a sweeping exposition of Article II's opening phrase, "The executive Power shall be vested in a president of the United States of America," Hamilton argued that only express provisions in the Constitution limited presidential authority. In numerous places, he referred to the president as the government, seeming to place not only control of foreign policy in the chief magistrate's hands, but by implication, other powers as well.

"For God's sake, my dear Sir," an alarmed Jefferson wrote to Madison, "take up your pen, select the most striking heresies, and cut him to pieces in the face of the public." Reluctantly, Madison agreed, and in his five "Helvidius" articles attacked the Hamiltonian doctrine, which he labeled "as no less vicious in theory than it would be dangerous in practice." The power to declare war and make treaties, Madison argued, is not solely an executive power, a doctrine that, he reminded his readers, had been forcefully expounded in *Federalist 69* and *75*, which Hamilton had written. "In no part of the Constitution," the fourth "Helvidius" paper asserted, "is more wisdom to be found than in the clause which confides the question of war or peace to the legislature," because war is the "true nurse of executive aggrandizement."

Although Jefferson pronounced himself well pleased with "Helvidius's" argument, Hamilton won the battle. The noted constitutional scholar E. S. Corwin later wrote that Hamilton's expansive doctrine that the "executive power" clause "embraces a prerogative in the diplomatic field which is plenary except as it is curtailed by more specific clauses of the Constitution has consistently prospered." Congress proved willing, for the most part, to leave the conduct of foreign affairs to the executive so long as it did not feel totally ignored or misled; in turn, presidents with few exceptions kept Congress informed and content and thus exercised practically unfettered discretion. This, however, led to assertions on the part of more recent presidents that their constitutional powers brooked no congressional interference, and a major issue in the last forty years has been the conflict between Congresses trying to reclaim coordinate authority against presidents attempting to preserve allegedly historic autonomy.

## Jay's Treaty

Washington saw Congress's role as quite limited, and he resisted any attempt by the legislators to go beyond their explicit constitutional responsibilities. In 1794, the president dispatched Chief Justice John Jay as a special emissary to Great Britain, with instructions to assure His Majesty's government that the United States did not seek war and to settle outstanding differences between the two countries. These included reparations for the losses of American shippers in the war, compensation for slaves carried away in 1783, and the continued British presence in western forts that they had agreed to abandon. Jay would also try to negotiate a commercial treaty, an effort in which Gouverneur Morris had failed five years earlier.

Jay arrived in London at an unpropitious time, and during the summer and fall of 1794, he conducted negotiations against the backdrop of British victories in the war against France. As a result, he had to cede much, including acceptance of British definitions of neutral rights, in order to secure agreement on other points. Although the British agreed to vacate the forts by June 1796 and to refer all outstanding claims on both sides to a joint arbitration commission, the treaty said nothing about reparations for slaves (whom the British considered "ex-slaves") or the impressment of American seamen. The commercial provisions permitted American ships into the West Indies, but little else. Considering the weakness of the United States as compared with the dominant position Great Britain held in world affairs, Jay's Treaty, in the eyes of many historians, may have contained the best terms the Americans could get at the time.

Washington kept the terms secret until the Senate could act, and that body ratified the treaty only after deleting the commercial provisions. The president, who detested political maneuvering, had to lobby extensively to secure approval. Opposing senators, moreover, leaked the text before the final vote, in hopes that a public outcry would force its defeat. News of the treaty shocked even Washington's strongest Federalist supporters, and the Republicans denounced the document and its author—Jay had sold out to the "Caligula of Great Britain" in his scheme of "starving a whole people out of their liberties." Charles Pinckney of South Carolina called on Washington to urge the impeachment of the chief justice, but Jay, before the treaty had been made public, had already resigned to accept the governorship of New York. Washington almost abandoned the treaty, but in the end he signed it, partly for political reasons and partly because he had believed all along that the treaty would prevent war with Britain.

Despite Washington's hopes that the controversy would now subside, Republicans in Congress felt they had a popular issue with which to attack the Federalists. In March 1796, the House of Representatives overwhelmingly adopted a resolution by Republican Edward Livingston of New York calling on the president to submit for its examination all documents relating to Jay's Treaty, with the exception of "such papers as any existing negotiations may render improper to disclose." The House intended to assert that it, too, had a legitimate role in the treaty-making process, because its control over appropriations gave it a discretionary power over implementation.

After taking counsel with Hamilton (who had resigned as treasury secretary a year earlier) and Secretary of State Timothy Pickering, Washington denied the House request. In his message, the president went further than some of his advisers deemed prudent. Under Article VI, treaties ratified by the Senate and signed by the president became the supreme law of the land. The constitutional silence on a role for the lower chamber had not been accidental. He had, he reminded the House, presided at the Constitutional Convention, and that body had explicitly rejected a proposal to give the House a voice in the treaty-making process.

To this point, James Madison attempted to cool Republican hotheads in the House, and he resisted another "For God's sake" plea from Jefferson to answer Hamilton's "Camillus" letters in defense of Jay's Treaty, which again had asserted extensive executive powers. But, as the recognized constitutional authority in the lower house, he now challenged Washington's analysis. Above all, he rejected the notion that the proceedings of the 1787 Constitutional Convention determined future interpretation. He described that piece of parchment as "nothing but a dead letter, and life and validity were breathed into it by the voice of the people" speaking, not in Philadelphia, but through the state ratifying conventions.

Madison expressed these views in a resolution William Blount of Kentucky introduced, which, while acknowledging that the House did not claim a direct role in treaty making, noted that "when a Treaty must depend for its execution . . . on a law or laws to be passed by Congress . . . it is the Constitutional duty of the House of Representatives to deliberate on the expediency of carrying such treaty into effect." The House need not explain to the president why it wanted to examine documents; that the chamber had expressed such a desire provided reason enough. And, if the House failed to agree on the merit of the treaty, it had the power to nullify it by refusing to appropriate the necessary funds.

The Blount resolution easily passed the House, 57 to 35, indicating that more than a few Federalists joined Republicans in asserting legislative authority against the executive. The next few weeks witnessed the first crisis of the new nation that could be attributed directly to party factionalism. Hamilton mobilized business sentiment behind the treaty; public meetings defended the president, and petitions flooded into the House urging support. The Senate, firmly in Federalist control, threatened to delay other business until the House acted favorably. Moreover, many Republicans wanted the benefits of Jay's Treaty, especially the abandonment of the western outposts, which would be forfeited if the House refused to vote the necessary funds.

By the end of April, the large majority behind the Blount resolution had melted away, and the House appropriated the funds on April 29, 1796, by a vote of 51 to 48. The Republican leader of the House, Frederick Muhlenberg, abandoned his party to support the bill; for his perfidy, he not only lost his bid for reelection that fall, but his brother-in-law, a rabid Republican, stabbed him. One month later, the British announced their readiness to surrender the western forts.

Historian Clinton Rossiter has described the debate over the implementation of Jay's Treaty as "a grand constitutional battle," but the outcome reflected a practical compromise. Despite the lopsided vote favoring the Blount resolution, the Republicans recognized that no constitutional authority existed to pry away the requested papers from a determined president. However, they stood on firm ground in arguing that when a treaty required monies to implement its terms, the Constitution gave the House a definite voice in the matter. Future chief executives would follow, as a matter of principle, Washington's denial that the House could "demand, and to have as a matter of course, all the papers respecting a negotiation with a foreign power." But in terms of expediency, when they needed House approval of a related fiscal bill, they gave the chamber the information it demanded. In the twentieth century especially, when so many treaties called for expenditures, the House came to play an important role in the nation's foreign affairs.

## Conclusion: Washington's Achievements

In 1796, Washington decided not to seek a third term. Sick of politics and hounded by a venomous Republican press, he wanted only to return to Mount Vernon and sit down to dinner alone with Martha—a pleasure, he told friends, he had not enjoyed for twenty years. Although his second term had been marked by partisan factionalism and contentious foreign problems, future historians would consistently rank him as one of the greatest of all American presidents. Deliberately yet surely, he had set government under the 1787 Constitution on a successful path, marking out the general outline for decades to come. Following Hamilton's advice, he had opted for an expansive interpretation of the Constitution, one that gave both Congress and the president sufficient power to deal with the critical issues facing the country.

The fears of the antifederalists regarding central authority provided the seeds for the growth of the Jeffersonian Republicans. Although Washington and others condemned partisan politics as a malignant force, the existence of two parties, both devoted to the welfare of the country even though opposed on means, would prove a beneficial aspect of the American experience. All told, the great experiment, thanks in large measure to Washington's efforts, had been launched with a fair start.

## For Further Reading

A good introduction to this period remains John C. Miller, *The Federalist Era, 1789–1800* (1960). More recently, see Stanley Elkins and Eric McKitrick, *The Age of Federalism* (1994). There are numerous studies on the beginnings of government under the Constitution. Leonard D. White, *The Federalists* (1948), is the initial volume in his administrative history of the federal government; see also Carl E. Prince, *The Federalists and the Origins of the U.S. Civil Service* (1977).

For the presidency, see James Hart, *The American Presidency in Action, 1789: A Study in Constitutional History* (1948); Forrest McDonald, *The Presidency of George Washington* (1974); and E. S. Corwin, *The President: Office and Powers* (1957). See also the two volumes by Thomas Flexner, *George Washington and the New Nation* (1967), and *George Washington: Anguish and Farewell* (1972). James Bryce's classic *The American Commonwealth*, 2 vols. (1888), has several interesting chapters on this period.

For the legislative branch, see Linda Grant Depauw et al., eds. *Documentary History of the First Federal Congress of the United States of America, March 4, 1789–March 3, 1791* (1972– ); George B. Galloway, *History of the House of Representatives* (1961; rev. by Sidney Wise, 1976);

and Ray Swanstrom, *The United States Senate, 1789–1801* (1962). On the creation of the courts, see Maeva Marcus, ed., *Origins of the Federal Judiciary: Essays on the Judiciary Act of 1789* (1992).

For Hamilton, see Clinton Rossiter, *Alexander Hamilton and the Constitution* (1964); and Gerald Stourzh, *Alexander Hamilton and the Idea of Republican Government* (1970). The dominant view of Jefferson as an advocate of negative government is set forth in Dumas Malone, "Jefferson, Hamilton, and the Constitution," in William Nelson, ed., *Theory and Practice in American Politics* (1964), and in Caleb Patterson, *The Constitutional Principles of Thomas Jefferson* (1953). See, however, Charles M. Wiltse, *The Jeffersonian Tradition in American Democracy* (1935), which portrays the Virginian as more of a nationalist. Edmund Randolph, often portrayed as a cipher of Hamilton, is shown as far more independent and useful to Washington in John J. Reardon, *Edmund Randolph* (1974). For ideological differences, see Richard Buel, Jr., *Securing the Revolution: Ideology in American Politics, 1789–1815* (1972); and John Zvesper, *Political Philosophy and Rhetoric: A Study of the Origin of American Party Politics* (1977).

Both Congress and the President were concerned with how to interpret the Constitution in this period. On the debates surrounding this important issue, see Joseph M. Lynch, *Negotiating the Constitution: The Earliest Debates over Original Intent* (1999); H. Jefferson Powell, "The Original Understanding of Original Intent," 98 *Harvard Law Review* 885 (1985); and Paul Finkelman, "The Constitution and the Intentions of the Framers: The Limits of Historical Analysis," 50 *University of Pittsburgh Law Review* 349 (1989). This article also fleshes out the constitutional issues surrounding the creation of the first Bank of the United States.

The best place to begin the Bill of Rights is Leonard W. Levy, *Origins of the Bill of Rights* (1999). On Madison's role, see Paul Finkelman, "James Madison and the Bill of Rights: A Reluctant Paternity," 1990 *Supreme Court Review* 301 (1991). On the debate over adding a bill of rights, see Ronald Hoffman and Peter J. Albert, eds., *The Bill of Rights: Government Proscribed* (1997); and Robert A. Rutland, *The Birth of the Bill of Rights, 1776–1791* (1955). For specific parts, see Leonard W. Levy, *Origins of the Fifth Amendment* (1968), and his various other books on specific clauses of the Bill of Rights. See also George Anastaplo, *The Constitutionalist: Notes on the First Amendment* (1971). On the religion clauses, see the early chapters of Edwyn A. Smith, *Religious Liberty in the United States: The Development of Church–State Thought Since the Revolutionary Era* (1972); a number of essays in Paul Finkelman, ed., *Religion and American Law: An Encyclopedia* (2000); and Michael McConnell, "The Origins and Historical Understanding of Free Exercise of Religion," 103 *Harvard Law Review* 1409 (1990). On the origin and meaning of the Second Amendment, see Michael A. Bellesiles, *Arming America: The Origins of a National Gun Culture* (2000); and the essays in a symposium on the Second Amendment edited by Carl Bogus, "The Second Amendment: Fresh Looks," 76 *Chicago-Kent Law Review* 1 (2000). A number of important essays on the Second Amendment, as well as significant cases, are reprinted in the three-volume collection in the series *Controversies in Constitutional Law*, Robert J. Cottrol, ed., *Guns and the Constitution* (1993). Also useful is Saul Cornell, ed., *Whose Right to Bear Arms Did the Second Amendment Mean to Protect?* (2000). A recent book by law professor Akhil Amar, *The Bill of Rights* (1999), provides interesting theoretical arguments about the Bill of Rights.

Leland D. Baldwin, *Whiskey Rebels: The Story of a Frontier Uprising* (1939), covers that incident well. For foreign affairs, Samuel F. Bemis's classic studies, *Jay's Treaty* (1923) and *Pinckney's Treaty* (1926), remain valuable, but can be supplemented by Jerald A. Combs, *The Jay Treaty* (1970). See also Lawrence S. Kaplan, *Colonies into Nation: American Diplomacy, 1763–1801* (1972); Felix Gilbert, *To the Farewell Address: Ideas of Early American Foreign Policy* (1961); and Alexander De Conde, *Entangling Alliances: Politics and Diplomacy Under George Washington* (1958). Harry Ammon, *The Genet Mission* (1973), explores the domestic impact of that farcical episode.

On slavery in this period, see Donald L. Robinson, *Slavery and the Structure of American Politics, 1765–1820* (1971); Paul Finkelman, *Slavery and the Founders: Race and Liberty in the Age of Jefferson* (2nd ed., 2001). See also David Brion Davis, *The Problem of Slavery in the Age of Revolution, 1780–1823* (1975); and William M. Wiecek, *The Sources of Antislavery Constitutionalism in the United States, 1760–1848* (1978).

For the birth of political parties see Stanley Elkins and Eric McKitrick, *The Age of Federalism* (1994); Doron Ben-Atar and Barbara Olberg, eds. *Federalists Reconsidered* (1998). See also Buel, *Securing the Revolution;* Zvesper, *Political Philosophy;* Joseph Charles, *The Origin of the American Party System* (1956); Richard Hofstadter, *The Idea of a Party System* (1969); Noble E. Cunningham, Jr., *The Jeffersonian Republicans: The Formation of Party Organization, 1789–1801* (1957); and Rudolph M. Bell, *Party and Faction in American Politics: The House of Representatives, 1789–1801* (1973). An older but still interesting study is Andrew C. McLoughlin, *The Courts, the Constitution, and Parties* (1912).

# 8

# The Supreme Court:
# The First Decade

*The Federal Court of Appeals • The Judiciary Act of 1789 •
The Process Act • The Jay Court Convenes • Separation of
Powers • Suing States in Federal Courts •* Chisholm v.
Georgia *• The Eleventh Amendment • The Debt Cases •
Judicial Review • The Ellsworth Tenure • Circuit Duties •
Conclusion • For Further Reading*

Aʀᴛɪᴄʟᴇ III ᴏғ the Constitution vests the judicial power of the United States in one
Supreme Court and such inferior courts as Congress shall establish. The Judiciary Act
of 1789 set out the basic outline of a federal court system, but just as Washington had
to fashion the executive branch, so the new courts and justices had to evolve procedures for the judicial arm of the government. Some of the precedents set during this
period would last for decades; others would vanish within a few years.

## The Federal Court of Appeals

In deciding to create a judicial branch as part of the new constitutional government,
the Framers recognized one of the major weaknesses of the Confederation, apparent
not only in the absence of a federal court system, but also in the confused record of
the only national court created under the Articles. As early as November 1775, George
Washington recommended that the Continental Congress authorize a prize court to dispose of captured British cargoes and vessels. Instead of establishing a federal court,
however, Congress suggested that each state set up a court, with a right of appeal to
the Congress itself. The states accordingly created prize courts, but jealous of their own
authority, they generally limited what appeals could be taken to Congress. New Hampshire, for example, permitted appeals only if the capturing ship had been an armed vessel fitted out by order of Congress; a few years later, it restricted appeals even further,

to cases in which the claimant was a subject of a foreign government "in amity with the United States."

Congress at first tried to handle appeals through a standing committee, but personnel and other problems led to a constant revision of both membership and responsibility. Finally, in January 1780, Congress created a three-judge court, any two of whom constituted a quorum, to try prize cases "according to the usage of nations, and not by jury." The Court of Appeals, which met originally in Philadelphia and later in New York, appears to have been plagued by frequent turnover of judges and by a lack of clarity in what it could or should do. Although it met throughout the Confederation period, the states, unwilling to cede any of their sovereign power, gradually reclaimed most of the appellate process, so that the state high courts reviewed prize court decisions. The weakness of the Court of Appeals, reflective of the Confederation as a whole, can be seen in the case of the sloop *Active*, in which the Pennsylvania court refused to acknowledge any review power of the Court of Appeals, and twice turned down requests from Congress that it abide by the federal court's decisions.

## The Judiciary Act of 1789

It is not surprising, therefore, that the first substantive bill introduced in the Senate proposed the establishment of a federal court system. But it took six months before the Congress could work out details acceptable to a majority in each house. The sticking point, as it would be in so many issues confronting the new government, involved how much power the Constitution transferred from the states to the nation. Both at the 1787 Constitutional Convention and in the state ratifying conventions, those fearful of central authority had argued that state courts should decide questions of federal rights and powers, with appeal to the Supreme Court as provided in the Constitution. If federal courts received original jurisdiction in these matters, that is, if issues could be argued directly in federal courts and bypass the state tribunals, then the power of the national government would be greatly augmented. George Mason warned that "the Judiciary of the United States is so constructed and extended as to absorb and destroy the Judiciaries of the several States."

The Senate appointed a committee on April 7, 1789, to draw up a court plan, and on June 12, it reported a draft, written primarily by Oliver Ellsworth of Connecticut and William Paterson of New Jersey, providing for a Supreme Court of six justices and for district and circuit courts to try criminal and admiralty cases as well as suits between citizens of different states. Richard Henry Lee of Virginia, an opponent of central authority, thought it a good plan, which avoided some of the more obvious dangers, but as he reminded Patrick Henry, "it must never be forgotten . . . that the liberties of the people are not so safe under the gracious manner of government as by the limitation of power." William Maclay of Pennsylvania, however, saw the bill as a "gunpowder-plot . . . a vile law system, calculated for expense and with a design to draw by degrees all law business into the Federal Courts. The Constitution is meant to swallow all the State Constitutions by degrees."

A similar debate raged in the House, especially over Section 25, which authorized writs of error to the Supreme Court, thus giving it appellate review over state court decisions. James Jackson of Georgia feared that "any suit or action brought in any State Courts but may under this clause be reversed or affirmed by being brought within the cognizance of the Supreme Court." Nonetheless, the proponents of the bill maintained that only a federal judiciary with sufficient powers could impose the order necessary under the Constitution. The domination of the Confederation by the states had led to its downfall. "If a State Court should usurp the jurisdiction of Federal causes," argued Roger Sherman, and "attempt to strip the Federal Government of its constitutional rights, it is necessary that the National tribunal shall possess the power of protecting those rights from invasion." Looking back, it is hard to envision how the supremacy of the Constitution provided for in Article VI could possibly have been sustained without federal courts empowered to review and, if necessary, overturn state court decisions. Otherwise, the country would have been saddled again with thirteen independent jurisdictions, each a power unto itself, with no means to conform them to a single national standard. The federal system, it is true, divided powers between nation and states, but the legal chaos of the articles could only be averted by a clear location of national power in federal courts.

The Judiciary Act received final approval on September 24, 1789. It provided for a Supreme Court with a chief justice and five associate justices. Each state would have one district court, except for Massachusetts and Virginia, where a second district judge would sit in the distant parts of those states which now constitute the separate states of Maine and Kentucky. As new states entered the Union, new district judges would be appointed. This much is familiar to Americans today, although now every state has more than one federal district judge, and many states are divided into numerous districts.

The circuit court system created by the act was quite complicated and differed substantially from our court system today. Congress created one circuit court for each state. A circuit court would consist of two Supreme Court justices, who were "riding circuit," and one district judge. The nation was divided into three circuits, and two Supreme Court justices were assigned to each circuit.

The jurisdiction of these courts was also quite different from today. The district courts were empowered to hear all admiralty cases and private lawsuits between citizens of different states where the value in question was at least $100. All criminal cases were tried in the circuit courts, as were private suits valued at more than $500. In admiralty cases where the judgment was more than $300, the losing party could appeal to the circuit court; smaller, nonadmiralty cases could also be appealed to the circuit court, but rarely were. Unlike today, most cases did not begin in the District Court and then move to the Court of Appeals. Indeed, the "Circuit Courts" were not primarily appellate courts, as the Courts of Appeals are today.

Section 25 of the 1789 act provided a relatively broad grant of power to the courts. It has remained a central aspect of federal jurisdiction ever since. Critics and some of the early judges condemned the legislation for its alleged inadequacies and because the circuit riding was particularly difficult for the Supreme Court justices. The system also lacked a grant of general "federal question" jurisdiction, which would have allowed the courts to hear any cases involving federal laws. Nevertheless, the 1789 act was an important first step in the development of a national judiciary and provided the basis and the general outline for what evolved into the modern court system.

The greatest powers of the Supreme Court, to pass on the constitutionality of state and federal legislation, as has so often been pointed out, are not to be found in the Constitution. The Court received the former by act of Congress and assumed the latter through textual extrapolation. Nonetheless, James Madison, who so often expressed himself as opposed to strong central authority, wrote in 1832 that the supremacy of the Constitution would have been impossible without such powers. "I have never been able to see," he asserted, that had the Courts not exercised this function, how "the Constitution itself could have been the supreme law of the land; or that the uniformity of Federal authority throughout the parts to it could be preserved; or that without the uniformity, anarchy and disunion could be prevented." Although there have always been limits on federal court jurisdiction, these basic powers are the minimum without which a federal system makes no sense.

## The Process Act

Opponents of a strong federal judiciary generally failed in their efforts to limit the powers granted by the Judiciary Act of 1789. These localists proved more successful in limiting the powers of the national courts in the Act to Regulate Processes in the Courts of the United States. Also passed by the First Congress, the so-called Process Act fleshed out and defined the authority granted earlier. For example, the Judiciary Act gave federal courts the power to issue writs of scire facias, habeas corpus, and "all other writs not specially provided for by statute, which may be necessary for the exercise of their respective jurisdictions, and agreeable to principles and usages of law." This vague mandate satisfied neither those who wanted to confer broad powers on the courts nor those seeking to restrict them. The twelve sections of the original bill constituted the first effort to create a uniform system of federal procedure. This, in turn, aroused local lawyers, whether they favored or opposed strong federal courts, because it impinged on the practices they knew and to which they were strongly attached.

All states had adopted some forms of English practice, but where New Jersey, New York, and South Carolina, for example, had clung to the common law of the Westminster courts, the New England states tended to follow the more informal rules of the inferior magistrates' courts. Further, in the course of nearly two centuries, the original English procedures had been modified by colonial practice, so that although the various practices in one state would not have been unfamiliar to a lawyer from another state, actual usage varied enormously from one jurisdiction to another. Although there had been no intention in Congress to supplant local rules—in fact, the district courts would for the most part follow state practices—the drafters wanted to set some standards, especially regarding due notice to defendants, which would be uniform throughout the system.

The debate over the Process Act came in the wake of the fight over the Judiciary Act, and at the same time that several states had submitted proposed amendments to gut Article III of the Constitution. As a result, the opponents of the bill proved able to cut out or water down practically all the sections they found objectionable; the final compromise might better have been tabled than passed, for it proved of little value. Even the section providing that writs would run in the name of the president had been eliminated, leaving unresolved what many considered an important constitutional issue. Without an identifiable source for their authority, writs technically had no legitimacy. Some of the questions would be answered by successive Process Acts that slowly, together with the court system's own actions, began to build a body of federal procedure. Congress did not enact a uniform set of rules for civil procedure in federal courts until the 1930s. In the meantime, the courts had to be organized and to start functioning, regardless of the confusion over the scope of their powers.

## The Jay Court Convenes

During the months in which Congress debated the Judiciary Act, President Washington had time to weigh carefully whom he would appoint to the federal courts, especially the six men who would sit on the Supreme Court. He consulted widely with members of Congress and friends, seeking persons who would carry out their duties in full sympathy with the nationalist tone of the Constitution. The Supreme Court, he declared, "must be recognized as the keystone of our political fabric." The importance of how the first Court would act did not escape his notice, for its actions, he told Edmund Randolph, would prove "essential to the happiness of our country and the stability of our political system."

For chief justice, Washington chose John Jay of New York, well known to the president both personally and as a strong nationalist. One of the authors of *The Federalist* and an ardent patriot, the forty-four-year-old Jay had greater prestige as a lawyer in 1789 than did Adams, Hamilton, or Jefferson. Prior to the Revolution, he had had a successful practice, with a reputation as a stickler for detail and as a shrewd, tenacious negotiator. Jay had also played a major role in drafting New York's first state constitution, generally acknowledged to be one of the better early documents. His judicial experience included a term as chief justice of New York, but most Americans probably knew John Jay best as a president of the Continental Congress, one of the American peace negotiators, and foreign minister of the Confederation. Some people wondered, in fact, if he would be content with the relative quietude of the Court after such extensive political and diplomatic activity.

For the five associate justices, Washington sought not only legal experience but a geographic distribution as well. From Massachusetts came William Cushing, who had sat for twelve years as chief justice of that state's highest court. John Blair of Virginia had been chief justice of the General Court and nine years a judge in chancery, while John Rutledge had also been a chancery judge in South Carolina. Washington wanted to name Robert Harrison of Maryland, who had served as chief justice of that state's highest court, but he declined the appointment. James Wilson of Pennsylvania and James Iredell of North Carolina lacked judicial experience, but contemporaries regarded Wilson as possessing perhaps the best legal mind in the country, while Iredell held a similar reputation in his home state. Perhaps of equal importance, all these men had been delegates to the Philadelphia Convention and/or had played an active role in securing state ratification of the Constitution.

Since the Judiciary Act provided for February and August terms, the Supreme Court met for the first time on February 1, 1790, at the Water Street Exchange in New

York, the former site of the Confederation's Court of Appeals. With only three justices present—Jay, Cushing, and Wilson—the Court adjourned until the next day, when, with the arrival of Blair, the Court had its quorum. Nonetheless, the Court again adjourned since it had no cases on appeal, no subpoenas to issue in cases of original jurisdiction, and no clerk to issue them. In fact, the only business of the Court that first term consisted of securing a clerk, John Tucker of Massachusetts; adopting a seal; and swearing in some two dozen lawyers for practice before it, of whom eleven were members of Congress. On February 10, the first term of the Supreme Court ended. At its second session, held on August 2 and 3, 1790, the Court again conducted no business other than admitting attorneys to practice.

Although they decided no cases and issued no writs, the justices did agree on one important question that first term. The failure of Congress to determine in whose name writs would run led to an absurd conclusion that a marshal could receive a command to arrest someone or seize some property without any named source for this authority. Senator William Smith of South Carolina introduced a resolution on January 29, 1790, calling on the Supreme Court to develop a plan to regulate the process in the federal courts and report on it to the House, but the majority tabled the proposal. Jay, however, acted on the assumption that Section 14 of the Judiciary Act, which gave the Court power to issue writs, also gave it power to determine the style of the process. He contacted his fellow appointees with the suggestion that all writs run in the name of the president, and at the February 1790 term, the Court ruled that "unless, and until, it shall be otherwise provided by law," writs would run in the president's name. Although as chief justice of New York Jay had refused to issue a writ of habeas corpus for one Thomas Hadden because the legislature had failed to fulfill a technical mandate of the state constitution, here he seems to have assumed that if the Court had a specific power (to issue writs), then, having the general delegation of Article III's judicial power, it could use all appropriate means to execute that power in the absence of enabling legislation. The Court has, on numerous occasions since, acted or refused to act in certain ways, thus informing Congress, as it did here, that the Congress may change the Court's procedure by statute or confirm it by inaction.

The history of the Court's first decade is, compared with later periods, far from clear. It kept no docket nor did it issue any official reports. A young Philadelphia lawyer, Alexander J. Dallas, compiled a series of cases much as had the early English reporters, partly from his own knowledge, partly from briefs and notes of counsel, and partly from those cases that led to written opinions. No list of cases in which the Court declined to act appeared, and the various volumes of the Dallas reports came out several years after the terms of the decisions. The reports covering the first decade include sixty-five cases, but at least forty-nine additional cases are known to have come before the Court, most on writ of error from state tribunals, in which the Court chose not to act. Nonetheless, the judges, in the cases they decided as well as in other areas, began to shape the contours of the judiciary.

## Separation of Powers

On at least two occasions, Jay's decisions not to act worked to strengthen the doctrine of separation of powers. In November 1790, the Virginia General Assembly adopted a resolution introduced by Patrick Henry condemning as unconstitutional Hamilton's plan to assume state debts. The treasury secretary heatedly wrote to the chief justice calling upon all branches of the national government to assert their opposition to the principle of states' rights embodied in Henry's resolution: "This is the first symptom," Hamilton fumed, "of a spirit which must either be killed, or will kill the Constitution." Jay, despite the intensity of Hamilton's plea, replied calmly, deeming it inadvisable for the Court or its members to engage openly in political disputes.

Jay was certainly not indifferent, as his previous struggles on behalf of the Constitution attested, but he considered it important for the Court to be untouched by partisanship. His close association with Washington, Hamilton, and other members of the administration left no doubt of his true feelings. We now also know that he gave advice quietly to the administration when asked. But he set the example that practically all justices have since followed. No matter how intense their feelings or extensive their involvement with other branches of the government, the appearance of total nonpartisanship must be maintained. When this has not happened, as it did in such cases as *Dred Scott v. Sandford* (1857) and *Bush v. Gore* (2001), the Court has lost prestige and public support.

The first Chief Justice and his Court bolstered the separation of powers more openly, again setting the precedent for their successors on at least two other occasions. In one provision of the Pension law of 1792, Congress required that circuit courts should pass on the claims of invalid veterans seeking pensions from the government, with review by the secretary of war and Congress. Justices Jay and Cushing, sitting in the Circuit Court for New York, ruled in *Hayburn's Case* (1792), the first litigation rising under this act, that "neither the Legislative nor the Executive branch can constitutionally assign to the Judicial any duties but such as are properly judicial, and to be performed in a judicial manner." Although this is the first instance involving the Court's power to invalidate an act of Congress, neither Jay nor Cushing wanted a direct collision between the legislature and judiciary. In a compromise move, they construed the act as in effect naming judges as commissioners to carry out nonjudicial responsibilities. They accepted the task, but maintained the principle, as did Justices James Wilson and John Blair sitting in the Pennsylvania circuit. Their decisions, however, went even further, and in effect they ruled the Pension law unconstitutional not only because it imposed nonjudicial duties on the courts, but also because it made their decisions reviewable by the other branches of the government.

If any doubt remained on the determination of the Court to stay out of the business of the other parts of government, Jay put it to rest, yet in a manner that indicates the bifurcation that has always seemed to attach to the justices in political matters. Jay had secretly written the first draft of Washington's 1793 Neutrality Proclamation, a clearly political act (see Chapter 7). The president, however, wanted to be sure he had the necessary constitutional authority to implement the program, since, following its issuance in April, a number of questions regarding neutrality and its effect upon commercial treaties had come to the government's attention. On July 18, at Washington's direction, the secretary of state sought the Court's opinion. The Neutrality Proclamation and its executive regulations, Jefferson wrote to Jay, involved delicate matters of treaty interpretation, and "the President would be much relieved if he found himself free to refer questions of this description to the opinions of the judges of the Supreme Court." Jefferson's letter included twenty-nine questions to which the President sought answers. Washington, recognizing that the Court might in the future have to rule on some of the matters he now posed in the abstract, proposed that the judges strike out any question that circumstances "would forbid them to pronounce on."

Several states not only permitted but constitutionally required their highest courts to provide advisory opinions to either the legislature or executive in particular circumstances; some states, most notably Massachusetts, still allow advisory opinions today. Washington, therefore, was not seeking to embarrass the Court, but merely expected that it would act according to an already established tradition. Jay, however, recognized the unintentional trap: if the Court rendered an advisory opinion on a hypothetical question, it would be bound to follow its decision when confronted with a real case whose particular circumstances might call for a completely opposite judgment. Jay also knew that the Philadelphia Convention had rejected a proposal allowing Congress or the president to require advisory opinions from the Court, based on the Massachusetts model, although the president had been given authority to require written opinions from heads of the executive departments.

Jay delayed responding until the full Court met for the August term, and on the 8th, with the full concurrence of his brethren, he turned down the request. The line of separation between branches drawn by the Constitution, he wrote,

> being in certain respects checks upon each other, and our being Judges of a Court in the last resort, are considerations which afford strong arguments against the propriety of our extra-judicially deciding the questions alluded to, especially as the power given by the Constitution to the President, of calling on the heads of departments for opinions seems to have been *purposively* as well as *expressly* united to the executive departments.

The Court's decision involved more than a rigid adherence to separation of powers. The whole country seemed divided between pro-French and pro-British factions, with feelings running quite high. Had the Court rendered an advisory opinion, it might well have plunged into the very political storms it sought to avoid. The wisdom of not answering abstract questions of law proved well founded when the following term, in *Glass v. Sloop Betsey,* it had to rule on one of the precise questions submitted by Washington.

The case involved a French privateer who, in violation of American neutrality, had brought a captured ship into an American port. The Court ordered the prize returned to its owners. Although the question had not been raised in argument, the Court went on to answer what had been one of the president's questions, holding that French consuls could not exercise admiralty jurisdiction over such prizes in the United States. "No decision of the Court," wrote Charles Warren in his classic *The Supreme Court in United States History*, "ever did more to vindicate our international rights [and] to establish respect amongst other nations for the sovereignty of this country." The force of the *Betsey* decision might well have been vitiated had the Court issued an earlier advisory opinion, for then it could have been seen merely as the political act of one branch of government in carrying out a policy that it had helped devise, and not as an independent decision of law.

Jay's actions sometimes ran against his firm espousal of strict separation. In 1792, he campaigned for the governorship of New York and lost to Republican George Clinton in a palpably fraudulent election. Future justices would resign from the bench if nominated for elective office. Two years after he lost the New York gubernatorial race and still chief justice, Jay acceded to Washington's request to undertake a diplomatic mission to Great Britain in an effort to resolve the outstanding issues between the two countries. No doubt existed that whatever terms he secured would stir up a political controversy bound to affect the Court. Yet neither Washington nor Jay evidently viewed the assignment as other than a patriotic duty; as Jay wrote to his wife, "the public consideration . . . and the manner in which it was pressed, strongly impressed me with a conviction that to refuse it would be to desert my duty."

By his lights, Jay did what he saw to be right, and after giving so much private counsel to Washington, he probably wanted to resume his former political activism. Shortly after returning from England, he resigned from the Court, and in 1794, ran successfully for governor of New York. But his diplomatic involvement exposed him to much criticism which, in terms of a rigorous separation of powers, he deserved. In the future, other justices would occasionally take on extrajudicial assignments. In 1877, five Supreme Court justices served on a commission to decide the disputed presidential election of 1876. After World War II, Robert Jackson served as a prosecutor at the Nuremberg trials. Similarly, Chief Justice Earl Warren headed the commission investigating President Kennedy's assassination. In these instances, critics charged that the integrity of the Court had been compromised. The general rule to which most judges have adhered is that whatever their private involvement in political matters, members of the Court should avoid nonjudicial assignments.

## Suing States in Federal Courts

Eventually, as government under the Constitution established itself, the Supreme Court began deciding cases of great import for both domestic and foreign affairs, and a body of precedents emerged that affected constitutional development for decades to come. The *Betsey* ruling, for example, governed a 1917 decision in which the Court ordered that the steamship *Appam,* captured by the Germans and brought into Norfolk in violation of American neutrality, be returned to its owners.

At its third term in February 1791, the Court again spent most of its time admitting lawyers to practice, but it also dealt, albeit inconclusively, with an issue that would soon erupt into a major constitutional and political fracas. Two rather innocent looking cases had been entered on the docket under the Court's original jurisdiction. In the first, two Amsterdam bankers, Nicholas and Jacob Van Staphorst, filed an action in assumpsit—a contractual remedy frequently used to collect debts—against the state of Maryland, whose attorney general, Luther Martin, appeared before the Court to respond. Although none of the records survive, it appears that the Court, relying for authority on Section 30 of the Judiciary Act, ordered a commission to take testimony, and continued the case. A docket notation for August 6, 1792, ordered the case discontinued because an out-of-court settlement had been reached.

The question of whether a private person could sue a state in federal court proved a vexatious one. In the same February 1791 term, a Pennsylvania newspaper editor, Eleazar Oswald, sued the state of New York for monies due to the estate of John Holt, of which he was the administrator. The writ had been served on Governor Clinton and Attorney General Aaron Burr, but the state refused to appear before the Court, and for the next three years, Oswald's counsel tried to convince the Court to use its full powers to compel appearance.

The fact that the Court had the power to hear such suits derived from Article III, Section 2(1), which declared that the "Judicial Power shall extend to all Cases, in Law and Equity . . . between a State and Citizen of another State," and Section 2(2), providing original jurisdiction in any case "in which a State shall be a Party." John Marshall, James Madison, and others had assured state ratifying conventions that in adopting the Constitution they would never open themselves to such suits, a position endorsed by Hamilton in *The Federalist*. The clauses, they had explained, would permit states to be plaintiffs in such suits, a rather sophistic argument, since it ignored the fact that if one state could sue another in the Supreme Court, then a state could obviously be a defendant.

But if the Court claimed jurisdiction, how could it force a state to comply? The Process Act gave it no power, and although it could read authority into Section 14, the all writs clause of the Judiciary Act, the Court hesitated to utilize various remedies available under common law. The states, hostile to growing national power, would hardly obey orders to appear in the Court or abide by its decisions. The attorney general of Massachusetts, James Sullivan, had already fired a broadside against the Court for hearing the Van Staphorst case, even though Maryland had consented to the suit. He rejected totally the notion that one sovereignty, that of the federal government, could be superior to another, that of a state. Sovereignty, Sullivan asserted, must by its nature be absolute. By January of 1792, Associate Justice James Iredell urged John Jay not to ride the southern circuit. In Iredell's home state of North Carolina, he told the chief justice, state courts had refused to obey a federal writ, and the North Carolina assembly had gone on record expressing its thanks to the state judges for doing so. Such an atmosphere, Iredell warned, could only embarrass and humiliate the federal judiciary.

With the Van Staphorst and Oswald actions still pending, the Court received two more suits in the August 1792 term, *Grayson v. Virginia* (later retitled *Hollingsworth v. Virginia*) and *Chisholm v. Georgia*. The Virginia case involved a suit in equity by shareholders of the Indiana Company for losses suffered when Virginia nullified the company's title to a large tract of western land that the state claimed. Governor Henry Lee and Attorney General Harry Innes refused to appear before the Court, even though the subpoena carried a $400 fine for nonappearance. The second suit, *Chisholm v. Georgia*, precipitated the constitutional crisis latent in all of these cases.

## *Chisholm v. Georgia*

The facts—which Alexander Dallas got wrong because he relied on a faulty newspaper report—did not involve Loyalist or British creditors, but rather, involved claims by the executor of a man named Farquhar, a South Carolina citizen and patriot, for cloth and clothing supplied to Georgia during the Revolution. The governor of Georgia, Edward Telfair, had originally entered a plea denying jurisdiction of the district court over a sovereign state. Errors in the original complaint led to a dismissal, and a new action in assumpsit, asking for nearly $70,000 in damages, was entered in the Supreme Court. Chisholm retained the attorney general of the United States, Edmund Randolph, in his capacity as a private lawyer; Jared Ingersoll and Alexander Dallas appeared for Georgia, and, acting on instructions, protested that the Court lacked jurisdiction and then declined to participate in the argument.

As a result, the Court heard only the plaintiff's side, and Randolph, in a far-ranging address, argued that the plain language of the Constitution left no possible doubts: under Article III the federal courts had jurisdiction in "Controversies . . . between a State and Citizens of another State." He did not deny the sovereignty of a state, but claimed it derived from the people, the same people who promulgated the Constitution and made it superior to the states in certain areas. When he finished, the Court asked if any member of the bar present wished "to take up the gauntlet in opposition to the Attorney General," but no one volunteered.

On February 18, 1793, the Supreme Court handed down the decision in its first great case. Following the English practice, the justices delivered their opinions seriatim; there appears not to have been a conference in which they tried to reach consensus or adjust their views. Only James Iredell, who spoke first, believed that the federal courts lacked sufficient jurisdiction in the matter, and that the sovereignty of a state could protect it against suit. The other five, for varying reasons, found that the Constitution permitted private citizens to sue a state in federal courts. The Court ordered Georgia to appear at the next term of Court and to show cause why judgment should not be entered against it, or judgment would be awarded in default.

To opponents of strong central authority, the majority holding confirmed their worst fears. Cushing and Blair took a fairly legalistic view; the Constitution said no state could abridge a contract, and the national government, in order to enforce that provision, could certainly exercise judicial supremacy over the states. Wilson declared the national government to be an assemblage, not of states, but of individuals, of the people in whom all sovereignty resided. He saw the states as analogous to the shires and counties of England, mere administrative subdivisions. "As to the purposes of Union," he concluded, "Georgia is not a sovereign state."

Chief Justice Jay, according to a contemporary newspaper, delivered "one of the most clear, profound and eloquent arguments perhaps ever given in a court of adjudicature." Modern students might not agree, for Jay rewrote history to serve his purposes, spoke at length and for the most part irrelevantly about differences among various types of government, and justified the suability of states on several grounds, some sound and one somewhat fanciful. A citizen, he explained, could sue any number of people upon whom he could serve process. He could, in fact, sue 40,000 or more, for in serving a corporation, all its members were sued even if not personally served. Thus, one could sue all the citizens of a state by serving process on the governor and attorney general, the legal representatives of the state as a corporation. Nor did Jay find any barriers to such suits in sovereignty. If one state could sue another, then obviously sovereignty did not bar a suit against a state, nor prevent it from appearing as a defendant.

Jay's strongest argument centered on the justice of the matter. At that time, Georgia had entered suit against two citizens of South Carolina. "The rule is said to be a bad one," Jay noted, "which does not work both ways." The preamble to the Constitution had set forth as one of its aims "to establish justice," and the document itself listed ten types of cases that could most effectively be dealt with by a federal judiciary. If the Constitution, so plain in this area, had meant states to be immune from citizen suits, it would have said so. Absent such a prohibition, the extension of the federal judicial power to such cases appeared to him "to be wise, because it is honest, and because it is useful." In an elegant and forceful conclusion, Jay declared that such an interpretation of the judicial power "leaves not even the most obscure and friendless citizen without means of obtaining justice from a neighboring State." Moreover, "it recognizes and rests upon this great moral truth, that justice is the same whether due from one man to a million, or from a million to one man."

## The Eleventh Amendment

Within a week, the Court also ruled that unless New York could show cause in the Oswald case it would enter a default judgment, and it issued a second subpoena in the Virginia case. The militant defenders of state sovereignty rose in protest. Georgia's lower house passed a bill imposing a penalty of hanging upon any person attempting to enforce the Supreme Court's decree, and Governor Telfair delivered a defiant address upholding the state's sovereignty against federal authority. When a Loyalist sued Massachusetts that June to regain confiscated property *(Vassal v. Massachusetts),* the legislature resolved that the *Chisholm* ruling threatened the safety and independence of the states, and instructed the Massachusetts delegation in Congress to secure an amendment removing any clause in the Constitution that might be construed to support the suability of a state. Virginia voted a similar resolution, attacking the *Chisholm* decision as tending "to a general consolidation of these confederated republics," that is, the states.

Within two days of the *Chisholm* decision, the Senate received a proposed amendment to prevent individuals from suing states in federal courts. An amended version passed the next session of Congress, receiving approval from the Senate on January 14, 1794, and from the House on March 4, both by lopsided margins. Four years later, on January 8, 1798, President Adams announced that a sufficient number of states had ratified the Eleventh Amendment to the Constitution. The amendment raised a number of issues that would plague the Court and the country for decades to come. In theory, it confirmed Justice Iredell's minority opinion that state sovereignty erected a well-defined barrier to the national authority, a view soon embodied in the Virginia and Kentucky Resolutions (1798), and later in the states' rights movements of the early nineteenth and mid-twentieth centuries. But at least temporarily, the amendment seemed to protect states, even for acts of questionable legal and constitutional basis.

Certainly in the years before the Civil War, it would confuse the issues of what federalism meant and where sovereignty resided. Madison, in *Federalist No. 45*, had declared that so "far as the sovereignty of the State cannot be reconciled to the happiness of the people, the voice of every good citizen must be, 'Let the former be sacrificed to the latter.'" Yet for many in the early Republic, indeed even for Madison himself a decade after he had written these words, the happiness of the people could only be protected through the sovereignty of the states. To demean the power of the state could lead only to a greater central authority that inevitably would become tyrannous and destructive of all liberty. Yet Chief Justice Jay's argument that justice required states to submit to suits also struck a powerful chord, and within a few years, the Court began whittling away at the barriers imposed by the Eleventh Amendment. Ultimately the nationalist position enunciated by Jay and Wilson would triumph.

## The Debt Cases

Articles IV and V of the 1783 peace treaty provided that no lawful impediments should be placed before the prosecution of claims by British citizens against American debtors, and that settlement should be made in full value in sterling money. Although the Congress had made the required recommendations to the states, the shortage of hard currency as well as resentment at Britain's failure to vacate the western outposts had prevented implementation of the agreement. During the 1790s, both the Supreme Court and the lower federal courts received dozens of suits from both British creditors seeking payment of debts as well as from Loyalists trying to regain their property.

In *Georgia v. Brailsford* (1794), the case Jay had adverted to in his comment that a good rule should work both ways, a state again raised the issue of its sovereignty as against the provisions of the peace treaty. Georgia relied upon two recent English cases, *Folliott v. Ogden* (1789) and *Wright v. Nutt* (1788), in which jurists had characterized American state confiscation laws as those of an independent country. As a result, Georgia claimed immunity from provisions of either the treaty or the Constitution in this matter. The unusual *Brailsford* case involved a number of complex issues of law, and proved one of the few cases tried in the Supreme Court before a jury. The Court never reached the broader issue of sovereignty, since the case involved only the specific question of whether sequestered debts vested in the state permanently or reverted to the original owner at the end of hostilities. Once the Court instructed the jury that sequestration, unlike confiscation, did not deprive the original owner of his property rights, the jury found against Georgia.

The Court decided the leading debt case, *Ware v. Hylton* (1796), before ratification of the Eleventh Amendment. The case had begun in the circuit court for the Virginia district in November 1790, and before its conclusion in March 1796, became beclouded in the political furor over Jay's Treaty. By the time the Court heard the case, in fact, Jay had resigned from the bench, believing that the storm over the *Chisholm* decision precluded the Court from ever becoming a major force in American life.

The case again involved the question (which had not been resolved in *Brailsford*) of whether treaty provisions took precedence over state laws. Public interest ran high, and in Virginia, where the debts amounted to over $2 million, several statutes operated to prevent British creditors from securing their claims. Interestingly enough, John Marshall made the lead argument for Virginia in his only appearance as an advocate before the Court. The future chief justice, who would do so much to strengthen national authority over that of the states, at this time argued that treaty provisions did not bind state governments. He referred to his opponents as "those who wish to impair the sovereignty of Virginia," the very phrase states' rights advocates would later use in attacking his own decisions on the Court.

Within two weeks of the arguments, the Court, with only Iredell dissenting, held that treaties made by the United States took precedence over state laws. Justice Samuel Chase's opinion, although acknowledging the unique sovereignty of each state and the right of a state to confiscate or sequester enemy assets during wartime, noted that the states in joining the Union had ceded some of their authority to the federal government. Article VI of the Constitution made it explicit that treaties duly made by the United States took precedence over state laws and even state constitutions. The peace treaty, even though made under the Confederation, had been negotiated and ratified by the then government of the United States, and therefore came within the reach of the Supremacy Clause. In meticulous detail, Chase demolished one argument after another that had been put forward to vitiate the clear meaning of the treaty: British creditors had the right to recover debts and could not be barred by state laws.

"Thus was settled forever," wrote Charles Warren, "one of the fundamental doctrines of American law." Although the Court on numerous occasions has interpreted how treaties affected state laws or the rights of individual citizens, the holding in *Ware* remains untouched; in the various building blocks that have erected a strong national government, it holds a place equivalent in many ways to *McCulloch v. Maryland* (see Chapter 11).

## Judicial Review

One day after upholding the precedence of treaties over state legislation, the Court handed down its decision in *Hylton v. United States* (1796), the first case testing the constitutionality of an act of Congress. As with so many of the Court's early cases, this one had more than its share of peculiarities. A 1794 U.S. statute imposed taxes on carriages kept by persons for their own use or let out for hire. In the House of Representatives, opponents had argued that the measure violated the Constitution's prohibition against direct taxes, since it had not been apportioned by population, but its supporters described it as an excise tax, which could be imposed without regard to population. Daniel Hylton of Richmond (the same man who had earlier contested the treaty debt provisions) and a number of other Virginians refused to pay the tax, and after the case had been removed from circuit court, Hylton informed the Supreme Court that his "object in contending the law" was "merely to ascertain a constitutional point and not by any means to delay the payment of a public duty." To prevent federal courts from becoming clogged with suits over petty claims, the 1789 Judiciary Act required that at least $2,000 be involved for a federal court to exercise jurisdiction over a suit. To meet this jurisdictional requirement, Hylton claimed to own 125 carriages "exclusively for the defendant's own private use and not to let out for hire," a fiction to which the government agreed, since the administration also wanted to test the law's validity.

In the lower court, ex-Senator John Taylor of Virginia, known as John Taylor of Caroline (for the county he lived in), a militant champion of states' rights, argued Hylton's case in such a diffuse and confused manner that hardly anyone understood his point. Taylor declined to represent Hylton in the high court, and the administration, in order to have the case fully argued, agreed to pay counsel for both sides. Alexander Hamilton, in his only appearance before the Court, presented the government's case along with Attorney General Charles Lee. Hamilton's "clear, impressive, and classical" argument predictably emphasized the legal doctrines supporting the tax through a broad reading of the Constitution's taxing power. But in a then unusual tactic, he also discussed the views of economists such as Sir John Steuart and Adam Smith to support the carriage duty as an excise rather than a direct tax.

Only three justices participated in the decision. Oliver Ellsworth had just been sworn in, William Cushing was ill, and James Wilson, having sat on the circuit court in the original case, recused himself. Chase seems to have thrown all his energies into *Ware,* for his opinion in *Hylton* carried little of the reasoning or force he had displayed the previous day. He accepted Congress's construction of the law as an excise, since Hylton's counsel had failed to prove otherwise. The power to lay and collect taxes reached into all areas except exports, with only two rules imposed by the Constitution: that taxes be uniform, and that direct taxes be apportioned by population. Since carriages were not necessarily distributed by population, it made no sense to insist that they be taxed that way.

Justice William Paterson, like Wilson, had been present at the Constitutional Convention, and his opinion argued that the Framers had intended Congress to have a broad taxing power, with the provision on direct taxes limited to capitation (a head tax) and land. He rejected Hylton's claim that apportionment constituted the proper rule for all taxation, since that reflected the unworkable requisition system of the Confederation. The fair tax system under the Constitution required uniformity, which should operate directly upon individuals without apportionment or even regard to the states.

*Hylton v. United States* has not received the attention given to *Marbury v. Madison* (1803), yet the great issue of the Court's power to nullify acts of Congress is implicit in its holding. Because the Court upheld the carriage tax, the justices evidently felt it unnecessary to explore the extent of this power. Chase, almost offhandedly, referred to the issue at the end of his opinion; he saw no need "at this time" to declare whether the Court had the power, but if it did, he would not use it except in a very clear case. Both sides in the litigation assumed the power existed. Counsel for the government did not argue that the Court lacked authority to nullify an act of Congress, but that it had no need to do so, since the statute fell within constitutional bounds.

The question of judicial review came up in the Court again two years later in *Calder v. Bull* (1798), this time in connection with state legislative powers. New England assemblies had for many years enjoyed the prerogative of ordering new trials by legislative resolve, a practice that, although not often exercised, now came under attack as violating the constitutional bar against ex post facto laws. The Connecticut legislature had set aside the decree of a probate court that had refused to record a will, and ordered a new trial with the right of appeal.

The four justices who heard the case agreed that the Connecticut resolution did not constitute an ex post facto law, since Blackstone and other authorities limited that definition to criminal proceedings. Chase seems to have been more troubled by a potential breach of the separation of powers, since the legislature appeared to be acting in a judicial manner. He also questioned whether the legislature's action affected vested property rights, and his comments on this would be cited three-quarters of a century later when the Court developed the doctrine of substantive due process (see Chapter 23). But if the law did not violate the federal Constitution, did it violate the state constitution? Here the Court laid down a rule that has endured to this day: Questions of conflict between state laws and state constitutions do not come within the jurisdiction of the federal judiciary but remain a matter solely for state courts to determine. In deciding this way, the Court strengthened the federal nature of the Union, and while up-holding the power of judicial review, it drew a clear line between the exercise of judicial review by the federal courts and state tribunals.

## The Ellsworth Tenure

Oliver Ellsworth succeeded Jay as chief justice, and during his tenure the work load of the Court slowly increased, although few of the cases had the significance of *Hylton v. United States*. A boundary dispute led to the first suit by one state against another, *New York v. Connecticut* (1799). In a nation so reliant on maritime commerce, it is not surprising that admiralty cases constituted a major part of the Court's business. These cases, although usually not of great constitutional significance, could raise important issues. In *United States v. La Vengeance* (1796), for example, the chief justice's opinion provided the basis for the later extension of federal admiralty jurisdiction to internal navigable rivers and the Great Lakes, as well as farther out on the high seas.

Nor did the political controversy surrounding the Court diminish, for then as now, its decisions related to the pressing issues of the day. In *Bas v. Tingy* (1800), the Court held that a state of "limited, partial war" existed between France and the United States, permitting salvage of ships "taken from the enemy" under a recent act of Congress. Federalists, who had denounced French attacks on American shipping, lauded the decision, while the Jeffersonians, who feared that the Adams administration wanted to involve the country in a war with France, denounced it. Ominously, one Jeffersonian paper, the *Aurora*, called for the impeachment of any justice who asserted the country was in a state of war, for only Congress had the power to declare hostilities.

The criticism that had attached to Jay when he went off to negotiate with Great Britain revived in 1798, when Oliver Ellsworth accepted a diplomatic assignment from John Adams. The chief justice, along with North Carolina Governor William R. Davie and the American minister to the Netherlands, William Vans Murray, went to Paris in an effort to avert all-out war between the two countries. While no doubt a laudable endeavor, it left the Court short-handed, and led to accusations that the federal bench had become little better than an adjunct to the executive. Congressional critics introduced several bills and at least one constitutional amendment to prohibit any federal judge from holding other appointments or offices.

Despite his short tenure (a little under four years), Ellsworth had grasped, as Jay had not, the potential for the chief justice to lead the Court. At a time when the Court followed the English practice of all judges delivering their opinions seriatim in every case, he managed to get his brethren to write shorter opinions. Toward the end of his term, it appears the justices agreed that if a consensus existed, the chief justice would deliver the opinion of the Court, a practice developed more fully during the Marshall years.

## Circuit Duties

In addition to hearing cases before the Supreme Court, the justices also heard cases while riding circuits. These proved arduous and unwelcome, especially because nearly all of the original justices suffered from some physical ailment. The southern circuit, for example, required travel of nearly 1,800 miles, twice a year, in a country that had poor roads or, in some places, none at all. The judges importuned Congress repeatedly to do away with circuit riding, and even offered to give up some of their salary if Congress would name separate circuit judges. But Congress proved willing only to reduce the circuits from two Supreme Court justices and a district judge to one of each, thus lightening the burden but not eliminating it.

Despite the hardships to the judges, Washington and congressional leaders had sound reasons for wanting the high court justices out on the circuits. District courts, while creatures of the federal government, dealt primarily with local matters and did not carry the majesty of the national government as did the Supreme Court. By having the justices in the countryside, the federal government could demonstrate its direct links to the people. In an era of poor communications, the Supreme Court would thus be viewed, not as some isolated tribunal in a remote city, but as a regular part of the ongoing legal life of the country. The wisdom of this policy can be seen in the general support of the people, many of whom opposed the growth of strong federal government, for the often controversial decisions of the circuit courts.

For example, *Hayburn's Case* (1792), in which several circuits declared an act of Congress in effect unconstitutional, met with no opposition in the states. Although this might be interpreted as the obvious approval of people wanting to see Congress reined in, the same people acquiesced in circuit decisions nullifying state laws. In June 1792, Jay and Cushing, together with District Judge Henry Marchant, sitting as the Circuit Court for Rhode Island, ruled in *Champion and Dickason v. Casey* that a state law impairing obligation of contract violated the Constitution. Although the decision received much publicity in Rhode Island—which more than any other state had opposed national authority—the next session of the state legislature amended the law to meet the court's objection. Circuit courts nullified a Connecticut statute in 1793, a Pennsylvania law in 1795, and a Vermont law (altering the terms of contract) in 1799. None of these cases aroused any objections to the circuits having this authority.

The power of judicial review appears to have been praised most by former Antifederalist newspapers that, at least at this time, saw the courts as brakes upon the growing central government. But although states' rights advocates seemed willing to concede that the power could also extend to state laws, they proved less receptive in instances where the circuits trod upon the toes of state courts. The North Carolina circuit removed by a writ of certiorari a case that had been pending in state court since before the adoption of the Constitution, but the state judges refused to yield jurisdiction. Why the circuit court did this is impossible to know, for there seem to have been no grounds for the action, and a number of persons feared that such arrogance would lead to a popular denunciation of the courts. Iredell had this case in mind when he counseled Jay against riding the circuit.

The major contribution of the circuits in developing respect for the federal judiciary lies in the extensive charges delivered by the Supreme Court justices to the circuit juries. As the *Farmer's Weekly Museum* of Walpole, New Hampshire, wrote:

> In these useful addresses to the jury, we not only discern sound legal information conveyed in a style at once popular and condensed, but much political and constitutional

knowledge. The Chief Justice of the United States [Ellsworth] has the high power of giving men much and most essential information in a style the very model of clearness and dignity.

Jay's charges always emphasized the need for a unified national government and the role of federal courts in binding the nation together.

# Conclusion

All told, the Court in its first decade could boast some significant accomplishments. The nation now had a functioning federal judiciary, with established appellate procedures. Just as the executive and legislative branches had begun to flesh out the constitutional skeleton, so too the courts had given shape to Article III's broad grant of the judicial power. By its actions, as well as by what it chose not to do, the Supreme Court defined its role, while at the same time strengthening the concept of separation of powers. Despite the nullification of *Chisholm v. Georgia* by the Eleventh Amendment, the Court gained significant powers through a broad reading of the constitutional mandate, and laid the basis for John Marshall's sweeping assertion of judicial review in the Marbury case. And, as we shall see in the next chapter, the growth of the federal judiciary paralleled robust developments in the daily legal life of the nation.

# For Further Reading

Henry J. Bourguignon, *The First Federal Court: The Federal Appellate Prize Court of the American Revolution, 1775–1787* (1977), is a careful study of the prize court. Dwight F. Henderson, *Courts for a New Nation* (1971) is very uncritical, but it has some useful information on lower federal courts. See also J. R. Saylor, "Creation of the Federal Judiciary," 8 *Baylor Law Review* (1956) 257; and Charles Warren, "New Light on the History of the Federal Judiciary Act of 1789," 37 *Harvard Law Review* 49 (1923).

For the Court during the Jay and Ellsworth tenures, see William Casto, *The Supreme Court in the Early Republic: The Chief Justiceships of John Jay and Oliver Ellsworth* (1995) and Julius Goebel, Jr., *Antecedents and Beginnings to 1801* (1971); the overly technical and massively detailed first volume of the Holmes Devise, *History of the Supreme Court of the United States*. Unlike later volumes, this one fails to relate the judiciary to contemporary political events and examines the Court in a judicial vacuum. Richard B. Morris, *John Jay, the Nation and the Court* (1967), has just the opposite problem. In three interpretive essays, Morris properly argues that we can understand Jay only in light of contemporaneous events, but the essays focus more on the events than on Jay. Charles Warren, *The Supreme Court in United States History*, 2 vols. (1932), still has some useful insights.

On the federal judiciary in this period, the best source remains chapter 1 of Felix Frankfurter and James M. Landis, *The Business of the Supreme Court: A Study in the Federal Judicial System* (1928). The volumes of Maeva Marcus et al., eds., *Documentary History of the Supreme Court* (1986– ) provide an amazing amount of new information on the work of the early Court and will eventually help to fill in some of the current gaps. Clyde Jacobs, *The Eleventh Amendment and Sovereign Immunity* (1972), argues that the Framers intended states to be subject to citizen suits in federal courts, and that the Eleventh Amendment failed to thwart that intent.

# 9

# *The Changing Face of the Law*

*Changes in the Common Law • Criminal Law • Property • Land and Water Usage • Contract • Procedure • Bench and Bar • Legal Literature • Lower Federal Courts • For Further Reading*

THE GREAT LEGAL changes precipitated by the Revolution, discussed in the last few chapters, took place in the area of public law, that is, in the creation of a system based on written constitutions establishing fundamental rules to govern the means and limits of governmental authority. The Constitution and the Supreme Court epitomized this process, but the legal system as a whole involved much more. Congress created lower federal courts, which together with the state courts took the lead in developing new law to meet the demands of a growing economy and a changing society. Property and contract law changed significantly in the late eighteenth and early nineteenth centuries, as did criminal law. These changes demonstrate the Americanization of English common law, as well as the privatization of particular areas that had previously been public.

## Changes in the Common Law

Blackstone, in his *Commentaries,* had praised the English common law as the great expression of natural law; judges, therefore, did not make law so much as *discover* it. As such, law supposedly remained neutral, favoring no one group in society against any other, but applying with equal impartiality to all who came into court seeking justice. Statute law, while articulating the will of ruling groups, also had to conform to natural law. Although Parliament could amend judge-made law by statute, common adherence to higher principles made this more a case of fine-tuning the legal and political system than one of conflict between law and politics.

In America, the colonists had long drawn a sharper distinction between English statutes and the common law, and had rejected much of the former as inappropriate to their situation. Following the Revolution, the reception statutes continued this practice: English common law would still be applied in American courts, but only those acts of

Parliament that embodied and did not alter common law and had been passed before a certain date would be accepted. As a young lawyer, James Kent, who later became chancellor of New York, emphasized the dichotomy between statutory and common law and noted that the common law "can only be discovered & known by searching into the Decisions of the English Courts . . . [which] are regarded with us as *authentic Evidence* of the Common Law."

For all the lip service paid to this ideal, Americans never adopted a strict allegiance to or reliance on English law. Beginning in the 1780s and culminating in the early nineteenth century, according to historian Morton Horwitz, "American jurists succeeded in dethroning the common law." When the Virginia law professor and jurist St. George Tucker published his American edition of Blackstone's *Commentaries* in 1803, he noted it would be "in vain" for Americans to "attempt, by any *general theory,* to establish an uniform authority and obligation in the common law of England, over the American colonies, at any period between the first migrations to this country, and that epoch, which annihilated the sovereignty of the crown of England over them."

This attitude is plainly revealed in the attack on the idea of a federal common law of crimes. In England, statutes proscribed a number of activities, but over the centuries the courts had designated many types of conduct as criminal without any legislative acts. Common law crimes included some types of moral and sexual behavior and the printing of antigovernment publications, known as seditious or criminal libel. Other crimes, like murder or battery could also be punished under the common law, if there were no specific statutes applicable to a particular set of facts. Judges exercised enormous discretion in defining criminal activities as well as in meting out appropriate penalties. Behind the American attack on common law crimes lay fears that if the federal judiciary could unrestrainedly define criminal activity without statutory authorization, then the national government would possess nearly unlimited powers.

Not all Jeffersonians shared that view, though. James Sullivan of Massachusetts believed that federal common law jurisdiction only reached so far as those areas over which Congress had authority, and if Congress wished to confer upon the courts common law jurisdiction in these matters, it could constitutionally do so. Congress, however, had not done so, and a growing number of people argued that the legislature and not the courts should define crime and punishment. As early as 1712, in the Connecticut trial of Daniel Gard for murder, the judges had petitioned the legislature to determine whether they had the power to set sentences, and the assembly had replied that they did, according to the rules of the common law. But in 1786, when Pennsylvania granted a similar discretion, lawyer and writer Francis Hopkinson attacked the law for "vesting [judges] with legislative authority."

It is also important to understand that most American lawyers had been trained in the common law and revered it. Jefferson believed states could, and should, use the common law to prosecute wrong doers. Indeed, as president he urged his allies to use state common law prosecutions for seditious libel against his critics.

## Criminal Law

As Hopkinson explained the problem, common law crimes and sentencing were *retrospective,* so that people did not know until they had been hauled into court whether they had acted criminally, and if so, what their punishment would be. A good example of this took place in Maine, in *Kanavan's Case* (1821), when a defendant was convicted of dropping the body of a dead child into a river "against common decency." Although no statute made this action a crime, the state's high court affirmed the conviction under common law. The court declared that "Good morals—decency—our best feelings—the law of the land—all forbid" the defendant's acts. Similarly, in *State v. Williams* (1808) the Tennessee Court upheld a conviction for eavesdropping, although the legislature had never addressed the topic. The court found the prosecution "agreeable to the common law." According to Hopkinson, "it is a distinguishing mark of a free government, that the people shall know before hand, the penalty which the laws annex to every offense." While the U.S. Constitution, Article I, Section 10, prohibited states from passing ex post facto laws, the courts here assumed that as a common law ruling, this was not an ex post facto law.

The common law was also a threat to political liberty. In 1735, for example, Governor William Cosby of New York arranged for the prosecution of the opposition printer John Peter Zenger for the common law crime of seditious libel—that is, defaming the government. In the 1790s, Federalist authorities in Pennsylvania used the common law of seditious libel to prosecute the editor of the Philadelphia *Aurora*, a Jeffersonian paper known for its sharp attacks on the Adams administration. Similarly, in 1803, at the behest of Thomas Jefferson, Republicans in New York indicted Harry Croswell for common law seditious libel for his criticism of President Jefferson. The danger of misusing common law prosecutions is perhaps best illustrated by the Jefferson administration itself. In 1806 and 1807, the U.S. attorney in Connecticut, who was appointed by Jefferson, initiated common law libel proceedings in *federal* court against Federalist publishers, Barzillai Hudson and George Goodwin. Even though the Jeffersonians claimed to oppose the idea of a federal common law of crimes, when in power they apparently could not resist using the common law to wreak political vengeance on their enemies.

Yet, even while using the common law to get at their political enemies, Jefferson and other opponents of common law prosecutions, especially at the federal level, argued that only through legislation could one secure a *prospective* system of criminal law spelling out specific criminal acts and their punishment. Without such a system of law no one could know, in advance, whether their, his, or her acts were criminal.

In 1793, Chief Justice Nathaniel Chipman in effect abolished common law capital crimes in Vermont. A few years later, Zephaniah Swift, a Connecticut legal scholar, cast the argument into constitutional terms by asserting that common law crimes in effect comprised ex post facto laws. In doing so, Swift implied what Blackstone and other natural law advocates had long denied, namely, that judges in fact did make law. Under a constitutional system, however, only the legislature possessed that power.

Ironically, a Federalist judge, and a leading target of the Jeffersonian attack on the judiciary, first ruled that there were no federal common law crimes. Justice Samuel Chase, on circuit in *United States v. Worrall* (1798), held that since the entire English common law had never been adopted in the United States and because the common law of one state differed from that of another there could be no general common law. In dismissing an indictment for bribing a federal official, Chase ruled that only Congress "should define the offenses to be tried, and apportion the punishments to be inflicted." In 1812, the full Supreme Court, in *United States v. Hudson and Goodwin,* agreed that federal courts had no jurisdiction over the actions of individuals unless Congress had first defined the crime, established the punishment, and assigned jurisdiction to the courts. Ironically, this case involved the use of the common law by the Republicans to prosecute the Federalist editors of *The Connecticut Courant*, who in 1806, had criticized President Thomas Jefferson.

The abolition of common law crimes in the federal courts and eventually in state courts as well comprised part of a larger reform movement in criminal law. The revolutionary generation had complained about the Crown's abuse of criminal law, and especially limits on jury trials; half of the Bill of Rights is devoted to protecting individual rights in this area. Beyond that, however, Americans were sympathetic to the ideas of Enlightenment writers such as Cesare Beccaria and Voltaire, with their calls for reform in criminal law. Reform sentiment affected numerous areas of criminal law, from efforts to abolish the death penalty to an abandonment of prosecution for most private sexual conduct. Although some changes can be discerned in the decades immediately following independence, one normally attributes many of the gains to the Jacksonian period. But the agitation began in the 1780s, with some results appearing fairly early.

Prosecution for moral offenses, for example, dropped off significantly after the Revolution. Massachusetts courts tried 679 cases of fornication between 1730 and 1769, but only 290 between 1770 and 1809, after which the offense practically disappeared from the courts. The statutes remained on the books, and the rising number of premarital pregnancies indicates that the activity did not cease. Rather, authorities abandoned the notion that private sexual conduct between consenting adults constituted a matter of public concern. The disestablishment of churches and the refusal of secular authorities to enforce church doctrines combined with a belief that private activities should be just that—private—and beyond the reach of the criminal process.

Ironically, some reform-minded judges and legislators used the common law to provide legal protections for slaves. Thus, in 1817, the North Carolina legislature declared that the "offence of Killing a Slave shall hereafter be denominated and considered homicide, and shall partake of the same degree of guilt when accompanied with the like circumstances that homicide now does at common law." The legislature left it up to the state judges to sort out what this meant, given that slaves were legally inferior to whites. But, in *State v. Reed* (1823) and *State v. Hoover* (1839) the North Carolina Supreme Court did uphold capital convictions for whites who had killed slaves, and in *State v. Hale* (1823) the same court upheld a common law indictment of a white for "having committed an assault on a slave," and for "inhumanly beating, wounding, &c." the slave.

Another reform involved the slow transfer of power from juries to judges, with the latter bound by new statutory penal codes. In theory, at the time of the Revolution, juries judged both the law and fact in criminal cases, and the memory of local juries thwarting arbitrary royal power remained strong for a number of years. But the great discretion of juries eventually led to attacks on jury verdicts that many considered as arbitrary as the king's justice. In South Carolina, according to one scholar, the same jury would change a murderer's indictment to manslaughter, while condemning a common thief to the gallows. With neighbors in the dock, juries often determined facts to their benefit, despite evidence to the contrary. One South Carolina juror declared that he "would not convict the defendant, or any other white person of murdering a slave," and when the judge refused to grant a mistrial, the jury came back with an acquittal.

Such jury "lawlessness" led to legal change. As popular notions against overly harsh penal statutes increased, jury reluctance to impose severe penalties or to find defendants guilty of unpopular crimes anticipated statutory changes that led to legal reform. In South Carolina, for example, the number of capital offenses dropped from 165 in 1813, to 32 in 1838, to 22 by 1850. In Massachusetts the number of capital offenses declined from a dozen or so at the time of the Revolution, to six by 1828 and to one—murder—by mid-century.

During this period, all the states codified their criminal law, replacing many of the vagaries of the older common law and providing the prospective system Hopkinson had called for in the 1780s. The new codes not only limited jury discretion, but they also restricted the power of judges to define crimes. Judges, however, did retain the authority to interpret the law, a power which, if they wished, they could use to circumvent its intent. For the most part, however, as judges developed rules of interpretation, the criminal justice system became marked more by uniformity than by eccentricity.

It is important to note, however, that even as the states codified the law, they often left open the possibility of recourse to the common law, when necessary. The 1817 North Carolina statute on the killing of slaves illustrates this. Both state constitutions in the eighteenth and early nineteenth centuries, as well as revised codes, often asserted that the common law of England, as it existed on July 4, 1776, remained in force, unless modified by a constitution or a statute. The common law thus remained available when statutory law was insufficient or unavailable.

# Property

A crucial area of law that departed from English common law was property law, or to be more precise, the rules governing the acquisition, use, and disposal of land. Property constituted the heart of English law, for ownership and control of land lay at the foundation of British society and government. The common law had begun in feudal times and developed in an agrarian nation where virtually all available land was either in use or assigned to particular owners. Because of the scarcity of land, English law had hedged the landowner or tenant with numerous safeguards.

The law, however, never allowed an owner complete control over his property. The old maxim, *sic utere tuo ut alienum non laedas*—use your own property so as not to injure another's—set outer limits on the freedom of landholders, although within those parameters the owner had enormous discretion. A complex series of laws had evolved regarding use, tenancy, inheritance, and conveyance, to protect the land and the social system that it undergirded. The language of English land law—feoffment with livery of seisin, contingent remainders, shifting and springing uses—traveled across the Atlantic and is still studied in first-year law classes. But the abundance of free land in America made English law an anachronism, and changes had begun well before the Revolution.

Primogeniture, in which the estate passed to the eldest son, had long been dead in New England; it had disappeared from the more traditional South by 1800. Feudal tenures and restrictions vanished in favor of simple, common sense rules designed to meet the needs of a society of settlers and speculators. Simplified documents evolved, and laws often required little more than that deeds be in writing with clear descriptions of the land involved. For land with clear title, the warranty deed became the norm, with the seller making certain guarantees to the buyer. When questions existed as to boundary or title, the seller gave a quit-claim deed, transferring whatever interests he had but providing no assurances to the buyer. Both in statute and custom, the law simplified the means to test title, with the older writ of entry giving way to the more streamlined action of ejectment. Only where English customs proved useful—or totally irrelevant—did Americans retain them. When New York and other states enacted general codifications of property law in the 1820s, they did not embark on new ventures, but merely summed up the changes of the previous decades.

Property law reform can be characterized as both procedural and substantive, the former dealing with the means by which property can be transferred, and the latter relating to its use. In both cases, however, reform shaped the law to meet the needs of a transient society. Transfer laws aimed at both democratizing and simplifying ownership. Liberalized property laws allowed married women to own land in their own name for the first time. In England, aliens could not inherit land, a common law rule that made no sense in a nation of immigrants, and just as feudal restrictions such as fee tail disappeared, other fetters on inheritance made no sense in a society with abundant land. In a country where nearly everyone speculated in land, transfer became so simple that a whole new problem arose, sorting out clear title to land, an issue that would keep frontier courts occupied for generations. Thus, most English restrictions on land disappeared before or shortly after the Revolution.

Traditionally, title to land required a precise description of boundaries. Surveyors marking out land would measure particular plots in "metes and bounds" or refer to lot numbers on master maps in the land offices; in less settled areas, they used recognizable natural features, such as boulders or river banks. But pioneers often outpaced government or private surveyors, and they identified the boundaries of their land by hatchet blazes on trees, or by referring to stumps with flowering berry bushes nearby. Many settlers presumed that building a cabin and cultivating the land provided sufficient evidence of their claim. American law in the nineteenth century is freighted with cases, many involving large estates, in which several parties put forward plausible claims to the same land. Government policy for the western lands envisioned a rational pattern of settlement, but political pressure from squatters and small holders with questionable claims could not be ignored.

## Land and Water Usage

The substantive changes in land law pertained to usage and marked a sharp departure from the English practices of "natural use" and "first in time." In a stable agrarian society, "natural" meant the normal use of land and its appurtenances, such as water. Any such use by one landowner, even if it inflicted some harm on a neighbor, protected the first owner from liability. The "first in time, first in right" principle held that if one property holder initiated certain activities that were natural to the land, the second could not at a later date begin a project that worked against the interests of the first. However, if technological innovations allowed the use of land and water for new purposes, both theories could be manipulated either to retard or advance the new activity. Courts began to use a balancing test, in which the priority rule gradually gained ascendance, and the natural use rule faded into obscurity. This pattern can be seen in the legal controversies generated by the use of water power for economic development.

Originally, the law viewed the flow of water in its natural channel as practicably inviolable and deemed any interference with the flow as unnatural. Everyone who bought land through which a stream flowed acquired rights to that water, but only to the extent that it did not diminish the riparian rights of his neighbors. A landowner could divert so much water as was necessary for his basic needs; exploitation of water for irrigation or for a mill dam, however, took such a large amount that downstream neighbors would be injured. The diverter could escape from damages only when a dam or other diversion had been established early on in the use of land, so that later neighboring owners took title with knowledge (the priority doctrine).

In the United States, with so much open land and a need to develop all available resources, courts soon discovered that efforts to apply the old laws raised issues unknown in England. In general, American courts pursued a policy of favoring development, balancing the economic good of the community against the inconvenience or injury to individual landowners. In *Shorey v. Gorrell* (1783), the Supreme Judicial Court of Massachusetts held that unless an owner had, through long usage, established his rights, he could not prevent a newcomer from obstructing a stream in order to build a mill dam. Other courts also developed various rationales to encourage development. New York, in *Palmer v. Mulligan* (1805), upheld the right of an upstream owner to dam a stream. While the court noted the common law proscriptions, it also believed that riparian owners had to suffer little inconveniences for the sake of the greater good. In *Palmer*, and a few years later in *Platt v. Johnson* (1818), the court introduced the idea that with property came the right to develop it for commercial purposes. The old doctrine of *sic utere* had to be balanced against the benefits the community would receive through such development.

This departure from tradition did not sit well with all jurists. Joseph Angell severely criticized the *Palmer* decision in his treatise on *Watercourses* (1824), and Justice Joseph Story's circuit court opinion in *Tyler v. Wilkinson* (1827) seemed to confirm the traditional limits on water diversion. Story's opinion, however, was filled with ambiguities. His criterion of "reasonable use" as a permissible departure from strict common law rules became the formula by which development-minded judges could justify extensive diversions.

To encourage the construction of mills, some states enacted statutes to compensate the adjoining landowners for damages. In doing so, they prohibited the traditional common law action of trespass or recourse to self-help (in which the afflicted landowner could take matters into his own hands and destroy the nuisance) and also denied any punitive damages. These laws came in time to aid the growth of the new textile mills, with their huge demand for water power. Although the mill acts generated new problems and eventually had to be modified, they did much to advance the notion of land as a commodity that could be used as any other asset in the pursuit of economic growth and profit.

The riparian cases provide but one example of how property law adjusted to meet economic needs. The law also had to be modified in cases in which traditional damage claims, such as those involving waste, would have prevented the development of land, or when the right of dower, in which widows held restrictive life interests on land, would have retarded the ease of transfer. The doctrine of prescriptive rights, in which a variety of property interests could be acquired by long usage, also had to be defeated. The owner of a house, for example, could claim after a number of years a prescriptive easement for "ancient lights" and thus prevent a neighbor from erecting a building on adjacent land that would interfere with his sunlight. English courts in the eighteenth century still entertained suits by merchants against customers of long standing who wanted to take their business elsewhere; the law held that the merchant had a prescriptive right in the customer's business!

This view of property, which gave the owner a type of monopolistic power not only over the use of his land but partially over that of his neighbors as well, stood opposed to the competitive drive of the new republic. In the early nineteenth century, state courts, despite the protests of conservatives, abandoned most prescriptive rights. New York, in *Parker v. Foote* (1838), canceled the "ancient lights" rule, and in the great *Charles River Bridge* case the U.S. Supreme Court denied that long usage without specific title established property rights (see Chapter 14). There, Justice Mclean noted that prescriptive rights made sense only in a fixed society, not one marked by "rapid growth in population and advance in improvements."

## Contract

Even greater changes reflecting the new business needs of the country took place in the area of contracts, which well into the eighteenth century had been considered a subsection of the common law of property. The idea of two parties negotiating an agreement reaches far back into history: the Codes of Hammurabi and Justinian, as well as the Torah and the Talmud, all dealt with matters of contract. The ancient maxim, *pacta sunt servanda*—"agreements shall be kept"—had long been accepted as involving legal and moral obligations. Contract developed primarily out of the equitable writ of assumpsit, which began as an action in tort. The underlying assumption seems to have been that breach of contract involved some deceit, and the wronged party had therefore suffered damages.

Equity, however, looked past the bargain for fairness, and although the existence of fraud or duress is still grounds for nullifying a contract, the courts of equity went further. If the judges believed that the agreement involved insufficient consideration paid by one party to the other, or if they did not like the terms of the bargain, they could cancel it. As commerce developed in England, merchants demanded far stricter standards, and the *law merchant*—the common and accepted practices of the marketplace—soon came to govern contract law. Lord Mansfield, who became Lord Chief Justice of the King's Bench in 1756, had played a key role in conforming the common law of contract to the law merchant and the needs of the marketplace. As in other areas, though, the innate conservatism of the law often kept changes in legal doctrine from proceeding as rapidly as changes in business practice, and English contract law retained outmoded technical vestiges well into the nineteenth century.

Although American judges continued to look to English developments, the spirit of independence permitted courts in this country to adapt more easily to current needs. As a result, the marketplace, whether of property or goods, did not find itself retarded by ancient rules. Part of this flexibility may be traced to the failure of Blackstone to develop contract law extensively. Writing primarily for the sons of gentry, he dealt with contract as it pertained to real property and included only two small sections on contract totaling a mere forty pages out of four volumes.

Eighteenth-century common law posited a title theory of contract, in which title to a particular piece of land or item changed hands; for breach of contract, the injured party could recover only the consideration tendered. Courts consistently rejected the idea of damages from the lost bargain, which is an essential part of modern contract law. With the growth of markets and speculation in fungible goods, the failure to live up to an agreement could cost a party not only the purchase price, which he could claim under the old law, but also expected gains, which the common law held unrecoverable. *Sands v. Taylor* (1810) involved a buyer who refused to accept part of a contracted shipment of wheat. The seller, under the old law, would have been required to hold the wheat, and then sue to force the buyer to accept the balance of the shipment and pay the agreed price. Instead, the seller sold the wheat on the open market and sued for the difference between the market price and the contract price. The New York court admitted that the case did not follow the traditional rules, but it saw no reason to let the wheat rot while the seller attempted to sue for the price. The old title theory, which related to specific goods, made no sense in markets in which, like wheat, one bushel was fungible with another, and both parties essentially speculated on changing prices for the goods. The court recognized that such exchanges reflected private desires by the parties of factors other than just the purchase price.

This awareness of the private nature of contract can also be seen in changing doctrine on consideration, the amount one party paid to the other for the goods or services. The eighteenth-century rule that defendants could offer evidence of insufficient consideration relied on the maxim that "a sound price warrants a sound commodity," and too high a price, even if contracted for, could be used as an excuse for breach. Since the market operated on economic rules of supply and demand, not on equitable laws of fairness, commerce would have been stifled had this rule prevailed.

The new rule did not judge the fairness of the contract (although courts could still act if fraud, duress, or overreaching existed), but rather facilitated and enforced private agreements reached between parties aware of the bargaining process and the value of the exchange. While adequacy of consideration remained an element of contract law, courts now left the measurement of adequacy to the parties, since they could best judge its value. The law set certain minimal standards to govern contract and did not question particular details. In general, written contracts could be offered as proof that both sides had agreed to the bargain; oral contracts, on the other hand, would not be enforced. Contract thus followed the general simplification taking place elsewhere in American law. Transfer of real property required only simple deeds; transfer of goods needed similarly simple, written contracts. Form followed function, since the market needed easy legal tools to facilitate trade between individuals. The law provided these and then left the parties to make the best bargain they could.

Changes in contract law constituted more of a functional than a substantive change in law. The triumph of contracts, in which the so-called "freedom to contract" became part of an individual's inherent freedom from restraint by the government, did not appear until the latter part of the nineteenth century. Late eighteenth- and early nineteenth-century contract law responded to an expanding economy, in which new forms of market transactions would have been hampered by adherence to older doctrines. The power of these new ideas would not be fully appreciated until the Supreme Court under John Marshall validated the sanctity of private contract in a number of decisions. The new rules adopted by the courts nonetheless represented common law jurisprudence at its best—the change of laws to reflect, as Justice Oliver Wendell Holmes later put it, "the felt necessities of the time."

# Procedure

The Americanization of English common law never meant the abandonment of that law, for it had become too embedded in American practice to be easily abolished. Nor, for that matter, did Americans want to do away completely with English legal custom, since they found much of it admirable, useful, and worth keeping. Even today, English cases are occasionally cited as precedents in American decisions, and some landmark opinions by American jurists are referred to by English courts. But the common law in England had evolved slowly to meet the needs of a particular society and economy, and when the nation underwent radical changes in the nineteenth century, great reforms took place in the mother country. In the United States, with its more open, democratic frontier society, the need for change manifested itself earlier.

Even in England, civil procedure badly needed reform by the late eighteenth century. The elaborate system of writs and pleadings that had developed over the centuries placed control of the system in the hands of a relatively small number of barristers who could find their way through the procedural intricacies. One error, even a small and inconsequential one, could lead to the dismissal of a case, and the necessity of starting all over again. Mastery of the technical aspects of the law kept enormous power in the hands of the legal profession, which viewed reform as an attack on its status.

In the United States, with its numerous jurisdictions and shortage of men trained in the law, procedures had to be simplified or else the system would have collapsed. Still, at least in the more settled seaboard states, the established bar often fought procedural reforms, and in many places a complete overhaul did not take place until the mid-nineteenth century. The generation of lawyers who practiced during and after the Revolution had been trained in English procedures and relied on English law books. Although Joseph Story's *Selections of Pleadings in Civil Actions* (1805) claimed to be an American manual, it mainly reprinted or adapted English sources; for many lawyers, English texts remained the standard sources of authority well into the Jacksonian era. But, as in other areas of the law, the roots of change took hold in the decades following independence.

Essentially, English pleading aimed at narrowing the litigation to a single issue, which could then be decided by judges according to the law. Although seemingly a laudable goal, the process had become so encrusted with technical minutiae that form rather than substance had become paramount; the issue had to be stated in a precise and time-hallowed manner, with no deviations. While litigants knew the issues at stake, they had to rely on lawyers to frame the pleadings properly and then wait upon the courts eventually to reach and resolve the matter.

Americans simply had no time for all this. To wait months, perhaps years (as often happened in England) to resolve a relatively straightforward matter made no sense and certainly did not benefit business. Merchants, landowners, planters, artisans, and even small farmers wanted their disputes settled quickly and at minimum expense, and they viewed with suspicion lawyers' arguments about arcane matters such as whether to use conjunctive or disjunctive traverses. Nor did they lightly dismiss the democratic argument for a simple and inexpensive justice. Ordinary citizens might never enter court as litigants, but they expected—in fact demanded—that if ever the occasion arose, justice would be swiftly and clearly delivered, without the intervention of expensive lawyers debating technical trivialities.

Many states moved toward reform either before or soon after the Revolution. In 1782, Alexander Hamilton noted that the fairly conservative New York court had "lately acquired a more liberal Cast" with the idea that "the end of Suits at Law is to Investigate the Merits of the Cause, and not to entangle in the Nets of technical Terms." In Georgia, the Judiciary Act of 1799 allowed plaintiffs to initiate civil suits merely by filing a petition setting out the case "plainly, fully and substantially," while the defendant would respond similarly, simply stating the "cause of the defense." The lack of qualified lawyers and judges led many states to abolish separate courts of law and equity, and the Constitution adopted this practice for the federal system. (It did not merge law and equity, but merely permitted the same court to try both types of law.) In the Judiciary Act of 1789, Congress permitted oral testimony in equity suits, even though traditionally only written evidence had been permitted. A few basic writs replaced the innumerable means of recourse for review by a higher court.

A typical effort attempting to clear away procedural obstructions can be found in a Massachusetts statute of 1784, which declared that judicial proceedings should not "be abated, arrested, quashed or reversed for any kind of circumstantial errors or mistakes . . . nor through defect or want of form only," and courts could now permit counsel, during the hearings, to amend their complaints. Even new counts could be added at the trial if they arose from the same cause of action as the original complaint. The Massachusetts Supreme Judicial Court later noted in *Kincaid v. Howe* (1813) that it gave little weight to "an objection . . . which was merely captious and dilatory in its nature, not at all affecting the merits of the action." In *Cole v. Fisher* (1814), the Massachusetts court held "a contest about the form of action . . . [to] be of little avail to the defendant," and left it to the jury to decide the issues solely on merit.

As historian William E. Nelson suggests, "what was new was the emphasis on substance over form and the rejection of British forms—that is, the writ system—as an intellectually acceptable mode of thinking about the law." Lawyers, however, often resisted change because it threatened their control of the system and because they understood that consistent procedures could protect their clients from arbitrary judges and capricious and often ignorant juries. Thus, in Georgia, for example, bench and bar effectively blocked the reforms of the 1790s for many years. But the trend could not be stopped, culminating eventually in the great code reforms of the 1840s.

## Bench and Bar

The changes in the law previously described did not result from decisions handed down from the Supreme Court; instead, they resulted from legislation passed by state assemblies and from common law interpretations made in state and lower federal courts. There, too, change took place not only in law but in bench and bar as well. Perhaps the most significant change might be termed the professionalization of the judiciary. The shortage of trained lawyers throughout the colonial and revolutionary periods saw many men appointed as judges who had little or no prior experience in the law. Armed with common sense and a few English texts, they learned on the job. In many ways, American judges occupied roles that were similar to local squires in England, and so long as the cases they tried involved relatively simple matters, the administration of justice did not suffer. American lawyers received nothing like the training English barristers had at the Inns of Court. The U.S. boasted only one law school at the time, that of Judge Tapping Reeves in Litchfield, Connecticut, established in 1784. A few colleges had chairs in law. The College of William and Mary appointed George Wythe to its law chair in 1779. Harvard University appointed Massachusetts Chief Justice Isaac Parker to its chair in law in 1815, and established a law school in 1817. Most lawyers, however, learned their craft by reading books and then serving an apprenticeship with a practicing attorney.

The early national period saw a new trend toward appointing only lawyers to the bench. When Nathaniel Chipman took his seat on the Supreme Court of Vermont in 1787, he was the only attorney of the five judges; but the following year, when Virginia established a Court of Appeals, all the appointees were active members of the bar. This trend continued even at the same time that a number of states provided greater popular control over judges by allowing for their election, since lawyers, who claimed to have the necessary expertise to be judges, became the only people to run for judicial office. The people wanted power to elect judges, but they also demanded competence in the office. The great swing toward democracy and popular control of state government in general that marked these decades also affected the judiciary.

There seemed to be no difference in ability or behavior between elected judges and appointees; both types energetically joined in helping transform the law to meet new needs. While stories abound of crude judges and even cruder justice on the frontier, in looking over the judges in this era, one is struck by the quality of many who served. Some collected the cases and prepared digests of state laws; others wrote significant treatises, such as Chancellor James Kent of New York. Harry Toulman edited the Kentucky statutes; he then moved to the Mississippi Territory, became a judge there, and edited its statutes. Still restless, he moved on to the Alabama Territory, and edited the laws there as well. Others displayed a breadth of learning equal to that of many judges in the mother country. Chancellor George Wythe of Virginia was known as the leading classical scholar in the state, and as professor of law and policy at William and Mary, he held the first chair in law at an American college. His successor, St. George Tucker, published the first American edition of Blackstone's *Commentaries* in 1803, before serving as U.S. District Judge in Virginia. Contemporaries knew Theophilus Parsons of Massachusetts not only as a judge, but as a Greek scholar, astronomer, and mathematician as well. When Joseph Story was appointed to the Supreme Court in 1812, at the age of thirty-three, he had already written a very mediocre volume of poetry and edited a handful of very excellent legal treatises.

Judges, in addition to interpreting the law, developed the judicial apparatus from its somewhat inchoate colonial origins into the modern system we know today. For example, although the Constitution, with its theory of separated powers, influenced all the states, legislatures continued to perform some judicial functions well into the nineteenth century. Until 1846, New York's highest court included all the members of the state senate. As late as the 1850s, some assemblies granted divorces; quieted title to property; legalized name changes; and, in some instances, granted new trials. Throughout the period, southern states passed special acts to emancipate slaves or to allow manumitted slaves to remain in the state. Gradually, however, most of these activities became the sole province of courts. Similarly, the difference between trial and appellate courts became sharper, so that ultimately state supreme courts handled only matters on review. No doubt some of the changes judges made in the common law resulted from their first-hand observations of the inapplicability of older doctrines in new settings. In the latter part of the eighteenth and early nineteenth centuries, many state supreme court judges, especially in the frontier states, still rode circuit where they tried cases. Memoirs of bench and bar in this era dwell on circuit riding, where lawyers and judges traveled from town to town to dispense justice and handle whatever legal business awaited their coming. This not only developed a sense of camaraderie, but just as in medieval England, it brought justice close to home.

Because most legal history has focused on the Supreme Court, we still have only fragmentary knowledge of the proceedings of state and lower federal courts. We do know that each state, while adopting a general form of trial and appellate courts, also set up specialized tribunals. In New Jersey, for example, the "ordinary" (a vestige of the ecclesiastical court system) probated wills, but other questions of estate were litigated in the orphan's court. Some states preserved separate courts of law and equity well into the nineteenth century, while others, following the federal example, soon vested jurisdiction over both in the same forum. Larger cities often had their own separate municipal systems. As the economy and society developed, however, the law system gradually eroded these idiosyncrasies, a process hastened by the growth in each state of a body of precedent governing procedure and content in all courts.

## Legal Literature

One important aspect of the creation of an *American* legal system was the development of law books and legal publications. On the eve of the American Revolution, with the exception of printed statutes, there were virtually no law books produced in the colonies. Systematic reports of cases were virtually unknown. However, pamphlet reports of famous or sensational trials, like the *Zenger Narrative*, abounded. They helped educate the public, as well as the bar, about law, but could hardly be relied upon for legal rules or precedents.

Most lawyers in America, if they had any access to traditional law books, relied on English books, primarily William Blackstone's four volume *Commentaries on the Law of England* (1765–1769) and occasionally on Sir Edward Coke's *First Part of the Institutes of the Laws of England; or Commentaries upon Littleton* (1628). Others used justice of the peace manuals and similar books.

There were reported cases in England, but at the end of the Revolution, only about one-fifth of all English reports were available *anywhere* in the new United States. Most places had few if any of these volumes. American lawyers and judges relied, for the most part, on notes taken in courtrooms by other judges and lawyers, pamphlet reports of cases, or simply the memories of judges and attorneys. As the Connecticut jurist and legal scholar Zephaniah Swift noted in his treatise, *System of Laws of the State of Connecticut* (1795), "The uncertainty" of the reported cases "has been the subject of much complaint."

In 1785, Connecticut authorized the publication of the decisions of its Supreme Court. Official, and semi-official reports soon appeared in other states. Some reporters went back to manuscript records to report older cases. Alexander Dallas, for example, went back as far as 1754 to find records of cases for his Pennsylvania reports. Dallas also served as the official reporter for the U.S. Supreme Court, for the 1790s, until the Court left Philadelphia and moved to Washington.

In addition to law reports, Americans began to publish specialized volumes on cases and laws. *Cases Adjudged in the Supreme Court of New-Jersey; relative to the Manumission of Negroes and Others Holden in Bondage* published by the New-Jersey Society for the Promotion of the Abolition of Slavery in 1793, is one example of how social change and law publishing were combined. More common were books for attorneys and civil servants, like *A Compilation of the Law of the State of Pennsylvania, Relative to the Poor* (1796). American treatise writing began with Zephaniah Swift's *System of the Laws of Connecticut* (1795).

The most important American treatise in these years was St. George Tucker's edition of *Blackstone's Commentaries* (1803), generally referred to as *Tucker's Blackstone*. His volumes would be the most important source for American law until James Kent's four-volume *Commentaries on American Law* (1826–1830) became the standard treatise for general American law.

Tucker's Blackstone was not simply a reprinting of Blackstone in America. That had been accomplished shortly after the volumes appeared in England. Rather, Tucker took Blackstone's four-volume commentaries and edited them to include American cases and notes that showed the differences between English law and the law of the new American republic. He ended up with a five-volume set explicitly designed to teach lawyers and law students the differences between English and American law. Part of this task was to integrate the republican Constitution of the United States and that of Virginia with the law of the English monarchy, as set out by Blackstone. As Tucker noted, the United States and Virginia both had a constitution and a bill of rights that changed the dynamic of law. He also noted that private law in America was different. "Many parts of the laws of England are also either obsolete, or have been deemed inapplicable to our local circumstances and policy; these it might be proper to recommend to the perusal of the student, rather as a matter of curiosity, than of necessary information to him as an American Lawyer." These changes, Tucker proclaimed, were all to the good. He was certain that "upon a candid investigation of the subject, that wherever the constitution of the United States departs from the principles of the British constitution; the change will, in an eminent degree, contribute to the liberty and happiness of the people, however it may diminish the splendour of government, or the personal influence of those who administer it."

## Lower Federal Courts

The Judiciary Act of 1789 spelled out the jurisdiction of the federal district courts. Besides admiralty and maritime cases, they had jurisdiction over inland seizures, suits for penalties and forfeitures incurred under federal law, suits involving consuls and vice-consuls (with the exception of criminal cases), and some patent infringements. At first, the district courts had limited criminal jurisdiction, being restricted to minor offenses involving fines of less than $100, jail sentences of less than six months, and punishments of no more than thirty stripes. In frontier Maine and Kentucky, where the district courts also served as circuit courts, the judges heard far more criminal cases.

District courts remained relatively inactive, at least in their first eight years; New York, the busiest district, had 269 cases in that period, averaging about eight cases in each of the four quarterly terms. This began to increase at the turn of the century, as lawyers and citizens became more familiar with the federal courts, and as the growth of interstate commerce led to more diverse suits. The criminal caseload also remained small, with only 147 cases in federal circuit courts between 1790 and 1797; over half of these arose in Pennsylvania as a result of the Whiskey Rebellion. Civil cases constituted the bulk of federal court work in the system's first decade, with many of the suits filed by British creditors against American citizens. Virginia, which had been notorious in its refusal to let British creditors sue in state courts, had the largest number of debt cases in federal circuit court.

The fullest examination we have of a lower federal court's operation is Mary K. Tachau's pioneering study of the Kentucky District Court. She relates how the first judge, Henry Innes, went on the bench in 1789, a year and a half before Kentucky became a state, and sat until 1816. During that time, the court decided 2,290 cases. For 98 percent of the litigants, the court's decision proved final, with only a handful appealing to the Supreme Court. Federal officers brought nearly a third of the caseload, and most suits reflected the difficulties in enforcing revenue laws on the frontier. Many of the private civil suits involved efforts to quiet title to property, indicating that in Kentucky, at least, the federal court became an essential factor in adjudication of private disputes.

The records deny the earlier wisdom that American courts warred with English common law. Rather, Innes and his colleagues were careful to conform to English practice when possible, though they gradually adopted changes in procedures and substance, as needs demanded. Kentucky, unlike some frontiers, was blessed with a large number of Virginians familiar with the law, and they demanded and received treatment by the court consonant with the established system they had left behind in the Old Dominion.

A careful balancing of various pressures in order to yield fairness marked the Innes court. Common law, new statutes, and state and federal constitutional constraints all had to be adjusted to the needs of a rapidly evolving society and economy. The idea of a simple, objective rule of law that could be discovered by the judges proved illusory; subjective considerations of bench, bar, and litigant led to a cautious adaptation of the common law. In doing so, the court not only helped Americanize the law, but also won acceptance of federal legitimacy in a time and place when many people suspected the national government of seeking to usurp their rights.

## For Further Reading

One of the most influential books on the legal history of this period is Morton J. Horwitz, *The Transformation of American Law, 1790–1860* (1977), which argues that the developmental necessities of American economic life required the abrogation or modification of the essentially precommercial and antidevelopmental doctrines of the older common law. Some of Horwitz's general statements must be modified by William E. Nelson, *The Americanization of the Common Law: The Impact of Legal Change on Massachusetts Society, 1760–1830* (1975). Nelson finds the same changes taking place but points to different causes and suggests that the process had started earlier. A more recent and important book arguing for a more humane legal system that is not focused on economics during in this period is Peter Karsten, *Heart Versus Head: Judge-Made Law in Nineteenth Century America* (1997). Many of the basic ideas of law as a positive force for economic development derive from the writings of the dean of American legal history, James Willard Hurst; see especially, his *Law and the Conditions of Freedom in the Nineteenth-Century United States* (1956). William J. Novak, *The People's Welfare: Law & Regulation in Nineteenth Century America* (1996) offers a sophisticated analysis of the interaction between the common law, legislation, and economic development in this period. Lawrence M. Friedman, *History of American Law* (2nd ed., 1985), remains valuable for its broad overview. Also useful is Kermit L. Hall, *The Magic Mirror* (1989). Students may also find the conceptual analysis of Grant Gilmore, *The Ages of American Law* (1977), both lively and stimulating. Less lively but still stimulating is Perry Miller's annotation to the documents in *The Legal Mind in America: From Independence to the Civil War* (1962). Wilfred J. Ritz, *American Judicial Proceedings First Printed Before 1801* (1984) is a comprehensive bibliography of early court cases and court reports. Covering all legal books but official reports of cases is Morris Cohen, *Bibliography of Early American Law*, 6 vols. (1998).

On the legal profession, see especially, Maxwell Bloomfield, *American Lawyers in a Changing Society, 1776–1876* (1976), which looks at both self-image and public perceptions of lawyers. Uncritical but packed with information is Anton-Hermann Chroust, *The Rise of the Legal Profession in America*, Vol. 2, *The Revolutionary and Post-Revolutionary Era* (1965). For the day-to-day business of an extremely successful attorney, see Julius Goebel, Jr. et al., eds., *The Law Practice of Alexander Hamilton*, 5 vols. (1964–1981). Paul S. Clarkson and R. Samuel Jett, *Luther Martin of Maryland* (1970), is a fine study of a man who served thirty years as attorney general of Maryland, maintained an extensive private practice, and headed the defense in both the Chase and Burr trials. On early legal education, see Robert Stevens, *Law School: Legal Education in America from the 1850s to the 1980s* (1983).

The work of an important frontier court is well analyzed in Mary K. Bonsteel Tachau, *Federal Courts in the Early Republic: Kentucky, 1789–1816* (1978), which examines the tenure of Judge Harry Innes. Carroll T. Bond's older book, *The Court of Appeals of Maryland: A History* (1928), is still useful, but there are far too few good studies of state courts in this period. *Tucker's Blackstone* (1803) remains the most important treatise for the period. A 1996 reprint by the Lawbook Exchange contains a scholarly introduction by David Cobin and Paul Finkelman.

# 10

# Adams, Jefferson, and the Courts

A KEY TEST OF the viability of the new nation would be whether it could peacefully transfer power from one faction to another. The growth of parties, along with the exaggerated political rhetoric common to the late eighteenth century, misled some foreign observers to conclude that the United States was tottering on the edge of chaos. They failed to appreciate that beneath the abusive campaign slogans, both Federalists and Republicans shared the basic tenets of the republican ideology. Problems did exist, however, because of differing views on the particulars of government, as well as from the tensions that were inevitable whenever a minority controls a key branch of the government. Adams and the Alien and Sedition Acts, Jefferson and his attack on the judiciary, and John Marshall and his development of the independent, powerful role of the Court all involved questions of power as well as of constitutional thought. Debates on *who* will govern and *how* they will govern dominated political discourse at the end of the eighteenth and beginning of the nineteenth centuries.

## The Alien and Sedition Acts

The rising strength of the Republicans had almost swept Jefferson into the presidency in 1796, but in the end John Adams won the office with 71 electoral votes, and Jefferson became vice president with 68. Adams stood philosophically between Jefferson and Hamilton, favoring a strong central government, while jealously protective of individual rights. He shared neither Hamilton's attachment to aristocracy nor Jefferson's faith in the common man. His three-volume *Defense of the Constitution of Government of the United States*, written in the 1780s, and the *Discourse on Davila* (1790), are nearly forgotten today, overshadowed by *The Federalist*. Although, as Adams biographer Joseph Ellis notes, "the sprawling, inchoate character of the work" led few to read it, both the *Defense* and the *Davila* reveal a man who had thought long and carefully on the problems of government.

Adams's greatest achievement as president, avoiding a full-scale war with France, led the Hamiltonian High Federalists on one side to condemn him for being pro-French, and the Jeffersonian Republicans on the other side for taking England's part. The patriotic fervor of the nation generated by the threat of war, however, gave the more extreme Federalists in Congress the opportunity to suppress what they considered treasonous criticism of the government by the Jeffersonian press. In 1798, with mixed support from Adams, they pushed through the Alien and Sedition Acts.

Three of the acts simply reflected hostility to foreigners, especially the French and Irish, many of whom, because of their anti-British feeling, had joined the Republicans. The Naturalization Act increased from five to fourteen years the period of residency before an immigrant could secure citizenship. The Alien Act gave the president power to expel "dangerous" aliens; the Alien Enemy Act authorized the president, in time of a declared war, to imprison or expel enemy aliens.

The Republicans could not constitutionally object to the Naturalization Act, since Article I, Section 8 gave Congress the power "to establish an uniform Rule of Naturalization." Nor did they object to the purpose of the Alien Enemies Act, and the bill received bipartisan support in the Congress. The Republicans did, however, oppose vesting so much control in the hands of the president, and they feared this power might be used against American citizens, as well as against aliens. They expressed these concerns even more strongly against the Alien Act, which they saw as a Federalist attack on their party, but to no avail. The wartime fervor carried all the bills through to passage.

The Republicans feared most the Sedition Act, which defined as a high misdemeanor any combination or conspiracy against the legal operations of the government, including interference with federal officers, insurrection, or riot. Furthermore, the law forbade writing, publishing, or speaking anything of "a false, scandalous and malicious writing . . . against the government of the United States, or either house of the Congress of the United States, or the President of the United States." Significantly, the act did not prohibit defaming the vice president of the United States. Although nominally passed as a war measure, the law was designed to silence the opposition in the coming election campaign. The Federalists made no attempt to disguise this purpose, and boldly provided that the statute would remain in force until March 3, 1801—which was the last day of Adams's administration. The expiration date cleverly allowed the Federalists to prosecute their opponents during the campaign, but if Jefferson won, he would not be able to turn the law around, and prosecute Federalists.

This was not the first time the Federalists had tried to muzzle opposition. On May 23, 1797, a grand jury in Richmond handed down a presentment against Samuel J. Cabell, the Republican representative from Albemarle, Jefferson's own district, for criticizing the Adams administration in letters to his constituents. The Virginia House of Delegates condemned the grand jury's action as a "violation of fundamental principles of representation . . . an usurpation of power . . . and a subjection of a natural right of speaking and writing freely." Although Cabell never stood trial on the charge, to Jefferson the incident foreshadowed an even greater attack. During the debate on the Naturalization and Alien bills, he told Madison, "there is now only wanting, to accomplish the whole declaration . . . by the Federalists, a sedition bill," to which Madison replied, "I hope the bridle is not yet upon the press."

The Jeffersonians argued that a free press constituted a bulwark of republican government. They remembered the role the prerevolutionary press had played in exposing the evils of royal government, and how newspapermen and pamphleteers had sustained patriotic fervor in the fight for independence. The Sedition Act seemed a return to the harsh English law, which made criticism of the government or of anyone in authority a criminal offense. Under the older English law, truth was no defense, and a jury in seditious libel cases considered only questions of *fact*—did the accused actually publish the offensive remarks? If yes, then the judge, a creature of the Crown, determined— as a matter of *law*—whether the material was seditious. As Blackstone explained, the truth or falsity of the remarks made no difference, "since the provocation, and not the falsity, is the thing to be punished criminally." Although the government could not censor a publication ahead of time and editors thus operated free of prior restraint, they could be penalized severely after publication if the court found the material seditious.

As early as 1735, in the famous trial of the journalist and printer John Peter Zenger, Americans had shown themselves unwilling to curb their press so drastically. In Zenger's case, the jury insisted on deciding not only the *fact* of publication, but the law as well, that is, the seditious nature of the material. The jury in that case ignored precedent, and acquitted Zenger, accepting the novel claims of his attorney that the defendant should be able to offer the truth of the publication as a defense. Zenger's case, which was really an example of jury nullification, set no legal precedent, but it did set an important political precedent. The Sedition Act of 1798 adopted this concept, and provided that a defendant could plead the truth of his statements, and that a jury could decide both law and facts in sedition cases. But "truth as a defense" was not much use in a politically charged prosecution, especially, as in the Sedition Act cases, when the judges were biased against the defendants, and the juries were often stacked with Federalists. More importantly, a zealous political debate does not lend itself to any easy objective test of truth. The claim that a government official is pompous or incompetent may be impossible to prove, since it is a subjective judgment. Whether a statement is "politically true" depends not on facts, but to which faction one belongs.

The administration of the new law proved as partisan as the Republicans had feared. Although editorial defenders of Jefferson often resorted to lies, innuendos, and misrepresentations in their attacks on the government, the Federalist press engaged in the same tactics against Vice President Jefferson and Republican members of Congress, yet the government did not charge a single Federalist editor under the law. It did secure fifteen indictments against Republicans, and the Federalist judges usually charged the juries in what today would clearly be seen as a politically biased manner. Ten cases resulted in convictions, despite the absurdly trivial nature of some of the allegedly seditious comments. Luther Baldwin of Newark, New Jersey, was convicted of libel for what was essentially barroom banter. While at a tavern, he heard a cannon being fired to salute President John Adams, who was passing through the town. Someone at the bar quipped, "there goes the President and they are firing at his a__." Baldwin answered that "he did not care if they fired thro' his a__." For this he was fined $150. Congressman Matthew Lyon of Vermont ridiculed Adams's "continual grasp for power" and "unbounded thirst for ridiculous pomp, foolish adulation, and selfish avarice," for which Lyon was fined $1,000 and languished four months in jail until he could raise the funds to pay the fine. The Constitution (Article I, Section 6) does provide immunity from prosecution for what members of Congress say in Congress, but the government prosecuted Lyon for the allegedly seditious articles he published in a Vermont newspaper.

## The Kentucky and Virginia Resolutions

Although Lyon and others argued that the Sedition Act was constitutional, none of the Federalist judges paid any attention to them, and no case testing the law reached the Supreme Court. Instead, the major constitutional attack came in resolutions drafted by Thomas Jefferson and James Madison, respectively, and passed by the Kentucky and Virginia legislatures in November and December 1798. The resolutions denounced the Sedition Act in part because it threatened freedom of expression. Madison, in the Virginia Resolution, declared that the attack on a free press "ought to produce universal alarm, because it is levelled against the right of freely examining public characters and measures, and of free communication among the people theron, which has ever been justly deemed the only effectual guardian of every other right."

But, despite this brief discussion of the right of freedom of expression, the main thrust of Madison's resolution as well as Jefferson's Kentucky Resolution was not a defense of free expression. The main issue for both men was on the limitations of congressional power and the argument that the law infringed upon the powers of the states. In essence, the resolutions were about states' rights. Madison and Jefferson argued that the Union had been formed by a compact among the states, and that rather than surrendering their sovereignty to the national government, the states preserved all the attributes of their autonomy save those they had specifically delegated through the Constitution. Therefore, whenever Congress passed any law that exceeded the very limited functions granted to it, the states had the power and the responsibility to interpose themselves between their citizens and the national government and to refuse enforcement of such laws within their borders. The states, according to the Virginia Resolution, "have the right and are duty bound to interpose for arresting the progress of the evil."

The Virginia and Kentucky Resolutions had far-ranging repercussions. Their key arguments—the compact theory of government, the authority of the states to judge for themselves the constitutionality of acts of Congress, and the power to nullify those acts they deemed illegitimate—would become the focus of the great constitutional debate preceding the Civil War. Madison would live to disclaim the nullification argument as developed by John C. Calhoun; Southern states, however, revived Madison's views on interposition again in the 1950s in their fight against school desegregation.

How far Jefferson and Madison intended to go with the Kentucky and Virginia resolutions is not clear. Neither state actually did anything to stop enforcement of the laws, but merely called upon other states to help win repeal. Jefferson advised against any violence, and assured other Republicans that "the reign of witches" would soon end. The rhetoric of the two documents did allow the Republicans to cast themselves as defenders of free speech and press, and it is possible that, at the time, they represented little more than the opening salvos of the 1800 election campaign. Unfortunately, the doctrines they proposed cast a lengthening shadow on the country in the following decades.

# The Election of 1800

The Republicans narrowly won the election of 1800, and the Federalists prepared to turn over the administration of government on March 4, 1801. Many European observers believed the United States would soon plunge into civil war, for history recorded no instance of one faction peacefully surrendering the power of government to another, especially to one that seemed so antithetical in purpose and beliefs. They misread the bitterness of the campaign, however, and did not understand that the strident rhetoric masked the deep commitment of both parties to republican government. The transition went peacefully, although not smoothly, confounding the critics, and the policies of the Jeffersonians in office confirmed rather than repudiated the general legacy of the Washington and Adams administrations. Before Jefferson could take the oath of office, though, two events of constitutional significance occurred: the lame-duck Congress changed the judiciary and then had to determine who would be president.

The Constitution had originally envisioned the president and vice president not as party representatives, but as the two individuals the people considered best qualified to lead the country. To choose the chief executive, electors in every state cast two ballots. Whoever had the largest total of all the ballots cast became president; the person with the next highest total became vice president. Since everyone expected Washington to be the first president, the first example we have of this system working in a competitive election is 1796, in which Adams and Jefferson vied for the highest office. Adams had the highest total of votes; Jefferson, his political adversary, had the second highest, and so they took their respective places.

Had the Federalists been more strategic in 1796, they would have all agreed to cast one of their ballots for a single presidential candidate (Adams) and their other ballot for another Federalist, who would have become vice president. Instead they scattered their votes among four Federalist candidates, which led to Adams being elected president with seventy-one electoral votes, but left the next Federalist candidate, Thomas Pinckney of South Carolina, with only fifty-nine electoral votes. The Democratic-Republicans were equally disorganized, casting sixty-eight votes for Jefferson, but scattering their second votes among eight candidates. The result was a divided administration with the Democratic-Republican Jefferson serving as vice president under the Federalist John Adams.

By 1800, however, the development of parties led each faction to nominate not only a candidate for president but a running mate as well. The Republicans forged a Virginia–New York alliance, with Aaron Burr as the nominee for vice president, while the Federalists named Charles Cotesworth Pinckney of South Carolina to run with Adams. But the Constitution did not provide for separate ballots for the two positions;

each of the seventy-three Republican electors cast one ballot each for Jefferson and Burr, resulting in a tie. Under Article II, Section 1, the lame-duck Congress, which the Federalists controlled, had to choose the president in the case of a tie in the electoral college. The intrigues that took place there need not be considered here. In the end, Jefferson's old foe, Alexander Hamilton, who hated his fellow New Yorker Aaron Burr more than he feared Thomas Jefferson, helped swing the balance in Jefferson's favor.

To prevent such a situation in the future, Congress drafted an amendment providing for separate ballots for president and vice president, and the states ratified the Twelfth Amendment on September 25, 1804. Like the Eleventh Amendment, it clarified a situation that the Founders had not anticipated; it would be the last technical change to the original Constitution. All the other amendments have been designed to expand individual rights or democratic involvement in government, meet new conditions in a changing society, or alter some clear constitutional provision to reflect current political notions of how government should work. One of the marvels of the 1787 document is that the basic political structure remains viable.

## The Judiciary Act of 1801

The lame-duck Congress also passed the Judiciary Act of 1801, which had been fully debated at the preceding session. The bill attempted to correct the deficiencies of the judicial system in the light of more than a decade's experience under the 1789 act. It created six new circuit courts to relieve the Supreme Court justices from the task of riding circuit, of which they had complained unceasingly. (In fact, after Chief Justice Ellsworth had resigned because of ill health, Adams had nominated John Jay in December 1800 to take his old seat; the Senate had confirmed the nomination, but Jay declined it on the grounds that Congress had not yet taken action to end circuit riding.) The new courts would be manned by a total of sixteen permanent judges, together with support staff of clerks, marshals, and attorneys. The bill also extended federal court jurisdiction by providing for a greater power of removal of certain types of cases from state to federal courts, and it created a new district court for the District of Columbia. In a gratuitous slap at Jefferson, the Federalists also reduced the size of the Supreme Court, a reduction that would take place with the next vacancy, thus depriving the new president of an opportunity to make a court appointment. On February 27, 1801, the Congress passed the Organic Act for the District of Columbia, under which President Adams appointed forty-two justices of the peace, including William Marbury.

Nearly all modern commentators have applauded the attempt in the Judiciary Act of 1801 to eliminate circuit riding and to create an intermediate appellate court. However, most scholars also recognize that the blatantly political nature of the two acts undermined the purposes of Judiciary Act. The increasing volume of business in the federal court system required more courts, and the growth of the country (Vermont, Kentucky, and Tennessee had joined the Union) made circuit riding not only physically draining, but practically impossible in light of the justices' other responsibilities. The Federalists, consistent with their philosophy, sought to strengthen the national government by binding the Union together through a cohesive judicial system. "There is no way to combat the state opposition," wrote Oliver Wolcott of Connecticut, "but by an efficient and extended organization of judges, magistrates, and other civil officers." Shortly after the bill's passage, Gouverneur Morris declared that it "answers the double purpose of bringing Justice near to Men's Doors and of giving additional fibres to the Roots of Government."

## John Marshall and the Midnight Judges

The real benefits of the Judiciary Act of 1801 have long been obscured by charges that the Federalists, ousted from authority by the people, sought to cling to power by expanding the court system and packing it with their allies. In Jefferson's words, the Federalists "retired into the judiciary as a stronghold." Had these appointments been available to the Republicans, their complaints might not have been so loud, for many in that party also recognized the need to correct the deficiencies in the system. On the other hand, had the goal of Adams and his party been only judicial reform, the retiring president might have been wise enough to leave some new judicial seats vacant, so Jefferson would have had an opportunity to make some appointments. But Adams made all the appointments, with great haste, and he did pack the judiciary with dozens of Federalists, many of whom, under terms of the law, would have tenure for life. Since the bill did not pass until February 13, 1801, and the Organic Act for the District of Columbia until February 27, Adams had to rush to fill all the positions. Those who received these offices have been stigmatized ever since as "midnight judges." Not all these men received their commissions before Adams left office, and one of them, William Marbury, in seeking to force the new administration to deliver his commission as a District justice of the peace, precipitated one of the landmark cases in our constitutional history.

Although John Marshall himself is often grouped with the "midnight judges," he actually received his own appointment considerably earlier. After Jay refused the office, Adams nominated Marshall to be Chief Justice of the United States on January 20, 1801, despite much grumbling in his own party. Many wanted Justice William Paterson elevated to the chief's position, while others preferred Charles Cotesworth Pinckney; both men had close ties to Hamilton. The Senate delayed its vote for a week, hoping Adams would change his mind, but the president held firm, and the upper chamber confirmed Marshall's nomination on January 27. "My gift of John Marshall to the people of the United States was the proudest act of my life," Adams later declared. "I have given to my country a Judge, equal to a Hale, a Holt or a Mansfield."

That Marshall would transform the Court, and by his vision forge it into an instrument of national unity, did not appear so clearly to his contemporaries. Although the forty-five-year-old Marshall had enjoyed a successful law practice in Richmond and was considered one of the leaders of the Virginia bar, he had no judicial experience. His contributions to public life had been primarily in foreign affairs, serving as special envoy to France and as secretary of state during the latter part of the Adams administration. The appointment evoked little enthusiasm among the Federalists. Oliver Wolcott believed that Marshall "will read and expound the Constitution as if it were a penal statute, and will sometimes be embarrassed with doubts." Federalist Fisher

Ames questioned Marshall's devotion to true Federalist principles because of the latter's disapproval of the Alien and Sedition laws. The Republicans, of course, had little use for him, and the *Aurora* characterized him as "more distinguished as a rhetorician and sophist than as a lawyer and statesman." Jefferson spoke of the "lax, lounging manner," "profound hypocrisy," and devotion to "English principles" of his distant cousin.

Marshall took his seat at the opening of the February 1801 term, and since the Court heard no cases that session, he continued to serve out the remaining weeks of the Adams administration as secretary of state; as such, his responsibility for delivering judicial commissions involved him with the midnight judges business. Jefferson also asked Marshall to continue as secretary of state for a short while into the new administration until James Madison could arrive to take up his duties. Cordially, Marshall swore in Jefferson as president on March 4, 1801, but within a short time they would be not merely on different sides of the political fence but implacable foes. Transcending the political storms of his first years in office, Marshall would become one of the greatest judicial statesmen in the nation's history.

## Jefferson Takes Office

In his inaugural, Jefferson appeared to want to calm the passions of the election and reach out to his opponents. "We are all Republicans, we are all Federalists," he declared. Rejecting the notion that speech could threaten the nation, and implicitly attacking the Sedition Act, he told his fellow citizens "If there be any among us who would wish to dissolve this Union or to change its republican form, let them stand undisturbed as monuments of the safety with which error of opinion may be tolerated where reason is left free to combat it." The new president even indicated his support for the policies of his predecessors. "Would the honest patriot," Jefferson asked, "in the full tide of the successful experiment, abandon a government which has thus far kept us free and firm?" He reassured his supporters of the principles he would follow: "Equal and exact justice to all men . . . freedom of religion; freedom of the press; and freedom of person, under the protection of the habeas corpus; and trial by juries impartially selected."

He struck a note of republican simplicity in his administration, abandoning the formal trappings of his predecessors and frequently riding about the new capital city alone on horseback. He installed a round table in the White House, so that no one could claim a place of honor, with the only rule of etiquette that women preceded the men into dinner.

Jefferson's first act as president was to pardon all people convicted under the Sedition Act. Some years later, Congress would remit their fines. "The reign of witches," as Jefferson called the period, at the federal level was over, and there would be no federal sedition prosecutions until the administration of Woodrow Wilson, more than a century later. But, newspapermen could still be charged under state law. Jefferson, who was notoriously thin-skinned, in fact privately urged the prosecution of his opponents in state courts. In 1803, Jefferson complained to a political ally about Federalists criticizing his administration, and urged "a few prosecutions of the most prominent offenders." In his second term, he condoned the act of a federal prosecutor, who charged opposition editors under common law. Ironically, this case would eventually lead to a Supreme Court decision, in *United States v. Hudson and Goodwin* (1812), declaring that there was no federal common law of crimes.

Meanwhile, Blackstone's common law principles on libel continued to be followed by many state courts until the 1820s, although a number of states began to provide for truth as a defense. In *People v. Croswell* (1804), New York's highest court was equally divided on whether truth should be a defense. Ironically, the prosecutor in this case was a Jeffersonian, who argued that the state should follow Blackstone and the conservative English rules, while Alexander Hamilton defended Croswell, an obscure Federalist publisher, arguing for freedom of the press. In *Commonwealth v. Clap* (1808), Chief Justice Parsons of Massachusetts drew a line between elected and appointed officials, anticipating in some ways the distinction later courts would draw between public and private figures. In the case of attacks on the former, the liberal rule of truth as a defense would be permitted. But in cases of libel against appointed officials, private reputation required greater protection, and the mere fact of the libel would be sufficient for conviction.

Perhaps because both the Federalists and the Jeffersonians prosecuted each other for seditious libel, its misuse as a political tool ended about the time Jefferson left office. Publicly, Jefferson had always supported a free press, and in the end, most Americans accepted that partisan political discussions should not be subject to legal restraints. Indeed, with one exception, political discussion remained vibrant until the Civil War. The one important exception involved slavery. Starting in the second decade of the nineteenth century and continuing until the end of the Civil War, frank discussions of slavery were impossible in the South, and could lead to legal sanctions, including arrest or expulsion from a southern state. During the Civil War, there would be a few arrests in the North, and a good deal of suppression of the press in the Confederacy. Following the Civil War, political discourse would face few restraints until World War I.

## Repeal of the Judiciary Act

Jefferson's conciliatory approach in his inaugural address did not last long. Shortly after taking office, he began to remove a number of public employees, such as customs collectors and postmasters, and replacing them with members of his own party. Jefferson claimed he would not be subject, as he wrote, to the embarrassment "of acting thro' men whose views were to defeat mine." But, of course, it is quite clear that customs inspectors and postmasters were hardly in a position to affect the implementation of Jefferson's policies.

In hindsight, it is clear that the president had the power to replace officeholders with people who favored his policies, yet at the time there was no precedent for doing so. Jefferson did not envision a wholesale ousting of Federalist officeholders. Some would have to go, and although he claimed no one would be dismissed merely for differing opinions, in fact, most of his dismissals were designed to make room for men of his own party. Thus, Jefferson removed public servants, including the most able diplomat in national service at the time, John Quincy Adams, simply because of their political affiliations.

The Constitution, aside from defining the terms of elected officials and establishing life tenure for federal judges, said nothing about other appointed officials; furthermore, Washington and Adams together had appointed some 600 officials, yet only six known Republicans could be found in the federal service at the time of Jefferson's inauguration. The realities of the new political party system did not originate with Andrew Jackson's famous dictum that "to the victor belongs the spoils"; it became a necessary adjunct of government with Jefferson's victory. While cleaning out Federalists from various national departments, Jefferson and his allies turned to the judiciary.

To Jefferson, the Judiciary Act of 1801, the Organic Act for the District of Columbia, and Adams's appointment of the midnight judges, represented nothing but court-packing. The Federalists, repudiated by the people at the polls, could now, he believed, thwart his democratic policies from the safety of the bench. In 1801, not a single Republican sat on a federal court, and nothing but death or resignation—both uncertain factors—would allow him to rectify that situation. Adams's appointment of John Marshall as Chief Justice did not please the new president at all, for there had long been ill will between them, and Marshall's federalism stood solidly opposed to Jeffersonian principles. Something had to be done, Jefferson believed, to prevent the Federalist bench from hindering democracy. As Republican William Giles asserted, "the revolution is incomplete, so long as that strong fortress is in possession of the enemy." Giles advocated that Jefferson remove "all of [the judges] . . . indiscriminately."

The solution raised interesting constitutional questions. Since judges served for life, no one knew if Congress could abolish judgeships in order to fire judges. Certainly if this were possible then the whole idea of life tenure for judges would be in doubt. Nothing would prevent Jefferson and his allies from abolishing all existing courts, including the Supreme Court, and then recreating them a short time later, so that the new president could appoint his allies to the bench.

Jefferson, who often claimed to be a strict constructionist when it came to reading the Constitution, nevertheless saw no constitutional problems. His plan was to abolish the new courts and, in the process, eliminate the judges. Shortly after his inauguration, Jefferson told a friend that "the judge of course stands till the law is repealed, which we trust will be at the next Congress." On January 6, 1802, John Breckinridge of Kentucky, who had been Jefferson's lieutenant in the Kentucky Resolution of 1798, introduced a bill in the Senate to repeal the Judiciary Act of 1801. After intense debate, the Repeal Act narrowly passed the upper chamber, 16 to 15, on February 3; the House, where the Republicans enjoyed a large majority, enacted the Senate bill without amendment a month later.

The real problems that the 1801 act had sought to resolve still remained, and in 1802, the Republicans attempted to deal with them. Although denounced by Congressman Thomas Bayard as a "miserable patchwork,' John Marshall, in *United States v. Daniel* (1821), declared the 1802 Amendatory Act a "great improvement of the pre-existing system." It increased the number of circuits from three to six, with each justice assigned to only one, where he would hold court with the local district judges on circuit twice a year. In addition, the new law provided for only one four-week term of the Supreme Court each year instead of the two terms in effect since 1789, thus further reducing the physical strain on the justices by eliminating an arduous trip to the capital. This provision, which certainly made sense in light of the Court's caseload, nonetheless provoked much criticism. Under the 1789 act, there would have been an

August 1802 term; the 1801 law had called for this to be moved to the following June. Now there would be no meeting of the nation's highest court until February 1803, a full fourteen months after its last session in December 1801.

Critics of the Amendatory law claimed that the Republicans feared that the Supreme Court at the anticipated June term would have found the Repeal Act unconstitutional. Jefferson's friend James Monroe, now governor of Virginia, argued that the Republicans should not fear the issue; far worse, he contended, if the public viewed the postponement as "an unconstitutional oppression of the judiciary by the legislature, adopted to carry a preceding measure [the Repeal Act] which was also unconstitutional." Monroe urged the president to veto the bill, but Jefferson never used the veto during his term. His biographer Dumas Malone suggests that although Jefferson would not willingly have sought a confrontation with the Court, he probably believed that the delay would work in the party's favor. By the time the Court met in 1803, the furor would have died down.

The Republicans thought the Court might hold the Repeal Act void, because under the Constitution judges were appointed for life. Although the Constitution specifically grants Congress the power to create new courts, it is not hard to imagine a court holding that once judges were appointed, they could not be summarily removed simply by abolishing a court. This after all, would allow a new majority in Congress to abolish an existing court and replace it with a new one. Such political tinkering with the courts strikes modern ears as unfathomable, but since the Republicans were in fact doing just that, it is not hard to see that they worried about the constitutionality of an act that fired judges.

On the other hand, it was reasonable to argue that one Congress ought to have the power to abolish a whole court structure and replace it with something new. As Robert Wright of Maryland noted in the Senate debate, "Are we to be eternally bound by the follies of a law which ought never to have been passed?"

Chief Justice John Marshall privately "doubted the constitutionality of the repeal." But, Marshall was shrewd enough as a politician to know when he could not win. He told Justice William Paterson that he would "be bound by the opinion of the majority of the Judges," knowing that in fact within the Court, only Justice Samuel Chase argued against the constitutionality of the repeal. When a specific challenge did reach the Court in *Stuart v. Laird* (1803), the Court, in an opinion by Paterson, affirmed the constitutionality of the repealing act. What had seemed so grave a question at the time passed quickly into obscurity. One reason for Marshall's acquiescence to the repeal of the 1801 act may have been his desire to avoid a direct confrontation with President Jefferson in a manner that would allow Jefferson to obstruct the Court's opinion. Shrewdly, Marshall found a better way to confront Jefferson in his opinion in *Marbury v. Madison*, which he delivered six days before the decision in *Stuart v. Laird*. Here Marshall was able to confront Jefferson—and beat him on a major jurisprudential point—in such a manner that Jefferson could not respond.

## *Marbury v. Madison*

While it was possible for Jefferson and his party to eliminate the new courts and judges, and simply return to the old court system, Jefferson had no interest in eliminating the new offices for the new city of Washington, D.C. However, the appointment of justices of the peace for that city created a major constitutional issue for the young nation.

When Congress created the national capital, the District of Columbia, it was divided into two counties, Washington (the present-day area of Washington, D.C.) and Alexandria (which is now Alexandria, Virginia). On March 2, 1801, Adams had nominated twenty-three men to be justices of the peace for the newly created Washington County and nineteen for Alexandria County. Of those nominated for Washington County, seventeen were Federalists, although only eleven were prominent in the party, and six were Jeffersonians. The Senate confirmed these nominations on March 3, and Adams signed commissions late into the last evening of the last day of his term. That night, James Marshall, the brother of the chief justice designate, delivered some of the commissions to men in Alexandria, who ultimately served their terms in office. But, none of the twenty-three justices of the peace for Washington County received their commissions before Adams left office.

When Jefferson took office he discovered the undelivered commissions. Jefferson then reappointed the six Republicans on Adams's list and six of the Federalists. He added a few more Republicans as well, but refused to reappoint the remaining eleven Federalists. Most of the Federalists accepted their fate passively. But William Marbury did not. Marbury was a proud public servant, stalwart Federalist, and wealthy investor who wanted the prestige that came with the office.

As secretary of state, John Marshall had been in charge of delivering the commissions to the last-minute appointments made by Adams. But, in the rush at the end of the administration, he had been unable to deliver the commission in time, and when Jefferson took office he ordered it withheld. The bill authorizing the positions had left the exact number to the discretion of the president, and Adams had chosen forty-two. Jefferson thought this number too high for the sparsely populated capital, and reduced it to thirty. The relative lack of partisanship in this decision is evident in that of the thirty appointments Jefferson made, twenty-five went to men originally nominated by Adams. William Marbury, however, was not one of them.

Jefferson later claimed that delivery was essential for a commission to be valid, just as for a deed or bond, and that by withholding the document, the entire nomination had been voided. Marbury, however, along with three others, filed suit at the December 1801 session of the Supreme Court seeking a writ of mandamus—an order

---

## SHOULD MARSHALL HAVE DECIDED *MARBURY V. MADISON?*

Some scholars have questioned whether Marshall should have removed himself from this case because of his prior involvement as secretary of state. Certainly, later judicial standards would have called for recusement, but at the time only financial connections to a case led judges to step aside, as Marshall did in the Virginia land suits. The Jeffersonians, always quick to criticize Marshall, did not even raise the issue of his sitting in the *Marbury* case.

from a court directing a person to perform a particular act or fulfill some obligation— to force the new secretary of state, James Madison, to deliver the commission. Marbury's lawyer, former Attorney General Charles Lee, argued that the signing and sealing of the commission completed the transaction, and that delivery constituted a mere formality. But formality or not, without the actual piece of parchment, Marbury could not enter into the duties of office. The Court, well aware of Jefferson's hostility, might well have dismissed the suit immediately for lack of jurisdiction (which it ultimately did), but instead it aroused Republican resentment by agreeing to hear the case at its next term. As it turned out, that would not be for over a year, but when Marshall convened the Court in February 1803, *Marbury v. Madison* stood on the docket.

The case, by any reasonable interpretation, can only be described as minor, for by the time the Court heard it, the wisdom of Jefferson's reduced number of justices of the peace to thirty had been confirmed, Marbury's original term was almost half over, and most people, like Jefferson, considered the issue moot. But Marshall, despite the political difficulties involved, recognized that he had a perfect case with which to expound a basic principle, and by his persistence, he utilized it to lay the foundation for the Court to assume the primary role in constitutional interpretation.

It is questionable if, in December 1801, when he decided to hear the case, Marshall had planned any grand strategy. Certainly, by the time he heard the arguments, he recognized the dilemma facing the Court. If it issued the mandamus, the Court had no power to enforce it, and Jefferson would certainly ignore it. If, on the other hand, the Court refused to issue the writ, it would appear that the judiciary had backed down before the executive, and this Marshall would not allow. The solution he chose has properly been termed a tour de force, in that he managed to establish the power of the Court as the ultimate arbiter of the Constitution, to chastise the Jefferson administration for its failure to obey the law, and yet to avoid having the Court's authority ignored by the administration.

Marshall, adopting a style that would mark all his major opinions, reduced the case to a few basic issues. Here, he asked three questions: Did Marbury have the right to the commission? If he did, and his rights had been violated, did the law provide him with a remedy? If so, did mandamus from the Supreme Court constitute the proper remedy? The last question, the crucial one, dealt with the jurisdiction of the Court in a particular case, and should normally have been answered first, since a negative response would have obviated the need to decide the other issues. But that would have denied Marshall the opportunity to criticize Jefferson for what the chief justice saw as a flouting of the laws.

For the most part, following the arguments of Marbury's counsel, Charles Lee, on the first two questions, Marshall held that the validity of a commission existed once a president signed it and transmitted it to the secretary of state for affixing the seal. Presidential discretion ended there, for the political decision had been made, and the secretary of state had only a ministerial task to perform—delivering the commission. In this, the law bound him, like anyone else, to obey. Marshall drew a careful and lengthy distinction between the political acts of the president and the secretary, in which the courts had no business interfering, and the simple administrative execution that, governed by law, the judiciary could review. "The province of the court," he wrote, "is, solely, to decide on the rights of individuals, not to inquire how the executive, or executive officers, perform duties in which they have a discretion. Questions in their nature political, or which are, by the constitution and laws, submitted to the executive, can never be made in this court."

Having decided that Marbury had the right to the commission, Marshall next turned to the question of remedy, and once again, it appeared that the Court would find for the plaintiff. Mandamus would require Secretary Madison either to provide the original commission or secure a copy from the record. So far, those sitting in the courtroom listening to the chief justice read the opinion in his hard, dry voice must have assumed that Marbury had won his case. But then, having lectured Jefferson and Madison for their sins in "sport[ing] away the vested rights of others," Marshall turned to the crucial third question. Now at last, he declared that Congress, in granting the Supreme Court the power of mandamus in original jurisdiction in Section 13 of the Judiciary Act of 1789, had violated the Constitution. That document, which laid out the original jurisdiction of the Court, did not grant it the power of mandamus, and therefore Congress could not do so. In effect, he told Marbury: "Plaintiff, your rights have been violated by Jefferson and mandamus is your proper remedy, but we are sorry; this Court cannot help you." Marshall thus had his cake and ate it also; he castigated the administration, but avoided a confrontation with Jefferson that the Court could not win.

The politics of *Marbury v. Madison* have been widely hailed. In view of the attacks the Jeffersonians had launched against the judiciary (discussed in the next section), Marshall had to make a strong statement to maintain the status of the Court as a coequal branch of government. By asserting the power to declare acts of Congress unconstitutional, a power that the Court would not exercise again for more than a half century, Marshall claimed for the Court the paramount position within the government in constitutional interpretation. Marbury set the abiding precedent for the Court's power in this area, and even today the case is cited as authority whenever a law comes before the Court for constitutional review.

The judicial logic of Marshall's argument, however, has been questioned over the years, especially at times when Court decisions have been unpopular. The proper initial question for any court to ask is whether it has jurisdiction over a particular case; if the answer is no, it need not—and should not—decide the merits. In essence, the Court decided it had no jurisdiction to decide the two questions it had already decided. Marshall stood the normal procedure on its head in order to make his political points.

There is also much support for the idea that Marshall wrongly interpreted the Constitution. Article III, Section 2 of the Constitution gives the Supreme Court original jurisdiction in a limited number of cases, and then gives the Court "appellate Jurisdiction" in "other cases" but "with such Exceptions, and under such Regulations as the Congress shall make." Many modern scholars argue that "such Exceptions" can be interpreted to allow Congress to *expand*, but not contract, the original jurisdiction of the Court. If this were so, then Congress did have the constitutional authority to give the Court the right to issue a writ of mandamus. Had Marshall been arguing from a position of strength, perhaps with a supportive president in office, he might have made such an interpretation. But, given the political realities of the case, he could not do so.

Beyond the immediate issue, Marshall also claimed for the Court two far-ranging powers. The first of these, judicial review of legislation, was not that revolutionary, despite the absence of a specific delegation of this authority in the Constitution. Marshall carefully justified the Court's power through a common-sense reading of Articles III and VI. Article III provided that "the judicial Power of the United States, shall be vested in one supreme Court, and in such inferior Courts as Congress may from time to time establish." The grant of judicial power provided a broad mandate, intended to include all functions normally performed by courts, and therefore had to be read in light of customary usage and other provisions of the Constitution. Article VI, the Supremacy Clause, established a hierarchy of law, with the Constitution at the apex, superior to acts of Congress. Whenever the two conflicted, the lesser (legislation) had to give way to the greater (the Constitution). Marshall also relied on English and American legal traditions, in which the power of courts to nullify legislative acts, while admittedly not exercised frequently, nonetheless existed, and sufficient examples, many fresh in memory, supported the power. Finally, the Constitution, although the fundamental law of the land, remained a law; as such, it had to be interpreted, and courts had always been the accepted interpreters of the law.

While these arguments supported Marshall's claim for the Court to decide the merits of the case, he assumed a second and even larger power. Not only did judges take an oath to support the Constitution, but the legislative and executive officers did so as well. Why did they not have an equal authority to decide on the constitutionality of a measure? Would not a major consideration of Congress in drafting a bill, and the president in signing it into law, be the validity of the statute in light of constitutional provisions? Marshall conceded that in certain areas the Court would defer to the other branches, but some agency had to decide which of the arms of government should pass on a specific measure. The question of "Who decides who decides?" is thus the most important of all, and Marshall assumed for the Court the power to determine when it would pass on the merits and when it would make the judgment that Congress or the president had the responsibility.

Although *Marbury v. Madison* has remained the key precedent for judicial review, the debate, even if diminished in volume, has continued for nearly two centuries. The Republicans condemned the decision, and Jefferson, until the end of his life, derided the opinion. In 1823, he told Justice William Johnson that the decision was "merely an obiter dissertation of the Chief Justice." Many years later, Justice John Bannister Gibson of the Pennsylvania Supreme Court, dissenting in *Eakin v. Raub* (1825), argued against Marshall's logic, claiming that courts lacked the power of judicial review unless it was specifically granted in a constitution.

The differences between Marshall and Gibson were mirrored in a debate in the 1950s between the noted constitutional scholar Herbert Wechsler and Judge Learned Hand. Wechsler argued for Marshall's interpretationist reading of the Constitution, finding judicial review solidly anchored in the text and in common assumptions about constitutional government, as well as in contemporary documents such as *Federalist No. 78*. There are, he claimed, legitimate processes of interpretation and decision making that elicit answers to constitutional questions even when the document does not address the issues directly. Moreover, since the Supremacy Clause is binding on state courts as well as on federal courts, and as the Supreme Court is the ultimate appellate tribunal in the land, judicial review is required to ensure both consistency and adherence to the Constitution.

Judge Hand, though, argued that since the Constitution, which is so clear in most areas, does not mention the review power, one cannot simply assume its existence as part of some larger judicial power. In fact, his argument was that judicial review runs counter to the whole theory of government in the Constitution, which did not envision a Supreme Court as a body of Platonic guardians with veto power over elected officials. Nonetheless, Hand conceded, even if this power is not authorized, the nation needs judicial review, so we must retain it, not on legal grounds, but for reasons of political expediency.

It is likely that the debate will never be fully resolved, and the literature about judicial review will continue to grow. But the fact remains that the Court has claimed and exercised the power through most of our country's history, and, as Hand noted, we are used to it by now. Moreover, it does fit into a government of checks and balances, as Hamilton had explained in *Federalist No. 78*. Finally, one can hardly argue with Marshall's statement of principle near the end of his opinion, "that a law repugnant to the constitution is void, and that courts, as well as other departments, are bound by that instrument."

*Marbury* received much less attention in 1803 than it did in succeeding years, in part because the result of the case—that Marbury did not get his commission—was uncontroversial. Jefferson had no intention of giving him the commission, and the Federalists, who believed he deserved it, were pleased enough with Marshall's deft handling of the case not to be too sorry about the result. Marbury himself remained a wealthy landowner and investor, who never could claim the title of justice of the peace. Meanwhile, lawyers, politicians, and concerned citizens who cared most about the judiciary focused their attention on two major actions of the Jefferson administration: the purchase of Louisiana and a broad attack on the federal judiciary.

## The Louisiana Purchase

In 1800, Napoleon Bonaparte secured the return of the vast Louisiana territory to France from Spain, to which it had been ceded in 1763. When Jefferson received word of this in May 1801, he recognized that France now held a noose around the neck of western American farmers, who floated their produce down the various tributaries of the Mississippi for transshipment from New Orleans. As he wrote to the new American ambassador in Paris, Robert R. Livingston, "the day that France takes possession of New Orleans . . . we must marry ourselves to the British fleet and nation." Jefferson sent James Monroe as an envoy to assist Livingston in trying to purchase West Florida and New Orleans; failing that, they had secret instructions to secure an alliance with Great Britain.

Napoleon, hard pressed for cash to resume his war against the English, decided to sell not just New Orleans, but the vast Louisiana territory as well, especially after the successful revolt against French rule by the slaves in Haiti doomed his dream of a North American empire. The treaty Monroe and Livingston signed with French representatives on April 30, 1803, called for the United States to pay France $11,250,000 outright, and to assume French debts owed to American citizens of another $3,750,000, for a total price of $15 million. A great bargain, in one stroke it more than doubled the size of the country.

Nothing in the Constitution, however, explicitly gave the national government power to purchase land beyond its original borders. As the strict constructionist he claimed to be, Jefferson could not justify the purchase, and he thought at first to propose a constitutional amendment. But such a procedure would take time, and his advisers warned that Napoleon might change his mind. Whatever else the sage of Monticello may have been, he was above all a pragmatist, and if it took an expansive reading of the Constitution to assure farmers' markets, protect the country's western frontier, and secure room into which his ideal of a nation of yeoman farmers could expand, then Jefferson could accept such a reading. Jefferson, as his biographer Dumas Malone notes, was always "less rigid in action than he appeared to be in theory."

Jefferson proved receptive, therefore, when his secretary of the treasury, Albert Gallatin, submitted a memorandum as liberal in interpreting the Constitution as anything Hamilton might have written. The United States, Gallatin argued, had inherent rights to acquire territory as part of its national sovereignty. This could be done by treaty, since the Constitution definitely granted the government treaty-making authority, and the content of treaties could be circumscribed only by specific constitutional prohibitions. Moreover, once the territory had been acquired, Congress had authority to dispose of it, either by admitting new states into the union, annexing it to existing states, or governing it in some other fashion. Gallatin suggested that constitutional difficulties be avoided by reliance on the treaty power, and the president soon accepted this approach. Although Jefferson continued to voice hopes that a constitutional amendment might be enacted for future acquisitions, he wisely did not press the matter.

Jefferson did call Congress into session three weeks ahead of schedule to secure a speedy ratification, lest Napoleon change his mind. As he told Madison, "the less we say about constitutional difficulties respecting Louisiana the better, and that what is necessary for surmounting them must be done *sub silentio*." Although Federalists in Congress took great glee in criticizing Jefferson for abandoning strict construction, the Senate quickly approved the treaty 26 to 6, and both houses voted the necessary funds. On December 20, 1803, the United States took possession of the territory from France, which had taken it over from Spain only three weeks before. The Louisiana purchase established the pattern for American expansion throughout the rest of the nineteenth century, with no one ever suggesting that a constitutional amendment would be necessary. Moreover, the Supreme Court in *American Insurance Co. v. Cantor* (1828), later upheld the acquisition of the territory through treaty.

## Republican Attacks on the Judiciary: The First Cases

The Republican attacks on the judiciary did not result from the Marbury case, although Marshall's tongue-lashing of the administration no doubt exacerbated the tensions. Even though the Repeal Act and a few new appointments had whittled down Federalist strength in the judiciary, Federalists still controlled a major branch of government. No relief to this predicament seemed in sight, for, as Jefferson said of officeholders in general, few died and none resigned. In his administration, Jefferson would ultimately make three appointments to the Supreme Court, but no vacancy occurred until 1804, the last year of his first term. The Republicans resented this situation, and beyond their hunger for office, feared that Federalist judges would use the power of the courts to undermine Republican programs. In fact, the only excuse for this otherwise indefensible assault on judicial independence is that some Federalist judges did indeed abuse their positions.

The opening round in the battle took place on the state level, with a Republican attack on Alexander Addison, the presiding judge of Pennsylvania's western district, who was known as the "transmontane Goliath" of federalism. Addison infuriated the newly elected Republican majority in the state legislature by his continued political harangues from the bench, while at the same time he denied a Republican colleague the right to address a grand jury. Although judges could be removed in Pennsylvania by a simple vote of both houses, the Republicans decided that his conduct warranted impeachment at the state level. The state Republicans hired Alexander J. Dallas to manage the Pennsylvania prosecution, and in late January 1803, he secured Addison's removal from office. At the time, Dallas was also serving as the U.S. district attorney, as an appointee of Jefferson.

One week later, Jefferson sent a letter to the House of Representatives. He had received complaints about the conduct of Federal District Judge John Pickering of New Hampshire, and since the matter did not lay "within Executive cognizance," he forwarded the materials to the lower chamber for whatever action it deemed appropriate. Pickering no doubt played politics from the bench. The incident triggering the attack involved the seizure of the ship *Eliza*, belonging to a Federalist merchant, by the Republican customs collector for allegedly carrying illegal goods. At the trial, an obviously drunken Pickering ruled for the owner and then verbally abused the Republican district attorney when he sought to appeal the decision. The elderly judge, who had given a number of years of distinguished service to his state, appeared mentally deranged as well as chronically inebriated. Pickering did not belong on the bench any longer and should have been removed, but this sad case became enmeshed in partisan strife.

Unfortunately, the Constitution made no provision for the removal of judges, or any official, in such a situation, and not until the Twenty-fifth Amendment, in 1967, did the nation address this problem for the presidency. In 1803, readers of the Constitution noted that judges "shall hold their Offices during good Behaviour" but could not find any definition of this phrase. Elsewhere, the document provided for the impeachment of the president and "all civil Officers of the United States" for "Treason, Bribery, or other high Crimes and Misdemeanors." But no one seriously suggested that Pickering's sad conduct fell into this category. At Jefferson's request, the judge's friends tried to persuade him to resign, but Pickering refused, in part because he was no longer mentally competent to make such a decision. The president considered impeachment "a bungling way" to remove judges, and he had earlier suggested a constitutional amendment to permit the chief executive, upon petition of Congress, to remove federal judges. Pickering's case might have offered the opportunity to amend the Constitution to provide for such cases, but the intense partisan bitterness over the judiciary at this time made any change impossible. In the end, Pickering was removed from office without much partisanship. Of the thirty-six Federalists in the House, only eight voted against his impeachment. Of the nine Federalists in the Senate, only one voted to acquit him. However, instead of voting him guilty of "high crimes and misdemeanors," the Senators voted that he was only "guilty as charged." Even the most partisan Republicans could not declare the obviously insane Pickering guilty of a "high crime."

## The Impeachment of Justice Chase

The Pickering case proved but a rehearsal for the next act of the drama, the impeachment of Supreme Court Justice Samuel Chase. A patriot and signer of the Declaration of Independence, Chase had enjoyed a long and distinguished career blemished, however, by more than one untoward incident. He had not been averse to rioting during the anti-British agitation, and during the war he had engaged in some questionable financial operations, leading Alexander Hamilton to condemn him as "universally despised." Chase had originally opposed the Constitution, then became a staunch Federalist. His combative nature was well known. As a state judge he barely escaped removal from the Maryland bench when the legislature failed to muster the two-thirds vote necessary for impeachment. Despite these liabilities, Washington had appointed him to the Supreme Court in 1796.

Of all Federalist officials, none had earned greater dislike from the Republicans than Chase, who had presided over the Sedition Act trials of Republican journalists Thomas Cooper and James Callender. Lawyers feared his frequent browbeating, and he often used jury charges to vent his spleen on political opponents. In fact, the impeachment stemmed directly from his charge to a grand jury in Baltimore in May 1803, in which he intemperately condemned the Repeal Act, as well as recent proposals to broaden the suffrage in Maryland, which he claimed would only lead to "mobocracy" and the destruction of peace, order, freedom, and property.

Jefferson originally tried to ignore Chase, and some of the party leaders, aware that Republican judges sometimes used state benches for political purposes too, hesitated to take action. But the groundswell of opposition, fueled by an aggressive Republican press, finally led Virginia Representative John Randolph of Roanoke to call in January 1804 for an investigation of Chase's conduct. At the request of Pennsylvania Republicans, the committee also looked into the activities of Richard Peters, a district judge in that state. No one expected Peters to be impeached, and in fact, the House committee rapidly cleared him, but Republicans hoped that the threat of impeachment would teach him and other Federalist judges some caution. The committee did, however, recommend impeachment proceedings against Chase, and on March 11, by a vote of 73 to 32, the House approved the report.

On March 12, 1804, on the same day that the Senate voted to remove Judge Pickering, the House impeached Justice Chase. It appeared the Republicans were going to dismantle the federal judiciary, one judge at a time. Chase's trial began in the Senate on February 4, 1805, presided over by Vice President Aaron Burr, amid a pomp that reminded many of the observers of a state trial before the House of Lords. Although the Republicans had been almost unanimous in their pursuit of Chase in the House, their ranks broke in the upper chamber. Senator William Giles of Virginia made no bones about what the proceedings meant: "A removal by impeachment [is] nothing more than a declaration by Congress to this effect: You hold dangerous opinions, and if you are suffered to carry them into effect you will work the destruction of the nation. *We want your offices,* for the purposes of giving them to men who will fill them better." Some Republicans, no matter how they despised Chase, feared such a bald attack on the independence of the judiciary, and Giles evidently hinted that once they removed Chase, they would go after Marshall and the rest. Events in Pennsylvania at this time, where Republicans were attempting to impeach all but one of the judges on the state's highest court, underscored the seriousness of the threat. The effort there failed, but only by a narrow margin.

These fears led enough moderate Republicans to defect, so that after a bitter and sensational trial, the Senate failed to master the two-thirds majority necessary to convict Chase. Unlike Pickering, who was too incompetent to mount a defense, Chase defended himself before the Senate with great vigor, arguing that "no judge can be impeached and removed from office for any act or offense for which he could not be indicted." Despite their overwhelming control of the Senate, the Republicans could only get a tiny majority, nothing close to the required two-thirds vote, on two of the eight charges of impeachment. On one count, only four Republicans voted to convict, and on another the Senate was unanimous in voting for acquittal. A motion by Federalist Senator Bayard, supported by several Republicans, called for each senator to answer whether Chase was guilty of "high crimes and misdemeanors" on each count, not merely whether he was guilty of the charge, as had been the practice at Pickering's trial. Chase had no doubt abused his office—he even admitted that his conduct on the bench had, on occasion, been "improper and dangerous," but he had not acted criminally, and that, in essence, became the standard for removal of federal judges.

It is worth noting that Vice President Aaron Burr presided over Chase's trial. At the time, Burr was under indictment in both New York and New Jersey for the murder of Alexander Hamilton in a duel. While the Republicans gleefully sought to remove Chase from the bench for his high-handed and partisan behavior, they were content to let their vice president serve out his term, while under indictment for murder.

Following Chase's acquittal and the failure to impeach the Pennsylvania judges, the Republicans' assault on the judiciary rapidly ebbed. The question of how to remove judges who were no longer capable of fulfilling their duties, or who abused the position but fell short of criminal behavior, remained unanswered. Shortly after Chase's trial, John Randolph proposed a constitutional amendment requiring the president to remove a federal judge on joint address of both houses of Congress. Although a majority of the Senate indicated its willingness to consider the motion, the idea never caught on. Jefferson, who did not take an active role in the proceedings, continued to worry about an irresponsible judiciary. Having found impeachment an empty threat, he wrote in 1820 that judges "consider themselves secure for life; they skulk from responsibility to public opinion. . . . A judiciary independent of a king or executive alone, is a good thing; but independence of the will of the nation is a solecism, at least in a republican government."

Jefferson underestimated the role public opinion would have on the judiciary and how, once the intense partisan passions of these early years subsided, most judges would usually eschew the openly political activities that both Federalists and Republicans engaged in at the time. The Chase affair did not make impeachment a "scarecrow"; had the party floor leaders handled the matter better, Chase might have been removed. Indeed, his high-handed partisanship from the bench might have made him deserving of removal. But Chase was superb in his own defense, and in the process shaped the law of impeachment for the next two centuries.

While losing the battle over Chase, Jefferson nevertheless made an important contribution to the development of American courts and constitutional law. Following the trial, federal judges began to avoid flagrantly partisan acts. If nothing else, the attack on the judiciary helped create a federal bench that concentrated on the law and left overt politics to the elected representatives of the people.

But it would be impossible for the bench to avoid the political fallout from all controversies. When such a situation arose, the judges had to exercise their political skills, as well as display their legal knowledge. Chief Justice Marshall would soon face such a challenge during the treason trial of Vice President Aaron Burr.

## Defining Treason

Burr had once been a close ally of Jefferson, but his unsuccessful machinations to secure the presidency in 1800 began his downfall from power. In 1804, he ended what little chance he had for any future political career by killing Alexander Hamilton in a duel. His fortunes in ruin, Burr embarked upon an ill-conceived filibustering scheme to capture and settle territory in Spanish-held western lands. His exact plans are shrouded in confusion, since he kept a number of options open. But whatever his plans may have been, the whole scheme fell apart when his chief confederate, General James Wilkinson, the governor of Louisiana (and secretly in the pay of Spain), denounced Burr to Jefferson. The army seized Burr as he floated downstream on a flatboat to New Orleans, and then brought him to Richmond to stand trial for treason in the U.S. Circuit Court.

By then, the conviction of Burr had become an obsession for Jefferson, and by extension, for the entire Republican party. The president publicly denounced Burr in a letter to Congress, identifying him as the "prime mover . . . whose guilt is placed beyond question" in a campaign to sever the Union and attack Mexico. Jefferson kept in close touch with the proceedings throughout the case, and personally directed the government prosecutor. His disdain for the guarantees of a fair trial, his suggestion that habeas corpus be suspended, and his veiled threats that if Burr went free the entire Supreme Court should be impeached all reveal what historian Leonard Levy has termed "the darker side" of a man venerated in history as the great apostle of individual liberty.

Jefferson's fury at Burr quickly encompassed John Marshall, who as circuit judge for Virginia presided over the trial. Since Burr was captured in a territory where there was no federal court, he was brought to the nearest site of a federal court that could hear the trial, namely Richmond. At that time, circuit courts had original jurisdiction to try treason cases; the Supreme Court has never had that power. Marshall presided because of his dual role—as a member both of the Supreme Court and of one of the circuits.

Painfully aware of the political ramifications of the trial, Marshall also recognized the serious legal issues involved. Historians have in general given him high marks for his handling of the case, as well as for the law he propounded during it. The chief justice, however, does not completely escape criticism. Several times during the proceedings he took the occasion to chastise the government for its apparent vendetta against Burr and its disregard for the essential safeguards of a fair trial. Rather indiscreetly, he even attended a dinner given by Burr's counsel in honor of the defendant! Little wonder then that Jefferson saw Marshall as attempting to coddle traitors and embarrass his administration.

Questions related to the Burr affair first came before the Supreme Court after General Wilkinson seized two of Burr's alleged coconspirators, Samuel Swarthout and Dr. Justus Bollmann, denied them hearing and counsel, and then sent them to Washington in January 1807 for indictment on charges of treason. The two Republican judges on the Circuit Court for the District of Columbia ruled that they should be imprisoned without bail, while William Cranch, the lone Federalist, believed they should be freed for lack of probable cause. The prisoners then appealed for a writ of habeas corpus to the Supreme Court, and Marshall directed the jailer to show cause why it should not be issued. Fearful that the Court would free the men, William Giles, Jefferson's lieutenant in the Senate, managed to get the upper house to pass, in one day, a bill suspending the privilege of habeas corpus for three months. A few days later, however, the House, despite its Republican majority, overwhelmingly rejected the bill.

Marshall well understood the importance of *Ex parte Bollmann;* he wanted above all to depoliticize the case, an effort doomed to failure from the beginning. He thus concentrated on the two crucial issues confronting the Court: Could it issue a writ of habeas corpus? and, What definition of treason should be used? On February 13, the chief justice, speaking for the majority, ruled that the Supreme Court had the power to issue the writ. In response to Justice William Johnson, a Jefferson appointee who believed the Judiciary Act's delegation of this power unconstitutional (following the lines Marshall had argued in Marbury), the chief justice conceded that if Bollmann and Swarthout had come directly to the high court seeking relief, they would have been turned down. But they had gone to a lower court, and now the Supreme Court, as an appellate tribunal, had the power to review decisions by an inferior court. The Court then heard arguments on whether the evidence of treason sufficed to keep the men in jail.

Treason against the United States, as defined in the Constitution (Article III, Section 3), "shall consist only in levying War against them, or in adhering to their Enemies, giving them Aid and Comfort." To support the charge of treason, therefore, war actually had to take place; conspiracy to make war, while certainly a crime, did not meet the definition of treason. In words that would later haunt him at Burr's trial, Marshall conceded that

> if a body of men be actually assembled for the purpose of effecting by force a treasonable purpose, all those who perform any part, however minute, or however remote from the scene of the action, and who are actually leagued in the general conspiracy, are to be considered as traitors.

Marshall had no need even to deal with this issue, which had not come before the Court; his ruling would later be used by the government at the Burr trial to justify its prosecution, while Marshall's later abandonment of this doctrine would lead to charges that he had changed his mind to spite Jefferson. But Marshall did make it clear in *Ex parte Bollmann* that although there had been "acts," and probably a conspiracy, war had not been levied, and absent war, there could be no treason. No doubt Marshall meant to rebuke the administration, but above all, the chief justice wanted to protect the rule of law. The Constitution defined treason, and both common and statutory law provided the process for prosecuting criminals and traitors. The law had to be obeyed and the legitimate processes followed. Wilkinson's heavy-handed seizure of the men and his denial of their rights could not be condoned.

Some Republicans recognized that Wilkinson—and Jefferson—had gone too far, but the more radical party members rose as a chorus to denounce the Court. Some urged a constitutional amendment to remove all criminal jurisdiction from the Supreme Court; others wanted to impeach the justices. A motion to redefine and restrict the habeas corpus privilege failed by only two votes in the House. But Bollmann and Swarthout were only minor cogs in the alleged conspiracy; the attention of the whole country now turned to Richmond, where Aaron Burr's trial, John Marshall presiding, opened in late March 1807.

## The Burr Trial

On April 1, Marshall dismissed the charge of treason against Aaron Burr. Despite a reference to the "hand of malignity," which must not be permitted to "grasp any individual against whom its hate may be directed, or whom it may capriciously seize, charge him with some secret crime, and put him on the proof of his innocence," the opinion displayed prudence and legal exactitude. A careful review of the evidence failed to prove treason, for actual war had not been levied against the United States. The government would be allowed to try Burr for assembling a military expedition against a country with whom the United States was then at peace, and if it could gather any evidence that Burr had intended to wage war against the United States, it could then seek a grand jury indictment for treason.

A furious Jefferson wrote to Senator Giles that the day could not be distant when the Constitution would be amended so as to remove "the error . . . which makes any branch independent of the nation." With more passion for vengeance than sensitivity to legal rights, the president personally took direction of the prosecution. Witnesses would be produced, he assured Giles, as well as evidence to "satisfy the world, if not the judges," of Burr's treason. He immediately sent out a call for anyone who could testify to the former vice president's guilt, promising pardons to anyone connected with the affair if they would cooperate. Jefferson even instructed George Hay, the government attorney, to introduce Marshall's opinion in *Marbury* and then denounce it "as not law." Ultimately, after much maneuvering on both sides, the jury found Burr not guilty. Although Marshall had to explain away his dictum in *Bollmann* (which had seemed to imply that just gathering an army would be treason) as inapplicable to the Burr case, he reaffirmed the definition of treason that had been developed earlier and that remains valid to this day.

## Presidential Privilege

The most potentially controversial issue in the Burr case failed to explode, however—that resulting from the defense's demand that the president be summoned as a witness and produce documents in his possession. Burr had discovered that Wilkinson had doctored some of the papers he had forwarded to Jefferson, in order both to magnify Burr's alleged guilt and to hide his own involvement in the affair. Burr had been denied access to the documents, and unless the government produced them voluntarily, he asked the court to issue a subpoena *duces tecum* to the president.

Surprisingly, Hay agreed that the court had the power to issue the order, and Jefferson subsequently turned over copies of the papers. The president evidently recognized that conflict between the executive and judicial branches existed here and told Hay that, as president, he would be the ultimate arbiter of what materials coming to his office could and could not be opened to public inspection. That is, he would provide documents other than those he believed should remain confidential. Jefferson may have anticipated that if he refused to turn over the papers on which he had initiated the prosecution, the public would believe charges that the attack on his former associate was little more than a political vendetta. There does not appear to have been any argument raised at the time that Marshall's order exceeded the court's authority or impinged on presidential prerogatives. Yet in many ways, this aspect of the trial may have been the most important.

Marshall's order laid the basis for the Supreme Court's decision 167 years later in *United States v. Nixon* (1974), when Chief Justice Warren Burger, quoting freely from Marshall, ordered Richard Nixon to turn over tapes in his possession, and the unanimous Court dismissed the president's claim to executive privilege. Marshall's various rulings in the Burr trial established the doctrine that although the court would give careful consideration to a presidential claim that certain documents were either immaterial or their exposure would endanger government policy, the materials had to be produced, and a court, in camera, would make the final decision as to their being opened or withheld. In criminal prosecution, the president had no right to withhold potentially material documents; if he did so, the court would direct that either the prosecution be dismissed or all inferences relating to the papers should be construed as favoring the defendant.

Although the Burr trial took place in circuit court, the ruling is properly viewed as part of John Marshall's tenure on the Supreme Court, for, as much as any case he participated in, it helped to develop the power of the judiciary and strengthen the rule of law. Despite Marshall's occasional slaps at Jefferson, he remained for the most part highly sensitive to the overcharged political atmosphere in which the trial took place. He worded his rulings carefully and displayed meticulous attention to legal principles; given the confusion that still exists regarding Burr's intentions, there is little doubt that treason, as defined by the Constitution, had not occurred. The Jeffersonians, as expected, reacted strongly to the acquittal. The president sent several hundred pages of supporting materials to Congress, urging it to consider the appropriate steps that should be taken—hoping that one would be the removal of John Marshall from the bench. But increased tensions with Great Britain and France soon diverted the administration's attention to other matters.

# For Further Reading

For the Court in this period, see William R. Casto, *The Supreme Court in the Early Republic: The Chief Justiceships of John Jay and Oliver Ellsworth* (1995); and the encyclopedic Julius Goebel, Jr., *Antecedents and Beginnings to 1801,* Vol. 1, *History of the Supreme Court of the United States* (1971). Extremely useful for the study of the early court is the ongoing project, Maeva Marcus, ed., *Documentary History of the Supreme Court of the United States, 1789–1800* (1985). For the Adams administration in general, see Page Smith, *John Adams,* 2 vols. (1962); Stephen G. Kurtz, *The Presidency of John Adams: The Collapse of Federalism, 1795–1800* (1957); and especially Martin J. Dauer, *The Adams Federalists* (1953), which distinguishes between the followers of Hamilton and Adams and suggests that the latter had much in common with their Jeffersonian opponents. For his political philosophy, see Joseph J. Ellis, *Passionate Sage: The Character and Legacy of John Adams* (1993). Also helpful are two older books, Zoltan Haraszti, *John Adams and the Prophets of Progress* (1952); and John R. Howe, Jr., *The Changing Political Thought of John Adams* (1966).

The literature on Thomas Jefferson is enormous, as befits his many-faceted personality. The best recent work on Jefferson is found in Peter S. Onuf, *Jeffersonian Legacies* (1996). Dumas Malone, *Jefferson and His Time,* 6 vols. (1948–1977), remains the standard biography. The presidential years are covered in volumes 4 and 5. Jefferson's hypocrisy on civil liberties, including his support of seditious libel prosecutions, is discussed in Leonard W. Levy, *Jefferson and Civil Liberties: The Darker Side* (1963). The best one-volume biography is Merrill D. Peterson, *Thomas Jefferson and the New Nation* (1970). Also useful for understanding the complexity of Jefferson's personality is Andrew Burstein, *The Inner Jefferson: Portrait of a Grieving Optimist* (1995). Paul Finkelman, *Slavery and the Founders: Race and Liberty in the Age of Jefferson* (2nd ed., 2001), discusses Jefferson's relationship to slavery, including his presidential years. See also Forrest McDonald, *The Presidency of Thomas Jefferson* (1976); and Leonard D. White, *The Jeffersonians: A Study in Administrative History, 1801–1829* (1951).

The Alien and Sedition Acts are well explored in James Morton Smith, *Freedom's Fetters: The Alien and Sedition Laws and American Civil Liberties* (1956); John C. Miller, *Crisis in Freedom: The Alien and Sedition Acts* (1951); and Levy's *Jefferson and Civil Liberties.* On the general issue of freedom of the press in this period, see Leonard W. Levy, *Emergence of a Free Press* (1985). For the Jeffersonian opposition, see Adrienne Koch and Harry Ammon, "The Virginia and Kentucky Resolutions: An Episode in Jefferson's and Madison's Defense of Civil Liberties," 5 *William and Mary Quarterly* 145 (1948), and also the relevant chapters of Adrienne Koch, *Jefferson and Madison: The Great Collaboration* (1950). For a case study of one related trial, see Ruth Wedgewood, "The Revolutionary Martyrdom of Jonathan Robbins," 100 *Yale Law Journal* 229 (1990).

The transfer of power from Federalists to Republicans is described from the Jeffersonian view in the last chapters of volume 3 of Malone's *Jefferson;* see also David Sisson, *The American Revolution of 1800* (1974); and John J. Turner, Jr., "The Twelfth Amendment and the First American Party System," 35 *The Historian* 221 (1973). On the Federalists themselves, see Stanley Elkins and Eric McKitrick, *The Age of Federalism* (1994); and Doron Ben-Atar and Barbara Oberg, eds., *The Federalists Reconsidered* (1998). For the Judiciary Act, see Maeva Marcus, ed., *Origins of the Federal Judiciary: Essays on the Judiciary Act of 1789* (1992); Wythe Holt, "'To Establish Justice': Politics, The Judiciary Act of 1789, and the Invention of the Federal Courts," 1989 *Duke Law Journal* 1421 (1989–90); Wilfred J. Ritz, *Rewriting the History of the Judiciary Act of 1789: Exposing Myths, Challenging Premises, and Using New Evidence* (1990); and Kathryn Turner, "Federalist Policy and the Judiciary Act of 1801," 22 *William and Mary Quarterly 3rd Sec.,* 3 (1965); see also Turner, "The Mid-night Judges," 109 *University of Pennsylvania Law Review* 494 (1961).

On the Marshall Court in general, see George Lee Haskins and Herbert A. Johnson, *Foundations of Power, 1801–1815* (1981); and G. Edward White, *The Marshall Court and Cultural Change, 1815–1835* (1988). Shorter studies include: Herbert A. Johnson, *The Chief Justiceship of John Marshall, 1801–1835* (1997); and Charles F. Hobson, *The Great Chief Justice: John Marshall and the Rule of Law* (1996). Also useful is Jean Edward Smith, *John Marshall: Definer of Nation* (1996). Still useful, but somewhat dated is R. Kent Newmyer, *The Supreme Court Under Marshall and Taney* (1968), which provides a fine sense of continuity and change over six decades.

The literature on *Marbury v. Madison* is as extensive as the debate over its meaning. A good place to start is Donald O. Dewey, *Marshall v. Jefferson: The Political Background of Marbury v. Madison* (1970); and Robert L. Clinton, *Marbury v. Madison and Judicial Review* (1989). Important background information to the case is found in David Forte, "Marbury's Travail: Federalist Politics and William Marbury's Appointment as Justice of the Peace," 45 *Catholic University Law Review* 349 (1996). Whether or not the Constitution envisioned judicial review is a problem that may never be solved to everyone's satisfaction. A good place to start is Jesse H. Choper, *Judicial Review and the National Political Process: A Functional Reconsideration of the Role of the Supreme Court* (1980). For good summaries of opposing positions on judicial review, see Raoul Berger, *Congress v. the Supreme Court* (1969), defending judicial review; and William W. Crosskey, *Politics and the Constitution in the History of the United States,* 2 vols. (1953), denying its legitimacy. An extensive evaluation of the case is in George L. Haskins and Herbert A. Johnson, *Foundations of Power: John Marshall, 1801–1815* (1981), the second volume in the Holmes Devise, *History of the Supreme Court of the United States.*

Everett S. Brown's *The Constitutional History of the Louisiana Purchase, 1803–1812* (1920) is still the only study of that subject; for a broader view of the purchase, see Alexander De Conde, *The Affairs of Louisiana* (1976). For the effect of the purchase on law in what had been a French and Spanish possession, see George Dargo, *Jefferson's Louisiana: Politics and the Clash of Legal Traditions* (1975). For the third president's troubles with the judiciary, start with Richard E. Ellis, *The Jeffersonian Crisis: Courts and Politics in the Young Republic* (1971). Ellis interprets the conflict less as a partisan battle than as a struggle between radicals and moderates within Republican ranks, for whom the judiciary became the focal point of ideological differences. See also Dewey, *Marshall v. Jefferson*; Richard B. Lillich, "The Chase Impeachment," 49 *American Journal of Legal History* 4 (1960); and Jerry W. Knudson, "The Jeffersonian Assault on the Federalist Judiciary, 1802–1805: Political Forces and Press Reaction," 14 *American Journal of Legal History* 55 (1978). On impeachment, see also Emily Van Tassel and Paul Finkelman, *Impeachable Offences: A Documentary History* (1999); and Peter C. Hoffer and N. E. H. Hull, *Impeachment in America, 1635–1805* (1984). More directly, on Chase's impeachment, see Richard Ellis, "The Impeachment of Samuel Case," in Michal R. Belknap, ed., *American Political Trials* (rev. ed., 1994); and Stephen B. Presser, "A Tale of Two Judges: Richard Peters, Samuel Chase, and the Broken Promise of Federal Jurisprudence," 23 *Northwestern University Law Review*, 26 (1978). An interesting take on these issues is developed in Stephen B. Presser, *The Original Misunderstanding: The English, The Americans, and the Dialectic of Federalist Jurisprudence* (1991).

The Burr conspiracy remains clouded in mystery; probably the best effort at unraveling it is Milton Lomask, *Aaron Burr: The Conspiracy and the Years of Exile, 1805–1836* (1982); and Robert Faulkner, "John Marshall and the Burr Trial," 53 *Journal of American History,* 247 (1966). For the debate over the meaning of treason, see Bradley Chapin, *The American Law of Treason: Revolutionary and Early National Origins* (1964). For Marshall's role, see Robert K. Faulkner, "John Marshall and the Burr Trial," 53 *Journal of American History* 247 (1966).

# 11

# *The Marshall Court and National Power*

THE EARLY NINETEENTH century witnessed a phenomenal expansion of the United States in physical size and population, a growth accompanied by an increasing national sentiment. The triumph of this spirit would not occur until the Civil War, however, and states' rights sentiments and sectional animosities remained strong throughout the Jeffersonian and Jacksonian eras. In the Supreme Court, however, nationalism dominated, as John Marshall and his colleagues developed the Constitution into an effective instrument of governmental power.

## The Attorney General

On March 4, 1809, Jefferson relinquished the "splendid misery" of the presidency to his close friend and colleague, James Madison, and returned to his beloved Monticello, where he spent the remainder of his years happily occupied with the affairs of the mind. With his departure, much of the tension between the executive and judicial branches vanished. Madison did not share his predecessor's personal animosity toward the chief justice; moreover, his own nationalistic views had much in common with those of Marshall, and the new president fully appreciated the value of the federal judiciary as a nationalizing force. By 1811, a majority of the justices on the high bench were nominally Republican, and even if they came under the influence of John Marshall, the partisan controversies of the early years between the president and the Court no longer mattered.

The conduct of the government's legal business took on a more professional and efficient character during the administrations of Madison and James Monroe. The Federalists had created the position of attorney general, but for the first quarter-century of government under the Constitution, the incumbent had neither office nor staff, had no control over the local federal attorneys, and had to earn the bulk of his income from private clients. Until 1814, the attorney general did not even have to be in the capital. Of the first attorney generals, Levi Lincoln spent much of his time in Massachusetts; Caesar Rodney stayed mostly in Delaware; and William Pinkney, during the two years he held the post, lived in Baltimore. During such absences, no legal business could be transacted except by mail, and in 1814, Madison asked Congress to consider requiring the attorney general to reside at the seat of government. Although the bill did not pass, Pinkney resigned, and his successor, Richard Rush, accepted the appointment with the understanding that he would live in Washington.

Although the attorney general had always been a member of the cabinet, his participation had been inconsistent, due to absence from town. Beginning with Rush, the post became an integral part of the government; his presence not only allowed him to join in cabinet discussions, but made him available for legal advice to the other department heads. But the office still remained little more than the occupant. As Monroe noted in 1817: "The office has no apartment for business, nor clerks, nor a messenger, nor stationery, nor fuel allowed. These have been supplied by the officer himself, at his own expense." Congress gradually began supplying these items, and under William Wirt (1817–1829), the office developed into a regular agency. Wirt, a true Republican, refused to undertake any function that was not specifically authorized by law, and he consistently fought off efforts by state officials, congressional committees, and lower federal officials to secure legal opinions from him. In response to one request, he wrote that "believing, as I do, that in a Government purely of laws, it would be incalculably dangerous to permit an officer to act, under color of his office, beyond the pale of the law. I trust I shall be excused from making any *official* report on the order with which the House has honored me."

Wirt had his hands full, however. The increase in the business of the Supreme Court, with many suits involving the federal government, kept him occupied with the preparation of briefs and arguments. He brought the federal attorneys under some control of his office and, for the first time, instituted a record-keeping system for the government's legal business. Instead of an adjunct and often ignored part of the executive branch, the attorney general would henceforth play an important role in the administration of government.

## Changes on the Court

Changes on the Supreme Court also affected the atmosphere in Washington. During Jefferson's entire administration, the Federalist majority of the Court willingly followed Marshall's lead. By 1811, although five members had been appointed by Republican presidents, the bench steadfastly clung to the strongly nationalistic views it had earlier espoused. William Johnson eventually become known as "the first dissenter," but in fact he averaged less than one dissent a year in the nearly three decades he served. A moderate nationalist, Johnson stood closer in view to Madison than to die-hard advocates of state sovereignty, like Judge Spencer Roane of the Virginia Court of Appeals, who condemned Jefferson's political pragmatism as a betrayal of the true faith. Johnson favored positive law—specific statutes as the source of law—and thus he sometimes opposed Marshall's inclination to broad and amorphous principles of natural law. Johnson believed that an elected Congress rather than an appointed Court should be the final arbiter of constitutionality. Thus, in any conflict between state and federal authority, he upheld the Congress, utilizing as broad a construction of Article I powers as did Marshall. He differed from the chief justice primarily in cases involving state powers and private property, and opposed Marshall's reading of the Constitution to limit state authority in this area.

Joseph Story, appointed associate justice by Madison in 1811, had, next to Marshall, the greatest impact on constitutional law in the early nineteenth century. Nominally a Republican, he nonetheless soon became Marshall's chief collaborator in expounding doctrines of strong national power. His extensive knowledge of international law and admiralty proved highly useful to the Court in his early years, but even more important, Story's great knowledge of law made him a perfect complement to Marshall's practicality. Story's scholarly three-volume *Commentaries on the Constitution* (1831), suffused with a strong nationalist spirit, remains one of the great treatises on the American constitutional system. In the two decades before the Civil War, it served as a central text for the training of lawyers, and in the process led many to have a nationalistic outlook. When the Court was not in session, Story taught at Harvard Law School, where he helped educate hundreds of lawyers from around the country.

In an era that prized oratory, some of the greatest forensic talents of the country argued before the Supreme Court. Leaders of Congress, like Daniel Webster and Henry Clay, regularly appeared in the first half of the nineteenth century, and in many important cases, Marshall and his colleagues adopted their arguments, stripped them of superfluities, and embodied them as part of the law of the land. Probably at no other time in our history have the arguments of counsel played so important a role. Although great lawyers would always be able to influence the Court, the lack of a large and historically validated body of precedent allowed bench and bar great leeway in developing law at this time.

# The Embargo Cases

Ironically, part of the reconciliation between the Marshall Court and the Jeffersonians resulted from the Court's confirmation of the federal government's broad use of the commerce power to support its foreign policy. Marshall's own experience as a diplomat and secretary of state underscored his and the Court's willingness to defer to the executive and legislative branches in what they regarded as essentially political matters. Marshall did not want to hamper the executive in its conduct of foreign affairs. While secretary of state, Marshall had asserted that "The President" was "the sole organ of the nation in its external relations, and its sole representative with foreign nations," and as such had broad discretion and extensive means at his disposal. On the Court, he took the same approach, often supporting Jefferson's foreign policy.

In his second term, Jefferson's foreign policy led to a rash of suits in federal courts. Desperately trying to avoid entanglement in the Napoleonic Wars, the president resurrected the colonial-era idea of an embargo. Completely failing to understand the European conflict, he naively believed that by denying American trade, he could force the belligerents to respect neutral rights. On December 18, 1807, Jefferson requested Congress to stop *all* trade to or from American ports, and four days later, Congress passed the first Embargo Act. The measure failed completely to influence either England or France, and succeeded only in crippling American commerce. But if the president recalled the efficacy of the colonists' embargo against the mother country, American shippers remembered the ingenuity they had shown in circumventing the earlier British Navigation Acts through smuggling and other means. Congress, like Parliament, could not statutorily anticipate all these stratagems, and as a result, the so-called Embargo cases, resulting from the 1807 act and its subsequent modifications, led the Supreme Court to develop a substantial body of case law on the subject.

In eleven cases between 1810 and 1815, the Supreme Court resolved several ambiguities in the statutes, while displaying a great willingness to tolerate executive discretion and prosecutorial flexibility, even against private property interests, in the conduct of foreign affairs.

In cases in which the statutes failed to be precise, the Supreme Court attempted to follow the spirit of the law. The acts included the traditional exception of "dangers of the seas," which permitted ships originally embarked on legitimate coastal voyages to put into foreign ports if forced to by storms or other hazards. In order to prevent the exception from swallowing the rule, the Court placed a heavy burden on the owner to prove that all possible efforts had been made to stay within coastal waters. In *The Brig James Wells v. United States* (1812), Justice Bushrod Washington found that the claimants had not sustained this burden, and he ordered the ship forfeited. The Court required an even higher standard of proof for exceptions claimed as a result of pursuit by warships or privateers. By thus placing the burden upon owners, the Court made prosecution easier, and also indicated that it did not view the Embargo laws as criminal statutes (in which the burden of proof lay on the government), but as regulations of trade.

Even with precise statutes, the Court permitted a fairly broad construction in order to uphold the law's intent. A cod-fishing vessel, the *Active,* had been seized in New London, Connecticut, her hold laden not with fish but with merchandise, and the owner argued that the seizure had not complied with the law. The local revenue officer had not been notified of the alleged violation, as required by the 1808 statute, nor had the boat left harbor; the law did not punish the *intention* to export goods, he claimed, but only the actual offense that patently could not occur until the ship left port. Marshall agreed that clearing harbor constituted a necessary precondition under Section 3 of the 1808 law, and the ship, therefore, could not be seized under the Embargo Acts. However, the *Active* had been registered as a fishing vessel under Section 32 of the 1793 act regulating coastal trade; since it had not been licensed to carry goods, it could be seized and forfeited under the Enrollment Act. Similarly, in *The Brig Eliza* (1812), the Court permitted a collector to seize a vessel upon its return from an illegal trip, rather than requiring him to go through the more cumbersome task of suing to recover the amount of the bond the owner had put up as assurance that he would not violate the embargo.

Despite the intensity of Federalist opposition to the embargo policy, federal judges, most of whom had been appointed by either Washington or Adams, did not play politics with these cases. They tried, as Marshall pointed out in the *Schooner Paulina* (1812), to carry out congressional intent to prohibit foreign trade. To implement this policy, the government had broad powers to prevent transactions directly related to this goal, and could even forbid other activities that indirectly undermined the national policy. Justices required the government to prove the appropriateness of its actions when it went beyond the specific authorization of statute; but if the government could carry that burden, the Court nearly always proved receptive to the argument. The limit came when government impinged on rights to private property without a clear rationale for doing so.

## United States v. Peters

Jefferson's policies hit especially hard in the northeastern states, whose economy depended heavily on oceanic commerce. These states had also been the traditional strongholds of the Federalist party, and as it suffered a string of defeats in national elections, the party gradually shifted away from the nationalism of Washington, Adams, and Hamilton toward an emphasis on states' rights. At the same time, the Jeffersonians, pursuing a strong foreign policy, moved ever closer to a broad nationalistic view of governmental powers, acutely aware that the legitimacy of the policy relied more and more on validation by the federal courts. With the partisan stridency that had characterized Jefferson's attitude toward the Court now muted, and Jefferson himself in retirement, the reconciliation between the executive and judiciary could proceed, and the change was seen in *United States v. Peters* (1809).

Since 1779, Pennsylvania had resisted an order of the Committee of Appeals of the Continental Congress reversing a decision of the state's admiralty court. In 1803, Federal District Judge Richard Peters had reaffirmed the committee's decision, but fearful of impeachment, he had refused to implement it. The state legislature, meanwhile, reasserted the state's paramount power to decide the matter and reaffirmed the earlier state court ruling. In 1808, a petition for mandamus reached the Supreme Court to compel Peters to execute his decision; by then, the case had assumed large and ominous implications for federal authority. If a state could successfully refuse to implement the order of a federal court or flagrantly ignore a federal law, the New England states, bitterly opposed to the embargo, would be able to nullify national policy. As one critic of the embargo wrote, such a course would send the Constitution "to the trunkmaker as a Damn'd Paper, Black as the ink that's on it: senseless bauble!"

In a powerful opinion, Marshall upheld the nation's authority to enforce its laws. "If the legislatures of the several states may, at will, annul the judgments of the courts of the United States," he wrote, "and destroy the rights acquired under those judgments, the constitution itself becomes a solemn mockery; and the nation is deprived of the means of enforcing its laws by the instrumentality of its own tribunals." The state, moreover, was not even a party to the suit, and therefore, "Pennsylvania can possess no constitutional right to resist the legal process which may be directed in this cause."

Although Pennsylvania had no constitutional right to resist, the state had already passed a statute authorizing its governor to do just that. The legislature also petitioned President Madison for redress, and when he refused, Governor Simon Snyder called out the militia to prevent execution of the decree. General Michael Bright arrived in Philadelphia with his troops and surrounded Peters's courthouse to block access to the federal marshals. The move lacked` popular support, however, and many of the recently naturalized militiamen, appalled at bearing arms against their newly adopted country, went home. A federal grand jury indicted Bright for resisting the laws of the United States, and ordered his arrest. Even the Philadelphia *Aurora*, which had been a vociferous critic of the federal judiciary, now supported Judge Peters, warning that only an independent judiciary could ensure the survival of the Constitution. Madison firmly upheld the power of the courts, and within a few weeks the so-called Pennsylvania Rebellion collapsed.

## The Hartford Convention

Opposition to the embargo and to the ensuing war with Great Britain, or "Mr. Madison's war" as New Englanders called it, continued. The region had initially kept aloof from the war and had even engaged in extensive illegal trading and privateering until the British extended their blockade up the coast. Instead of rallying to the flag, New England Federalists demanded an end to the war. In October 1814, the Federalist Massachusetts legislature called for a convention of New England states to plan independent action, because the Constitution "has failed to secure to this commonwealth, and as they believe, to the Eastern section of this Union, those equal rights and benefits which are the greatest objects of its formation."

On December 15, twenty-two delegates from Massachusetts, Rhode Island, Connecticut, Vermont, and New Hampshire met in Hartford. Although the more extreme Federalist Essex Junto of Massachusetts, led by Timothy Pickering, wanted to secede, the moderates in control secured resolutions reminiscent of Madison's Virginia Resolution, calling for seven constitutional amendments that would, among other things, have severely limited the national government's power in foreign affairs, and eliminate the three-fifths clause, which they believed led to an unfair domination of the nation by slaveowners like Jefferson and Madison. The delegates also called for a later meeting in Boston, with the clearly implied threat that unless the government met their demands, the states would secede. But when the messengers from Hartford reached Washington, they found the capital celebrating both the military victory at New Orleans and the peace treaty just signed at Ghent. The secession movement collapsed, and the Hartford Convention signaled the death of the Federalist party.

Still, the Federalists had raised several constitutional questions about the war powers of Congress. The Constitution (Article I, Section 8) gives Congress the power to call out the militia, and "To provide for organizing, arming, and disciplining, the Militia, and for governing such Part of them as may be employed in the Service of the

United States." Several New England states refused to let their militia be commanded by federal officers or become part of the regular army. The state supreme court of Massachusetts, invoking the narrowest literal interpretation of the Constitution, held that neither the president nor Congress had been given the power to determine when the militia should be called out—and therefore could not call them out at all! The Connecticut legislature resolved that the Constitution did not authorize the use of militia in an offensive war, but reserved their use for defense only. All the New England states, in fact, tried to prevent their militias from being sent outside their respective states.

The Supreme Court did not rule on this issue until *Martin v. Mott* (1827); it then upheld the power of the president, when acting pursuant to congressional authorization, to be the sole judge of when circumstances warranted calling out the state militia. According to the Court, the militia, once in federal service, came under the authority of federal officers. The decision did not eliminate all state responsibility for or power over the militia, but it did settle when and whether Congress and the president could act.

## The Court and Nationalist Sentiment

Although the Treaty of Ghent passed over in silence issues such as neutral rights and the impressment of American seamen, the alleged causes of the War of 1812, Americans basked in a sense of victory. If the United States had not defeated Great Britain, it had at least fought the world's mightiest power to a draw and confirmed the independence won some three decades earlier. A spirit of energy invigorated the nation, and there could be no doubt that a nation now existed. An unusual wave of prosperity fed the sense of well-being, and even Jefferson's hated embargo proved to have some long-term beneficial results. The limits on commerce had caused capital in the mid-Atlantic and New England states to shift into manufacturing; many Americans now believed that the strength of the nation required a balanced economy, in which domestic factories would free the country from dependence on European products. Although this Era of Good Feelings lasted only a short while, it provided the context for the Marshall Court to expand its rulings in two areas that would be crucial for the later development of the Union—the supremacy of a powerful national government and the protection of private property rights.

---

CALLING OUT THE MILITIA: THE MODERN PROBLEM

Many constitutional issues reemerge, years after they appear to have been settled. Thus, in *Perpich v. Department of Defense* (1990) the Supreme Court unanimously reaffirmed the concept, first articulated in *Martin v. Mott*, that the president has the power to call up a state militia, or national guard, when he deems it necessary. In this case, the governor of Minnesota tried to prevent the deployment of his state's national guard in Central America for training purposes. The Supreme Court affirmed the right of the president to overrule the state governor.

The nationalistic wave that began with the 1807 attack on the *Chesapeake* and swelled during and immediately following the War of 1812 is but one factor in understanding the expansion in the Court's prestige and power. John Jay's gloomy prediction in 1801 that the Court lacked and would never acquire "energy, weight and dignity" had failed to anticipate a number of factors. John Marshall's immense energy helped make the Court into a clear partner within the government, even if not quite a fully equal partner. Lacking the power of either the purse or the sword, the power of the Court depended on its prestige and the perception of its importance to the success of the nation. Marshall's astute sense of what was politically possible, as well as his sometimes brilliant opinions, affirmed the Court as the supreme arbiter of constitutional issues.

Usually, the chief justice picked out a political path that led to the widespread acceptance of this role. Only rarely did he challenge the other branches of the national government. Although famous for declaring a federal law unconstitutional in *Marbury v. Madison* (1803), this decision did not directly challenge either branch of the government. By deciding that the statute was unconstitutional, Marshall in effect ruled in favor of Jefferson, who was thoroughly hostile to the Courts. Thus, as we have seen, Jefferson could not oppose the use of judicial review, because he won the case. While establishing the precedent of judicial review of congressional acts, Marshall never again used the precedent, thus avoiding any direct conflict with Congress. Similarly, with the one exception of his opinion in *Worcester v. Georgia* (1832) siding with the rights of the Cherokee Nation (see Chapter 14), Marshall also avoided challenging the power of the president. Some of his most powerful opinions in this period challenged the powers of particular states, but these were always written from the perspective of patriotic nationalism. This placed Marshall in a position stronger than that of the states' rights politicians who opposed him.

Furthermore, as the nation increasingly saw the value of a written Constitution, the Court was perfectly placed to rise in prestige. No other agency of government, either state or federal, could compete in this area. Although a number of states tried, in a variety of ways, to assert power superior to that of the national government, all faltered because of the anarchy or disunion implicit in such claims and the lack of support from other states. Even at the Hartford Convention, which is famous for its secessionist overtones, a large number, perhaps an actual majority, of the people involved did not want to dismember the Union, and recognized that some connection existed between the federal judiciary and the national government under the Constitution. Similarly, in 1832–1833, during the Nullification Crisis (see Chapter 14), the rest of the South refused to support South Carolina's challenge to the national government.

Step by step, case by case, the Court developed its authority and saw its acceptance—admittedly at times over bitter opposition—by the other branches and the public. The united bench delivering a single opinion—the growth of *obiter dicta* (judicial commentary beyond the holding of the case), the refinement of techniques of constitutional and statutory interpretation—supported the growing power of the Court, a power made attractive and acceptable because Marshall always appeared to be exercising power, not in the name of party or state, or the Court itself, but on behalf of the people as the ultimate source of sovereign authority.

## Martin v. Hunter's Lessee

Several of these factors were at play in *Martin v. Hunter's Lessee* (1816), Joseph Story's first great opinion. Story stands second only to Chief Justice John Marshall as an advocate of judicial nationalism. He believed that for the United States the judiciary should provide a "strong and stringent link" between the national government and the states in order "to promote the harmony of States, and cement the Union," which he believed was "already too feebly supported." His whole judicial career, as well as his scholarship, exemplified by his *Commentaries on the Constitution* (1831), was based on his view "that the Government of the United States is intrinsically too weak, and the powers of the State Governments too strong; that the danger always is much greater of anarchy in the parts, than of tyranny in the head." Similarly, one of his last major opinions, *Prigg v. Pennsylvania* (1842), nationalized the return of fugitive slaves, as part of Story's lifelong goal to create a strong central government. His opinion in *Martin* would be his first major effort at nationalizing American law.

*Martin v. Hunter's Lessee* began as a case interpreting the common law rights of property and inheritance in Virginia. Ultimately, however, it involved the constitutionality of Section 25 of the 1789 Judiciary Act, giving the Supreme Court appellate jurisdiction over state court decisions. Lord Fairfax, the original owner of substantial tracts of land in Virginia's Northern Neck fled to England during the Revolution, and died in 1781, bequeathing the property to his nephew Denny Martin, a British subject. One condition of the bequest, which Martin readily agreed to, was that he change his name to Fairfax. In 1782, however, Virginia passed an act voiding the original grant, contending that, under her laws, aliens such as Denny Fairfax could not inherit real property in the state. Furthermore, the various confiscation measures enacted (but never implemented) during the war had transferred the property from Lord Fairfax to the state. David Hunter obtained a grant of nearly 800 acres of the Fairfax land from the state of Virginia, and brought an action of ejectment against the Fairfax interests. Virginia's highest court decided for Hunter, but by then Jay's Treaty had reaffirmed title to the original holders of land confiscated by the states. The case dragged on through years of litigation, and in 1813, reached the Supreme Court on a writ of error, under the title of *Fairfax's Devisee v. Hunter's Lessee*.

John Marshall was an investor in the Fairfax lands, and his brother was involved in the suit. Thus the chief justice recused himself from the case. Story, writing for the Court, reversed the Virginia court, claiming that the common law rules of property and inheritance had been incorporated by the states at the time of the Revolution. While states could certainly amend the common law through statute, Virginia had not done so. The state could have seized Fairfax's property during the war, but it had not done that either, and this left Denny Fairfax in full legal possession of the property. Virginia argued that it had, in fact, changed the common law, but Story disagreed, noting that the 1782 statute had failed to indicate the exact intention of the legislature. Story thus dismissed Virginia's laws, as well as their interpretation by the state's highest court. In doing so, according to one scholar, he implied that the state had no separate legal identity or jurisdiction from the United States and was scarcely more than an administrative unit of the central government.

There is no doubt that Marshall agreed with Story's conclusion, but the chief justice's political tact contrasts sharply with Story's arrogance. Such an attitude, even during a time of high nationalism, invited retaliation, and the Virginia judges, after consulting with Jefferson and Madison, ignored Story's order requiring them to enter judgment for the Fairfax interests. Instead, they challenged the validity of the Court's jurisdiction over state court decisions, which relied on the Judiciary Act of 1789. Section 25 provided for Supreme Court review of final judgments in state supreme courts involving the validity of any federal statute, treaty, or clause of the Constitution. The Virginia judges claimed that although they, like other state judges, had to obey the Constitution, laws, and treaties of the United States, they were not bound to obey the Supreme Court's interpretation of those items. State and federal judges represented two distinct sovereignties, and therefore, one could not be required to follow the decisions of the other. In *Hunter v. Fairfax's Devisee* (Va. 1810), the Virginia court bluntly asserted: "The appellate power of the Supreme Court of the United States does not extend to this court."

By this time, Denny Fairfax was long dead, and his brother and heir, General Philip Martin, now began a new lawsuit, which reached the Court in 1816 as *Martin v. Hunter's Lessee.* Speaking for a unanimous Court (with Marshall still recusing himself), Story, who had been appointed to the Court by the Republican president, James Madison, castigated Virginia for pursuing the states' rights doctrines similar to those of Federalists in Massachusetts, who had opposed the embargo and the War of 1812. He rejected outright any contention of equal sovereignty between the states and the federal government. The Constitution, he reminded Virginia, had not been formed by the states, but by "the people of the United States." As such, the people had the right and the power to cede to the national government "all the powers which they might deem proper and necessary."

The people had lodged the judicial power of the nation in the federal courts, especially the Supreme Court. Story conceded that although nowhere in the Constitution could one find an express grant of appellate jurisdiction over state courts, "this instrument, like every other grant, is to have a reasonable construction, according to the import of its terms; and where a power is expressly given in general terms, it is not to be restrained to particular cases, unless that construction grows out of the context expressly, or by necessary implication." By this rule, Story deduced that the judicial power of the government had to be coextensive with the legislative, so that it could decide every question that grew out of the Constitution and laws, a principle first enunciated in *Federalist No. 18.*

Article III, Section 2 of the Constitution expressly declares that the "judicial Power shall extend to all Cases" arising under the "Constitution, the Laws of the United States, and Treaties" made by the United States. Furthermore, the Constitution granted the Supreme Court original jurisdiction in a handful of circumstances, and that "in all other Cases," the Supreme Court "shall have appellate Jurisdiction, both as to Law and Fact." The *case,* Story concluded, and not the *court,* provides jurisdiction, and if a proper case originating in a state court involves the Constitution, laws, or treaties of the federal government, then the Supreme Court had the necessary jurisdiction. How else would it be possible to secure a uniform system of law for the entire land or carry out the mandate of the Supremacy Clause? Indeed, Story noted that judges in different states might interpret federal law or the Constitution in different ways.

> If there were no revising authority to control these jarring and discordant judgments, and harmonize them into uniformity, the laws, the treaties, and the constitution of the United States would be different in different states, and might, perhaps, never have precisely the same construction, obligation, or efficacy, in any two states. The public mischiefs that would attend such a state of things would be truly deplorable.

Thus, the very nature of the American system required that "the absolute right of decision, in the last resort, must rest somewhere," and following Marshall's reasoning in *Marbury*, Story found that "somewhere" could only be the U.S. Supreme Court.

*Martin* was among Story's most important opinions in his thirty-four years on the bench. It affirmed, in unusually powerful and sweeping language, the Supreme Court's power to override state courts. Justice Oliver Wendell Holmes, Jr., concurred in this sentiment a century later, when he noted that the real power of the Court lay, not in its review of federal legislation, but in its review of state decisions. Without this power, the Supremacy Clause would be meaningless, for there would be no way to conform the laws of the several states to a single constitutional standard. As the legal historian Charles Warren wrote, *Martin* provided the "keystone of the whole arch of Federal judicial power."

Story's opinion also dealt with implied powers, and *Martin* was the first case to utilize this means of constitutional construction. Chief Justice Marshall would perfect this method a few years later in *McCulloch v. Maryland*. Of equal importance was the denial of the compact theory of government and the espousal of the doctrine that the Union derived its authority directly from the people. The compact theory did not die easily, however, and it would take a civil war to confirm Story's view. Finally, Story departed radically from the Jeffersonian view that the national government was one of limited powers. Even John Marshall never went as far as Story in giving the central government such widespread authority. The Hamiltonians, including Marshall, saw the Constitution as providing ample power to meet the governmental necessities of the Union, but still conceded a fair degree of authority to the states. In the *Fairfax* and *Martin* cases, Story claimed almost unlimited power for the national government, and relegated the states to little more than administrative units. He would offer a fuller exposition of this theory in his *Commentaries on the Constitution* (1831).

## Madison's Proposals

The Court's assertion of federal power meshed with the programs then being proposed by James Madison. The War of 1812 had taught many Republicans that Jefferson's theories of government, while admirable in the abstract, fell short of the mark when confronting the actual needs of the country. Madison, who had collaborated with Jefferson in the Virginia and Kentucky resolutions, now seemed more like the nationalist who had coauthored *The Federalist* with Hamilton and Jay. Recalling the total lack of preparedness to fight the war, he now supported a standing army and navy. Once a fervent opponent of the Bank of the United States, he now wanted it to have a new charter, because when the old one had run out in 1811, the Republican Congress had not rechartered it. Madison had seen that the lack of a central bank had caused the administration serious problems in financing the war. The cutoff of European goods had led to the rise of new American industries, which now sought tariff protection against the revived flood of cheaper British products that threatened to swamp their markets. Westward expansion had revealed the need for better internal transportation, and Madison agreed that the federal government should play a role in developing new roads and canals.

In his first annual message to Congress after the war, Madison proposed several measures to strengthen the nation. He called for better fortifications, a standing army and larger navy, a new national bank, protective tariffs for infant industries, a system of canals and roads for commercial and military use, and a great national university. All these, he maintained, fell within the constitutional prerogatives of the government, with the exception of internal improvements, and there he urged an amendment to enable Congress to act. More than a few old-line Jeffersonians expressed shock at the plan, while Josiah Quincy, a staunch Massachusetts Federalist, joyfully proclaimed that "the Republicans had out-Federalized Federalism." Congress, in the flush of national fervor following the war, gave the president most of what he suggested. It authorized a standing army of 10,000 men, strengthened the navy, enacted a tariff to provide protection as well as revenue, and chartered a new national bank. Congress also voted funds for internal improvements, but Madison, showing a burst of his old scruples, vetoed it until a constitutional amendment could be secured. Only in his request for a national university did Madison fail to get his way.

The three planks of a national economic program—the bank, a protective tariff, and internal improvements—inspired the great political and constitutional controversies that would occupy the country for the next generation. Beneath all three, however, was the ongoing division between states' rights proponents and advocates of a strong national government that traced back to the debates over ratification of the Constitution. Deeply tied to states' rights was the relationship between the states, the national government, and slavery. The southern states were most concerned about their powers because they wanted to protect slavery; similarly, the New England delegates to the Hartford Convention had flirted with states' rights in part because they felt the federal government was dominated by proslavey forces. Within a generation, of course, all of these issues would be swallowed up by the intractable problem of slavery, which would ultimately lead to civil war.

## The Second Bank of the United States in Court

The charter of the first Bank of the United States expired in 1811. By the end of the War of 1812, the country's finances were truly muddled. State-chartered banks mushroomed, but few states imposed regulations to ensure prudence in banking operations, while state bank notes, rarely worth their face value, flooded the avenues of commerce. Gold and specie remained rare, and most of it drifted to the New England banks, increasing the commercial prosperity of that region. During the war, the administration had been embarrassed by the lack of a national bank, both as a source for borrowing and as a means of transferring funds from one part of the country to another.

Despite his earlier arguments that the bank was unconstitutional, Madison now believed it was a necessity. The issue, he told Congress, had been settled "by repeated recognitions . . . of the validity of such an institution in acts of the legislative, executive and judicial branches of the Government . . . accompanied by . . . a concurrence of the general will of the nation." Congress agreed, and in 1816 issued a twenty-year charter for a new Bank of the United States, modeled after Hamilton's original, but capitalized at $35 million instead of $10 million.

The debate on the charter predictably aroused the ire of unreconstructed Jeffersonians, but it also featured three men who would play commanding roles in the nation's politics for the next three decades—John C. Calhoun of South Carolina; Henry Clay of Kentucky; and Daniel Webster, then of New Hampshire and afterward of Massachusetts. Calhoun, later to be the chief advocate of states' rights but then still a War Hawk nationalist, introduced the bank measure and saw it through to passage. The constitutionality of the bill, he argued, derived from congressional power to regulate money. Clay, who had helped kill efforts to recharter the First Bank of the United States in 1811, admitted he had failed to see the problems that would arise from the absence of a central bank. Webster, on the other hand, argued against the Bank, reflecting the New England Federalists' hostility to Madison, as well as a reluctance to see the nation's banking center shift from Boston to Philadelphia.

No one doubted that a court challenge to the new Bank would eventually arise, for despite Madison's assertion, the Supreme Court had never passed on the legitimacy of the first Bank. States' rights advocates still insisted that Congress had no authority to issue the charter, and they feared the effect that a powerful and financially sound bank would have on their local institutions. These fears seemed confirmed in 1818, when the Bank, anticipating an economic downturn, called in many of its loans, and in doing so, caused a number of overextended banks in the South and West to fail. By the next year, the country was in the midst of its first full-scale depression, known as the Panic of 1819. With many people claiming that the Bank itself had caused the panic, and under pressure from jealous local banks, seven states passed laws restricting the Bank's operations within their borders; in some instances, they taxed any notes issued by nonstate chartered banks. When James McCulloch, the cashier of the Baltimore branch of the Bank, refused to pay Maryland's claim to a $15,000 tax on its notes, the state sued and won in the Maryland high court, thus setting the stage for an appeal by the Bank to the U.S. Supreme Court.

The Court had to resolve two questions: Did Congress have the power to charter the Bank? And if so, did Maryland have the right to tax its operations within the state? Although the questions appeared simple enough, the answers—and the form they took—would have far larger implications. Few people expected the Court to rule against congressional authority to charter the Bank. In arguments before the bench, counsel for both sides apologized about repeating contentions that had now grown "threadbare" since the debate between Hamilton and Jefferson more than a quarter-century earlier. Why should the Court adopt Jefferson's claims when even his own party had abandoned them? Madison had certainly been right when he noted the "concurrence of the general will of the nation" in the Bank's legitimacy. For most observers, only the constitutionality of the state tax on a valid organ of the national government seemed in doubt.

John Marshall's opinion in *McCulloch v. Maryland* (1819) went far beyond the two basic questions. His "state paper," as it has been properly called, expounded theories of national supremacy and federal power that over the next century and a half would be used to justify the growth of the central government and its involvement in nearly every aspect of national life. Justice Story considered the national bank, along with national military academies, a great navy, and a strong judiciary, necessary for creating the "great National interests which shall bind us in an indissoluble chain." Marshall's opinion in *McCulloch* set out the legal theory that supported this nationalist goal.

Speaking for a unanimous Court, Marshall quickly demolished Maryland's assertions of state sovereignty. While conceding that the federal government had limited powers in a Union of divided sovereignty, Marshall asserted that within its assigned spheres of power, the national government reigned supreme. Whenever legitimate federal power conflicted with state authority, the latter had to give way. The federal government took precedence over the state, because it derived its mandate from the people: "It is the government of all; its powers are delegated by all; it represents all, and acts for all."

But if the state could not restrict a legitimate act of Congress, did Congress have the power to charter a bank in the first place? Such authority had admittedly not been included among the enumerated powers of Article I, Section 8, but Marshall held that it still came within the parameters of the Constitution. Relying on William Pinkney's argument for the Bank, and even more on Alexander Hamilton's defense of the first bank, Marshall set out a broad interpretation of constitutional power.

To begin with, he noted that "We must never forget that it is a constitution we are expounding," a flexible instrument sufficient to the "exigencies of the nation." If every power necessary to the federal government had to be listed, the Constitution would be nothing more than a legal code, whose prolixity "could scarcely be embraced by the human mind." The enumerated powers merely pointed out certain obvious traits of government, but they had to be interpreted liberally, so that the government could act without undue restraint in any area of its responsibilities. The Framers had been too wise to attempt anticipating all contingencies, and so had provided, along with enumerated powers, the power to pass "all laws which shall be necessary and proper for carrying into execution the foregoing powers."

The word "necessary" should not be construed, as Maryland urged, as a restriction, but rather as an addition to the enumerated powers. Congress thus had discretion over which means it would choose to implement "those great powers on which the welfare of the nation essentially depends." "Let the end be legitimate," Marshall declared in one of his most oft-quoted passages, "let it be within the scope of the constitution, and all means which are appropriate, which are plainly adapted to that end, which are not prohibited, but consist with the letter and spirit of the constitution, are constitutional." Any other reading would reduce the Constitution to a "splendid bauble," and not a great charter of government "intended to endure for ages to come, and, consequently, to be adapted to the various crises of human affairs."

But could the Bank (which had barely been mentioned so far) be taxed? Marshall had made clear the supremacy of the national government when operating within its broadly defined parameters; now he set about preventing the state's conceded sovereignty from clashing with that of the federal government. The Constitution, Marshall noted, did not expressly limit the state's power to tax, but by a series of inferences, he solved that problem. If the government had the power to create an agency, then it obviously had the means to preserve it. But "the power to tax involves the power to destroy . . . and render useless the power to create." How could the federal government be supreme within its area of competency if another sovereignty could exercise a power capable of reaching into and destroying creations authorized by the Constitution? The chief justice did not discuss whether the Maryland tax in fact threatened the Bank with destruction—although in fact it did. For Marshall, the potentially injurious power of the tax alone invalidated it on constitutional grounds. Declaring it as a broad principle, Marshall concluded that "States have no power, by taxation or otherwise, to retard, impede, burden, or in any manner control the operation of the constitutional laws enacted by Congress to carry into execution the powers vested in the general government."

The impact of *McCulloch* lay less in its specific holding than in the bold and expansive manner in which the chief justice interpreted federal power. The decision heartened the Bank, but did not prove decisive. Within a few years, the exact same issue came back before the Court in *Osborn v. Bank of the United States* (1824), when Ohio, in defiance of a circuit court injunction, levied and collected a tax on the Bank. Once again, Marshall (this time with Justice Johnson dissenting) upheld the constitutionality of the Bank and gave another strong lecture on national supremacy. Moreover, he ensured the Bank access to the federal courts even against state opposition, thus ignoring the spirit of the Eleventh Amendment. Even more important, he ruled that agents of the state were personally liable for damages inflicted while executing an unconstitutional statute.

There could not have been much surprise at the ruling. After all, the first bank had been around for twenty years, and the second bank, despite intense hostility from some local interests, had already gained recognition as an important and useful feature of the nation's economic life. Charges that the Bank had caused the Panic of 1819 had led to an attempt in the House of Representatives to revoke the charter, but a majority in Congress considered the Bank too valuable for such a severe action. So "the Bank Case" would never have become "the Great Case" just for its validation of the bank's legitimacy.

It became a great case because the chief justice justified the Bank's legitimacy on the basis of a broad and flexible interpretation of the Constitution, arguing that a constitution could not be expected to list every power of government and that Congress enjoyed large discretion in determining the means it would use to achieve its ends. His analysis provided the foundation for broadly conceived national action that has been drawn upon ever since as the government expanded its activities. Moreover, Marshall's decision came at a time when the postwar euphoria had begun to ebb and Congress had withdrawn from the strong nationalism with which it had greeted Madison's expansive program.

To many Republicans, however, *McCulloch* sounded an alarm, and although they grudgingly conceded that the Second Bank of the United States might be a necessary evil, they recognized in Marshall's abstractions the legitimation of an all-encompassing national power against which they had fought for decades. The clearest statement of this view can be found in a series of newspaper articles published in the influential Richmond *Enquirer* by Judge William Brockenbrough, writing as "Amphictyon," and by one of the most potent states' rights philosophers of his day, Spencer Roane of Virginia's Court of Appeals, under the name of "Hampden." These statements appeared so powerful that Marshall himself, writing pseudonymously, felt compelled to answer and elaborate on the analysis of national supremacy in *McCulloch.*

## Cohens v. Virginia

Virginia, although Marshall's home state, had long been the chief opponent of a strong national government. Patrick Henry, Roane's father-in-law, had led the fight against ratification of the Constitution. James Madison, in the Virginia Resolution of 1798 and the Committee Report of 1799, had attacked the Alien and Sedition laws and asserted the right of a state to interpose itself against excessive national authority. Even though Jefferson and Madison had tempered their principles when confronted with the problems of governing the nation, men like John Randolph of Roanoke and John Taylor of Caroline still clung to the old orthodoxy and, together with Roane, refused to abandon it. When the Virginia legislature met after the Bank decision, it condemned the Supreme Court and instructed its congressional delegation to introduce constitutional amendments to put the Court in its proper place. Before long, Virginia had its chance to make the argument directly to Marshall and his brethren in *Cohens v. Virginia* (1821).

The Cohens had been convicted of selling District of Columbia lottery tickets in Virginia in violation of state law against lotteries. They appealed directly to the Supreme Court, claiming that they had acted under a congressional statute authorizing the lottery in Washington, D.C. At the heart of the case, as Marshall noted, lay questions "of great magnitude" concerning the nature of the Union and the role of the Court itself in a federal system. Virginia argued that the general sovereignty of states, as well as the specific immunity of the Eleventh Amendment, prohibited the Court from hearing the case. In addition, counsel rehearsed every states' rights argument of the previous twenty-five years.

In a strongly worded opinion upholding the supremacy of the national government, Marshall declared that the Constitution had made the Union and had made it supreme; both that supremacy and therefore the Union itself now stood endangered by state jealousy. In a slight variation on *McCulloch,* Marshall noted not only the paramount authority of the national government over the states but the necessary corollary to this proposition—the supremacy of the federal departments in their appropriate spheres. Judges interpreted the law, and, therefore, the federal judiciary stood as the ultimate arbiter of the law. "The exercise of the appellate power over those judgments of the state tribunals which may contravene the constitution or laws of the United States is, we believe, essential to the attainment of these objects." Within the Union, there could be no division between the state and federal judicial systems. The states had jurisdiction in all cases involving their own laws, but any federal question required appellate jurisdiction by the federal bench as provided for in Section 25. The Eleventh Amendment merely prohibited suits by individuals against states without the latter's consent, but it did not prevent federal courts from properly deciding legitimate federal questions. Marshall also noted that Virginia had instituted this prosecution and therefore could not invoke the Eleventh Amendment.

After this powerful lecture on the nearly unlimited power of the Supreme Court to review state court decisions, Marshall, once again displayed his prowess as a judicial politician, by ruling for Virginia on the grounds that the lottery statute applied only in the District of Columbia and had not been intended to apply to the states. Thus there would be no danger of Virginia defying the Court's decision, since it had technically won the case, just as Jefferson had technically won in *Marbury*. But states' rights advocates were appalled at the chief justice's opinion, especially his argument that in forming the Union, the people had transferred large measures of state sovereignty to the national government. Marshall's "immortal national address," they feared, would eventually win acceptance over their own claims of state power.

## The Steamboat Case

In *McCulloch* and *Cohens,* the chief justice read the *implied* powers of the national government in an expansive manner. The Constitution also gives Congress *explicit* powers, and in these instances—especially in the Commerce Clause—the Marshall Court also expanded national power. Restrictive state economic regulations had nearly crippled the nation under the Confederation and led to the call for the Philadelphia Convention. There the Framers had specifically intended to promote full and free intercourse between the states. For Marshall, there was no need for specific statutes authorizing trade, for commerce between the states "derives its source from those laws whose authority is acknowledged by civilized man throughout the world." The Constitution merely acknowledged this natural right, and gave Congress the power to regulate it to promote the general welfare.

The strongest exposition of the commerce power came in *Gibbons v. Ogden* (1824). The case illustrates how the early state governments used their power to expand the economy, as well as the importance of the Marshall Court's development of the commerce power.

In 1798, the state of New York gave Robert R. Livingston an exclusive fourteen-year franchise to operate steamboats "within" the state. In 1803, Livingston and his partner Robert Fulton successfully launched the nation's first steamboat. In 1808, the New York legislature extended the franchise for another twenty years, until 1838. The franchise gave the Livingston and Fulton exclusive rights of steamboat navigation on all state waters, including the adjacent coastal waters and the Hudson River between New York and New Jersey. The New York courts upheld this monopoly in *Livingston v. Van Ingen* (1812), after James Van Ingen began operating steamboat service from New York City to Albany.

In 1815, Aaron Ogden, a former governor of New Jersey, purchased rights from the Livingston-Fulton group to operate a steamboat between New York City and New Jersey. Thomas Gibbons later started his own company to operate on this route, and Ogden secured an injunction from Chancellor James Kent to prevent Gibbons from operating his steamboats in violation of the franchise. Kent also refused Gibbons's request to move the suit to federal court. Gibbons then secured a coasting license under the Coasting Act of 1793, and went back to the state court, arguing that the federal license took precedence over New York's power to regulate the lower Hudson River.

Once again, in *Gibbons v. Ogden* (New York, 1820), Kent upheld the monopoly, refusing to believe that a simple coasting license, obtained "as a matter of course, and with as much facility as the flag of the *United States* could be procured and hoisted" could enable its holder to flout an act of New York's sovereign legislature. But Gibbons now had his federal question, and he retained Daniel Webster to appeal the case to the U.S. Supreme Court.

Webster began by noting that New York's law, which had invited retaliatory legislation by Connecticut and New Jersey, imposed just those barriers to interstate commerce that had befuddled the Confederation. Unlike taxation, in which the federal and state governments enjoyed concurrent power, the Constitution had granted full power to the national government in this area. If Congress failed to exercise its authority, then the states remained free to act. But Congress had not been silent on this issue; through the 1793 Coasting Act, it had stated its intention to bring coastal trade under federal control. The New York assembly went beyond its acknowledged power to police trade within its borders, and in effect regulated commerce between states, a power reserved exclusively to Congress. Webster claimed that Gibbons's license gave him a right to "navigate freely the waters of the United States," a right that New York now attempted to take away from him.

On behalf of Ogden, former congressman Thomas J. Oakley urged the Court to view the regulation of commerce as a concurrent power. While not going as far as Virginia had in defending states' rights, Oakley also maintained that in 1787, the states had reserved certain powers and had not ceded their sovereignty in all matters to the federal government. Moreover, interstate commerce had always been viewed as the transportation of goods and not, as in this case, the movement of passengers. Oakley's associate, Thomas A. Emmet, the longtime counsel for the Livingstons, then proceeded to list numerous areas that affected interstate commerce and that had always been considered within the purview of the states, such as quarantines, pilotage, lighthouses, turnpikes, and even Indian trade. These had all been pursued for the general welfare of the people, and not only as police measures to protect their health and safety.

Emmet's arguments led Webster's colleague, Attorney General William Wirt, to suggest that Webster had never intended that the state had no powers in regulating trade. Although Wirt appeared in court in a private capacity, as counsel to Gibbons, he also spoke for the federal power, and he urged the Court to draw a line between those activities deriving from the commerce power, which were exclusive to the federal government, and those regulations over primarily intrastate commerce growing out of the police powers, which might indirectly affect interstate trade. This compromise position pleased the Fulton-Livingston interests, which drew the bulk of their income from activities north of New York City, where the Hudson flowed entirely within state borders. Ogden's license between New York and New Jersey could easily be sacrificed, providing the monopoly remained intact elsewhere.

Marshall initially approached this decision with caution. He had great respect for Chancellor Kent, who had been a leader of the Federalists in New York, and was probably the most prominent and able state judge in the nation. His lower court opinion could not be cavalierly brushed aside. The Commerce Clause itself had received practically no judicial explication, and no one knew how far it reached. Nonetheless, Marshall casually stated it as a "well-settled rule" that the enumerated powers had to be construed both by the language of the Constitution and in light of the purpose for which they had been conferred. The Article I powers had been granted to further the "general advantage" of the whole American people. Although not infinite in its reach, in delegated areas the "the sovereignty of Congress, though limited to specified objects, is plenary as to those objects."

Commerce, a vital aspect of national life, included not just the exchange of goods, but "every species of commercial intercourse" among the states. The key word "among" meant not only between, but intermingled with, so that the power of Congress did not stop at state lines, but extended into the interiors of the states as well. The congressional power to regulate this commerce meant it could reach all aspects of trade; "complete in itself, [it] may be exercised to its utmost extent, and acknowledges no limitations other than are prescribed in the Constitution." Other than constitutional prohibitions, only the wisdom of Congress and the electorate in choosing appropriate policies restrained its exercise.

Marshall no doubt sympathized with Webster's view of the commerce power as exclusive, but he recognized that some nod had to be made to at least a limited claim of state sovereignty. His opinion thus held that both state and national governments had concurrent powers over commerce but that the former always had to give way to the latter in case of conflict. Through a broad reading of the Coasting Act of 1793, the chief justice ruled that the statute constituted a guaranty against state interference with interstate commerce. The New York law contradicted this intent, and was therefore void. In an aside, Marshall hinted that the mere grant of the commerce power might have been sufficient to reach this result, even in the absence of a specific congressional statute.

The *Gibbons* decision had both immediate and long-range consequences. In the short run, it proved to be extremely popular, since it broke up what had become an unpopular monopoly and prevented a looming transportation war between the states. Although it diminished state power, it did so in an area in which most Americans, even states' rights localists, wanted a free market. The case treated the nation as a single commercial entity, and prevented states from fragmenting the national economy. The broad interpretation of what constituted interstate commerce permitted the government to adapt its policies to new technologies in transportation and communications, and except for a relatively brief period in the early twentieth century, allowed the continuous expansion of federal regulation over the nation's commerce, banking, industry, and labor. Beyond that, the analysis applied to the commerce power could be used to expand the scope of the other enumerated powers as well.

Three years later in *Brown v. Maryland* (1827), the Court again emphasized the national character of commerce when it voided a Maryland statute that imposed a tax on importers of out-of-state goods. Although Congress had not addressed itself to this issue (as it supposedly had in the steamboat case), Marshall enlarged on his earlier *obiter dicta* that the commerce power by itself might preclude a state from any interference in interstate trade. Although the states still enjoyed authority over primarily intrastate activities, the new demarcation line would be the original package doctrine. So long as goods crossing state lines remained in their original packages, they could not be taxed or otherwise regulated by the states, a doctrine that remained in effect for over a century.

But if Congress had the broad power, the Supreme Court retained the ultimate authority to determine when and if that power had been applied. In *Willson v. Black Bird Creek Marsh Co.* (1829), Marshall sustained a Delaware law authorizing the damming of a creek to keep out marsh waters, even though the creek was navigable and had at times been used in coastal trade. Willson had registered his boat under the same 1793 law as had Gibbons, and following the reasoning of the earlier cases, Marshall might have held that the mere existence of either the commerce power or the statute invalidated the Delaware law. But Congress had not acted specifically in this matter, and thus the Court reserved the right to determine whether congressional silence permitted state action or if the commerce power precluded it.

## Conclusion: The Marshall Court's Legacy

In the thirty-four years that John Marshall served as chief justice, the Supreme Court invalidated statutes of more than half the states; despite the unflagging assertion of states' rights, the constitutional nationalism expounded by the Court flourished. Although each state protested when one of its laws had been struck down, at no time did a majority of them band together to curtail the power of the Court, as they had after *Chisholm v. Georgia*. In spite of the theoretical assertions of Jefferson, Roane, and others about the supremacy of the states in the federal scheme, states acted on immediate economic interests rather than on broad theoretical concerns. Moreover, a general consensus was emerging that the Court, and not the states or the Congress, should act as the final arbiter of constitutional questions.

There were, it is true, efforts to curb the power of the Court. In both statehouses and the Congress, numerous resolutions railed against the Court's alleged usurpation of a power that was not mentioned anywhere in the Constitution, attacked Marshall and his brethren for emasculating state sovereignty, and complained about the Court's lack of accountability to the people. Senator Richard Johnson of Kentucky proposed that the Senate should be a court of last resort in any case involving a state statute or in which a state would be a party. Others suggested expanding the size of the Court, so that justices more sympathetic to states' rights could be appointed and dilute the nationalists' strength. Although the House passed a bill increasing the number of justices to ten and redrawing circuit boundaries, the measure failed in the Senate. Growing sectional tensions, the absence of party discipline, public faith in the Court, as well as agreement by many groups with the Court's decisions—all undermined the various attacks on the tribunal. The virtually unanimous popularity of the decision in *Gibbons v. Ogden* (1824) also enhanced the prestige and popularity of the Court. Most Americans correctly viewed that decision as a democratic expansion of economic opportunity that would in fact lower the cost of transportation for all Americans. By the late 1820s, moreover, changes in the Court's personnel made it only a matter of time until Marshall's strong nationalism would give way to newer philosophies.

Nonetheless, one can hardly question the enormous legacy of constitutional nationalism left by the Marshall Court. Although some of its interpretations would later be abandoned or modified, much of its judicial philosophy has become permanently embedded in the nation's constitutional fabric. Later Supreme Courts and other justices might be less nationalistic or less inclined to read the Constitution as such a broad grant of power, but none ever renounced the Marshall Court's claim to be the ultimate arbiter of constitutional questions.

The times no doubt encouraged a broad reading of the Constitution, but Marshall did not invent his doctrines out of whole cloth, nor did he have to teach nationalism to his colleagues, certainly not to Joseph Story nor even to William Johnson. Marshall's force of personality undoubtedly carried the Court further along these lines than some of his colleagues occasionally wished to go, but the unanimity of the bench in many of its great cases indicated a basic agreement among the brethren that was independent of Marshall's views. Part of his genius consisted in articulating this consensus in a manner that expanded the prestige of the Court and the power of the federal government under the Constitution. Although he claimed, as have other chief justices, to be no more than "first among equals," he personified the Court and gave utterance to some of its greatest constitutional decisions. He has remained *the* chief justice.

Later schools of jurisprudence that valued judicial restraint would argue that the Marshall Court came perilously close to, if not actually overstepped, the boundary between the review of constitutional power and making policy. The Marshall Court believed judicial review could and should be used as an instrument of national purpose. Yet the Court could never reach beyond those questions that came before it; the Court never spoke on many of the issues that would soon transfix the country, because these had not yet entered the judicial process. But the chief justice and his colleagues left a legacy of a willingness, adopted for better or worse by nearly all subsequent Courts, to face up to the issues of the day that came before the bench.

Some critics have dismissed Marshall's assertions of national supremacy as a failure, and have blamed him in part for exacerbating the tensions that led to the Civil War a generation after his death. To do so places on the Court a power to control events that it never had, while ignoring the divisiveness of slavery, which proved beyond the grasp of the entire political system. It would be more accurate to say that Marshall contributed enormously to the validity of the ideas that animated the defenders of the Union, and ultimately proved successful in putting down the forces of disunion. In doing so, Marshall helped transform the entire notion of a union into a nation, an idea whose power still remains vital.

# For Further Reading

The most thorough study of the first part of Marshall's tenure is the second volume of the Holmes Devise *History of the Supreme Court of the United States,* George Lee Haskins and Herbert A. Johnson, *Foundations of Power, 1801–1815* (1981). This is really two books, with Haskins emphasizing the interplay between the Court and the Jeffersonians, and Johnson analyzing the workaday business of the Court. The rest of Marshall's career is covered in the same series in G. Edward White, *The Marshall Court and Cultural Change, 1815–1835* (1988). Shorter studies include Herbert A. Johnson, *The Chief Justiceship of John Marshall, 1801–1835* (1997); and Charles F. Hobson, *The Great Chief Justice: John Marshall and the Rule of Law* (1996). Also useful is Jean Edward Smith, *John Marshall: Definer of Nation* (1996). Still useful, but somewhat dated, is R. Kent Newmyer, *The Supreme Court Under Marshall and Taney* (1968), which provides a fine sense of continuity and change over six decades.

For specific cases, see Gerald Gunther, ed., *John Marshall's Defense of McCulloch v. Maryland* (1969); and Maurice G. Baxter, *The Steamboat Monopoly: Gibbons v. Ogden, 1824* (1972). Baxter's *Daniel Webster and the Supreme Court* (1966) is also quite useful. Webster argued 168 cases before the Court between 1814 and 1852, and Baxter claims that no other attorney did so much to develop the legal rules and constitutional doctrines of the Court in this formative period. On Madison's changing view of the bank, see Paul Finkelman, "The Constitution and the Intentions of the Framers: The Limits of Historical Analysis," 50 *University of Pittsburgh Law Review* 349 (1989).

The Lockean elements in Marshall's philosophy are emphasized in Robert K. Faulkner, *The Jurisprudence of John Marshall* (1968); for Marshall's nationalism, see Samuel J. Konefsky, *John Marshall and Alexander Hamilton: Architects of the Constitution* (1964). Madison's nationalism, as well as his presidency, is detailed in Ralph L. Ketcham, *James Madison* (1971).

There are a number of works on the commerce power, but good places to begin remain Felix Frankfurter, *The Commerce Clause Under Marshall, Taney, and Waite* (1937); and E.S. Corwin, *Commerce Power Versus States Rights* (1936).

# 12

# The Marshall Court and Economic Development

LAW HAS ALWAYS been closely connected with commerce, and rules of property, contract, and damages play an important role in shaping the forms of business arrangements, as well as the means by which society enforces or refuses to enforce private commercial agreements. John Marshall shared many of Alexander Hamilton's views on the need for a prosperous economy to undergird a strong Union, and he believed the Constitution gave the federal government authority to support national economic development. Not surprisingly, the theme of states' rights versus national power that we examined in the last chapter is present in this area as well.

## Law and Economic Development

Commercial growth in the United States proceeded along two intermingled paths, activity within individual states, as well as interstate activity. The Framers understood this distinction, but believed that as the nation grew, the economic ties developed through interstate business would form a powerful cement to bind the Union together. Recognizing that local interests would try to hamper this growth, they wrote into the Constitution specific limits on state regulation and activity in Article I, Section 10, and gave over the power to control interstate commerce to the national government.

Many of the cases discussed in the preceding chapter not only strengthened the U.S. Supreme Court and the national government in general, but also reflected the Marshall Court's determination to pursue the commercial policy it believed had been propounded by the Framers. In *McCulloch v. Maryland* (1819) it not only upheld the right of Congress to create a powerful bank monopoly that spanned the nation, but it also prohibited the states, sensitive to the demands of local banks, from interfering with the national policy. *Brown v. Maryland* (1827) added a barrier to state taxation, by striking down a state law requiring importers of foreign goods to get a special license. The Court found that the license both infringed on Congress's power to regulate foreign commerce, and also constituted a state tax on imported goods, in violation of Article I, Section 10 of the Constitution. *Gibbons v. Ogden* (1824) gave Congress the authority to override state policies in pursuit of a national scheme of commerce. Indeed, the broad mandate of *Gibbons* would have permitted Congress to embark on an extensive program of internal improvements, but political dissension over this issue delayed Congress from acting until the Civil War.

In numerous commercial cases, the Court invariably chose rules of law that would promote rather than retard national economic development. Since many of these decisions involved constitutional rather than statutory interpretation, accusations arose, and continued for more than a century, that the Court was going far beyond its professed role of impartial arbiter and was assuming decisive policy-making functions that exceeded the limit of judicial authority. That the Court created economic policy through decisions is obvious; that in doing so the justices expressed their personal views, as opposed to those of the people acting through democratically elected legislatures, is also arguably true. But as French author Alexis de Tocqueville wrote in 1835, "Scarcely any political question arises in the United States that is not resolved, sooner or later, into a judicial question." Just as business and politics cannot be separated, so neither can law and commerce.

In part, this resulted from the muddled legal legacy of independence. Although all states derived their law from common English sources, the particular form of government peculiar to each colony, as well as local idiosyncracies and conditions, made each state's law uniquely different in particular respects from those of its sister states. Little had been done during the Confederation and early national periods to impose any consistency on this muddle, and the federal system created in the Constitution permitted each state to establish its own law in matters in which it had sole or primary responsibility. From the beginning, there had been tension between state law and national policy, but in the early nineteenth century, this friction intensified as the economy took on a more national character, marked by the growth of interstate business.

Marshall and his brethren certainly favored this development, for they believed that a national economy would prove a significant counterweight to the local prejudices they feared could subvert the Union. In the early twentieth century some scholars claimed the Marshall Court justices conspired with an exploitative capitalistic elite against the democratic wishes of the people. This rather unsophisticated charge simply does not hold up.

The Marshall Court shared with both Hamilton and Jefferson, as well as John Quincy Adams and Andrew Jackson, the vision of the United States as a great nation—even a great empire. The details of this vision, of course, differed among them. For Jefferson and Jackson, this greatness would be achieved by territorial expansion—the Louisiana Purchase, for example—and the subsequent expulsion of native peoples from the land. Marshall and his colleagues never resisted the acquisition of new land, but, for Hamilton, Adams, and most of the Marshall Court, the promise of a great nation would be redeemed through a commercial republic, in which local interests were subordinated to national economic goals. Most Americans in this period shared both visions, to lesser or greater extent. Thus, Marshall's decision in *Gibbons v. Ogden* was enormously popular because it created commercial opportunities for most people at the expense of a monopoly. Less popular was *McCulloch v. Maryland*, because it seemed to favor large investors at the expense of the masses. But, jurisprudentially, both were similar in that they upheld federal power at the expense of state power.

Marshall and his colleagues—including most of the justices appointed by the Virginia Republicans, Jefferson, Madison, and Monroe—did bring particular economic and political views to their deliberations, but many American shared these views. At no time could the Court create policy out of whole cloth; it had to work within the legal rules of the game that the Framers had provided, rules that supported development of a national economy.

The wide range of economic questions coming before the Court, the disparity in views among the people, and the competing interests of many factions meant that no matter which way the Court decided a particular issue, some groups would be displeased and others frustrated. *Brown v. Maryland* (1827), for example, displeased some Maryland merchants, but cheered Baltimore importers who resented state regulation of their businesses.

Many scholars have recognized the necessarily close ties between law and commerce without imputing a conspiratorial tone. Willard Hurst, for example, saw law as a vehicle for the "release of energy" that allowed Americans to be creative in their use of land, water, and other resources. More recently, William J. Novak has demonstrated how law in nineteenth-century America was "not created to protect preexisting private rights, but to further the welfare of the whole people and community." As Chancellor James Kent of New York wrote at the time, "Private interest must be made subservient to the general interest of the community."

At the same time, nineteenth-century thought held that the individual and the protection of his or her rights and property constituted the primary justification for society; the individual, in turn, animated social progress. Behind the individual's efforts to achieve there is private property, the single most important denominator of status. "Man yearns," declared the nineteenth-century legal scholar Francis Lieber, "to see his individuality expressed and reflected in the acts of his exertions—in property." Property, according to John Locke and William Blackstone in England and James Madison and James Kent in America, led men to create, to overcome barriers, to produce communal wealth. Therefore, individual and collective progress could not be separated, for one fed the other. The individual entrepreneur created the climate for national growth, and the government, in turn, had to support such efforts, by either eliminating barriers or providing positive assistance.

Business interests, or at least those with a national viewpoint, welcomed the Court's efforts to clarify the laws with which they had to deal. The essence of commercial law is reliability, so that all parties to a transaction may count on a rational, stable set of rules, applied equally and impartially. A unified law system, applicable to business transactions all over the nation, appeared infinitely preferable to navigating the shoals of multiple and often conflicting state laws. These state laws, however, did serve the interests of local business, which jealously guarded them against infringement by the national government. Some merchants, through either choice or inability to compete in the national market, preferred local rules designed for their benefit, and utilized the rhetoric of states' rights and popular democracy in an effort to thwart the development of a law system supportive of a national economy.

The Marshall Court had two sets of tools at its disposal. The commerce power, as demonstrated in *Gibbons,* could be utilized to expand congressional authority, even to override local policy. But the power, although articulated, could only be exercised if Congress chose to do so, and, as in the case of internal improvements, political stalemate blocked its use. But the Constitution also provided a set of restraints upon the states, and here the Court could act, at least to prevent local passions from undermining national interests. Article I, Section 10, set out a list of activities that were forbidden to the states, such as coining money, impairing contracts, or laying duties on imports or exports. The Court would use these tools skillfully and effectively.

## *Fletcher v. Peck*

A good example of the Court at work in this area is one of the most important and controversial cases of the time, *Fletcher v. Peck* (1810). In 1789, the Georgia legislature authorized the sale of 35 million acres to several land companies. When the speculators tried to pay in near worthless scrip, the state refused to accept payment. Some of the grantees then brought suit to compel performance of the sale, with one case, *Chisholm v. Georgia* (1793), leading to the adoption of the Eleventh Amendment, which prohibited suing a state in federal court. In 1795, the state granted an additional 35 million acres in what were known as the Yazoo tracts (located in what is now Alabama and Mississippi) to four land companies for $1^1/_2$ cents an acre. Nearly all the legislators had been bribed with stock in the companies, and numerous other officials, including two senators as well as state and federal judges, had some connection with the fraud. The angered populace turned out the crooked legislators at the next election, and in 1796, the new assembly repealed the grant, publicly burned the original bill, and voided any property rights deriving from it.

But between the enactment of the grant in January 1795 and its repeal in 1796, the four companies had sold off millions of acres. In one transaction, dated the same day as the rescinding statute, the Georgia Mississippi Company sold 11 million acres at 10 cents an acre in a complex transaction that included the formation of the New England Mississippi Land Company, whose stockholders counted some of the leading citizens of the Northeast. The sale and the rescission gave rise to loud controversy throughout the nation, both for the fraud surrounding the original act and fear of how the sale might affect the powerful Indian tribes in the Yazoo. The Washington administration, which had wanted to secure these lands for the national government, claimed that only the federal government could deal with the Indian tribes and their lands. After protracted negotiations, Jefferson secured cession of these lands to the United States for $1,250,000. The administration, however, set aside 5 million acres to settle claims resulting under the 1795 grant.

New England investors who had bought land in good faith wanted to settle title to determine if they had valid claims. The Eleventh Amendment prevented them from suing Georgia, and the rescinding act forbade Georgia's courts from hearing suits concerning the Yazoo lands. In 1803, Robert Fletcher of New Hampshire brought suit against John Peck of Boston, who had sold him land in the Yazoo, and as citizens of different states, they entered federal court under the diversity of citizenship rule. Fletcher sued for breach of warranty of title, claiming that Peck had sold him land that he did not actually possess. Both Fletcher and Peck had been shareholders in the New England Mississippi Company, which had been involved in the bribery in Georgia, although there is no evidence of their personal involvement in the bribery scheme. Almost all scholars agree that the sale took place solely to test the Georgia law, and that the suit itself was collusive between the two from the start. Collusive suits are not uncommon in property matters, since it is to the benefit of all parties in land transactions to have title quieted. Nevertheless, had the Court decided to duck this issue, it might have done so on the grounds that this was not a true "case or controversy" as required by the Constitution. Indeed, in his concurring opinion Supreme Court Justice William Johnson all but accused the attorneys, one of whom was Joseph Story, of bringing a phony suit before the Court.

But the parties and the courts seemed determined get a final resolution of the case. Even after the circuit court held Fletcher's title to the land valid, he appealed to the Supreme Court in 1810; the lower court decision could not undo the Georgia rescission, but the Supreme Court could.

The issues, aside from the fraud and chicanery marking the entire Yazoo scheme, were far from one-sided. In repealing the grant, the state had done its duty, for few would have argued that a state could not remedy a fraud, even when agencies of its government had been party to it. On the other hand, permitting states to revoke previous grants at will would have undermined faith in state obligations, especially in regard to disposal of public lands, the fuel behind western expansion. Moreover, in addition to Georgia and the four companies that had received the grants, third parties, who had purchased land in good faith reliance that the companies had clear title, also had to be protected. Although common law had long held that one cannot sell what one does not own, a related rule in transactions of negotiable instruments protected the rights of third parties, the holders in due course, who bought in good faith, even over the rights of the original owners.

Marshall could easily have decided that the Court should not hear this case. The fraud surrounding the case, the collusion between the parties, defects in the pleadings, and the fact that the federal government had already acquired most of the Yazoo lands and had provided a remedy for claims, allowed ample room to duck the case. Furthermore, the general antagonism of states toward the Supreme Court for impinging on states' rights made it a politically volatile case. To uphold the original grant, as the Court would inevitably do, meant to affirm a land transaction based on fraud and bribery. Moreover, by upholding the original sale the Court would strike down the Georgia rescission, which was popular because it represented a clear rejection of dishonest government. No matter how the Court ruled, influential groups would be offended. In addition, other states also faced challenges to their disposal of public lands, and while a definitive rule would remove the clouds of uncertainty from these transactions, several of the justices, including Marshall, owned stock in speculative land companies (as did many wealthy and politically powerful Americans), and thus they could be open to charges of acting in their own self-interest.

As he so often did, Marshall picked a careful path through the political briar patch. Title raised in a private contract between individuals, he averred, constituted the only question before the Court. "It would be indecent in the extreme, upon a private contract between two individuals, to enter into an enquiry respecting the corruption of the sovereign power of a State." By declining to look behind legislative motives, the Court exercised a judicial restraint that reinforced the growing notion that one branch of government should not encroach upon another except when constitutionally required. To have examined the Yazoo frauds would have inundated the Court with suits from hundreds of dissatisfied interest groups, each claiming it had been done in by corruption. A later chief justice, Morrison Waite, succinctly summed up the Court's view in *Munn v. Illinois* (1877): "For protection against abuses by legislatures, the people must resort to the polls, not to the courts."

But if the Court would not consider legislative motive, it could look at the constitutional implications of the results. A legitimately elected assembly had approved, for whatever reasons, certain grants of land; a subsequent legislature, for its own reasons, had rescinded the grants. The second act had destroyed the validity of bona fide contracts made in good faith reliance upon the original grants. The purchaser, Marshall wrote, "has paid his money for a title good at law, he is innocent, whatever may be the guilt of others, and equity will not subject him to the penalties attached to that guilt. All titles would be insecure, and the intercourse between man and man would be very seriously obstructed, if this principle be overturned." The Georgia land grants, once accepted by a grantee, constituted a contract, and the Section 10 prohibition against impairment of contract forbade the state from revoking the grant, as it had done in the 1796 law.

The Supreme Court had previously invalidated a state law, and Marshall's opinion also had precedent in its interpretation of how the Contract Clause would limit state action; the circuit court decision in *Vanhorn's Lessee v. Dorrance* (1795) had utilized the clause to void a legislative act. The importance of *Fletcher v. Peck* lay in its impact on the vast land speculation then rampant throughout the country. With settlers streaming westward, land changed hands frequently, and clear title depended on the validity of original grants. Virginia, for example, had granted large tracts of land in what later became Kentucky, and the original grantees moved quickly to sell off the lots. The lack of decent survey maps, the absence of local land offices to register deeds, the shortage of qualified conveyancers, and the large number of squatters would clog federal and local courts in Kentucky with property cases for decades to come. *Fletcher* at least provided a rule by which the courts could try, even if not always successfully, to clear away the morass of disputed claims.

Marshall's opinion went beyond the simple defense of contract, however, and invoked the natural law doctrine of vested rights, thus raising the issue above the relatively simple level of enforcing an agreement. When "a law is in its nature a contract, when absolute rights have vested under that contract, a repeal of the law cannot divest those rights." The Constitution not only protected rights long acknowledged as inhering in the possession of property, but through the Contract Clause, it also assured the right to acquire property. Justice William Johnson, in his concurring opinion, disagreed with Marshall over the breach of contract, but supported the result because rights had been vested under terms of the original grant that could not be taken away.

Much of the import of the case seems to have been lost on contemporaries, who claimed that once again the Court had impinged on states' rights, and thus validated, in effect, the fraud perpetrated on the people of Georgia. Only in later years did the larger issues emerge. The Court had explicitly stated that it would defer to the legislature in terms of policy and would not look behind the face of the statute to examine reasons or conditions, even if corrupt, that had impelled the state to act. This of course might be read as supportive of state legislatures. This support of legislation, however, had to be complete. Thus, once having acted, the legislature through its contract had vested rights not only in the original parties, but in subsequent holders as well, and here the Court would restrain state action. By its recognition that commerce, in land or goods, would be disrupted if parties could not rely on the validity of a state's word, Marshall helped smooth the way for the growth of an interstate economy in which parties to transactions in one state could rely on deeds done elsewhere.

## Public Land Cases

In *Federalist No. 44*, James Madison had predicted that the Contract Clause would "inspire a general prudence and industry, and give a regular course to the business of society." The Marshall Court shared this hope, and its various decisions provided certain rules upon which the growing commerce of the nation could depend. One knew after *Fletcher*, for example, that a legislative grant, no matter how bad a bargain, bound the state to its word. The Court emphasized this point in several decisions that helped transform contract from an aspect of private law into a central constitutional tenet of the nineteenth century.

Two years after *Fletcher*, the Court had to deal with whether states could be bound by the terms of colonial grants. In 1758, the colonial government of New Jersey had awarded a tax exemption to lands owned and occupied by the Delaware Indians. In 1801, the Indians sought and received permission to sell these lands, and in 1803, they sold the property and moved to western New York. Neither the statute authorizing the sale nor the deed of transfer mentioned the tax exemption, but in 1804, the state repealed the exemption and assessed the new owners for taxes dating to the time they had taken possession. In *New Jersey v. Wilson* (1812), Marshall determined that there had been a valid contract between the Delawares and the colony and that the tax exemption had been granted, at least in part in consideration of the tribe's cession of lands it claimed in southern New Jersey. Although the exemption had been for their benefit, it adhered not to the persons of the Indians but to the land itself. Although New Jersey could have conditioned its approval of the sale upon surrender of the exemption, it had not done so, and the purchasers had taken the land with all its rights attached, including the exemption from taxes.

The Marshall Court's devotion to protecting land grants was, in part, a function of the importance of land speculation at the time. Many people, including justices of the high court, speculated in land. Justice James Wilson had wrecked his career through his failed speculations, and Chief Justice Marshall owned extensive holdings both in Virginia and New York land companies. Wilson has been criticized for the Court's excessive zeal on behalf of land speculators at the expense of the state's inherent right to tax property within its borders. In fact, New Jersey ignored the decision and continued to collect taxes on the former Indian land. Other cases also found the Court upholding property rights against the states. In *Fairfax's Devisee v. Hunter's Lessee* (1813), as we have seen, Justice Story voided Virginia's confiscation of Tory lands, which, in addition to permitting an alien to inherit, confirmed the claims of speculators to 300,000 acres of the finest land on the eastern coast. A few years later, Story again invalidated a Virginia property law. In colonial days, Virginia had granted lands to the Anglican Church for its support; following the Revolution, the state had disestablished the church and repealed the grants. In *Terrett v. Taylor* (1815), Story followed Marshall's fusion of the Contract Clause and vested rights to strike down the repealing act, fearing it would "uproot the very foundations of almost all the land titles in Virginia."

In denying states the right to tax or control certain properties, the Court can be said to have sided with agrarian capitalists—or vested economic interests—against the democratic will of the people acting through their legislatures. The undemocratic consequences of the land contract cases can be seen in *Green v. Biddle* (1823). In 1791, when Kentucky separated from Virginia, the new state promised not to invalidate land titles granted under Virginia law. But the Old Dominion had by then developed a complex land law designed, in part, to protect the interests of absentee owners. As pioneers streamed across the Appalachians, neither they nor the few lawyers in Kentucky understood the intricacies of that law, nor did they find any evidence that the virgin lands in Kentucky that they settled belonged to someone else. Some farmers purchased what they believed to be valid titles, settled on the land and improved it, only to discover they owned neither the land nor the improvements. Untutored in the arcane mysteries of conveyance, they easily fell prey to unscrupulous speculators. Other settlers, believing the untouched wilderness to be free, took up land without benefit of deed, assuming that their success in taming the forests provided sufficient evidence of their ownership. The Kentucky legislature soon found itself caught between its earlier promise to Virginia and the political pressure of thousands of its citizens who demanded protection from absentee claimants. Kentucky enacted a series of laws prohibiting claimants with Virginia titles from taking land unless they reimbursed the actual settlers for improvements made on the land.

The constitutionality of these laws had been argued several times, and became a focal point for both states' rights sentiment as well as for anti-Court feelings in the South and West. Although sensitive to the frontier opposition, the Court nonetheless believed the constitutional issue clear and, following the economic and legal arguments of its earlier decisions, invalidated the Kentucky laws in *Green*. Kentucky had undoubtedly broken its word to Virginia, but the records of the Constitutional Convention were silent on whether the Contract Clause extended to agreements between sovereign states. Nor did anyone, with the exception of the Virginia landowners, question the irrationality and unfairness of that state's convoluted property laws.

For once, Marshall's famed political intuition failed him. He permitted the case to be decided with three of the seven justices absent, and could only win over two of his brethren in voiding the statutes. Justice Johnson, much to Jefferson's satisfaction, entered a strongly worded separate opinion that, although avoiding the word, amounted to a dissent. Given the Court's apparent failure to provide a definitive decision, Kentucky refused to abide by *Green,* and passed further legislation to uphold squatters' rights. Other frontier states followed suit, since failure to protect the interests of their inhabitants against the claims of eastern titleholders would have seriously impaired western expansion.

*Green* is of a piece with the Court's insistence in other cases that a state's pledged word could not be broken, or else the fabric of national commerce would be fatally weakened. The fact that such promises resulted from fraud or a misunderstanding of the consequences made no difference; the Court would not look into the circumstances surrounding the decision, nor did it exist as a superlegislature to remedy current inequities.

The Court's refusal to look behind the terms of the contract, while certainly sound judicial practice, nonetheless opened it to continued charges of favoring large speculators against the interests of the common settlers. A good example can be seen in *United States v. Arrendondo* (1832), one of a series of cases growing out of the Adams–Onís Treaty of 1819, which transferred control of the Floridas from Spain to the United States. The treaty called for the United States to recognize any land grants in the ceded territory made by the king of Spain prior to January 24, 1818. Before the Senate could ratify the treaty, Spanish officials issued a host of back-dated grants to American speculators. Recognizing the precarious nature of these claims, the new grantees went into federal courts to confirm their titles. Applying the rule of *Fletcher v. Peck,* the Supreme Court upheld their claims and refused to acknowledge the patent fraud involved, although fraud had long been an accepted reason in common law to void contracts. In the related case of *United States v. Clarke* (1834), the Court put the burden of showing such fraud on the plaintiff; the Court itself would deal only with the record presented to it. Without proof of fraud in that record, the claimants' titles remained, and they ultimately took possession of several million acres of land in Florida and the Louisiana Purchase.

The public land cases made up a relatively small portion of the Court's business during the Marshall years, yet they exerted an influence out of proportion to their numbers. The land market constituted one of the most important outlets for venture capital in the early republic and involved many of the "better" people, including a number of government officials. Marshall and his brethren, although sensitive to the needs of the individual settler, expressed more concern with developing national commercial ties and in upholding the rights of men engaged in interstate commerce against what they saw as the arbitrary political maneuverings of the states.

When property rights were not at stake, however, the Court proved fairly flexible in its public land decisions. In *Marshall v. Currie* (1807), the Court melded Kentucky law and Virginia practice in validating a land claimed registered with only vaguely marked boundaries. Justice Johnson noted "the necessity of liberality" in order "to save the early estates acquired in that country." In *Bodley v. Taylor* (1809), the Court took judicial notice of the primitive conditions of settlement and the legal illiteracy prevalent on the frontier. But, as in so many cases involving state laws, those that restricted state legislatures drew the most attention and enhanced the portrait of the Court as an advocate of property rights against the common man.

# The Emergence of the Corporation

The development of the business corporation stood second only to land enterprise in the commercial growth of the country. The corporate form traced back to medieval times, and by the sixteenth century, it had assumed its basic character—an association of private individuals who were desirous of achieving specific goals, usually private, political, or charitable in nature. Several of the colonies had been settled under the aegis of a corporation, and some cities, like New York, were created as corporations, and some institutions such as hospitals and colleges were founded as corporations. But the use of a corporate charter for purely business purposes in both Great Britain and America dates only to the late eighteenth century. In 1780, barely a handful of business corporations existed in the United States; twenty years later, American states had chartered 317 corporations, primarily to build turnpikes, canals, and bridges. Indeed, only sixty-seven of these early corporations were banks and insurance companies.

In the early nineteenth century, the growth of the corporate form mushroomed; nearly 1,800 had charters by 1817, with most of them for public utilities, like roads, or for banks or insurance companies. While a few states passed "general incorporation laws" in the early part of the century, most states required special legislative acts until after the Civil War. In Pennsylvania, for example, the legislature granted 2,333 corporate charters between 1790 and 1880. But as William J. Novak notes, "only 8 percent went to manufacturing or general business firms," while 88 percent went to "transport, utility, and financial corporations."

The corporation proved remarkably appropriate to the economic needs of the new nation. In a country perennially short of capital, it allowed numerous individuals to pool limited resources, while at the same time limiting each person's liability to his share of the original investment. Alexis de Tocqueville perceived the corporation as the ideal instrument for a democratic society. In an age of relatively weak government, at both the state and federal level, the government could not always perform various economic functions, nor could it call upon an aristocracy to do so, as Europe could, since no established hereditary elite existed. But the government, through the grant of corporate charters with specified powers and privileges, could encourage private individuals to band together and undertake socially desirable activity, promising them the opportunity to share in the potential rewards purchased by their risks. Often, state governments invested in these corporations in a sort of public/private joint effort.

The corporate charter provided an interface between public policy and private activity, and in order to work properly, needed the sanction and protection of law. Although the corporation per se extended back several centuries, the new business form had very little in the way of established law to guide its activities; moreover, it had to fit into both the needs of a federal system of government, as well as into those of a democratic society. In developing from a rather primitive and limited associational activity into the dynamic linchpin of American economic expansion and growth, the corporation benefited from one of the most creative periods of legal development in history. Legal tradition collided with and then merged with new interests to form the basis of a corporate law that helped fuel the nation's transformation from an agrarian outpost to an industrial giant in the late nineteenth century.

During the Marshall years, both the law and the economy underwent rapid change.

The reliance on English law, already weakened by the Revolution, eroded further as American judges and legislators looked more and more to their own precedents and social needs than to the earlier cases and treatises of the mother country. While the Supreme Court served as a powerful force in the development of an American law, state courts during this period did not view Supreme Court decisions as necessarily binding. As often as not, they cited cases in other state courts to buttress their own decisions. It would be several decades before all state courts willingly accepted the judgment of the nation's highest tribunal as even equal to their own in defining American law. In many areas of private law, the law of domestic relations and most criminal law, there was little federal jurisprudence or jurisdiction. To this day, the states reign supreme in these areas.

Since states issued virtually all the new corporate charters, most of the litigation and resulting creativity in fashioning new law occurred in state courts (a phenomenon we shall examine further in the next chapter). Questions of the internal governance of the corporation—sale and transfer of its property, liability of its agents and shareholders, its relation to the chartering legislature—was usually determined by state law in state courts. The Supreme Court, the forum of ultimate appellate review, heard many of these issues, and thus joined with state courts in fashioning corporate law. In some instances, the high court confirmed doctrines previously enunciated in state courts; at other times, it took the lead in espousing new doctrines. The Court's greatest influence, of course, could be found in those areas involving corporate activities in interstate commerce, where the power of the national government took precedence, or where actions of the states seemed to contradict the contract clause of Article I. Thus, as Professor R. Kent Newmyer has suggested, in making corporate law, the Court fused nineteenth-century notions of politics, economics, and morality into an "authoritative ideology . . . the ground rules for free enterprise."

## Defining Corporate Rights

One of the first corporation cases to come before the Marshall Court raised the issue of whether a corporation derived its legal nature from the individuals who had joined in the enterprise or from the legislature that had granted the charter. If the former, then the rights of private property would shield its operations from public scrutiny and control; if the latter, then the legislature retained power to oversee the activity, and the corporation could be viewed primarily as an instrument of political purpose. In *Head and Amory v. Providence Insurance Company* (1804), Marshall explicitly defined a corporation as public in character, and thus affirmed legislative dominance. The corporation, he wrote, "is the mere creature of the act to which it owes its existence; its powers are only those which the legislature granted to it." The opinion reflected the historic experience under mercantile governments of corporations designed primarily to effect quasi-public activities such as colonization or road-building. It also reflected the fact that corporations were in fact created by the legislature, and could only exist if the legislature chose to create them. As corporations shifted to production of goods and services—that is, toward what had traditionally been considered private activity—the Court would eventually change some of its jurisprudence in this arena. But, as

William Novak has demonstrated, until after the Civil War, the Supreme Court, as well as most state courts, followed the general rule that corporate charters be construed "in favor of the public." Of course, that still left enormous latitude in determining what was in the best interest of the "public."

In *Bank of the United States v. Devaux* (1809), the Court faced the question of what was the "citizenship" of a domestic corporation. In circumstances that are practically identical to those of *McCulloch v. Maryland* a decade later (see Chapter 11), Georgia had taxed a local branch of the first Bank of the United States, and upon refusal of bank officials to pay, it had seized the cash. The bank sued in federal court, claiming that the company and its officials were citizens of Pennsylvania. Georgia pleaded that the bank, as a body corporate and politic, did not constitute a "citizen" under terms of the Judiciary Act of 1789, and therefore could not avail itself of the diversity of citizenship jurisdiction of federal courts. After losing in lower court, the bank appealed to the Supreme Court.

Marshall first established that the bank could sue as an entity by virtue of its incorporation; then he addressed the "much more difficult" question of whether it had access to federal courts on the basis of diversity of citizenship. Under English law, corporations could be treated as inhabitants of cities for certain purposes, and in *Mayor of London v. Wood* (1702), the judges had ruled that courts could look beyond the corporation to identify its individual members.

Marshall noted the silence of the Constitution as well as the Judiciary Act on the legal status of corporations. But a "constitution, from its nature, deals in generals, not in details. Its framers cannot perceive minute distinctions which arise in the progress of the nation, and therefore confine it to the establishment of broad and general principles." As an abstract legal creature, the corporation would have to be "excluded from the courts of the Union." Only by looking beyond the charter to the individuals comprising the corporation could jurisdiction be permitted, and this Marshall proceeded to do. Although it is an artificial and invisible creature of the law, a corporation is also an association of individuals. While their citizenship does not transfer to the corporation, common sense as well as common law made it clear that they had legal rights both as individuals and in association. Since they had the right to sue as individuals, they retained that right as corporate members, and could invoke diversity jurisdiction in federal courts if they resided in a state other than that of their adversary in litigation.

The idea of looking behind the charter to the individuals eventually proved unworkable, and corporations ultimately secured a citizenship of their own for purposes of federal jurisdiction. But initially, the concept of transfer of rights enabled the Court to extend other privileges as well.

One troublesome area was the extent to which a state could revise, or abolish, a corporate charter. This raised a federal question, because Article I, Section 10 of the Constitution prohibited the states from "impairing the Obligations of Contracts." If a corporate charter was a "contract" between the state and those who formed the corporation, then this clause might prevent the state from altering the corporate body after the charter was granted.

In *Terrett v. Taylor* (1815), the question arose whether a state legislature could revoke a charter. In 1784, the parishes of the Episcopal Church in Virginia had incorporated, partially in order to administer the glebe lands whose revenue had been used prior to the Revolution to support the parsons and charitable work. Two years later, Virginia revoked the charter, and ordered the parishes to appoint trustees to sell the lands and use the proceeds to support the poor.

Writing for the Court, Justice Story differentiated between public and private corporations, a distinction hitherto unrecognized in American law. Public corporations included counties, towns, and cities, and as little more than administrative conveniences for the state, the legislature could revoke or modify their charters practically at will. But private corporations enjoyed the protection of both natural and constitutional law, and therefore, once chartered, their property and their rights extended beyond the legislative reach. To allow otherwise, Story maintained, would be "utterly inconsistent with a great and fundamental principle of a republican government, the right of the citizens to the free enjoyment of their property legally acquired." "We think ourselves standing upon the principles of natural justice," he observed, "upon the fundamental laws of every free government, upon the spirit and the letter of the Constitution of the United States, and upon the decisions of most respectable judicial tribunals, in resisting such a doctrine."

The Court could hardly have held otherwise, for if it had allowed the legislature to revoke the charter, it would have called into question the validity of title to large tracts of land in Virginia. Story's reasoning, though, received scant attention, especially the distinction he made between public and private corporations. In another 1815 case, *Town of Pawlett v. Clark,* Story enlarged on these ideas. In this case, a Vermont town was attempting to recover land it had been given by the state, which had originally been bestowed by the king to the Anglican Church. A voluntary association of Episcopalians, without a charter, claimed the land, but since no church had been consecrated in Pawlett at the time of the royal charter, Story reasoned that the property remained in abeyance. The state, therefore, as successor to the Crown, could legitimately dispose of it by granting the land to the town. Without a charter, the church had none of the legal rights afforded to incorporated groups. Without ever mentioning the Contract Clause, Story in effect brought corporate charters within the protection of Article I, Section 10. These two cases set the stage for one of the great corporate and contract cases of the Marshall Court, *Trustees of Dartmouth College v. Woodward* (1819).

## The *Dartmouth College* Case

In 1754, the Congregational clergyman Eleazer Wheelock founded a school to train Christian missionaries for Indians, as well as to provide advanced education for Indians. He secured support from English benefactors—including Lord Dartmouth—who became trustees of the institution, and in 1769, he received a royal charter from King George III, incorporating Dartmouth College. By the terms of the charter, Wheelock became president for life, with the right to name his successor. The college trustees, however, retained the power to remove the president and to fill subsequent openings on the board. When Wheelock died in 1779, his son John succeeded him and successfully ran the school until 1810, when the trustees rejected his choice for a faculty appointment. By this time, the autocratic John Wheelock had lost the support of the trustees, which over the three decades of his presidency had become more assertive. In 1816, the trustees fired Wheelock. By this time, the controversy had become highly politicized, with Republicans backing Wheelock and Federalists arrayed behind the trustees.

In 1816, under the prodding of the newly elected Republican governor of New Hampshire, William Plumer, the legislature amended the royal charter, reorganized the board of trustees, and created Dartmouth University, with Wheelock as president. New Hampshire's resolution of the controversy agitated colleges throughout the country. It had been bad enough to have Wheelock and the trustees airing dirty linen in public, but to have the legislature intervene boded nothing but ill; no college could be sure that tomorrow a hostile legislature would not annul its charter.

In 1817, the old trustees operated Dartmouth College, with ninety-five students, while the new trustees operated Dartmouth University, with only fourteen students. The old trustees then hired attorneys, including the school's most famous alumnus, Daniel Webster, to challenge the new law. The trustees sued William Woodward, the college's secretary and treasurer, who had gone over to the new university, to recover the college's seal, charter, and record books, which Woodward had taken with him. The state superior court found for Woodward and the new trustees and rejected the college's arguments that the legislature had violated vested rights, the New Hampshire constitution, and the Contract Clause of the federal Constitution. Attempting to follow Story's dichotomy, it held the college to be a public corporation and therefore subject to state regulation. The old trustees then turned to the U.S. Supreme Court in 1819.

Marshall's opinion for the majority is one of his most audacious, and at the same time, one of the most poorly reasoned of all his major decisions. He relied heavily on Story's differentiation in *Terrett v. Taylor* between public and private corporations; in fact, Justice Bushrod Washington, concurring with the chief justice, thought the doctrine laid down earlier by Story answered the questions so completely as to render further discussion practically superfluous. Story, however, had never mentioned the Contract Clause explicitly, but had relied on a vested rights theory, recognizing the difficulty of proving corporate charters to be contracts within Section 10.

Marshall's proof involved more fancy legal footwork and obfuscation than sound analysis. He ignored the strong argument of counsel for the new trustees that gratuitous charters lacked consideration, a universally recognized element of any contract, and assumed, without proof of any sort, that all the necessary conditions for a contract existed. He had to concede that the constitutional prohibition "never has been understood to embrace other contracts than those which respect property"; those involving civil institutions and marriage, for example, stood outside the constitutional pale. Nonetheless, Dartmouth College, as a "private eleemosynary institution" constituted a private corporation, and its charter was a contract within the protection of Article I, Section 10. New Hampshire could, therefore, neither amend, repeal, nor in any way abridge the rights conferred by that charter.

Although Marshall's sweeping language would ultimately be used to bring all private corporations within the protection of the Contract Clause, its manifest weaknesses led Story to take the unusual step of writing a concurring opinion. To begin with, he knew and understood the case far better than did the chief justice; Governor Plumer had, in fact, named Story to the new board of trustees, a position that the justice had never accepted. Story evidently believed he would have a chance to decide the case in the first circuit, and together with Daniel Webster, counsel for the old trustees, he had devised a plan by which all the issues would be tried. Webster filed three separate suits in New Hampshire federal district court, any one of which would have allowed the district judge to rule on the repealing legislation. Story and the district judge would then disagree in circuit so that the case could be taken to the Supreme Court, but with Story's opinion there to guide its decision. Before any of these cases came to trial, however, the Supreme Court had accepted the original case from the state court and decided the issues.

Story, as he told Webster, wanted to frame the opinion in its broadest possible application, involving not just the impairment of contract, but natural law and vested rights as well. Story evidently anticipated many of the weaknesses in Marshall's argument, especially his confusion over what constituted a contract, and there is evidence that Story made a number of suggestions to the chief justice that the latter incorporated in his final written opinion, which differed considerably from what he delivered orally. Nonetheless, the argument remained so weak that Story felt constrained to write a separate concurrence; taken together, the two opinions effected their joint purpose— to erect legal barriers against arbitrary state interference with rights granted by charter to private corporations.

The two opinions, in fact, tell us much about the two men and their approach to the law. Marshall, bold and assertive, glossed over technical problems. His statement of constitutional principles, while forceful and broadly construed, lacked substantiation; he could not, for example, cite a single precedent to justify his equation of a corporate charter with a private contract. Marshall had been a successful practicing attorney, and there is no doubt as to his ability as the chief justice, but he apparently did not understand common law development in a number of areas. Although a brilliant legal tactician and writer, Marshall was a weak legal scholar. Story, on the other hand, proved the perfect complement to his chief's boldness. His opinion, calm and detached, lacked Marshall's powerful rhetoric, but it covered every weakness in Marshall's exposition of contract with copious detail and full citation to English commentators and appropriate English and American precedents. The introductory section provided a miniature treatise on the nature of corporate charters and the rules governing corporations.

Once a king had created a private eleemosynary corporation, Story asserted, the Crown had no more control over it except for what had been expressly or implicitly reserved in the charter. This key point provided the escape clause that made Dartmouth College palatable to the state legislatures. Marshall's opinion implied that once a state granted a charter, it could never exercise any influence or control over corporate activity, a condition that might well have led states to refuse to issue new charters, and thus retard economic growth. Story told the states that if they wanted to retain some authority over their corporate creations, they only had to pay attention to basic common law principles and include the powers they wished to reserve as explicit terms of the charter itself. This was less a suggestion than part of his overall explanation of the rights of existing corporations. Yet, this off-hand comment was powerful. "Ironically," as Herbert A. Johnson concluded his study, *The Chief Justiceship of John Marshall, 1801–1835*, this minor point "alerted states to include such reservations in their future issuance of corporate charters."

Story expressed himself as well pleased with the opinion, and he predicted

> the vital importance, to the well-being of society and the security of private rights, of
> the principles on which that decision rested. Unless I am very much mistaken, these
> principles will be found to apply with an extensive reach to all the great concerns of
> the people, and will check any undue encroachments upon civil rights, which the pas-
> sions or the popular doctrines of the day may stimulate our State Legislatures to adopt.

Neither Story nor Marshall believed that the legislatures had no power over corporations; rather, once having determined the relationship through the terms of the
charter, they could not alter it at will. Story's escape clause assumed that assemblies
would carefully determine the limits as well as the powers they wished to confer on
private corporations, and those seeking charters would recognize that they had to accept such restraints as part of the cost of securing the grant.

In an ideal world, perhaps, such deliberation would occur, but political reality
hardly conforms to a legal paradigm. Legislatures wanted to encourage economic
growth; they wanted corporations to undertake tasks for the benefit of society, and
those seeking charters soon discovered that a little lobbying could usually eliminate
any undesirable features in the charters. Once having secured the legislative grant, they
had all the power of Marshall's rhetoric and Story's reasoning to protect them constitutionally from further legislative interference. The economic history of the country
shows that business learned this lesson well. Both the excesses and the achievements
of American industry trace, at least in part, to the contract protection Marshall and
Story wrought in *Dartmouth College.*

## Bankruptcy

The 1819 term saw three great probusiness decisions that reined in the power of the
states. As we have seen, *Dartmouth College* brought corporate charters within the protection of the Contract Clause, while *McCulloch v. Maryland* upheld the Constitutionality of the Second Bank of the United States, curtailed state taxing powers, and
gave the federal government powers, if it ever chose to use them, to undertake internal improvements. The third case, *Sturgis v. Crowinshield,* involved the validity of a
New York bankruptcy law, and when the Panic of 1819 developed later that year, the
case proved of more than passing interest to the business community.

Richard Crowinshield, an old acquaintance of Story's from the days when they
had both been Jeffersonian activists, had moved to New York, where he led a rather
spectacular life before eventually failing in business. In November 1811, he invoked
the aid of a recently enacted state bankruptcy law, listed his creditors, assigned his
property, and secured a discharge from his debts. One of the creditors, Josiah Sturgis,
who had lent Crowinshield over $1,400 a few weeks before the insolvency statute had
been enacted, opposed the discharge. Crowinshield returned to Salem, Massachusetts,
where he recouped his fortune in textiles. Meanwhile, however, Sturgis filed suit to recover on the note at the October 1816 term of the circuit court in Boston, claiming that
the bankruptcy law, when applied to debts made prior to its passage, unconstitutionally impaired the obligation of contract. Sturgis was not the first to challenge the law.

In 1814, Justice Bushrod Washington had delivered a circuit court opinion holding that a similar law did not apply to contracts made prior to passage. Then, in April 1817, Justice Brockholst Livingston, on circuit in New York, ruled that the law could be applied retroactively. Story, aware of the conflicts, arranged that he and the district judge would divide in the Sturgis case without an opinion, and thus carry it to the Supreme Court for resolution of the issues.

The business community agreed on the need for clear and equitable rules governing insolvency, but the Court had to determine whether Congress or the states should enact bankruptcy laws. Article I, Section 8, gave Congress the power to establish "uniform Laws on the subject of Bankruptcies throughout the United States," but the Constitution did not specify whether Congress had sole power in this area, or if the states shared concurrent powers. Congress had so far failed to act, but the states, responding to commercial needs, had passed legislation. If the Court decided that Congress had exclusive power, then all state bankruptcy laws would be invalid; if, in the absence of a federal statute, the states enjoyed concurrent power, then the Court had to determine if the New York law applied retroactively to contracts that were made before its passage.

Both justices Bushrod Washington and Joseph Story believed that the Constitution reserved bankruptcy powers solely to the federal government, while justices William Johnson, Brockholst Livingston, and Gabriel Duvall maintained that the states could legislate, so long as Congress chose not to do so. (Justice Thomas Todd did not participate in the case due to illness.) On February 17, 1819, Marshall delivered the opinion of a unanimous Court, holding that the grant of national bankruptcy power did not void state legislation. Nonetheless, the Constitution did set a limit on state powers. The Contract Clause did not permit states to alter the substance of a contract, but only the remedy for its breach. Specifically, the New York law could not affect contracts made prior to its passage.

Marshall's forceful words on the Contract Clause led many to misinterpret what he meant. Some observers believed he practically prohibited state bankruptcy laws, and Story hoped that the ambiguity would speed passage of a federal statute then being debated in Congress. Others interpreted the chief justice's opinion to mean that state laws remained valid until or if Congress acted, which is undoubtedly what he intended. To have voided all state laws without a federal statute in place would have seriously disrupted commerce, a prospect Marshall could not have countenanced. But too many questions, such as the effect of state laws on future debts, remained unanswered, and despite Marshall's sermon on the sanctity of contract, these issues would have to be resolved by the Court before long. That opportunity came in *Ogden v. Saunders* (1827).

The *Ogden* case signaled the beginning of the Court's retreat from the militant economic nationalism that had marked the first quarter-century of Marshall's tenure, and it found the chief justice for the first time in dissent from his brethren on a major constitutional issue. Marshall's emphasis in *Sturgis* on the Contract Clause's prohibition against retroactivity led many states, following the Panic of 1819, to enact insolvency laws specifically applying only to debts contracted after passage. Presumably, this would place a restriction on all future debts, and thus escape Marshall's holding that the states could not alter the substance of a contract. In *Ogden*, by a 4 to 3 vote, the Court endorsed this interpretation, but the six opinions filed displayed not only the divisions of the bench on this case, but, as Justice Johnson admitted in his majority opinion, that they had existed at the time of *Sturgis* as well. Story and Bushrod Washington had muted their argument for sole federal power in return for striking down retroactive application; Johnson and the other Jeffersonians had agreed on condition that nothing be said about the effects on future debts.

The four majority justices arrived at their conclusion by somewhat different paths. Washington argued that contracts incorporated existing law as part of the contract itself; bankruptcy statutes, therefore, provided not only remedies, but became part of the substance of the contract. Johnson and Robert Trimble (who had replaced Todd) argued that states always had the authority to prescribe the nature of obligations of contracts made under their jurisdiction. Johnson wrote: "The rights of all must be held and enjoyed in subserviency to the good of the whole. The state construes them, the state applies them, the state controls them, and the state decides how far the social exercise of the rights they give us over each other can be justly asserted." A decade later the Court would apply this logic to the development of state "police powers."

To Marshall and Story, this smacked of heresy, undermining the whole structure of vested rights and the sanctity of contract that they had labored to erect. While conceding that the Contract Clause permitted states to amend the means by which contracts could be enforced, the chief justice attacked the majority position for destroying the substance of contract and warned that it would virtually eliminate any meaning of the Contract Clause. Marshall derived scant satisfaction when Johnson joined the conservatives to rule that a state's bankruptcy law could not apply to a debt owed to a citizen of another state, since this would result in a "conflict of sovereign power, and a collision with the judicial powers granted to the United States." In essence, *Ogden* did not overrule *Sturgis*. States could still pass bankruptcy laws in the absence of a federal statute, but they could not apply them retroactively to contracts made before their passage. Future obligations (which had been skirted in *Sturgis*) would be encompassed by the laws, but not those owed to citizens of another state.

## Conclusion: The Marshall Court's Legacy

With *Ogden,* the Marshall Court began a slow retreat from the unrestrained judicial nationalism and probusiness attitudes it had espoused in the first quarter of the nineteenth century. The Court, despite the opposition of the Jeffersonians, had utilized the Constitution as an instrument of national unification and provided the federal government with tools it could use effectively to manage the growing country. Its interpretations of the Commerce and Contract Clauses had been of a piece with its nationalism, since Marshall and Story, like Hamilton, saw commerce as a cement binding the various interests of the country into a unified, dynamic whole. The foundation had been established for both the states and the federal government to promote massive corporate expansion, but the strictures of protecting private property limited interference with or regulation of corporate enterprise. Liberated by free trade and aided by uniform commercial laws, economic development would, they hoped, erase sectional interests while at the same time preserving the liberty that derived from the vested rights of property.

No doubt the times were right for the early Marshall Court's nationalism and expansive view of the Constitution. The War of 1812 and western expansion amplified the glow of independence. Starting in 1819, however, economic adversity and sectional conflict initiated four decades of growing tension, straining the bonds of the Union beyond the breaking point. In the last years of his tenure, Marshall faced increased opposition both from within the Court and from the political forces unleashed by Jacksonian democracy. Many of the tools he forged lay unused as the country sank ever deeper into sectional strife, but they remained available, to be called on after the Civil War, when the nation burst forth in a new surge of nationalism and economic expansion.

# For Further Reading

For a short history of the Marshall Court, see Herbert A. Johnson, *The Chief Justiceship of John Marshall, 1801–1835* (1997). Many of the sources cited in the previous chapter, especially on the Marshall Court, are relevant here as well. In addition, see C. Peter Magrath, *Yazoo: Land and Politics in the New Republic, The Case of Fletcher v. Peck* (1966); and Francis N. Stites, *Private Interest Public Gain: The Dartmouth College Case, 1819* (1972), both of which have excellent analyses of the cases and their backgrounds. Benjamin F. Wright's older work, *The Contract Clause of the Constitution* (1938), is still useful. One should also look at R. Kent Newmyer's fine biography of *Supreme Court Justice Joseph Story: Statesman of the Old Republic* (1985).

On the issues of property, see Jennifer Nadelsky, *Private Property and the Limits of American Constitutionalism: The Madisonian Framework and Its Legacy* (1990); and James W. Ely, *The Guardian of Every Other Right: A Constitutional History of Property Rights* (1992). On regulation in America, an important revisionist work is William J. Novak, *The People's Welfare: Law & Regulation in Nineteenth-Century America* (1996). Novak shows that despite protection for corporations in cases like *Dartmouth College*, throughout the next half century the states successfully subjected corporations to the police power, just as they regulated other aspects of society. Peter Karsten, *Heart Versus Head: Judge-Made Law in Nineteenth Century America* (1997), meanwhile, argues that at the state and local level judges often used their "heart" as well as their "head" in cases involving the human costs of industrialization and economic growth.

For the growth of the corporate form, see the appropriate sections of Lawrence M. Friedman, *History of American Law;* and Morton J. Horwitz, *Transformation of American Law.* Some specialized studies reflect the larger patterns, such as Louis Hartz, *Economic Policy and Democratic Thought, Pennsylvania, 1776–1860* (1948); and John W. Cadman, Jr., *The Corporation in New Jersey: Business and Politics, 1791–1875* (1949). Land speculation is explored in Shaw Livermore, *Early American Land Companies* (1939). See also, E. M. Dodd, *American Business Corporations Until 1860* (1954); and Oscar and Mary Handlin, "Origins of American Business Corporations," 5 *Journal of Economic History* 1 (1945).

# 13

# A Law Made for the Times

ONE OF THE most famous sentences in legal literature is Oliver Wendell Holmes's statement in his book *The Common Law* (1881), that law resulted not from logic, but from "the felt necessities of the times." No better example can be found of this thesis than in American law in the first half of the nineteenth century. Enormous changes in the economy necessitated alterations in traditional legal doctrine to accommodate the spirit of entrepreneurial expansion. While statutes outlined broad public policies, they usually lacked the means for enforcement or for applying the vague goals to specific circumstances; these tasks, as a result, often fell upon the courts. Law did not, of course, create new markets or industries, but it facilitated and legitimized the vast transformations taking place. The law created the circumstances that allowed for what the great legal historian J. Willard Hurst called "the release of creative energies."

## Debate over the Law

The general anti-British sentiment following the Revolution had extended, as we have seen, to English law as well (see Chapter 9); initially, some states forbade litigants from even citing English precedents or writings in their arguments. But in the years immediately following the Revolution, most American lawyers knew only English law. Even in the early nineteenth century, most lawyers learned their craft by reading Blackstone, either in a British version or in the Americanized version edited and expanded by the Virginia jurist St. George Tucker and published in 1803. Thus, for better or worse, English law remained the starting point for American law, although for fifty years it faced hostility from both Anglophobes and democratic radicals, the latter objecting strenuously to a court system staffed by professionally trained judges, in which plaintiffs and defendants could only argue their cases through hired attorneys.

At the other end of the spectrum, conservatives viewed law as the only foundation for civilization and the protection of private property. For them, the common law represented the accumulated wisdom and experience of the ages, and although they agreed with the radicals that law was often mysterious, they saw it as the mystery that accompanied majesty. Since only men learned in the law could interpret it properly, conservatives applauded the necessity of lawyers and exalted the role of an independent judiciary.

The majority of Americans recognized the need for a "rule of laws not of men" in a democratic society, and since the vast majority of free American families owned some property, or expected to later in life, they saw law as the protector of both an individual's rights and possessions. Rather than throw away their English heritage in a fit of patriotism, they supported change that would adapt the law to American conditions; in English precedents and writings, they found the tools they needed. Great Britain had begun a vast commercial expansion at the same time as its American colonies sought independence, and in the latter part of the eighteenth century, the great Lord Mansfield and his colleagues had initiated their own attack on the Blackstonian tradition. Mansfield exerted great influence in America. Many American jurists, including Joseph Story, revered the efforts of the chief justice of the King's Bench to modernize the law, especially his willingness to disregard precedent in the light of changed conditions. Other American jurists revered Mansfield for his ruling in *Somerset v. Stewart* (1772) that slaves brought into a free jurisdiction would immediately be able to gain their liberty.

## An American System

The search for a viable law system occupied a great deal of energy and thought in the early nineteenth century. St. George Tucker's edition of *Blackstone's Commentaries* (1803) began with the premise that English common law, rooted as it was in a monarchy, had to be reconciled with the emerging law of the American Republic. Similarly, James Kent's four-volume *Commentaries on American Law* (1826–1830) reflected the maturing of American law in this period.

Much of this maturing took place at the state level. By 1820, every state but Rhode Island had amended, revised, or totally rewritten its revolutionary constitution. Although variations could be found from state to state, reflecting local social, political, and economic predilections, some scholars believe that by the 1820s, an American system of law existed. It was one in which the similarities among the states far outweighed the differences.

Most states expanded their court systems in an effort to make prompt, inexpensive justice available to free adults. The typical state had at least fifteen trial court districts, each of which had three or more judges exercising civil and criminal jurisdiction. By the 1820s, the people expected that men trained in the law would occupy the bench, and the importance of lay justices of the peace diminished. Above the local court was an intermediate appellate court, which met on a schedule in the different parts of the state. Almost all states also had a "supreme" appellate court, with final judgment in matters of state law. By 1820, all but a few states provided for the publication of the decisions of their highest court, and some also printed various lower court proceedings. To remove political influence from the courts as much as possible, most states provided for an independent judiciary, if not through life tenure, then either through long-term appointments or tenure during good behavior. The principle of judicial review, attacked so vehemently by Jeffersonians in the federal courts, escaped such criticism on the state level, possibly because it was so rarely invoked before the Civil War.

The most significant aspect of this emerging American system may have been the enormous variety of subjects that came before the courts for adjudication. In the 1830s, the French intellectual Alexis de Tocqueville perceptively observed in his book *Democracy in America*, that "scarcely any political question arises in the United States that is not resolved, sooner or later, into a judicial question." A century and a half later, Grant Gilmore noted in his book *The Ages of American Law*:

> from the beginning our courts, both state and federal, seem to have been willing to answer any conceivable question which any conceivable litigant might choose to ask. And from the beginning—which is even more curious—the American people, which throughout most of our history has distrusted lawyers, seems to have acquiesced in, indeed to have enthusiastically welcomed, the arrogation of unlimited power by the judges.

The resolution of this apparent paradox derives from several factors. First, any society, even a primitive one, needs rules to govern its members' behavior and a system for peacefully resolving conflicts between them. The more complex the society, the more complex its laws, so that eventually only specialists are able to interpret the myriad rules. Although some people resent this, the majority see it not only as necessary, but as a beneficial means of ensuring uniformity and stability. These latter qualities are especially important as commerce grows, because legal predictability is an essential feature of business transactions. Finally, such widespread acquiescence in a professionally dominated legal system indicates that judges and lawyers are meeting the needs of the society; people perceive the system as operating equitably and to the general advantage of the country.

## Legal Instrumentalism

Judges did more, however, than merely dispense justice. They created law, a function common law judges had always exercised, but now in a new and dramatic manner. According to historian Morton Horwitz, during the nineteenth century, judges increasingly affected the course of social change in ways that distinguished them from earlier jurists. Rather than merely reflecting the conditions surrounding them, they consciously used the law to advance the commercial interests of the country. In doing so, they abandoned the Blackstonian concept of a common law derived from immutable principles of natural law and adopted in its place what Horwitz terms an instrumental conception of law.

Many scholars have criticized the political conclusion of this thesis—that judges were essentially the allies of the new industries and corporations. Some judges certainly tried to use their heart, as well as their head, in their decision making. And often, judges were troubled by the outcomes of some cases, which seemed to favor the powerful over the powerless. Justice William Johnson, for example, complained in *The Rabid* (1814), that "It is the unenvied province of the Court to be directed by the head, and not the heart." But, whether serving the powerful or the powerless, nineteenth-century jurists were innovators. Where eighteenth-century jurists saw their task as discovering essentially changeless general rules, American judges now sought to determine what best served the public interest in a society characterized by ceaseless change.

This, of course, had been Mansfield's goal, and had dismayed critics such as Jefferson, who noted in 1785 that judges had previously sought "to render the law more & more certain," but Mansfield had sought "to render it more uncertain under pretense of rendering it more reasonable." Reasonability, a subjective judgment, Jefferson thought belonged in the province of legislators, not that of judges. The former had responsibility for determining the consensual will of the people and enacting it into statutes; for judges to arrogate such power destroyed the distinction between the legislative and the judicial.

Yet, there could be found in the common law tradition strains that sought to enforce the popular will as perceived by the courts. Jesse Root, who edited the Connecticut reports, argued that one branch of the common law "derived from certain usages and customs, universally assented to and adopted in practice by citizens at large . . . [which] courts of justice take notice of . . . as rules of right, and as having the force of laws." Courts should notice how people conducted their daily affairs, and unless contradictory to statute or simple justice, they should conform the law to meet the expectations of society. The common law thus served as an instrument of popular will, and as that will changed, courts needed to adjust the law accordingly. Chief Justice Nathaniel Chipman of Vermont, although in many ways a conservative, reflected this view when he claimed that in England, precedent served to support a static society; in America, new conditions required new law, based on reason and principle, two extremely subjective criteria.

This instrumentalism expressed itself in a number of areas. The highly technical forms of pleading gave way to simple statements of litigants' claims or defenses, with forms of action correspondingly streamlined. Where colonial judges had deferred to juries in determining questions of both law and fact, they now either gave more specific charges on what the law required or reserved questions of law wholly as their own decisions. For the first time, courts ordered new trials when judges decided that jury verdicts ran counter to the weight of testimony. More and more, counsel argued that precedent provided no guidance from the past, since the issues confronting the court had previously not existed. Lawyers sought, successfully, to have judges abandon older precedent and create new law—and new precedent—responsive to current needs. Ironically, these judges were often masters at using common law reasoning and analysis, even as they abandoned common law precedent.

## Changing Views of Land

Perhaps in no other area could change be seen so clearly as in the rules governing property. In England, land had been the scarcest of commodities, and therefore the most valuable. It had served as the cement binding loyalty of vassal to lord in feudal times, and in the more recent past, it had become the mark of power and status. Land, of course, had to be used somewhat; tenants grew food on it or grazed herds, and some lumber might be cut from the forests. But ideas of developing land for commercial purposes, or trading it as one might grain or cloth, had remained foreign to the English mind and to English law.

In America, land was a resource available in seemingly boundless supply, and from the beginning, settlers viewed land as a commodity to buy, sell, or trade. As public policy facilitated the removal of Indians, either by treaty or war, Americans moved on to new land, often ahead of any kind of territorial government. In the generation following the Revolution, the arcane mysteries of land conveyancing gave way to simple, mass-produced instruments of transfer. The quit-claim deed, which made no promises about good title or quiet enjoyment, proved handy in wide-open frontier markets, where people often bought land, not to build homes on, but for speculation. They expected to sell it just as soon as prices rose, possibly within a few days, and they cared not if there were clouds upon their title, since they passed on the title—and the clouds—as quickly as they could. This is one example of how a changing law allowed for the "release of energy," as western migrants cleared forests and plowed fields with only marginal concerns about the niceties of land titles.

Property, more than any other branch of the law, is local in its nature; land does not move, its *situs* is fixed. As a result, one would expect to find more local variations here than in commercial law, where uniformity across broad markets is desirable. While all states saw some reform, older, more settled areas, such as Massachusetts and Virginia, could cling to traditional forms so long as they did not disturb the market. On the frontier, the older forms never gained a toehold. For example, the common law prohibited aliens from inheriting land, a rule that made no sense in a nation of immigrants. The dynamics of the market in land required as many people as possible to invest in order for prices to rise. As a result, strictures against property owning by aliens and women fell quickly; land law in all states, no matter what form it took, had the primary aim of keeping the market open.

The market in land remained a constant throughout the nineteenth century, but the major focus of speculation moved steadily westward with the line of expansion. The settlers came behind, and while viewing land as a commodity, they also saw it as a means of livelihood, as a resource on which to build. If common law rules regarding transfer made little sense on the frontier, the restrictions on use proved equally irrelevant. Americans did not want to preserve land in its pristine state; they demanded a law that permitted them to exploit the one resource they had in abundance.

## Water Usage

One area in which the reform of property law can be clearly seen is in water law, what lawyers call riparian rights. Water, and water power, were essential for agriculture, as well as for manufacturing, mining, and transportation. In England, the law of water rights had developed over centuries, with the clear aim of guaranteeing all owners along a stream their fair share of water. While any owner could take water for natural needs, no owner could obstruct or divert the flow, thus depriving his downstream neighbors of their supply. The only exceptions to this rule were when all owners consented to the diversion or when so-called prescriptive rights existed, in which a blockage or diversion of long standing sanctioned its continuation. This perfectly reflected the English view of land not as a productive asset, but as an estate to be quietly enjoyed by its owner.

Americans however, had different needs from those of the English landed gentry. They required water to irrigate fields where the natural flow was insufficient, and they needed water to power mills to grind their grain, saw their lumber, and by the 1830s, run their factories. By mid-century, they also needed water to facilitate mining in the West. But to divert water for irrigation or block it to drive a mill wheel ran against English precedent. Almost from the beginning, American courts, faced by a choice between the older law and economic development, decided in favor of development.

As early as 1783, in *Shorey v. Gorrell,* the Supreme Judicial Court of Massachusetts held that even without long usage conferring a prescriptive right, the law could not prevent a newcomer from blocking a stream. Although the Commonwealth temporarily backed away from this radical doctrine, other states soon took it up. In *Palmer v. Mulligan* (1805), New York's court held that an upstream owner could dam up water for mill purposes, even if it caused "inconveniences" to an entrepreneur who had previously built a mill downstream. Speaking for the New York court, Judge Brockholst Livingston, who would soon to be appointed to the U.S. Supreme Court, clearly recognized that preserving the common law, reserving only to the lowest downstream owner the right to erect a mill, would hinder development. As a result, "the public, whose advantage is always to be regarded, would be deprived of the benefits which always attend competition and rivalry." In this analysis, the court can be understood as instrumentalist, as it helped create a competitive economy and refused to allow a vested interest (the old mill owner) to prevent new industries from developing.

However, this case also illustrates the emerging notion that all waterways belong to the public. Under English law, waterways were "public" only if navigable and affected by the ebb and flow of the tide. Inland waterways were subject to wholly private control and usage. As William Novak has noted, the United States moved away from this rule, as "courts and legislatures moved steadily toward making most American rivers, navigable *in fact*, susceptible to public jurisdiction and state power. In some jurisdictions, mere 'floatability'—the ability of a stream to carry logs or other products—became the measure for public easements and regulatory claims." This was particularly important as development moved further inland, away from the ocean.

*Palmer v. Mulligan* illustrates this concept. The New York court noted that "The erection of both dams are nuisances," and thus the court doubted that one nuisance creator could "complain that the defendant's nuisance is injurious to their nuisance." The key to the New York decision was the right of the public to the waterways. Anyone might build a dam on a public waterway, if it did not interfere with the public's use of the river; similarly, all dams might be prohibited as nuisances, if they interfered with the public's use of the river.

The developmental view of property did not go unchallenged. In his 1824 treatise *Watercourses,* for example, Joseph Angell denounced the New York decisions as "contrary to authorities, and obviously unjust." In *Tyler v. Wilkinson* (1827), Justice Joseph

Story, while riding circuit, seemingly reaffirmed the traditional rules of natural flow, and a number of subsequent decisions cited *Tyler* in supporting an eighteenth-century conception of undisturbed property rights. But Story, although he may have agreed in principle with Angell, nonetheless recognized the need for some development in order not to stifle growth. He did not, therefore, hold that there could be "no diminution whatsoever, and no obstruction or impediment whatsoever . . . for that would be to deny any valuable use." Story articulated a utilitarian view of legal rules: law had to meet the social and economic needs of the people it served. By seizing upon his concession that the law permitted diversion or stoppage for "valuable use," judges could, and more often than not did, find the justification needed to depart from the traditional prescriptions. By the Civil War, nearly all state courts had adopted a reasonable use test to support development.

The utilitarian view dominated the Massachusetts Supreme Judicial Court during the tenure of Chief Justice Lemuel Shaw, one of the most influential of the pre–Civil War state judges. In *Cary v. Daniels* (Mass. 1844), Shaw spoke not of the quiet enjoyment of property, but of the "beneficial uses of a watercourse." In the balancing of rights, Shaw looked not only to the competing claims of rival landowners, but more importantly, to the "usages and wants of the community." If the community benefited from development, then some owners might have to suffer losses, but as far as the law was concerned, this would be *damnum absque injuria,* "damage without legal remedy."

Most of the early cases involving diversion or mill blockage imposed, as some judges saw it, mere inconvenience upon downstream owners. The states, and even earlier, the colonies, recognizing the economic value of mills, passed a variety of statutes to encourage their construction. But mills affected not only the flow of water, they often flooded neighboring lands, rendering them useless. Many of the statutes included procedures to compensate owners of the flooded property, but in the eighteenth century, courts normally refused to interpret the statutes as barring the traditional common law remedies for trespass and nuisance. In the late 1700s, Massachusetts passed legislation in response to mill owners' pleas that common law remedies imposed too heavy a penalty upon them, and other states soon copied the Bay State's laws. The legislature not only encouraged development of water power, but also turned its back on traditional notions of property. The act allowed only for compensation of damage to the productive value of the land; owners could not recover for loss of quiet enjoyment of their property.

The mill laws blurred the distinction between public and private interests. The mills, owned entirely by private entrepreneurs, had been given the protection of public policy against suits by other landowners for the loss of traditional, albeit nonproductive, values that were associated with property. "Such an invasion of private property," argued Boston lawyer Benjamin Rand, "can only be defended in a case of great public necessity and utility." As water power came to be used for manufacturing as well as agricultural purposes, the state's favoring of particular interests at the expense of others accelerated the trend to view property rights as relative rather than absolute, with the balance nearly always being struck in favor of those uses that promoted economic growth.

As we have seen, for the most part the states took the lead in the development of water law. But there is also a parallel in the federal story. The Northwest Ordinance declared that the "navigable waters leading into the Mississippi and St. Lawrence, and the carrying places between the same, shall be common highways, forever free. . . ." This was a recognition of the public interest in the waterways, but did not overturn the common law rule for any other waterways, and did not give the national government full admiralty jurisdiction even over these waters. Initially, the federal courts stuck to the English rule requiring that public waters be affected by the tides. But in *Propeller Genesee Chief v. Fitzhugh* (1851), the U.S. Supreme Court adopted the rule that federal admiralty jurisdiction was not limited to waters affected by the tide. Chief Justice Taney said such a rule made sense in England where "there was no navigable stream in the country beyond the ebb and flow of the tide" and thus "tide water and navigable water are synonymous terms." Explicitly recognizing that inland expansion and steamboats had altered the nature of water commerce, Taney rejected the Marshall Court precedent in *The Thomas Jefferson* (1825), and declared that it would be "inadmissible" to accept a definition of commerce that limited "public rivers in this country to the tide-water rivers." Thus, admiralty jurisdiction was to "depend on the navigable character of the water, and not upon the ebb and flow of the tide." Navigability did not depend on the tide, but on the reality of the waterway.

It is also worth noting that in the Rocky Mountains and Far West, a new kind of water law developed. The doctrine, sometimes called the Arid Region Doctrine, allowed for the private development of water resources without regard to the needs of other users or the public. This did not affect large rivers, but it did affect streams and smaller water sources, some of which might have been "navigable" under the floatation principle. The notion in the West was that water was so scarce that the first user had the right to take all he needed, even if that left no water for a subsequent user. Without such a rule there would never be enough water for any economic development. But under such a rule, first users would be able to develop land and mining resources, which would benefit the community as a whole, even if it limited or harmed other users.

Illustrative of this rule was the California Supreme Court's decisions in *Irwin v. Phillips* (1855). Here the court allowed Irwin to divert a stream from its natural course to facilitate his mining operation. The court understood that this violated traditional notions of water rights. This was appropriate, the California justices argued, because "Courts are bound to take notice of the political and social condition of the country which they judicially rule." California, with its rich mineral resources and poor water resources, had to allow for new rules. The miner staking out a claim "must take it [the land] as he finds it, subject to prior rights." If water existed he could use it, as Irwin did, and no subsequent settler could undermine the rights he acquired through this usage, as Phillips had tried to do.

# Taking of Land

Public policy and its implementation by the courts did not just passively favor one set of claims against another; rather, the law changed positively to give developers tools to aid them in their enterprises. By allowing builders the use of the powerful legal weapon of eminent domain, for example, the law permitted entrepreneurs to force landowners to give over portions of their property in the name of the public good. Where eminent domain had previously been applied only to takings by the state, it could now be used by private developers as well.

The now familiar concept, embodied in the Fifth Amendment, that private property should not be taken for public use without just compensation, was then a relatively new invention. In the eighteenth century, so little property had been taken for public development that it hardly mattered, and only colonial Massachusetts seems to have paid owners for land taken to build roads. As late as 1800, only three state constitutions had provisions analogous to the Fifth Amendment, and in 1800, a majority of states still did not provide compensation for the taking of private land for public use.

Although not required by the Fifth Amendment, and in most cases not required by their own constitutions, many states nonetheless began to provide for some compensation in their turnpike acts. Still, at least until the 1830s, compensation for public takings remained not a legal obligation, but rather an expression of legislative kindness or political expedience. Even where statutory provisions allowed for compensation, courts interpreted them narrowly, arguing that all property existed only at the sufferance of the sovereign, and therefore could be taken to further the public good.

The problem of taking land became more widespread and important with the construction of canals and railroads and involved not only rights-of-way, but also damages suffered by landowners adjacent to the undertaking. The building of the Erie Canal, for example, gave rise to hundreds of suits both during and after construction. The courts eventually extended a sovereign-like protection to private companies, relieving them of liability for damages that were incident to economic development. In nearly all cases, traditional doctrines gave way to tests of social utility. As one judge put it later, in *Losee v. Buchanan,* (N.Y., 1873), the older rules of quiet enjoyment and undisturbed use "are much modified by the exigencies of the social state. We must have factories, machinery, dams, canals, and railroads. They are demanded by the manifold wants of mankind, and lay at the basis of our civilization."

Economic advances, however beneficial they might be, involve costs. Investment capital and its attendant risks lie with the promoter, but new enterprises affect others who have not asked for the undertaking, and who, despite incidental benefits, suffer damages to their property. Who will pay these costs? And what formula will be derived to evaluate the damages? The common law answered these questions by placing responsibility squarely on the trespasser and required nothing more than proof that the act had in fact occurred; it permitted no excuse on grounds of social utility. Nonetheless, in the early nineteenth century, American courts threw over this doctrine, and in effect immunized entrepreneurs from liability for most injuries to land resulting from development activity.

Typifying this approach was New York's Chancellor Rueben Walworth, who declared in *Lansing v. Smith* (1829), that:

> every great public improvement must, almost of necessity, more or less affect individual convenience and property; and when the injury sustained is remote and consequential, it is *damnum absque injuria,* and is to be borne as part of the price to be paid for the advantage of the social condition. This is founded upon the principle that the general good is to prevail over partial individual convenience.

The great public necessity here was the construction of the Erie Canal, which revolutionized the state and the national economy. This necessity allowed the state to regulate rivers, harbors, and private lands for the public welfare.

By this reasoning, nearly all damages, both immediate and consequential, could be charged not to the offender, but to the social good. In effect, the state acting on its own, or through private developers, could regulate or take property to enhance the welfare of the general public. Illustrative of this was Chief Justice Lemuel Shaw's ruling in *Commonwealth v. Tewksbury* (1846). The defendant had removed sand from his own property, which included an ocean beach, in violation of a law passed to protect Boston harbor. Shaw upheld the law as a reasonable police regulation. As historian William Novak summed up the case: "Shaw held that the beaches and embankments of public ports and harbors were 'of great public importance,' subject to extensive regulation."

## Emergence of Tort Law

Economic development affected all types of property. Just as the law regarding real property changed to encourage growth, other traditional rules on damages and compensation also had to be altered in the face of new social and economic imperatives. In this process, what had hitherto been a relatively minor branch of the law mushroomed; tort law in America is the child of industrialization.

A tort is a civil wrong by one person against another or against another's property; prior to the mid-nineteenth century, it involved primarily issues of trespass, assault and battery, and libel and slander. Torts constituted such a minor area of law that not a single treatise—English or American—appeared on the subject before 1850. Negligence, which eventually came to be the dominant form of tort action, received barely a nod from Blackstone, and Nathan Dane's *General Abridgement and Digest of American Law* (1824) casually treated it as a residual category, those torts that could not be "brought conveniently under more particular heads."

Machines changed all this. Not only could they damage property, but human beings as well. According to Lawrence Friedman, "one specific machine, the railroad locomotive, generated, on its own steam (so to speak), more tort law than any other in the nineteenth century. The railroad engine swept like a great roaring bull through the countryside, carrying out an economic and social revolution; but it exacted a toll of thousands, injured and dead." No developed body of law existed in regard to this type of activity, so judges did not have to worry about rejecting precedents. They had a relatively clean slate to write on, and their efforts clearly reflected a commitment to fostering entrepreneurial growth.

Negligence law began with cases of damage to land, and at the beginning of the nineteenth century, English courts ruled that recovery could not be made for public officials' damages to land that resulted from public works authorized by Parliament, even though similar acts by private citizens would make them liable. American judges initially resisted this idea, apparently unwilling to draw such a distinction between public and private acts. But the first step down this road eventually came when American courts began extending immunity to private companies acting under a mandate from the state, or in which the state held a portion of the stock (a not infrequent occurrence, since states and municipalities often bought stock as a means of encouraging and subsidizing desirable undertakings). In *Spring v. Russell* (Me. 1831) the Maine Supreme Court granted a wholly private canal company full immunity from damages. Just because "a plaintiff may have sustained a serious injury to his property, consequent upon the voluntary act of a defendant," did not lead to the conclusion that "he has a right to recover damages for that injury." Such acts, according to the court, operated to the benefit of the community, even if some individuals suffered as a result. By the 1840s, courts routinely ruled that when private companies acted to carry out a legislatively authorized task, they enjoyed immunity from the inevitable injuries caused by such work. Theodore Sedgwick, an influential New York law writer, declared in his *Treatise on Damages* (1847) a "general rule . . . that where the grantees have not exceeded the power conferred on them, and when they are not chargeable with want of due care, no claim can be maintained for any damage resulting from their acts."

This new attitude of damages as being incidental to the advancement of the social good differed markedly from previous views of tort as antisocial behavior that could rarely, if ever, be justified. The goal of earlier law, to regulate and control in a noncriminal manner actions frowned upon by society, now had to be rethought if one declared such damages to be a necessary cost of progress. In some instances it would have been so unjust to force deprived parties to bear the whole cost of communal advance that states provided for compensation. But negligence proved to be a far more important means for balancing progress and private rights. If parties acted with due care, as Sedgwick maintained, they enjoyed immunity; but if they behaved negligently, even in pursuit of a worthwhile goal, they would be liable for damages.

This distinction wrought a revolution in legal thinking. Earlier tort law had not allowed for excuse; a person either did or did not do a particular proscribed act. If proven guilty of committing the act, he or she remained strictly liable for the consequences, regardless of intent or lack of it. Under common law, a person acts at his or her peril. The new doctrine looked to the cause of the injury and the intent behind the action, and held parties liable only for damages resulting from fault. If one took reasonable precautions, or if an accident occurred that could not have been foreseen or prevented by exercise of due care, the law imposed no liability. "No liability without culpability" became the rule, and it seemingly met the need for a moral justification of rules, as well as provided a means to sustain economic growth.

This rule had important consequences in several areas. First, by relying on concepts such as reasonable care and reasonable use, it introduced objective criteria into tort suits. How would, to use the famous phrase, "the average man, the man of ordinary intelligence and prudence," be expected to act? This led to the transfer of many issues in tort cases from the hands of juries, which would normally be sympathetic to the claims of their aggrieved neighbors, to judges, who were attuned to the needs of entrepreneurs, and who made the determination as questions of law. Damages caused by negligence led to compensation for the injured party, though the law often limited the extent of liability.

The determination of damages now became a central issue for the courts. The rule soon developed that "the extent of the injury is the legal measure of damages," and lawyers devoted enormous energies to the mathematical calibration of how much harm had been caused by particular acts. A plaintiff injured by a defendant's negligence could recover what had been lost, but could not profit from the injury. This concept also led courts to deny punitive damages, even in cases where it could be shown that the defendant had acted not only negligently, but maliciously as well. While such a punishment would satisfy one's natural desire to secure retribution against those acting immorally, the nineteenth-century legal writer and jurist Theron Metcalf noted, "it is impracticable to make moral duties and legal obligations, or moral and legal liabilities, co-extensive." Punishment for immoral behavior remained a matter of public concern, and therefore had no place in private law.

This new regime did not, however, leave people wholly unprotected in their property. A rising insurance industry provided at least some protection for property owners. A New York case, *Ryan v. New York Central Railroad* (1866) illustrates this point. In 1854, the railroad negligently caused a fire in its own woodshed. Sparks from that fire eventually caused Ryan's house to burn down. The New York court held that the railroad was not liable, because it was unforeseeable that a spark on the railroad's property could cause a fire 130 feet away, where Ryan's house had stood. The court noted that a fire could spread from house to house to house, and it would be intolerable to make the railroad financially responsible for all such losses. The court noted and "a man may insure his own house or his own furniture, but he cannot insure his neighbor's building or furniture." The answer to urban growth, and industrialization, was insurance, in which individuals took precautions to protect themselves from the dangers that came with progress.

## Master and Servant

In the early and mid-nineteenth century, most judges and legislators accepted that some types of property bore a higher proportion of the costs of economic progress than others, or that individuals had to protect themselves from remote dangers caused by the negligence of people distant from themselves. These concepts were acceptable, perhaps, because relatively few people were harmed by them. But far greater social cost was involved when progress was measured in terms of life and limb. One might resent the loss of one's property, but such losses rarely proved disastrous, and in terms of overall benefits, the community (including those who bore the costs) came out ahead. But how could one replace an arm or leg or eye? How did a family cope with its breadwinner disabled or killed by injury? How did the law provide in these instances for those who paid such a terrible price for progress?

Prior to industrialization, tort law never had to deal with such problems. In an agricultural society, few personal injuries could be attributed to the negligence of employers, since most farmers, even tenants, worked for and by themselves. Accidents, of course, happened on farms and in small shops, but any negligence was usually on the part of the victim; there was no one else to blame, and therefore no need for legal remedies. The old law of master and servant did make the master responsible for any harm perpetrated by an employee while acting in the capacity of an agent. "If an inn-keeper's servants rob his guests," wrote Blackstone, "the master is bound to restitution."

The idea of a master (or employer) being responsible for the acts of his employee survived into modern law insofar as it affected innocent third parties. But not until the twentieth century, as a result of Progressive reform, did employers assume liability for the injuries suffered by their workers on the job (see Chapter 26). In the period of industrialization, judges fashioned a trio of defenses that served generally to immunize employers from liability for job-related accidents: the fellow servant doctrine, contributory negligence, and assumption of risk.

Under the fellow servant rule, a worker stood responsible for the negligence of other employees that resulted in his own injury, on the theory that he should acquaint himself with the bad habits of his coworkers and even encourage them to behave more prudently. This might have made sense in small, preindustrial workshops, but it seemed totally divorced from reality in large mills or railroads that employed hundreds, perhaps thousands of people. The second employer defense, contributory negligence, served to shift liability if any fault could be found in the conduct of the worker. For example, in a later case in Arizona, a railroad engineer had been forced to work thirty hours straight, in violation of a state law, and as a result, had fallen asleep on the job, causing an accident in which he had been injured. The engineer had continued to work only because of the threat of dismissal, but the court held him contributorily negligent anyway. He had a free choice, the judges said, of cooperating or terminating his employment, and by choosing to cooperate, he became responsible for the results. Dangerous or even illegal conditions did not vitiate the third defense, assumption of risk. If a worker knew of dangers related to the job and still accepted employment, the law held that he had assumed any attendant risks. *Volenti non fit injuria* ran the ancient maxim, "that to which a person assents is not an injury."

Massachusetts Chief Justice Lemuel Shaw forcefully expressed these doctrines in *Farwell v. Boston & Worcester Railroad* (1842), a case that influenced judges in every other state. Farwell, an employee of the railroad, had lost his hand in an accident when a switchman had failed to do his job properly, which caused Farwell's train to run off the tracks. Farwell sued the railroad because of the negligence of its agent. Shaw denied recovery: "he who is engaged in the employment of another for the performance of specified duties and service for compensation, takes upon himself the natural and ordinary risks and perils incident to the performance of such services, and in legal presumption, the compensation is adjusted accordingly." In modern parlance, the two parties had, through the labor contract, bargained out the various risks, and the worker, in return for higher wages had agreed to assume all responsibility for his safety and welfare, with the exception of those injuries that he could prove had been caused by the gross negligence of the employer, or from risks that the employer had hidden from him. If injured, the workman was thrown onto his own resources, or if he had none, his family could apply for the pittance provided by the poor relief.

Shaw also developed the theory that the workers were better able to police the dangers of the job than management. Shaw believed it was up to the conscientious or "watchful workmen," in Shaw's language, to report negligence. Peter Karsten argues that, in fact, many workers did this. But, such watchfulness was not always possible, and many workers doubtless did not want to report on their neighbors and friends, and see them fired. Watching was also often not possible. Farwell hardly could have stopped his train at every switch to inspect the work of the switchman.

There was a danger, however, both in taking the law literally and in ignoring its consequences. These doctrines socialized the economic impact of railroads and factories by theoretically spreading the cost across the wider community. In fact, the costs fell upon a particular group that was ill equipped to bear them and that had little political power with which to protest. As a result, during the latter half of the nineteenth century, laboring groups came to see the courts as their enemy and the law as a tool of the industrial interests that exploited them. The support for entrepreneurial development that marked American law before 1850 grew into a powerful ideology after the Civil War, and labor's perception that it had been forced to pay, both in sweat and blood, for the industrial growth of the country was not totally wrong.

While many American judges consciously shaped the law to support development, harsh doctrines did not always operate as mercilessly as in the *Farwell* case. Many judges created exceptions to the rule, finding that various fellow servants were actually more like the agents of the employers. Moreover, courts allowed injured workers to sue supervisors, who often had some assets or whose losses might be covered by the employer. As Peter Karsten has argued, courts created exemptions based on such categories and concepts as the "vice principle," the "superior servant," the "different department," and the "subcontractor" to reduce the impact of the fellow servant rule. Similarly, judges modified the notion of assumption of risk with exception based on the failure of employers to provide "safe tools," a "safe worksite," a "competent servant," or for "extraordinary risks." The modifications were not universally applied, and were less common in New England than elsewhere, but they do illustrate the complexity of both legal change and the categorization of judge-made law.

Legislatures also reacted to the harsh laws of industrialization. As early as 1855, Georgia statutorily modified the fellow servant rule, and over the next half-century, a number of other states reformed judge-made law and imposed a limited liability on the employer. Moreover, the growth of large corporations, with absentee owners, combined with the steep rise in industrial accidents after 1865, led many judges to seek more equity in the law. In *Parker v. Hannibal & St. Joseph Railroad* (Mo., 1891), a Missouri judge spoke of the "hardship and injustice" of the fellow servant rule, and approvingly quoted a federal judge, who in *Gilmore v. Northern Pacific Railroad* (C.C.D. Ore., 1884) noted the modern tendency to mitigate the rule whenever possible, so as to place upon the employer "a due and just share of the responsibility for the lives and limbs of the persons in [his] employ." By then, industrial accidents were claiming 35,000 lives a year and inflicting two million injuries. For far too many people, this enlightened attitude developed too late.

In general these rules, especially fellow servant and assumption of risk, favored entrepreneurs at the expense of workers, and certainly shifted some of the costs of industrial accidents from investors to workers. If an unskilled worker was injured by the negligence of a fellow unskilled worker, the injured worker could not seek compensation from the employer, and while he could sue his fellow worker, that worker would be unlikely to have any assets—he would be, in modern language, judgment proof. Thus the cost of the injury would be borne entirely by the worker and his family.

Ironically, this rule was less useful to the industries in the South, which depended heavily on slave labor. If the slaves were rented, as was often the case, the courts usually allowed the owners to sue the renters for the value of any injured slaves. Thus, the cost of the injury was borne by the industry—often a railroad, steamboat, or mining company, or an iron manufacturing operation. On the other hand, if the industrial employer owned the slave, then of course the loss of the slave was borne entirely by the stockholders. The slave states also could not implement the concept of "watchful workmen" for slaves, because slaves could never be allowed to report on the poor behavior or skills of fellow workers if they were white.

## Commercial Law

Businessmen and their lawyers in this era, responding to the needs of the market, fashioned a commercial law to facilitate their transactions, creating new legal devices or altering older tools, resulting, as one observer noted, in "a law made for the times." In fact, it went beyond that, laying the foundation for the growth and triumph of industrial capitalism.

Underlying commercial law is the concept of a market that, simply defined, is a forum in which particular goods or services can be exchanged, either for money or for other goods and services. A market may be local or international, depending on the commodities and those seeking them. In the eighteenth century, most American markets could be characterized as local, involving limited, identifiable goods and limited, identifiable traders. The nineteenth century saw the emergence of national and international markets in fungible commodities, and the rules that had governed local trade had to be altered or abandoned to fit new demands. Few statutes existed, since legislators preferred to leave the workings of the marketplace to those engaged in it. When merchants turned to the law to enforce or negate their agreements, judges looked at market customs and essentially ratified them through common law. In some areas, such as credit and banking, the political process exerted great influence, but for the most part, the courts fashioned commercial law not in the light of great, immutable principles, but rather, to facilitate merchants in pursuit of their business.

## The Corporation

The law facilitated the rapid growth of the era's most important business device, the corporation. Nineteenth-century entrepreneurs had quickly realized that the corporate form provided an efficient structure for organizing and financing their ventures. It facilitated raising funds from a larger pool of investors, an especially attractive feature for those engaged in banking and insurance. The firm could continue in business despite the death or withdrawal of individual members, and under the law, it enjoyed many of the rights and privileges of real persons. The *Dartmouth College* case, for example, extended the protection of the Contract Clause to corporations. The main roadblock in the early development of the corporate form involved the time limits common to most charters, as well as restrictions on corporate activities. Early charters often did not give equal voting rights to each share of stock; some grants, moreover, placed a limit on the number of votes by any one stockholder regardless of the amount of stock controlled.

Eventually, the corporate charter assumed the characteristics and powers that have remained common to this day. The principle of one vote for each share became the norm. Limited liability, which restricted the obligation of investors to the amount of capital they paid in, was not universal; the 1814 charter of the Mystic Manufacturing Company of Connecticut held stockholders responsible in their private capacity for corporate debts. But limited liability, the greatest attraction of a corporation to potential investors, came to be a standard feature. Standardization of the means of doing corporate business, in fact, led to the great change in securing charters. As the corporate form adopted general practices in terms of proxy voting, liability, unlimited duration, and modes and times of meetings, these could all be embodied in standard clauses in standard charters. State legislatures, besieged with hundreds of requests for charters, began passing general incorporation acts that made it possible to secure a charter from an administrative officer by filing an application and paying a fee. New York passed the first general incorporation law in 1811, and some other states soon followed suit. However, many important industrial states, such as Pennsylvania and Illinois, did not adopt such laws until after the Civil War.

Moreover, late in the century, many legislatures annually passed hundreds of special acts to create companies or give existing companies special rights and franchises. These special incorporation acts not only made the creation of businesses more costly than under general incorporation acts, but they also set the stage for corruption of the legislative process.

Even after the advent of the general incorporation acts, many entrepreneurs continued to press legislatures for special charters with additional benefits or privileges. Before the Civil War, special charters remained the rule, even in those states with general incorporation laws. But in the 1840s, public alarm led many states to pass constitutional provisions severely limiting legislative power to grant special charters. The Louisiana constitution of 1845, for example, prohibited special charters except for political or municipal purposes. Nonetheless, corporations had no dearth of friends who viewed them as extremely beneficial to the public interest. When New Jersey debated tightening up its charter rules, one delegate declared that corporations "have done more to increase the prosperity of our State than anything else. Let the legislature grant all that may apply, if the object is to benefit the community."

As corporations undertook ever more varied operations, the law sought to adapt. The rather thin law relating to corporations in the eighteenth century had reflected the reality of corporations created for a single purpose, either quasi-public or charitable in nature. Charters, therefore, had been strictly construed, and any venture beyond the specific purposes allowed were declared *ultra vires*, beyond authorization, and could subject the company to forfeiture of its charter. But as companies expanded the scope of their operations, courts correspondingly expanded their interpretation of the powers granted in the charters. Initially, judges read implied powers into clauses nominally restraining corporate activity. Before long, however, lawyers began drafting more expansively worded provisions that imposed few if any restrictions on the firm's activities.

# Sales

Other areas of the law also responded to changing economic conditions. The law of sales had been fairly simple in the eighteenth century, since most sales took place in local markets between a small number of merchants, and the law dealt primarily with the time and manner in which the title, or ownership, of specified goods passed from one hand to another. The intent of the parties governed the law; title passed when they intended it to pass, even if delivery or payment had not yet been made.

Such law worked well in local markets, where people who knew each other dealt at arm's length with identifiable goods; the law assumed that both parties understood the workings of the market as well as the governing customs and documents. The law did favor the seller to a small degree, but not to a disproportionate extent. The common law of sales, for example, included the doctrine of caveat emptor, "let the buyer beware"; the rule grew out of the not unreasonable assumption that buyers, being knowledgeable about the market and its customs, would normally exercise caution. In Pennsylvania, a buyer had accepted a horse with a "defluxion from the nose at the time of the bargain," since the seller had assured him that it was a minor ailment that was typical of colts. The horse, in fact, was seriously ill, and the buyer sued to recover the price. In *McFarland v. Newman,* (Pa., 1839), Judge John B. Gibson refused the plea, sternly declaring that "he who is so simple as to contract without a specification of the terms, is not a fit subject of judicial guardianship."

Caveat emptor as thus applied may have seemed a harsh rule, but as Judge Gibson noted, otherwise there "would be a stop to commerce itself . . . [through] the terror of endless litigation." As markets expanded, any particular buyer or seller would in all likelihood be a middleman, a link in the chain of distribution from original producer to the ultimate consumer. While it undoubtedly favored sellers, the rule put a stamp of finality on each transaction in the link. Caveat emptor, although long known in the common law, did not gain its preeminent place until the nineteenth century. Older doctrines of sales had held that "a sound price warrants a sound commodity," an equitable notion that supported an implied warranty by the seller of the quality of the goods. Around 1800, both English and American courts abandoned this doctrine; only express warranties could be the basis for recovery, and the Supreme Court gave its imprimatur to this doctrine in *Laidlaw v. Organ* (1817).

It should be noted that caveat emptor did not reign supreme everywhere. Louisiana maintained its civil law tradition of an implied warranty of soundness when goods were sold.

## Negotiable Instruments

The necessity for finality in commercial transactions can also be seen in relation to negotiable instruments, which became crucial elements in the development of a national economy. A negotiable instrument is a promise by one party to pay money or goods to another, the bearer, and that can be transferred to a third or subsequent party. Money is the most negotiable form of bearer paper, but checks, notes, and bills of lading also serve as media of commerce. The valid transfer to a third party terminates all obligations between the original parties. Thus if A promises to pay B $100 and signs a note to that effect, and B sells the note to C, A now owes the $100 to C, and has no further duty to B. In other types of assignments, the buyer can never receive more than the seller has; a buyer of land, for example, takes only as good a title as the previous owner, and inherits any charges or claims against the title. The good-faith buyer of a negotiable instrument, known as the holder in due course, however, takes full and unobstructed title. In the preceding example, assume B had borrowed money from D and had pledged A's note as collateral. If C then bought the note from B without knowledge of D's interest, he would still have clear title. D would have no recourse against C on the note, although he could always sue B on the debt.

English common law had traditionally been hostile to assignment, because it violated one of the central tenets of contract law, privity of contract. How could A be sued by C on a note originally given to B, when A and C had never bargained on the matter? Moreover, how could C ever have a better title to the note than B, the original holder? If contracts supposedly represented the will of the bargaining parties, then negotiability ran beyond the intent of the contractors. 'A' may have given the original note to B because of personal relations between them, and may never have intended that B could sell it to a third party.

The colonies had always been more sympathetic to assignment than the mother country, since the lack of hard money made it easier to do business through various forms of assignment. Courts, however, frowned upon promissory notes until the end of the eighteenth century, and held that subsequent purchasers assumed all the risks and liabilities attached to the notes. By 1800, only five states provided for full negotiability, and most continued the common law distinction between bonds (sealed promissory notes) and regular notes, with only the former enjoying full negotiability.

The Supreme Court did not originally prove receptive to negotiability either. In *Mandeville v. Riddle* (1803), John Marshall declared that without a state law making notes negotiable, federal courts could not enforce them. The chief justice treated the issue as one of applying state law and did not suggest that federal courts could independently develop a common commercial law. But William Cranch, whose lower court decision had been overruled, wrote a lengthy essay on the history of negotiable instruments that he then published as an appendix to the volume of Supreme Court cases in which Marshall's opinion appeared. There Cranch argued, contrary to nearly all historical evidence, that negotiability had always been a common law doctrine that needed no statutory authorization. "The custom of merchants," he declared, "ought not to be considered as a system contrary to the common law, but as an essential constituent part of it, and . . . it always was of coequal authority." Moreover, he added, almost as an aside, even if negotiability had not existed at common law, it had been recognized at equity.

With this weighty, although historically doubtful argument, Riddle appealed again to the Supreme Court, and in *Riddle & Co. v. Mandeville & Jameson* (1809), Marshall reversed the earlier decision, stating that a subsequent holder could recover in equity, based on "the general understanding of the transaction." The Marshall Court ignored Kentucky case law against negotiability in *Bank of the United States v. Weisiger* (1829) to validate a note on equitable grounds. No doubt Joseph Story, who would publish his influential *Commentaries on the Law of Promissory Notes* in 1845, had much to do with this decision.

More than any other jurist of his time, Story believed in the need for a uniform commercial law to promote the national economy, and in *Swift v. Tyson* (1842), he finally secured the Supreme Court's approval for federal courts to apply general commercial law as part of an alleged federal common law. This fit with Story's lifelong desire to federalize all law. As a young justice, he had favored the creation of a federal common law of crimes. Moreover, in the same term that Story decided *Swift*, he also wrote the majority opinion in *Prigg v. Pennsylvania* (1842), creating a federal common law for the return of fugitive slaves.

By this time, the need for negotiable instruments in national commerce could not be denied. Even in prosperous times, hard money remained scarce, and promissory notes offered a medium of exchange and credit that the burgeoning economy badly needed. Nonetheless, a number of states, especially in the West, distrusted the practice and hedged the use of notes with restrictions that seriously reduced their value. Surprisingly, the U.S. Supreme Court, in *Withers v. Greene* (1850), refused to override an explicit Alabama statute limiting negotiability. The state, according to Justice Peter Daniel, had the right to set limits on a contract, and new rights could not be created in violation of state policy.

*Withers v. Greene,* if allowed to stand, could have seriously blocked the arteries of commerce. As Story had conceded in his treatise, "in some States the circulation of Promissory Notes still remains clogged with positive restriction . . . which greatly impede their use and value." Under the impetus of *Swift v. Tyson,* Justice Daniel reversed himself only five years later in *Watson v. Tarpley,* holding that federal courts could impose general commercial law even if it ran counter to state statutes. Daniel seemed to elevate this general commercial law, which had never been recognized before *Swift,* to a near parity with the Constitution and federal laws and treaties under the Supremacy Clause. "Any state law," he declared, "must be nugatory and unavailing" if it denies rights secured under commercial law. In fact, Daniels went even further than Story, who in *Swift* had permitted enforcement of general commercial law only in the absence of contrary state statutes. In *Watson,* such a Mississippi law existed, but now evidently federal courts could impose general law regardless of state policy. "The question is one of general law," Daniel asserted, "and depends nowise for its solution upon local laws and usages."

The Supreme Court justices, like state judges, thus helped fashion law to meet commercial needs. A majority of states, through either statute or case law, had accepted full negotiability prior to the Civil War. The Supreme Court may have had a broader view of national commerce than did state judges or legislators, and rulings such as *Watson* may have been necessary to ensure the free flow of negotiable instruments throughout the country. But in essence, the high court justices did nothing different from what dozens of state court judges were doing—ratifying through case law the evolving practices of the market.

## Contract

The developing law in sales and negotiable instruments highlighted one of the major economic transformations of the first half of the nineteenth century—the emergence of national markets. But nowhere did the dynamics of the new economy make itself so felt in law as in the hitherto minor field of contract.

Blackstone had devoted but a handful of pages to privately negotiated bargains, and until the 1790s, contract law had been devoted to equitable remedies in tort. The action of assumpsit dealt with deceit: the plaintiff had relied upon a promise by the defendant, who had refused or failed to carry out his or her part of the agreement, whether it involved payment of monies or performance of particular duties. Equitable remedy called for the defendant either to pay the sum or to perform the duty, which in many cases called for the transfer of title to property. The law provided no damages, but merely insisted that, in the old Latin phrase, *pacta sunt servanda,* "agreements shall be kept." Some ancillary doctrines gradually arose, such as the requirement for consideration (i.e., some kind of payment) and that the agreement be in writing. Consideration bound together the crucial elements of a contract, an offer by one party and an acceptance by the other; there had to be some quid pro quo to make the bargain enforceable. The 1677 English Statute of Frauds, one of the few legislative guides to contract, provided that all agreements of certain types or involving more than a certain sum of money had to be in writing; evidence of oral agreements could not alter the terms of a written document. Although all the states reenacted the Statute of Frauds, eventually it ceased to be a strict rule and served primarily as a guide to judges in interpreting the law. Contract, more than any other branch of the law at this time, remained common law, made by judges to reflect market needs.

There is some debate among historians as to when contract as an equitable remedy for unfulfilled promises came to involve the enforcement of executory (future) agreements. Although many of the elements of present contract law can be found in sixteenth-century English decisions, the equitable concept seems to have been alive and strong through most of the next two centuries. The shift required two economic developments, the growth of extensive markets and trade in fungible commodities. So long as local merchants dealt in specific goods, a suit for specific performance met business needs. 'A' agreed to buy a horse from B for *x* dollars; B later changed his mind, and A sought a court order to require B to deliver the animal.

By 1800, however, some merchants negotiated future deals in fungible goods. *Sands v. Taylor* (1810) is one of the earliest cases demonstrating the new trend in executory contracts. The sellers had agreed to deliver a certain amount of wheat, but the buyer, after accepting part of the shipment, had refused the rest. Under the old theory, the seller would have been required to hold the balance and go to court to force the buyer to take and pay for the wheat in this particular shipment. The sellers, however, fearful that the grain would go bad, sold the remainder of the wheat in the open market and then sued the buyer for the difference between what they had received and what the buyer had contractually agreed to pay. The New York court acknowledged that no precedents existed to guide them, but found for the sellers. "It is a much fitter rule," said the court, than to require the seller "to suffer the property to perish, as a condition on which his right to damages is to depend."

*Sands v. Taylor* presaged the great change in contract law. The court recognized that merchants no longer exchanged just particular goods but speculated on future prices of fungible commodities. It made no difference whether sellers delivered one particular shipment of wheat or another; the bargain revolved around the future price of wheat. To allow the party that had guessed wrongly to renege on the deal would have been unfair. As a result, law abandoned the title theory of contract and accommodated itself to the reality of executory contracts in speculative markets. The case also indicated that equitable notions of contract no longer applied. Prior to this time, courts could set aside contracts if they found the bargain unfair, or for lack of sufficient consideration. If A agreed to sell a $100 wagon to B for $20, then changed his mind, he could often find relief in the courts. The rule of inadequacy of price, a variant of a sound price for a sound commodity, governed many suits in the eighteenth century. Now judges would not, except in cases of fraud, duress, or overreaching, interfere with private agreements, leaving it to the parties to negotiate what they considered an acceptable bargain, the proof of which would be in the written contract.

The "will theory" revolutionized contract law, since it broke away from a property-oriented theory of title exchange and from equitable remedies for tort. The purpose of contract would now be to enforce what the parties had agreed to in the context of national markets in fungible goods. Damages would no longer be specific performance or restitution but expectation damages, that is, what the aggrieved party would have gotten had the defendant not breached. The rule set forth in *Sands v. Taylor* won confirmation from the Supreme Court only eight years later in *Shepherd v. Hampton* (1818). Recognizing the existence of a national futures market in cotton, the Court held that the measure of damages when the seller failed to deliver was the difference between the contract price and the market price at which the buyer could cover his requirements. The older idea of objective or fair price gave way to a market price, no matter how high or low, if that expressed the will of the parties. Contract law existed not to promote equity but to enforce the agreement of private individuals who were freely bargaining with an eye to the future fluctuations of the market.

The influential law writers of the period soon expanded upon the will theory. Daniel Chipman, Nathan Dane, Joseph Story, and Gulian Verplanck all agreed that only subjective values could be assigned to goods. "Price depends solely upon the agreement by the parties," wrote Verplanck, "being created by it alone." Dane and Story also departed drastically from earlier notions that law should embody morality to the exclusion of other considerations. While ideally, law and morality went hand in hand, law had other mandates, including the peace of society, for which it had to look, not to virtue, but to what is practicable. The law could not enquire into the fairness of every bargain but must assume that the parties, more familiar with the customs of the market, negotiated from a relatively equal basis; if a particular agreement benefited one person more than the other, that did not concern the courts.

Unfortunately, not all contracts expressed everything that the parties intended. Poorly drawn instruments often left loopholes that one party or the other could exploit. More important, contracts assumed the customs of the market, and did not reduce them to writing. At first, courts proved reluctant to allow mercantile usage to dictate legal decisions, but by the 1820s, courts seemed more willing to take account of the business context in which contracts had been drawn. Usage could not supplant law but might serve as a guide to courts in determining the will of the parties.

## Conclusion

To look back at the revolution in commercial law prior to the Civil War is to see clearly the influence of changing economic conditions and relations upon a law created in ear-

lier, nonindustrial times. Critics may charge that the law favored the wealthy and powerful against the poor and weak, corporate entrepreneurs over individual rights. There
is no denying this, but one must recognize that the law did not create these imbalances,
and that, for the most part, judges did little more than reflect the prevailing sentiment
of the country.

Americans did not see the law as a tool for social reform or for redressing economic grievances. In an era in which laissez faire began its long domination of American political thought, courts adapted the law to permit private parties to negotiate their
business matters by and for themselves. Reflecting the social demand for economic development, the courts also struck down the remnants of agrarian legal rules that not
only did not make sense in nineteenth-century America, but that would have seriously
hindered what a vast majority of the people saw as progress. When courts did not act
fast enough, or failed to go far enough, social pressure led to legislative enactments
favoring business needs. Neither the American polity nor the free enterprise system it
encompassed ever proclaimed itself as egalitarian, and it therefore should not be surprising that courts ratified the resulting imbalances that an expanding market capitalism created.

# For Further Reading

The idea of the release of energy in law was propounded by the great legal historian J. Willard
Hurst, in *Law and the Conditions of Freedom in the Nineteenth Century United States* (1956).
This book remains a classic and is the best place to start in reading about nineteenth-century
law. Legal instrumentalism is set forth in Morton J. Horwitz, *The Transformation of American
Law, 1780–1860* (1977). This work has been modified or challenged by the work of William J.
Novak, *The People's Welfare: Law and Regulation in Nineteenth Century America* (1996);
Peter Karsten, *Heart Versus Head: Judge-Made Law in Nineteenth Century United States* (1997);
Gary T. Schwartz, "Tort Law and the Economy in Nineteenth-Century America: A Reinterpre-
tation," 90 *Yale Law Journal* 1717 (1981); and Harry N. Scheiber, "Instrumentalism and Prop-
erty Rights: A Reconsideration of American 'Styles of Judicial Reasoning' in the 19th Century,"
1976 *Wisonsin Law Review* 1 (1976). Useful discussion of contract law can be found in Grant
Gilmore, *The Ages of American Law* (1977).

For general work on this period, see Kermit L. Hall, *The Magir Mirror* (1989); Lawrence
M. Friedman, *A History of American Law* (2nd ed., 1985); and George Dargo, *Law in the New
Republic: Private Law and Public Estate* (1983).

The interaction of government and entrepreneurship to affect law is detailed in J. Willard
Hurst's classic *Law and Economic Growth: The Legal History of the Lumber Industry in Wisconsin, 1836–1915* (1964). See also the fine case studies by Stephen Salbury, *The State, the Investor and the Railroad: The Boston & Albany, 1825–1867* (1967); and Harry N. Scheiber, *Ohio
Canal Era: A Case Study of Government and the Economy, 1820–1861* (1969). Richard H. Kil-
bourne, Jr., *Louisiana Commercial Law: The Antebellum Period* (1980), does a less satisfactory
job in exploring how law furthered commercial growth.

Leonard W. Levy, *The Law of the Commonwealth and Chief Justice Shaw* (1957), is an excellent work examining the influence of a creative state judge on legal development. Wythe Holt,
ed., *Essays in Nineteenth-Century American Legal History* (1976), touches on several aspects
of this chapter. The lineage of the buyer beware concept is traced in Walton Hamilton, "The
Ancient Maxim Caveat Emptor," 40 *Yale Law Journal* 1133 (1931). Frederick Beutel examines

state legislation in "The Development of State Statutes on Negotiable Paper Prior to the Negotiable Instruments Law," 40 *Colorado Law Review* 836 (1940).

Some general works that cover more than this period are Lawrence M. Friedman, *Contract Law in America* (1965); Charles Warren, *Bankruptcy in American History* (1935); and G. Edward White, *Tort Law in America: An Intellectual History* (1980). On the business law of slavery, see Jenny Bourne Wahl, *The Bondsman's Burden* (1998); and the October 1987 issue of the *American Journal of Legal History*, which has a symposium on the business law of slavery, with articles by Robert Cottrol, Andrew Fede, Paul Finkelman, and Judith Schafer.

# 14

# Politics, Nationalism, and Competition

*The "Era of Good Feeling" • Georgia, Jackson, and the Indians • Georgia, the Indians, and the Court • Calhoun Responds to the Tariff • The Webster–Hayne Debate • The Nullification Crisis • Internal Improvements • Jackson Versus the Bank • Monopoly and Economic Expansion • The* Charles River Bridge *Case Begins • The Last Years of the Marshall Court • Chief Justice Taney • The* Charles River Bridge *Case Is Decided • Conclusion: The New Departure • For Further Reading*

THE GREAT CHANGES in constitutional and common law of the first half of the nineteenth century reflected the dramatic economic transformations taking place in the country at the time. Change often brings disappointment and controversy, and during the 1820s and 1830s, it caused much dissension. Competing interest groups needed different types of law, and until clear policies could be adopted, economic development would be retarded. But, even after such policies were developed, there would be controversies. Moreover, every policy choice had its costs. For example, the nation's emerging manufacturing sector needed economic protection, which led to higher tariffs. Tariffs were certainly constitutional for raising revenue, but were they constitutional for the purpose of protecting the economic interests of one section while perhaps harming the interests of another section? Ultimately, the debate over tariffs sparked a new interpretation of states' rights that threatened the Union.

## The "Era of Good Feeling"

The surface of good will following the War of 1812 hid dangerous problems, of which only a few could then be discerned. Slavery and sectionalism alarmed the nation during the debate over admission of Missouri into the Union, and even after the immediate crisis subsided, the issue remained a potent threat to the Union. We will examine this issue in detail in Chapter 17. However, when reading this chapter and the one that follows, it is important to remember that slavery lurked in the background of many, perhaps most, constitutional issues during this period.

The collapse of the Federalist party at the national level after 1816 led for a while to one-party rule, a state of affairs that is never healthy in a democracy. Nevertheless, party factionalism, sectional disagreements over economics and slavery, and personal rivalries and ambitions kept politics lively and vibrant. The Panic of 1819, although only a momentary interruption in general prosperity, nonetheless exposed structural weaknesses in the economy. The panic led manufacturers to demand a higher tariff, which eventually led to a constitutional crisis, which anticipated the most critical event in the nation's history—the Civil War.

Monroe's virtually uncontested reelection as president in 1820 led scholars to dub this an "era of good feeling." In reality, however, bad feelings and fears that threatened the future of the nation were readily apparent. The two most obvious issues involved slavery in the West and economic policy. One would lead to a crisis in 1819–1821 and the other in 1832–1833.

In 1819, before Monroe's reelection, Missouri sought to come into the Union as a slave state. Northern Congressmen argued that almost all of Missouri was located both north and west of the southern boundary of the Ohio River, and thus should enter the Union as a free state under the requirements of the Northwest Ordinance. Southerners argued that the Northwest Ordinance applied only to the lands of the old Northwest, and the force of the Ordinance terminated at the Mississippi River. Debate over the status of Missouri spanned two sessions of Congress before the Missouri Compromise led to the admission of Maine as a free state in 1820 and Missouri as a slave state in 1821, and to a prohibition of slavery in the territory west and north of Missouri.

The fact that Congress was able to reach a compromise on this divisive issue might have been viewed as a positive sign. However, the passionate language employed by both Southern and Northern members of Congress, as well as the sectional voting in Congress, troubled many in the nation. Thomas Jefferson wrote that the debate affected him, "like a fire bell in the night, awakened and filled [him] with terror." Jefferson might have been speaking for the majority of Southerners in Congress as well, who were shocked to learn how deeply many Northerners hated slavery.

Southern fears about slavery were further heightened a year later, when South Carolinians discovered the Denmark Vesey conspiracy in Charleston. As many as 8,000 slaves may have been ready to join Vesey, a free black who planned to seize the city, and initiate a full-scale slave rebellion in the state. Authorities in Charleston discovered the plot before it could be implemented, and scores of slaves were arrested and either executed or transported out of the state. The magnitude of the plot, combined with a series of mysterious fires in Charleston during the rest of the decade, made Southerners especially edgy.

Politics also undermined the "good feeling" of the era, as jockeying for the election of 1824 began shortly after Monroe's reelection. In 1822, the Tennessee legislature nominated Andrew Jackson; Kentucky soon put forward Henry Clay, and Massachusetts endorsed John Quincy Adams. The deep South favored Secretary of the

Treasury William Crawford of Georgia, although a paralyzing illness ultimately ended his presidential hopes. Only Crawford and Clay had what might be called specific platforms; Jackson ran as a war hero, while Adams stood as the heir to Monroe, whom he had served brilliantly as secretary of state. In the 1824 election, no candidate received a majority of the electoral or popular vote, although Jackson, with 153,544 popular votes (43%) and 99 electoral votes (38%), led the pack. Adams, running second, had 108,740 popular votes and 84 electoral votes. As mandated by the Constitution, the House of Representatives decided the election between the three candidates with the highest number of electoral votes. Clay, who had come in fourth in the election, used his position as Speaker of the House to secure the presidency for Adams against Jackson, whom he regarded as unfit for the nation's highest office.

Immediately, the Jacksonians raised cries of a corrupt bargain, which intensified when Adams named Clay as secretary of state. The bargain was probably not corrupt, in part because Adams was too honest a man, and perhaps too poor a politician, to make any useful political bargain. Clay sided with Adams because he hated Jackson; Adams chose Clay because he thought him the best man for the job.

The animosity split the old Republican party into two factions: those supporting Clay and Adams eventually became known as Whigs, while Jackson's followers styled themselves as Democrats. Still, for all their outrage, the Jacksonians never questioned the constitutionality of the procedure. Adams, undoubtedly one of the most gifted public servants in the history of the country, lacked the common touch necessary to rally great popular support, as Jackson did. At the same time, Adams lacked the skill and the stomach for political maneuvering. As a result, his broad, Hamiltonian vision of national growth led by a strong central government never had a chance of success.

The Democrats hounded Adams at every turn, and defeated nearly all his proposals. His presidency was generally uninspired and his legacy as the nation's chief executive was unimpressive. In 1828, Andrew Jackson, of Tennessee, easily defeated Adams. Jackson was the first president from the West, but in other ways, he fit in well with the presidents who preceded Adams. Like them, Jackson was a Southerner, a planter, a slaveowner, and an advocate of western expansion. Unlike all previous presidents, however, he was a self-made man, who had been born poor but risen to the highest offices of his nation.

## Georgia, Jackson, and the Indians

The dispute between Georgia and the Native Americans living in that state illustrates the difficulties confronting Adams. In 1825, a federal Indian commissioner negotiated the fraudulent Treaty of Indian Springs, by which Creek chiefs ceded some 4.7 million acres in Georgia to the federal government. Adams signed the treaty, but upon learning of the trickery, he withdrew it and secured the less stringent Treaty of Washington the following year. The Georgia legislature declared that Adams's annulment of the earlier treaty was invalid, and characterized his action as a violation of states' rights. In the agreement ceding its western lands to the national government, Georgia had been promised that the federal government would, as soon as possible, secure for the state all the Indian lands within its borders. The Cherokee and Creek tribes had resisted efforts to be moved, and Georgia used the false treaty as the lever to get Indian lands that white settlers had long coveted. Governor George M. Troup threatened to call out the militia if Adams sent in federal surveyors or did anything to prevent enforcement of the Indian Springs Treaty. Adams caved in and left the Creek to their fate.

Andrew Jackson's position on Indian affairs reflected the attitude of the West in general—Indians should get out of the white man's way. In the earlier Creek and Seminole wars, he had shown both his valor as a fighter as well as his inclination to drive the natives off their ancestral lands. By 1828, Jackson had fully endorsed the notion that a "just, humane, liberal policy" required that Indians be moved as far west as possible, to the "great American desert" beyond the Mississippi. There the land, according to common wisdom, would never accommodate cultivation by the white man, but would serve perfectly the needs of "primitive" Indian tribes.

This policy had been crystallizing since Jefferson's time, and the purchase of Louisiana and had been fully articulated by Secretary of War John C. Calhoun as early as 1823. But as president, Jackson made it the official policy of the government, and in the Indian Removal Act of 1830, Congress appropriated a half-million dollars to facilitate massive tribal transfers. The administration negotiated over ninety treaties in the next few years, and in 1836, the president announced that with the exception of a few tribes, the program had been effected.

In all these negotiations, the national government failed to bargain with the tribes in good faith and never carried out its obligations or fulfilled its promises to them. Furthermore, the federal government made little or no effort to control the states, whose citizens could not wait for the Indians to move before rushing in to grab their lands. In the North, weak tribes either gave way before the white settlers or were tricked or bribed by federal Indian commissioners to give up what little they had. The struggle they occasionally put up often ended in disaster, as in the Black Hawk War of 1832, with its gruesome massacre of Sauk and Fox women and children trying to flee across the Mississippi.

Stronger tribes in the Southern states put up a stiffer resistance. The Florida Seminoles fought a guerrilla war in the Everglades swamps from 1835 to 1842, and were never actually defeated, although military engagements dissipated after white soldiers treacherously seized their chief, Osceola, under a flag of truce. The Cherokee, more than any other tribe had adopted aspects of white culture. The Cherokee had a written constitution, had divided tribal land into individually owned farms, and had even adopted the Southern practice of slaveholding. They grew cotton and corn, and tried to blend in to the South, while occupying large tracts of land in northern Georgia and western North Carolina that had been guaranteed to them by a 1791 treaty. In 1827, the Cherokee adopted a constitution, based on their treaty rights, which not only affirmed their claims to the land, but also insisted that, as an independent nation, they were not subject to the laws of any other state or nation. Georgia responded the following year with a statute declaring that after June 1, 1830, state law would extend over all the Cherokees living within the state's borders. With the discovery of gold deposits in 1829, white settlers and prospectors began crowding into Indian country.

As we have seen, Georgia had forced John Quincy Adams to back down from his efforts to revise the Indian Springs Treaty, which had pushed the Cherokee into a narrow strip of land on the western and northern borders of Georgia. Georgia had no constitutional right either to claim jurisdiction over the Indians or to negotiate with them on land or other matters. Under the Articles of Confederation, the states had negotiated directly with Indian tribes, but the Constitution ended this. Article I, Section 8 reserved the power to regulate trade with the Indian tribes to the Congress, and treaties negotiated by the United States took priority, under the Supremacy Clause, over state laws.

Since the adoption of the Articles of Confederation, American governments had dealt with various tribes as autonomous nations, and even while trying to remove the Indians from the path of settlement, they had at least heeded these formalities. But the status of the tribes remained vague at best, and the manner in which the federal government tried to manage Indian policy depended on whether the vigor of a president in exercising federal prerogatives outweighed the determination of the states to gain control of tribal lands.

In President Jackson, the Southern states recognized a man who sympathized with their desire to remove the Indians, and who, they correctly anticipated, would not oppose them if they did not directly challenge his authority. Jackson made no comment on the 1830 Georgia law extending state control over Indian territory or on the state's subsequent seizure of much of that land. The state found the Supreme Court somewhat less sympathetic, but it did not really matter; Georgia, in this case, successfully defied the judicial power of the United States.

## Georgia, the Indians, and the Court

The first case involved the state murder prosecution of a Cherokee named Corn Tassel, under Georgia's newly proclaimed jurisdiction over the Indians. Corn Tassel argued that Georgia had no jurisdiction over him. The Supreme Court issued a writ of error to bring the case to Washington, but Georgia refused to acknowledge the writ. Governor Troup, backed by the legislature, declared that he would fight off any attempt to interfere with the state's court system. Corn Tassel, who may or may not have been guilty, was soon executed.

Although Jackson refused to interfere, Georgia's actions and the breach of treaty obligations to the Cherokee outraged some whites, who sought an injunction to prevent the state from seizing Indian lands or enforcing its law over the tribes. An aging John Marshall tried once again to walk the political tightrope he had so successfully traversed for three decades. In *Cherokee Nation v. Georgia* (1831), the Court held on the one hand that the Indian tribes constituted neither a state of the Union nor a foreign nation, and they therefore could not pursue an action in the federal courts. On the other hand, the chief justice defined the Indians as "domestic dependent nations" under the jurisdiction of the United States, who could not be forced to give up their lands except through voluntary cession. But the cautious opinion carefully skirted the main issues, so Georgia ignored it.

The issue of Indian sovereignty came back to the Supreme Court a year later in *Worcester v. Georgia* (1832). Samuel Worcester, a missionary, had been arrested for inhabiting Indian land without a license from the state, and the case thus tested Georgia's right to extend its jurisdiction over the Cherokee lands. No doubt annoyed at the state's contempt for his previous decision, this time the chief justice laid out the Court's view succinctly. The Cherokee constituted a distinct political entity with full control over their territory, over which "the laws of Georgia can have no force, and which the citizens of Georgia have no right to enter but with the assent of the Cherokees themselves." The state refused to send counsel to argue the case before the Court and then openly flouted the decision.

Marshall strongly implied in his opinion that the president had a duty to enforce federal law and treaty obligations, to which Jackson supposedly replied: "John Marshall has made his decision, now let him enforce it." The president did, as a matter of law, enjoy some discretion in how he interpreted and applied federal law and, having little sympathy for the Cherokee, pressured the tribe into signing a new treaty. In 1835, the Cherokee agreed to vacate their land in exchange for land in a newly designated "Indian Territory" in present-day Oklahoma, along with $5 million and expenses for transportation. In the next few years, they departed on their "trail of tears," with thousands dying along the way or shortly after their arrival in the Indian Territory. Inadequate food and shelter, as well as the strenuous journey, caused most of these deaths. On the trail, the Cherokee were subjected to humiliating treatment by the soldiers supposedly guarding their way, to pilferage from civilian contractors on whom they relied for supplies, and to the open scorn of whites along the route. A few Cherokee, known as the eastern band, remained, and eventually settled on a reservation in North Carolina.

The Cherokee removal illustrates how whites as individuals and collectively through the federal and state governments, maltreated the Indians in the nineteenth century. It remains a blot on the national heritage. It also pointed up one of the gray areas of the Constitution, which at this time provided little protection for Indians or other minority groups. The inherent racism of whites toward Indians influenced policy and actions from the time of the early settlements until well into the twentieth century, despite the efforts of a few whites to secure justice and fair treatment for the tribes. Most of the states supported Georgia's flouting of the Supreme Court, as well as Jackson's policy to force the tribes, against their will, to give up fertile lands that they had inhabited for centuries to move to the barren reaches of the Great Plains. Just as ominously, Georgia's assertion of state sovereignty against the federal judicial power anticipated a major constitutional crisis involving federal tariff policy.

## Calhoun Responds to the Tariff

President Jackson had little personal interest in the tariff. Government revenues had to be raised, and the Constitution specifically gave Congress the power to levy import duties. The success of the Hamiltonian tax plan could hardly be denied, with the once staggering national debt now practically retired. Nevertheless, the level of tariff rates engendered great controversy, and tariff laws, together with slavery, banking policy, and internal improvements, constituted the most bitter political issues dividing the country prior to the Civil War.

In 1828, Congress passed a tariff with record high rates. The tariff resulted from a political miscalculation, as Southerners who opposed the tariff, tried to kill the bill by offering amendments to raise tariffs beyond what even the most ardent advocates of the tariff wanted. These Southerners assumed that most Northerners would oppose the whole bill because the duties on all goods would be too high. The goal, led by supporters of Jackson, was to defeat the tariff, isolate New Englanders, and set the stage for Jackson's election. Congressman John Randolph of Roanoke, a quirky but astute Virginia politician, suggested that the bill was more concerned with "manufacturing a president" than manufactured goods. The immediate plan backfired, however, as Congressmen from all over the North voted for the high rates. The end result, known as the "Tariff of Abominations," had rates that were unjustified by either revenue needs or the protection of domestic goods. The long-range goal of electing Jackson was successful, but it is unlikely the outcome would have been any different if the tariff had not been an issue.

The tariff infuriated the South, and led Vice President John C. Calhoun to abandon his nationalistic position. A War Hawk in 1812 and a backer of federally funded internal improvements, he had earlier supported tariff protection to foster American industry. He had also supported rechartering the Second Bank of the United States in 1816. In the early 1820s, his native South Carolina had expected to attract cotton mills and other factories to become the Southern counterpart of Massachusetts, then the most prosperous manufacturing state in the Union. That dream had died stillborn, however, and the virtually total dependence on growing cotton and other staple crops left South Carolina, like most Southern states, with an economy especially vulnerable to market fluctuations. It also fed a growing sense of persecution, a belief that national policies benefited the North at the expense of the South. The hostility to slavery expressed during the Missouri Compromise debates, the abortive Denmark Vesey rebellion, and rising opposition to slavery, including an incendiary pamphlet by a free black named David Walker urging slaves to rebel, further exacerbated the sense of fear and isolation growing in the slave states, especially in South Carolina.

Compounding this feeling was an apparently permanent agricultural depression. In the 1820s, 70,000 South Carolinians migrated west, and nearly twice that number left in the following decade. Sometime in the late 1820s, Calhoun dropped his Hamiltonian views (which had always been somewhat at odds with the prevailing sentiment in his native state) and began advocating a strong states' rights doctrine, derived from the Virginia and Kentucky resolutions and the more radical strain of early Jeffersonian Republicanism (see Chapter 10).

The "Tariff of Abominations" of 1828 forced Calhoun to bolster his political base in South Carolina by joining with those who opposed the tariff. Many in South Carolina—and in the South in general—protested that they were being forced to pay higher prices for imported goods to benefit Northern manufacturers. They also resented what they saw as the growing power of the national government at the expense of the states. Calhoun secretly wrote the *South Carolina Exposition and Protest,* which denounced the alleged economic exploitation of the South by measures such as a protective tariff, and asserted the right of individual states to interpose themselves between their citizens and unjust, unconstitutional federal laws. Issued as a pamphlet by the South Carolina legislature in December 1828, the *Exposition,* however, should not be seen as a radical call to dissolve the Union, a position already being advocated by some Southerners. Nullification of congressional statutes was not equivalent to secession;

rather, it provided a device to protect the rights of a minority against imposition by the majority. It could not be undertaken lightly, and Calhoun suggested that a state convention should notify the national government of its objections, after which Congress could either repeal the law or submit a constitutional amendment to the states embodying the proposal. If the amendment passed, the objecting state would have to accept it; if not, Congress would have to abandon the plan. Calhoun was seeking, by these means, to preserve the Union, but the heart of his argument provided the philosophical wedge soon to be employed by states' rights advocates in their call for secession. Although the Constitution, by its opening phrase, placed sovereignty, and therefore the authority for government, in the hands of all the people, Calhoun argued that the Union was a compact of states, with ultimate sovereignty remaining in the hands of the individual states, and not with the national government.

Since Calhoun recognized Congress's authority to establish tariffs, he attacked the 1828 tariff on the constitutional grounds that this power had been granted for revenue purposes only, and not to provide protection for manufacturers. The South Carolina legislature issued the anonymously written *Exposition* along with several resolutions condemning the tariff, but it took no further action, awaiting the results of the election that year, in which Calhoun ran for vice president with Andrew Jackson. The state believed that with Jackson in office and Calhoun at his side, Congress would lower the rates. Aware of Southern resentment, Jackson did, in fact, call on Congress in late 1829 for a reduction in rates on goods "which cannot come in competition with our own products." In the spring of the following year, Congress lowered duties on some consumer items such as tea, coffee, and salt, and reduced the total tariff revenue by about one-fourth. Although this appeased some South Carolinians, the more ardent nullifiers condemned it as a meaningless gesture. Furthermore, by endorsing only a cut on taxing imports that did not compete with American producers, Jackson was implicitly endorsing the policy that Calhoun thought was unconstitutional: using a tariff to protect industries.

## The Webster–Hayne Debate

In this context, one of the great constitutional debates in American history took place—the tilt between senators Daniel Webster of Massachusetts and Robert Y. Hayne of South Carolina in January 1830. Although the tariff controversy loomed in the background, the immediate trigger was a proposal by Senator Samuel A. Foot of Connecticut for an investigation looking toward the restriction of western land sales. The West, led by Thomas Hart Benton of Missouri, denounced the move as an effort to cripple western growth so that eastern states could retain a large, cheap labor supply.

Hayne, hoping to strengthen the alliance between the West and the South that had elected Jackson, jumped to Benton's support. The national government, he charged, presented the greatest danger to perpetual union whenever it undertook to benefit one part of the country at the expense of another. Not only had the national government dealt unfairly with the West, Hayne asserted, but the revenue from western land sales led to corruption, "fatal to the sovereignty and independence of the states."

The heart of Hayne's argument was a defense of the South Carolina *Exposition*;

for historical support, he appealed not only to the Virginia and Kentucky resolutions, but to the Hartford Convention, in which New Englanders, during the War of 1812, had affirmed the compact theory of states and claimed that the states possessed the right of interposition (see Chapter 11).

Webster denied that the East had ever shown a hostile attitude toward the West. Nor did he fear a strong central government; he waxed poetic in describing a Hamiltonian vision of the benefits that a great national government would secure for the people by developing the country's resources. In his justly renowned second reply to Hayne, Webster dismissed the Hartford Convention as a relic of the past; New England, he claimed, no longer thought in terms of sectional selfishness, but rather, in terms of the good of the entire nation. He then denounced nullification as a false doctrine that could only end in disaster. The federal government represented not the will of the states, as the compact theorists claimed, but of the people, with their expanding national interests. Before the packed galleries, Webster closed his speech with one of the great passages in American political literature, urging the Senate and the nation to support the "sentiment, dear to every true American heart—Liberty *and* Union, now and forever, one and inseparable!"

Hayne was partially correct in his claim that the states, through the ratification process, had brought the Constitution into being. But he failed to consider that the people had directly elected the ratifying conventions, rather than having the state legislators adopt the Constitution. More importantly, by 1830 he was speaking for a states' rights sentiment that had become the province of a minority—a Southern minority—of the country. Webster's vision of the Union reflected the growing pride in the United States, a vision, still imperfect, of a mighty nation, which he and others of his generation had labored to build.

Jackson, if not totally in accord with the Massachusetts senator, nonetheless shared much of his vision, and he had no intention of presiding over the dismantling of the Union. He displayed these sentiments in a postscript to the Webster–Hayne debate. States' rights advocates arranged for a banquet on Jefferson's birthday (April 13) to broaden their support, and the two dozen arranged toasts glorified state sovereignty and the Virginia and Kentucky resolutions, as well as Georgia's defiance of John Quincy Adams. After listening to these, Jackson rose to give the first impromptu toast. With emphasis in his voice, he raised his glass: "Our Federal Union. It must be preserved." The crowd stood in response, but the previous gaiety disappeared. Calhoun, attempting to regain the initiative, responded with the next toast: "The Union—next to our liberty, the most dear." Jackson thus gave notice that while he served as president, he would defend the Union. The vice president, his political standing already undermined by Jackson's distrust, probably recognized then, if he had not already known, that his chances of succeeding Jackson in the White House had evaporated. In his remaining years, Calhoun became an ever more ardent and forceful advocate of states' rights.

## The Nullification Crisis

The president, an astute politician, fully recognized that so long as the Southern states perceived the tariff as unfair, the canker of dissatisfaction would eat away at the Union.

Toward the end of 1831, Jackson called for further reductions in the tariff, and the resulting bill, guided through Congress by former president and now Representative John Quincy Adams, the Tariff of 1832 cut revenues another $5 million. Although the new rates averaged 25 percent, those on cotton, woolens, and iron stayed at 50 percent, thus protecting key emerging industries. Jackson thought it a reasonable measure and hoped the controversy would die down; he failed to reckon with the intransigence of the South Carolina hotheads.

By now the actual rates mattered less than the tariff's political symbolism. The 1832 Tariff cut overall revenues to about half those of the Tariff of Abominations, but the nullifiers still damned it as unconstitutional. In the election of 1832, the "Nullies" inflamed states' rights passions. Calhoun, no longer Jackson's running mate, openly rejected nationalism. "The Constitution is the work of the people of the States, considered as separate and independent political communities," Calhoun wrote. "The Union, of which the Constitution is the bond, is a union of States, and not of individuals." He conceded that the Constitution imposed obligations on the people, but he maintained that the states determined the extent of these duties. If a state believed Congress had gone too far, it could declare such acts null and void, and this action of the state, not federal law, bound the state's citizens.

Although Calhoun had moved closer to the more radical supporters of states' rights, he still argued for nullification, not secession. But the Union he sought to preserve was not the shining ideal of Webster's vision; it was a mere confederation, with each state holding an effective veto over the acts of Congress. Whatever his intent, Calhoun's theory cut out the substance of the Union and left it a hollow shell, subject to the whims of each component. Such a theory pointed unerringly toward one logical conclusion— secession.

In 1832, Andrew Jackson was swept into a second term with a new running mate, Martin Van Buren of New York. Meanwhile, South Carolina was mesmerized by one and only one issue—nullification. The Nullies swept every county, and won a two-thirds majority in both houses of the legislature. Governor James Hamilton called a special session, which in turn voted for a popular convention. On November 19, 1832, 136 nullifiers met in Columbia, easily outnumbering the 26 hapless Unionists. The convention quickly adopted an ordinance that declared the 1828 and 1832 tariffs void, forbade the appeal of the ordinance to the U.S. Supreme Court, and prohibited the federal government from collecting the duties in South Carolina ports after February 1, 1833. Should Washington try to enforce the tariff, the state's allegiance to the Union would be dissolved. The legislature then reassembled, elected Robert Hayne as the new governor, with Calhoun to succeed him as U.S. senator. Calhoun promptly resigned as vice president (he still had three more months in his term) and prepared to defend the nullification ordinance.

The Nullies dismayed even the other Southern states which, to some degree, shared South Carolina's dissatisfaction over the tariff. Georgia, which had earlier resisted the federal government, called for a Southern convention, but dismissed nullification as "rash and revolutionary." Mississippi would have nothing to do with it, and Alabama denounced it as "unsound in theory and dangerous in practice." Andrew Jackson fulminated in private against the traitors and threatened to hang them all, starting with Calhoun. Later on, he expressed regret that he had not at least hung his former vice

---

## THE FIRST NATIONALLY ELECTED OFFICIAL TO RESIGN

In 1832, John C. Calhoun became the first nationally elected official to resign his office. He left office to protest President Jackson's policies over the tariff and nullification. The next resignations—two in one administration—came in 1973 when Vice President Spiro Agnew resigned as part of a plea bargain to avoid prosecution for various felonies, including accepting bribes and tax fraud. A year later, President Richard M. Nixon resigned to avoid certain impeachment, and almost certain conviction, for his involvement in the cover-up of the Watergate break-in.

---

president. But in public he adopted a more temperate, though no less firm approach, a form of "carrot and stick."

In his annual message to Congress on December 4, 1832, the president called for a substantial reduction in tariffs. With the national debt soon to be extinguished, the government would have no need for the revenue, and protection should only be extended to articles that were essential for the nation's safety in time of war. As for the situation in South Carolina, Jackson regretted the excitement, but federal laws could adequately deal with the matter. Assured by congressional leaders that they would back him fully in defending the Union, Jackson had Secretary of State Edward Livingston of Louisiana draw up a "Proclamation to the People of South Carolina." In it, the president sounded like a sorrowful father admonishing his wayward children. The South Carolina ordinance, he declared, would in the end lead to the destruction of the Union, because it contradicted every principle on which the government had been founded. The Constitution represented the will of the people, not of the states; therefore no state could secede, because that would destroy the unity of the people. "To say that any state may at pleasure secede from the Union," he argued, "is to say that the United States is not a nation."

Nullification, Jackson warned, could only end in failure or worse, and he, as president, had a duty to see that this did not happen. "The laws of the United States must be executed. I have no discretionary power on the subject; my duty is emphatically pronounced in the Constitution." Those leaders who said that the laws could be peacefully flouted had lied to the people; only forcible opposition could prevent the execution of the laws, "and they know that such opposition must be repelled. Their object is disunion. But be not deceived by names. Disunion by armed force is *Treason.* Are you really ready to incur its guilt?" Jackson's stick included more than just words; in January 1833, he asked Congress to enact the Force Bill, giving the president additional powers for the collection of import duties and for the enforcement of other federal laws, along with military reinforcements.

On the carrot side, the administration supported a bill to reduce immediately many of the rates and to lower the entire tariff revenue by 50 percent within a year. For political reasons, however, Henry Clay opposed the administration measure, and after consulting with Calhoun and John Tyler of Virginia, he introduced his own bill, which became the Compromise Tariff of 1833. The Clay bill called for a series of reductions at two-year intervals, so that by July 1, 1842, the top rate would be 20 percent, about that of the Tariff of 1816. The South and West supported this bill enthusiastically, while New England and the Middle Atlantic states opposed it; there could be no clearer sign of the sectional nature of the tariff controversy.

The Tariff and the Force bills passed Congress at the same time, and Jackson signed them into law on March 2, 1833. Defiant to the end, South Carolina symbolically nullified the Force Act, but the compromise tariff allowed the Palmetto State to claim victory over the original tariff, and thus back away, for the time being, from civil war. But the entire nullification controversy portended little good for the future, even though the forces of nationalism and majority will had triumphed. Webster's arguments for the Union had widespread support, not only in the North, but throughout much of the South as well; none of her sister slave states rallied to South Carolina's defense. The compact theory put forward by Calhoun and Hayne had seemingly been defeated not only in debate but also in practice.

Nonetheless, the episode pointed to a growing conflict between the free, diversified, and expanding economy of the Northern states and the slave-labor, agrarian South. It also underscored the growing cultural differences between the two sections. The North was becoming a region where a diversity of ideas, interests, and viewpoints constantly clashed. In the South, there was an increasing desire to shut off debate, particularly over slavery. Although the philosophy of the Constitution as the expressed will of the entire people had won a resounding triumph, Calhoun's theory of the Union as a compact among sovereign states had only been temporarily stilled.

## Internal Improvements

Internal improvements continued to be a vexatious political and legal question right up to the Civil War. As Americans expanded westward, the demand arose for roads, canals, and later, railroads, to link the interior to eastern markets. The expense of building this transportation network, however, exceeded the resources of many states and localities, so that the West turned toward the federal government for aid. Madison had called for such a program in his postwar address to Congress in 1816, but he had vetoed the ensuing bill because he believed that the Constitution, unless amended, did not grant this power to the federal government. Southerners, for the most part, also opposed internal improvements, shrouding their policy goals in a strict and narrow interpretation of federal powers under the Constitution.

Henry Clay, however, believed the government had the constitutional authority to help develop the nation. An intellectual descendant of Alexander Hamilton, Clay, in what he termed the "American system," advocated a strong government utilizing its powers to further the country's growth, building an extensive network of roads and canals to tie the nation together. The Constitution, written to create that nation, had to be interpreted broadly, and Clay saw no impediments to funding works, which, even if wholly within the borders of a single state, contributed to the general welfare.

Jackson, like most Westerners, favored improvements in general, and during his first term, the government doubled its spending for developing transportation. But he also had some constitutional scruples about the extent of federal power, which found an outlet in his political animosity toward Clay. In 1830, Congress appropriated money to buy stock in a road from Maysville, Kentucky, to Clay's hometown of Lexington. Some twenty miles long, the road lay entirely within Kentucky, but its advocates argued that it constituted part of the National Road through the Cumberland Gap. Jackson, to much popular support, promptly vetoed the bill. As Van Buren pointed out, this road affected only a few people directly, so a veto would not cause widespread protest. In fact, it received near universal approval. New York and Pennsylvania, wealthy enough to finance their own projects, saw no reason why other states should benefit from federal largesse, while the South applauded Jackson's denial of the national government's authority in this area. In his veto message, the president maintained that government should be as economical as possible, and such expenditures blocked the rapid retirement of the national debt.

Although couched in constitutional terms, the veto is better seen as a political slap against Henry Clay, for Jackson signed other bills fully as local in nature as the Maysville Road. But it did reflect Jackson's belief, which many people shared, that states and localities, not the federal government, had the responsibility for the construction of roads and canals. The national government, although it had to be strong within its proper sphere of activities, was nevertheless a government of limited powers. Jefferson's views thus became a cardinal tenet of Jacksonian democracy. But one has to be careful in distinguishing rhetoric from action. Like other politicians both before and afterward, Jackson could justify often contradictory policies by appeal to constitutional philosophy; in practice, Old Hickory continued to do the politically expedient or what reflected his personal prejudices and passions.

## Jackson Versus the Bank

Expediency, reinforced by distrust of eastern and urban institutions, and by Andrew Jackson's limited understanding of basic economics or finance, marked the administration's attack on the Second Bank of the United States. The overriding issue in the 1832 election proved to be neither internal improvements, Jackson's Indian policy, nor South Carolina's nullification ordinance, but rather, what many people called "The Monster"—the Second Bank of the United States. Jackson, like many Westerners, feared and despised the Bank, whose policies had punctured a land boom and caused, at least in part, the Panic of 1819. Jackson never understood the need for a central bank, and despite the Supreme Court's decision in *McCulloch v. Maryland,* he considered the national bank unconstitutional. The president made no secret of his feelings. "I think it right to be perfectly frank with you," he told the Bank's president, Nicholas Biddle. "I do not dislike your bank any more than all banks. But ever since I read the history of the South Sea Bubble I have been afraid of banks." This news undoubtedly puzzled Biddle, since his conservative policies had been designed precisely to frustrate speculative ventures such as the great English land fraud of the previous century.

At first, Biddle tried to placate Jackson, and appointed a number of the president's friends to branch office positions. But Jackson continued to denounce the Bank as unconstitutional, and despite all evidence to the contrary, he charged that it had failed to maintain a sound currency. With the Bank's charter due to expire in 1836, Biddle, trying to eliminate uncertainty, decided to apply for a renewal before the 1832 election. Senator Daniel Webster, who also served as counsel to the Bank, agreed with Biddle on this strategy, as did Henry Clay; they doubted that Jackson would veto a recharter bill during an election year. If he proved foolish enough to do so, then the National Republicans (the predecessors of the Whigs) would be able to capitalize on the veto as a campaign issue that fall. None of them recognized the depth of prejudice against the Bank, especially in the South and West, and thus handed Jackson not only a chance to strike out at the hated Monster, but to make it a key issue in his bid for reelection.

Both houses of Congress passed a recharter bill by comfortable margins in June 1832. As amended, the bill met some of the objections of Jackson and other critics by limiting the Bank's ability to hold real estate and establish additional branches, and by giving the president the power to appoint one member of each branch's board of directors. The power to regulate currency, however, which conservatives saw as one of the Bank's most important functions, was increased. Once again, the vote manifested the growing sectional nature of American politics. The slave states voted solidly against the bill; the rest of the country overwhelmingly endorsed it. Proponents of the Bank felt they had Old Hickory trapped; a veto, they believed, would cost Jackson support in key states that he needed for reelection.

If Jackson worried about the political consequences, he gave no sign of it in the stinging veto message he sent to Congress. Dismissing the amendments as "of little value," he pilloried the bank on one count after another, claiming its great power threatened the states. He also claimed that the large number of foreign stockholders jeopardized American control of its own financial affairs. Turning the attack to his political advantage, Jackson denounced the bill as a sellout by the government to the rich and powerful, and promised always to stand against "the advancement of the few at the expense of the many."

The veto message, drafted by Jackson's attorney general, Roger B. Taney, read like a Supreme Court opinion. Despite Chief Justice Marshall's opinion in *McCulloch v. Maryland*, the president condemned the bank as unconstitutional because, as he said in his veto message, it was "an attempt to amend the Constitution by an act of legislation." In essence, Taney, speaking through the voice of President Jackson, overruled Marshall's interpretation of the Constitution in *McCulloch*. The bank, in Jackson's mind, was neither "necessary" nor "proper" for the functioning of the national government.

From a political point of view, there is no question that Jackson got the better of his enemies. Congress failed to override the veto, and in the election that fall, people rallied to Old Hickory against those whom he depicted as tools of privilege, reelecting him overwhelmingly over Henry Clay in 1832.

Economically, the destruction of the bank proved a disaster, since much of the recent prosperity had been made possible by a strong central bank. Moreover, the Jacksonians' characterization of the Bank as a monopoly made no sense. At its peak, it never held more than a third of the nation's specie deposits nor issued more than one-fifth of loans or notes; its charter had a limited life, during which Congress could revise the terms. But the Bank had kept irresponsible local banks in line, and by its opposition to speculation, it had incurred the wrath of Westerners who needed cheap money to fuel both settlement and land speculation. No doubt the Bank could be a force for privilege and corruption; it kept Daniel Webster on a healthy retainer and made generous loans to public officials. Such abuses, however, could have been controlled. The Jacksonians, rightly or wrongly, saw the Bank as imperiling the republic, and they, and henceforth the Democratic party, argued that political and social democracy could not survive without an underpinning of economic democracy. Because of this perception, the country would suffer without a central bank for the better part of a century.

Jackson's constitutional argument was more complicated. Others had attacked opinions of John Marshall as erroneous; indeed, the Supreme Court had been criticized for various decisions almost from its inception. Beginning with *Marbury v. Madison,* though, the Court had carefully built up its claim to be the final arbiter of those constitutional questions that came before it. The idea that there had to be some ultimate authority, and that authority was the Court, had won numerous adherents by 1830.

In his veto message, Jackson did not actually challenge the right of the Court to decide on the constitutionality of legislation, once it was passed and signed into law. He simply argued that members of the other branches of government had to make a constitutional determination for themselves, whether or not to support a bill. In this case, Jackson's strict construction of the Constitution led him to conclude that he should not sign the bank bill. In this manner, he was exercising a perfectly reasonable constitutional power—the power of the president to sign or veto bills.

Jackson did not, in this instance, assert that he was not bound by decisions of the Supreme Court, but only that when a bill reached his desk he was bound to make a constitutional determination, on his own, about the soundness of the bill. Jackson had in fact already flouted the Court in *Worcester v. Georgia*, but his disregard for the Court went largely unnoticed because of the popularity of the Indian removal, and the inability of the Cherokee and other Indian nations to affect national policy. Had Jackson and subsequent presidents regularly followed the path taken after *Worcester* of refusing to implement the Court's decisions, there could well have been constitutional anarchy. But this did not occur.

What is perhaps most striking about both the bank controversy and the Maysville Road bill, was Jackson's desire to constitutionalize them. He might have simply vetoed both bills on policy grounds. No one could have argued that Jackson lacked the constitutional authority to veto a bill simply because he did not like it. That Jackson made his case on constitutional grounds illustrates the importance of the Constitution in American political culture at the time.

Jackson proved in many ways to have been the first modern president—a strong political leader who was determined to exercise independent leadership in the nation's affairs. He made free and potent use of tools that had hitherto lain dormant, such as the veto and the power over appointments and removals, and he also showed the strength of political party discipline in effecting policy. His actions reflected his self-perception as a champion of the people against vested privilege, an attitude reinforced by his strong temperament and his previous experience as a military commander.

After the veto, the Bank still had four years to run on its charter, but Jackson was determined to kill it off even sooner and thus rid democracy of a great threat. In November 1832, Jackson informed the cabinet that he believed the Bank to be insolvent, and he then requested Congress to investigate the safety of government deposits in the

Bank. The House looked into the matter and found them secure, an opinion that the president ignored. At the urging of some of his advisers, he decided to shift government funds out of the Bank of the United States and into local banks. But Secretary of the Treasury Louis McLane argued that Congress opposed this idea and would not go along with the plan. Jackson shifted McLane to the State Department and replaced him with William J. Duane, a Philadelphia attorney who detested the Bank almost as much as Jackson did. But Duane also hated state banks, which had already issued notes far in excess of their specie holdings; the transfer of funds would only increase inflation, so he too refused to shift the funds. Now the president fired Duane and moved Roger Taney from the Justice Department to the Treasury. At last, Old Hickory had a man willing to do his bidding. The government drew down its holdings in the Bank to pay its current expenses, and put all new deposits into so-called pet banks, often controlled by Jackson supporters, in cities around the country.

Jackson's actions, which eventually drove the nation into the most severe economic downturn prior to the Great Depression of the 1930s, did not go unnoticed. The U.S. Senate passed a resolution of censure directed at the president, declaring that his reasons for removing the bank deposits were "insufficient and unsatisfactory." Jackson was deeply stung by this resolution and vigorously argued that it was unconstitutional. He argued that a motion of censure did not give him an opportunity to defend his policies and his honor. Jackson, in fact, challenged Congress to impeach him, if he deserved punishment, rather than censure him.

Meanwhile, as Jackson removed the deposit, Biddle did the reasonable thing; he began to wind up the Bank's affairs by calling in notes and restricting its discount activities (that is, he refused to lend money to other banks on the basis of their securities and loans as collateral). Biddle probably hoped that the resulting contraction of credit would lead to a demand for recharter, and indeed, hundreds of petitions flooded Congress asking for relief from economic instability through a new charter. But Jackson would not be moved. Those in trouble deserved it, he declared. "The failures that are now taking place are amongst the stock-jobbers, brokers, and gamblers, and would to God, they were all swept from the land! It would be a happy thing for the country." In the end, not just the stock-jobbers, but many ordinary people suffered in the Panic of 1837. By then, however, Old Hickory had retired to Tennessee, and his chosen successor, Martin Van Buren, who had helped mastermind the war against the Bank, inherited the problems and the odium for four years of financial misery.

The Second Bank of the United States episode still had a few, last scenes to play. With so many of the pet banks failing in 1837, Van Buren proposed a system of subtreasuries to receive, transfer, and pay out government funds. As he explained, the Constitution granted no power for the government to engage in private banking, but it could provide for its own financial operations through a wholly public agency. In 1840, Congress approved the subtreasury plan, but in the election of that year, the Whigs won the presidency and control of Congress. Under Henry Clay's leadership, Congress repealed the subtreasury plan and created a Fiscal Bank of the United States, a reincarnation of the old Bank, but located in Washington rather than in Philadelphia. By then, however, the new president, William Henry Harrison, who would have been amenable to Clay's proposal, had died, and his vice president, John Tyler, a states' rights Virginian and strict constructionist, sat in the White House. Tyler indicated his willingness to approve a bill if it contained a clause requiring state approval for the location of branch offices within their borders. But Clay and other Whig leaders responded that Congress had the power to locate branches where it wished—a power that had been affirmed by the Supreme Court. Instead, they added a section that assumed a state's consent unless it promptly registered its objection.

Tyler vetoed the bill, arguing that Congress did not have the power to create a national bank. He conceded that Congress and some presidents had differed over this issue in the past; unlike Jackson, he did not set himself up as the ultimate arbiter of the matter. But, as he told Congress, he had long believed that the government had no constitutional power to create such a bank, and without an express safeguard for states' rights, he would not assent. The Whigs could not override the veto, and later in the year they passed another bill, which, while meeting some of Tyler's objections, still did not require state approval for the creation of branches. The president vetoed the second bill as well, sealing his break with the Whig party, in which he had never felt particularly comfortable. When the Democrats regained control of Congress, they reenacted the subtreasury system in 1846, and left control of the banking system to the states.

## Monopoly and Economic Expansion

A larger context in which to place the Bank fight was the Jacksonian attack on privilege and monopoly, whose legal expression can be found in both state courts and the Supreme Court. The United States was far from a privilege-ridden society in the 1830s, nor had big business taken over control of the economy. But the rush for development had led many legislatures to grant special rights through corporate charters and franchises, which gave some entrepreneurs the power to freeze out competitors. The Jacksonians did not speak for an exploited proletariat, but rather, for young men on the make who sought unlimited entry into new markets and access to the new technology that created them.

English common law had a built-in disposition against monopoly, but it also recognized the power of the Crown to grant exclusive franchises or even to grant monopolistic control over whole markets, as it had done in the tea business with the East India Company. In America, a state's right to grant a monopoly had never been questioned until the New York steamboat controversy, and the Supreme Court decision in *Gibbons v. Ogden* (1824) had rested on the interstate nature of the business rather than on questions of monopoly. In the early part of the century, in fact, courts had looked favorably on exclusive franchises. The New York court had upheld the steamboat charter in *Livingston v. Van Ingen* (1812), and confirmed the state's power to grant monopolies. When James Kent, one of the nation's foremost legal authorities, became chancellor two years later, he set about creating rules of equity to support both explicit and implied grants of exclusive franchises.

Kent, according to some, practically single-handedly developed American equity jurisprudence, especially the use of the injunction. He himself wrote: "I had nothing to guide me, was left at liberty to assume all English chancery powers and jurisdiction as I thought applicable under our constitution. . . . I most always found principles suited to my views of the case." An early example is *Croton Turnpike Co. v. Ryder* (N.Y., 1815), in which Kent, despite specific wording in the statute permitting other parties to secure turnpike franchises, issued an injunction preventing a potential competitor from entering the field. The rival road, he declared, would be "a material and mischievous disturbance of the plaintiffs in the enjoyment of their statute privilege." By assuming that a franchise necessarily implied exclusivity, Kent invested it with an inviolable property right that often went beyond the original legislative intent. Following Kent, other courts read the common law rule of prescription to give the earliest franchise holder protection against future competitors. Given the scarce resources at the beginning of the nineteenth century, these decisions made good economic policy. Without some protection against later entries, it might have been difficult to secure investment for badly needed transportation facilities.

A new question arose, however, when the state consciously decided to license competitors. Most of Kent's cases arose when an existing franchise owner sought protection against nonlicensed newcomers. But as areas grew more densely settled, a single road or bridge often proved insufficient, and states began to license new roads to compete against existing franchises. The equity decisions fostered by Kent, as well as contract cases such as *Fletcher v. Peck* and *Dartmouth College,* seemed to rule against this policy; but in the second quarter of the century the states nonetheless began issuing new charters to competitors, and courts, recognizing the need for these enterprises, soon abandoned the doctrine of exclusivity. In 1830, for example, the Cayuga Bridge Company lost an important battle in the New York courts. The company had held exclusive rights to build and maintain two toll bridges across a lake, but in 1825, the legislature granted local citizens the right to build a free bridge in the immediate vicinity of one of the existing structures. Chancellor Kent had been forced to retire because of age, and his successor, Reuben H. Walworth, by strictly construing the terms of the company's charter, found against an injunction. "Such injudicious grants of exclusive privilege," he argued, "should not be farther extended by construction" (*Cayuga Bridge Co. v. Magee* [N.Y., 1830]).

## The *Charles River Bridge* Case Begins

The great case on the subject of monopolies involved the Charles River Bridge, which had been built in 1785 to connect Boston with Charlestown, then a hamlet of only 1,200 souls. By 1827, Boston's population had expanded to 60,000, that of Charlestown to 8,000. The accompanying increase in traffic gave the proprietors of the bridge company unexpectedly large profits; on an investment of $70,000, they collected annual tolls of $30,000. To relieve the congestion caused by growth, the legislature in 1827 authorized the construction of a second bridge, the Warren Bridge, less than one-quarter mile from the original crossing. The investors would be able to collect tolls until they had recovered their costs plus a fixed return, but in any event, six years after it opened, the Warren Bridge would revert to the state and become toll free. Within a year after completion of the new bridge, the revenues of the Charles River Bridge had dropped by more than half, and by the time the case reached the U.S. Supreme Court, they had fallen to practically nothing.

The Charles River Bridge proprietors claimed that their charter had given them exclusive rights to build and maintain a crossing between Boston and Charlestown; the new license, therefore, impaired the state's obligation. Counsel for the plaintiffs, Daniel Webster and Lemuel Shaw, put forward the traditional arguments for vested rights, which had, until this time, carried great weight with the courts. Public enterprise, they warned, would come to a halt if private investors could not rely on the government to keep its word. Responding for the new bridge company, Richard Fletcher attacked the monopoly that had led the legislature to grant a new charter. Monopoly, he charged, restricted enterprise, and for continued growth and prosperity, the community needed competition. Progress always took a toll on older, established agencies; while this might be regrettable, it was the price to be paid for advancement.

The state court split, 2–2 in January 1830, thus upholding the new charter. Justice Marcus Morton, one of the most prominent Jacksonians in Massachusetts, endorsed Fletcher's arguments and dismissed the fears that private capital would not be forthcoming unless given ironclad guaranties. One could only ask for a fair field and a promise that the legislature would not blatantly sacrifice the property of one portion of the community for the benefit of another. Samuel Wilde, a Federalist, not only joined Morton, but went even further in approving the legislative response to popular need. The original grant had been for the public accommodation. If the legislature determined that the public was no longer properly accommodated, it had the power to make alternate arrangements.

On the other side of the issue, Chief Justice Isaac Parker and Associate Justice Samuel Putnam voted for the Charles River Bridge proprietors. Putnam, an old Federalist who had been Joseph Story's law tutor, came down heavily for protecting vested rights. Parker, much more of a political realist, found himself torn between his legal attachment to property rights and his appreciation that public controversies of this sort reflected political and economic considerations as much as constitutional questions. He recognized the legislature's need to respond to new needs, but wanted, as much as possible, to protect individual security. The split vote in effect upheld the rights of the new company, and the losers, the Charles River Bridge Company, appealed to the U.S. Supreme Court.

Had this case concerned only competing bridges over the Charles River it could easily have escaped public notice. But the contest between existing franchise holders and newcomers spoke to similar conflicts in other areas as well. Just as Fulton's demonstration of steam power ushered in a new era for water transportation, George Stephenson's development of the steam locomotive, in 1826, opened new vistas for land travel. Investors who had sunk millions into canals did not view kindly the prospects of a new technology—the railroad—that could render their enterprises obsolete. In 1828, the first evidence of what might occur came when a group of Baltimore businessmen, complaining of high rates extracted by the canal monopolies, petitioned the legislature for a charter to build the Baltimore & Ohio Railroad. The Supreme Court's decision in *Charles River Bridge* would have far-reaching implications for the future of American transportation.

The Supreme Court's handling of the case, however, kept the outcome in doubt for several years. When it first heard arguments in March 1831, John Marshall still presided, and a majority of the justices had sat together for more than twenty years;

only two of the brethren, John McLean of Ohio and Henry Baldwin of Pennsylvania, were Jackson appointees. One might have expected, as did Daniel Webster, that a Marshall-dominated Court would support the contract argument; but five days after the initial argument, the Court announced that it could not reach a decision. Since there are no minutes of the Court's deliberations, one can only guess at the reasons from other evidence. Story seems to have been the strongest supporter of the old bridge, but questions of jurisdiction led some justices to believe that the Court should just leave the Massachusetts opinion in place. Since the original bridge charter did not promise exclusivity, other justices suggested that a strict construction did not preclude later competition.

The Court, however, permitted reargument in 1833, again with no result. Soon after, the Marshall Court disintegrated. Justice William Johnson died in August 1834, Gabriel Duvall resigned a few months later, and the chief justice himself passed away in July 1835. Andrew Jackson, with three additional appointments, determined to make the Court more "democratic." James M. Wayne of Georgia, a staunch Unionist, succeeded Johnson. Old Hickory then named his loyal treasury secretary, Roger Brooke Taney, to replace Duvall, but the Senate, irate over Taney's removal of federal funds from the Bank of the United States, refused to confirm him. When Marshall died, however, Jackson renominated Taney, this time to be chief justice, and applying party discipline, he secured approval of Taney along with that of Philip Barbour of Virginia to succeed Duvall.

## The Last Years of the Marshall Court

By the time of Marshall's death, virtually all Americans, including President Jackson, accepted the idea of judicial review and respected the general prestige of the Court. Despite Jackson's high-handed response to Marshall's opinion in *Worcester v. Georgia,* and their disagreement over the constitutionality of the national bank, Jackson never actually openly defied the court.

By the time Marshall died, the Court had moved away from some of the high judicial nationalism displayed in *Fletcher v. Peck, Martin v. Hunter's Lessee,* and *McCulloch v. Maryland.* In *Barron v. Baltimore* (1833), for example, Marshall refused to apply the Bill of Rights to the states, and in that case allowed the city of Baltimore to destroy the economic value of Barron's property without any compensation. Similarly, in *Cherokee Nation*, Marshall refused to challenge state power, even though it seems clear that the federal government had the power, and the responsibility, to protect the rights of Native Americans. Even where Marshall did assert expansive federal power, as in *Gibbons v. Ogden,* his decisions were popular because they dovetailed with the national mood.

## Chief Justice Taney

With the swearing in of Chief Justice Roger Brooke Taney, the Democrats anticipated a revolution in constitutional interpretation—now that the old guard had finally been ejected from its last bastion of power. One Jacksonian predicted that Taney's appointment, "together with those of his present democratic associates, will provide a revolution in some important particulars in the doctrines heretofore advanced . . . highly favourable to the independence of the States and the substantial freedom of the people." Yet Marshall, before he died, spoke well of Taney, while John C. Calhoun, still furious at Jackson over nullification, voted against his confirmation. The Taney Court, in general, did not reverse but rather modified, or even confirmed, the doctrines laid down during Marshall's long tenure, and when Taney died in 1864, one could find little evidence of a judicial revolution.

Even in the *Bridge* case, the Taney Court did not depart radically from Marshall's views. The various contract cases decided by the Marshall Court, although emphasizing the binding nature of agreements, nonetheless recognized the power of the state to change its mind. In *Dartmouth College,* Story had explicitly told the states they could reserve the power to alter or repeal charters, a suggestion quickly taken up and written into nearly all special and general charter laws. In *Charles River Bridge,* Taney applied this logic, noting that the failure of the state to explicitly grant a monopoly to the original bridge company meant that the state had reserved the right to charter bridges.

Always an astute politician, Marshall was not blind to the conflict that often arose between contractual charter rights and changing community needs. The majority opinion in *Dartmouth College* represented the broadest application of the Contract Clause; afterward, the Court retreated somewhat in recognition of the need to preserve legislative flexibility. In *Beaty v. Knowles* (1830), the Court ruled that corporate charters should be strictly construed, limiting the company only to those powers that are explicitly given by the legislature. That same year, in *Providence Bank v. Billings,* the chief justice pursued this line even further and gave Taney the precedent he used in the bridge case.

Rhode Island had chartered the Providence Bank in 1791. Thirty years later, the state imposed a bank tax of fifty cents for every $1,000 of capital stock, a rate afterward raised to $1.25. The stockholders sued to prevent payment of the tax, claiming it impaired the obligation of contract created by the charter. Marshall summarily dismissed this argument, noting that the charter contained no express provision exempting the bank from taxation. The plaintiff also claimed an implied immunity—otherwise the state might tax away all the profits. The chief justice not only refused to consider such abstractions, but he declared that federal courts could not correct every abuse of power by the states; for that relief, the people had to rely on the political process. Finally, the ability to tax constituted one of the great powers of the state and could not be alienated except through express provision. Government had to retain the ability to act for the benefit of the community. When it vested particular rights, the Contract Clause bound it to honor such obligations; but individuals could not limit the state by trying to read implicit immunities where they did not exist.

Taney undoubtedly knew of this opinion and, in fact, had used similar reasoning in an advisory opinion he had rendered as attorney general to a New Jersey turnpike company that wanted to build a railroad over its right of way. Part of the route ran parallel to another rail line, which had secured an exclusivity clause from the legislature a few years earlier. Taney denied that one legislature could bind future sessions, and thus prevent the proper exercise of sovereign powers for the benefit of the community. To let a monopoly prevail would inhibit development and prevent the people "from using the means necessary to promote the prosperity and happiness of the community." Taney's opinion also reflected Jeffersonian and Jacksonian views on popular sovereignty, with the people, through their elected representatives, capable of responding to changing needs. If one legislature could bind its successors, then periodic elections meant nothing.

## The *Charles River Bridge* Case Is Decided

The Supreme Court's decision in *Charles River Bridge v. Warren Bridge Company* surprised few people. Webster, still counsel for the old proprietors, appeared in ill humor through most of the reargument in early 1837, and he presented his case for vested rights and contractual sanctity in a petulant manner. Arguing for the Warren Bridge, Simon Greenleaf, Royall Professor of Law at Harvard, emphasized the inherent sovereign power of a state to respond to new conditions, as well as the need for strict construction of charters. To interpret charters too liberally, he claimed, would inhibit the ability of states to meet the changing needs of their citizens. Greenleaf, referring indirectly to Taney's earlier advisory opinion, warned that any decision favoring the old proprietors would severely crimp future development of new modes of transportation, and thus inhibit economic development.

The decision, upholding the legislature's right to grant new and competing charters, marks a division between the Marshall and Taney eras. Taney's majority opinion did not overturn thirty-five years of previous doctrine; strict construction of charters had been maintained by Marshall in several cases. Rather, the tone of the decision reflected greater understanding of a changing political and economic situation, as well as an emphatically more flexible reading of both the Contract Clause of the Constitution and the text of particular corporate charters. The legislature could not be bound, causing it to ignore new considerations, but had to remain free to cultivate the greatest good for its citizens. The decision also did not overthrow the Contract Clause, but limited it somewhat, a trend well underway after *Dartmouth College*.

Perhaps of greater institutional significance is the strong dissent entered by Joseph Story and concurred in by Smith Thompson, the only other pre-Jacksonian members of the Court. Story believed in the near absolute rights of private property, and his dissent summed up his philosophy. He brought every weapon in his formidable intellectual arsenal to bear against the new and, as he conceived it, pernicious doctrine that sacred promises by a state could be casually dismissed. Warning the Court against hasty innovation, he declared: "I stand upon the old law . . . in resisting any such encroachments upon the rights and liberties of the citizens, secured by public grants." As to the argument that support of the old bridge would fetter development, he said he knew of "no surer plan to arrest all public improvements, founded on private capital and enterprise, than to make the outlay of that capital uncertain and questionable." But such economic and political policies did not matter, he argued; the Court's obligations did not include oversight of legislative policy decisions. "It seems to me to be our duty to interpret laws, and not to wander into speculations upon their policy."

This avowal of what would later be termed judicial restraint seems somewhat odd coming from Story, whose constitutional views did in fact embody a clear-cut policy favoring business enterprise. One of his great later opinions, *Swift v. Tyson* (1842; see Chapter 16), created a federal common law for commerce without the support of any express constitutional provision, and ignored state policies with which he disagreed. Whatever can be said in favor of judicial restraint, the fact remains that judges and courts did create policy, and some of the Marshall Court's greatest opinions went beyond the strict limits of constitutional interpretation to establish the prodevelopment climate so necessary for American growth. Despite the intellectual merits of Story's opinion, Taney's decision rested on solid ground. Moreover, just as the Marshall Court's early decisions had met the economic needs of the first quarter of the century, so Taney's opinion responded to a new climate, in which competition would be the favored standard of a burgeoning enterprise.

## Conclusion: The New Departure

Although the arrival of Taney and four other Jacksonians on the Supreme Court marked the end of one era of constitutional history and the beginning of another, it would be far too simplistic to assume that the Taney Court set about dismantling its predecessor's doctrinal structure. In many areas, the new Court confirmed Marshall's rulings; in others, it reined in some of the excesses, especially Marshall's overly broad view of the Commerce Clause. But in no area did it actually repudiate earlier decisions, and despite Taney's sympathy for states' rights, he proved as much a nationalist as Marshall had been.

The differences between the two Courts was more in tone than in differing views of national development. Marshall had a very eighteenth-century view of wealth, and his great decisions often dealt with property as land, which he well understood as a device for fostering growth. Property rights dominated his thinking because he shared the Federalist notion that property undergirded society and secured all other rights. Yet even while protecting vested rights, Marshall never made them sacrosanct; he never denied the need of the state to respond to changed conditions. Taney valued property as much as Marshall, but the Jacksonians were creating new modes of wealth, and as a result, they needed a law that allowed entrepreneurs or a sponsoring state government greater flexibility in promoting new ventures.

The Massachusetts bridge decision is, therefore, a great transitional case, relying on earlier precedents but supporting new directions in business. For all the rhetoric, the Jacksonians proved as conservative as their erstwhile opponents in favoring robust economic expansion. If one seeks more dramatic evidence of change, one must look at social and political developments that also had their impact on the law.

The *Charles River Bridge* case also illustrates three interpretive themes of law in this period put forward by Morton Horwitz, James Willard Hurst, and William J. Novak. The bridge case can be seen as an instrumentalist opinion, in which the Court used its power to push economic development forward in a particular way. It also can be seen as a decision that allows for the release of energy, so that Americans could create new institutions and use new technologies to enhance their own lives. Finally, it is a decision that keeps what Novak calls the "people's welfare" in mind. Thus, Taney interprets the original charter not to the benefit of one party to the case or the other, but rather, fundamentally, to the benefit of the people. Taney asserts: "The object and end of all government is to promote the happiness and prosperity of the community by which it is established; and it can never be assumed, that the government intended to diminish its power of accomplishing the end for which it was created."

# For Further Reading

A good overview of the period is Glyndon G. Van Deusen, *The Jacksonian Era, 1828–1848* (1959), which should be supplemented by Edward E. Pessen, *Jacksonian America: Society, Personality and Politics* (1978). See also Robert V. Remini's three-volume biography of *Andrew Jackson* (1977–1984). For an extraordinary study of the opponents of Jackson, see Michael F. Holt, *The Rise and Fall of the American Whig Party: Jacksonian Politics and the Onset of the Civil War* (1999). Still useful and readable, although perhaps over-sympathetic to Jackson, is Arthur M. Schlesinger, Jr., *The Age of Jackson* (1946). Good constitutional overviews are provided in Harold Hyman and William M. Wiecek, *Equal Justice Under Law: Constitutional Development, 1835–1875* (1982); and Bernard Schwartz, *From Confederation to Nation: The American Constitution, 1835–1877* (1973). Also useful for understanding Jacksonian politics is Robert V. Remini, *Henry Clay: Statesman for Union* (1991).

Jackson's Indian policy is dissected in Ronald Satz, *American Indian Policy in the Jacksonian Era* (1975); and Michael P. Rogin, *Fathers and Children: Andrew Jackson and the Subjugation of the American Indian* (1975). The Supreme Court's involvement is examined in detail in Jill Norgren, *The Cherokee Cases: The Confrontation of Law and Politics* (1995). A good documentary history of the removal, with a fine introduction, is Theda Perdue, *The Cherokee Removal: A Brief History with Documents* (1995). Older, but still useful, are Joseph Burke, "The Cherokee Cases: A Study in Law, Politics, and Morality," 21 *Stanford Law Review* 500 (1969), and Edwin A. Miles, "After John Marshall's Decision: *Worcester v. Georgia* and the Nullification Crisis," 39 *Journal of Southern History* 519 (1973). On Jeffersonian notions of empire and the Indians, see Peter Onuf, *Jefferson's Empire: The Language of American Nationhood* (2000).

For the nullification crisis, see William W. Freehling's excellent work, *Prelude to Civil War: The Nullification Controversy in South Carolina, 1816–1836* (1966). Freehling examines the relationship between the state's opposition to the tariff and its fear that federal power would be used to end slavery. Equally important is Richard Ellis, *The Union at Risk: Jacksonian Democracy, States' Rights, and the Nullification Crisis* (1987). Freehling's *The Road to Disunion: Secessionists at Bay, 1776–1854* (1990) puts nullification in an even larger context. Merrill D. Peterson, *Olive Branch and Sword: The Compromise of 1833* (1982), contains no new information, but is a fine analysis of the complexity of Jacksonian politics. For Calhoun's thought, see August O. Spain, *The Political Theory of John C. Calhoun* (1950). See also Paul C. Nagle's interesting study of an idea in *One Nation Indivisible: The Union in American Thought* (1964). Useful for understanding the slavery background to the nullification crisis is Edward A. Pearson, *Designs Against Charleston: The Trial Record of the Denmark Vesey Slave Conspiracy of 1822* (1999).

To understand the economic background of the Bank War, see Bray Hammond, *Banks and Politics in America from the Revolution to the Civil War* (1957). For Jackson's views, see Robert V. Remini, *Andrew Jackson and the Bank War* (1967), which interprets the conflict in political terms; Thomas P. Govan's biography of *Nicholas Biddle* (1959) shows the anti-Jacksonian side. On the attempts to censure Jackson, see Emily Van Tassel and Paul Finkelman, *Impeachable Offenses: A Documentary History from 1787 to the Present* (1999).

Stanley I. Kutler, *Privilege and Creative Destruction: The Charles River Bridge Case* (1971), is a model case study integrating law, economics, and politics. See also R. Kent Newmyer, "Justice Joseph Story, the Charles River Bridge Case and the Crisis of Republicanism," 17 *American Journal of Legal History*, 232 (1973). The continuity between the Marshall and Taney Courts can be studied in R. Kent Newmyer, *The Supreme Court Under Marshall and Taney* (1968); and Gerald Garvey, "The Constitutional Revolution of 1837 and the Myth of Marshall's Monolith," 18 *Western Politics Quarterly* 27 (1965). Finally, on Story, see R. Kent Newmyer's masterful, *Supreme Court Justice Joseph Story: Statesman of the Old Republic* (1984). On the lower federal judiciary in this period, see Kermit L. Hall, *The Politics of Justice: Lower Federal Judicial Selection and the Second Party System* (1979).

# 15

# *Jacksonian Democracy*

*A Sense of Mastery • State Constitutional Development • Constitutional Flexibility • The Political Party and Its Function • Family Law • Women's Rights • Children and the Law • Early Labor Movements • Debtor Imprisonment • Pauper Relief • The New Prison • Code Revision • Race Relations and Antislavery • Conclusion • For Further Reading*

THE 1830s MARKED the beginning of three decades of enormous ferment in America. Throughout the period, especially in the North and West, countless groups, organizations, and individuals clamored for "reform" and improvement in society. Vast economic, social, and political changes both stimulated the calls for reform and also made them possible. The South generally rejected social reforms (temperance was an exception), in part because slavery chained Southern society to existing social relations, even as it chained African Americans in servitude.

The era we call the Age of Jackson saw rapid strides in economic development; major steps in social and political activity also transformed laws of personal status and affected the practical workings of constitutional government. And, as in all periods of change, failure accompanied success.

## A Sense of Mastery

Americans in the middle of the nineteenth century seemed in constant motion. Foreign and domestic observers noted the restless energy that fueled economic development and encouraged civic and cultural enterprises, religious crusades, and movements aimed at improving the lot of paupers, ameliorating conditions in prisons and asylums, fighting the abuse of alcohol, gaining political and legal rights for women, and, most of all, ending slavery. From coastal urban centers to interior hamlets, Americans appeared to be ceaselessly working, exhorting, building, or dreaming. Amazingly, many of these dreams came true—as canals and railroads tied the nation together and public schools, at least in the North, provided education for children of all social classes. A surge of democratic sentiment took the vision of government by the people several steps forward, and it is little wonder that Americans of this period viewed the world with a sense of mastery.

Not all the gains attributed to Jacksonian democracy, however, took place during Old Hickory's eight years in office. Many had been developing since the early days of the republic, but came to fruition in the late 1820s and 1830s. Others, such as labor reform, nearly died during this era, only to emerge and triumph many decades later. Although historians like to describe things in neat periods, it is impossible to put definite dates on the Jacksonian era; it started well before Jackson took office, and on the eve of the Civil War, men who considered themselves Jacksonian Democrats still held major offices in state and national government. The Jacksonians ushered in a new era in American politics, which in turn had a profound effect on how government operated under the Constitution.

Virtually all of Founders despised political parties, believing that they sapped the national will and engendered strife. In *Federalist No. 10*, Madison had assumed that politics would lead to the formation of "factions," but he argued these would be temporary groupings of people concerned about particular objectives, not permanent coalitions. Ironically, in the 1790s, Madison was instrumental in forming the Republican party which sent Jefferson (and then Madison himself) to the presidency.

To Madison's surprise, rather than hindering the task of leading the nation, parties proved an efficacious means of enacting desirable legislation. Under Jackson, party effectiveness increased significantly, and national elections thereafter represented not just the choice of a candidate, but also popular endorsement of his party and the ideas it propounded. It also led to a dramatic increase in the use of political patronage, which rewarded party loyalists and punished the opposition. As Jackson would say, "to the victor go the spoils."

The expansion of the electoral base dramatically affected the emergence of party politics. In the 1780s, universal adult male suffrage hardly existed, even though a greater percentage of the populace had access to the polls in America than in any European country, including England. Women, slaves, minors, Indians, and propertyless males had limited or no suffrage rights, although the record is not clear on just how stringently officials enforced property qualifications; in some states, free blacks could not vote, but in others they could. Although there were no religious restrictions on voting in the 1790s, all but a few states prohibited Jews from holding office and a majority also prohibited Catholic officeholders. By Jackson's time, almost all states had abolished property requirements for voting and religious tests for officeholding. In addition, the country had grown enormously, from roughly three million at the time Washington took the oath of office to eighteen million by 1840. Millions of white men could now vote, and if nothing else, sheer numbers dictated some form of political organization. Black voting on the other hand, declined during the Jacksonian era as Pennsylvania, North Carolina, and Tennessee took the vote away from free blacks.

The growth of the electorate went hand in hand with the breakdown of class distinctions. Although America was never a classless society, the country had been marked by social fluidity since colonial times. The existence of a large domain of inexpensive or even free land gave most white Americans the opportunity to become freeholders—

to secure that highly prized property stake in society. Moreover, the traditional markings of an aristocracy, birth and inherited status, meant little on the frontier; the ability to survive and prosper or the talent to lead created new and constantly changing elites.

Only in the Northeast and coastal states of the South could one find semblances of hereditary elites, and even there fresh infusions of blood took place in every generation. If few Americans made the journey from log cabin to White House, many made the trip from rude huts to farms and plantations or to careers as successful businessmen and professionals. Symbolically, the first and last presidents elected in the Jacksonian era—Andrew Jackson and Abraham Lincoln—were born in poverty and grew up in log cabins on the frontier.

Government policy encouraged settlement, giving those with ambition and the willingness to work hard an opportunity unknown in the Old World. Through most of the first half of the nineteenth century, the federal government offered eighty acres of good land for $100; some states disposed of their public lands on even more generous terms. For those unwilling to farm, the East also provided a variety of economic opportunities, as new businesses rose to serve a rapidly expanding population. In a nation that was still plagued by chronic labor shortages, workingmen, although far from well off, could earn a decent living. Altogether, these groups formed a large pool of potential political support, eager to back candidates who caught their imaginations or whose program promised them more and better chances to improve their condition.

Politics became a national mania. Foreign observers noted with amazement American preoccupation with political affairs, and how rude farmers and laborers would stand alongside businessmen for hours listening to political speeches. In taverns afterward, they would debate endlessly on the pros and cons of one candidate against another. Parties hastened to organize their supporters from village precincts upward. In September 1831, the Anti-Masonic party held the first national nominating convention and adopted a formal platform, devices soon copied by the National Republicans and the Democrats.

## State Constitutional Development

On the state level, the democratic impulse led to the wholesale rewriting of most state constitutions at least once between 1800 and 1860. Some states overhauled their governmental framework two or three times. Most states held conventions to write new constitutions, with the general electorate choosing delegates to represent them as a committee of the whole. The conventions dealt with a variety of topics, some peculiar to one state, others common across the country. States did not write their constitutions on a tabula rasa, but drew upon their own experiences as well as on those of sister states; a clause in one document would often wind up being copied, sometimes verbatim, in others. New states drew heavily on older ones as they drafted constitutions for the first time; Michigan and Wisconsin relied on New York, while California and Oregon borrowed liberally from Iowa and Indiana. In 1798, Tennessee copied from the North Carolina constitution, just as Kentucky had borrowed from Virginia. This influence reflected the common heritage and values that frontier states shared with their elder siblings, but no state copied another's constitution either in whole or slavishly.

Each state always had to adjust for local values and concerns, but expediency suggested it was prudent to learn from another's experience.

Apportionment and suffrage proved persistent themes, since changes in electoral distribution and who could vote determined who would rule. Western states tended to be more liberal in granting the suffrage to whites, but with a few minor exceptions, refused to grant it at all to blacks. Indiana, Illinois, Mississippi, Alabama, and Missouri, for example, provided for universal white male suffrage in their first constitutions and also made all voters eligible to hold public office. In Ohio after 1849, if localities chose to create a segregated school system, blacks were allowed to vote for board members; similarly, in Michigan blacks could vote in school bond elections. Other new states followed these examples. In more settled states, established power blocs hesitated to disturb the status quo. In Rhode Island, for example, a narrow suffrage and an outdated apportionment scheme kept power in a few hands, and conservatives stubbornly resisted the call for greater democracy. Dorr's Rebellion in 1842 proved an unsuccessful, partially violent, protest against the lack of reform (see Chapter 16). Later that year, the state finally modernized its government and opened the ballot to all adult males without regard to property or race. Similar, though bloodless, battles took place in Pennsylvania, Virginia, and New York; often a halfway compromise substituted tax paying for property owning as a voting qualification.

The dominance of legislative over executive branches, so marked in the state constitutions of the late eighteenth century, gradually gave way to a more equitable sharing of responsibility and power between the governor and the assembly. Governors secured the veto power, and many appointments previously under the control of the legislature became the prerogative of the executive. As a result, strong governors now had the means to serve as forceful and effective state leaders. If the postrevolutionary generation had feared executive arbitrariness, Americans in the second quarter of the nineteenth century worried about too much lawmaking. They were also reacting to repeated legislative scandals, in which large property holders and moneyed corporations gained favorable dispensations, often through outright bribery, as in the Yazoo land scandal. In many cases, efforts to write protections against legislative abuse into constitutions made these documents cumbersome and unworkable, and as conditions changed, their inflexibility required further revisions.

Restrictions on the legislature constituted part of a wider movement to give the people more control over their government. A greater portion of state and local officials would now be elected rather than appointed, so that even minor functionaries would be accountable to the public. On the negative side, the voter confronted a ballot with an often bewildering list of offices and candidates, about whom he often knew little. Political parties, by using slates for these myriads of office-seekers, simplified the process at the same time as they built up their influence.

Fear of the judiciary seemed nearly as prevalent in some states as fear of the legislature, and was reflected in constitutional provisions providing for the periodic election of judges in place of appointment for life. This trend had its roots decades earlier. Vermont provided for the election of local magistrates in 1777, even though it was not officially recognized as a state until 1791. In 1803, Ohio gave the legislature the power to elect the state's judges to seven-year terms. Georgia and Indiana elected some of their judges as early as 1812, while Mississippi first elected all its judges following the constitutional revision of 1832. By the time New York adopted this provision in 1846, the pattern had been set. Scholars have seen this development as part of the general democratization of political life, in which the Jacksonians built upon the ideological base of the Jeffersonians a generation earlier. The distrust that Jefferson and his followers displayed toward the judiciary had not been limited to John Marshall and the federal courts, but took in judges as a whole. So long as the Federalists and their successors retained sufficient power in the states, they had been able to block judicial election, but the tide of Jacksonian democracy swept away the last vestige of resistance. Judges, just like other government officials, went the argument at that time, ought to be responsive to the public will and accountable for their actions.

Such a view ran counter to the Framers' notion that courts should be above the daily rough and tumble of politics, and that an independent judiciary required that judges be free to implement the law without first considering the political implications of their decisions. Similarly, the Founders believed that judges should be chosen, not for their political views or ideological positions, but for their legal acumen. By midcentury, however, such standards for choosing judges were rare. The consequences could be dramatic. One example makes this clear. In 1850, a jury in St. Louis, Missouri found that the slave Dred Scott was entitled to his freedom, based on his residence in free jurisdictions. This result was consistent with numerous Missouri precedents. In 1851, Missouri went from an appointed to an elected Supreme Court, and a majority of the newly elected judges reversed this result for blatantly political reasons. This set the stage for the U.S. Supreme Court's opinion in *Dred Scott v. Sandford* (1857) (see Chapter 18).

A perusal of state constitutions of this period provides insight not only into political ideals but social and economic values as well. Clauses forbidding states to charter banks, such as those in Indiana (1816) and Louisiana (1845), reflected the antibank sentiment that Andrew Jackson exploited in his veto of the bill to recharter the Second Bank of the United States. The effort to restrict corporations took the form of constitutional prohibitions against all special charters, restrictions of general charters to a specific term of years, or prohibitions of the state's purchasing shares in joint stock companies. On the other side, states protected debtors by adopting homestead clauses, which exempted a set amount of land as well as some personal property from forced sale to repay debts. In addition, the idea of free common schools caught on rapidly, especially in the free states, and many state constitutions provided for free public education.

## Constitutional Flexibility

The democratic impulse manifested itself on the national level as well, although not in the form of constitutional revision. Despite Jefferson's dictum that every generation should amend the Constitution to reflect prevailing popular sentiment, the U.S. Constitution has proven remarkably resistant to change. The requirement that two-thirds of Congress must approve an amendment, which three-quarters of the states must ratify, makes change enormously difficult. In the modern United States, it takes only 13 states to prevent the ratification of any amendment. Because of the difficulty of amending the Constitution, at various times Congress, the executive branch, and the federal courts have all met new conditions by reinterpretation rather than by amendment.

---

### THE DIFFICULTY OF AMENDING THE CONSTITUTION

A striking example of the difficulty of amending the Constitution is seen by the constitutional status of slavery. In 1861, there were fifteen slave states. Thus, had the Civil War not intervened, it would, to this day, be impossible to end slavery through a constitutional amendment unless three slave states also voted to end slavery.

---

There were, of course, proposals for change; between 1804 and 1860, Congress received over 400 suggested amendments, but none were ratified. Several states asked Congress to call a new constitutional convention, but they could never muster the support of two-thirds of the states required under Article V. Many of the proposals called for changing the method of choosing the House of Representatives, whose members were then elected on a general, or at large, basis rather than by district. In 1842, however, Congress passed the Apportionment Act, which mandated the election of representatives by district. Another proposal called for the direct election of senators, instead of having state legislators choose them, but this reform did not occur until ratification of the Seventeenth Amendment in 1913. Similarly, the electoral college came under attack, especially following Jackson's defeat in the House of Representatives in 1825, after he had won a plurality of the popular vote. Jackson himself called for such an amendment, but he could never gather the necessary majorities in Congress. Even had such an amendment passed, it is doubtful the states would have ratified it. The slave states, for example, fully understood that the electoral college gave them added power through the three-fifths clause, while a direct election of the president would undermine their power because the North had so many more free people and hence more voters than the South. In fact, the only amendment to secure congressional approval would have stripped American citizenship from persons who accepted foreign titles or honors. It passed Congress in 1810, and came within a single vote of ratification by the states; for many years, in fact, the public believed it had been adopted.

Several reasons explain the failure to amend the Constitution. Although the Framers had wanted to do away with the impossible amendment mechanism of the Articles of Confederation, which required unanimous consent of all the states, they did not intend that the Constitution be easily altered. The processes they chose, proposal either by a two-thirds majority in each house of Congress or by a convention assembled upon the petition of two-thirds of the states, and then ratification by three-fourths of the states, ensured that only important measures with widespread support would gain acceptance. Sectional or political differences, then as now, could block not only frivolous or partisan suggestions, but vital ones as well.

## The Political Party and Its Function

Inability to amend the Constitution did not prevent reform on the federal level. The wide latitude given the national government in its organization and powers allowed the democratic impulse to effect many changes, often through the most significant extra-constitutional feature of American government—the political party system. Although periodically maligned, especially by radicals at the extremes of the political spectrum, political parties have proven wondrously effective in determining the needs and desires of the people and in marshaling support to enact specific programs. Although not perfect, the party system has complemented constitutional government, reinforcing the abstract system of checks and balances and, through competition for votes, providing an additional set of restraints on government leaders. By grouping candidates who were pledged to particular ideas, parties enabled the growing electorate to use the ballot effectively. Parties also permitted voters to choose officials at every level of government, from local justices of the peace to the president of the United States. The party system has served as the chief tool for resolving national conflicts. With the exception of slavery, where the party system could not develop a compromise acceptable to all sides, the system has been able to reconcile differing viewpoints on controversial issues and develop solutions acceptable to a majority of the electorate.

During the Jacksonian era, the party system developed a fully vertical organization, from local through national levels, committed to particular candidates and programs. This organization enabled national nominating conventions to replace the older caucus system, in which small groups of congressional leaders had chosen presidential candidates. The adoption of party platforms strengthened ties between local party workers and the national organization and candidates, and thus bolstered the party in its bid for votes. While all parties are coalitions of various interest groups, they now had to find common ground on which they could unite. Extreme and minority demands could be excluded, since only general proposals could expect to gain a majority of the votes. Critics have pointed out that since major parties often appeal to the middle of the political spectrum, there is in effect little distinction between them. In normal times, this is frequently true; differences are often of degree rather than of kind. But this ignores the process by which conflicting demands are reconciled, or the defusing of radical schemes that could disturb the social equilibrium. Moreover, when it has mattered, the parties have responded and given the people clear-cut choices; significant differences existed between Democrats and Republicans, for example, in 1860, 1864, 1868, 1896, 1936, 1964, 1972, 1980, 1996, and 2000.

Parties exist not just to organize voters or rationalize choices, but above all to win elections, so that candidates can carry out the will of the people and enact their programs. This demands leadership, both in symbol and in fact, and also requires that party workers share in the rewards of victory. Only so many people can hold elective office, but as government grew in the nineteenth century, appointive positions in government administration became more plentiful. Early presidents had sought to appoint men sympathetic to their goals, but they did not always make party loyalty a test for officeholding. For all Jefferson's complaints that Federalists dominated the federal bureaucracy, he did not turn them out wholesale when he took over in 1801. He retained some capable Federalists, fired others, including John Quincy Adams, and appointed Republicans whenever vacancies occurred.

Jackson, however, regarded rotation in office as "a leading principle in the republican creed." He believed that few jobs in the government required skills beyond the competence of the average person, and that, by constant turnover, the government would be assured of honesty and the people given greater control over their affairs. Although Jackson gave lip service to the idea that "to the victor belong the spoils," he proved far more restrained in practice. During the first eighteen months of his admin-istration, he removed only 919 men out of 10,093 government employees, or about 9 percent. In his entire eight years in office, he turned out far less than one-fifth of all federal officeholders.

Nonetheless, patronage became a fixture of American political life for the next fifty years, on both the state and national levels. Although never the motor that drove the party system, as some critics have claimed, patronage did serve as a powerful im-petus for those seeking advancement in politics, as an incentive to work for party vic-tory, and as a tool of party discipline to encourage support of presidential programs. Rotation in office also fit in well with the prevailing democratic ethos, which assumed that the common man had the ability to perform duties of government service and a right to the opportunity. Not only should the people have power over elected officials, but rotation theoretically gave them control over the machinery of government as well.

## Family Law

The democratic impulse could not fail to affect the legal status of many groups in so-ciety, although not all of them; nothing occurred for example, to improve the place of the Indian within the framework of American law. The great majority of African Amer-icans remained bound to perpetual slavery in the South. In the North, free blacks faced social, economic, and political discrimination, but except in the right to vote, gained in legal rights throughout the period. The spirit of reform did more to improve, in vary-ing degrees, the status of other groups.

Changes in the law of family relations led to some improvement for women and children. Because of their scarcity, women had always enjoyed greater freedom in America than in Europe, and in the seventeenth and eighteenth centuries, there was ev-idence that practice often diverged from the strict ideal of total male supremacy em-bedded in the common law. The family supposedly embodied in miniature the ideal-ized traits of the larger society, a small community with clearly delineated authority that imposed the prevailing social values upon the individual. Woman merged with man when married, and the two became legally one; but that one was the husband, who assumed control over his wife's person and property.

In the nineteenth century, the law began slowly to change. Until then, divorce had been uncommon, and even rarer were those instances in which the wife filed suit. In most states, divorce could be granted only by the legislature; in others, courts could dissolve marriages on their own authority; in still others, judicial proceedings had to be validated by the assembly. Starting in the early 1800s, one state after another es-tablished judicial procedures permitting divorce, although the grounds for the action varied enormously. Adultery, desertion, impotence, "gross misbehavior and wicked-ness," even joining the Shaker sect (a community that practiced celibacy) provided, in one state or another, reason to terminate a marriage.

The change in law did not necessarily reflect a more tolerant attitude toward divorce. Congregationalist clergyman Timothy Dwight, for example, fulminated against the practice, warning that Connecticut would become "one vast Brothel; one great province of the World of Perdition." Rather, it reflected the reality that a number of marriages had not worked out to the satisfaction of the partners; in a nation that believed people should and could better themselves, many people saw no good reason why one should not seek a happier marriage, just as one sought more fertile land or a higher-paying job. As legislators became burdened with mounting demands for bills of divorce, they reacted as they had done to increased pressure for private corporate charters—they passed general laws assigning the responsibility to the courts.

Judicial divorce certainly appeared cheaper and easier than legislative divorce, and some states facilitated the process by adding grounds such as habitual drunkenness, cruelty, and conviction of a felony. But divorce still remained expensive, and in poorer areas many marriages dissolved through the simple expedient of desertion or the partners going their separate ways. This raised questions of the individuals' future status, putting more pressure on the states to liberalize the law. Settled areas with more of a defined class structure resisted this pressure. New York maintained adultery as the only grounds for divorce, leading, as Chancellor Kent noted, to collusive arrangements in which the husband committed, or confessed to having committed, adultery, for the sole purpose of securing a divorce. In the West, with looser class structure, legislatures proved more amenable to liberalizing their laws.

## Women's Rights

Still another small gain for women came with the revision of property laws. The traditional view, expressed by Chief Justice Zephaniah Swift of Connecticut in *Griswold v. Penniman* (Conn., 1818), held that "the husband, by marriage, acquires a right to the use of the real property of his wife, during her life. . . . He acquires an absolute right to her chattels real, and may dispose of them. . . . He acquires an absolute property in her chattels personal in possession." There were numerous ways to circumvent such rules, such as premarital settlements or trust arrangements, but these were of value only to the wealthier classes. Persons of limited property neither understood nor could use them. But beginning in the 1830s, several states tentatively reformed their statutes to give married women rights over their own property.

In 1839, Mississippi permitted women to own and sell slaves, although the husbands retained control of the slaves' labor. A few years later, Michigan excluded a wife's earned or inherited property from liability for her husband's debts. Altogether, seventeen states passed some form of a married women's property act by 1850, permitting women to hold property and to contract for its sale independently of their spouses. Even in states without married women's property laws, it appears that women still enjoyed some degree of autonomy. A study of the free women of Petersburg, Virginia, indicates that despite the traditionally paternalistic mores of the time, women owned and dealt extensively in various types of property.

Even where legislation existed, though, its intent was hardly to grant women equality with their husbands. The bulk of litigation over these laws rarely involved spouses; more often, the husband's creditors were suing to reach the wife's property to satisfy a debt. By allowing women some control over their property, the state, at least in part, sought to stabilize the family; in the case of economic failure, the wife's property could help the family make a new start. Economic and legal pressures, not egalitarianism, propelled these changes.

A number of eastern states refused to pass such laws, and unsympathetic courts often construed the statutes so as to nullify their intent. A jumble of moral, ethical, and economic factors often confused the issue. "To enable the wife to leave her husband at pleasure," complained counsel for one irate husband, "and to take with her, all her property . . . to be enjoyed by her, and managed and disposed of as her own . . . in total disregard of the marital rights, is a monstrous proposition, that, among all the wild theories of improvements. has never yet been advocated in a civilized, Christian community."

If women had few legal rights, they had even less to show elsewhere. The Seneca Falls Convention gathered in 1848 to discuss "the social, civil and religious condition and rights of women." It issued a Declaration of Sentiments, mainly the work of suffragist Elizabeth Cady Stanton, which cleverly paraphrased Jefferson's Declaration of Independence, and declared the self-evident truth that "all men and women are created equal." All laws that placed women in positions inferior to men "are contrary to the great precept of nature, and therefore have no force or authority." The suffrage movement gained a number of adherents, but made little headway before the Civil War; its final triumph did not come until ratification of the Nineteenth Amendment in 1920.

Women's legal status changed surprisingly little during this age of reform. They remained excluded from most higher education and professions and could do little else than teach primary school or work in factories or in stores catering to other women if they left the domestic scene. Women nonetheless began their campaign for equal rights that, when compared with other groups, has been agonizingly slow. The opportunities that reformer Margaret Fuller sought, "as a nature to grow, as an intellect to discern, as a soul to live freely and unimpeded," represented the dreams of many in the Jacksonian era, but they would be denied to most women of that generation, as well as their daughters and granddaughters. The few steps taken so hesitatingly in the law reflected the reluctance of society in general to accord women their full rights.

## Children and the Law

One can also perceive some marginal changes in family relations law affecting children during this period. The common law had posited near total parental authority; colonial Massachusetts, in fact, had made filial disobedience a capital crime, although no one appears to have ever been executed under the law. Just as the husband assumed control over his wife's property, the father claimed the earnings of a minor child as well as use of any property the child might inherit. As Chancellor Henry De Saussure of the South Carolina equity court asserted in *Prather v. Prather* (S.C., 1809), the father was the child's "natural guardian, invested by God and the law of the country with reasonable power over the child. Unless his parental power has been monstrously and cruelly abused, this court would be very cautious in interfering with the execution of it." Thus, it would be misleading to talk of children's rights as they later developed, but courts did anticipate the modern doctrine of the best interests of the child in litigation affecting custody and property rights.

With the increase in divorce, courts had to determine not only the division of property, but also who would get the children. They gradually abandoned the older doctrine of the child as the property of the father to inquire into what would best meet the young person's needs. In many cases, judges ruled that small children had greater need for maternal care and awarded custody to the mother. Thus, in the *Prather* case quoted above, Chancellor De Saussure gave a mother custody of an infant daughter, but gave the rest of the children to Mr. Prather, even though he was openly living in adultery with another woman. As Michael Grossberg observed, the judges realized that even this seemingly sensible ruling was "treading on uncertain legal ground."

The change in custody rulings is dramatically illustrated in two New York cases only a few years apart. In *People v. Nickerson* (1837), Mrs. Nickerson had "withdrawn herself from the protection of her husband" and returned to her father's house, taking their infant son with her. Her husband sued for custody; the state supreme court, following traditional common law rules, awarded him custody. It found no reason to doubt his ability to act as "a fit and proper person to have the care and education of the child," and chastised Mrs. Nickerson for abandoning her marital duties and "living in a state unauthorized by the law of the land." In passing, however, the court noted that under some circumstances, if the father could be shown not to be a fit parent, custody might be given to the mother.

Three years later, the New York Senate, acting in its role (akin to that of the British House of Lords) as the state's court of highest appeal, totally ignored both the *Nickerson* decision as well as common law precedents in *Mercein v. The People ex rel. Barry* (1840). In the discussion preceding the vote, Senator Paige argued that "it is the benefit and welfare of the infant to which the attention of the court ought principally to be directed." As to the prevalent notion of parental supremacy, Paige declared that "the interest of the infant is deemed paramount to the claims of both parents." Examining the circumstances, the Senate overwhelmingly decided that the child, who was not in good health, would be better off with his mother.

Most interesting in the *Mercein* case is the view Paige put forward of the child's relation to the state. "The moment a child is born," he said, "it owes allegiance to the government of the country of its birth, and is entitled to the protection of that government. And such government is obligated by its duty of protection, to consult the welfare, comfort and interests of such child in regulating its custody during the period of its minority." Common law had long recognized the concept of *parens patriae,* or the state as parent, but it had been used primarily to preserve an infant's property from "waste" by parents or guardians. American courts expanded the *parens patriae* doctrine to allow intervention to protect a child's person or morals. In this beginning, there exists the legal basis for later laws requiring compulsory education, prohibiting child labor, and eventually extending to children the right to be free from abuse, neglect, or exploitation.

These small steps constituted part of a larger move away from the view of children as miniature adults and toward a recognition of childhood as a distinct stage of life, with its own psychological, physical, social, and ultimately, legal characteristics and needs. Since today's child would be tomorrow's adult citizen, a democratic government had an imperative interest in ensuring fair treatment of its future citizens and protecting them from conditions over which they had no control or responsibility. In the case of illegitimacy, for example, Blackstone described a child born out of wed-lock as *filius nullius,* the child of nobody, with no rights at law. But these children had not created their status, and gradually courts and legislatures reduced the legal stigma of bastardy by allowing unwed mothers and children some rights of custody and inheritance.

By 1850, the legislatures in New York and Massachusetts had altered the com-mon law of child custody, as the outcome in the *Mercein* case reflected. But, most states still almost automatically gave fathers custody of children. Not surprisingly, the "Declaration of Sentiments" issued by the nation's first woman's rights convention in Seneca Falls, New York, in 1848, protested this situation, complaining that the law ig-nored "the happiness of women" by "in all such cases going upon the false supposi-tion of the supremacy of man, and giving all powers into his hands."

Courts also began to regularize the status of orphans and deserted children who had been thrown upon the charity of the community or the good-heartedness of neigh-bors or relatives. Under common law, they had no clear legal status, and no matter how much their new, albeit irregular, families loved them, they had no rights to in-herit, nor did the families have clear legal custody. Judges began to rationalize these informal relations, establishing some limited rights between the de facto parents and children. Then, in 1851, Massachusetts passed the first statute establishing adoption procedures, which the other states soon followed. In such limited ways, children also benefited from the democratic impulse.

## Early Labor Movements

The reform impulse to make society over affected many groups. Alexis de Tocqueville noted with amazement the large number of "intellectual and moral associations" ded-icated to improving society in general and the lot of its less fortunate citizens in par-ticular. Ralph Waldo Emerson epitomized this mindset when he asked: "What is man born for, but to be a Reformer, a Remaker of what man has made?" Societies advo-cating temperance, prison reform, the abolition of slavery, dietary changes, and nu-merous other causes sprouted across the land; there were also dozens of utopian ex-periments, such as John Humphrey Noyes's Oneida Community and Robert Owen's New Harmony. As Emerson noted, "we are all a little mad here with numberless pro-jects of social reform."

Reform seemed particularly active in matters relating to working persons. There had long been associations of skilled workers, most of which met for social reasons or to provide mutual benefits, a tradition that reached back to the medieval guilds. Some-time in the late eighteenth century, these associations began to concentrate on eco-nomic matters, and in some cases they had been able to effect closed shops or even secure higher wages; for the most part, though, they had had little success. The most long-lived of these groups, a union of bootmakers, the Philadelphia Federated Society of Journeymen Cordwainers (the name was derived from the Cordovan leather the cob-blers worked), had been organized in 1794. The society wanted to prevent employers from reducing wages; it also sought a more uniform pay scale among those engaged in making shoes. In the fall of 1805, the society struck for higher wages, and the city's merchants had the leaders arrested and indicted for conspiracy. In *Commonwealth v. Pullis* (1806), the jury found the defendants guilty, the first time the old common law crime of conspiracy had ever been used in American courts. The judge's charge to the jury came down heavily against the union, which he characterized as "a government unto themselves," imperiling public safety and private property. The defense's argument must certainly have struck the city's conservatives as radically dangerous. The employers' freedom to cut wages, the union claimed, constituted an exercise of arbitrary power that denied workers their common rights of man, and the union constituted an appropriate means to resist.

The conviction broke the union, and for a number of years it served as a warning that courts would treat unions unfavorably. During Jackson's administration, however, widespread union activity, usually confined to single crafts, began appearing in major cities, followed by federations that attempted to unite different unions in common purpose. In the 1830s, a number of local craft unions—of printers, shoemakers, and carpenters, for example—joined together in national organizations, and in 1834, the National Trades' Union sought to unite the various local federations. All these groups collapsed in the Panic of 1837. For a while, some unions hoped to win their goals through direct political action. A Working Men's party captured enough seats on the Philadelphia City Council to give it the balance of power; similar organizations sprang up in about fifteen states. Although they all faded quickly, many of the activists gravitated to the Democratic party, especially the more radical wing, ultimately known as Locofocos, where they made their presence felt. Their efforts, in part, led Jackson to establish a ten-hour work day at the Philadelphia Navy Yard in 1836, and four years later, Van Buren extended it to all government workers and projects.

Although early attempts at unionization failed, the unions did not disappear. On the eve of the Civil War, there were still about twenty national groups as well as dozens of local societies. The Democratic party would be their natural home for the next century, and many of their demands would ultimately be enacted into law, such as mechanics' liens, limitations on monopolies, the restriction of leased convict labor, and the elimination of child labor. As a larger percentage of the population worked for wages, unions garnered more sympathy for their cause, although large parts of the business and professional communities have always been hostile to unions. Occasionally, they even found a sympathetic hearing in court.

By the 1840s, a loose characterization would have put the Democrats on labor's side, and the Whigs as favoring merchants and employers. The Whig district attorney of Boston brought an indictment charging conspiracy against the Journeymen Bootmakers' Society, when members threatened to quit an employer who had hired a nonunion employee. Judge Peter O. Thacher, who had previously ruled unions to be common law conspiracies, even absent a state statute to that effect, practically ordered the jury to find the labor leaders guilty. On appeal to the Massachusetts Supreme Judicial Court, however, the highly respected Chief Justice Lemuel Shaw, who could hardly be termed a radical—he was in fact a conservative Whig—overturned the decision in *Commonwealth v. Hunt* (Mass., 1842). Shaw held that unions were not by themselves illegal, nor were their demands that employers hire only union members.

In part, Shaw ruled that employees were free to leave an employer just as an employer was free to fire them. Hunt could not be prosecuted merely for urging his fellow workers to quit their jobs.

Unfortunately for the unions, other courts ignored *Commonwealth v. Hunt* and pursued their antiunion bias in one case after another, citing the Philadelphia cordwainers' decision. Even after some states specifically approved the legality of unions, court injunctions restricted nearly all the unions' most effective tools, such as strikes and boycotts.

# Debtor Imprisonment

Workingmen and reformers in general proved more successful in abolishing imprisonment for debt. Here developments in the United States mirrored changes in England, which limited the practice to relatively high amounts of debt in the Imprisonment for Debt Act of 1827, and virtually abolished imprisonment in the Judgments Act of 1838 and the Debtors Act of 1868.

Traditionally, both law and society frowned on insolvency. The Puritans in New England considered bankruptcy a sure sign of moral degeneration. After the Revolution, all states, following the British custom, had jailed debtors who defaulted on their obligations.

In England, imprisonment for debt reflected the seriousness with which society viewed contractual duties, as well as three complimentary assumptions about debt. First, was the idea that, with the exception of tradesmen and entrepreneurs, most men who went into debt did so knowingly, and with fraudulent or malicious intent. As Blackstone wrote, "If a gentleman, or one in a liberal profession [such as law or medicine], at the time of contracting his debts, has a sufficient fund to pay them, the delay of payment is a species of dishonesty, and a temporary injustice to the creditor; and if, at such time, he has no sufficient fund, the dishonesty and injustice is greater." Second, was the notion that most debtors hid assets or stubbornly refused to use their assets to pay their debts, and the complexities of the writ system made it difficult for creditors to exercise judgments on these assets. A jailed debtor, however, would quickly reveal his assets to pay his debts in order to get out of jail. Third, was the belief that even if the debtor had no assets, his friends and relatives would pay his debts to get him out of jail, and thus the creditor would be satisfied.

These rules may have made some sense in medieval England, when most people were not involved in commerce, most people did not own land, and few people, especially poor people, participated in a market economy or even in a cash economy. As trade and commerce developed, the English government recognized that men involved in trade and commerce might go bankrupt through no fault of their own—such as a warehouse burning down—and thus as early as the reign of Henry VIII, England passed bankruptcy statutes that allowed merchants and only merchants to declare bankruptcy. These laws were later extended to "bankers, brokers, and factors," and others involved in commercial activities.

Such concepts may have made sense in England, where commercial activity was limited to a small class of individuals, and where debt was rarely incurred by most people. Americans thus adopted imprisonment for debt, but unlike England, did not develop bankruptcy laws for those merchants and traders most likely to become bankrupt. The inertia of the English practice lived on in America long after it made any sense.

Furthermore, in America debt was more common, stimulated in part by land speculation. The theories that made imprisonment plausible in England, such as the idea that debtors had hidden assets, made little sense in America, where debtors were likely to be people who failed in the their attempts to raise their status, as well as rich speculators who might have lost everything when their investments failed to pan out. From the end of the Revolution until the Jacksonian period, the law simply ignored the practical reality that a person in prison could hardly pay what he or she owed.

As commerce developed, however, the moral stigma surrounding bankruptcy gave way to a realization that impersonal market forces, rather than the innate goodness or evil of an individual, often dictated the difference between success and failure, and that the same person under other circumstances might prosper. A ship lost to a storm could ruin a merchant; fair winds would make him wealthy.

Congress, under its constitutional authority, passed two short-lived bankruptcy laws before the Civil War, one in 1800 and the other in 1841; the latter reflected this changing attitude and tried to be fair to debtors as well as creditors. States also began applying a morally neutral policy, and the move to abolish debtor imprisonment had started well before Jackson's time. But horror stories still abounded to enrage public sentiment. In 1820, Massachusetts imprisoned 1,442 debtors; in 1827, a sick and elderly man spent four months in jail for a debt of $1.00 and court costs of $3.22. And in 1830, Rhode Island imprisoned a widow for a debt of 68 cents!

Some, but not all, states, wrote prohibitions against debtor imprisonment into their new constitutions. In other states, courts began relaxing the laws or finding loopholes through creative construction to mitigate their severity. They had to, because according to one study, one householder in five in the early nineteenth century became insolvent at some point in his working lifetime. This problem hit not just workers, but also farmers, artisans, small businessmen, and even professionals. Two Framers of the Constitution, Robert Morris and James Wilson, died in prison for debts after their land speculations collapsed.

Thus by the early 1840s, imprisonment for debt had practically disappeared from the scene, although the more general laws that were developed to resolve debtor–creditor relations still remained confused and irrational. Had Congress passed a permanent federal bankruptcy law, there would at least have been uniform procedures throughout the country. In the absence of such law, as John Marshall had ruled in *Sturges v. Crowinshield* (1819), the states remained free to act. Some states treated debtors more liberally than others, but none neglected the rights of creditors. They tried to balance the needs of people who, for whatever reason, could not meet their obligations and needed a fresh start against the legitimate demands of those who had lent them money in good faith expecting to be paid, if not in full, then as much as could be secured from the debtor's assets. No state solved the problem satisfactorily, and the nation had to wait until after the Civil War to get a workable and uniform scheme.

# Pauper Relief

Most debtors, even if scorned by some in society, surmounted their problems, and sufficient sentiment existed by the 1840s to overcome the older notions of debt as immoral. There was no such sympathy for paupers, those who could not make their way in a society in which opportunity seemed so abundant. Something had to be done for the poor, of course, and ever since Elizabethan times, this responsibility had rested on localities. America followed the English pattern, with various state statutes charging communities to provide relief. The federal government had nothing to do with this subject; when social reformer Dorothea Dix lobbied for federal land grants to help the insane, President Franklin Pierce vetoed the bill she secured because the national government should not act as "the great almoner of public charity." Only in treating disabled veterans and sailors did strict Jacksonians like Pierce see a legitimate federal role.

Reform proposals for paupers showed little compassion and seemed grounded on a crude cost and benefit analysis. In the eighteenth century, states had required towns to provide what came to be known as "outdoor" relief: the poor residents of a town received a small dole, and how they lived did not concern the authorities. Where possible, officials put them to work to pay off these sums, usually by having their labor auctioned off to a local farmer or businessman. In 1845, for example, one Emaley Wiley "bought" all the paupers of Fulton County, Illinois, for $594. If the poor moved to another town, the officials there could bill the "home" town for reimbursement of the dole and could go to court in their efforts to collect. Public opinion ran strongly against using taxpayers' money to support the allegedly able-bodied, yet idle poor, even if conscience would not permit them to let the wretches starve.

The concept of asylum originated in numerous sources, but ideas on the treatment of the poor—and to some extent of the criminal—owe a great deal to the writings of the great English philosopher, Jeremy Bentham (1748–1832). Trained as a lawyer, Bentham had read Blackstone's lectures equating the common law with justice and social welfare; yet looking at the real world, he saw crime, injustice, and poverty. He also rejected Blackstone's notion of an immutable natural law. There is no such thing as *Law*, he declared, but thousands of *laws*, made by man, and therefore, changeable by him. Utilizing his pleasure/pain calculus (in which good behavior would be rewarded and bad action punished), he argued that the law could be used to effect specific social policies. He applied this analysis to the British Poor Laws, especially the Elizabethan Era Act of 1601, which had established that every Englishman had a right to relief, and directed the localities to provide it. He suggested instead a "panoptican," a house of industry where the poor would live and labor, all the time learning habits of thrift and industry. Bentham's influence can be seen in the British Poor Law of 1833 and in the almshouse movement in the United States.

During Jacksonian times, provision for helping the poor shifted to "indoor" relief—almshouses, or, as they were commonly called, poorhouses. There the paupers, following the Benthamite model, were subjected to mandatory moral education and required to work, in the hope that once having learned the immorality of poverty, they would become self-sustaining members of society. The sponsors of this movement undoubtedly harbored humane sentiments; they sought not just to alleviate poverty but to cure it. They saw the very poor as victims, not of society, but of their own moral infirmity; the proper "cure" was to awaken them to the need to change their ways.

Hard-headed economic considerations also figured in these proposals, as Bentham had also pointed out. Indoor relief would reduce costs and end the problem of paupers wandering the countryside, begging from door to door and causing friction between townships over who had responsibility for them. The Quincy Report in Massachusetts in 1821 and the Yates Report in New York three years later urged indoor relief as the most efficient means of dealing with the problem. As New York reformer John Yates claimed:

> The average annual expense *in* an almshouse having a convenient farm attached to it, will not exceed 20 to 35 dollars for the support of each pauper, exclusive of the amount of labour he may perform; while *out* of an almshouse, it will not be less than from 35 to 65 dollars, and in many instances where the pauper is old and infirm, or diseased, from 80 to 100 dollars, and even more.

In practice, the poorhouse removed the problem from the sight of an indifferent public. Yet instead of becoming schools for moral and manual training, they became dumping grounds for the unfortunate; instead of showing paupers how to live cleanly and comfortably, they quickly degenerated into hellholes. But the poor had no choice. State laws usually conditioned aid upon their entering the almshouse; those states that still permitted some form of outdoor relief limited the amount so severely that the poor had no real alternative. As for rights, paupers had none. Most statutes gave local authorities the power to send beggars to the poorhouse without any formal hearing, and courts rarely, if ever, intervened in the process.

The poorhouse and its cousin, the insane asylum, nonetheless represented another aspect of Jacksonian era reform. The sponsors of almshouses originally conceived of such institutions not only as expedient but also as providing the best hopes of "curing" the problem of poverty. For the insane, reformers sought a more enlightened environment to deal with a problem few people understood. There were, to begin with, few hospitals in the country at the time, and of these, only a handful had facilities to care for "lunaticks." For the most part, families took care of the mentally ill at home as best they could, and if that proved impossible, they had them confined in jails or almhouses. Starting in 1815, states established asylums for the insane, separating them from criminals. Advocates of the insane asylum also hoped for cures; a report to the Massachusetts legislature in 1832 optimistically asserted that with the right treatment, "insanity yields with more readiness than ordinary disease."

Like poorhouses, mental asylums proved little more than warehouses to keep their unfortunate inmates out of sight. Dorothea Dix, the remarkable woman who spearheaded the drive to provide more humane treatment for the insane, told the Massachusetts legislature what she had seen—inmates confined in *"cages, closets, cellars, stalls, pens! Chained, naked, beaten with rods, and lashed into obedience!"* More effective than many reformers, she got twenty states either to increase their support for public institutions or to create new ones, in which more humane policies would govern. She convinced Congress to establish St. Elizabeth's Hospital in Washington, D.C., and even lectured the Pope on the Church's responsibility for taking better care of the insane in Rome. But the problem proved far beyond the medical or psychological knowledge of her day; she pricked the legislative conscience to at least provide better care, but little else could then be done. As with paupers, the mentally ill had no rights, and few had even a chance ever to leave the asylum to which they could be so easily consigned. It would be well over a century before the idea that mentally ill persons retained the minimal rights of due process would make a dent in American law.

## The New Prison

Bentham also applied his utilitarian ideas to criminals. Joliet Prison in Illinois became the first penitentiary in the United States to be modeled directly on the panoptican; several others reflected the new idea that incarceration should serve not only as a punishment but also as an aid to rehabilitation. In Joliet, as well as in Auburn in New York and Cherry Hill in Philadelphia, prisoners would be subject to a harsh but fair discipline in which they would learn the error of their ways, ultimately emerging as useful, law-abiding citizens. These prisons emphasized solitary confinement and strict adherence to minutely detailed codes of conduct. Prisoners remained silent at all times and had to listen to numerous sermons urging them to repent of their evil ways.

As with the poor and the insane, the idea of asylum failed for criminals as well. In effect, prisons got criminals off the streets, at least those criminals caught and convicted, but fear governed their administration far more than did humane impulses. The English novelist Charles Dickens, visiting Cherry Hill, exclaimed in horror that "the benevolent gentlemen who carry [this discipline] into execution, do not know what they are doing." In his book *American Notes*, Dickens described the regimen, which drove some prisoners insane, as "immeasurably worse than any torture of the body." Not surprisingly, discipline soon broke down, and within a few years, officials at Cherry Hill had to resort to strait jackets, beatings, and iron gags. Conditions in other facilities proved just as bad, with legislatures reluctant to spend the money needed to run them as the reformers had intended. The public, with few exceptions, did not care: as with the poor and the insane, criminals out of sight were out of mind.

Once in prison, convicts had no rights, other than to be released when they had served their time. How many rights they had enjoyed during their trials is hard to determine. Criminal law remained a question of state law, and not until the twentieth century did the Supreme Court begin to apply the guarantees of the Fourth, Fifth, and Sixth amendments to the states (see Chapter 29). A few states had bills of rights modeled after the federal list; at a minimum, there had to be a jury trial and proof of guilt and, in some cases, poor defendants had access to lawyers. The law itself did not really change that much; it still emphasized property crimes, and a number of regulatory infractions reflected local economic predilections rather than any attempt at reform.

## Code Revision

One of the most striking efforts at legal reform in this time stemmed, at least in part, from the ever-increasing caseload of state courts, which in many cases doubled in the mid-nineteenth century. The drive to simplify the procedural mechanisms of the law burst into flower in the 1840s, but, as in so many "revolutions," its origins dated back a number of years.

The ancient common law and equity pleadings had, by the end of the eighteenth century, ceased to facilitate the search for justice, and had become a quagmire that only skilled and expensive lawyers could traverse. Originally, the various pleadings had the purpose of eliminating all secondary matters from a civil dispute, so that by the time a case came to trial, the judge and jury could focus on the one critical issue at dispute. As the law grew more complex, however, so did the pleadings, and attorneys, aware of weaknesses in their client's case, manipulated technicalities to delay a trial for years. Charles Dickens parodied this situation in *Bleak House,* describing "Jarndyce and Jarndyce," as a "scarecrow of a suit," which had "in course of time, become so complicated, that no man alive knows what it means."

In England, Jeremy Bentham aimed some of his sharpest barbs at this procedural morass, and while despairing of reform in his native land, he hoped that the United States would prove a more fertile ground for reform; the new nation, after all, had already taken the radical step of merging law and equity in the federal courts, and in some of the states. In October 1811, Bentham wrote to President James Madison, offering to draw up for the United States a code of law, or as he called it, a *Pannomion,* reducing all legal principles to statute. Bentham rejected Blackstone's veneration of common law and its reliance on previously decided cases; such unwritten law, interpreted at whim by judges, seemed to Bentham worse than no law, because one could not rely on securing similar results in all cases. In place of the tradition-bound vagaries of common law, Bentham proposed a European-style civil code, reflecting the ideas of positive law. Because of the War of 1812, Madison did not respond until May 1816. While admitting that Bentham had outlined noble goals, he declined the offer, doubting its practicability.

Bentham's ideas, however, did have great impact not only on Great Britain but in the United States as well. Edward Livingston, who drew up the civil code of Louisiana (the only state that, because of its French origins, never adopted common law), acknowledged that Bentham's works had inspired and guided him. By the 1830s, a number of positivists (those who believed in statute or positive law) could be heard calling for reform. In 1825, the Massachusetts House of Representatives called for a complete revision of the common law, with its essential principles codified in statute. "Let the obsolete, unconstitutional, frivolous and iniquitous parts of the common law be abolished," the report urged, "and whatever is good and useful be passed into statute law," expressed in language so clear that even high school students could understand it.

New York, and not the Bay State, gave codification its greatest boost when its 1845 constitution called for the establishment of a commission "to revise, reform, simplify, and abridge the rules and practices, pleadings, forms and proceedings of the courts of record of this State." The people got more than they anticipated when David Dudley Field, a New York lawyer and legal reformer, joined the commission in 1847. Field had long called for codification, and the resulting New York Code of 1848, popularly called the Field Code, reflected his obsession with statute law, and streamlined procedure in nearly every one of its clauses. The heart of Field's procedural reform can be found in Section 69:

> The distinction between actions at law and suits in equity, and the forms of all such actions and suits, heretofore existing, are abolished; and, there shall be in this state, hereafter, but one form of action, for the enforcement or protection of private rights and the redress of private wrongs, which shall be denominated a civil action.

Later sections mandated that all complaints initiating a civil action, as well as defendants' responses to them, should be brief and precise; requested relief should be spelled out and, if in money, with the exact amount.

The New York Code embodied numerous other reforms. It reduced the pleadings in civil suits to complaint, answer, reply, and demurrer (an admission that the facts stated are true but do not support a legal cause of action), and it liberalized the procedure for amending complaints. The purpose of common law pleading had been to reduce the dispute to a single *issue;* the Field Code emphasized revealing the underlying *facts* on which the claim rested, as well as the defense to it. With the facts thus exposed, judge and jury would then have a better understanding of which law to apply.

Other states quickly copied the New York code, among them California, where Field's brother Stephen practiced; then several western states modeled their codes on that of California. Ultimately, the basic ideas of the Field Code would be adopted in the Federal Code of Civil Procedure enacted in 1938; this provided that federal pleadings should emphasize facts rather than issues, but it also aimed at ensuring *notice* of a claim or defense, so that adequate discovery could be made in the course of trial preparation. At present, most states adhere to the purpose and general form of the federal rules; although a handful of states still retain common law pleadings, they bear little resemblance to the ancient forms.

The Field Code, despite its rapid adoption in several states, did not go uncontested. Lawyers for the most part opposed it bitterly, some because they did not want to give up the forms of pleading that they saw as sanctified by time and usage, others because they believed that simplified pleadings would either reduce their business or possibly allow clients to do without attorneys altogether. Some lawyers no doubt genuinely believed that the existing system, however cumbersome, was better—or at least safer—than the new and untried code system. Since they could not stop the demand for reform outright, many opponents of reform adopted the tactic of killing the new procedures through amendment. The New York bar managed to restrict the reach of Field's reforms by securing additional code revisions in 1851, 1876, and 1880. By then, Field's brief and efficient proposal had swollen to 3,356 sections, and a new demand for reform arose to do away with this monstrosity and to adopt a simplified procedure!

The courts also resisted change, and advocates of simplification claimed, with some truth, that judges deliberately sabotaged the code. Some judges refused to believe that law and equity could ever be merged; others cherished the arcane mysteries of the old pleadings as much as the lawyers who practiced before them.

Perhaps the real reason for the hostility lay not in the specifics of the new codes, but in the philosophical differences between common law and code jurisprudence. The strength of the common law was its grounding in experience; at their best, common law judges responded to changing circumstances, fashioning new and relevant rules of law out of older principles. Conversely, the common law valued precedent and stability, and in its less creative periods, judges seemingly ignored the world around them, applying ancient and outmoded cases. Advocates of statutory law and procedural reform saw only the latter situation, and claimed that legislatures, politically responsive to popular needs, could continuously modernize the law by the simple expedient of enacting new legislation. They failed to see any benefit in tradition and so discarded the old pleadings, ignoring the importance of form as well as substance in law. Deriving their principles from abstract reasoning, reformers often seemed to know little of the actual workings of courts or the cases that came before them. In the end, the reformers won, but only after the revisions had a chance to be absorbed into the common law mode.

The bulk of the opposition could be found in the East, where legal tradition had strong ties to English antecedents. In the West, acceptance came much more easily, partly because of the lack of a strong pleadings tradition, partly because of the more open and eclectic atmosphere of bar and bench, partly because of the scarcity of trained and experienced lawyers, and partly because some of the problems they faced did not fit into the neat pigeonholes of the old law. Land registration cases constituted a large portion of all court business west of the Appalachians, yet where did one classify it— equity or law? In fact, it fit into neither of these categories, and a reform that abolished the distinction made eminent sense. Courts adopted laws that fit local needs, and when the forms of common law interfered with need, the Field Code provided the means to circumvent the roadblock.

Statutory law, which the positivists believed better reflected current needs, also had its drawbacks. It lacked flexibility, for, once written, it froze the law into static form and could be changed only by additional legislation, a process rarely as easy as the reformers believed. Moreover, the sword cut both ways: positive law too could prevent judges from adjusting the law to rapidly changing conditions. This may have appealed to reformers in the more settled East; it proved less attractive in the West, where change often seemed the only constant. The nation ultimately adopted simplified procedures, and more law would be statutory than judge-made; but the need for flexibility and creativity ensured that American law would always retain a large measure of common law jurisprudence.

## Race Relations and Antislavery

The most important reform movement of this period was the antislavery or abolitionist movement. We will discuss the law of slavery and abolition Chapter 17. However, the reform impulses of Jacksonian America cannot be fully understood without some discussion of slavery and antislavery.

The antislavery movement began as a reaction to the formation of the American Colonization Society in 1817. That organization advocated that blacks be recolonized in Africa. Some members of the ACS were dedicated to the abolition of slavery, and saw colonization as a way to stimulate masters to voluntarily free their slaves. Over the next three and a half decades, about 5,500 slaves would in fact get their freedom so they could be repatriated by the ACS to Liberia. Some of these conditional manumissions were the subject of litigation, often brought by heirs trying to defeat wills that freed slaves on the condition that they were sent to Africa. In *Elder v. Elder's Executor* (1833), the Virginia court upheld a will directing that slaves be given the choice of freedom in Liberia or continued slavery in Virginia. However, in *Bailey v. Poindexter's Executor* (1858), the Virginia court struck down a similar will.

Most free blacks in the United States vehemently objected to expatriation and saw the ACS as a proslavery tool to remove free blacks from the society, and thus further strengthen slavery. The harsh criticisms of blacks, especially by the Boston pamphleteer David Walker, led a white opponent of slavery, William Lloyd Garrison, to organize the American Anti-Slavery Society in 1831. Garrison called on whites to take immediate steps to begin the emancipation of all slaves.

Although never attracting more than a small percentage of the Northern population as members of their societies, abolitionists had an enormous impact on Northern society. By the 1840s, most Northerners were thinking about slavery, and once they thought about it, most opposed it. Most Northerners did not demand the immediate end to slavery, as Garrison and his followers did, but they did want an end to new slave states. Lincoln, who in many ways truly represented the North, argued that slavery should be put on the road to ultimate extinction. By the late 1850s, this sentiment against slavery would coalesce around Lincoln and the Republican party.

Until the Civil War, the opponents of slavery were thoroughly unsuccessful at the federal level. In the Northern states, however, they achieved success in four general areas.

First, they succeeded in getting their states to eliminate whatever remnants of slavery still existed within the North. For example, in 1827, New York freed all the remaining slaves in that state. In 1847, Pennsylvania finally emancipated those few people, all born before 1780, who were still slaves. Abolitionists were not totally successful in New Jersey, which still had a few hundred slaves as late as 1845, when a new constitution converted these blacks, all born before 1804, into indentured servants.

Second, through litigation and political activism, opponents of slavery convinced most of the free states to immediately emancipate any slaves brought within their jurisdiction. Thus, in response to a suit brought by the Boston Female Anti-Slavery Society, Chief Justice Lemuel Shaw ruled in *Commonwealth v. Aves* (Mass., 1836), that slaves brought into Massachusetts by the voluntary actions of their masters became immediately free. Connecticut followed suit in 1837. In 1841, New York, responding to antislavery pressure, repealed a law that had allowed visiting masters to keep their slaves in the state for up to nine months. In 1847, Pennsylvania passed a similar law, repealing its six-month transit law. This issue had important implications for the national Constitution, and will be discussed in greater depth in Chapter 17.

Third, starting in the 1820s and continuing until the Civil War, opponents of slavery successfully convinced Northern legislatures to pass personal liberty laws to help prevent the kidnaping of free blacks by Southerners hunting for fugitive slaves. These laws were also designed to frustrate the implementation of the fugitive slave clause of the Constitution, and the federal laws of 1793 and 1850, which had been passed to implement this clause. We will also return to this issue in Chapter 17.

Finally, opponents of slavery also worked to improve the conditions of free blacks in the North. In 1849, for example, a coalition of Free-Soilers and Democratic state legislators repealed Ohio's black code, provided for public education for blacks (with segregated schools as a local option), and sent a dedicated opponent of slavery, Salmon P. Chase, to the U.S. Senate. By 1860, blacks could find some form of public education open to them in almost all of the North. This was not equal education, but compared to the South, where in some places it was illegal for even free blacks to attend schools, this was huge step forward. In *Roberts v. Boston* (Mass., 1850), Chief Justice Shaw found that segregation in the state's public schools did not violate the Massachusetts constitution. But five years later, the state legislature banned the practice. By the end of the decade, Maine and Vermont had also eliminated all forms of state-created racial discrimination.

## Conclusion

We have seen how the democratic impulse that accompanied and propelled Andrew Jackson to power affected the political and legal contours of the nation in numerous ways. In some areas, it proved successful, as in the democratization of political life; in others, despite great effort, society took only small steps to improve the status of groups that were suffering from a variety of disabilities. Perhaps the most important achievement of some of the programs that failed is that they indicated a trail for future reformers to follow. But all these conflicts soon paled before the greatest reform movement of the nineteenth century—the drive to abolish slavery.

## For Further Reading

State constitutional changes are detailed in Merrill Peterson, ed., *Democracy, Liberty and Property: The State Constitutional Conventions of the 1820s* (1966). Relatively little has been written on the subject in recent years, other than an isolated article or two, such as William E. Nelson, "Changing Conceptions of Judicial Review: The Evolution of Constitutional Theory in the States, 1790–1860," 120 *University of Pennsylvania Law Review* 1166 (1972). One has to refer to older works such as Fletcher M. Green, *Constitutional Development in the South Atlantic States, 1776–1860* (1930); or James Q. Dealey, *Growth of American State Constitutions, 1776–1914* (1915).

Political parties, on the other hand, have been the subject of far more scholarly attention. See, for example, Richard P. McCormick, *The Second American Party System: Party Formation in the Jacksonian Era* (1966); Lee Benson, *The Concept of Jacksonian Democracy: New York as a Test Case* (1961); Richard Hofstadter, *The Idea of the Party System* (1969); James S. Chase, *Emergence of the Presidential Nominating Convention, 1789–1832* (1973); and Michael F. Holt, *The Rise and Fall of the American Whig Party: Jacksonian Politics and the Onset of Civil War* (1999). See also Kermit L. Hall, *The Politics of Justice: Lower Federal Judicial Selection and the Second Party System 1829–1861* (1979).

For the wide range of reforms during this era, Alice Felt Tyler, *Freedom's Ferment: Phases of American Social History to 1860* (1944), is still good; while Ronald G. Walters, *American Reformers* (1978), looks at the limits of the reform impulse. On mental and penal reform, see Gerald N. Grob, *Mental Institutions in America* (1973), and David J. Rothman, *The Discovery of the Asylum* (1971). For the poor laws in action, see Martha Branscombe, *The Courts and the Poor Laws in New York State, 1784–1929* (1943); for prisons, see Negley K. Teeters and John D. Shearer, *The Prison at Philadelphia: Cherry Hill* (1957); and W. David Lewis, *From Newgate to Dannemora, The Rise of the Penitentiary in New York, 1796–1848* (1965). Dickens's observations are in his *American Notes* (1842). See also Edward L. Ayres, *Vengeance and Justice:*

*Crime and Punishment in the 19th Century American South* (1984), which claims that prior to the Civil War, not too much difference in criminal patterns and incidence existed between North and South.

The changes in family law and the status of women are documented and discussed in several sources. The leading work on family law, including child custody issues, is Michael Grossberg, *Governing the Hearth: Law and Family in Nineteenth-Century America* (1985). On adoption, see Jamil Zainaldin, "The Emergence of a Modern American Family Law: Child Custody, Adoption, and the Courts, 1796–1851," 78 *Northwestern University Law Review* 1038 (1979). The most important starting point for the status of women in the nineteenth-century United States is Sandra VanBurkleo, *"Belonging to the World": Women's Rights in American Constitutional Culture* (2001). Also useful is Carl Degler, *At Odds; Women and Family in America from the Revolution to the Present* (1980); or Gerda Lerner, *The Woman in American History* (1970). Suzanne Lebsock, *The Free Women of Petersburg: Status and Culture in a Southern Town, 1784–1860* (1984), suggests that women experienced increasing autonomy in the sense of "freedom from utter dependence on particular men." Legal rather than feminist pressures led to the Married Women's Property Acts, according to Norma Basch, *In the Eyes of the Law: Women, Marriage, and Property in Nineteenth-Century New York* (1982). Changes in divorce law are recounted in Nelson M. Blake, *The Road to Reno, A History of Divorce in the United States* (1962). The early women's rights movement is assessed in Ellen Dubois, *Feminism and Suffrage: The Emergence of an Independent Women's Movement, 1848–1869* (1978).

For labor's role and response to economic growth, see, among others, Edward E. Pessen, *Most Uncommon Jacksonians: The Radical Leaders of the Early Labor Movement* (1967); Joseph G. Rayback, *A History of American Labor* (1966); and Bruce Laurie, *The Working People of Philadelphia, 1800–1850* (1980). Peter J. Coleman, *Debtors and Creditors in America: Insolvency, Imprisonment for Debt, and Bankruptcy, 1607–1900* (1974), is uneven, but is useful for its compendium of state laws, and has very good essays on imprisonment for debt and the evolution of bankruptcy laws. There are numerous journal articles on restrictions of employer liability; for the fellow servant rule, see Lawrence M. Friedman and Jack Ladinsky, "Social Change and the Law of Industrial Accidents," 67 *Columbia Law Review* 50 (1967).

Procedural reform, and especially the Field Code, are examined in Maxwell Bloomfield, "William Sampson and the Codifiers: The Roots of American Legal Reform, 1820–1830," 11 *American Journal of Legal History* 234 (1967); Mildred Coe and Lewis Morse, "Chronology of the Development of the David Dudley Field Code," 27 *Cornell Law Quarterly* 238 (1941); Robert W. Miller, *Civil Procedure of the Trial Court in Historical Perspective* (1952); and Lawrence M. Friedman, "Law Reform in Historical Perspective," 13 *St. Louis University Law Journal* 351 (1969). See also Charles M. Cook, *The American Codification Movement: A Study of Ante Bellum Legal Reform* (1981).

On legal change for free blacks, see Robert Cottrol, *The Afro-Yankees: Providence's Black Community in the AnteBellum Era* (1982); Paul Finkelman, "Prelude to the Fourteenth Amendment: Black Legal Rights in the Antebellum North," 17 *Rutgers Law Journal* 415 (1986); on social discrimination against blacks, see James Oliver Horton and Louis Horton, *Black Bostonians* (rev. ed., 1999); James Oliver Horton, *Free People of Color* (1993); and Leon Litwack, *North of Slavery: The Free Negro in the North* (1961).

# 16

# The Taney Court:
# Change and Continuity

THE SURGE OF Jacksonian democracy, as we have seen, played a major role in the legal reforms of the era. Like their Jeffersonian predecessors, the Jacksonians initially saw the judiciary as a conservative bastion preserving property rights against the popular needs of the community. On a constitutional level, the Supreme Court under Roger Brooke Taney generally emphasized the idea of public power, expressed through statute, as a counterweight to the Federalist and Whig concern for property. But despite some significant departures from the ideas of John Marshall, Taney built upon his predecessor's work, and continued to expand and protect the Court's influence.

## The New Chief Justice

Taney succeeded as chief justice a man who, in Joseph Story's words, "cannot be equalled." Together with five other Jackson appointees to the Court, Taney had the opportunity to extend the ideas of the Democratic party through the judiciary as they already had been in the legislative and executive branches. Taney had been among Old Hickory's most devoted followers. He had drafted key portions of Jackson's veto of the national bank, and then as secretary of the treasury had carried out the disastrous transfer of government funds to local pet banks. Admirers of the Court under Marshall could hardly view his appointment with equanimity, for it had been Taney who had written, in the veto message, that "the opinion of the judges has no more authority over

Congress than the opinion of Congress has over the judges, and on that point the President is independent of both." Indeed, Taney had aroused such animosity that the Senate had previously refused to confirm him as an associate justice of the Court, but in March 1836, Jackson had the votes to successfully appoint him chief justice.

Taney would serve for twenty-seven years, longer than any chief justice but Marshall, and he would see the Union severed during that tenure; in fact, his opinion in *Dred Scott v. Sandford* (1857) hastened the advent of Civil War. A Catholic during a time of intense anti-Catholic sentiment, a man psychologically marked by electoral defeats and the refusal of the Senate three times to confirm his appointment to high office, Taney's judicial career has sometimes been interpreted in the light of one case— his majority opinion in *Dred Scott v. Sandford*. Such an interpretation fails to recognize the great accomplishments of Taney and his Court. Yet, Taney's opinion in *Dred Scott* was fully consistent with his overwhelmingly proslavery jurisprudence, his deep hostility to free blacks, and his opposition to the expansion of federal power and the nationalization of rights, *except* when such an increase in power was useful to protect slavery. A Southerner (from Maryland) and a defender of states' rights, he nonetheless did not intend to preside over the dismantling of the Supreme Court. The fact that the tribunal would now take a different approach could hardly be doubted; but if Taney proved to be less nationalistic than his predecessor, the Court continued the work of elaborating the Constitution as the supreme law of the land.

Observers of the Court in Taney's first term in 1837, thought that the evidence of new directions was unmistakable. *Charles River Bridge* certainly departed from the vested rights direction of the Marshall Court toward support of new and dynamic capital (see Chapter 14). The Court's decisions on two other cases involving the continuing issue of state powers—*Briscoe v. Bank of Kentucky* (1837) and *Mayor of New York v. Miln* (1837)—also differed from what might have been expected under Marshall.

The Constitution (Article I, Section 10) prohibited states from issuing bills of credit, and in *Craig v. Missouri* (1830), Marshall had struck down a state scheme that allowed state loan office certificates to serve as a form of currency. *Craig* especially hurt the South and West, where hard currency remained scarce and the states lacked capital for economic development. Kentucky attempted to get around the constitutional problem by chartering a bank wholly owned by the state, which issued notes that circulated as currency. As a Southerner, Taney sympathized with the economic needs that had led to the Kentucky Plan, and he assigned Justice John McLean, who had dissented in *Craig*, to write the majority opinion in *Briscoe v. Bank of Kentucky* (1837), upholding the law. McLean avoided the substantive issue of whether notes issued by a state-created bank in fact constituted state notes by looking only at the form; the bank had issued the notes, not the state, and therefore the Constitution had not been violated. The decision was consistent with the Jacksonian goal of allowing states to set their own economic and banking policy. Indeed, the destruction of the Bank of the United States, which Taney had helped accomplish, seemed to require that the states be allowed greater latitude on banking and currency issues. Joseph Story dissented alone, and, evoking Marshall, claimed that "had he been living he would have spoken in the joint names of both of us."

*Briscoe v. Bank of Kentucky* had little lasting significance, and is important primarily as an indication of the Taney Court's willingness to shift the federal balance away from Marshall's nationalism toward the states. Yet Taney did not intend to destroy what his predecessor had built; for all his states' rights sympathies, he understood the need for a strong central government, as well as the necessity of protecting property rights in order to sustain economic growth. He showed this side of his judicial philosophy in *Bronson v. Kinzie* (1843).

The Panic of 1837 had led a number of states to enact debtor relief laws to help prevent foreclosure of mortgages. These statutes usually involved some sort of stay, giving debtors additional time to meet their obligations; they also established minimal amounts, usually a percentage of market value, below which the property could not be sold at foreclosure sales. Creditors naturally objected to these laws, and in *Bronson,* Taney ruled that they unconstitutionally impaired the obligation of contract. But Taney did recognize the legitimate problems confronting the states, and like Story in *Dartmouth College,* he pointed out to the states a way in which they could act properly. In fact, he relied on an earlier Story opinion on *Green v. Biddle* (1823) to note that although the substantive obligation could not be impaired, the states retained the power to adjust the remedies, so that proper legislation could change future debtor-creditor relations.

Another major case of the 1837 term, *Mayor of New York v. Miln,* involved a state law requiring all vessels docking in New York City to provide a list of passengers and to post security against these passengers from becoming public charges. Miln, the master of the ship *Emily,* had not done so, and the city sought to collect the statutory penalty for his failure to file the report. Miln argued that the state had no power to pass such a law, since it violated the Commerce Clause, which vested all powers over interstate and foreign commerce in the Congress. Justice Philip J. Barbour, whom Jackson had named to the Court at the same time as Taney, avoided the Commerce Clause argument, and instead invoked, for the first time, what later came to be called the state police power—the right of a state to take all necessary steps to protect the health, safety, and welfare of its citizens. A state, according to Barbour, is as competent "to provide precautionary measures against the moral pestilence of paupers, vagabonds, and possibly convicts, as it is to guard against the physical pestilence, which may arise from unsound and infectious articles imported."

Although the reasoning in *Miln* may have been novel, the common law had restricted the free movement of paupers for centuries. While limits on the right to move about, based solely on a person's economic status, offend modern notions of civil liberty, few judges of the nineteenth century saw anything wrong; society had the right to limit the actions of those who drained away its resources.

While not apparent at first glance, the subtext to the decision in *Miln* was the growing sectional tension over slavery and the rights of free blacks. While *Miln* was the first case in which the Supreme Court had articulated the police power in this way, the concept had been articulated by lawyers for the state of South Carolina in the Circuit Court case of *Elkison v. Deliesseline* (1823), which tested the validity of South Carolina's "Negro Seamen's Act." Since 1820, South Carolina and other southern coastal states had been arresting free black sailors who entered their ports. In *Elkison,* Justice William Johnson, while riding circuit, heard a case involving a West Indian sailor on a British ship who was arrested and jailed while his ship was in the port of Charleston. Justice Johnson, who was a native of South Carolina and a staunch Jeffersonian, nevertheless denounced South Carolina's law. However, because of the procedural posture of the case, Justice Johnson declared he had no jurisdiction in the case. After that decision, officials in Massachusetts and other northern maritime states tried to get South Carolina to stop enforcing its "black seamen's law" against sailors from the free states. However, in *Miln,* the Supreme Court indirectly supported South Carolina on this issue. If New York could control immigrants, then, South Carolina and other slave states argued, they could control the influx of free blacks, who they believed threatened slavery.

In the 1840s, Massachusetts would attempt to negotiate directly with South Carolina and Louisiana to resolve the problem. But, with precedents like *Miln* to fall back on, the Southern states with major seaports all insisted on the right to arrest free black sailors. Ultimately, the Fourteenth Amendment, adopted after the Civil War, would resolve this issue. When introducing what would become the Fourteenth Amendment in Congress, John Bingham of Ohio would make a direct reference to the refusal of the slave states to allow free black sailors to enter their ports. Meanwhile, a number of states, relying on *Miln,* enacted laws restricting indigents. In *Crandall v. Nevada* (1868), the Supreme Court would recognize a constitutional right to travel, based on the Fourteenth Amendment. In *Edwards v. California* (1941), *Memorial Hospital v. Maricopa* (1973), and *Saenz v. Roe* (1999), the Supreme Court ruled that economic status cannot be used to limit freedom of movement.

## The Court and Codification

The Supreme Court, although primarily concerned with national and constitutional questions, must also be sensitive to trends in local law, for there is a significant connection between what the states are doing and the powers of the federal government. State commercial law, for example, must always be viewed with an eye to the reach of the Commerce Clause. The codification movement exercised its greatest vigor, appropriately, in the individual states, but the interaction of national and state law in the federal system led to at least a marginal impact on the Supreme Court and its justices. Joseph Story, for example, had been an early advocate of codification, and had applauded Louisiana's civil law system, but he became less enthusiastic in light of what he perceived as democratic excess among the Jacksonians. In 1836, he chaired a Massachusetts committee to study the practicability of codifying that state's common law, and his report took an ambiguous position: although some areas, such as civil rights, property, contract, and criminal law could be codified, in other areas the common law should not be stifled by strict rules. The report said nothing about practice or pleadings. As Story told a friend, "We have not yet become votaries of the notions of Jeremy Bentham."

No other justice of the Court at the time seems to have taken much interest in the subject. Congressional statutes governing procedure called for federal courts to use the rules of the state in which they were located, as fixed at the time the state entered the Union. As a result, federal rules remained fairly static. In 1842, Congress gave the Court power to promulgate federal rules for both law and equity, but the justices, evidently satisfied with the existing situation, took no action. As more and more states enacted procedural reform, however, the disparity between federal court practices in the new and the older states became extremely confusing. Thus in 1872, Congress passed the Conformity Act, calling for federal courts to use the state rules that were currently in effect.

In the few cases involving procedural changes that did come to the Court, the justices showed little sympathy for reform. Part of the problem grew out of the confusion that inevitably accompanies a changeover from one system to another. But the conservatism of some of the high court's members—at least in this area—can hardly be disguised. Justice Robert C. Grier of Pennsylvania spoke for a unanimous Court in several minor cases involving problems arising from the new codes, and in each one he disparaged the innovations. "It is no wrong or hardship to suitors who come to the courts for a remedy," he declared in *Farni v. Tesson* (1862), "to be required to do it in the mode established by the law. State Legislatures may substitute, by code, the whims of solicitors and inventors for the experience and wisdom of the ages; but the success of these experiments is not such as to allure the court to follow their example." Not until the appointment of men from the code states in the 1860s did the nation's highest court finally accept the ideas of codification and procedural reform. By then, the early state efforts had matured, and through experience, had produced at least some of the efficiency for which they had been designed.

## Federal Common Law: *Swift v. Tyson*

The Supreme Court, of course, has always been a tribunal of both common law and statutory jurisdiction. The Constitution, as Marshall pointed out, is a law, but at the same time, it is far more than a mere statute; it is the organic law of the nation, designed for the ages, and therefore in constant need of reinterpretation. In time, the Court as the expositor of the Constitution would exercise enormous influence on the practice of the state courts, but as is clear from contemporary law journals and commentaries, in the mid-nineteenth century the greater part of the legal community's attention remained fixed on the highest state courts. The federal court system had relatively little to do with the everyday business affairs of the country. In addition, the state courts, like their legislative counterparts, jealously preserved their prerogatives against federal, or "alien," influences.

In effect, the nation had as many law systems as it had states, plus the federal courts, which had no constitutional power to impose national uniformity. In *United States v. Hudson and Goodwin* (1812) the Court declared that in the area of criminal law, there was no federal common law. Thus, after *Hudson and Goodwin,* a criminal prosecution in federal courts could take place only if Congress had passed a statute criminalizing the act of the defendant. In the states, on the other hand, many crimes were still prosecuted under the common, or unwritten, law. The ruling in *Hudson and Goodwin,* while reining in the power of the federal government, only affected the criminal law.

With commercial firms increasingly doing business in two or more states, entrepreneurs began to demand consistency across state lines. The rules of the market did not vary significantly from state to state; why then should businesses have to work with a multitude of often conflicting legal rules? Joseph Story, who had opposed the holding of *Hudson and Goodwin*, sympathized with this complaint, and through much of his career sought to achieve a uniformity of decisional rules in federal courts. In 1825, he finally managed to get Congress to pass a limited version of a federal criminal code he had drafted, but his greatest triumph came in 1842, in a case that had enormous impact on American commercial law, *Swift v. Tyson*.

Section 34 of the Judiciary Act of 1789 provided that cases coming into federal courts "in trials at common law" should, with certain exceptions, follow the decisional rules of "the laws of the several states." Historian Charles Warren later discovered draft materials showing, he claimed, that the Framers intended but did not specify that federal courts should also follow state "unwritten or common law." Warren believed that the final phrasing had not been intended to exclude common law, but merely served to compress the language. Story, however, took just the opposite view; since the statute referred specifically to "the laws," he argued, federal courts need not be bound by state common law.

In *Swift,* the Court had to decide whether a federal district court in New York had to follow the common law of that state on a question of commercial law, or whether it could look elsewhere. For a unanimous bench, Story held that federal courts were bound only by local laws, "that is to say . . . by positive statutes of the state, and the construction thereof adopted by the local tribunals." Otherwise, federal judges could be guided by "the general principles and doctrines of common jurisprudence." Story, whose various treatises had attempted to create a national body of accepted common law, assumed that such a corpus in fact existed, the product of centuries of experience. A judge merely had to seek the relevant principle and apply it, an idea Justice Oliver Wendell Holmes later derided when he insisted that the common law was not a "brooding omnipresence in the sky."

"Old Swifty," as the case eventually came to be called, had a rather checkered career during its near century of existence, until Justice Louis D. Brandeis finally laid it to rest in *Erie Railroad v. Tompkins* (1938) (see Chapter 31). Initially, the case gave federal courts a tool by which they could forge a somewhat coherent body of national rules in various areas of commercial law. Swift aroused practically no attention in its own time, since most people assumed that commerce that is national in scope required uniformity in commercial law. Even Justice Peter V. Daniel, normally a staunch defender of states' rights, recognized that too rigid an application of federalism could damage credit, negotiability, and other aspects of a national market. Later on, however, *Swift* opened the door to forum-shopping, by which essentially local firms evaded state law by going into federal courts.

Although overshadowed by other decisions of the Taney Court, such as *Charles River Bridge* and *Dred Scott, Swift v. Tyson* proved of major importance in constitutional interpretation. Too often, the Taney Court is seen as merely trying to overrule earlier opinions of the Marshall era, and certainly *Swift* and *Charles River Bridge* can support that interpretation. It is more accurate, however, to recognize that the Taney Court built on the experience gained under Marshall; that many of the earlier decisions had never been cast in stone, but represented initial efforts to deal with complex and novel issues; that Marshall's nationalism had often led him to sweeping decisions that caused confusion when judges attempted to apply them in different circumstances.

Taney, a good Jacksonian, placed more emphasis on the states than did his predecessor, but some of Taney's decisions necessarily corrected the overreaching interpretations to which Marshall was prone. The new chief justice did not intend to turn the clock back to 1801.

*Swift* must also be understood as a triumph for Justice Joseph Story, who remained the last representative of the Marshall era. Story was even more of a judicial nationalist than Marshall, and throughout his career he tried to create a strong Court and, where possible, to strengthen federal law. Story had opposed the ruling in *Hudson and Goodwin* (1812), and forever after tried to create a federal common law. Throughout his career he urged Congress to pass statutes to adopt what would have amounted to a federal common law. In *Swift*, he managed to accomplish this for commercial law.

In the same terms in which he wrote the majority opinion in *Swift*, Story also spoke for the Court in *Prigg v. Pennsylvania* (1842), which upheld the federal fugitive slave law of 1793, and struck down the personal liberty laws of the Northern states, which had been adopted to protect free blacks from being removed from the state under the lax evidentiary standards of the federal fugitive slave law of 1793. Story also used this decision to create a federal common law right of recaption, allowing the seizure of alleged fugitive slaves to bring them back to the South without any judicial hearing. We will examine the details of this case in the next chapter, but for the moment it is important to see that *Swift* should not be read in isolation, but as part of a lifelong attempt by Story to nationalize law. Story's opinion in *Prigg* illustrates this jurisprudence.

Although nominally opposed to slavery, Story wrote a strongly proslavery decision in *Prigg* because it was also strongly nationalist. Story was willing to sacrifice the liberty of free blacks who might be seized under this ruling for the sake of strengthening national law. Story also privately urged members of Congress to pass a new fugitive slave law, creating federal commissioners throughout the nation for the purpose of enforcing such a law. Story hoped to nationalize law enforcement in a way that would be acceptable to the South. A few years after Story's death, Congress would do just that, in passing the Fugitive Slave Law of 1850.

## The Police Power

The emergence of the state police powers doctrine must be considered one of the most important legacies of the Taney era. The chief justice invoked it in the *Charles River Bridge* case, declaring that courts could not take from the state "any portion of that power over their own internal police and improvements, which is so necessary to their well being and prosperity." In *West River Bridge Company v. Dix* (1848), the Court upheld a state's abrogation of a charter on the basis of the state's inherent police powers. Vermont had granted a franchise to a bridge company, authorizing it to collect tolls; when the legislature later decided to build a free public road, it revoked the charter. The state compensated the bridge company for lost property but not for anticipated profits, and the company sued. The Court, through Justice Daniel, upheld the taking as within the sovereign powers of the state; the Contract Clause did not apply in situations of eminent domain. But despite the relatively strong language of this decision, it would be inaccurate to say that Taney and his colleagues had developed a fully articulated doctrine on state police powers; rather, an inchoate series of assumptions were jostling for a place in the constitutional sun.

Much of the decisional basis for the police power doctrine grew out of state court decisions exploring the extent to which a state could override both individual and property rights in order to preserve public order and maintain minimal standards of health, safety, and welfare for its people. The power is nowhere spelled out, but is assumed as part of a state's sovereignty; as Justice Joseph McKenna later wrote, the police power "is but another name for government." In many ways, the entire doctrine is a product of common law and was created by courts in an effort to harmonize the needs of a dynamic society with the strictures of written constitutions and statutes. The police power was—and is—essentially what the courts declare it to be.

The police power was sometimes used to balance the so-called higher law doctrine that conservatives invoked for the protection of property and individual rights. The higher law advocates claimed that legislatures could not enact statutes that violated more potent sources of authority, such as divine law, or as some termed it, natural law. For example, Justice Samuel Chase had declared in *Calder v. Bull* (1798) that neither the federal government nor state government could override "vital principles," although he never spelled out these principles. Under Marshall, higher law had been used to protect property, but after his death, Joseph Story remained the only justice to cling to the doctrine. On the state benches, however, conservative judges still invoked it to thwart some of the era's reforms, such as temperance legislation or married women's property acts. But as the idea of democracy spread into the courts, judges ignored the higher law arguments advanced by aggrieved property owners, and increasingly used the police power to support legislative reforms.

The most cogent definition of the power during this time came from the chief justice of Massachusetts, Lemuel Shaw, in *Commonwealth v. Alger* (1851). The police power, he declared, permitted the legislature to make "all manner of wholesome and reasonable laws . . . not repugnant to the constitution, as they shall judge to be for the good and welfare of the commonwealth." The rights of property are never absolute; they can never be used to harm the community, and "are subject to such reasonable limitations in their enjoyment, as shall prevent them from being injurious, and to such reasonable restraints and regulations established by law" as the legislature saw fit.

For the next ninety years—until the Great Depression—the battle raged between the advocates of police power justifying various reform measures and the defenders of property invoking constitutional and higher law arguments in an effort to stave off governmental interference.

## Bank of Augusta v. Earle

The Taney Court took a few hesitant steps in explicating the police power, and attempted to fit this new idea into a constitutional framework alongside the broad doctrine of the federal commerce power, inherited from the Marshall Court. Could, for example, a state under its police power exclude a corporation chartered elsewhere from doing business within its borders, or did that violate the comity among states and interfere with interstate commerce? The Court dealt with this issue in *Bank of Augusta v. Earle* (1839), which arose when an Alabama citizen declined to pay the bills of exchange of a Georgia bank, claiming that a bank chartered in one state—a foreign corporation in the language of corporation law—had no right to make a contract in another state. The bank argued that under the Constitution's Privileges and Immunities Clause, a corporation can do business in another state, just like a natural person.

Taney's decision acknowledged the power of a state to control intrastate business, even to the point of excluding corporations from other states—foreign corporations— if it chose, but he also noted the right of a corporation to engage in interstate business under the comity among states guaranteed by the Constitution. He denied, however, that a corporation had all the rights of a natural person. Its legal existence and rights remained defined by the chartering state, and it could do business elsewhere only if other states gave their permission. This consent, however, need not be explicit; if a state did not expressly prohibit an out-of-state corporation from doing business, its silence implied consent. Since Alabama had not forbidden foreign banks from selling bills of exchange, the Georgia firm could infer its right to do so, and the bills had to be honored.

The decision left states free to regulate business within their borders, and many states did adopt statutes controlling out-of-state corporations. In the absence of federal regulation of interstate firms, these regulations probably had an overall beneficial influence, although they frequently proved confusing. Eventually, however, after the adoption of the Fourteenth Amendment in 1868, the Supreme Court began to treat corporations as having the same rights as natural persons, and thus vitiated much of the force of *Bank of Augusta*.

## The *License* and *Passenger* Cases

The conflict between state powers and interstate commerce also turned up in the *License* cases (1847), which resulted from the efforts of three New England states to control the sale of liquor, the first fruits of the new prohibition movement. Massachusetts upheld its state law, with Chief Justice Shaw invoking the police power rationale. But prohibition unquestionably interfered with property rights, and business stood to lose both current property rights and future profits that had previously been legitimate. Moreover, Daniel Webster, speaking for the liquor interests, drew a parallel with South Carolina's Negro Seamen's Act and similar laws in most other slave states, which had caused a furor in New England at the time. South Carolina could no more try to control the importation of ideas as Massachusetts could attempt to control liquor, Webster argued.

The Supreme Court produced six opinions, all upholding prohibition laws, but no doctrinal consensus emerged. Taney relied to some extent on the police power, as did John McLean; justices Peter V. Daniel, Robert C. Grier, and John Catron of Tennessee all emphasized states' rights, while Justice Levi Woodbury of New Hampshire wrote a lone opinion suggesting that the reach of the Commerce Clause depended on the local or national character of the commerce. There seems to have been little correlation between the personal views of the justices on temperance and their opinions, but it is likely that the furor over the seamen's acts may have played a part in their thinking; they could hardly prevent Massachusetts from regulating the importation of liquor without striking down Southern laws that clearly violated the rights of citizens of other states who engaged in interstate commerce. Given the Taney Court's overwhelmingly proslavery stance, it was unlikely to set a precedent that might be used against slavery.

The Court still lacked a coherent doctrine when in the *Passenger* cases (1849), it reviewed New York and Massachusetts laws taxing incoming passengers and authorizing the inspection and exclusion of diseased or mentally incompetent immigrants. The case produced eight opinions occupying 180 pages; by a 5 to 4 vote, the Court ruled that the laws violated the Commerce Clause. Taney wrote in dissent this time, along with Daniel, Samuel Nelson of New York, and Woodbury, and again the backdrop of the slavery controversy could not be ignored; the dissenters undoubtedly felt that in order to preserve the right of the Southern states to forbid free blacks from entering their jurisdiction, the Court had to allow the Northern states to exclude undesirable aliens. Justice James Wayne, a slaveowner from Georgia, one of the majority, argued that the two had nothing to do with each other, but Levi Woodbury warned that one could not separate the categories: nationalism in commerce and states' rights in controlling blacks were just not compatible. Southern newspapers for the most part agreed; whatever fine lines of legal reasoning may have existed in the various opinions, the seamen's acts were clearly threatened by these cases. According to the *Charleston* [S.C.] *Mercury,* the decision would "strip the South of all power of self-protection, and make submission to its rule equivalent to ruin and degradation."

In fact, however, Southerners need not have been worried. At issue in the *Passenger* cases was a tax, which the Court denied the states had the power to institute. Indeed, one of the original reasons for calling the Constitutional Convention in the first place had been to prevent state taxation of interstate and international commerce. The *Passenger* cases did not go to the issue of whether a state might completely exclude a class of migrants. Most of the states had banned the African slave trade before 1808, and by this time, virtually all the Northern states freed slaves brought within their jurisdiction. Thus, it would seem, if Massachusetts or New York could ban slaves as a class, then South Carolina or Georgia could equally ban free blacks.

In *Strader v. Graham* (1851), the Court indirectly faced a variant of the *Passenger Cases* as well as the *Miln* case. However, in this case, slavery was directly at issue. This case is usually, and correctly, seen as part of the jurisprudence of slavery. As such, we will examine it more closely in the next chapter. However, the facts of the case illustrate the way in which the regulation of interstate transportation was connected to slavery, and also why Southerners were deeply concerned about the right to control numerous local aspects of interstate commerce.

Graham was the owner of three slaves who escaped to Indiana, aboard Strader's steamship. Graham successfully sued him under a Kentucky law making shipowners liable for the value of slaves taken out of the state against the wishes of the master. Plausibly, this law could have been seen as an unconstitutional burden on interstate commerce by requiring every steamboat owner or ship captain to check the identify of every paying passenger. But, this was a road the Court was not about to take. While Taney's opinion for the Court and the two concurring opinions mentioned the importance of interstate commerce to the national compact, the justices steered clear of the implications of the commerce power for this case and other cases involving transportation and slaves.

## Defining State and Federal Powers

In a number of cases, the Taney Court wrestled with the same problem that had confronted Marshall—where to draw the line between state and federal powers. While Marshall leaned toward a broad interpretation of federal powers and Taney showed greater consideration for the states, it would be wrong to see the Taney Court as timid about the reach of the Commerce Clause. Rather, it sought an acceptable line that would provide guidance over when and how each sovereign could act.

In some areas, such as admiralty law, Taney actually extended federal court jurisdiction. In 1825, in the case of *The Thomas Jefferson,* the Marshall Court had adopted the English rule that admiralty law applied only in tidal waters. The expansion of river and canal commerce led Congress in 1845 to provide that admiralty forms and remedies could apply to matters of contract and tort resulting from traffic between states or territories on inland lakes and navigable waterways. In *Genesee Chief v. Fitzhugh* (1851), the Court upheld this enlarged federal jurisdiction, and Taney overruled Marshall's earlier decision, holding it to be no longer useful or appropriate.

The Court finally found what it considered an acceptable compromise to the tension between the state police power and the Commerce Clause in *Cooley v. Board of Wardens of the Port of Philadelphia* (1852). Pennsylvania had enacted regulations governing local harbor pilotage, which had been attacked as interfering with Congress's sole jurisdiction over interstate and foreign commerce. No one questioned that pilotage involved more than local commerce, but the state claimed that it had to regulate pilots and their fees for the proper operation of traffic in the port of Philadelphia. The state argued that the Commerce Clause did not totally forbid the states to act in this area. If Congress had passed appropriate legislation, that would have governed; but since Congress had not acted, states could pass necessary laws under their police power, even if they affected interstate commerce.

Six justices thought this a sensible approach and upheld the state. Commerce that is truly national in scope, Justice Benjamin R. Curtis of Massachusetts explained, and that called for a single uniform system of regulation, belonged solely to Congress. But some aspects of interstate and foreign commerce remained primarily local in nature. While Congress had the power to regulate these activities, if it chose not to do so, then the states could act.

Although states' rights advocates may have claimed *Cooley* as a victory, Curtis's opinion did little more than propose a commonsense solution to some gray-area situations in which state regulation seemed to contradict the Commerce Clause. However, in an age when debates over slavery clouded everything, *Cooley* reaffirmed for Southerners the important power of local authorities to control the "police power," which included the power to regulate local institutions and people. *Cooley* neither restricted congressional powers nor enlarged those of the states, and in terms of doctrine, it had limited significance, as can be seen in a later case that term, yet another of the famous bridge cases.

## The *Wheeling Bridge* Case

*Pennsylvania v. Wheeling & Belmont Bridge Co.* (1852) involved not only state laws affecting interstate commerce, but also reflected the growing rivalry between railroad and water transportation. In 1847, Virginia had authorized a railroad bridge across the Ohio River, connecting Wheeling, Virginia (now in West Virginia), and Bridgeport, Ohio. Wheeling, then the western terminus of the B & O Railroad, could thus divert much of the traffic carried on river barges onto trains headed for Baltimore. Pittsburgh, a major center of river traffic, objected to the prospect of losing much of its commerce, and the State of Pennsylvania moved to stop construction, claiming that the bridge obstructed interstate commerce, specifically goods traveling on barges down the Ohio River.

The case is significant for marking out some of the legal and economic perplexities facing the Court and the country. The bridge, by connecting two states, definitely fell within the purview of interstate commerce, yet Congress, despite repeated urging by Virginia to declare the bridge an instrument of interstate commerce, had refused to act in the matter. Under *Cooley,* in the absence of congressional action, states had the right to legislate on matters of primarily local nature, even if they affected interstate commerce. Pennsylvania had entered the controversy to protect its interests in extensive river and canal networks, in which it had invested millions of dollars. Yet using the reasoning of *Charles River Bridge,* the Wheeling bridge represented not only dynamic capital, but competition that would benefit the entire community as well.

A majority of the Court, speaking through Justice McLean, acknowledged that Pennsylvania had no basis for suing at law in the absence of a federal statute. Nonetheless, McLean ruled that resort to equity could provide relief; since a special master (the factfinder appointed by the Court) had determined that the bridge obstructed steam navigation (steamships had to lower or remove their smokestacks to pass under the span), he ordered the company either to remove the bridge or to raise it. Taney's dissent invoked not only *Cooley* to justify Virginia's authorization of the bridge, but Marshall's opinion in *Willson v. Black Bird Creek Marsh Co.* (1829), in which the Court had upheld a Delaware statute permitting a dam across a navigable stream. However, the applicability of *Willson* was questionable. The Black Bird Creek was not even big enough to qualify as a river but, because of its location, was navigable. But Virginia had built its bridge across the second most important river in the nation. Stopping traffic on the Ohio could in fact have had a substantial impact on interstate commerce.

Taney, and Justice Daniel in an even stronger dissent, also questioned how equity could be invoked when obviously the community benefited from the increase in commerce caused by railroad expansion. This part of their opinions, however, went to state and sectional interests. The real split on the Court derived from economic experience as much as from judicial philosophy. McLean, from Ohio, acknowledged that railroads would eventually bring great benefit, but his state had over 12,000 miles of navigable rivers and canals, and he wanted to preserve their value. Daniel, from Virginia, while sensitive to the value of water networks, saw railroads as the future, bringing prosperity to areas, including much of his own state, that lacked easy access to rivers or canals.

Had the decision stood, railroad expansion might have been greatly retarded, but several events led to its reversal within a short time. Pressure from local interests seeking rail expansion led Congress later, in 1852, to approve a rider to a post office bill declaring the Wheeling bridge to be a lawful structure in its existing elevation and position and naming it as a post road for the passage of mail. Sentiment against the Supreme Court decree was so strong that Pennsylvania abandoned efforts to have the decision enforced. However, when a severe windstorm toppled the bridge in May 1854—to the great delight of Pittsburgh residents—Pennsylvania, claiming that the original ruling remained in effect, secured an injunction to prevent the company from building a new structure. The company ignored the order, and by midsummer had a new bridge in operation. Pennsylvania still insisted on pursuing the matter, and the case came back to the Supreme Court in December 1854.

The final opinion did not come down until eighteen months later, and in the second *Wheeling Bridge* case (1856), the majority of the Court upheld the power of Congress, acting under the Commerce Clause, to legitimize the bridge. Justices McLean, Wayne, and Grier, previously in the majority, now dissented. McLean argued that once the Court had declared the bridge a nuisance, Congress did not have the power to alter its status, and he took an extremely narrow view of the Commerce Clause, holding it to mean that Congress could do little more than remove obstructions to navigation. But for the majority, the *Cooley* decision seemed vindicated. Congress had acted, and no more needed to be said.

Unfortunately for the courts, a great deal more remained to be said. As railroads expanded, they built one bridge after another across navigable streams. Drawbridges became the rule, for once opened they allowed steamships to pass freely; but opening the draws required time, and thus impeded the flow of river traffic. Whenever a bridge spanned an interstate boundary, a case almost always resulted, and the federal courts had to handle dozens of suits. The intense competition between railroads and water navigation did not abate until after the Civil War, and despite *Wheeling Bridge,* not all decisions favored the railroads. In those instances in which Congress had authorized construction, railroads would usually win; but where states had acted on their own, judges sympathetic to water traffic, would, on occasion, still declare the structures nuisances. *Cooley* provided a rough rule of thumb, but so long as the economic issues remained unresolved, so too did the legal questions.

## The "Political Question" Doctrine

The "political question" doctrine is another enduring legacy of the Taney era. Essentially, it holds that some questions coming before a court are beyond the judicial capacity to answer within the accepted parameters of constitutional decision making or separation of powers. These may involve questions of policy, expediency, and, not the least in importance, the recognition that if the judiciary decides, other branches of government may refuse to enforce the ruling. Taney did not originate the general idea, but he elevated it to the level of constitutional doctrine.

He initially elaborated the idea in his dissent in *Rhode Island v. Massachusetts* (1838), one of those rare cases in which the Supreme Court exercised original jurisdiction under Article III, Section 2 (suits between two states come directly to the high court). The case involved a boundary dispute dating from the colonial period. A majority of the Court voted to take jurisdiction, with Justice Henry Baldwin asserting that the Constitution had intended the Court to hear just this type of dispute. In the end, after a number of hearings exploring the claims, the Court dismissed Rhode Island's claim.

Taney dissented from the original decision accepting jurisdiction. The Court, he conceded, could certainly decide questions of boundaries, but not if they involved larger questions of sovereignty, as he thought existed in this instance. "The powers given to the courts of the United States," he explained, "are judicial powers; and extend to those subjects only which are judicial in their character; and not to those which are political." The questions in this case just did not belong in the judicial department, he argued. Although alone in his dissent here, Taney carried the Court with him in a far more important case a few years later.

## Dorr's Rebellion

Staring in 1776, all of the thirteen new states except Connecticut and Rhode Island adopted a constitution with a representative government. Connecticut adopted a constitution in 1818. Most of the states had some limitations on voting, but these decreased over time. Rhode Island, however, continued its government under the royal charter issued by Charles II in 1663, with no changes in its allocation of representation in the legislature or changes in voting rights. By the 1840s, the document badly needed revision—among other things, to expand the extremely narrow suffrage and to provide more equitable representation in the legislature. But entrenched interests managed to defeat every effort at modification. In October 1841, frustrated reformers under the leadership of Providence lawyer Thomas W. Dorr called a convention to draft a new constitution, which an extralegal gathering approved two months later. On April 18, an unofficial balloting led to the election of a new slate of state officers pledged to democratize state government, with Dorr as governor.

In the meantime, the Whig governor, Samuel King, and the Whig legislature continued to function under the charter. The struggle between the two governments received national attention, and in May, Dorr, believing he would receive wide popular support, attempted to seize the arsenal at Providence. The effort failed, Dorr's followers disbanded, and he fled from the state. But rumors that he would soon launch an invasion led Governor King to declare martial law and to ask President Tyler for military aid under Article IV of the Constitution. Tyler said he could do nothing until an actual insurrection occurred, but he promised that aid would be forthcoming in the event of violence. The president's position led to the final collapse of Dorr's Rebellion, but the turmoil it had engendered eventually produced democratic reforms in Rhode Island. Dorr, in the meantime, had been arrested, tried for treason, and sentenced to life imprisonment at hard labor.

The rebellion generated two cases for the Supreme Court to consider. In *Ex parte Dorr* (1845), the Court denied a petition for habeas corpus that Dorr's friends had sought on the grounds that he had been illegally tried and imprisoned; treason could only be committed against the nation and not an individual state, and therefore only the United States could try someone for that crime, the argument went. Speaking through Justice McLean, the Court ruled unanimously that no federal court or judge could issue a writ of habeas corpus to free a prisoner in state custody for any purpose other than to bring him as a witness in a federal proceeding. Although this effort failed, the popular sentiment in his favor did lead to a general amnesty, and Dorr left prison in June 1845.

## Luther v. Borden

The second case arising from Dorr's Rebellion to reach the Supreme Court involved Martin Luther, a Dorrite leader in Warren, Rhode Island, who sued Luther Borden and others, who had invaded and searched his house without a warrant during the period of martial law. Luther, who had escaped by fleeing the state, evidently hoped that the case would serve as a vehicle to air the Dorrite grievances and gain public exoneration of their deeds. They received attention—but not quite as they had intended. The two judges sitting on circuit, Joseph Story and District Judge John Pitman, had both expressed their strong opposition to the rebellion, and could have been expected to dismiss the suit out of hand. Instead, they agreed to disagree, so that technically unable to reach a decision, they could file a certificate of division to have the Supreme Court resolve the matter.

The case came to the high court in 1846, but because of illnesses on the bench and other postponements, argument was delayed until January 1848. Despite the absence of three justices and an overcrowded docket, the Court allowed six full days for argument. During that time, counsel for Rhode Island, led by Daniel Webster, mercilessly attacked the idea that government reform could take place through illegal actions. Luther's lawyers, on the other hand, sought to have the Court declare that Rhode Island's actions before and during the rebellion had been illegal, claiming that Article IV, Section 4, of the Constitution guaranteed to every "State in this Union a Republican Form of Government."

The chief justice delivered the opinion of the Court in January 1849, with only Levi Woodbury dissenting on one minor point of interpretation. *Luther v. Borden* remains a landmark case in the establishment of the political question doctrine. Taney began by listing the enormous difficulties that would ensue if the Court declared the Rhode Island government and its actions for the past seven years invalid. Were the Court to do so, it would first have to examine closely its own powers in such a situation, and Taney could find no grounds for such authority. Certainly, the power did not exist under Article IV, at least not for the courts. The authority "belonged to the political power and not to the judicial; it rested with the political power to decide whether the charter government had been displaced or not; and when that decision was made, the judicial department would be bound to take notice of it as the paramount law of the State." Responsibility for the Article IV guaranty, therefore, lay with Congress and not the Supreme Court.

Meanwhile, real-life politics solved the problems of Rhode Island. In 1851, Rhode Island's governor pardoned Dorr. This governor was elected under a new constitution with expanded suffrage, including equal suffrage for blacks.

While *Luther v. Borden*, did not, in the end, settle the issues arising from the Dorr Rebellion, it did leave the Court with a valuable weapon for future cases. The decision firmly established the principle that courts would not inquire into certain types of activities of the political branches of government. It would prove a particularly useful tool after 1865, enabling the Court to avert a destructive battle with Congress over the constitutionality of Reconstruction legislation. For well over a century, the Court deliberately avoided what Justice Felix Frankfurter later called the "political thicket," and despite some weakening of the doctrine by the Warren Court in the 1960s, it still retains much of its vigor. It accounted, at least in part, for the disinclination of federal courts to rule on the constitutionality of the Vietnam War. Even if lacking a clearly defined doctrinal base, it serves the useful purpose of permitting judges to defer ruling on issues they sense are immune to judicial resolution.

## Conclusion: The Taney Court's Balance

Before the election of Lincoln, Congress exercised but a fraction of its commerce power. Thus, during most of the Taney chief justiceship, many potentially divisive issues never reached the Court. During this period, with one or two exceptions, the major Taney decisions concerning state and federal control of commerce struck few sparks, as compared with the major cases handed down by John Marshall a few decades earlier. But Taney, aside from his states' rights and proslavery views, also supported what would later be termed judicial self-restraint. He remembered too well the opprobrium heaped upon the Court during Marshall's tenure, and especially the Court's impotence when Jackson had refused to enforce Marshall's ruling on Cherokee rights (see Chapter 14). Under Taney, the Court deliberately assumed a lower profile, and until *Dred Scott,* managed to avoid any major political controversies. Taney preferred to decide constitutional questions on as narrow a basis as possible, looking always to positive law for guidance. Discretion, he believed, should be exercised by the legislature and not the judiciary.

In part, Taney was able to avoid political controversies because, for most of his career on the bench, he was in sympathy with the political majority. From the time of his appointment until the inauguration of Lincoln in 1861, a Democrat was in the White House for all but the one month of William Henry Harrison's term (before he died in office) and the combined four years of Taylor and Fillmore. As a confirmed defender of slavery, Taney did not see an antislavery president until Lincoln took office, and in fact saw mostly Southern slaveowners in the White House. The only Northerners, Van Buren, Fillmore, Pierce, and Buchanan, were considered Northern doughfaces—Northern men with Southern principles.

Congress mirrored the presidency in this period, generally dominated by Southerners, Democrats, and slaveowners, or their doughface allies. Most of the states were controlled by Democrats as well, and their legislation rarely threatened federal power.

Judicial restraint and deference to the states might lead to the conclusion that the Taney Court's accomplishments were all of a negative type, that it did its best work in refusing to exercise power. Such an interpretation would fail to acknowledge the real achievements of Taney and his colleagues. The ability to draw clear lines of authority is critical to the success of a government of shared authority. The Marshall Court's excessive use of the judicial power to further nationalistic goals often led it into conflict not only with the states but with other branches of the central government as well. Until the Civil War, with the exception of *Dred Scott*, and to a lesser extent *Prigg v. Pennsylvania*, the Taney Court managed to strike a laudable balance in its exercise of power, rarely calling down the wrath of the public or its partners in government. The development of the political question and police power doctrines proved as important in many ways as some of the Marshall Court's rulings, while *Swift v. Tyson*, whatever problems it later caused, helped the federal courts in creating a relatively uniform system of commercial law. On one point Taney and his Court differed little from that of Marshall, despite Taney's earlier views on the bank veto: the Supreme Court remained the ultimate arbiter in interpreting the Constitution.

# For Further Reading

The most comprehensive study of the Taney Court is the fifth volume of the Holmes Devise *History of the Supreme Court,* Carl Brent Swisher, *The Taney Period, 1836–1864* (1974). Unfortunately, it often suffers from outdated generalizations; published posthumously six years after Swisher's death, it lists only four works after 1960 in the bibliography. It should be read in conjunction with Harold Hyman and William Wiecek, *Equal Justice Under Law* (1982); or R. Kent Newmyer, *The Supreme Court Under Marshall and Taney* (1968). Also useful for this period is R. Kent Newmyer's *Supreme Court Justice Joseph Story: Statesman of the Old Republic* (1984).

On codification, see Charles M. Cook, *The American Codification Movement* (1981). Randell Birdwell and Ralph U. Whitten, in *The Constitution and the Common Law: The Decline of the Doctrine of Separation of Powers and Federalism* (1977), claim that modern scholars, blinded by positivist and realist concepts of common law, do not understand or appreciate *Swift.* Tony Freyer, *Harmony and Dissonance: The Swift and Erie Cases in American Federalism* (1981) provides a useful history of the case. Also helpful is Charles A. Heckman, "The Relationship of *Swift v. Tyson* to the Status of Commercial Law in the Nineteenth Century and the Federal System," 17 *American Journal of Legal History* 246 (1973). The Charles Warren article is "New Light on the History of the Federal Judiciary Act of 1789," 37 *Harvard Law Review* 49 (1923). On the importance of *Prigg v. Pennsylvania* and its connection to the nationalization of law, see Paul Finkelman, "Story Telling on the Supreme Court: *Prigg v. Pennsylvania* and Justice Joseph Story's Judicial Nationalism," 1994 *Supreme Court Review* 247 (1995). Some of the implications of commerce clause jurisprudence for slavery are discussed in Paul Finkelman, *An Imperfect Union: Slavery, Federalism, and Comity* (1981).

Elizabeth Brand Monroe, *The Wheeling Bridge Case: Its Significance in American Law and Technology* (1992) is a useful study of that important case. For the Dorr episode, see Marvin E. Gettleman, *The Dorr Rebellion: A Study in American Radicalism, 1833–1849* (1973); and George M. Dennison, *The Dorr War: Republicanism on Trial, 1831–1861* (1976). See also William M. Wiecek, *The Guaranty Clause of the U.S. Constitution* (1972); and John S. Schuchman, "The Political Background of the Political Question Doctrine: The Judges and the Dorr War," 16 *American Journal of Legal History* 111 (1972).

# 17

# The Peculiar Laws of America's Peculiar Institution

*Slavery in the New Nation • The Missouri Compromise • Black and White Opposition to Slavery: Slave Rebels and New Abolitionists • Abolitionist Theories and the Constitution • Abolitionist Use of the Law • Slaves in Transit • Antebellum Race Discrimination • Federal Fugitive Slave Laws •* Prigg v. Pennsylvania *• Law and Conscience • Southern Slave Codes • Controlling the Bondsmen • Slaves and Criminal Law • Manumission • Free Blacks • Conclusion • For Further Reading*

Despite growing nationalism and prosperity, the United States still had a long way to go before it could realize Daniel Webster's vision of a country bound by a common allegiance to particular ideals and loyalty to a single government. The old debate between national supremacy and states' rights had assumed a new lease on life in the nullification crisis of 1832. Even more important—and more dangerous to the stability of the Union—was the emergence of slavery as the central political, social, and constitutional problem of the nation. Starting with the Missouri Compromise debate of 1819–20, the South's "peculiar institution" came under increasing attack. Slavery ultimately put an intolerable strain on the political system and constitutional order, and raised profound questions about the nature of American government.

The rise of slavery as a political issue was due to a number of factors. These include the end of slavery in the North, the Missouri Compromise debates, the response of blacks to slavery, the emergence of the abolitionist movement in the 1830s, the ossifying of attitudes among white Southerners on race and slavery, the maturing of the Southern slave culture, the realization throughout the North that the South would *never* end slavery on its own, and the conflict between the North and South over the return of fugitive slaves.

## Slavery in the New Nation

At the time of the American Revolution, slavery existed in all the colonies. Slaves made up about 50 percent of Virginia, more than half of South Carolina, and a large portion of the populations of North Carolina, Maryland, and Georgia. About 12 percent of New Yorkers were black, and probably three-quarters of these were slaves. In other Northern states, the slave population varied from 8 percent in New Jersey to 4 percent in Connecticut, Rhode Island, and Pennsylvania, and much less than that in Massachusetts and New Hampshire. During the Revolution, Pennsylvania passed a gradual emancipation act, which provided that the children of all slaves born after March 1, 1780, would be free, subject to an indenture. Connecticut and Rhode Island adopted similar laws in 1784, and New York and New Jersey followed in 1799 and 1804, respectively. Meanwhile, starting in 1780, Massachusetts, New Hampshire, and the fourteenth state, Vermont, ended slavery in their constitutions. Even without these laws, however, the slave populations dropped during the Revolution, as thousands of slaves gained their liberty by fighting for the patriots, siding with the British, or simply using the chaos of war to escape their bondage. Many northern masters also took the words of the Declaration of Independence to heart, and manumitted their slaves. Some of the drop in the slave populations in these states was also due to masters who removed their slaves from the states, to sell them south. Some masters, in violation of Northern state law, also removed the children of slaves to prevent them from becoming free.

Before 1820, Northern opponents of slavery focused their energies on four issues: insuring the implementation of their state laws ending slavery; preventing the kidnaping of free blacks or the illegal removal of indentured blacks to the South; creating institutions, especially schools, for free blacks to make sure that emancipation did not simply substitute for slavery some new form of oppression; and working to limit or end the African slave trade.

Known as the "first emancipation," this reform movement was amazingly successful. By 1820, slavery was all but dead in most of the North, although as late as the 1830s and 1840s, a few aging slaves could be found in Pennsylvania, Connecticut, New Jersey, and Illinois. In this period, Northerners mostly ignored the question of slavery in the South. That was a Southern problem over which they had little power or influence.

In the South, slavery boomed. Some Southern masters manumitted their slaves in the wake of the Revolution. Most of these Southerners were devoutly religious, like the Virginia Quakers John and Jonathan Pleasants, or deeply committed to the ideology of the Revolution, like South Carolina's Henry Laurens. The most famous manumitter in this period was George Washington, who prepared his hundreds of slaves for freedom, which he bequeathed them, along with much of his land, in his will. James Madison's private secretary, Edward Coles, freed his far smaller number of slaves by taking them to Illinois after the War of 1812. In Virginia, the free black population grew from about 2,000 in 1782 to about 30,000 by 1810. Most of this growth was due to private manumissions. This is a tribute to the many Virginia masters who found slavery inconsistent with their new world of liberty and their faith in God. However, these private actions between 1775 and 1820 had hardly any effect on the growth of slavery in the South.

Most of the Southern Founders did little, if anything, to either encourage an end to slavery or personally to resolve the conflict between their adherence to revolutionary principles of "liberty" and their continued ownership of human beings. Thomas Jefferson was typical of his age. He freed three slaves during his lifetime and another five in his will. All eight were members of the Hemings family, and some were his own children. His hundreds of other slaves lived and died in bondage. When he died, these slaves were auctioned off to pay his debts.

Many factors kept the South tied to bondage. Slaves were valuable possessions, whose labor produced valuable crops. Economic self-interest made manumission unlikely for most masters. The cotton boom, beginning in the late-1790s, made already valuable slaves even more valuable. Slaves were also racially different, and after the Revolution, Southerners increasingly adopted notions of race to justify slavery. Jefferson, for example, understood, at some level, the fundamental injustice of slavery. He also recognized that in the long run, slavery was dangerous to society. In 1797, for example, commenting on the successful slave rebellion in Haiti, he wrote: "if something is not done, and soon done" about slavery, "we shall be murderers of our own children." But he could never bring himself to work publicly to end slavery, even in the most gradual way. Nor would he free his own slaves. His fear of blacks, which verged on paranoia, paralyzed him. He wrote that blacks were mentally and physically inferior to whites, that they lacked judgment, and were sexually immoral. Compounding his racism was his economic dependence on slavery. Jefferson's beliefs, fears, and economic needs made it impossible for him to do anything, or even to say anything, to encourage emancipation. In this sense, the Master of Monticello was similar to most other Southern white slaveowners at the time.

As we have seen, at the Constitutional Convention many Southern delegates aggressively defended slavery and made no apology for owning slaves. As Charles Pinckney of South Carolina told the Convention, slavery was "justified by the example of all the world."

Thus, revolutionary era Southerners did little to deal with the problem of slavery. In 1782, Virginia allowed manumitted adult slaves to remain in the state after gaining their liberty. South Carolina and Maryland passed similar laws, but North Carolina and Georgia did not. Allowing private manumission was consistent with the reverence for private property in the ideology of the Revolution. These laws essentially allowed masters to dispose of their property as they wished. The refusal of Georgia or North Carolina to allow this reflected the belief that free blacks were inherently dangerous to the society. By the 1850s, all of the states that would secede had made manumission difficult or absolutely banned it.

In the early national period, some states also mitigated the harshness of their colonial slave codes. Virginia, for example, reduced the number of capital offenses for slaves, while North Carolina attempted to criminalize the murder of a slave. However, the statute was so poorly drafted that the state supreme court struck it down in *State v. Boon* (N.C., 1801).

At the national level, the Founders did little about slavery. In the Northwest Ordinance of 1787, Congress, acting under the Articles of Confederation, banned slavery in the federal territories north of the Ohio River. After the adoption of the Constitution, the new Congress reaffirmed this law. However, the national government did little to enforce the provision. Slaves were legally held in Indiana until that territory achieved statehood in 1816, and as late as the 1840s, some blacks would still be held in bondage in Illinois. Meanwhile, slavery spread rapidly throughout the southwestern territories.

Most Americans, including many Southern whites, agreed that the African slave trade was fundamentally immoral, but the Constitutional Convention caved in to the demands of South Carolina and Georgia and allowed the trade to continue, at least until 1808. By then, about 100,000 new slaves had been brought into the country. In the 1790s, Congress weakly regulated the trade, and in 1808, it banned the trade outright. However, at no time before the Civil War did Congress appropriate enough money to stop the illegal trade, which may have brought an additional 30,000 slaves into the United States before 1861. Meanwhile, in 1793, Congress passed the first fugitive slave law, placing the power of the federal courts behind masters seeking runaway slaves. In the same decade, Congress refused to consider petitions from free blacks who feared they would be kidnaped and taken South.

From 1800 until the eve of the Civil War, the constitutional compromises over slavery helped secure political hegemony for the South. Northerners complained bitterly, with some justice, about the application of the three-fifths clause to the electoral college. In the extremely close election of 1800, the electoral votes created by counting slaves for representation provided the margin of victory for Thomas Jefferson, who owned about 200 slaves at the time, over John Adams, who had never owned a slave. From 1801 until 1850, a slaveowner served as president for 42 years, while a non-slaveowner (John Quincy Adams and Martin Van Buren) served for only eight years. Furthermore, Van Buren, although from New York, was a proslavery Democrat. From 1801 until 1864, two Southerners served as chief justice of the Supreme Court, and with the exception of a few years, Southerners constituted a majority of the Court. Southerners disproportionately held high and powerful positions in Congress and in the executive branch. Uncompromising proslavery advocates, like John C. Calhoun, Jefferson Davis, and Robert Toombs, were cabinet officers, while no antislavery advocates were ever in such positions of power and influence.

At the beginning of this period, Northern opponents of slavery concentrated their efforts in their own region, naively hoping that Southern whites would eventually see the danger and immorality of slavery, or that the closing of the African trade would undermine the institution. Northern attitudes would change after the Missouri Compromise debates revealed the depth of Southern commitment to slavery and the danger that slavery posed to national expansion.

## The Missouri Compromise

Shortly after John Marshall's expansive opinion in *McCulloch v. Maryland* (see Chapter 11), the Virginia states' rights advocate John Taylor of Caroline published an attack on the chief justice's views in a slim volume entitled *Construction Construed and Constitutions Vindicated* (1820). Probably no purer statement of an extreme agrarian, states' rights philosophy can be found, and it is suggestive that the book ended with a reference to slavery; if Congress could incorporate a bank, then would it not also have power to free slaves? Taylor's concern went beyond hypothetical speculation, for Congress had already begun to debate the issue as it related to the admission of Missouri into the Union.

Slavery had existed in the area of the Louisiana Purchase, which included Missouri, long before the territory had been acquired from France in 1803. The Northwest Ordinance of 1787, had, as we have seen, prohibited slavery in the territory north and west of the Ohio River, which would have included most of the Louisiana Territory. However when the United States acquired Louisiana, Congress did not consider the status of slavery in that region. Nor did the issue arise in 1812 when Louisiana became the first state to enter the Union from this region. Louisiana had a large slave population and was south of the Ohio River, and would have been open to slavery under the Ordinance. Thus, no one questioned allowing Louisiana to enter the Union as a slave state.

The legitimacy of slavery in Missouri, however, was less clear. Almost all of Missouri was north and west of the Ohio River's most southern point. Thus, in February 1819, Congressman James Tallmadge of New York proposed an amendment to the Missouri statehood bill, prohibiting the further introduction of slaves into the would-be state and emancipating all children born to slaves there once they reached age twenty-five. At the time, about 10,000 slaves resided in Missouri, out of a total population of 66,000. Slavery had been entrenched in the region since the settlement of St. Louis, and most of the territory's leading citizens were slaveowners. Moreover, by 1819, Southern slaveowners were streaming into the state.

The Tallmadge amendment passed the House on an almost entirely sectional vote. Only two Southern representatives, both born in free states, voted for it, while only a handful of Northerners voted against it. In the Senate, a solid slave-state bloc joined by a few Northerners who had either constitutional or political doubts about the legislation defeated the Tallmadge amendment. When Congress adjourned on March 4, Missouri remained a territory, but everyone recognized the significance of what had happened. Thomas Jefferson likened it to "a firebell in the night," and "considered it at once as the [death] knell of the Union." However, in his typical fashion, he refused an invitation by a congressman from the Maine district of Massachusetts to weigh in *against* the expansion of slavery into the West. Instead, he merely bemoaned the fact

## JEFFERSON OPPOSES THE DEBATE OVER SLAVERY

During the debates over the Missouri Compromise, Jefferson wrote Congressman John Holmes of the Maine district of Massachusetts, arguing against prohibiting slavery in the West: a "geographical line, coinciding with a marked principle, moral and political" would stir the "angry passions of men." "I regret," he wrote, in response the Missouri debates, "that I am now to die in the belief, that the useless sacrifice of themselves by the generation of 1776, to acquire self-government and happiness to their country, is to be thrown away by the unwise and unworthy passions of their sons." Thomas Jefferson to Congressman John Holmes, April 22, 1820.

that white Americans were wasting their energies, and jeopardizing the Union, over the fate of blacks.

Although Tallmadge's amendment was aimed only at limiting the expansion of slavery, many Southerners saw it as the opening wedge in attacking slavery elsewhere. Beyond that, the precarious political balance seemed in danger of collapsing. Population had already shifted in favor of the North, which had 105 votes in the House of Representatives to 85 from the slave states. The South was thus even more determined to preserve parity in the Senate. If Missouri came in as a free state, the South feared a future in which, politically, it would be at the mercy of the North.

In December 1819, congressional leaders worked out a compromise. Missouri would be admitted as a slave state, while Maine, until then part of Massachusetts, would come in as a free state. Slavery would also be excluded in the rest of the Louisiana Territory north of 36⁻30', the southern border of Missouri. This left only the present day Florida, Arkansas, and Oklahoma open to slavery. Most of the South saw the compromise as a victory, although a hard core of adamant proslavery Southern extremists, led by the senators from South Carolina and Virginia, considered any ban on slavery in the territories both unconstitutional and insulting to Southerners. Most Northerners in Congress opposed the compromise as a violation of the Northwest Ordinance. In the end, however, Henry Clay's manipulation of the conference committee cleared the way for its passage on March 2, 1820.

Almost immediately, however, a new problem arose. The Missouri constitutional convention adopted a clause excluding free Negroes and mulattos from the state, in violation of the federal Constitution's guarantee that "[t]he Citizens of each State shall be entitled to all Privileges and Immunities of Citizens in the Several States" (Article IV, Section 2). Free blacks held citizenship in many states, and in addition to political rights in most of the Northeast, free blacks could even vote in North Carolina and Tennessee, although both of these states, as well as Pennsylvania, rescinded this right as part of the "reforms" of Jacksonian democracy in the 1830s.

To save his original agreement, Clay worked out a second compromise, by which the Missouri legislature promised never to construe the clause to deny citizens privileges they held under the U.S. Constitution. Perhaps tired from nearly a year of wrestling with the question, Northern Congressmen agreed to Missouri's assurance that its constitution did not mean what it clearly said. On August 10, 1821, Missouri entered the Union as the twenty-fourth state.

The Missouri debates touched on a number of constitutional issues, all tied to the nature of slavery within the governmental system. It also marked a further evolution of the Southern assertion that slavery was a positive good for both the master and the slave. Senator William Smith of South Carolina, for example, offered a religious justification for bondage, pointing out, as many Southern ministers would do in the coming decades, that both the Old and New Testaments condoned slavery and even provided elaborate rules for the governing of slaves. Representative Nathaniel Macon of North Carolina noted that the Declaration of Independence's assertion that "all men are created equal," was "no[t] part of the Constitution or of any other book," and concluded "There is no place for free blacks in the United States."

Macon spoke not just to the relation of master and slave in the South, but to the broader question of race relations in the North as well as the South. While many Northerners attacked the immorality of slavery, few were ready to argue for full racial equality. Nevertheless, whatever their personal prejudices, a majority of Northern Congressmen were prepared to take a stand against the spread of slavery into new states and against new states blatantly discriminating against free blacks. Southerners found both these Northern positions utterly unacceptable.

## Black and White Opposition to Slavery: Slave Rebels and New Abolitionists

While the Missouri Compromise ended Congressional debate over slavery in the short run, it had the opposite effect outside of Washington. In 1822, a planned slave uprising in South Carolina organized by a former slave named Denmark Vesey provoked Southern charges that abolitionist agitators in the North were stimulating slave unrest. South Carolinians were especially disturbed because among Vesey's books and papers were copies of antislavery speeches given by Northern Congressmen during the Missouri debates. In 1828, David Walker, a free black living in Massachusetts wrote and began secretly distributing in the South his own antislavery tract known as *David Walker's Appeal* (1828). Walker called on Southerners to free their slaves, as a matter of Christian duty, but if they did not, he urged blacks to rebel to win their own freedom. Never before had an African American urged slaves to seek their own liberty, with arms if necessary, just as the American patriots had done against the British in 1775. Southern officials contacted the mayor of Boston, urging him to have this "incendiary" arrested. Massachusetts authorities refused to impose slave state law on their free society, and Walker continued to publish his book until he mysteriously died, perhaps as many believe, murdered by agents of the South.

Both the Vesey conspiracy and the Walker affair illustrated the evolving differences between the South and the North. After the Vesey conspiracy, South Carolina began to enforce its black seamen's law, arresting free black sailors entering its ports. In *Elkison v. Deliesseline* (1823), Justice William Johnson, while riding circuit, condemned these laws, but also concluded that he lacked the power to interfere with them. Other Southern states soon passed similar laws, and issues of the interstate movement of free, Northern blacks simmered until the Civil War. One goal of the Fourteenth Amendment was to forever end such conflicts.

The debate over abolition also illustrates the differences between the North and South on the right of freedom of expression. The South wanted to shut off all discussion of slavery, even for whites, because of fears that slaves would revolt if they knew some whites opposed human bondage. By the 1850s, the South would in fact have evolved into a virtually closed society, where any debate on slavery was impossible, and whites faced arrest merely for the possession of antislavery literature. Northerners, meanwhile, began to see that the South's peculiar institution not only curtailed the liberties of blacks, slave and free, but also of whites.

Although South Carolina authorities arrested Vesey before he could start his rebellion, Virginians were caught off guard in 1831, when Nat Turner initiated the bloodiest slave rebellion in that state's history. Following this rebellion, which led to the death of about 65 whites and more than 100 slaves, the Virginia legislature debated, but failed to pass, a gradual emancipation statute. This would prove to be the last time any Southern state considered ending slavery until the Civil War forced the issue. The South's future, and fate, was to be inextricably tied to white supremacy and black slavery.

Meanwhile, stimulated by the arguments of free blacks like David Walker, a new abolitionist movement developed in the North, marked by the establishment of the New England Anti-Slavery Society (1831) and the American Anti-Slavery Society (1833), and the appearance of the most vocal and radical of all the abolitionist organs, William Lloyd Garrison's *The Liberator*, in 1831. Nat Turner's revolt in Virginia later that year rekindled Southern fears that abolitionists wanted to destroy not only slavery, but the South with it.

## Abolitionist Theories and the Constitution

The abolitionist movement began as a moral and religious crusade, directed at convincing Southerners of the sin of slaveowning. Nevertheless, opponents of slavery ultimately focused great energy on the Constitution and the political system it had created. But just as the abolitionists did not agree on the best strategy to achieve complete emancipation, they also differed in their constitutional views. Three main bodies of antislavery constitutional thought emerged.

The first critique of slavery and the Constitution emerged from William Lloyd Garrison and his closest colleague, Wendell Phillips, who had studied at Harvard Law School under Supreme Court Justice Joseph Story. The Garrisonians condemned the Constitution as a proslavery compact, which they called a "covenant with death" and "an agreement in Hell." The posthumous publication in 1840 of Madison's *Notes of Debates in the Federal Convention of 1787*, which revealed the depths of the compromises over slavery at the Constitutional Convention, underscored the Garrisonian critique. Garrison, and many of his followers, refused to vote or participate in politics under the proslavery Constitution. Instead, they urged Northerners to renounce the Constitution and secede from the Union.

While seeming almost insane from the perspective of post–Civil War America, Garrison's idea was rooted in a clearly thought-out strategy. If the North seceded, then the boundary of freedom would have been moved from the St. Lawrence River to the Ohio River. The Mason-Dixon line would have truly marked the boundary between slavery and freedom, and as slaves escaped across it and the Ohio River, they would have been immune from slave hunters, because the fugitive slave laws would no longer mandate their return. Furthermore, Garrison and his followers believed that without Northern funds, industries, and military protection, the slave system would collapse.

Garrison's argument was intellectually coherent. Most scholars accept the idea that the Constitutional Convention made huge concessions to slavery—although scholars disagree on the necessity of these concessions. Nevertheless, Garrison's impractical solution—withdrawal first from politics and then from the Union—appealed to almost no northerners. Most modern scholars interpret it as a radical proposal, which successfully attracted attention to his movement, while infuriating Southerners.

More practical was the moderate antislavery argument that the Constitution could be used to limit slavery, and that law, politics, and constitutional theory should be applied to attack slavery where it could be reached. First in the Liberty party, then in the Free Soil party, and finally in the Republican party after 1854, the political abolitionists worked to stop the spread of slavery and to undercut the fugitive slave laws.

These more moderate antislavery activists, and to a lesser extent the Garrisonians, also litigated in court, brought test cases on segregation, and sought to protect fugitive slaves and their abolitionists allies who were charged with helping fugitive slaves. The most successful of the political abolitionists was Salmon P. Chase of Ohio, often called "the attorney general for fugitive slaves." In addition to representing numerous free blacks, fugitive slaves, and abolitionists, he served as a U.S. senator and governor of Ohio before the Civil War, and as secretary of the treasury (1861–1864) and then chief justice of the United States during and after the war.

The political abolitionists never claimed that the federal government had the power to abolish slavery, until Lincoln was able to use the war powers in this way. The moderates, many of whom joined the Free Soil party in 1848 and the Republican party after 1854, focused more on preventing the spread of slavery into the territories than wiping it out in the South. The corollary to their view that the federal government lacked the power to abolish slavery was that it also lacked the power to establish it or protect it with such measures as the fugitive slave laws of 1793 and 1850. Without the shelter of federal protection, and with slavery bottled up in the existing slave states, they believed the institution would ultimately collapse and die.

Finally, a small group of radical antislavery lawyers and politicians, associated with the Liberty party, claimed slavery was illegal everywhere, since it violated the Fifth Amendment's guarantee of due process, the promise of equal protection in Article IV, and other clauses in both federal and state constitutions. Led by Alvan Stewart of New York, Lysander Spooner of Boston, and the reform editor William Goodell, the radicals argued that the Constitution did not protect slavery, but had been perverted by continued acquiescence in the evil. Their most ambitious project was an unsuccessful law suit, *State v. Post* (N.J., 1844), argued by Alvan Stewart, in which they tried to free the few hundred elderly slaves who had been born in New Jersey before that state passed its gradual emancipation statute in 1804. They wanted the federal government to use its powers to eradicate slavery everywhere. While never politically or legally successful, they helped frame useful arguments for political abolitionists and lawyers, like Chase and William H. Seward of New York.

From the 1830s on, abolitionists presented their various theories to state and federal jurists, ranging from obscure justices of the peace to the justices of the U.S. Supreme Court. Cases testing the status of free blacks and runaway slaves ran into a variety of judicial responses. Most judges proved unsympathetic to the abolitionist cause. Proslavery and racist attitudes guided the thinking of most federal judges, especially when Democrats like Andrew Jackson were able to apply a litmus test of support for the fugitive slave law to any judicial nominee. By relying on strict adherence to statutory law, most state and nearly all federal jurists easily rejected abolitionist arguments about fundamental justice and natural rights. Nevertheless, a few judges appeared determined at least to stop the South from utilizing Northern courts to enforce slave laws.

## Abolitionist Use of the Law

Antislavery activists were skilled propagandists, speakers, and agitators. They were also creative litigators who effectively used the legal system to combat an entrenched social and economic system. While not always successful in their litigation strategy, even when they lost, antislavery lawyers and activists managed to use their cases to educate the Northern public about the evils of slavery and the dangers it posed, not only to blacks, but also to whites. In many ways the abolitionists provided a model that civil rights activists would use a century later. They did not develop their litigation strategy out of whole cloth, however. Rather, they drew on a tradition of using law to fight slavery that began in England. As such, they often turned to common law concepts and English constitutional principles in their assault on slavery.

The most important legal case for American abolitionists was *Somerset v. Stewart* (G.B., 1772) decided by the Court of King's Bench in London before the American Revolution. Charles Stewart, a minor colonial official had brought his slave, James Somerset, to England, and held him in bondage, until Somerset escaped. Stewart then seized Somerset and placed him in the care of an English sea captain, with instructions to take the slave to the West Indies and sell him. In 1772, English lawyers, working for the famous abolitionist Granville Sharp, obtained a writ of habeas corpus to test the status of a slave in England. The chief justice, Lord Mansfield, urged the parties to settle the case, but when they did not, he dramatically ruled that no person could be forcibly held as a slave in England because there was no positive law—that is, a statute—to create the status of slavery. Thus, Somerset went free.

From the 1780s until the War of 1812, the Pennsylvania Society for the Abolition of Slavery, the New York Manumission Society, and similar revolutionary era antislavery organizations, followed the lead set out by Granville Sharpe. These organizations maintained active legal committees and brought numerous, and often successful, suits to free slaves illegally held in bondage and to protect the rights of free blacks. They also successfully lobbied for gradual emancipation statutes that put slavery in the North on the road to extinction.

The societies that brought these suits had begun to wither away by 1812. The new abolitionist movement that emerged in the 1830s was primarily a moral crusade. Nevertheless, even though some of these abolitionists spurned traditional political action, they lobbied their state legislatures for laws that would protect free blacks and confront slavery. They also made effective use of the courts to free slaves in their midst, to defend blacks seized as fugitive slaves, to defend abolitionists arrested or sued for helping slaves escape, and to challenge segregation and race discrimination in some parts of the North.

## Slaves in Transit

Starting with the Pennsylvania Gradual Emancipation Act (1780) the Northern states acknowledged the importance and power of the *Somerset* precedent, even as they modified it. Pennsylvania's 1780 statute allowed masters to keep their slaves in that state for up to six months before they would become free. New York, in 1799, gave visiting masters a nine-month extension. But where there were no such laws, the rule throughout the new nation was that if a slave lived in a free jurisdiction, the slave became free forever.

The South as well as the North accepted the *Somerset* rule. In *Harry v. Decker & Hopkins* (Miss., 1818), Mississippi's highest court ruled that Harry was free because his master had taken him to a free state. Kentucky reached the same conclusion in *Rankin v. Lydia* (Ky., 1820), as did Louisiana in *Lunsford v. Coquillon* (La., 1824), and Missouri in *Winny v. Whitesides* (Mo., 1824).

The issue was most fully discussed in *Commonwealth v. Aves* (Mass., 1836), decided by the most important state jurist of the time, Chief Justice Lemuel Shaw of Massachusetts. Although titled a prosecution by the state, in fact this habeas corpus action was initiated by members of the Boston Female Anti-Slavery Society. While only men could practice law, the enterprising women of this society did everything but appear in court. They gathered evidence, hired an attorney, and helped the attorney prepare his arguments.

The case involved a six-year-old slave girl named Med who was accompanying her mistress, Mrs. Samuel Slater, who was visiting her father, Thomas Aves, in Boston. Med was not a runaway, which would have brought her under federal law, but a transient or sojourner, just as Somerset had been in England. Lawyers on her behalf argued that the Massachusetts constitution, which held that "all men are born free and equal," prohibited slavery in the state, even for sojourners.

Shaw had little trouble agreeing with the abolitionist attorneys. In fact, he was surprised to find that this issue had not long been settled. "Until this discussion," he wrote, "I had supposed that there had been adjudged cases on this subject in the Commonwealth; and it is believed to have been a prevalent opinion among lawyers, that if a slave is brought voluntarily and unnecessarily within the limits of this State, he becomes free, . . . because by the operation of our laws, there is no authority on the part of the master, either to restrain the slave of his liberty, whilst here, or forcibly to take him into custody" to remove him from the state. Shaw was surprised there was no reported "case on this subject," but he quickly remedied this deficiency.

Shaw offered a detailed legal history of slavery in Massachusetts, as well as in England and the United States. He cited *Somerset*, and a number of other English cases, some U.S. Supreme Court cases, the relevant precedents from Louisiana and Kentucky, and even the French *Code Noir*. The conclusion was clear: slaves brought to Massachusetts "become free, not so much because any alteration is made in their *status*, or condition, as because there is no law which will warrant, but there are laws, if they choose to avail themselves of them, which prohibit, their forcible detention or forcible removal." Shaw made it clear that this rule would not apply to fugitive slaves, whose status was controlled by the U.S. Constitution.

The only complication to this outcome was Med's age. She was only six-years-old, and Mrs. Slater's attorneys argued that she should be allowed to return to Louisiana, where her mother was also a slave of the Slaters. Shaw rejected this notion. As attorneys for Med pointed out, it was slavery, and not the law of Massachusetts, that separated Med from her mother. Furthermore, as everyone realized, under Louisiana law, slave parents had no rights to their children. Louisiana law prohibited selling a child under ten-years-old away from his or her mother. But the Slaters could sell Med's mother whenever they wished, and in two years, when Med was eight, she could also be sold. Thus, Med was given over to an abolitionist woman, who renamed her Maria Somerset, in honor of the chief instigator of the case, Maria Weston Chapman, and the English precedent that helped lead to her freedom.

Following *Aves*, virtually every Northern state adopted the rule that slaves became free the moment they entered a nonslave jurisdiction, unless their status was preserved by the Fugitive Slave Clause of the U.S. Constitution. In 1841, New York repealed its "nine months law," and in 1847, Pennsylvania did the same for its "six months law," thus providing no exemptions for visiting masters. A number of slave states, meanwhile, began to back away from their earlier decisions supporting freedom for slaves who had lived in free states. The Kentucky court modified, but did not completely reject, its rule. In 1846, the Louisiana legislature specifically prohibited a judicial recognition of freedom based on transit or sojourn in a free state. In *Scott v. Emerson* (Mo., 1852), a case that led to the more famous U.S. Supreme Court case, *Dred Scott v. Sandford* (1857), the Missouri court rejected nearly three decades of state precedents, declaring that it would no longer recognize freedom gained by living in a free state. Mississippi rejected such claims as well, and in *Mitchell v. Wells* (1859) asserted that it would not recognize freedom even if the master had purposefully taken the slave to a free state and formally manumitted the slave.

In *Lemmon v. The People* (N.Y., 1860), New York's highest court would rule that a slave brought into that state for only one day became free. Many in the North feared that Virginia would take this case to the U.S. Supreme Court, where observers expected the Taney Court to rule that Southerners had a constitutional right to carry their slave property into any state in the nation, and as long as they did not become residents of a free state, they would be able to keep their slaves with them. The Civil War, however, prevented any appeal in this case.

## Antebellum Race Discrimination

While antebellum Northerners generally opposed slavery, their views on race were far more complex. Most Northerners opposed social mixing of blacks and whites. Thus, on the eve of the Civil War, interracial marriages were illegal in much of the North,

---

### THE IRONY OF LEGAL REPRESENTATION

In Med's case, Mrs. Slater hired a very able young attorney named Benjamin Robbins Curtis. He vigorously, but unsuccessfully, argued that Mrs. Slater had the right to temporarily bring her slave into a free state. Twenty-one years later, as a justice of the U.S. Supreme Court, Curtis would write a lengthy dissent in *Dred Scott v. Sandford* (U.S., 1857). Part of his dissent would be based on the precedent in *Aves*, as Curtis argued that Dred Scott had gained his freedom by living in the free state of Illinois, as well as the free territory that encompasses the state of Minnesota.

and segregated schools could be found in many places. On the other hand, the very fact that blacks were allowed to attend schools in the North, and the fact that Northern taxpayers funded schools for blacks, illustrates the huge chasm between the sections on the issue of race. In much of the South, it was illegal even to educate free blacks, and no slave state provided public schools for blacks.

Most abolitionists tried to overcome the racist ideas of their society, although on a personal level they did so with mixed success. Wendell Phillips, William Lloyd Garrison, and the more radical John Brown regularly had social interactions with blacks. Garrison employed some at his newspaper, *The Liberator*. Other abolitionists, however, were clearly uncomfortable mixing with blacks on a social level, even though in public meetings and in the struggle against slavery they worked side-by-side with blacks.

Education was a key issue for blacks, and abolitionists used use the courts and legislatures to secure changes. The first important case involving black education, ironically, involved the prosecution of a white woman.

In 1832, Prudence Crandall, a Quaker abolitionist, began to accept black students in her school for girls in Canterbury, Connecticut. When white parents objected, she converted the school into one for blacks only; her neighbors continued to harass her and persuaded the state legislature to pass a law forbidding anyone from maintaining a school for nonresident blacks without obtaining local approval. Crandall refused to close her school and continued to enroll students from other states. Thus, she was convicted of violating the statute. The Connecticut Supreme Court later overturned the conviction on a technicality, but by then mob violence had forced her to close the school.

The abolitionists who supported Crandall based their legal case on the Privileges and Immunities Clause of the U.S. Constitution, claiming that free blacks were citizens within its meaning. Citizenship, however, proved a difficult concept to define, since prior to the passage of the Fourteenth Amendment in 1868, it remained primarily a matter of state law. A person could be a citizen of both a state and of the nation, but it did not follow, at least in law, that citizenship in one automatically conferred the other. Abolitionists argued that the Connecticut law, by abridging the rights of free blacks to an education, violated their constitutional rights as citizens. The issue proved

## THE *AMISTAD* CASE

Andrew T. Judson, a Democratic politician, prosecuted Prudence Crandall. The Jacksonian Democrats were particularly hostile to the rights of free blacks, and the prosecution was popular. A party loyalist, President Andrew Jackson appointed Judson as the U.S. District Judge for Connecticut in 1836. In this capacity, he presided over the *Amistad* trial. The lawyers assumed Judson would rule against their clients, as did President Martin Van Buren, who had ordered a U.S. Coast Guard ship to New Haven to transport the Amistads to Cuba. However, to almost everyone's surprise, and to Van Buren's consternation, Judson properly put law above politics, and ruled, correctly, that the blacks on the *Amistad* had been illegally imported from Africa and had never been slaves.

too difficult, both legally and politically, for the judges to resolve, so they evaded it, and reversed Crandall's conviction on a technicality. Within a few years, however, sentiment had changed in Connecticut. In *Jackson v. Bulloch* (Conn., 1837), the state court adopted the precedent set in *Commonwealth v. Aves* (Mass., 1836), and emancipated a slave brought into Connecticut for a short time. At about this time, the legislature also repealed the law under which Prudence Crandall had been prosecuted.

Similar change took place in Ohio. Before 1849, blacks had few rights in the state, and those entering it were required to prove their freedom and find a white person to sign a surety bond, promising to pay for the maintenance of the black migrant if he or she should need public assistance. With the exception of a few Quaker settlements and the northeastern section of the state, known as the Western Reserve, blacks in Ohio rarely had access to the public schools. However, in 1849, as part of a political bargain that sent Salmon P. Chase to the U.S. Senate, the Ohio legislature repealed these black laws, and required that localities provide public schools for blacks. The localities were allowed to choose whether or not the schools would be integrated or segregated, but at least the legislature now guaranteed that blacks could get a public education.

The struggle for black education in Massachusetts was also complex. By 1830, Massachusetts provided public education for all its children, but Boston maintained separate schools for blacks. In *Roberts v. City of Boston* (Mass., 1850), blacks challenged this system. The facts of the case were much like those in *Brown v. Board of Education* (1954) a century later. Sara Roberts, like Linda Brown, was forced to pass by a number of white elementary schools before she reached the black primary school in the city. Charles Sumner, who would later become a U.S. senator, argued before the Massachusetts Supreme Judicial Court that segregation violated the state's constitutional guarantee of equal protection under the law. Anticipating future arguments against segregation, Sumner charged that segregation inflicted psychological damage on both races and that separate facilities could never meet the constitutional test of equality. Joining Sumner in this case was Robert Morris, one of the first black attorneys in the United States.

Chief Justice Lemuel Shaw nonetheless upheld the power of the school board to segregate children by race. In his opinion in *Roberts v. City of Boston* (Mass., 1850), Shaw dismissed Sumner's argument that the law required all citizens to be treated equally, and instead interpreted equal protection to mean that each citizen had to be treated according to his or her existing circumstances. The legislature could take such conditions into account in giving or withholding rights—and could do so on the basis of race if it chose. Shaw's argument is generally considered to be the first articulation of the concept of "separate but equal." In his opinion, Shaw noted that the schools were "equal" in terms of facilities and funding.

The growing abolitionist sentiment in the Bay State led to popular denunciation of the *Roberts* ruling. The General Court finally prohibited racial segregation by statute in 1855. Nevertheless, echoes of Shaw's decision would be found in segregation cases well into the twentieth century and would not be fully silenced until *Brown v. Board of Education* in 1954 (see Chapter 35).

The extent of racial prejudice in the courts can be seen in cases involving black voting. In 1837, Chief Judge John Gibson of Pennsylvania disenfranchised that state's black citizens in *Hobbs v. Fogg* (Pa., 1837), on the grounds that a black did not meet the definition of a "freeman" under the existing state constitution. Gibson relied on no authority and frankly confessed that his own racial views had determined the case. It proved to be a popular opinion; a convention then meeting to revise the state constitution immediately adopted Gibson's views and restricted voting in the state to whites only. By contrast, the Rhode Island constitution of 1844 enfranchised blacks in that state, and in *Anderson v. Milliken* (Ohio, 1859) the Ohio Supreme Court ruled that the state's constitutional prohibition on black voters did not apply to mulattoes.

## Federal Fugitive Slave Laws

Unlike Med and other slaves in transit, fugitive slaves came under the coverage of the U.S. Constitution and federal statutes passed in 1793 and 1850. Article IV, Section 2 of the Constitution provided for the return of runaways: "No Person held to Service or Labour in one State, under the Laws thereof, escaping into another, shall, in Consequence of any Law or Regulation therein, be discharged from such Service or Labour, but shall be delivered up on Claim of the Party to whom such Service or Labour may be due." Congress passed the first Fugitive Slave Act in 1793, providing for enforcement by summary process before any federal or state magistrate. Proof of the runaway's obligation could be made either in person or by deposition, but the Fugitive Slave law contained no guidelines on how states should implement the procedure.

From the beginning, opponents of slavery, and especially Northern free blacks, were concerned that lax standards of proof would lead to the kidnaping of free blacks. In the 1820s, New Jersey, New York, and Pennsylvania passed personal liberty laws designed to guarantee that free blacks would not be taken from the state and that fugitive slaves would not be removed without a fair hearing and clear evidence.

Antislavery lawyers used the personal liberty laws to protect free blacks and fugitives in their states. They also mounted a broad attack on the law and proved that, on this issue at least, they could be as ardent defenders of states' rights and strict construction as their Southern brethren. They questioned the power of the federal government to pass such a law, since the Constitution did not specifically give Congress authorization to implement the Fugitive Slave Clause. The Constitution, they claimed, made it clear when Congress could and could not act; the Necessary and Proper Clause gave Congress the power to implement only its delegated powers, and the Full Faith and Credit Clause called for congressional action. Relying on the rule of construction of *expressio unius est exclusio alterius*—the expression of one thing is the exclusion of other things not mentioned—they challenged the constitutionality of the Fugitive Slave Act.

The response to the challenge was mixed. Before 1820, Chief Judge William Tilghman of Pennsylvania and Isaac Parker of Massachusetts upheld the constitutionality of the law. But in the 1830s, the highest courts of New York, New Jersey, and Pennsylvania all adopted the view that Congress lacked power to pass such a law. In an unpublished opinion, Chief Justice Joseph C. Hornblower of New Jersey also argued that the lack of a jury trial in the federal law undermined its constitutionality. In 1837, Salmon P. Chase, then a young Cincinnati lawyer, took on the case of the runaway slave Matilda Lawrence; he developed an elaborate attack on the 1793 Act, claiming that it violated the protection against unreasonable search and seizure of the Fourth Amendment, the procedural Due Process Clause of the Fifth, and the guarantees of jury trial and habeas corpus in the Northwest Ordinance. Chase also argued that Congress had no power to pass the law, and finally appealed to *Somerset*: Matilda had become free by escaping into free territory. The local Ohio court rejected the argument, and before any appeal could be filed, slave catchers dragged her and her children off to the New Orleans slave auction. But the abolitionist James Birney, with whom she had sought refuge, had Chase's brief printed and distributed widely, and it soon entered the arsenal of abolitionist literature.

## *Prigg v. Pennsylvania*

In the same year that Chase made his futile arguments in Ohio, a case emerged in Pennsylvania that posed a more serious challenge to the federal law of 1793. Under Pennsylvania's personal liberty law, anyone claiming a fugitive slave was required to obtain a certificate of removal from a state magistrate or judge. In 1837, Edward Prigg and three other Marylanders brought Margaret Morgan, her husband, Jerry, and their children before a York County justice of the peace to obtain such a certificate. He refused to grant it, because of doubts about the status of these blacks. Jerry had been born free in Pennsylvania; Margaret's parents had been slaves, but she had always lived as a free person, was listed as such in the 1830 census in Maryland, and had never been claimed as a slave by anyone. Furthermore, at least one and possibly more of the Morgan children had been born in Pennsylvania, and were thus free under the state's laws, no matter what Margaret's status was. When the justice of the peace refused to issue the certificate, Prigg and his cohorts removed Margaret and her children without proper authorization, and they were subsequently indicted for kidnaping by a York County grand jury. Meanwhile, Margaret and her children, including those born in Pennsylvania, were sold to slave traders and never heard from again.

Initially, Maryland refused to extradite the kidnapers, even though the governor acknowledged in private correspondence that they had violated Pennsylvania's law. After much negotiation, Maryland returned only Prigg for trial, with the assurance that if convicted he would not be punished until after the Supreme Court had ruled on the matter. What began as a fairly straightforward kidnaping prosecution had evolved into a complex interstate controversy. As expected, a York County jury found Prigg guilty of kidnaping, and the Pennsylvania Supreme Court summarily affirmed this result. The case then went to the U.S. Supreme Court.

Seven justices wrote opinions in *Prigg*, which tied it for the most opinions up to that time in any Supreme Court case. The sheer number of opinions suggests the difficulty of the case. Justice Story of Massachusetts clearly spoke for the Court. Everyone else on the Court except Justice John McLean agreed with the outcome—that Prigg's conviction was invalid—and with Story's major points that (1) the Fugitive Slave Act of 1793 was constitutional; (2) state personal liberty laws that interfered with the rights of slaveowners under the Constitution were unconstitutional; (3) the Constitution gave masters a common law right to recapture a fugitive slave without resorting to any legal process, if it could be done without a "breach of the peace"; and

(4) no fugitive slave was entitled to any due process hearing or trial beyond a summary proceeding to determine if the person seized was the person described in the affidavit or other papers provided by the claimant. Most significantly, Story's opinion effectively made the law of the South the law of the nation. In the South, race was a presumption of slave status and by giving masters and slave hunters a common law right of recaption, Story nationalized this presumption. As a result, slave catchers could operate in the North without having to prove the seized person's slave status. The consequences for the nearly 175,000 free blacks in the North could have been dire.

The only controversy among the majority justices centered on the role of the states in the return of fugitive slaves. Justice Story believed that state officials *ought* to enforce the fugitive slave law, but could not be forced to so, and that state laws authorizing state officials to act under the law were entirely constitutional, but more general supplementary laws were not. Story, in what was probably the earliest use of the "preemption doctrine," asserted that because Congress had passed legislation on this subject, the states were preempted from acting. This ruling dovetailed with Story's lifelong goal of nationalizing law and allowing for the development of a federal common law. Chief Justice Roger B. Taney, on the other hand, argued that states must help enforce the law, and they could enact more elaborate legislation as long as it was supportive of the recapture of runaways.

In dissent, Justice McLean noted that this opinion would lead to the enslavement of free blacks. Indeed, Justice Story's refusal to consider the status of the Pennsylvania-born children of Margaret Morgan illustrates the inherent dangers in McLean's opinion.

In his opinion, Justice Story misrepresented the importance of the Fugitive Slave Clause at the Constitutional Convention, and contradicted the analysis of the clause he had presented in his *Commentaries on the Constitution of the United States* (1833). In *Prigg,* he asserted that the Fugitive Slave Clause was the most important slavery compromise at the Convention, when in fact he knew it was the least debated and least important at the time.

Story doubtless hoped that his opinion would reduce sectional tensions and give the South a greater sense of security in the nation. This goal, however, backfired. The failure of *Prigg* to settle the issue manifested itself in Boston, in the case of a runaway

---

## MULTIPLE OPINIONS AND SUPREME COURT JUSTICES

Today we take for granted that controversial cases may produce multiple opinions. This was not true in the nineteenth century. In 1832, for example, the Supreme Court decided fifty-five cases. Forty-six were unanimous opinions; eight had a single dissent, and one, *Worcester v. Georgia*, involving the status of the Cherokee in Georgia, had a majority opinion, a concurrence, and a dissent. In the year *Prigg* was decided, thirty-eight cases had only an opinion of the Court; three other cases had a single dissent. In only one other case before *Prigg*, or indeed, until *Dred Scott v. Sandford* (1857), were there more than six opinions. That was *Groves v. Slaughter* (1841), which like *Prigg* and *Dred Scott*, involved slavery.

slave named George Latimer. Initially, Latimer was confined in the local jail while his owner, James B. Gray, waited for proper documentation of Latimer's status to arrive from Virginia. Abolitionists appealed to Chief Justice Shaw for a writ of habeas corpus, but Shaw refused, claiming that Latimer was legitimately held under the Fugitive Slave Law of 1793. Local abolitionists, however, successfully argued to the local sheriff that he could not hold a slave in a Massachusetts jail. Faced with the prospect of trying to keep Latimer in a Boston hotel, Gray agreed to sell Latimer—for far less than the slave was worth—to agents of his defense committee, who immediately freed him.

In *Prigg,* Story had in fact held that state officials could not be forced to implement a federal law, since they were not paid to do so. This was the earliest articulation of the modern notion that Congress cannot compel the states to spend money for "unfunded mandates." Story in fact noted, in passing, that the states might even legally prohibit their officials from acting in such cases. This idea led to a new series of personal liberty laws in Northern states, in which legislatures prohibited local agents from enforcing the Fugitive Slave Act. In 1843, Massachusetts passed the "Latimer Law," which prohibited the use of any state facility for holding a fugitive slave and prohibited all state employees from participating in the return of a slave. In 1855, Massachusetts passed the most radical and comprehensive of these new personal liberty laws, which gave runaway slaves the right to appointed counsel, jury trials, habeas corpus, and even the writ of personal replevin, an old procedural device to free a person from prison or from the custody of another. Even more important, the Latimer incident highlighted the growing dilemma for abolitionists and lawyers between obedience to law and adherence to what many perceived as a higher moral duty. The moral repugnance of slavery led the abolitionists, especially the Garrisonians, to mount an outright attack on the Constitution and those federal and state laws that enforced its slavery provisions. A majority of lawyers and judges, however, opted for obedience to the law, taking refuge in strict adherence to the letter of the statute. This formalistic view permitted some of them to find, in the absence of positive law, the means to free some individual fugitives. Most, however, even when pronouncing their personal opposition to slavery, argued that they could do nothing until the laws had been changed.

## Law and Conscience

The conflict between law and conscience on the slavery issue reached the Supreme Court in *Jones v. Van Zandt* (1847), which involved the conviction of a white man for violating the 1793 Act by helping slaves escape from Kentucky. Salmon Chase defended Van Zandt, expanding the approach he had first used in Matilda Lawrence's case, and making the fullest argument heard until then that slavery could not exist without the sanction of positive local law. If a slave escaped to free jurisdiction, Chase urged, he "leaves behind him the force of law." The Fugitive Slave Act should be declared unconstitutional because the federal government had no power to enslave anyone, the law violated various provisions of the Bill of Rights, and it intruded into the domain of powers reserved solely to the states. Justice Levi Woodbury, who had taken Story's seat on the Court in 1845, dismissed Chase's arguments in his majority opinion, and reaffirmed *Prigg's* ruling on the constitutionality of the Fugitive Slave Act.

But he also addressed the question of conscience, and his opinion clearly indicated how a reliance on formalism permitted evasion of the moral question. Slavery remained essentially a matter for each state to decide in its own laws, Woodbury wrote, but in order to secure Southern allegiance to the Union, a sacred compromise had been made in the Constitution, protecting the South's peculiar institution. "This court has no alternative," he concluded, "while they exist, but to stand by the constitution and the laws with fidelity to their duties and their oaths." This rationale would be repeated by numerous Northern judges when confronted with the choice between strict adherence to statute and claims for obedience to a higher moral duty.

## Southern Slave Codes

Cases and laws involving fugitive slaves, slavery in the territories, and the right of free blacks in the North made great headlines and increased sectional tensions. They put great stress on the constitutional order. But on a day-to-day basis, the law of slavery was most important in the South.

Slaves were the most valuable form of personal property held in the South. They were sold, rented out, inherited, and seized for debt. Slaves were the victims of crimes and also the perpetrators of crimes. There are literally thousands of reported cases on the law of slavery from the fifteen slave states. There are also thousands of statutes that these states passed. What follows is a brief introduction to this area of legal history.

Laws regulating the status of slaves and blacks reflected the conceptual and practical difficulties of treating people as property. The Alabama code of 1852 illustrates this. One clause characterized the slave as property, and confirmed the right of the owner to the slave's "time, labor and services." The other recognized slaves as persons and required their masters to treat them humanely, furnish them with adequate food and clothing, and provide for them in sickness and old age. The one clause justified the harsh measures necessary to keep slaves obedient and under control; the other imposed obligations on the owners in dealing with their human property. The conflict between these two clauses was more apparent than real. Owners, legislators, and judges, never doubted that slaves, whether looked at as property or people, were to be always subservient to their masters and other whites, and that the sole purpose of their very existence was to make life easier and more profitable for the master class.

With minor exceptions, the Southern states defined bondsmen as moveable property, what lawyers called "chattels personal." According to the Louisiana Slave Code, the master "may sell him, dispose of his person, his industry, and his labor; he can do nothing, possess nothing, nor acquire anything but what must belong to his master." Slaves could not acquire property or be a party to a contract. They could not testify in court, except in cases involving other slaves. They had no rights, and the owner's ability to sell, give away, or devise by will the disposition of this "property" was virtually unrestricted. Although individual owners might refuse to sell slaves away from their families or make provisions in their wills to this effect, they did so from compassion and not from legal obligation.

Often, in order to meet the terms of a will or to settle an estate and debts, slaves were sold. In such cases, courts and executors treated slaves as any other personalty. The North Carolina Supreme Court conceded that it might be harsh to separate members of families, but in *Cannon v. Jenkins* (N.C., 1830), the court declared "it must be done, if the executor discovers that the interest of the estate requires it, for he is not to indulge his charities at the expense of others." Advertisements for estate sales often listed slaves along with cows, horses, and farm implements, all chattels personal. In one suit involving a buyer's claim that the seller had misled him over the condition of a slave, the opposing lawyer referred to prior decisions regarding what "unsound" meant in horses to bolster his case.

The various codes to regulate the behavior of slaves had much in common, since colonies and states often copied from one another. In 1712, South Carolina adopted much of the code of Barbados; Georgia later copied that of South Carolina. Alabama and Mississippi borrowed heavily from these two states, while Virginia served as a model for Kentucky and Missouri. The codes varied somewhat in detail and degree of severity. After the Revolution, most states began to abolish many of the barbaric punishments of the colonial period and reduced the number of capital offenses for slaves. A Georgia law, for example, prohibited "cutting, or wounding, or . . . cruelly or unnecessarily biting or tearing with dogs." In the early national period, most states allowed some masters to free their slaves although by 1860 most slave states had repealed or severely restricted this right. The increasing number of slave uprisings in the first third of the nineteenth century led to laws designed to further restrict blacks, slave and free, while at the same time getting rid of some harsh punishments, such as branding and mutilation (including castration), that could only serve to incite slaves to rebellion. After Nat Turner's rebellion in 1831, for example, the Virginia legislature adopted stern measures to prevent future insurrections and to keep the slave population under strict control. During this period, the slave states also prohibited free blacks from entering their domains and limited or prohibited private manumissions.

While all the laws relating to slaves were designed, above all else, to sustain the system, most states mandated some basic levels of treatment for slaves. In *Ford v. Ford* (Tenn. 1846), the Tennessee court, in explicitly affirming that the laws do not "extinguish [a slave's] high-born nature nor deprive him of many rights which are inherent in man," referred to the various statutes and constitutional provisions in all Southern codes designed to ensure minimal humane treatment. These included requirements of adequate food and clothing, protection from abuse, and care when sick or elderly. Nor could whites willfully murder or torture slaves, and by 1850, most states made cruelty an offense as well.

White supremacy clearly informed all the codes, leaving no doubts as to the proper relationship between master and slave. The Louisiana code declared that the slave's "subordination to his master and to all who represent him is not susceptible to modification or restriction. . . . He owes to his master, and to all his family, a respect without bounds, and an absolute obedience." Insolence in any form deserved swift punishment, and both owners and courts freely interpreted what this meant. As the North Carolina court declared in *State v. Bill, a Slave* (N.C., 1852), "A look, the pointing of a finger, a refusal or neglect to step out of the way," violated rules of propriety, "and if tolerated, would destroy that subordination upon which our social system rests."

# Controlling the Bondsmen

The codes hemmed in slaves on all sides, to ensure that they had neither the time nor the resources to make trouble. Slaves could not be away from the plantation without a pass, be out after dark, or even if their master were willing, hire out their own labor. Slaves could not gather in groups of more than five without a white person in attendance. Even on the plantation, they were always to be under the supervision of resident whites, either the owner or an overseer. Slaves could not own guns, possess liquor, or trade without a permit from their owners. The codes forbade whites, even owners, from teaching bondsmen to read or write or providing them with books—even the Bible. The law proscribed any conduct that could conceivably lead to "a spirit of insubordination." Other rules kept slaves and free blacks "in their place"; a Richmond ordinance required all blacks to step aside when whites passed and forbade slaves from riding in carriages, except in their role as servants.

The harshest parts of the codes dealt with any action that might lead to discontent, and these laws affected whites in some ways as well. Almost all Southern states forbade the publication or circulation of abolitionist materials; local postmasters and public officials frequently seized and destroyed abolitionist literature; mobs sometimes attacked post offices, to destroy "incendiary mail" from the North, with state and local officials refusing to intervene. Louisiana made it a capital offense to preach insubordination among slaves, and laws throughout the South emphasized the need to maintain a line of discrimination. The District of Columbia adopted similar laws, as did federal territories in the South, such as Florida before statehood, where an abolitionist was branded by court order for helping slaves escape. Such laws and punishments in federal jurisdictions had obvious constitutional implications. So too did state actions that allowed for the destruction of mail from the North or prevented the interstate circulation of antislavery newspapers or books, such as *Uncle Tom's Cabin*. But the U.S. Supreme Court never ruled on any of these issues, while Congress never enforced constitutional norms in federal territories or the District of Columbia.

These measures were intended not only to prevent insubordination, but to reduce the temptation to escape. Here of course they were bound to fail. The problem of runaways plagued all owners, so state law also provided assistance in recovering their property. Every Southern state required public officials to assist in seizing runaways, and any white person could arrest and detain a black suspected of being a fugitive. Owners, in turn, were required to compensate the captors, and some professionals made a living tracking down runaways. In most cases, the law called for the captors to treat the slave, not gently, but only in such a manner as not to diminish his or her worth as property. "Vicious" runaways, however, or escaped black felons, could be hunted down and even killed. Most colonies and states provided statutory protection from criminal prosecution or civil liability for anyone who killed an escaping or rebellious slave. State statutes exempted masters from any criminal liability if they inadvertently killed their slaves through "normal" punishment.

Some states made it a crime to beat a stranger's slave. In upholding the conviction of a white man for "inhumanly beating [and] wounding" a slave, the North Carolina court in *State v. Hale* (N.C., 1823) gave the slave some protection against battery. The court was motivated, not by compassion for the slave, but rather by the

## "THE MAN WITH THE BRANDED HAND"

In July 1844, authorities in the Florida territory captured Captain Jonathan Walker, near Key West, where he was charged with "stealing" for attempting to transport a number of slaves to the British Bahamas, where they would be free. By the time his ordeal was over, authorities had forced him to give up his ship, incarcerated him in leg irons for four months, then branded him, with a hot iron brand, on the hand, with the letters S.S. for "slave stealer." He was then jailed for another six months. He subsequently returned to his native Massachusetts, where he published *The Trial and Imprisonment of Jonathan Walker* (1845), became known as the man with the branded hand, and lectured throughout the North on the evils of slavery. In his narrative, Walker noted that his treatment and punishment violated the Eighth Amendment to the U.S. Constitution, which bans "cruel and unusual punishment." Like many other attempts to punish the opponents of slavery, this incident backfired on the South, as Walker's ordeal helped convince Northerners of the dangers of slavery to the liberty of all people.

economic interest of the master. Thus, the Court noted that vicious attacks on slaves were "usually committed by men of dissolute habits, hanging loose upon society" who lacked the means to compensate a master for the diminished value of his slave. Thus, the fear of prosecution was the only way to prevent such crimes. However, masters or their overseers were free to beat slaves as much as they wished, as long as they did not kill them. In *State v. Mann* (N.C., 1829), the North Carolina court overturned the conviction of a white man for shooting, but not killing, a slave over whom he had temporary legal control. Chief Justice Thomas Ruffin declared that "we cannot allow the right of the master to be brought into discussion in the Courts of Justice. The slave, to remain a slave, must be made sensible, that there is no appeal from his master; that his power is in no instance, usurped; but is conferred by the laws of man, if not by the law of God."

Murdering a slave was another matter. Most states prohibited the murder of a slave, even by a master. Such laws did not affect accidental killings, or even killings caused during "reasonable" punishment. But when masters tortured slaves to death, or brutally punished them beyond community standards, to the point where the slave died, then the law might step in. In *Souther v. Commonwealth* (Va., 1851), the Virginia court upheld a five-year sentence for a man who had literally tortured his slave to death during a three-day orgy of sadism. In *State v. Hoover* (N.C., 1839), the North Carolina Supreme Court upheld a death penalty for a man who had tortured a female slave over the course of many months. His punishments including burning her, making her stand outside in the winter with almost no clothes on, and inflicting five potentially fatal wounds to her head, including one that was one and a half inches long and reached to the bone.

Such cases illustrate the utter horror of slavery, and also the great latitude masters had in their treatment of slaves. As long as the slave did not die, the law would ignore whatever sadistic punishments the master might invent.

Although professional slave hunters existed in all states, slave patrols carried the primary burden, after the owner, of ensuring that slaves did not escape, or if they did, of recapturing them. The law required both owners and nonslaveholders to serve terms on the patrol, although the evidence suggests a somewhat sporadic enforcement of this obligation. In times of trouble, whites carried out their patrols diligently; in quieter times, they tended to shirk what many considered an irksome duty. At times, patrols exceeded their authority, whipping slaves indiscriminately or turning the pursuit of runaways into a brutal sport, complete with liquor, guns, and trained slave hounds.

What Southerners feared most was slave rebellion. Despite constant indoctrination by whites that God had intended the African for slavery, the bondsmen never willingly accepted that role. Nat Turner's uprising is only the best known of literally hundreds of local incidents. The law punished harshly—either by execution or forced sale to some remote slave jurisdiction—all those involved, and rebellion usually led to a rigorous enforcement of the slave codes. Slave patrols could be sure to ride regularly after the troubles, and courts were more likely to hand down harsh sentences against all blacks accused of misdemeanors or felonies. On the plantations, masters took extra efforts to ensure that their slaves showed no signs of insubordination.

## Slaves and Criminal Law

Although slaves were legally deemed to be property, with no rights or human attributes, Southern law recognized that slaves were human beings, with a will and the ability to know right from wrong. Thus, the law saw the slave as simultaneously property and as a person, and therefore liable for his or her misdeeds. All the Southern states had laws designed to try slaves accused of crimes and to punish those convicted of misdemeanors and felonies. Criminal regulations supported the slave system, but they did attempt to apply Anglo-American concepts of criminal procedure to ensure some semblance of fair treatment. The resulting system, fairly similar from state to state, operated for nearly 200 years.

While masters could not legally murder their slaves, all regulations of slave punishment included the significant exception of "moderate correction," and if such correction resulted in death, it would not be deemed homicide. Even severe chastisement, according to the Tennessee Supreme Court, in *State v. McCarn* (Tenn., 1851), did not justify a slave in resisting, "because the law cannot recognize the violence of the master as a legitimate cause of provocation." Only rarely can one find a case in which courts exonerated a slave for killing an overseer (never a master) while resisting brutal treatment that might have caused death. In *State v. Caesar (a slave)* (N.C., 1849), the North Carolina court reversed the murder conviction of a slave who accidently stabbed and killed his overseer while fleeing from the overseer and a number of slaves the overseer had ordered to chase him. The court was in part influenced by the fact that the overseer had shot and wounded the slave, and was apparently bent on killing him. Chief Justice Thomas Ruffin of North Carolina objected to this ruling, claiming that if one permitted slaves to decide when they could resist, it would encourage the bondsmen to denounce "the injustice of slavery itself, and upon that pretext, band together to throw off their common bondage entirely."

Slaves could not initiate action against whites who violated the law, and as a result, the vast majority of white crimes against blacks went unreported and unpunished.

Even when whites were charged with harming slaves, neither slaves nor free blacks could testify against whites, which severely limited prosecutions. Courts and prosecutors refused to examine the measures owners took to discipline their slaves; only the most heinous assaults came to the notice of authorities. For example, as noted above, in *State v. Hoover* (1839), the North Carolina Supreme Court upheld a death penalty sentence for Hoover, who was convicted of systematically beating and torturing a female slave to death. Shortly after, the sentence was carried out. Altogether, about a dozen cases can be found of states executing whites for murdering slaves, and of this handful, most involved the wanton murder of slaves belonging to other people. More often, courts either convicted masters of lesser offenses or let them go altogether.

We can find more of an outward semblance of procedural justice in cases involving slave defendants, although the law gave blacks less protection than that accorded to whites. Blacks, slave and free, could give testimony for and against slaves, and virtually all states provided counsel for slave defendants charged with felonies, if their masters did not do so. Indeed, in this one area, slaves had a right that poor whites did not have. But this should not be misunderstood as a desire to be fair to slaves. Nineteenth-century defendants often represented themselves, especially in minor cases or noncapital trials. But the courts could not allow a slave to act as his or her own lawyer because that would have undermined the entire racial etiquette of the South. Nor could lawyers and judges trained in the common law participate in a trial in which a defendant could neither defend him or herself, or hire a lawyer. In this area, slaves were treated like children or the mentally incompetent. Like people in those groups, no blacks sat on juries. In many states, special "Negro courts" dispensed summary justice in noncapital cases involving slave defendants. In Alabama, for example, a single judge heard minor cases; in Georgia, three judges; and in Mississippi, two judges and five slaveholders. For felonies involving the death penalty, most states required trial by jury—albeit an all-white jury. Despite constant criticism of the system in general and of the Negro courts in particular, no reforms took place. The trial of a slave, even with the outward trappings of judge, jury, and counsel, remained the trial of an inferior person, more property than human being.

Even when tried as a person, the property attributes of a slave were never far from the court's mind. Despite the large number of capital crimes for which they could be tried—murder, arson, rape or attempted rape of a white woman, and especially rebellion—dead slaves had no value. To prevent masters from hiding their slaves' crimes to protect their investment, several states provided compensation to owners for slaves who were executed or, as punishment for serious crimes, transported from the state to be sold out of state. Preserving the value of their slaves also served as some check upon the cruelty of masters, although many owners had difficulty with harsh overseers who brutalized slaves, against the owners' wishes, in order to secure larger crops.

In the end, most slaves accused of a crime never saw the inside of a courtroom. Justice, if it can be called that, began and often ended with the owner. The slave codes relied on the master to keep his chattels under control and within the law, and left discipline for all but the most serious infractions to the plantation head. Just as local barons had dispensed justice to their serfs in feudal days, so the owners served as judge, jury, and the inflictor of punishment to their slaves. Even from a benevolent and fair master, slaves could never expect real justice, since in the eyes of law and society, they were inferior beings.

## Manumission

The contradiction between the dual status of slaves as people and as property became obvious when masters sought to free their slaves. Motivations for manumission—the legal term for voluntarily freeing a slave—varied. Some masters, like George Washington, thought slavery violated the ideology of the American Revolution. In the 1790s, Robert "Councillor" Carter came home from a Baptist church meeting and manumitted his more than 500 slaves, and provided them with land and housing. Similarly, John and Jonathan Pleasants, following their Quaker principles, manumitted nearly 200 slaves. Thomas Jefferson, on the other hand, freed only eight of his many slaves. All of them were either his children, fathered with his slave mistress Sally Hemings, or her relatives. While Jefferson did not free Sally, the slaves most often freed were the mistresses of the masters. The exact number of slaves freed by their owners in the peculiar institution's nearly two and a half centuries of existence is impossible to determine; about all one can say with any certainty is that although owners released only a minute portion of slaves from bondage, the practice was sufficiently widespread to warrant legal attention.

In the upper South, at least in the early years, states put few obstacles in the way, usually just that creditors' claims could not be evaded by emancipating a slave pledged as collateral, and that the freed bondsman should not be a burden on the public because of age or infirmity. A number of states further required that the newly freed slave leave the state within a set period of time: Tennessee called for immediate departure and North Carolina gave them ninety days. From 1782 until 1806, Virginia allowed most manumitted slaves to remain in the state. After 1806, Virginia allowed a year, although before 1852, the legislature or the courts could, in special circumstances, allow exceptions.

In the Deep South, states gradually made manumission more difficult, and in some cases, impossible. Louisiana, which originally had a very liberal policy, adopted one restriction after another, and in 1857, forbade private emancipation completely. By then, in most states of the Deep South, only the legislature could grant freedom, and then only upon petition of the owner in recognition of meritorious service. These states also denied emancipation by last will and testament, and courts frequently blocked efforts to get around this restriction. The South Carolina Court of Appeals noted in *Gordon v. Blackman* (S.C., 1844), that the attempted manumission in this case was simply one more example "in which the superstitious weakness of dying men . . . induce them, in their last minutes, to emancipate their slaves, in fraud of the . . . declared policy of the State."

The idea of manumission for meritorious service revealed one of the inherent contradictions of slavery. By the 1830s, most Southerners argued that slavery was a "positive good," not only for the master but the slave as well. Southerners argued that slavery was sanctioned by the law of God and supported by science. Inferior blacks, they asserted, were better off as slaves. Yet, when a slave gave some truly outstanding service to a master or the community, the reward might be freedom—the very thing most Southerners claimed slaves were unfit for and incapable of truly enjoying.

If masters really wanted to free their slaves, they could always take them to a free state and release them there, but the available evidence does not indicate that this happened frequently. Although there were notable examples of owners emancipating some or even all of their slaves during their life or by testament, the inescapable fact is that voluntary manumission made hardly a dent in the slave population in most states. In no year did the total of emancipated slaves even begin to approach the number of new bondsmen who were born into servitude. In 1859, a year for which we have fairly precise data, 3,000 slaves were freed in the entire South; in Virginia, which had the largest slave population of any state, owners freed only 277 bondsmen out of a slave population of a half million. Virginia allowed manumission by deed or will, but required that the former slaves leave the state. Such a rule often forced a slave to choose between living near his or her family, including a spouse or child owned by another master, or gaining freedom. Moreover, in *Bailey v. Poindexter* (Va., 1858), the Virginia court, following the lead of other slave states like Mississippi and Georgia, interpreted the state's laws in a manner as unfavorable to manumission as possible. But even without such legal impediments, it is doubtful that large numbers of masters would have freed their slaves. By the late 1850s, almost all Southern whites accepted the fundamental justice and propriety of enslaving blacks, and these ideas were reinforced by teachers, scientists, doctors, ministers, legal theorists, lawyers, and jurists.

## Free Blacks

Free blacks had some opportunity for a better life, but they still faced inordinate legal, social, and economic barriers. Nearly all Southern whites feared and detested free blacks. A South Carolina judge in *Morton v. Thompson* (S.C., 1854) voiced the popular sentiment when he declared that "a free African population is a curse to any country." This only reflected Jefferson's assertion in *Notes on the State of Virginia*, that free blacks were "pests" on society. Nor should one believe that this attitude was limited to the South. Although the North might object to slavery as an institution, few Northern whites, even among the abolitionists, considered the black man equal to the white man. In 1830, only four New England states gave free blacks the same voting rights as whites. Most Northern states prohibited intermarriage between the races, and others took steps to discourage free blacks from settling within their borders. Throughout most of the antebellum period, blacks entering Indiana, Illinois, and Ohio had to prove their free status and find sureties to sign bonds guaranteeing their self-sufficiency and good behavior.

Throughout the North, free, or as one scholar has termed them, "quasi-free" Negroes, found numerous state and local restrictions on where and how they could live and work. At a time when states were liberalizing white male suffrage, they restricted the voting rights of free blacks. By the 1850s, only New England (where blacks made up less than 1 percent of the population) allowed a relatively free vote. New York allowed blacks to vote, but imposed a heavy property qualification that effectively disenfranchised most of them, other Northern states simply excluded them altogether. By the 1850s, all Northern states did, however, provide some education for free black children. Like all the Southern states, a few Northern states prohibited black testimony in cases involving a white person. Legal disabilities, however, apparently weighed less heavily on free blacks than did social patterns, which denied them economic opportunity and political participation in the life of the community.

The situation was even worse in the South, where more than half of all free blacks lived. On the eve of the Civil War, Virginia had 60,000 free blacks, while another 25,000 lived in Baltimore. Louisiana, Maryland, Missouri, and Kentucky had large free black populations, and a fair number lived in Charleston, South Carolina. Although they had legal rights—that is, formal protection under the law—in practice, they had little or no power to enforce their rights. Furthermore, state legislatures hemmed them around with rules similar to those applied to slaves. In Maryland, they could not own dogs; in Georgia, they could not possess or use guns or dispense medicine. Free blacks who were convicted of crimes often faced harsher penalties than those meted out to whites for the same offense. Several states prohibited free blacks, like slaves, from being taught to read or write, and legislated against any fraternization between the races: a South Carolina law condemned any white man who was found gambling with a black, free or slave, to a whipping. Most cities had established separate burial facilities for the two races, as well as other forms of legalized segregation. Free Negroes also faced restrictions on their movements; if for any reason they left their own state, they could not return. Local authorities often arrested black seamen in seaports and kept them in custody until their ships got ready to sail.

Perhaps worst of all, several states had laws permitting the reenslavement of free blacks. Arkansas, which had only a few free blacks, attempted to expel them from the state in 1859; those who refused to leave were to be hired out as slaves for a year, and if they still remained after that, they could be sold into permanent bondage. In the 1850s, several Southern states, fearful that free blacks served as abolitionist agents, adopted laws for voluntary enslavement, which "generously" allowed free blacks to select their new masters. Virginia permitted free blacks who were convicted of crimes that called for imprisonment to be sold into slavery instead; Florida applied a similar statute to those who were found dissolute or idle.

These harsh laws accurately reflected whites' fear of free blacks. Free blacks affronted the Southern consciousness; by casting doubt on the basic assumption that blacks by character and intellect were unfit to be anything but slaves, the existence of free blacks called into question the very legitimacy of slavery as an institution.

## Conclusion

By 1850, the controversy over slavery had become the dominant issue facing the country. Just as the political system proved unable to effect a compromise acceptable to both North and South, so the legal system also failed to resolve the slavery question. What had begun as a labor system common to all European colonies in the New World, had, by the 1820s, become a racially based system of social control and repression, as well as a valuable form of labor and property. This system also meant that the American South was increasingly legally, culturally, and socially isolated, not only from the rest of the United States, but from Western Europe as well.

By the 1820s, Southerners saw slavery as the central feature of the economic, political, and social fabric of their lives. For Northerners, thanks in part to the tireless efforts of abolitionists and the heart-rending plight of recaptured slaves, the involuntary servitude of black people had emerged as the paramount moral problem of the day. Just as slavery paralyzed politics, it also adversely affected the law, stultifying the creativity and flexibility hitherto associated with the common law tradition. Efforts to resolve the issue failed and brought increasing public condemnation on the courts for their defense of slavery.

# For Further Reading

The literature on American slavery is immense, and there is also a wealth of information on slavery, the law, and the Constitution. The best place to start for a general overview of slavery as an institution, although dated, remains Kenneth M. Stampp, *The Peculiar Institution* (1956).

The study of the law of slavery has become something of cottage industry since 1975. On the law of slavery in the South, see Thomas D. Morris, *Southern Slavery and the Law, 1619–1860* (1996); Paul Finkelman, *Slavery in the Courtroom* (1985); Paul Finkelman, ed., *Slavery and the Law* (1998); Mark V. Tushnet, *The American Law of Slavery, 1810–1860: Considerations of Humanity and Interest* (1981); William Wiethoff, *A Peculiar Humanism: The Judicial Advocacy of Slavery in the High Courts of the Old South, 1820–1850* (1996); and A. E. Keir Nash, in "A More Equitable Past? Southern Supreme Courts and the Protection of the Antebellum Negro," 48 *North Carolina Law Review* 199 (1970); Two excellent state studies are, Judith Kelleher Schafer, *Slavery, The Civil Law, and the Supreme Court of Louisiana* (1994); and Philip J. Schwarz, *Twice Condemned: Slaves and the Criminal Laws of Virginia, 1705–1865* (1988).

For legal aspects of slavery at the time of the Revolution, see William M. Wiecek, "The Statutory Law of Slavery and Race in the Thirteen Mainland Colonies of British America," 34 *William and Mary Quarterly* 258 (1977); A. Leon Higginbotham, *In the Matter of Color: Race and the American Legal Process: The Colonial Period* (1980); and Paul Finkelman, *Slavery and the Founders: Race and Liberty in the Age of Jefferson* (1996).

On antislavery and the law, see Robert M. Cover, *Justice Accused: Antislavery and the Judicial Process* (1975), a provocative indictment of judges, whom Cover believes resorted to legal formalism in order to avoid the moral dilemmas confronting them. A. E. Keir Nash, in "Fairness and Formalism in the Treatment of Blacks in the State Supreme Courts of the Old South," 56 *Virginia Law Review* 64 (1970), and in other articles shows that although Southern judicial behavior varied considerably from state to state, one could find a fairly high degree of concern for fairness, at least in the appellate decisions. One should also see the comparative study by Michael S. Hindus, *Prison and Plantation: Crime, Justice and Authority in Massachusetts and South Carolina, 1767–1878* (1980).

Glover Moore, *The Missouri Controversy, 1819–1821* (1953) remains the standard work on this issue. William M. Wiecek, *The Sources of Antislavery Constitutionalism in America, 1760–1848* (1977) provides a rich analysis of the complexities on antislavery constitutional theory. Also useful for antislavery ideas and are David Brion Davis, *The Problem of Slavery in the Age of Revolution, 1770–1823* (1975); and Harold M. Hyman and William M. Wiecek, *Equal Justice Under Law: Constitutional Development, 1835–1875* (1982). The defense of slavery can be found in William S. Jenkins, *Pro-Slavery Thought in the Old South* (1935); and Jesse T. Carpenter, *The South as a Conscious Minority* (1930).

Free blacks are the subject of Leon F. Litwack, *North of Slavery: The Negro in the Free States, 1790–1860* (1961); Ira Berlin, *Slaves Without Masters: The Free Negro in the Ante-Bellum South* (1974); Paul Finkelman "Prelude to the Fourteenth Amendment: Black Legal Rights in the Antebellum North," 17 *Rutgers Law Journal* 415 (1986); and James Horton and Lois Horton, *Free People of Color* (1993). There is a fine chapter on Indians, slaves, and free blacks in James H. Kettner, *The Development of American Citizenship, 1608–1870* (1978).

The issue of slaves in transit is covered at great length, and for the entire nation, in Paul Finkelman, *An Imperfect Union: Slavery, Federalism, and Comity* (1981). The role of Chief Justice Shaw in the *Aves* and *Latimer* cases in set out in Leonard W. Levy's masterful biography, *The Law of the Commonwealth and Chief Justice Shaw* (1957).

For the *Prigg* case, see Paul Finkelman, "Story Telling on the Supreme Court: *Prigg v. Pennsylvania* and Justice Joseph Story's Judicial Nationalism," 1994 *Supreme Court Review* 247 (1995); and Paul Finkelman, "*Prigg v. Pennsylvania* and the Northern State Courts: Anti-Slavery Uses of a Pro-Slavery Decision," 25 *Civil War History* 5 (1979). For runaway slaves, the federal statutes, and personal liberty laws, see Stanley Campbell, *The Slave Catchers* (1968); Thomas D. Morris, *Free Men All: The Personal Liberty Laws of the North* (1974); and John Hope Franklin and Loren Schweninger, *Runaway Slaves: Rebels on the Plantation* (1999). An excellent example of a more specialized study of the interaction between race and criminal law in this period is Christopher Waldrep, *Roots of Disorder: Race and Criminal Justice in the American South, 1817–1880* (1998). On the free speech and freedom of expression issues, see Michael Kent Curtis, *Free Speech, "The People's Darling Privilege": Struggles for Freedom of Expression in American History* (2001). Clement Eaton, *The Freedom of Thought Struggle in the Old South* (1964), remains a classic study of overall intellectual suppression in the slave states, while Russell B. Nye, *Fettered Freedom: Civil Liberties and the Slavery Controversy, 1830–1860* (1963), provides a still-valuable discussion of the suppression of antislavery speech in the North.

# 18

# A House Dividing

Dᴜʀɪɴɢ ᴛʜᴇ 1820s and early 1830s, slavery grew from a nagging but secondary issue to a major concern in American politics, and by extension, in American law as well. In the next two and a half decades, the peculiar institution would become the central question of American life and gradually cripple the political process. Just as the country could not deal politically with the moral questions raised by slavery, the nation's courts were unable to resolve constitutional problems in a manner acceptable to both the North and South. Chief Justice Taney's major effort to impose a judicial solution on a political and moral controversy—his opinion in *Dred Scott v. Sandford* (1857)—proved disastrous and helped set the stage for the Civil War.

## The Gag Rule

Starting in the 1790s, opponents of slavery took advantage of the First Amendment right "to petition the Government for a redress of grievances." These reformers asked Congress to hem in the slave trade and to protect free blacks. Their pleas generally fell on deaf ears, and the only significant slavery-related act of the first few congresses was the adoption of the fugitive slave law in 1793. After the end of the African slave trade, which Congress banned in 1808, most Northern opponents of slavery looked inward, to reform their own states, lobbying for schools and other institutions for free blacks. Southern opposition to slavery, meanwhile, withered away.

Starting in the early 1830s, however, a new abolitionist movement emerged, dedicated to confronting slavery in the South and at the national level. The abolitionists inundated Congress with remonstrances attacking slavery wherever the federal government had jurisdiction, as in the territories and Washington, D.C. The abolitionist petitions grew from a small trickle to a giant flood. In 1837–38, for example, the abolitionists sent more than 410,000 petitions to Congress, signed by more than one million Northerners.

Southerners, who dominated Congress, responded to these attacks on their most important social institution with outrage and a tactic that in the end proved more dangerous to slavery than the petitions ever were. In 1836, Congressman Henry L. Pinckney of South Carolina, the son of a signer of the Constitution, Charles Pinckney, proposed a "gag rule," which provided that all petitions relating to slavery "shall, without being either printed or referred, be laid upon the table, and that no further action whatever shall be taken thereon." The rule passed by a large majority, but not without opposition—especially from John Quincy Adams, who, after leaving the White House, had been elected to Congress from his home district in Massachusetts. "I hold the resolution to be a direct violation of the constitution," he declared during the debate, and of "the rules of this House, and the rights of my constituents." The House renewed the Pinckney gag at each new session until 1840, when it became a standing rule. And, at every session, Old Man Eloquent, as Adams was nicknamed, protested, sometimes almost alone, that the rule was unconstitutional. Despite threats of censure and expulsion from his proslavery colleagues, Adams gradually gained support from a few other Northern Congressmen.

Adams did not fully agree with the substance of the petitions; in response to one abolitionist, Adams argued that neither the will of God, as he understood it, nor practical politics would permit the immediate emancipation of slaves. But he considered it his duty, as he told the House, to present any petition from any citizen. "It is for the sacredness of the right of petition that I have adopted this course." The right to petition could be traced back to Magna Carta, and in 1669, the House of Commons had resolved that every English citizen possessed "the inherent right to prepare and present petitions . . . in case of grievances." The English Bill of Rights of 1689 had confirmed this right, as had resolutions of the Stamp Act Congress of 1765 and the First Amendment. The right did not carry a requirement that the government act, but for the right to petition to be more than an empty form Congress at least had to read and consider the documents. Otherwise, as Daniel Webster wrote, "the whole right of petition is but a vain illusion and a mockery."

Even Adams's personal stature as a former president did not protect him from the power and anger of the proslavery forces. In 1842, he received a petition from abolitionist followers of William Lloyd Garrison, who urged a break-up of the Union to prevent Northerners from having to support slavery. Adams was totally opposed to such a petition, and said so on the floor of Congress, but he also believed he had a constitutional obligation to present it. This secessionist petition, however, gave his enemies in Congress the pretext to censure him. The ex-president then began a defense of his actions, which he turned into a wholesale attack on slavery. After six days of Adams's wit, lawyerly skills, and barbed attacks, the Congress tabled the motion of censure. By this time, most newspapers in the North, and even some in the South, had condemned this insulting attack on a venerated ex-president.

In constitutional terms, the gag rule and the censure attempt helped create in the North a public sense of the value of the right of petition, while exposing the danger slavery posed to all Northerners. Slavery not only oppressed African Americans, but it threatened the political liberty of all free people, since supporters of the institution refused to allow opponents of slavery to speak.

Shortly after the censure of Adams failed, the House passed a censure motion against the avowedly abolitionist Representative Joshua Giddings, an Ohio Whig, after he offered resolutions attacking American policy in the *Creole* incident. This incident developed when slaves being transported within southern waters seized the ship they were on—the *Creole*—and successfully reached a safe harbor in the British Bahamas. The American government demanded the return of these slaves, or payment of their value, which Great Britain refused to do.

Rather than listen to Giddings defend his resolutions, the Whig majority, with the support of Southern Democrats and many Northern Democrats, passed a censure motion. Giddings then resigned from Congress and returned to Ohio for a special election. Giddings won with a larger electoral majority than any other sitting Congressman had received in the previous election. Censure had failed, although the gag rule would remain in force until 1844, a symbol of the danger slavery posed to constitutional rights.

When Giddings returned to Congress, after his impressive victory in the special election, he introduced his Creole Resolutions, condemning Secretary of State Daniel Webster, a fellow Whig, for carrying out the proslavery policies of the Tyler administration, and threatening British-American relations over the return of slaves. Giddings's resolution stated that slaves became free once they crossed out of a state in which positive law kept them in bondage.

In the meantime, John Quincy Adams had kept up his attacks, and although succeeding Houses repassed the gag rule, the majority in its favor steadily eroded. Finally, in 1844, Adams's perennial resolution calling for the rule's elimination carried the day. "Blessed, forever blessed," he exclaimed, "be the name of God!"

The gag rule never stilled the slavery debate, and in the end did slaveowners little good; enforced silence in the House merely served to increase the volume of abolitionist agitation elsewhere, while making Northerners see that slavery threatened the liberty of whites as well as blacks. The sight of the elderly Adams arguing, not against slavery but for the rights that his father had helped secure more than a half century earlier, evoked an enormous response in the North. People who had little sympathy with the crusade against slavery came to see that the suppression of speech for free whites was linked to the suppression of human rights for enslaved blacks.

## The *Amistad* Case

Swirling around the gag rule, the censure of Adams, and the *Creole* case, was the first great slavery case to reach the Supreme Court, *The United States v. The Amistad* (1841).

The *Amistad* case is a classic example of how political and social issues in the United States are often transformed into legal and constitutional questions.

The *Amistad* was a Cuban ship being used to transport slaves from one part of that Spanish colony to another. The slaves on the ship had been recently, and illegally, imported into Cuba. The illegal slave trade thrived in Cuba, where Spanish authorities often ignored violations of the international prohibitions on the trade, and where a few well-placed bribes could smooth over the illegal importation and sale of slaves fresh from Africa. The slaves on the ship were owned by two Cuban planters, Pedro Montez and José Ruiz. On June 28, 1839, the ship left Havana with the two owners, three other whites, two slaves native to Cuba, and fifty-three recently imported Africans. Four days later, the Africans, led by a man named Cinque, broke out of their chains, killed three whites and the slave cook (who had cruelly mocked the bewildered Africans). They spared Montez and Ruiz, in hopes that the two men could take them back to Africa.

For the next two months, the ship wandered the waters north of Cuba. During the day, the ship sailed east, toward Africa, as the Africans demanded. At night, Montez and Ruiz headed north and west, hoping to reach the American South. Instead, by late August the *Amistad* had reached Long Island Sound, where a coast guard commander, Lt. Thomas R. Gedney, boarded the ship and brought it to safe harbor in Connecticut.

Immediately, legal disputes arose over who owned the ship, and its cargo, including the Africans. Local Connecticut fishermen, who had already traded briefly with the Africans for food and water, filed for salvage in order to get the value of the ship and its cargo, which they claimed included the slaves on board. Lt. Gedney and his crew did the same, which at the time coast guard and naval crews were allowed to do. Both the Connecticut fishermen and Gedney argued that the Africans were slaves, and thus as salvaged property, they should be auctioned off for the benefit of the owners and those who saved the ship. Ruiz and Montez, meanwhile, claimed the Africans as their slave property. The U.S. attorney made numerous and inconsistent claims. At various points, the U.S. attorney asked that the Africans be prosecuted for murder on the high seas, be returned to Ruiz and Montez as slaves, be returned to the Spanish government, and that they be handed over to the president of the United States so that he could return them to Africa. Meanwhile, the "Amistads," as the Africans were soon called, were jailed for mutiny, piracy, and murder on the high seas.

Abolitionist attorneys, led by Roger Sherman Baldwin (the grandson of Roger Sherman, the Framer who had signed the Constitution), intervened on behalf of the "Amistads." Baldwin and his co-counsel, which included the prominent Boston abolitionist lawyer Ellis Gray Loring, opposed awarding salvage for the blacks, arguing that free persons enslaved illegally could not be the subject of a property claim under admiralty law. He also argued that they could not be charged with murder because the United States had no jurisdiction over an offense committed on a Cuban ship in international waters. The New York philanthropist Lewis Tappan immediately began raising funds for the cause. Yale professors soon joined the defense, working to teach the Amistads English and instructing them in Christian doctrine. Most importantly, the Yale professors helped find someone who could communicate with the Africans, who spoke no Spanish. Eventually the defense team found an African-born British sailor, James Covey, who spoke both English and Mende, the West African language that the Amistads spoke. He was able to translate for the Africans, so their story could be heard.

The case was first heard in the U.S. Circuit Court, presided over by Supreme Court Justice Smith Thompson and District Judge Andrew T. Judson. This case was a habeas corpus action, brought by New York attorneys, Seth P. Staples and Theodore Sedgwick. On the third day of the case, Baldwin joined them. This case was a preemptive strike against the government's attempt to prosecute the Amistads for murder. During this hearing, the court, sitting in Connecticut, ruled that the Amistads could not be sold for salvage, because slavery could not exist in Connecticut. While this case was going on, a federal grand jury was considering whether to indict the Amistads for murder. After hearing the facts of the case, Justice Thompson instructed the grand jury not to indict the Africans on that charge, declaring that "the Courts of the United States have no jurisdiction in the case." Thompson declared that "if it was an offence," it was not an offense against either the laws of the United States or international law.

With this issue out of the way, the case went to the U.S. District Court, which also had admiralty jurisdiction. In 1840, as *Gedney v. L'Amistad*, to the surprise of everyone involved, Judge Andrew T. Judson, ruled: (1) that the Amistads could not be tried for murder because the United States had no jurisdiction over their crime; (2) that because of their African birth and illegal importation they were never legally slaves in Cuba; and (3) that under U.S. law they had to be returned to Africa. He awarded Lt. Gedney one-third of the value of the ship and its remaining, nonslave cargo, as salvage for saving it, and ordered the surviving Cuban-born slave returned to his master. He then ordered the president of the United States to return the Amistads to Africa. In the meantime, he ordered the Africans released from the jail they had been in since the case began.

The U.S. government appealed Judson's ruling, arguing that under its treaty with Spain it had a right to return the Africans to their "rightful" owners in Cuba. The U.S. government simultaneously argued that if the Africans were not to be returned as slaves, they should still be turned over to Spanish authorities for criminal prosecution.

Joining Baldwin before the Supreme Court was Congressman John Quincy Adams, who brought his prestige as a former secretary of state and former president to the case. Baldwin and Adams argued that the federal government lacked the power to enslave any person, which would be the practical result if American authorities handed the blacks over to the Cubans. Moreover, the Court had to look at the background facts; if the Africans had been illegally captured, then they were free men and should be let go. U.S. Attorney General Henry D. Gilpin responded that since the *Amistad*'s papers

## JUDGE JUDSON AND THE AMISTADS

Before going on the bench, Judge Judson had prosecuted an abolitionist woman, Prudence Crandall, for opening a boarding school for free black girls from other states. Thus, the abolitionists were surprised when he ruled in their favor in the *Amistad* case. In his opinion, Judson, referring to the leaders of the revolt, declared: "Cinquez and Grabeau shall not sigh for Africa in vain. Bloody as may be their hands, they shall yet embrace their kindred."

had been in good order, the United States, under international law and the Pinckney Treaty with Spain, had no choice but to return the schooner and its cargo without inquiring into the legal status of the Africans. The case aroused much comment, not only because of the appearance of a former president before the bench, but because of Southern fears that if the Court decided against the slaveowners, it would not only foster further mutinies, but would encourage domestic slave rebellions as well.

Because of the death of Philip Barbour of Virginia and the illness of John McKinley of Kentucky, only seven justices heard the arguments, which took up eight days of the Court's time. To nearly everyone's surprise, Joseph Story, speaking for all his brethren save Henry Baldwin, decided not only that the Africans had indeed been illegally enslaved, a fact that even Gilpin conceded, but that this fact had to be recognized. Free men trying to regain their liberty could hardly be considered pirates, and nothing in the Spanish treaty required their restoration. Although the lower courts had ordered the blacks deported to Africa, the Supreme Court cynically refused to do this, and instead set them free in the United States. This cheap slap at the abolitionists actually worked to the benefit of their cause, since it allowed them to fundraise for another year, until in 1842, when Cinque and his brethren were returned to their homeland.

From a constitutional viewpoint, the case by itself broke no new ground. Story wrote a circumspect opinion, being careful not to offend his proslavery colleagues on the bench. He indicated that if the Amistads had legally been slaves, he would have ordered them returned to their masters. The case was, in the end, decided on interpretations of international law, not on the moral issue of slavery. The abolitionists, nevertheless, saw it as a great victory. In reporting the case Richard Peters, the official Court reporter, did not print Adams's 135 page polemical argument, although he did print all of the other arguments of counsel. Nevertheless, the New York committee that had financed the defense circulated Adams's argument as an abolitionist tract.

The *Amistad* case, however, did not end with the Court decision. The Spanish government continued to demand reparations, and in February 1843, President Tyler vainly recommended to Congress that some payment be made. In 1846, Secretary of State James Buchanan, acting for the Polk administration, renewed the request, in effect telling Congress and the Spanish ambassador that the executive branch of the government had repudiated a decision of the judiciary. Although the Senate voted an appropriation of $50,000, John Quincy Adams, by then quite ill, led the opposition in the House, and defeated the measure. In the 1850s, President Franklin Pierce renewed the request, again to no avail, as did Buchanan, after he became president. Not until the election of Lincoln, with a civil war in sight, did Buchanan and Spain finally concede defeat.

## The Lone Star Republic

During most of this period, only a small number of Northerners demanded the immediate abolition of slavery; the majority showed more concern with preventing the peculiar institution from spreading into the western territories. Many believed that slavery would eventually end if it was not allowed to expand. The Missouri Compromise temporarily quieted the sectional debate over slavery in the West, but changing circumstances led to a growing dissatisfaction among slaveowners, who believed they had been shortchanged. The so-called great American desert proved to be remarkably fertile, and settlers also streamed into the rich lands on the Pacific Coast. But the spark for renewed tension was set off by Texas, an enormous area hospitable to traditional Southern, plantation-based agriculture. Texas was, as many on both sides of the sectional debate realized, "a great empire for slavery."

Some Americans claimed, with little evidence, that Texas had been part of the Louisiana Purchase and had been abandoned when Secretary of State John Quincy Adams signed a border agreement with Mexico in 1819, setting the boundary at the Sabine River. As president, Adams had tried to buy Texas for $1 million; Andrew Jackson later upped the ante to $5 million, but Mexico refused both times. Meanwhile, by selling land for a tenth of what it cost in the United States, and giving large land grants to some Americans, including Moses Austin, Mexico encouraged Americans to settle in Texas, its sparsely populated northern province. By 1830, 20,000 white American settlers were living in Texas, bringing with them, in violation of Mexican law, about a 1,000 black slaves. These "Texans" had established a thriving community, growing cotton and other crops on the lush coastal Gulf plain. Americans outnumbered Mexicans in the region 10 to 1, and friction rose perceptibly between the settlers and the government. In 1834, General Antonio Lopez de Santa Ana seized power in Mexico, abolished the federal government, and attempted to extend control over what had been, in many ways, a self-governing American community in Texas. The Texans reacted by declaring independence on March 2, 1836, and after a short but bloody war, secured their independence by the end of April.

The Lone Star Republic drafted a constitution, named Sam Houston, a protege of Andrew Jackson, as president, and sought annexation to the United States. President Jackson certainly wanted Texas in the Union, but he feared that the admission of another slave state would upset the tenuous political balance and might also lead to war with Mexico. He delayed recognition of the Texas republic until his last day in office, and his successor, Martin Van Buren, beset by one economic or political crisis after another, avoided the issue throughout his term. Unable to secure admission to the Union, and afraid that Mexico might try to reconquer it, Texas looked overseas for help. England, intrigued by this new source of cotton, also recognized a potential political base from which to stop American expansion. But Great Britain, which had emancipated slaves in its colonies in 1833, insisted that Texas abolish slavery as the price for protection against Mexico.

## Annexing Texas

The idea of Texas—a free Texas—allied with Great Britain alarmed the South, for such an arrangement would deprive the slave states of any hope for further expansion in the Southwest, while providing a safe harbor for runaway slaves from Arkansas, Louisiana, and the Indian Territory (Oklahoma). In 1843, Tyler's secretary of state, Abel Upshur, opened secret negotiations with Texas, which his successor, John C. Calhoun, completed; Tyler sent the treaty to the Senate later in the year for ratification. Whether the treaty by itself might have been approved at the time is difficult to say; certainly a spirit of Manifest Destiny pervaded the entire country, and many Northerners saw Texas as a logical addition to the Union. But Calhoun, annoyed at British intrigue in Texas, sent the British ambassador, Richard Packenham, a letter extolling the blessings of slavery and declaring the annexation of Texas by the U.S. necessary to thwart the machinations of British abolitionists. Publication of the letter changed the whole tone of the debate, so that the proposed annexation appeared less as a matter of national interest and more as a scheme to extend slavery. The Senate overwhelmingly rejected the treaty.

Then came the election of James K. Polk in 1844, on an outright expansionist platform calling for "the reoccupation of Oregon and the reannexation of Texas." Although Polk's margin of victory was razor thin, it emboldened Tyler to make one last effort to secure Texas before he left office. He hit upon the expedient of asking Congress, which had also read the election results as a mandate for expansion, to annex Texas by joint resolution, which required only a simple majority in each house, rather than by treaty, which needed a two-thirds vote in the Senate. After a bitter debate over slavery, Congress approved, and Tyler signed the joint resolution on March 1, 1845. Texas would keep its public lands, have to pay its own public debt, and with its consent, might be divided into as many as five states in the future. The Texans approved the offer in October, and finally entered the Union as a slave state on December 29, 1845.

## Constitutional Questions over Annexation

The admission of Texas to the Union, and the ensuing war with Mexico, raised a number of constitutional questions. The United States had previously added territory by the purchases of Louisiana in 1803 and of the Floridas in 1810 and 1819, but these had all been colonial possessions of another country. Texas, however, was an independent republic, and opponents of annexation argued that the Constitution did not authorize the absorption of another nation. As in so many issues affected by slavery, normal roles often became reversed. Southerners such as Tyler and Calhoun, who had advocated strict and narrow construction for decades, derided the annexation issue as a mere technicality. Thomas Gilmer of Virginia declared that he was "a strict constructionist of the power of our federal government," but as to annexing Texas, "the power conferred by the constitution over our foreign relations, and the repeated acquisitions of territory under it, seems to me to leave this question open, as one of expedience." On the other hand, Northerners such as Webster and John Quincy Adams, who had always espoused a broad, Hamiltonian interpretation of constitutional power, now took a Jeffersonian stance, failing to see anything in the Constitution to allow transforming an independent republic into a territory or state.

Force of reason as well as precedent rested with the annexationists. It is true that the Constitution did not provide for acquiring an independent nation, but neither did it refer to acquiring any other sort of territory. Vermont had claimed to be an independent republic when it entered the Union as the fourteenth state in 1791. Both President Jefferson, when he bought Louisiana, and Chief Justice Marshall, in *American Insurance Co. v. Canter* (1828), believed that the power to acquire territory of any kind, by purchase or treaty, rested in the government's inherent sovereignty. Since the Constitution gave the government power to wage war and to make treaties, Marshall declared in an expansive opinion that the "government possesses the power of acquiring territory, either by conquest or by treaty."

Tyler's tactic of securing Texas by joint resolution rather than by treaty raised another problem, however. Because Mexico still considered Texas part of its territory, annexation evoked important questions of foreign policy, which the Framers had believed required the advice and consent of two-thirds of the Senate. Admittedly, Congress had the power to admit new states (Article IV, Section 3), and a procedure to that effect had been provided in the Northwest Ordinance. But Texas would not come in under that method, and the idea of a shortcut did not appeal to Southern conservatives any more than to Northern opponents of expansion. Senator William Rives, a Virginia Whig, warned his Southern colleagues that the slave states should be wary of giving up the conservative features of the Constitution, lest such practices be used later to attack slavery. But the joint resolution passed, and Texas entered the Union without any constitutional infirmity for not having come in, as did other new states, under the usual process.

## Presidential War Powers

The squabble over how Texas would be admitted paled before the larger issue of presidential power invoked to protect the new state. Mexico had warned that it would consider annexation equivalent to a declaration of war, and Tyler, over a year before the joint resolution was passed, ordered army and naval units to take up positions in case of hostilities between Texas and Mexico. Naval units patrolled the Gulf, and army patrols camped near the Texas border, but Tyler carefully avoided sending American troops onto Texas soil, much less into Mexico. When the American chargé d'affaires, William S. Murphy, gave assurances to the Texas government that the United States would provide military assistance, Tyler rebuked him in terms that showed a fine regard for the constitutional distribution of power. The president could not authorize such a commitment, for "the employment of the army or navy against a Foreign power, with which the United States are at peace, is not within the competency of the President."

Upon taking office in 1845, President Polk proved less restrained, especially since he was so eager to seize new territory. He backed Texas's rather tenuous claim for land, not only to the Nueces River, the historic boundary of the province, but down to the Rio Grande, taking in part of the Mexican state of Tamaulipas. On his own authority, Polk ordered General Zachary Taylor to march to a site south of the Nueces, while naval patrols sailed along both Mexico's Gulf and California coasts. The president also dispatched General John C. Frémont to survey California, with implied instructions to start military action if war should break out. Finally, Polk demanded that Mexico agree to sell California and much of present-day New Mexico and Arizona to the United States.

When Polk's arrogant diplomacy failed, he obtained the support of his cabinet to ask for a declaration of war. The cabinet vote took place on a Friday. Conveniently for Polk, on Saturday he received news that Mexican and American troops had fought a minor skirmish in the disputed area between the Nueces and Rio Grande. On Monday, Polk demanded a declaration of war, telling Congress that Mexico "has invaded our Territory and shed American blood upon American soil." In the meantime, he ordered Taylor to march into Mexico, and Frémont to take California.

The war resolution passed Congress easily enough in May 1846, but opposition to "Mr. Polk's War" soon arose from Whigs, abolitionists, and various factions within the Democratic party. The opposition increased as the expected "short" war dragged on until late in 1847. Abraham Lincoln, elected to the House from Illinois, introduced the "Spot Resolutions," demanding to know the "spot" on American soil where American blood had been shed and questioning the constitutionality of war-making by the president. In January 1848, the Whig majority in the House of Representatives passed a resolution terming the war with Mexico "unnecessarily and unconstitutionally begun by the President of the United States." Congress, it is true, had voted for the war, but Polk had presented it as a fait accompli; Congress could not refuse Polk's request without repudiating General Taylor and the men who were already engaged in hostilities.

The president had undeniably ridden roughshod to get his war; by committing American troops to fighting, he had denied Congress any discretion. Polk thus focused attention on the constitutional gray area between the president's role as commander-in-chief and the congressional war power. Could a president, without sanction from Congress, commit troops to combat on foreign soil? The question is as old as the Republic and as current as today's news. In 1793, in their "Helvidius" and "Pacificus" letters, Madison and Hamilton had debated the powers of the president in foreign affairs. John Marshall, as secretary of state, had declared the president "the sole organ of the nation in its external relations," yet as chief justice he initially asserted in *Talbot v. Seeman* (1801) that the entire war power rested in Congress. Three years later, however, in *Little v. Barreme*, Marshall found that "it is by no means clear" what limits existed on the president in his role as commander-in-chief to order the army and navy to act. Congress did little to clarify its own role. On several occasions, it authorized presidents to take all necessary actions they thought justified, thus leaving the executive a great deal of discretion. There had been a full debate before the War of

---

## CIVIL DISOBEDIENCE

The Mexican-American War was unpopular in much of the nation. Many Southerners doubted the constitutionality of the war, and believed it would only exacerbate sectional conflict. The war also led to the nation's most famous single act of civil disobedience, when the Concord, Massachusetts philosopher Henry David Thoreau refused to pay his taxes to protest the war, and instead briefly went to jail. While in jail, Thoreau began his famous essay "On Civil Disobedience," which argued for peaceful refusal to support immoral laws. In the 1940s, the book influenced the Indian independence leader Mohandas K. Gandhi. In the 1950s and 1960s, civil rights demonstrators, especially Rev. Martin Luther King, Jr. followed Thoreau's philosophy in opposing segregation through nonviolent civil disobedience.

1812, but Madison and congressional leaders had agreed on their policy. No similar debate occurred in 1846, and before the Whigs could organize their opposition, hostilities had ended and the two countries had signed the Treaty of Guadeloupe Hidalgo in early 1848.

Two cases resulting from the war and the peace treaty eventually came to the Supreme Court. In *Cross v. Harrison* (1853), the Court upheld Polk's actions in establishing a military government for occupied California. The president had assumed from the start that he had the authority to do so, but the Whigs had disagreed. Daniel Webster, back in the Senate, did not challenge the government's ability to administer conquered territory, but he argued that Congress, and not the president, had that authority. The Court confirmed Polk's policy; he had done no more than exercise the belligerent rights of a conqueror. The Constitution and the laws of nations validated his actions, as did those of the army and navy commanders in the field. As to whether the United States could acquire territory through war, the issue raised by the second case, Chief Justice Taney thought that the answer was obvious. "The United States may extend its boundaries by conquest," he ruled in *Fleming v. Page* (1850), "and may demand the cession of territory as the condition of peace."

## The Wilmot Proviso

In the early part of the Mexican-American War, Representative David Wilmot, a Pennsylvania Democrat, offered an amendment to a military appropriations bill that "as an express and fundamental condition to the acquisition of any territory from the Republic of Mexico by the United States, . . . neither slavery nor involuntary servitude shall ever exist in any part of said territory, except for crime, whereof the party shall first be duly convicted." The familiar language had been part of the Northwest Ordinance, but now it exploded as a bombshell, setting off a political and constitutional crisis. Within a short time, every free-state legislature but one had directed its congressional delegation to support the Wilmot Proviso. Northern Democrats rallied to it. The Proviso allowed Northern Democrats to support the war, while avoiding the accusation in the next election that they had helped expand slavery. The Proviso, however, split the party. Southern interests killed it in the Senate, but the damage had already been done. For the first time, the antislavery movement had a focal point that attracted militant abolitionists, mainstream politicians, and a wide cross section of the Northern population.

## Free Labor and Free Soil

Abolitionists, of course, did not want to see the expansion of slavery beyond its current borders. Believing that slavery was fundamentally immoral, they opposed anything that aided or expanded the institution. Many whites who were less concerned about the morality of the peculiar institution nevertheless thought slavery was a form of unfair economic competition. Congressman Wilmot himself called upon white citizens to "keep what remains for ourselves, and our children . . . for the free white laborers."

The idea of free labor was becoming a powerful ideology in the North. It delineated not only the economic differences between wage earners and slaves, but the social gulf as well. Southerners derided Northern "wage slaves" as being no better, and possibly even worse off, than black slaves. But Northern workmen owned their own labor, could contract for it, change jobs, and move on to seek better opportunities. Moreover, they could also hope that their children would be better off in the future. And unlike slaves, Northern workers knew that no one could take their children from them and sell them to a new owner. Northerners fully understood that even the poorest white laborer had a freedom and a dignity denied to any black slave. "Our paupers today," declared *The New York Times*, "thanks to free labor, are our yeoman and merchants of tomorrow." Despite the many political, social, and economic differences in the antebellum North, the free labor doctrine seems to have been accepted by nearly all strata of Northern society.

Free labor, however, needed a free land in which to expand and prosper, and its advocates believed that free and slave labor could not exist side by side. To open the newly acquired territories to slavery meant not only the expansion of the slave power, but the diminution of freedom for everyone else. The concept of free labor would have important constitutional consequences later in the century, forming a core element of the freedom of contract doctrine developed after the Civil War era (see Chapter 23). But before the Civil War, it had already become a focus for the free soil movement, which aimed to keep slavery limited to where it already existed and to allow free laborers unrestricted entry to the new "Empire of Liberty" in the West.

Many political pragmatists viewed the free soil doctrine as unworkable because of the limitations it placed on the South. Whatever their personal views on slavery, they believed any effort to block its expansion westward would alienate the Southern states and lead to the disintegration of the Union. Since the South had been willing to live with the Missouri Compromise for a generation, the simplest solution might have been to extend the Missouri line due west. Representative William Wick of Indiana proposed this on August 8, 1846, the same day that Wilmot introduced his resolution, but the House promptly voted it down; the old compromises no longer appealed to either section of the country. The North feared it would give too much potential slave land to the South. In addition, Northerners were tired of the seemingly endless demands of the South for more land, and more power for slavery. Southerners, meanwhile, insisted that all U.S. citizens had the right to bring their property—including their slave property—into any federal territory.

Another proposal, called "territorial sovereignty" or "popular sovereignty," generated a fair amount of enthusiasm, and Senator Stephen A. Douglas of Illinois, a rising star in the Democratic party, later adopted it in his effort to resolve the Kansas–Nebraska controversy (see pp. 384–385). Under popular sovereignty, the issue of slavery would be left to the settlers, acting through their territorial legislatures. The constitutionality of this plan was questionable, however, since it invested the people of a territory with sovereign powers that had never before been allowed. Under the Northwest Ordinance, the territorial legislatures exercised some authority, but their acts were subject to ultimate congressional approval. In order to get this vexatious issue out of Congress, Senator Lewis Cass of Michigan and others tried to shift the responsibility to the people to whom the issue meant the most—the actual inhabitants of the area.

The ambiguity of the proposal won some support both in the North and South. If enough free labor advocates settled a region, they could exclude slavery; conversely, if a majority of the population approved of slavery, they could enact the positive laws that were necessary to protect and preserve it.

## Calhoun's Southern Ideology

At the opposite end of the spectrum from free soil stood John C. Calhoun and the Southern bloc, who steadfastly maintained that Congress had no authority to exclude slavery from the territories. Calhoun also argued that territorial legislatures, as creatures of Congress, similarly lacked any power to exclude slavery. Only actual states already in the Union could constitutionally deal with slavery within their borders. Southerners could, therefore, migrate to any territory, taking their property, including slaves, with them, just as citizens from other states could move with their goods. By this reasoning, the Missouri Compromise, its proposed extension westward, and even the Northwest Ordinance violated the Constitution, since they represented unlawful exercises of congressional power. Calhoun's negative conception that Congress could not legislate against slavery gradually shifted into a positive demand that the national government pass a slave code to protect slavery in the territories. For Calhoun and the South, only positive state law could abolish slavery; everywhere else it not only could exist but also claimed protection under the Constitution.

Spurred on by the Wilmot Proviso and the awareness of his impending death, Calhoun set out his mature political thought in two treatises, *A Disquisition on Government* and *A Discourse on the Constitution and Government of the United States*, both published soon after his death in 1850. In some ways, they relied on Madison's arguments in *The Federalist* concerning the self-seeking nature of man and the fear that the majority would oppress minorities. But where Madison would use the power of republican government to keep interest groups in check, Calhoun relied on the factions to keep government under control, by giving each faction a veto over action inimical to its interests. In the 1840s, he recognized two such factions—the free states and the slave states—and proposed limiting the government only to those policies that were simultaneously acceptable to both. There would be two presidents, one representing the North and the other the South, each with a veto over legislation harmful to his section. Only legislation approved by a concurrent majority, that is, by a majority in each section, would be allowed.

Calhoun had long recognized that the South would be a permanent minority in the Union, never able to catch up with the North's rapidly growing population. Unless a constitutional change occurred, the South could expect increasingly hostile legislation from a Northern-dominated national government. The trend could already be seen in measures Calhoun believed were designed to undermine slavery such as the tariff and the Missouri Compromise.

But there remained one last weapon to fight off Northern domination. The Union had been created through a compact of states, with the federal government exercising power only within the terms of that agreement. If the government exceeded its powers and abused its trust by working against the interests of any state, the compact could be dissolved. Just as states had voluntarily entered the Union, so they could now leave it. From the Texas controversy on, more and more Southerners began to consider this option seriously. As a result, the country was polarized between two inflexible and totally contradictory positions: the free soilers demanding that the federal government act to keep slavery out of the territories and the slave states insisting with equal fervor that slavery be admitted and protected by the government in the new lands. As Senator Thomas Hart Benton of Missouri said, Wilmot and Calhoun had fashioned a pair of shears. Neither blade could cut very well alone, but between them they would cut the ties that bound the Union.

This impasse led Senator John Clayton of Delaware to propose a compromise designed to quiet the troublesome question of slavery in the territories. In 1848, as the Senate debated how to organize California and the New Mexico territories, he suggested that the legislation should make no mention of slavery at all and that questions concerning slavery be referred to the territorial high court, whose decisions could be appealed directly to the Supreme Court. Clayton believed that the judiciary could solve this complex problem more easily than the political branch of government. Perhaps because all the other proposals had potential constitutional defects, a final determination by the country's highest tribunal would be accepted by everyone. By then, however, slavery constituted far more than just a political or a legal question; it had become a burning moral issue, one incapable of resolution by the normal processes of political compromise or adjudication. Some people already recognized this, but most political leaders hoped that a new settlement might help the country ride out the storm. In 1850, the miracle they sought seemingly happened.

## The Compromise of 1850

The election of 1848 gave no hint of a solution to the territorial problem. The regular Democrats nominated Lewis Cass, a proponent of popular sovereignty. Antislavery Democrats—known as barnburners—bolted, and joined by some abolitionists and "conscience Whigs," formed the Free Soil party. They nominated former president Martin Van Buren, a Democrat, for president and Charles Francis Adams, a conscience Whig and a son of John Quincy Adams, for vice president, on a slogan of "Free Soil! Free Labor! Free Speech!" The Whigs ignored the issues and nominated General Zachary Taylor, the apolitical hero of the Mexican-American War. Taylor, who had never even voted in an election, was a slaveholding sugar planter who opposed the extension of slavery into the territories he had helped acquire with his military success. Taylor won by only a 100,000 vote margin in the popular vote, but he had a comfortable plurality in the electoral college. Both Whigs and Democrats still retained a national base; Taylor took eight slave and seven free states, Cass seven slave and eight free states. The Free Soilers finished a distant third, with only 10 percent of the popular vote, though they did capture fifteen seats in the House of Representatives, giving them the balance of power between the almost evenly divided major parties.

In his first annual message, on December 4, 1849, Zachary Taylor endorsed statehood for California and urged Congress to "abstain from . . . those exciting topics of sectional character which have hitherto produced painful apprehensions in the public mind." Unfortunately, those exciting topics could not be ignored. In the Senate, Henry Clay, who had fashioned the Missouri Compromise in 1820, attempted to construct a new compromise to hold the Union together. He looked to fellow Whigs and moderate Democrats to accomplish this.

He put together a package with various provisions designed to please both the North and the South. For the North, the bill immediately admitted California as a free state, ended the slave trade in Washington, D.C., and settled the Texas boundary east of what the state claimed. The slave states gained a stronger fugitive slave law, with draconian penalties for those who helped runaways, and the promise of vigorous federal enforcement. The federal government promised to pay off Texas's massive debt, left over from its years as a republic, and finally, the law allowed slavery in the Utah and New Mexico territories. Clay called this an "omnibus bill," and expected Northerners to support it because of California statehood and the other provisions they liked, and Southerners to support it because of the new fugitive slave law and the other provisions they liked.

Southern moderates, like Thomas Hart Benton of Missouri and Sam Houston of Texas, supported the bill, as did most Northern Democrats, led by Stephen A. Douglas of Illinois. Daniel Webster, in his famous "Seventh of March Speech," surprised Northerners by supporting the compromise, which his Massachusetts constituents considered too proslavery.

President Taylor threatened to veto the compromise, in part because he was furious at Texas for its aggressive stance, including a threatened invasion of the New Mexico territory, to push its boundary further west. Despite his status as a sugar planter, he did not want to extend slavery into any new territories. Shortly after July 4, 1850, Taylor unexpectedly died, and was replaced by Millard Fillmore, a New York "doughface"—a Northern man with Southern principles—who had no moral qualms about the new fugitive slave law or the expansion of slavery into the territories. Fillmore stood ready to sign the bill, but no bill reached his desk.

Rather, on both sides of the sectional divide, Clay's strategy backfired. A dying Calhoun had himself carried into the Senate chamber where he listened as Senator James Mason of Virginia read his "sentiments," essentially calling for a radical restructuring of the nation, along the lines of his concurrent majority. Less philosophical Southerners simply stood firm against California admission and the "insult" of banning the slave trade in Washington, D.C. Northern opponents of slavery, like Salmon P. Chase of Ohio and Roger Sherman Baldwin of Connecticut, who had argued the *Amistad* case, were unwilling to compromise. New York's William H. Seward spoke for many of them when he called the compromise "radically vicious." Thus, Southerners and Northerners voted against what they opposed, rather than jumping on Clay's "omnibus" to support what they liked in the bill. The bill died in the Senate, Clay went on vacation, and Webster resigned from the Senate to become secretary of state.

What happened next was a remarkable political tour de force by Stephan A. Douglas that indicated the new constitutional politics of the era. Douglas revived the compromise, bill-by-bill. Working with a core of Northern and Southern moderates, he put together a new coalition for each part of the compromise. Northerners joined the centrists to bring California into the Union and end the slave trade in the national capital; Southerners joined the centrists to pass the fugitive slave law and open up the territories to slavery. Thus, the compromise passed, with Fillmore signing each bill as it reached his desk. All in all, the political system, seriously weakened by a decade of stress, still seemed to work, and a large number of Americans greeted the Compromise of 1850 with relief. Millard Fillmore, in his message to Congress later in the year, called it "a final settlement." However, the settlement was false, and would fall apart soon after it was implemented. In the end, the series of laws that created the compromise might more properly be called the Armistice of 1850.

## The Slave Trade in the Nation's Capital, California Statehood, and Slavery in the Territories

Three parts of the compromise were particularly important: the ban on the slave trade in Washington D.C.; the admission of California as a free state; and allowing slavery in the New Mexico and Utah territories. However, the most critical part of the compromise was the Fugitive Slave Law of 1850, which in the end came to symbolize the failure of the compromise.

The ban on the slave trade in Washington, D.C., was a symbolic victory for the North. The sight of slave coffles and auctions in the nation's capital had appalled Northern congressmen for years, even though, in comparison to other Southern cities, the volume of trade in human flesh was small. As a political concession, therefore, it seemed a small loss. But to enact such a law affirmed that Congress could exercise control over the interstate slave trade, since the law provided that no slave could be brought into the District for the purpose of sale or be held in a depot there for sale or transfer elsewhere. Southerners had long argued that Congress lacked this power. Moreover, this was a psychological and rhetorical slap at the South. The most extreme Southern nationalists, like Jefferson Davis of Mississippi and Robert W. Barnwell of South Carolina, rejected any such assaults on the "honor" of their section, but more practical Southern politicians understood they could always buy and sell slaves across the D.C. line in Maryland or Virginia.

The admission of California as a free state gave the North a majority in the Senate, and with no new slave state likely to enter the Union for some time, a permanent free state majority seemed likely. But, at the same time, Southern fear of such a result might lead to demands for new slave states, even where existing populations did not justify them. Some Southerners were less worried about this situation than others. After all, they reasoned, there were always a few Northerners in the Senate, like Cass of Michigan, Douglas of Illinois, or Buchanan of Pennsylvania, who sided with the South.

The act creating the New Mexico and Utah territories on the other hand, clearly pleased the South and troubled the North. The act did not mention slavery, but gave the territorial legislature authority over "all rightful subjects of legislation," though individuals could challenge these statutes by appealing to federal courts. In effect, Congress had married territorial sovereignty to the Clayton proposal in a deliberately ambiguous manner. Nevertheless, the result was transparently clear to everyone: with no prohibition on slavery, the old Missouri Compromise line was gone, as was the Wilmot Proviso. Slavery would now be legal in the new territories.

## The Fugitive Slave Law

The Fugitive Slave Act, the centerpiece of the Compromise, was designed to still Southern complaints on this issue forever. A supplement to, rather than a replacement for, the 1793 statute, it immediately inflamed the North—and with good reason. The act totally favored the slave catcher or owner, and denied the alleged runaway even minimal due process protections. Southerners considered this the most important law since the Missouri Compromise. A Georgia convention declared that "upon the faithful execution of the Fugitive Slave Bill by the proper authorities, depends the preservation of our Union." Congressman George W. Julian of Indiana, on the other hand, spoke for many Northerners when he declared that "a more heartless and cold-blooded" law had "never disgraced the legislation of a civilized people."

Among its many provisions, the act provided the following:

- Owners or professional slave catchers could seize a black without a warrant.
- Warrants and rendition certificates could be issued by either a federal judge or a new class of commissioners named by the federal courts.
- The alleged slave could not testify on his own behalf.
- No legal process, including habeas corpus, could interfere with returning a captured slave.
- The federal judge or commissioner would make the determination if the person before him was a slave, and this could not be appealed.
- An alleged slave was not allowed to test his freedom, or even his identity, before a jury.
- Federal marshals and commissioners could form a posse, asking all "good citizens" to help catch a runaway slave.
- Commissioners would be paid a fee of $5 if they ruled that the alleged slave was either not a runaway or not the person claimed in the warrant, but $10 if they found for the owner.
- Obstruction of the law, or rescue of a runaway, could be punished by a fine of $1,000 and six months in jail.
- Once in custody, federal marshals would be responsible for the slaves and could be liable for the slave's full value in case of escape.
- To help capture slaves or to prevent their rescue, federal commissioners or judges could call on the state militias or the U.S. Army, Navy, or Coast Guard.

The terrible one-sidedness of the law gave abolitionists their greatest propaganda weapon since the gag rule. Denouncing "this filthy enactment," the philosopher Ralph Waldo Emerson urged his neighbors to break it "on the earliest occasion." Clergymen across the North echoed these sentiments, and many Northerners needed little encouragement; although in the first six years of the law, abolitionists took only three runaways away from slave catchers, owners recovered fewer than 200 escapees through the law's process. Moreover, vigilance committees formed by free blacks, fugitive slaves, and their white allies made enforcement dangerous or impossible in many places in the North. The great black abolitionist Frederick Douglass noted in his memoirs that after the successful Jerry Rescue in Syracuse, New York in 1851, the law was a "dead letter" throughout upstate New York. In that incident, a mob, which included the mayor and the city's leading minister, removed the fugitive slave Jerry McHenry from the custody of a U.S. Marshal. Abolitionists later successfully took Jerry to Canada.

The Fugitive Slave Act had its greatest impact, one evidently unforeseen by the South, in spreading revulsion against slavery throughout the North, and in politicizing Northerners who had previously ignored the issue of slavery. Both moral and legal considerations governed the views of many Northerners. When Senator William H. Seward of New York attacked the territorial aspects of the Compromise, he declared: "There is a higher law than the Constitution!" That phrase, plucked out of context, became the rallying cry for opposition to the Fugitive Slave Act, but the law also had substantive constitutional problems that opponents seized on to bolster resistance to its operation.

Opponents denied the power of the federal government to enact such a law. The Fugitive Slave Clause of the Constitution, as Salmon P. Chase had argued in the *Van Zandt* case in 1847, resided in Article IV, which dealt primarily with relations between the states. The Clause conceivably placed an obligation on the states to return runaways, but it did not give the federal government the enabling authority found in its Article I, Section 8 powers.

Northerners also focused on the act's open violation of rights guaranteed in the Constitution, such as jury trial, the right to testify in one's own defense, and habeas corpus. In *Barron v. Baltimore* (1833), the Supreme Court had ruled that the Bill of Rights did not apply to the states. But the Fugitive Slave Act was a federal law, and the protections of the Constitution should have applied to this statute.

The final objection was to the power of the commissioners. The law allowed federal judges to appoint one or more commissioners in every county in the United States. Although vested with considerable judicial power, these commissioners were neither nominated by the president nor confirmed by Congress. Yet they had the power to call out the militia to enforce their commands and to order that someone be sent to slavery, without a trial or even a fair hearing. The appointment of a commissioner in every county was a massive and unprecedented expansion of federal power, in an era when the only representative of the federal government found in most communities was the local postmaster.

The act led to a variety of responses. The Chicago City Council passed a resolution declaring the law null and void. The Ohio legislature passed a resolution declaring the act unconstitutional because Congress lacked the power to pass such a law and because it violated the Bill of Rights. However, initially, the states took a wait-and-see attitude toward the law. Between 1854 and 1858, in response to both increasingly vigorous federal enforcement and the Kansas–Nebraska Act of 1854, all six of the New England states, as well as Ohio, Michigan, and Wisconsin, passed new personal liberty laws. A Massachusetts act of 1855 prohibited any lawyer in the state from representing a slaveowner, and prohibited any state official from acting under the law. Most of the federal commissioners in Massachusetts were also state officeholders and lawyers, and thus acting under the law as commissioners could cost them their regular job, as well as their right to practice law. Most of these states also closed their jails to slave catchers.

Free blacks, fugitive slaves, and their white allies did not wait for the political system to respond; they acted on their own to protect themselves and their neighbors from the new law. Some Northern-born blacks moved to Canada, fearful that even though born in a free state, they were now likely to be "kidnaped" under the law. In many communities, blacks and their white allies formed "vigilance committees" to warn when strangers, especially those with Southern accents, were in the community. Many of these vigilance committees evolved into armed self-defense organizations. Between 1850 and 1852, a number of dramatic clashes between federal officials and Northern opponents of the law electrified the nation. This resistance illustrates the difficulty of enforcing a law that violates fundamental notions of fairness and due process.

## The Kansas–Nebraska Act

The initial hostility to the fugitive slave law died down by 1853. In 1852, the overwhelming victory of the Democratic candidate for president, Franklin Pierce, virtually destroyed the Whig Party, while the Free Soilers had all but disappeared from the political scene. In 1853, no fugitive slaves were rescued from custody, and about 30 were returned to their owners. However, as if determined to prevent national peace on the issue, in 1854, Congress was hard at work undoing aspects of both the Missouri Compromise and the Compromise of 1850. In the Kansas–Nebraska Act, adopted in 1854, Congress opened to slavery most of the remaining portions of the Louisiana Purchase. With this new law, the great settlement in 1850 to save the Union came crashing down, the victim of political blunder and local ambition. After 1854, all that seemed left of the Compromise of four years earlier was the fugitive slave law, which proved to be an increasing irritant to the nation.

The collapse of the compromises over slavery in the territories began with the Gadsden Purchase in 1853. In this transaction, the United States purchased from Mexico some 30,000 square miles south of the Gila River to provide a southern route for a transcontinental railroad. The idea of linking up the western domain of the country to the older, more populous regions via rail had been discussed for years, but resistance from Indians, sectional conflict, and other problems had stalled the project. Senator Stephen A. Douglas of Illinois wanted Chicago to be the eastern terminus of the line, and in 1854, he utilized his position as chairman of the Senate Committee on Territories to secure congressional support for his plan. He offered a bill creating a new territory west of Missouri and Iowa, to be called Nebraska. His bill also provided for the organization of the rest of the Louisiana Purchase and, to win Southern support for his scheme, he wrote the idea of popular sovereignty into the measure. "All questions pertaining to slavery in the territories," the proposal read "and in the new states to be formed therefrom are to be left to the people residing therein, through their appropriate representatives."

Southerners immediately protested that since the Missouri Compromise prevented them from bringing slaves into the area, the territorial legislatures would organize and vote on slavery before slaveholders had a chance to establish themselves. So Douglas agreed to two further concessions: he offered an amendment repealing the slavery provisions of the Missouri Compromise outright and agreed to organize two territories,

Kansas, west of Missouri, and Nebraska, west of Iowa and the Minnesota territory. Whatever Douglas's motives—his ambition to be president, his need of Southern support for a rail route, or the misplaced belief that this would finally settle the problem of slavery in the territories—this blunder rekindled the sectional flames that the 1850 Compromise had dampened.

Douglas never expected slavery to gain a foothold in the new territories, because plantation culture could not flourish there. He no doubt saw the gesture as meaningless, but this illustrated his failure to grasp the moral issue of slavery expansion for Northerners and its political importance for Southerners. Moreover, if slavery was profitable in western Missouri, and it was, then it could be equally profitable in eastern Kansas. Between about 1680 and 1720, South Carolina masters had made great profits using slaves in raising cattle. In the 1780s and 1790s, Virginia planters had made substantial profits using slave labor to grow wheat. Anyone who knew this history understood that slavery might be profitable in Kansas as well. Thus, Douglas's law in fact opened Kansas to slave settlement, and this touched off a roar of protest in the North and a mini–civil war in Kansas. It also led to the creation of a new political organization, the Republican party, that could challenge both the South and the Democratic party for control of the nation.

With the aid of President Franklin Pierce, Douglas pushed the measure through Congress behind a nearly solid Southern phalanx. One of the few exceptions, Senator Sam Houston of Texas, objected that the bill broke not only the Missouri compact but also treaties with the Indians, who had been promised the land "as long as grass shall grow and water run." Federal agents, however, had already been sent in by the administration to extinguish Indian land titles.

The Kansas–Nebraska Act destroyed sectional peace and led to a variety of responses. Northern states began electing more opponents of slavery to their state legislatures, which in turn passed new personal liberty laws to obstruct enforcement of the law. Opposition to the fugitive slave law also increased at the local level, as dramatic rescues in Wisconsin and Ohio, a failed rescue in Boston, and many smaller rescues and attempts elsewhere gained national publicity. Finally, after Congress passed the Kansas–Nebraska Act, a new political party, initially called the Anti-Nebraska party, emerged. Dedicated to prohibiting slavery in all the territories, by the end of 1854, the organization had a new name: the Republican party.

## Obstructing the Fugitive Slave Act

The Kansas–Nebraska bill wiped out not only the Missouri Compromise but the 1850 settlement as well. In the North, the growing antislavery movement reasoned that since the territorial aspects of the agreement had been scuttled, the Fugitive Slave Act also should be ignored. State after state passed personal liberty laws going far beyond the earlier statutes. States openly defied the federal statute by reaffirming rights to habeas corpus and jury trial and prohibiting state officials from participating in recaptures. Massachusetts disbarred any attorney representing a slaveowner in a rendition case, vacated the office of any state official granting a certificate of removal, and prohibited them from holding state office in the future. Many states barred the use of jails for holding fugitives, forcing the slave catchers to try to rent rooms in hostile communities.

Northern judges already had their hands full even before the Kansas–Nebraska Act triggered the new wave of revulsion against the Fugitive Slave Act. The building that housed both the U.S. District Court and the Massachusetts Supreme Judicial Court had to be cordoned off and protected by armed guards when a federal commissioner heard the case of escaped slave Anthony Burns in the spring of 1854. For Northerners, this symbolized how slavery chained liberty, even in the North. The sight of the dignified and nationally respected Chief Justice Lemuel Shaw practically having to crawl under the chains to get into his own courtroom drove home the dangers of slavery to Northern liberty.

Starting in 1851, celebrated riots and rescues occurred in New York, Pennsylvania, Massachusetts, Wisconsin, and Ohio. In 1854, it took a company of armed marines to get recaptured slave Anthony Burns out of Boston, at a cost to the federal government of as much as $100,000. That spring also saw the rescue of the slave Joshua Glover by a mob led by Sherman Booth. When U.S. Marshal Stephen Ableman arrested Booth, the Wisconsin Supreme Court issued a writ of habeas corpus and forced Ableman to release Booth. This set the stage for a major confrontation between the Wisconsin court and the U.S. Supreme Court.

No federal judges challenged the law outright, as the Wisconsin court did in *Ableman v. Booth*. Those Northern federal judges who did not like the law took refuge in a formalistic approach. In *Miller v. McQuerry* (1853), Justice John McLean, while riding circuit, wrote that "The hardship and injustice supposed," by the 1850 law, "arises out of the institution of slavery, over which we have no control. Under such circumstances, we cannot be held answerable." Like McLean, who truly hated slavery, most other Northern federal judges who disliked slavery also put aside their personal feelings and supported the law. Some Northern leaders, though not particularly supportive of slavery, nevertheless became so obsessed with enforcing the law that they lost a sense of perspective on it. Thus, after he became President Fillmore's secretary of state, Daniel Webster asserted that rescue of a fugitive slave would be "an act of clear treason."

The Fillmore administration took this argument to heart, indicting forty-one men for treason in Pennsylvania in the aftermath of the Christiana incident in 1851. Most of these men had not actually aided the fugitive slaves, one of whom, in the process of resisting capture, had killed his former master. Rather, the men indicted for treason had simply refused to aid the federal marshal in enforcing the 1850 law. Nevertheless, District Judge John Kane, who was notoriously hostile to blacks and abolitionists, directed the grand jury to indict the men for treason for their refusal to cooperate in the execution of a federal law.

To his credit, Justice Robert Grier, a Northern Democrat sympathetic to slavery, nevertheless instructed the jury to reject the use of a treason charge in this case. Grier, who presided over the case as part of his circuit court duties, instructed the jury that the escaped slaves' resistance had been a private and not a public rebellion, and thus the accused's act did not qualify as treason. After the jury acquitted the first defendant, the government dropped all the remaining charges.

A few weeks after the Christiana affair, the Jerry Rescue took place in Syracuse, New York. Here thousands of local residents, as well as visiting abolitionists attending a convention in the city, rescued the fugitive slave, Jerry, from federal custody. A handful of rescuers were tried under the 1850 law, but local juries refused to convict most of them. The only defendant actually convicted died while his case was on appeal.

Other rescues took place in Boston (1851, 1855), Sandusky, Ohio (1852), Milwaukee, Wisconsin (1854), Norristown, Pennsylvania (1855), Dayville, Connecticut (1855), Mechanicsburg, Ohio (1857), Blaisville, Pennsylvania (1858), Oberlin, Ohio (1858), Ottawa, Illinois (1859), and Chicago, Illinois (1860).

During this period, masters successfully recovered nearly 300 slaves. The handful of dramatic rescues, however, gained national publicity, and focused attention on hostility to the law. Southerners came to believe that almost all Northerners opposed enforcement. By 1861, many in the South were convinced that the North would never keep its part of the constitutional bargain to return fugitive slaves.

## "Bleeding Kansas"

While Southerners complained about the failure of 1850 act, Northerners soon found a new cause for their own complaints. The Kansas–Nebraska Act of 1854 repealed the Missouri Compromise's ban on slavery in most of what remained of the Louisiana Purchase. Moreover, the law openly invited slaveowners into the new territory, and the contest for control of the area brought free-staters in as well. The result, "bleeding Kansas," presaged the greater combat soon to follow.

When the election for the first Kansas territorial legislature took place in March 1855, thousands of "border ruffians" crossed into the territory from Missouri, illegally voted, and carried the day for proslavery candidates. The territorial governor, Andrew H. Reeder of Pennsylvania, condemned the fraudulent election, but refused to invalidate the results. When the legislature met, it expelled the few antislavery members, adopted a severe slave code, and made it a capital crime to aid a fugitive slave and a felony even to question the legality of slavery in the territory!

The Kansas free-staters labeled the territorial government "bogus," and held their own rump convention. By March 1856, a free state "government" had set up office in Topeka and applied for statehood. The battle of ballots soon gave way to one of bullets. In the winter and spring of 1856, proslavery forces ambushed and killed a number of free state settlers. In May, a proslavery mob sacked Lawrence, burned the free state "governor's" home, stole everything in sight, and destroyed the Free State Hotel. Fortunately, there was only one casualty, but the attack sparked the free-stater John Brown to lead a retaliatory raid at Pottawatomie, killing five proslavery men, some of whom had previously threatened to do the same to Brown and his fellow free state settlers. The events at Lawrence and Pottowatomie, as well as other acts of violence throughout the territory, sparked a mini-civil war, which lasted through the summer and fall of 1856, when the new governor, John Geary, restored order with the use of federal troops. By then, more than 200 people had lost their lives, and $2 million worth of property had been destroyed.

The violence in Kansas found a disturbing parallel in Congress. The day after the sack of Lawrence, Congressman Preston S. Brooks of South Carolina snuck up behind

Senator Charles Sumner of Massachusetts while he was sitting at his desk. Brooks then beat Sumner senseless with a cane for alleged insults to his uncle, Senator Andrew P. Butler of South Carolina, during a vituperative attack on slavery and its defenders. Brooks may have felt that he had satisfied Southern honor, but he had also created a martyr for the abolitionists. Northerners who disliked Sumner's intemperate tongue nonetheless defended him, while Southerners who would never have stooped to caning a defenseless man energetically justified the act in light of the purported provocation. Bleeding Kansas and bleeding Sumner augured ill for the Union's future.

## The Republican Party

There was yet one more casualty of the Kansas–Nebraska Act—the old political party system. In 1852, the Democrats, led by Franklin Pierce of New Hampshire, won a decisive victory over the Whigs, who were once again led by a military hero, General Winfield Scott. Pierce easily carried both the North and the South. Flush with this victory, and with strong majorities in Congress, the Democrats, led by Stephen A. Douglas, passed the Kansas–Nebraska Act in 1854.

Northern reaction to the act was overwhelmingly negative, and politicians of all stripes—Democrats, defeated Whigs, former Free Soilers, and radical members of the Liberty Party—led a grass roots movement against the new law. Initially known as "anti-Nebraska men," they soon became known as Republicans. In 1854, they competed for seats in Congress along with another new party, the Know-Nothing, or American party, which was devoted to stopping foreign, especially Catholic, immigration. Although initially successful—for example, the Know-Nothings carried the entire Massachusetts congressional delegation—by 1856, most Northern Know-Nothings had moved into the Republican party.

The Republicans were not a single-issue party, and they took positions on the tariff question, banking, and federal land policy. But the central issue of the party was the determination to repeal the Kansas–Nebraska Act and to stop, once and for all, the spread of slavery, which the party labeled a "relic of barbarism." The new party attracted a variety of people who did not have all that much in common, but by 1856, the Republicans had worked out an ideological program on which most antislavery groups could cooperate.

In constitutional terms, the Republicans adopted two principles that by then had become familiar staples in the legal attack against slavery. First, only positive law could support slavery, and where positive law did not exist, then neither could slavery; as Lincoln put it, "no law is free law." Second, the national government had no power to establish, protect, or even abolish slavery; only states could enact such measures. The Republicans granted the legitimacy of slavery in the Southern states, but denied the federal government any power to promote it in the territories. The two principles quickly became popularized in the slogans "Freedom National" and "Divorce." The first derived from an interpretation that Salmon P. Chase had given to *Somerset* during the debate over the 1850 Compromise: "Freedom is national; slavery only is local and sectional." Divorce, a remnant from the old Liberty party of 1844, meant the total separation of the national government from anything having to do with slavery, including the recapture and rendition of runaway slaves.

Thus stated, the Republicans could hardly hope to win adherents in the South. Meanwhile, the South's increasing control of the Democratic party, with its extreme proslavery constitutional ideas, had begun to alienate large numbers of Northern voters. The Republicans might be a sectional party, but because of the disparity in population, they could well become the majority party. This was clear in the 1856 presidential election. In that election, the Republicans carried eleven of the sixteen free states, and ran strongly against the Democrats, led by Pennsylvania's James Buchanan, in the rest of the North. In the South, there was no Republican opposition, and Millard Fillmore, running on the Know-Nothing ticket, posed only a minor threat to the Democrats.

To win the next presidential election, the Republicans needed only to carry a few more free states, including Buchanan's home state of Pennsylvania. Since "Old Buck" would be too old to run in 1860, prospects looked good. Furthermore, as the 1850 fugitive slave law and the Kansas–Nebraska act showed, the Southerners and their increasingly desperate Northern Democratic allies were fully capable of causing some incident or passing some law that would outrage the rest of the North, and bring a Republican victory. It needed only one event to throw into stark relief the irreconcilable differences between the defenders of slavery and those who sought to limit the peculiar institution. On March 6, 1857, Chief Justice Roger Taney handed the Republicans this gift with his decision in *Dred Scott v. Sandford*. As if to put icing on this Republican cake, Southerners and President Buchanan would team up in 1858 to once again bring Kansas to the headlines in a way that would underscore the antidemocratic nature of slavery.

## Dred Scott's Case

The *Dred Scott* decision holds a unique place in American constitutional history as the worst example of the Supreme Court trying to impose a judicial solution on a political problem. No other case called down such opprobrium upon the Court in its own time, nor has this criticism abated since. A later chief justice, Charles Evans Hughes, characterized the decision as the Court's great "self-inflicted wound," although at the time, Taney thought he had, in a single opinion, solved the nation's most intractable problem.

Born in Southampton County, Virginia, around the turn of the century, Dred Scott came with his master, Peter Blow, to St. Louis in 1830; a few years later, John Emerson, an army physician, bought him. Scott traveled with his new master to an army fort in the free state of Illinois and then to Fort Snelling, then in the Wisconsin territory (now in Minnesota), where slavery was prohibited under the Missouri Compromise. Around 1836, while living at Fort Snelling, Scott married Harriet Robinson in a legal ceremony. The judicial officer who performed this ceremony had previously been the owner of Harriet Robinson. Since slaves could not legally marry in any jurisdiction, this formal marriage can be seen as evidence that while at Fort Snelling, Scott had gained his freedom. However, Emerson and the Scotts subsequently returned to Missouri.

In 1843, Emerson died, leaving Scott as the property of his widow; three years later, Scott sued for his freedom on the grounds that his earlier residence in a free state and in free territory had liberated him. It is impossible to tell exactly who advised the illiterate Scott on this strategy, although evidence points to a white abolitionist lawyer, Francis B. Murdoch, and a former slave, the Reverend John R. Anderson, pastor of the black Baptist church to which Scott's wife belonged, as well as to the sons of Scott's former owner, Peter Blow, who were now actively trying to secure the freedom of their boyhood friend and his family. Members of the Blow family posted the necessary bonds, hired lawyers, and saw the case through the Missouri courts.

Scott's supporters believed they had a solid legal argument. In *Winny v. Whitesides* (Mo., 1824), the Missouri Supreme Court ruled that slaves gained their freedom if they lived in free states. The Missouri court sustained this precedent in more than a dozen subsequent cases, including *Rachel v. Walker* (Mo., 1836), which had a fact pattern similar to Scott's. The Missouri Supreme Court had ruled in favor of Rachel's freedom claim because her owner, an army officer, had taken her to live on army bases in free territories. This residence, even on military bases, had freed her. These cases followed a line of precedents that began with the English case of *Somerset v. Stewart* (1772), which held that slavery could be created only by positive law, and if a slave was taken to a place where the statutes did not recognize slavery, the slave was free. Most American jurisdictions accepted this ruling well into the 1830s. In addition to Missouri, courts in Louisiana, Kentucky, and Mississippi had freed slaves who had lived in free states, territories, or countries.

In *The Slave, Grace* (1827), a British court had modified the *Somerset* rule, by asserting that while a slave would be able to claim freedom while temporarily in a free jurisdiction, if the slave voluntarily returned a slave jurisdiction, the courts of that place could decide the status of the slave. In his *Commentaries on the Conflicts of Laws* (1834), Justice Joseph Story had accepted the idea that the law of the forum state took precedence over that of "foreign" jurisdictions. However, Missouri, Kentucky, and Louisiana, continued to free slaves who had lived in the North, even though under the precedent of *The Slave, Grace* or the theories of Story, they might have reenslaved them.

In *Strader v. Graham* (1851), Chief Justice Taney affirmed the right of a slave state to refuse to recognize the liberating effect of free state residence. However, this was not a binding precedent on the slave states, and these states were free to continue to recognize freedom gained by free state residence. Certainly, this seemed to be the rule in Missouri, and in 1850, a Missouri jury ruled that Dred Scott was a free man, having lived in a free state and a free territory.

Scott's owner, the widow of Dr. John Emerson, appealed this result. The ownership of Scott, his wife, and their two daughters was at stake. In addition, since the litigation had begun in 1846, Scott had been hired out and all his wages were being held in escrow. This was a tidy sum, and Mrs. Emerson wanted it. So, she appealed to the Missouri Supreme Court.

The case reached the court in 1852, and was tied to the political issues surrounding the Compromise of 1850. The court was dominated by recently elected judges who were hostile to the Compromise and who were aggressively proslavery. They were prepared to reject the rulings in *Winny v. Whitesides* and *Rachel v. Walker*, and did so in

*Scott v. Emerson* (1852). Speaking for the Missouri court, Chief Justice William Scott emphatically rejected the doctrine of "once free always free," and held that regardless of the laws in Illinois or Wisconsin, the policy of Missouri would govern. The judges not only defended slavery but also vigorously attacked those who would destroy the peculiar institution. "It does not behoove the State of Missouri to show the least countenance to any measure which might gratify this spirit [of abolition]. . . . [And] we will not go to them to learn law, morality or religion on this subject." What had started out as a simple freedom suit had led to a sea change in Missouri law. It was about to evolve into a major political and legal issue.

Scott's story might have ended in the Missouri courts. The case had been decided by a state court under state law, and no issue involving the U.S. Constitution had been raised. Section 25 of the Judiciary Act of 1789 permitted appeal from a state court if the appellant could show it had impinged on a federally guaranteed right. It is true that in determining that Scott was still a slave, the Missouri court had blatantly ignored a federal statute: the Missouri Compromise of 1820. But at the time, there was no general, federal question jurisdiction, and it seems unlikely that the U.S. Supreme Court would have considered an appeal based on Missouri's interpretation, or misinterpretation, of the Missouri Compromise, without a more specific constitutionally based claim. Clearly, Scott did not have such a claim. Thus, the case seemed over.

However, in 1850, Mrs. Emerson remarried, and sometime after that she transferred ownership of Scott to her brother, John F. A. Sanford, who had business interests in St. Louis, but lived in New York. The Blows helped Scott find a new lawyer who, in May 1854, sued Sanford in federal court for battery and false imprisonment against Scott, and demanded $9,000 in damages. This federal court suit was possible because of the diversity of citizenship of the parties. Scott claimed to be a free citizen of Missouri, while Sanford was clearly a citizen of New York. Scott did not expect to win such a large sum of money, but merely hoped the suit would establish his freedom.

Hugh Garland, representing Sanford, filed a "plea in abatement," arguing that the case should be stopped because Scott was "a negro of African descent," and as such could never be a citizen of the United States, and therefore could never sue in diversity. Judge Robert W. Wells, a Virginian by birth and proslavery by inclination, nevertheless ruled that if Scott were free, then he was enough of a citizen of Missouri to sue in diversity in federal courts. After hearing the case, however, Wells instructed the jury that Scott's status under Missouri law had been determined by the Missouri Supreme Court, and the federal courts were bound to accept that result. Wells did not consider whether the Missouri courts had improperly interpreted the Missouri Compromise. The jury found for Sanford, and Scott appealed to the U.S. Supreme Court. The case, now called *Dred Scott v. Sandford*, reached the Supreme Court in 1856.

## The Self-Inflicted Wound

At the presentation of oral arguments before the Supreme Court in 1856, Senators Henry S. Geyer of Missouri and Reverdy Johnson of Maryland joined Sanford's lawyers. They claimed that blacks could not be citizens and that Congress had no power

A SUPREME SPELLING ERROR

The defendant in the *Dred Scott* case spelled his name "Sanford." However, the clerk of the U.S. Supreme Court misspelled John F. A. Sanford's name, by adding a "d." Thus, forever after, the name of the case is *Scott v. Sandford*, even though the defendant's name is Sanford.

to enact legislation affecting the status of slaves as private property in the federal territories. The Missouri Compromise (which had been partially repealed by the Kansas–Nebraska Act) had, therefore, never been constitutional, and Scott's tenure in free territory did not affect his status as a slave at all.

The Court could not reach agreement after the first hearing, and in December 1856, heard reargument on the constitutionality of the Missouri Compromise. This argument went beyond the 1820 act, however, and by extension, dealt with the power of Congress to legislate on slavery in all the territories. If the 1820 act was unconstitutional, so were the acts banning slavery in the Minnesota and Oregon territories. Furthermore, the whole idea of popular sovereignty was at stake, because if Congress could not ban slavery in the territories it was possible to argue that territorial legislatures, created by Congress, were also precluded from banning slavery.

Since 1857, many commentators have argued that if ever a case called for judicial restraint, this one cried out for it. Although framed in constitutional terms, the questions confronting the Court had already torn gaping holes in the political and social fabric of the Union. The tense national atmosphere precluded any definitive judgment of the Court from being accepted by a large part of the nation. Yet, there were many in the nation who prayed for a final ruling by the Court. The political system seemed incapable of handling the issue of slavery in the territories, but a Court ruling might end debate and allow the nation to get back to the business of building railroads, settling new lands, and bringing prosperity to its white inhabitants. Taney and his brethren had an opportunity, so they thought, to render a great service to the nation by finally ending the debate over slavery in the territories.

At first, the Court leaned toward evading the territorial issue. Justice Samuel Nelson of New York drafted an opinion that, relying on *Strader*, affirmed the Missouri court's interpretation of state law and reaffirmed that states had the power to determine the status of all people within their jurisdiction. But Southern justices insisted that the Court decide the issues Nelson had deliberately avoided—black citizenship, the constitutionality of the Missouri Compromise, and the power of Congress to legislate on slavery in the territories. Taney agreed with the other four Southerners on the Court, and the chief justice drafted an opinion that dealt with every one of the major slavery issues.

The importance of the case led President-elect James Buchanan to write to Justice Catron of Tennessee, asking if the Court would reach its decision in time for him to refer to it in his inaugural address. In mid-February, Catron told Buchanan that the Court would address the constitutionality of the Missouri Compromise, and he suggested that in his inaugural the president tell the nation that the issue of slavery in the territories should be settled by the "appropriate tribunal,"—the Supreme Court. In his inaugural address, Buchanan would do just this, asserting that the issue of slavery in the territories was a "judicial question, which legitimately belongs to the Supreme Court of the United States."

Catron also asked Buchanan to bring pressure on his fellow Pennsylvanian, Robert Grier, to join the majority so that the final decision would have less of a sectional character. Buchanan promptly did so, praying fervently that a definitive ruling from the Court would spare his administration the problems that had plagued his predecessor.

## The *Dred Scott* Decision

On March 6, Taney handed down the decision of the Court, although each of his eight colleagues also wrote an opinion. While the opinions differ in many respects, the following is clear. Seven of the justices agreed that Scott was still a slave, six agreed that blacks could not be citizens of the United States, and five or six agreed that the Missouri Compromise was unconstitutional. Two justices, John McLean of Ohio and Benjamin R. Curtis of Massachusetts, dissented from all these positions.

Taney's opinion is one of the worst he ever wrote; he ignored precedent, distorted history, imposed a static construction on the Constitution, ignored specific grants of power in the document, and tortured meanings out of other, more obscure clauses.

Taney's logic on the citizenship issue was perhaps the most convoluted. He admitted that blacks could be citizens of a particular state, that they might even be able to vote, as they did in some states. But he argued that state citizenship had nothing to do with national citizenship, and that blacks could not sue in diversity because they could not be citizens of the United States. He dismissed Scott's suit, therefore, for lack of jurisdiction. On this point, Taney stood on shaky constitutional ground; if one state considered a black person a citizen, then the Constitution required that all states, and by inference, the federal government, had to accord that person "all Privileges and Immunities of Citizens in the several States" (Article IV, Section 2), which included the right to sue in federal court. Furthermore, Article III gave the courts jurisdiction over suits "between Citizens of different States," and did not talk about federal citizenship at all. But even with this weak argument, Taney could have been accused of no worse than faulty reasoning, if he had stopped there; if Scott was not a citizen, he could not sue in federal court, and therefore the Court could dismiss the case.

But Taney had determined to impose a judicial solution on the slavery controversy. Although later courts would adopt the policy of deciding constitutional questions on the narrowest possible basis, the pre–Civil War Courts often decided all issues that could support their rulings. So Taney continued, holding that Scott had never been free. Congress had exceeded its authority in the Missouri Compromise, Taney stated, because it had no power to forbid or abolish slavery in the territories. The Missouri Compromise, which had served as the accepted constitutional settlement for nearly four decades, also fell. Even the substitute of territorial sovereignty that Douglas had written into the Kansas–Nebraska Act also lacked constitutional legitimacy. "The only power conferred [on Congress] is the power coupled with the duty of guarding and

protecting the owner in his rights." Free soil, territorial sovereignty, indeed every aspect of antislavery constitutional thought had been attacked and declared void. Nor
could Scott claim freedom based on his residence in Illinois. Whatever status Scott
might have had while in a free state or territory, once he had returned to Missouri, his
status depended entirely on local law. The Missouri court had declared him to be a
slave and therefore property, and no federal court could challenge that ruling. The doctrine of once free always free had no validity.

The South could not have asked for more. "The Southern opinion upon the subject of Southern slavery," trumpeted one Georgia newspaper, "is now the supreme law
of the land," and opposition to it is "morally treason against the Government." The extreme doctrine of Calhoun—that the federal government had a positive obligation to
defend slavery—had apparently triumphed.

The North, of course, exploded in denunciations of Taney's opinion. Several sober
appraisals in the Northern press decimated the chief justice's tortured legal reasoning.
The press and pulpit echoed with attacks on the decision as heated as Southern defenses of it. Taney's hopes of settling the issue lay smashed; if anything, *Dred Scott*
inflamed passions and brought the Union closer to the breaking point. As for Scott
himself, Taylor Blow, one of his champions throughout the long legal battle, purchased
him from Sanford and emancipated him; he died a free man two and a half years after the Supreme Court had pronounced him a slave.

## The Aftermath

For all practical purposes, Northern courts and politicians rejected *Dred Scott* as binding. In an advisory opinion, Maine's high court declared that blacks could vote in both
state and federal elections. The Ohio Supreme Court ruled that any slave coming into
the state with his master's consent, even as a sojourner, became free and could not be
reenslaved upon returning to a slave state; the New York Court of Appeals handed
down a similar ruling in *Lemmon v. The People* (N.Y., 1860). In several states, legislatures resolved to prohibit slavery, in any form, from coming onto their soil, and enacted legislation freeing slaves coming within their borders.

The case also raised fears in the North that the decision would impose slavery on
the free states. Indeed, some extreme Southern spokesmen argued that the Constitution would protect them in taking their slaves anywhere, even for sale in the North;
Senator Robert Toombs of Georgia supposedly declared that one day he would call the
roll of his slaves at Boston's Bunker Hill. In the Lincoln–Douglas debates in Illinois
in 1858, Lincoln several times referred to the possibility that the Supreme Court could
nationalize slavery by forbidding states to exclude slavery within their borders. At
Galesberg, he spelled out the reasoning that to many Northerners now seemed well
within the realm of the possible:

- Nothing in the Constitution or laws of any state can destroy a right distinctly and
  expressly affirmed in the Constitution of the United States.

- The right of property in a slave is distinctly and expressly affirmed in the Constitution of the United States.

- Therefore, nothing in the Constitution or laws of any state can destroy the right of property in a slave.

Lincoln's opponent in the 1858 senatorial race, Stephen A. Douglas, appeared to be the major political loser as a result of *Dred Scott*. He had gambled his career on popular sovereignty, hoping that the ambiguity of the formula would win him enough support in both North and South to propel him into the White House. The Supreme Court's ruling had removed that ambiguity; in fact, it had destroyed the entire basis of his proposed constitutional settlement. Yet he continued to insist that popular sovereignty would still work. In their debate at Freeport, Lincoln asked him how he could reconcile popular sovereignty with *Dred Scott*; Douglas responded that it did not matter what the Supreme Court said on the abstract question of slavery in the territories. The people would still decide, for "slavery cannot exist a day or an hour anywhere, unless it is supported by local police regulations." The territorial assemblies could, therefore, adopt unfriendly legislation to discourage slaveowners from bringing in their slaves. The so-called Freeport Doctrine, with its open invitation to disregard *Dred Scott*, infuriated the South, which now insisted that the Court's decision meant Congress and the territorial legislatures had to protect slavery. Douglas won the senatorial election, but lost any chance he might have had for the presidency. Probably, however, Douglas's fate had already been sealed earlier that year, when he had prevented the Buchanan administration from bringing Kansas into the Union as a slave state. Douglas, who did not care if Kansas was free or not, objected because the proposed Kansas constitution—known as the Lecompton Constitution because the convention met in Lecompton, Kansas—had been written by an unrepresentative convention and then endorsed by a fraudulent ratification process. Neither Douglas nor his Illinois constituents would accept this parody of popular sovereignty. Thus, the Buchanan administration opposed Douglas when he ran for reelection in 1858. To understand this, we must return to Kansas.

## Kansas, Once Again

While the North was reacting to *Dred Scott*, the struggle in Kansas intruded on national affairs. In June 1857, the proslavery government in Kansas, which President Pierce had installed and Buchanan had supported, held an election to choose delegates to write a state constitution. Settlers from the free states boycotted the election because of past instances of vote fraud and ballot box stuffing, and because the allocation of delegates unfairly favored the proslavery minority in the territory. Only 2,200 of the territory's 24,000 eligible voters participated in the election, which chose an overwhelmingly proslavery convention. The convention met in Lecompton in September 1857 and drew up a constitution that protected slaveowners' rights, guaranteed forever the right of all masters who then held slaves in the territory, and prohibited any amendments for seven years. The Convention allowed the voters the right to choose between permanent slavery in the territory or banning the introduction of new slaves, but settlers could not vote on the clause allowing existing slaves to be kept in the new state. More importantly, the voters were not given the right to vote for or against the entire new constitution.

President Buchanan supported this approach, claiming that it focused attention on the one critical issue involved. Douglas, Buchanan's chief rival in the Democratic party, opposed it as a perversion of popular sovereignty. In December, the referendum took place with 6,226 voters (including many illegal voters who crossed into the territory from Missouri) supporting permanent slavery in Kansas and 569 opposing it. Free staters, who could not vote against the entire constitution, boycotted the referendum. However, in January the legislature, dominated by free state representatives, held a referendum on the whole constitution, and the free state settlers voted it down 10,226 to 162. Clearly, the majority of the settlers in the territory opposed the new constitution.

Nonetheless, Buchanan wanted to force the Lecompton Constitution on Kansas. This failed, however, when the House of Representatives passed a substitute motion to resubmit the entire Kansas constitution to the territorial electorate on an up-or-down vote. Although in the Senate at the time, Stephen A. Douglas of Illinois masterminded this administration defeat. Congress ultimately enacted an measure supported by Buchanan to resubmit the document for a third vote; if the people rejected it, then Kansas would have to remain a territory until its population reached 90,000. This stupid ploy so angered Kansans that they overwhelmingly voted the constitution down, 11,300 to 1,788. Kansas would remain a territory until 1861, when it entered the Union as a free state.

In retaliation for opposing the administration, the Democrats in the Senate removed Douglas as chairman of the powerful committee on the territories, and in 1858, undermined his reelection campaign. As we have seen, Douglas won reelection to the Senate, but at great cost not only to his own political career, but to the Democrats in the North. Lincoln, his opponent, emerged from the 1858 election as a national figure who had carefully dissected and exposed the nature of Taney's decision in *Dred Scott*. The two issues—*Dred Scott* and Kansas—would soon catapult Lincoln to the White House.

## *Ableman v. Booth*

With Kansas and *Dred Scott* still on the political agenda, the fugitive slave issues once again came before the nation and the courts. In Ohio, the governor threatened to use the state militia to remove abolitionists from federal custody after they were arrested for helping fugitive slaves escape in what is known as the Oberlin-Wellington Rescue. However, by a one-vote margin, the Ohio Supreme Court refused to interfere with the case, and the U.S. attorney worked out a compromise that let the rescuers out of jail.

The case of Sherman Booth, which came out of Wisconsin, raised greater tensions, led to one of the most important challenges to federal law in our constitutional history, and forced the Court to confront the doctrine of state sovereignty. The case, *Ableman v. Booth* (1859), rejected the arguments, asserted by the Wisconsin Supreme Court, that states could overrule the federal courts in the implementation of federal law. Thus the strongly abolitionist court in Wisconsin forced Chief Justice Taney to take a strongly nationalist position, not merely on slavery, but on the power of the federal courts to overrule actions of the states. Ironically, a century later, in *Cooper v. Aaron* (1958), in a case growing out of attempts to desegregate the Little Rock, Arkansas schools, the Supreme Court would resurrect the *Booth* decision to support racial integration. There, the Court quoted Chief Justice Taney, noting that the Supremacy Clause of the Constitution obligated state officials to support federal laws, because the Framers of the Constitution were anxious "to preserve it [the Constitution] in full force, in all its powers, and to guard against resistance to or evasion of its authority, on the part of a State. . . ." Thus, the Warren Court would concluded that "No state legislator or executive or judicial officer can war against the Constitution without violating his undertaking to support it."

The *Booth* case began in March 1854, when a mob, purportedly led by Sherman Booth, an antislavery newspaper editor, rescued a fugitive slave, Joshua Glover, from a jail in Milwaukee, Wisconsin. A few days later, federal authorities arrested Booth for violating the fugitive slave law, but Booth secured a writ of habeas corpus from Justice Abram D. Smith of the Wisconsin Supreme Court. Justice Smith declared the 1850 fugitive slave law to be unconstitutional, and released Booth. United States Marshal Stephen R. V. Ableman then appealed to the full Wisconsin Supreme Court, which in *In re Booth* (Wis., 1854) upheld the writ.

In July, the federal grand jury indicted Booth under the 1850 law. After the indictment, the Wisconsin Supreme Court refused to issue another writ of habeas corpus to free Booth, asserting that it could not interfere with a case before the federal courts. In January 1855, Booth was convicted under the 1850 law, and sentenced to thirty days in jail and a $1,000 fine. At this point, however, the Wisconsin Supreme Court issued a second writ of habeas corpus, in *In re Booth and Rycraft* (Wis., 1855), and at the end of January freed Booth and a codefendant, John Rycraft, from federal custody.

The U.S. attorney appealed this decision, as well as the early one in *In re Booth*, to the U.S. Supreme Court. The Wisconsin Supreme Court, however, ordered its clerk to ignore any communications from the U.S. Supreme Court, and to refuse to send a record of the case to Washington. Thus, the U.S. high court did not get to hear the case until January 1859.

Neither Booth nor representatives of Wisconsin appeared, since they refused to recognize the proceedings. Taney's opinion for a unanimous Court in *Ableman v. Booth* (1859) is considered one of his finest. The heart of the case was the proper relation between state and federal judiciaries. In tones Marshall and Story would have applauded, Taney upheld the supremacy of the federal court system over that of the states as a necessary ingredient for the successful working of constitutional government.

This part of *Ableman* has stood the test of time, and has been cited and reaffirmed in cases testing the federal judicial power. But the case has also been stigmatized because of its defense of an unpopular and discredited cause. The Supreme Court had upheld the Fugitive Slave Law of 1793 in an elaborate opinion in *Prigg*, and reaffirmed this in *Jones v. Van Zandt*. The 1850 law was technically just a refinement of that law, and the earlier decisions had settled the main constitutional issue of federal power. Furthermore, in two minor cases, *Norris v. Crocker* (1851) and *Moore v. Illinois* (1852), the high court had affirmed the constitutionality of the 1850 law. Thus, in *Booth*, Taney simply referred to the constitutionality of the 1850 law in dictum. By then, however, the widely evaded law had become practically a dead letter, and if Southerners thought about it, they might have concluded that it had done their cause more harm than good. The law remained on the books, and on the political agenda, however, until the Civil

War. Ironically, even after the war began, some Southerners would seek to gain fugitive slaves who had escaped to the security of the U.S. Army. In 1864 Congress would repeal the laws of 1793 and 1850.

# Conclusion

By 1859, the political process had failed. As the two major parties became more sectional in ideology, the center fell apart. The South generally interpreted the election of Abraham Lincoln as president in 1860 as proof of Northern determination to destroy slavery, although Lincoln had said time and again that he had no intention of tampering with slavery where it existed, but only to stop its spread into the territories. Just as slavery had not been settled politically, so too it remained unresolved constitutionally. The Supreme Court's decisions on slavery in the territories and on the Fugitive Slave Act failed to win widespread support except in the South, and its invalidation of the Missouri Compromise destroyed the one constitutional settlement that both sides, however reluctantly, had seemed willing to live with. The scheme of constitutional government that the Framers had drafted to ensure perpetual Union now faced its severest crisis.

A final exclamation point to the whole decade came on October 16, 1859, when John Brown and eighteen other men seized the federal arsenal at Harpers Ferry, Virginia. Brown planned to seize weapons at the arsenal, rally slaves to the cause of freedom, and then melt into the rugged mountains to begin a guerrilla war against slavery. His mad plan failed when he was trapped in the arsenal, and two days later captured by U.S. Marines led by Colonel Robert E. Lee of the U.S. Army. Implementing the "Domestic Insurrections Clause" of the Constitution, President Buchanan had acted swiftly in sending Lee and the marines to crush this rebellion against both slavery and the national government.

Although the attack was on a federal facility, the Buchanan administration allowed Virginia to prosecute Brown and his few surviving raiders. The charge, oddly enough, was treason against Virginia, which Brown vehemently denied he had committed, since he had never owed any allegiance to that state. The court put such legal technicalities aside, and put Brown on trial on November 2. Although Brown was still recovering from wounds he incurred when captured, and his lawyer was unable to reach the courtroom because of a storm, Virginia would not delay the proceedings even for a day. The trial was speedy, and the result a foregone conclusion. Nevertheless, throughout the North, people were shocked at the rush to judgment of an old, wounded man, who many people thought was insane. On December 2, 1859, a month after the trial began, Brown was hanged.

Brown's raid, and its aftermath, underscored the political and constitutional crisis of the nation. Southerners saw Brown as the embodiment of abolitionism, the Republican party, and the North itself, even though the overwhelming majority of Northerners, including virtually all prominent Republicans and most abolitionists, condemned Brown's actions and methods. Northerners, on the other hand, saw in Virginia's actions a vengeful society, rushing to execute a wounded man without offering a fair trial, on a charge—treason against Virginia—of which he was clearly innocent.

Brown himself went calmly to the gallows. He understood the value of his martyrdom. The North was electrified after reading Brown's statement to the court just before his sentencing: "Now, if it is deemed necessary that I should forfeit my life for the furtherance of the ends of justice, and mingle my blood further with the blood of my children and with the blood of millions in this slave country whose rights are disregarded by wicked, cruel, and unjust enactments,—I submit; so let it be done!" As Brown told his brother, "I am worth inconceivably more to hang than for any other purpose."

In this he was right, as millions of Northerners saw Brown as a martyr, a Christlike figure willing nobly to die to save people from slavery. John Andrew, the Republican governor of Massachusetts, summed up the feelings of many Northerners when he refused to endorse Brown's tactics or the wisdom of his raid, but declared that "John Brown himself is right." Southerners, meanwhile, saw in Brown the ultimate terror: whites ready to join slaves in a fight to the death over human bondage. With the memory of Brown fresh in their memories—as either a horrible sinner or a wonderful, martyred saint—Southerners and Northerners faced the presidential election year of 1860.

# For Further Reading

For a general introduction to the prewar years, see David M. Potter, *The Impending Crisis, 1848–1861* (1979); William R. Brock, *Parties and Political Conscience: American Dilemmas, 1840–1850* (1979); William W. Freehling, *The Road to Disunion: Secessionists at Bay, 1776–1854* (1990), and the older but still useful Roy F. Nichols, *The Disruption of American Democracy* (1948). For the "Gag Rule," see Samuel Flagg Bemis, *John Quincy Adams and the Union* (1956); Russell B. Nye, *Fettered Freedoms: Civil Liberties and the Slavery Controversy* (1963); and the classic Gilbert Hobbs Barnes, *The Antislavery Impulse: 1830–1844* (1933).

To understand American expansion, one can start with Randolph Campbell, *An Empire for Slavery* (1989). Still useful are older works, including Frederick Merk, *Manifest Destiny and Mission in American History* (1963); and Norman A. Graebner, *Empire on the Pacific: A Study in American Continental Expansion* (1955). Merk's *Slavery and the Annexation of Texas* (1972) is a useful supplement to Campbell's book on slavery in Texas. Resistance to adding Texas territory is explained in Champlain Morrison, *Democratic Politics and Sectionalism: The Wilmot Proviso Controversy* (1967).

A good introduction to the free labor doctrine and how it formed the ideological basis for the new party system is Eric Foner, *Free Soil, Free Labor, Free Men: The Ideology of the Republican Party Before the Civil War* (1970). The legal implications of free labor are analyzed in Charles McCurdy, "The Roots of Liberty of Contract Reconsidered: Major Premises in the Law of Employment, 1867–1937," *1984 Yearbook of the Supreme Court Historical Society* 20 (1984).

Holman Hamilton, *Prologue to Conflict: The Crisis and Compromise of 1850* (1964), explores the political alignments leading to the Compromise. Forces that led to its failure are explored William W. Freehling, *The Road to Disunion: Secessionists at Bay, 1776–1854* (1990), which offers a detailed background of the history leading up to the 1850s. See also, Michael F. Holt, *The Political Crisis of the 1850s* (1978), which traces the demise of the Whigs; and Frederick J. Blue, *Free Soilers: Third Party Politics, 1848–1854* (1973). Robert W. Johansen, *Stephen A. Douglas* (1973), offers a good analysis of popular sovereignty. The disaster in Kansas is detailed in James C. Malin, *The Nebraska Question, 1852–1854* (1953); and James A. Rawley, *Race and Politics: "Bleeding Kansas" and the Coming of the Civil War* (1969). For the violent incident in the Senate, see William E. Gienapp, "The Crime Against Sumner: The Caning of Charles Sumner and the Rise of the Republican Party," 25 *Civil War History* 218 (1979). John Brown is dealt with in a number of biographies, most importantly, Stephen Oates, *To Purge This Land with Blood: A Biography of John Brown* (1970). The aftermath of his raid and its political impact throughout the nation, is dealt with in Paul Finkelman, ed., *His Soul Goes Marching On: Responses to John Brown and the Harpers Ferry Raid* (1995).

Stanley W. Campbell, *The Slave Catchers: Enforcement of the Fugitive Slave Law, 1850–1860* (1970), provides some facts, but has little analysis and a narrow view of the issues. Thomas D. Morris, *Free Men All: The Personal Liberty Laws of the North, 1780–1861* (1974), suggests that Northerners started out in good faith to keep their bargain, but conscience got the better of them. The very complex constitutional and legal issues of slave transit are analyzed in Paul Finkelman, *An Imperfect Union: Slavery, Federalism, and Comity* (1981). On the problem of runaway slaves, see the prize winning, John Hope Franklin and Loren Schweninger, *Runaway Slaves: Rebels on the Plantation* (1999). The controversy surrounding Sherman Booth is covered in Jenni Parrish, "The *Booth* Cases: Final Step to the Civil War," 29 *Willamette Law Review* 237 (1993).

Dred Scott's case has drawn extensive scholarly attention. Don E. Fehrenbacher, *The Dred Scott Case: Its Significance in American Law and Politics* (1978), puts the case in its broader social, political, and economic context, seeing the Taney decision as the result of eight decades of turmoil. Walter Ehrlich, *They Have No Rights: Dred Scott's Struggle for Freedom* (1979), provides a careful and detailed narrative of the case, with a useful reminder that whatever other people made of it, Scott only wanted to be free. Paul Finkelman, *Dred Scott v. Sandford: A Brief History with Documents* (1997), provides a short analysis and explanation of this case. Both Finkelman and William M. Wiecek, "Slavery and Abolition Before the United States Supreme Court, 1820–1860," 65 *Journal of American History* 34 (1978), claim that the *Scott* decision was not an anomaly, but emerged from doctrines the Court had been expounding for twenty years.

Harry V. Jaffa, *Crisis of the House Divided: An Interpretation of the Lincoln–Douglas Debates* (1959), is a good analysis of the political and constitutional issues of these debates. See also Don E. Fehrenbacher, *Prelude to Greatness: Lincoln in the 1850s* (1962), for the Republicans and territorial issues. For a single volume study of Lincoln, see Stephen Oates, *With Malice Toward None* (1977).

# 19

# The Union Sundered

*The Election of 1860 • Secession Winter • "And the War Came" • The Provisional Confederate Constitution • The Permanent Confederate Constitution • Defects in the Confederate Scheme • The Political Party as a War Tool • Lincoln Takes Control • Ex Parte Merryman • Judicial Reorganization in Wartime • The Adequacy of the Constitution • War Powers and the Rebellion • Defining Rebel Status • The Growth of National Power • The Emancipation Proclamation • The Thirteenth Amendment • For Further Reading*

SOUTHERN SECESSION AND the Civil War provided an opportunity for the United States to resolve the seemingly intractable constitutional issues that had plagued the nation since the Founding. In the end, secession and the war set the stage for the abolition of slavery—something that would never have been politically or constitutionally possible if the slave states had remained in the Union. Battlefield victories made these fundamental changes possible, while President Lincoln's practical political sense, steely resolve, and rhetorical skill shaped their implementation. At the heart of the fundamental changes brought about by the war, stood the question that Lincoln posed so eloquently at Gettysburg: whether the government "conceived in Liberty, and dedicated to the proposition that all men are created equal" could endure.

In important ways Lincoln's persistent return to the Declaration of Independence reshaped American culture and politics by making equality the central meaning of American democracy and by reinterpreting the Declaration as the most important "text" of American society. In doing this, Lincoln relied on an idealized and historically inaccurate understanding of the Founders, and their views on race, equality, and slavery. Nevertheless, rhetorically, Lincoln provided a usable past, however misleading, to help justify the carnage of the Civil War and help rally Northerners to the cause of both perpetuating the Union and ending slavery.

The Civil War also raised issues of how a constitution, designed for a limited government, could function during what amounted to total war, complicated by the fact that this was also a civil war. The Founders had never anticipated such a situation, and the Constitution did not address it.

Many people thought the Constitution could not survive an internecine struggle and that for the United States to prevail militarily, it would have to destroy the limited governmental framework that had served the nation for seven decades. But Lincoln proved otherwise, and while he sometimes stretched the Constitution to meet the demands of war, in the end he left as his legacy to the country the Constitution preserved, although fundamentally altered, and the Union intact and stronger than ever. Slavery—the root cause of the War—lay defeated and destroyed.

## The Election of 1860

Four candidates vied for the presidency in 1860. This unusual number of parties reflected the disintegration of the old political system. The Republicans bypassed the leading contenders, Senators William Seward of New York and Salmon P. Chase of Ohio, and named Abraham Lincoln of Illinois, which strengthened their appeal in the lower Midwest and among moderates throughout the North. Lincoln had come to national prominence in his debates with Stephen Douglas two years earlier, and was something of a hero among Republicans for his articulate critique of the *Dred Scott* decision and his unwavering stand against allowing slavery in the territories. But as he explained in 1860, in his Cooper Union address in New York City, while the evil of slavery should not be extended, it had to be tolerated and protected where it already existed, because "that toleration and protection [is] a necessity." In an effort to reassure the South, the party's platform promised the "maintenance inviolate of the right of each state to make and control its own domestic institutions."

The Democrats met in April 1860 in Charleston, South Carolina, a hotbed of Southern extremism. When the delegates refused to adopt planks promising congressional protection of slavery in the territories, most Southerners walked out. The convention reconvened in June in Baltimore, without much of the Southern bloc, and nominated Stephen A. Douglas on the 1856 platform of popular sovereignty. The Charleston secessionists later gathered, first in Richmond and then in Baltimore, and named Buchanan's vice president, John C. Breckinridge of Kentucky, on a strong proslavery platform. The Constitutional Union party, made up of diehard Whigs and border state delegates who feared that their states would bear the burden of any intersectional strife, nominated John Bell of Tennessee and Edward Everett of Massachusetts, on a platform that simply endorsed "the Constitution of the Country, the Union of the States, and the Enforcement of the Laws."

Only the Douglas Democrats and the Constitutional Unionists—the two weakest parties—ran a national campaign. Lincoln received only 40 percent of the popular vote, but a clear majority in the electoral college; he carried all eighteen free states, and would have been elected even if the votes of the other candidates had been combined. Although many Southerners denied Lincoln's legitimacy because of his supposed antislavery views, no one claimed that he had not been legally elected. With that issue firmly settled, the South now had to decide on its future course of action: would it stay in a Union supposedly controlled by an antislavery government, or would it secede?

When he learned that Lincoln had won, Stephen A. Douglas performed the noblest act of his career, personally traveling to several Southern states appealing for the Union.

## Secession Winter

Urged on by the fire-eaters, South Carolina led the way to secession. A specially elected convention met in Charleston on December 20, 1860, and unanimously voted an Ordinance of Secession, repealed the state's earlier ratification of the Constitution, and dissolved its ties to the other states. Six other states—Georgia, Florida, Alabama, Mississippi, Louisiana, and Texas—followed suit in the next few weeks. Slavery lay behind their actions, and the secessionists did not try to hide it. The South Carolina ordinance claimed that the Northern states had reneged on their constitutional obligations by fostering abolitionist agitation, aiding runaway slaves, and keeping slaveholders out of the territories.

The idea of secession had been discussed for so long in the South that it had acquired the patina of legitimacy. Following Calhoun's arguments, Southern theorists claimed that by its very nature sovereignty could never be relinquished; the states, therefore, could never give up their sovereign powers. In this view, the federal government constituted little more than an arrangement of convenience that, when it ceased to be convenient, could be discarded. Senator Jefferson Davis of Mississippi claimed that the Framers had denied the national government powers to coerce the states to remain in the Union; if the government lacked that power, as Davis argued, then a state could withdraw from the arrangement at will.

The secessionists also attempted to bolster their political theory with historical arguments. The Tenth Amendment referred to retained state powers; the revered Madison and Jefferson, in the Virginia and Kentucky resolves, had charted the path of residual state authority; and the New England states at the Hartford Convention had proposed secession in order to preserve their state interests against alleged depredations by the national government. Spencer Roane, John Taylor of Caroline, John Randolph of Roanoke, Thomas Dew, Beverley Tucker, Thomas Cooper, and others had over the years elevated states' rights doctrines into a widely shared consensus in the South, which then received its most elaborate exposition in the hands of John C. Calhoun. From the time of the nullification controversy until his death, Calhoun articulated the idea of state sovereignty as the keystone of the federal system. The peoples of the several states, not "We the People of the United States," had formed the Union, and so they had the right to nullify federal statutes that violated their rights or impinged on their interests; if this proved ineffective, they retained the ultimate right to secede from the Union.

In the months between the South Carolina convention in December 1860 and Lincoln's inauguration in March 1861, the fate of the Union remained unclear. Virginia, whose sons had developed so much of the states' rights doctrine, adopted a cautious attitude, as did several other slave states. Paralysis gripped the North, especially in Washington, where Buchanan, while calling for the preservation of the Union, claimed he lacked power to forestall secession. His attorney general, the doughface Jeremiah S. Black of Pennsylvania, had given the president his official opinion in late November 1860, setting out the constraints on presidential authority. If states seceded, only Congress could act, and if Congress took military steps to coerce a state, that would absolve the state's constitutional obligations to the Union.

In December 1860, in his last address to Congress, Buchanan adopted much, but not all, of Black's argument. He blamed the Northern states, with their personal liberty laws and abolitionist agitation, for the crisis, and he proposed a constitutional amendment to protect slavery in the territories and secure the recapture of runaways. On the other hand, the Constitution did not permit secession, and Article II, Section 3 required the president to "take Care that the Laws be faithfully executed." As for preventing secession, however, Buchanan took Black's thesis completely: the Constitution did not provide coercive authority to prevent the states from leaving. William Seward sarcastically summed up Buchanan's position: "It is the duty of the President to execute the laws—unless somebody opposes him—and that no state has the right to go out of the Union—unless it wants to."

Although the fire-eaters extended their influence in the South, several groups vainly sought new constitutional provisions to keep the Union intact. In the Senate, a Committee of Thirteen proposed four different alternatives. Two of them, written by Jefferson Davis of Mississippi and Robert Toombs of Georgia, embodied Southern demands for strict protection of slavery. Stephen Douglas tried to meet some of the Southern demands, but he went too far to satisfy the North and not far enough to placate the South. Senator John J. Crittenden of Kentucky came up with a set of proposals that attracted some attention. In addition to protecting slavery where it existed and softening personal liberty laws elsewhere, he proposed applying the Missouri Compromise line not only to present territories but to future accessions as well.

In the House of Representatives, a Committee of Thirty-three called for the immediate admission of New Mexico, presumably as a slave state, and an unamendable constitutional prohibition against interference with slavery in the states. The Republicans went along with this plan, believing it meant nothing, since they doubted slavery could establish itself in the desert regions. Both houses of Congress approved the proslavery amendment, which, ironically, would have been the Thirteenth Amendment, and three states actually ratified it before events made it meaningless.

Meanwhile, Virginia called for a Peace Conference, which met at Willard's Hotel in Washington in February; ex-President Tyler presided, and twenty-one states sent delegates. Technically, the Peace Conference did not meet the Article V requirements for a constitutional convention, because Congress had not called for it on petition by two-thirds of the state legislatures. The conference adopted many of Crittenden's proposals, but despite extensive debate, Congress never adopted them. Congress went home at the end of February with little to show for its efforts other than, perhaps, that war had been delayed. Even as Congress debated, the seven secessionist states were meeting in Montgomery, Alabama, and on February 7, the delegates adopted a provisional constitution for the Confederate States of America. They also elected Jefferson Davis as president and Alexander Stephens of Georgia as vice president, and on February 18, the two men took the oath of office. All eyes now turned to Washington, where Abraham Lincoln had come to be sworn in as the sixteenth president of the United States.

## THE SUPREME COURT DURING THE SECESSION WINTER

For most of the secession winter, Chief Justice Taney, who by this time had become an ardent Southern nationalist, could only watch the momentous political events swirl around him. However, *Kentucky v. Dennison*, decided in February 1861, allowed him to weigh in on these issues. The case had begun some years earlier when Willis Lago, a free black from Ohio, helped a slave woman, perhaps his future wife, escape from Kentucky to Ohio. The Kentucky governor asked that Lago be returned for stealing. But, Governor Salmon P. Chase refused, arguing that Ohio did not recognize the crime of "stealing" a person, because Ohio did not recognize property in human beings. When Chase's successor, William Dennison, also refused to extradite Lago, Kentucky sued. In normal times, the Taney Court might have sided with the slave state. But February 1861 was not a normal time. To side with Kentucky, the Court would have to set the precedent that the Court, or the national government, could force a state governor to act. Taney avoided handing the incoming president—Abraham Lincoln—such a powerful weapon. Thus, in an opinion reminiscent of John Marshall's in *Marbury v. Madison* (1803), Taney chastised Ohio for not extraditing Lago, but then ruled that the national government could not force a state governor to act.

## *"And the War Came"*

During the four months between his election and inauguration, Lincoln had steadfastly refused to comment publicly on the rapid tide of events. He had, however, reiterated his opposition to the extension of bondage in the territories, and repeated that he had no desire, intention, or constitutional power to interfere with slavery in the states where it existed. He had tacitly approved the Committee of Thirty-three's constitutional amendment, but had ignored other efforts at compromise. No one knew what he would do; Lincoln kept his options open, while assuring the South that he would not interfere with its domestic policies. In his inaugural address, he emphasized this point again: "I have no purpose, directly or indirectly, to interfere with the institution of slavery in the States where it exists. I believe I have no lawful right to do so, and I have no inclination to do so."

But by March 1861, secession, not slavery, had become the focus of public concern, and Lincoln unequivocally denied the right of any state to leave the Union. Unlike Buchanan, who claimed he had no authority to act, Lincoln assumed he had the necessary power and promised to hold areas belonging to the government, deliver the mails, and collect taxes. Above all, he appealed for harmony and promised the South that "there will be no invasion, no using of force against or among the people anywhere." After the long secession winter, when many Northerners seemed willing to buy peace at any price, Lincoln still put forward no specific plans; but he strongly implied that he would take any steps necessary to preserve the Union.

Once in office, Lincoln at first appeared to be playing Buchanan's game. Although he had promised to act, he did nothing—for he had determined that if war came, the South would fire the first shot. On March 5, 1861, the new president received word that Fort Sumter in Charleston harbor had been surrounded by a Confederate "ring of fire." Major Robert Anderson reported that he had between four and six weeks of supplies and would not be able to hold the fort without resupply. Events now moved swiftly to their climax. Lincoln informed the governor of South Carolina on April 6 that only provisions would be sent to Sumter. Three days later, Jefferson Davis and the Confederate cabinet decided not to let Lincoln maintain the status quo. On April 11, General Pierre G. T. Beauregard demanded the surrender of the fort; when Anderson refused, he opened fire the following morning. Anderson's troops held out for thirty hours, until their ammunition was spent; then they lowered the flag. As Lincoln noted in his second inaugural: "Both parties deprecated war, but one of them would *make* war rather than let the nation survive, and the other would *accept* war rather than let it perish. And the war came."

## The Provisional Confederate Constitution

The South had always avowed its allegiance to the Constitution, claiming that the North had distorted the original intent of the Framers. The war would ultimately invalidate Southern constitutional theories, but in the beginning, the Confederacy set out to show what it considered proper construction. The Southerners adopted two constitutions, a provisional one at their organizational meeting in early February 1861, and a permanent document the following month.

The secessionists established a provisional government cautiously, for prior to Lincoln's inauguration, they did not know what the new Republican administration would do. Some delegates at the Montgomery Convention opposed creating a new government, unsure what effect it would have on those slave states that had not seceded; they also feared imposing a structure on states that had not taken part in its formulation. So long as adequate state governments existed, they reasoned, due concern for state autonomy should preclude further action. Realism, however, soon overcame this idealistic view. Most Southerners had no doubt that Lincoln would do something, even if they did not know what course he would follow, and the South had to be prepared to respond swiftly. By opting for a provisional government, some structure would be in place; then, when the other slave states joined in, a permanent government could be created.

The Montgomery Convention served as a constitutional convention, a temporary legislature, and even functioned as an electoral college. For chief draftsman, the delegates chose Christopher Gustavus Memminger of South Carolina, formerly an opponent of secession who had not adopted the radical view until late 1859, and who later served the Confederacy as secretary of the treasury. Although Memminger introduced a number of ideas to alter the older organization of government under the Constitution, the drafting Committee of Twelve insisted on sticking close to the original. They did not want a new scheme, but merely the old one altered to protect slavery and states' rights; only this type of constitution, they believed, would attract the still uncommitted slave states.

The Committee of Twelve worked feverishly; in four days it drafted a provisional constitution and saw it debated and adopted by the convention. Of course, the drafters' burden was made lighter by the fact that they merely had to alter the U.S. Constitution rather than start from scratch. Some of the differences between the provisional constitution and the U.S. Constitution represented sacrifices to exigencies, but others addressed some of the concerns expressed by the South in the previous three decades:

- The preamble specifically located the authority of the Confederacy in the sovereignty of the states, not in the general sovereignty of the people. As Jabez Curry of Alabama explained, the preamble intended "to assert the derivative character of the Federal Government and to exclude the conclusion which Webster and others had sought to draw from the phrase, 'We the people of the United States.'"

- A unicameral Congress exercised the legislative powers of the provisional government. Although wide sentiment existed for two chambers, exigency ruled for the moment. The committee believed that a single house could act more quickly; moreover, until a president could take office, the Congress would have to exercise executive responsibility as well.

- The president and vice president were to be chosen by Congress, with each state casting one vote. The president had all the powers granted in the original Constitution, plus a line item veto, so he could strike out particulars to which he objected without killing the entire bill.

- Congress had the power to determine if a president could no longer perform the duties of office, and could remove him from office by a two-thirds vote, in which case the vice president succeeded.

- Each state would constitute a single judicial district (there would be no circuit courts), and the Supreme Court would consist of the district judges.

- Congress, not the states, could amend the provisional constitution by a two-thirds vote.

- The document lacked the prohibition in the original forbidding congressmen from holding any other office in the government. Some of the South's outstanding leaders sat in the Congress, and the framers did not want the president, the legislative arm, or the military to be deprived of their services.

From the beginning, the Committee of Twelve had seen its work as an interim measure; one member candidly admitted that their document was but the Constitution "with such changes and modifications as are necessary to meet the exigencies of the times." The committee's aim was to give the constituent assembly some cloak of legitimacy rather than to establish a permanent form of government. In fact, the provisional constitution included its own death sentence: it would continue in force for one year from the inauguration of the president, or until a permanent constitution could be drafted, whichever occurred first. Curiously, the provisional constitution completely omitted any reference to slavery, the issue that had led the seven states to secede in the first place. Evidently, the Committee of Twelve felt no need for an immediate statement on the subject and preferred that the guarantees Southern states had been demanding should be left until a permanent document could be drafted.

## The Permanent Confederate Constitution

On February 9, 1861, two days after the adoption of the provisional constitution, Robert Barnwell Rhett of South Carolina moved that the Montgomery Convention, now acting as the Congress of the Confederacy, appoint a committee to draft a permanent document. That same day, a second Committee of Twelve began its labors. For this document, the key draftsman was Thomas R. R. Cobb, a cofounder of the Lumpkin Law School, which was the precursor of the University of Georgia School of Law, and the author of *An Inquiry into the Law of Negro Slavery* (1858), the only treatise on slave law written by a Southerner. Like his predecessor, Cobb used the federal Constitution as a guide, but he also looked to the provisional Confederate constitution as an indicator of some of the changes his colleagues believed were important. Once again, the framers worked quickly, completing their draft in nineteen days. In the meantime, Jefferson Davis took the oath of office as president of the provisional government, named a cabinet, dispatched emissaries to the government in Washington, and named ambassadors to France and Great Britain to seek recognition of the Confederacy. The Confederate Congress also voted to keep in force all the laws of the old Union that were not inconsistent with the provisional constitution. Thus a working government, acting under a constitutionally claimed legitimacy, had been erected by the time Lincoln entered the White House; it was far more than their revolutionary forebears had enjoyed when they decided to cast loose from Great Britain.

The permanent constitution of the Confederate States of America, adopted on March 11, 1861, not only paralleled the Constitution of the United States in form and content, but in many places copied it word for word. The South wanted to keep the familiar scheme under which it had lived for more than seventy years, but with mostly propagandistic modifications to give even greater protection to slavery. The constitution had some phrases that dovetailed with traditional states' rights theory. For example, the preamble began "We, the people of the Confederate States, each State acting in its sovereign and independent character," indicating the emphasis on state rather than on national sovereignty. This phrase is also the only one that might be considered as legitimizing secession, for like the original, the Confederate constitution contained no clause enabling a state to withdraw from the "permanent federal government." However, overall, the document created a central government that was potentially as strong, or stronger, than the one created in 1787.

Article I established the legislative power, this time in a bicameral Congress. Nearly all the powers given to the U.S. Congress, often in the same words, devolved upon its Confederate counterpart. Although Southerners and states' rights advocates had often objected to the "necessary and proper" clause in the U.S. Constitution, the Confederate framers retained it, fully understanding that their Congress would need flexible powers as the new government grew. Similarly, the Confederate framers retained, word for word, the supremacy clause of the U.S. Constitution. The retention of these clauses suggests that Southern nationalism, and not a desire for greater state autonomy, was the driving force behind secession.

Despite the continuities, the Confederate framers did make some significant changes in the constitutional order. The most important were:

- The Southern antipathy toward internal improvements had not faded over the years, and Section 8, which listed the legislative powers, specifically prohibited the appropriation of money for internal improvements. The drafters also omitted a general welfare clause, so that the Congress could not use it as a back door into this field.

- The House had the power of impeachment, but state legislatures could also impeach federal officials or judges acting solely within their boundaries.

- The Constitution specifically banned the African slave trade; Congress also had the power to prohibit the importation of slaves from any state or territory not part of the Confederacy.

- The clause in the provisional constitution allowing members of Congress to serve in other offices was abandoned; instead, Congress could give the principal officers of each department a seat on the floor of either house, as well as the right to participate in discussions relating to their business.

- The line item veto established by the provisional constitution carried over into the permanent document.

- An appropriations bill could include only one item.

Executive power was defined in the second article, which differed only in a few particulars from the U.S. Constitution:

- The president would serve a six-year term, and could not succeed himself.

- The president had explicit, rather than implicit, powers to remove the principal officers, such as department heads or members of the foreign service, at his pleasure. He could also remove all other appointees, but had to inform the Senate of his reasons.

Article III copied the judicial section of the Constitution almost verbatim. One sop to the Southern states' rights tradition was the minor change, vesting the judicial power "in one Superior Court," rather than in a "Supreme Court." The Confederate document also allowed for the creation of "such inferior courts as the Congress may from time to time ordain and establish." The article also incorporated the essence of the Eleventh Amendment, explicitly prohibiting a citizen of one state suing another state in federal court.

The most significant aspect of the judiciary provision was what the constitution omitted. It did not contain any clause abolishing, modifying, or even limiting judicial review. Despite the attacks on judicial review by such Southern leaders as Spencer Roane and Thomas Jefferson, the Southern framers, led by Thomas R. R. Cobb, implicitly accepted the idea of judicial review. In the hands of a proslavery Southern nationalist like Chief Justice Taney, the leaders of the secessionist movement had come to see that judicial review was valuable and useful.

The major changes to Article IV, concerning relations among the states, dealt primarily with slavery:

- A citizen of any state had the right of transit and sojourn, with his slaves, into any other state of the Confederacy.

- The fugitive clause referred explicitly to slavery.

- In any new territory acquired by the Confederacy, slavery would be recognized and protected by the Congress and the territorial governments, and citizens would have an unfettered right to take their slaves with them into the territory.

Article I of the constitution retained the three-fifths ratio for representation and taxation.

Amendment, the subject of Article V, differed from the older process. Any three states could petition Congress for a constitutional convention, and proposals from such conventions needed approval by two-thirds of the states, either by the legislatures or by special conventions. Congress did not have the power to propose amendments to the states. Ratification of the permanent constitution required the assent of five states, and it took place on March 26, 1861, after Mississippi joined Alabama, Georgia, Louisiana, and Texas in approving it.

Article VI included both the Ninth and Tenth amendments to the Constitution, which retained rights not otherwise enumerated or delegated to the people and to the states. (The other parts of the Bill of Rights appeared as restrictions on the Congress in Article I.) The last article also included, word for word, the Supremacy Clause. The secessionist leaders were, in the end, Southern nationalists trying to create their own nation under difficult circumstances. Thus, they fully recognized and endorsed the need for some hierarchy of authority.

## Defects in the Confederate Scheme

Placing the Confederacy's permanent constitution alongside the original Constitution, one is immediately struck not by the differences but by the similarities, indeed by the many identical clauses they shared. Only in areas relating to slavery were there significant departures. On paper at least, Jefferson Davis and Abraham Lincoln had virtually the same constitutional tools to work with. Indeed, with his six-year term, Davis had the advantage of not having to run for office during the war. But where Lincoln used the Constitution as an effective instrument in prosecuting the war, Davis could not. The reasons are not to be found just in the differences, but in the spirit that was manifested in those changes. In the early years of the Republic, a battle had raged over the division of powers between the state and national governments. Over the years, what might be called the Hamilton/Marshall view of a strong central government had gradually won acceptance in the North, which was now able to accept Lincoln's expansion of the federal government's powers as a necessary part of waging war. The South, ever the bastion of states' rights, had always resisted this trend toward nationalization, except when it benefited slavery. The Confederate constitution did not elevate state sovereignty over the national government, and in some ways the Confederate government was constitutionally stronger than its counterpart in Washington. But, ideologically, many Confederate leaders were fierce defenders of states' rights and equally fierce opponents of a central government, even one of their own creation. For example, during the war, governors in Georgia and North Carolina refused to send food to the Confederate Army, but would only supply it to troops from their own states. Despite the words of the Confederate constitution and the pressing needs of the war effort, war or no war, the Confederacy was ideologically a compact of states and never achieved that critical mass of nationalistic spirit necessary to emerge as a new union.

In the midst of the war, for example, the Confederate attorney general, Thomas Hill Watts of Alabama, declared in an official opinion that "the Confederate Government is one of limited and specific powers" in which "a strict construction of the Constitution is essential to preserve the rights of the States, the sovereign parties to the Constitutional compact." A few months later, he described the constitution as nothing more than "a power of attorney creating a Government and giving a few and well-defined powers to its Departments."

The jealousy of states over their prerogatives can be seen in the fact that although the constitution prescribed a Supreme Court, the Confederacy never established a high tribunal. The way John Marshall had used the Court's appellate jurisdiction to enhance national power remained a bitter memory in Southern minds and fueled resistance to giving any court power over the state high courts. A uniform law system, however, is an essential ingredient of a nation state, so the Confederacy suffered for the lack of a single, final expositor of constitutional law. Although it is true that the various state courts for the most part sustained the acts of the government, the Confederacy had no recourse when, for example, North Carolina's chief judge ruled the national draft law invalid in 1864. The secretary of war, James Seddon, threatened to arrest any state judge who interfered with conscription, hardly an edifying solution, but as Seddon wrote to North Carolina's governor, "the want of a Supreme Court in the Confederate States leaves [us] impotent against the . . . action of state judges by the regular and accustomed course of review by an appellate tribunal."

## The Political Party as a War Tool

The ideological commitment to states' rights also adversely affected the Confederacy by thwarting the growth of a viable political party system. Despite the fears of Washington's generation that the rise of factions would undermine the new government, the party process had become an invaluable support of the Union. By the 1830s, the party system had developed basically into the form we know today, with interconnected local and national organizations, nominating conventions, and platforms stating the party's general philosophy. Politics allowed strong leaders like Jefferson, Jackson, and Polk to steer the country along the philosophical lines they espoused and became the means by which Americans debated and resolved national issues. The inability of the political system to mediate the problem of slavery had eventually caused the war.

A successful party system helped create a stronger national government, which the two general factions struggled to control. Although the federal government had nothing like the budget or programs it has today, it did have considerable benefits to confer on states and localities through the disposition of western lands, support for internal improvements, and tariff protection of industry. State governments as well as local party organizations vied to affect national policies. What had once appeared as a dangerous tension in fact worked to strengthen the hold of the Union on local loyalties.

During the war, the Lincoln administration always had a strong opposition in the northern Democratic party, and Lincoln—one of the greatest politicians ever to inhabit the White House—used the threat of a Democratic victory at the polls to organize Republican sentiment as a tool of war. The state and local party organizations loyally supported administration policy not only because they perceived it as necessary for the war, but also for the far more mundane but nonetheless important reason of maintaining political control of the government.

In the South, however, nominal unity over issues such as secession, states' rights, and slavery masked the lack of an informal infrastructure that could be harnessed to support the rebellion. Davis could not rally political support with the threat of an opposition victory, because no opposition was allowed to exist. Opponents of the war were stifled, threatened, jailed, and sometimes lynched. Thus, the Southern leadership was not forced to grow and develop in response to a viable opposition party. Nor could Jefferson Davis exert pressure on the states by withholding patronage or governmental support, because the Confederate government had few benefits to dispense. The official line, supported by lethal violence when necessary, silenced doubters and never allowed the development of a multiparty system that, by working out compromise solutions, could have secured a broad base of committed support. Governmental activity in the South, especially in response to war problems, took place primarily in the states. Davis had to do many of the things Lincoln did—declare martial law, suspend habeas corpus, and implement conscription laws—all of which grated on the Southern devotion to state autonomy. But the South, unlike the North, never developed formal and informal relations to make these measures palatable. Davis never called a conference of governors, had virtually no patronage to dispense, and could exercise no political pressure. There was no Provost Marshal's office to soften the impact of abrasive policies, and the constitutional requirement that all appropriations bills have only one item made it difficult for the various factions to trade votes and eventually unite on broader issues of policy.

All this resulted from a constitution that looked like the Union document, but whose differences deprived the South of political tools essential to effective governance, and from a nation led by politicians who had been schooled in states' rights doctrine and could not easily develop a new rhetoric or ideology to fit their new circumstances. Many Southern politicians continued to act as though their national Congress was dominated by Northerners, who might at any moment strike at slavery. Furthermore, their ideological commitment to the Jeffersonian insistence on literal construction and the preoccupation with, indeed fixation on slavery and states' rights narrowed the limits of acceptable political discourse. White Southerners thought that writing their earlier demands into the constitution would solve their problems; instead, it weakened their cause, and would have dire effects after the war, especially in the inability to develop acceptable race relations.

## Lincoln Takes Control

Many of the problems confronting Lincoln resembled those with which Davis had to deal—mobilizing public and military support, organizing resources, raising money, and maintaining internal security—but Lincoln faced the additional and far more difficult problem of putting down a rebellion. The Confederacy only had to survive to achieve success; the Union had to crush the rebellion utterly. The Constitution did not address the problem of an insurrection by states seeking to secede, but from various clauses, Lincoln evoked the explicit and implicit powers necessary to preserve the United States.

Lincoln's apparent sluggishness between his inauguration and the firing on Fort Sumter drew vigorous criticism from contemporaries, who expected him to act immediately. We can now see that Lincoln was buying time through this alleged inaction—time to assess his options, time for pro-Union sentiment to crystallize, and time to bolster Unionist factions in the border states. Moreover, by patiently waiting until Southern hotheads forced the issue and fired the first shot, he put the onus of starting the war on the Confederacy and thus energized Union loyalty in the North. Once war broke out, Lincoln sprang into action, and his policies led to a more expansive interpretation of governmental powers.

Congress had adjourned before the war began, and although Lincoln could have called it into special session immediately, he chose not to do so. He had not yet attained uncontested leadership of the Republican party, and he feared that a recalcitrant Congress, with its vocal Democratic minority, would hinder rather than advance a coherent war policy. He recalled that during the secessionist winter of 1860–61, many in the North had seemed willing to buy peace at any price, and he worried that such sentiment might still be strong enough to let the South go rather than embark on a civil war. Perhaps most important, Lincoln needed the flexibility of action that would be his so long as he alone directed affairs. Congress, in which the Constitution lodged the war power, would properly demand a voice in running the war, but if he could delay its meeting until some semblance of a policy took shape, then the president, and not Congress, would control affairs. Lincoln won support from the congressional Republican leaders, who agreed on the need for a single policymaker at this stage of events; they promised that Congress, when it met, would confirm the actions he had taken until that time. This arrangement reflected the political realities of the crisis, and while not something set out by the Constitution, it did not violate any formal constitutional requirements or structures.

Between the attack on Fort Sumter and July 4, 1861, when Congress convened in special session, Lincoln proclaimed a blockade of ports in the secessionist states, provided funds to pro-Union forces in the border states, called for volunteers, and brought 75,000 state militia troops into federal service for ninety days—all to put down an insurrection he described as "too powerful to be suppressed by the ordinary course of judicial proceedings." The attack on Fort Sumter unified the North, but Lincoln's response, to call for troops, also sent Virginia, North Carolina, Tennessee, and Arkansas into the ranks of the Confederacy. Unionists from parts of Tennessee and Virginia refused to abide by this decision, however; Andrew Johnson of Tennessee remained in the Senate, the only senator from a seceding state to do so, while pro-Union congressmen from eastern Tennessee and western Virginia kept their seats in the House.

Lincoln could do little about the four newly seceding states, but he determined to back strong Unionist factions and prevent secession in the border states of Kentucky, Maryland, Delaware, and Missouri. When public pressure forced the Unionist governor of Maryland, Thomas Hick, to call the legislature into session to vote on secession, Lincoln sent troops to occupy Baltimore and other strategic points and suspended habeas corpus, thus virtually imposing martial law. The tactic worked, and a cowed legislature rejected secession.

## Ex Parte Merryman

The suspension of habeas corpus in Maryland and elsewhere allowed the government to round up and hold people suspected of disloyal activities and prevented their release by court order until a determination could be made on their potential to cause future trouble. All told, the military arrested about 18,000 civilians during the war, nearly all of whom regained their freedom within a few days of taking an oath to abstain from further secessionist activities. Although the action shocked many, the government did not abuse its extraordinary power; not a single person suffered torture or execution.

Lincoln resorted to this drastic tactic because of substantial sympathy for the secessionists, especially in the border states, and because he could not rely on local law enforcement officials, many of whom shared secessionist sentiment, to keep order. Local officials, for example, made no effort to control the arson and rioting by Confederate sympathizers in several states in the early weeks of the war. There were few *federal* criminal laws, and none of them applied in this situation, so Lincoln had to act swiftly and decisively to preserve internal order and prevent further losses to the Confederacy.

In Baltimore, local mobs, abetted by officials, attacked troops passing through the city to Washington. Acting on Lincoln's orders, the army began arresting some of the troublemakers, including one John Merryman, a well-known Baltimore social figure, a member of the state legislature, a colonel in the militia, and an ardent secessionist who was organizing a military unit to fight for the Confederacy. Merryman had immediate access to counsel, who quickly filed for a writ of habeas corpus. Since the local military commander had ignored a similar writ issued by District Judge William F. Giles (in the case of a minor who had enrolled in the Union forces without the consent of his parents), Merryman's attorney decided to present the petition directly to Chief Justice Taney. On May 26, 1861, when Taney arrived in Baltimore to sit as circuit judge, he learned that Merryman had been charged with various acts of treason, and that, in light of the current crisis, the president of the United States had suspended habeas corpus in the area. The commander of the Fort McHenry military district, General George Cadwalader, ignored the writ and refused to present the prisoner.

Two days later, Taney delivered an impassioned opinion asserting that the suspension of habeas corpus, while permitted by the Constitution (Article I, Section 9), belonged within the powers of the Congress, and that the president could not suspend the writ on his own authority or authorize any military officer to do so. Before an amazed and crowded courtroom, Taney declared that he would write out his opinion fully, have it delivered to the president, and call on him "to perform his constitutional duty to enforce the laws. In other words, to enforce the process of this Court."

Taney worked over his opinion, hoping to make it so persuasive that the full Court would agree with him and thus pit the power of the federal judiciary against Lincoln. He had it ready within a week, and saw to it that it received wide distribution. Taney implied, by copious references to sources—some of which had little reference to the issue—that habeas corpus had been readily available as a protection against unjust imprisonment since at least 1789. In fact, the use of habeas corpus in federal courts had been negligible, because there were so few federal crimes for which a person could be arrested. Primarily a state court remedy, habeas corpus had not been widely used even there. The only time the Supreme Court had ever examined its use in a conflict between state and federal jurisdiction had been in *Ableman v. Booth* (1859), and that case had dealt not with the appropriateness of the relief but with the Supreme Court's power as the final arbiter of constitutional issues (see Chapter 18).

Antiadministration newspapers in the North hailed the Chief Justice as the defender of the Constitution; the South greeted the decision as equivalent to a military victory. Lincoln's supporters, on the other hand, criticized Taney severely and pointed out the inconsistencies in his career: for example, he had supported strong executive action, except when such actions might harm slavery. They also quoted his earlier opinion in *Luther v. Borden* (1849), that "power in the President [is said to be] dangerous to liberty, and may be abused. All power may be abused if placed in unworthy hands. But it would be difficult, we think, to point out any other hands in which this power would be more safe and at the same time equally effectual."

Since a majority of the Court realized that Lincoln would not obey its order, his associate justices refused to go along with Taney in his demand that the Court confront the president. Hostilities had begun, and Lincoln had wide support in the North for his measures taken to prevent the rebellion from spreading. Lincoln would suspend habeas corpus again, from time to time, in some parts of the North, especially those areas harboring pro-Confederate sentiment or exposed to invasion, and in March 1863, Congress finally enacted a habeas corpus statute, retroactively authorizing the president's actions back to the start of the war.

As for Merryman himself, it appears that he might have been released earlier had the chief justice not intervened. Criticism of his arrest had harmed the Union cause, and the administration, unsure about what course to follow, had even considered backing off from habeas corpus suspension. Taney's attempt to turn Merryman's case into a conflict between the executive and judiciary stiffened the administration's resolve and led to widespread support for the policy. In the end, the administration got rid of the problem by having Merryman indicted for treason in civil court. He was released on bail in July 1861, and his case, like that of many others similarly indicted, hung in the fire for the rest of the war.

## Judicial Reorganization in Wartime

Because Lincoln had sharply criticized the *Dred Scott* decision, some Republicans hoped that once in office he would move to eliminate what they perceived as lingering Southern power in the judiciary, much as the Jeffersonians had viewed the Marshall Court as a bastion of repudiated Federalism to be overturned. The Chicago *Tribune* termed the Court "the last entrenchment behind which Despotism is sheltered," and Senator John P. Hale of New Hampshire proposed abolishing the current Court and putting another one in its place. Other Republicans suggested increasing the bench to thirteen members, with the new appointees all to be fervent Unionists and able to outvote the pro-Southern bloc. Lincoln, however distressed he may have been at its pro-slavery decisions, had too much respect for the Court as an institution to consider such radical proposals, just as he had no intention of engaging in the confrontation Taney had invited. The Court, Lincoln declared, had been established to decide constitutional questions, and the president termed it "the most enlightened judicial tribunal in the world." Moreover, by this time, Lincoln could see the possibility of remaking the Court. Justice John Campbell had followed his native Georgia out of the Union, and Peter Daniel, the fanatical proslavery jurist from Virginia, had died in 1860, but Buchanan had been unable to fill his seat. McLean's death a month after Lincoln took office assured the president of three quick appointments. Other vacancies were sure to follow on a Court with only one justice under 60, four in their seventies, and Chief Justice Taney, Lincoln's greatest nemesis, in his mid-80s. Indeed, before the end of his first term, Lincoln would put five new justices on the bench, more than any other first-term president except Washington.

Nonetheless, in his first annual message to Congress in December 1861, he did address a number of longstanding problems without, it should be noted, proposing any diminution of judicial power. In particular, he sought reform of the circuit court system, which had become increasingly inefficient; he offered Congress several alternatives, ranging from total abolition to thorough reorganization. As for the Supreme Court, he suggested that the number of justices might be made more convenient, but although Congress expanded the Court to ten members in 1863, Lincoln did not seek to pack the bench to ensure judicial support of the war.

The resulting Judicial Reorganization Act of 1862 did not significantly alter the basic judicial structure, but it did bring some necessary changes. The statute equalized the circuits and brought the newer states, several of which had not previously been included in any circuit, wholly into the system. Prior to the war, for example, eight of the new western states had not been assigned to any circuit. The Ninth Circuit had consisted of Mississippi and Arkansas, with about one million people, while the Seventh, comprising Ohio, Indiana, Illinois, and Michigan, had over six million. In terms of business, the Second Circuit (New York, Connecticut, and Vermont), with its enormous commercial litigation, had more cases on its docket than all five Southern circuits combined. The new plan provided for ten circuits, three of them in the South and a new Tenth Circuit for the western states; and while some population imbalance remained, the act eliminated the great discrepancies that had existed before the war.

Although Roger Taney's truculence remained a thorn in the side of the administration until his death in 1864, the Court as a whole did not impede the war effort. The justices had the difficult task of interpreting the Constitution in a time of crisis, trying to balance the needs of a Union struggling for its life against the guaranteed rights of individuals, many of whom had actively aided the rebellion. Despite the widespread Northern criticism of the Court after *Dred Scott* and continued charges that Taney and his brethren supported secession and slavery, the reputation of the Court as an institution appears not to have suffered either before or during the war. Of the Southerners on the bench in 1861, only John A. Campbell of Alabama resigned and went home to become an official in the Confederate government. James M. Wayne of Georgia and John Catron of Tennessee, both staunch Unionists, remained on the bench, while Chief Justice Taney, who as we have seen supported slavery and secession, also retained his seat. Taney may have stayed on the bench because he fully understood that from that position he could best serve slavery and Southern nationalism.

Although there is no evidence that the justices, aside from Taney, tried to use their position to hamper the administration, Republicans continued to see the Court as a bulwark of Calhounian theory. Republicans also hungered for patronage, another reason that in 1863, Congress, with little debate, increased the number of justices from nine to ten, ostensibly to match the number of circuits. The resignation of Campbell and the deaths of Peter Daniel and John McLean had given Lincoln the chance to name three new justices in his first year; he chose Noah Swayne of Ohio, David Davis of Illinois, and Samuel Miller of Iowa. The first two were all solid Republicans who received widespread editorial acclaim. Miller was an unknown quantity appointed to placate representatives from the West. As it turned out, he was hostile to blacks and was lukewarm, at best, in his opposition to slavery. During Reconstruction, he would emerge as a strong opponent of civil rights and black freedom. In 1863, Lincoln used the new, tenth seat to nominate the first man from the Pacific coast, the Democrat Stephen J. Field, who would become one of the giants of the nineteenth-century Court.

These four appointees significantly shifted the political and geographic balance of the Court from Southern and Democratic to Northern and Republican. Finally, with Taney's death in 1864, Republicans rejoiced that their opportunity had come, in Charles Sumner's words, to change the Supreme Court from one in which "the Constitution has been interpreted for Slavery" to one in which "it may now be interpreted wholly for Liberty." To the great joy of antislavery Republicans, Lincoln nominated Salmon P. Chase of Ohio, the abolitionist attorney and politician known as the "attorney general for fugitive slaves"—to replace Chief Justice Taney. As secretary of the treasury, Chase was one of the most capable men in the administration. The transition from Taney to Chase, more than any other appointment, symbolized the shift in power and attitude that the Republicans sought.

Yet for all the attacks on proslavery justices and the desire to place Union men on the bench, the Court itself continued to enjoy widespread approbation. One cannot find, for example, the bitter polemics that were directed against the judicial power during the Jeffersonian and Jacksonian eras. *Dred Scott* may have been, as twentieth-century Chief Justice Charles Evans Hughes noted, a "self-inflicted wound," but it apparently had not cut too deeply, and most of the opprobrium fell on its architect. The Republicans detested Taney, but they evinced no desire to undermine the Court or its power. Throughout the war, for example, no one suggested reducing the Court's appellate jurisdiction to bar it from hearing attacks on administration policies. In fact, the opposite view prevailed: key legislation should be tested before the Court to assure that it met constitutional standards, since then it would also have popular support. If the fight to preserve the Union were to be successful, not only would the rebellion have to be crushed, but it would have to be done in a constitutionally acceptable manner, and that meant with the approval of the Supreme Court.

## The Adequacy of the Constitution

By refusing to join in Taney's condemnation of Lincoln's suspension of habeas corpus, the Court in effect legitimized the policy by not invalidating it. Lincoln's other early measures also fared well. In *Ex parte Stevens* (1861), Justice Wayne had to consider the plight of a U.S. soldier who had originally enlisted for three months, but learned, at the end of that time, that his term had been extended to three years as a result of presidential proclamation. Congress had, by an act of August 6, 1861, retroactively ratified the president's actions, though a stickler for detail might well have found the procedure wholly irregular. Hearing the case in chambers, Wayne ruled that Congress had acted within its powers "to legalize and confirm Executive acts, proclamations, and orders done for the public good, although they were not, when done, authorized by any existing laws."

Wayne's opinion not only reassured the administration, but reflected a new thinking about the powers of government under the Constitution. Until the war, the accepted view held that the Constitution had created a government of restricted powers, which could act only in those areas specifically ascribed to it. Under John Marshall, the Court had broadly interpreted the reach of these delegated powers, but even Marshall often referred to the government as one of limited authority. Although Southerners had emphasized limitations more than Northerners had, the latter nonetheless shared this conceptual framework, and as a result, many in the North feared that the Constitution would prove inadequate to meet the demands of a nation at war. Lincoln's early actions, therefore, troubled some of his supporters not because they disagreed with his policy, but because he went far beyond what had previously been considered the limits of governmental power. If such actions were indeed necessary to preserve the Union and the Constitution, then the Constitution would either have to be amended to provide power explicitly, or reinterpreted to find hitherto undiscovered latent authority. Since amendment with eleven states in rebellion and without a clear idea of what would be needed seemed impractical, a close reexamination of the Constitution appeared in order.

To support Lincoln's prosecution of the war, Northern legal writers developed what abolitionist legal scholar Timothy Farrar called the "adequacy-of-the-Constitution" theory. Farrar and others argued that the Southern emphasis on the Constitution as a framework of negative restraints on the government had hidden the positive commandments for the government to act effectively to sustain and preserve the Union. Such clauses as the guarantee to every state of a republican form of government (Article IV, Section 4) and the General Welfare Clause (Article I, Section 8), as expounded by Hamilton, Marshall, and Story, required the government to take the necessary steps to carry out the general purposes of the Framers as enumerated in the Preamble. As Sidney George Fisher, another legal writer of the time, explained, the president and Congress had the power to react to concrete situations—such as the rebellion—and they also had discretion to choose the most effective means at their disposal. One might question the wisdom of Lincoln's policy in the spring of 1861, but it had been effective; the Union still endured. Preserving the Union unquestionably constituted a positive requirement of government, even if the particular means had not been spelled out in constitutional detail.

The old debate on the division of power between state and national governments, which had occupied three generations, now gave way to a newer, and more vital, concern over the role of the central government as the preserver of national unity and the protector of individual liberties. That there would be tension between these roles seemed inevitable, and resolution of this conflict would determine not only if the Union survived, but what type of Union it would be. No one wanted, for the sake of a nominal unity, to substitute autocracy for democracy, and many feared that a broad reading of governmental power could not be sustained except at the expense of individual free-dom. Northern Democrats, especially, damned Lincoln for what they perceived as the destruction of civil liberties, and cheered Taney when he lent his prestige to this at-tack. But gradually the adequacy-of-the-Constitution approach prevailed, and if early decisions on the nature of constitutional power seemed confused, that resulted in part from the unprecedented and unique situation.

## War Powers and the Rebellion

Unlike the suspension of habeas corpus and the proclamation on enlistment time, Lin-coln's blockade of southern ports received a full hearing before the Supreme Court. From the beginning Lincoln had denied the power of any state to leave the Union; the Confederate states had rebelled, and the insurrection had to be put down. The Consti-tution did not deal extensively with internal revolts, although Article I did provide for Congress "calling forth the Militia to execute the Laws of the Union, suppress Insur-rections and repel Invasions." Nevertheless, critics claimed this clause could not be used against the states, or that if the clause was applicable to the states, it could only be implemented by Congress. If Lincoln accepted these interpretations, he would have had to accept the idea that secession was not an attack on "the Laws of the Union" and that the president, when Congress was not in session, was powerless to act to enforce the laws of the United States. Not surprisingly, he rejected both ideas. Critics further argued that Lincoln could not act as commander-in-chief under the war powers, be-cause those powers referred only to foreign enemies. If Lincoln had accepted this in-terpretation, he would either have had to admit the legitimacy of the Confederacy as a foreign nation in order to utilize the war powers, or given up the power to sustain the argument that the rebellious states remained in the Union. Not surprisingly, Lin-coln rejected this argument as well.

The nature of the rebellion first came to the full Court in *The Prize Cases*, argued in February and decided in March 1863. This litigation dealt with a dozen different suits involving ships seized under the proclamation blockading southern ports. The at-torney for the shipowners, James Carlisle, delighted Taney with his argument denying the legitimacy of the blockade. If war did exist, only Congress—and not the presi-dent—could invoke the war powers, and Congress had not confirmed the blockade un-til July 13, 1861. If not war but rebellion existed, then neither Congress nor the pres-ident had the power of blockade. Whatever interpretation might be placed on the facts of the situation, necessity created no constitutional powers; to allow the president to claim them arbitrarily would make him a dictator. In response, counsel for the gov-ernment argued that the Constitution provided for defense not only against foreign in-vaders but against internal enemies as well. This war was not theory, it was fact. Rebels had attacked forces of the United States, and the president had the necessary power to repel the attack and put down the rebellion.

The Court's decision supported the administration, but by a bare 5 to 4 vote. Jus-tice Grier agreed with the government that one never declared a civil war, but one still had to recognize its existence. While war against a foreign power undoubtedly required congressional approval, the president's obligation to support the laws empowered him, and not the Congress or the Court, to recognize and act on the threat of domestic insurrection, and this meant he could decide on the appropriate measures. Taney could hardly have been happy with Grier's resort to judicial restraint when the latter termed this a political rather than a justiciable issue: the seizure of enemy property proceeded not from rules of law, but from principles of public policy. So long as the Confederate states remained in rebellion, their citizens, technically enemies of the United States, could have their property seized.

Although the administration took comfort from the decision, the closeness of the vote as well as the cogency of Justice Nelson's dissenting opinion proved disturbing. A war certainly existed, Nelson declared, but lacking a congressional declaration, it could be considered neither legal nor constitutional—it was, in effect, no more than a personal war by the president. Taking a narrow view of executive authority, he denied that the president had any war powers until Congress invested him with the necessary authority. Nelson's opinion did not deny that the government had the power to act, nor did it openly confront the president as Taney had done in *Merryman*. But the four dissenters—Taney, Catron, Nelson, and Clifford—two Southerners and two proslavery Northern doughface Democrats—needed only one more vote to call into question the administration's ability to act forcefully by stretching the Constitution to meet the crisis. With the Southerner Wayne and the Northern doughface Democrat Grier still on the bench, a change in jurisprudence was still possible.

But the four dissenters never persuaded a fifth justice to join them. In *Roosevelt v. Meyer* (1863), the Court refused to take jurisdiction in a case questioning the constitutionality of the government's issue of paper currency as legal tender to help finance the war. Again the following year, in *Ex parte Vallandigham* (1864), the Court refused to interfere with the prosecution of the war. Vallandigham, an antiwar Democrat, had been arrested by the army for violating an order banning pro-Confederate expressions of sympathy. After the trial and conviction, Lincoln changed the military court's sentence of confinement for the duration of the war to banishment to the South. Vallandigham subsequently ran the blockade to Canada and then slipped back into Ohio; from there he appealed to the Supreme Court to void the military court's proceedings, on the grounds that he had been unlawfully arrested. The judge advocate general informed the Court that it could inhibit neither the Congress (which had authorized such proceedings in the Habeas Corpus Act) nor the president in prosecuting the war. The brief opinion by Justice Wayne did not reach the merits of Vallandigham's appeal, but it declared that justification for relief through a writ of certiorari could be found neither in common nor statute law. By then a dying Chief Justice Taney confessed that he no longer had any hopes that the Court would act to stop what he believed was the destruction of the Constitution. Ironically, of course, Taney never saw secession, massive disregard for federal law, or military attacks on the United States as a threat to the Constitution.

## Defining Rebel Status

Very few questions concerning the conduct of the war came before the Supreme Court before Appomattox, a fact that probably relieved a majority of the justices, as well as the administration. The suspension of civil authority and numerous presidential proclamations, plus congressional acts concerning treason, confiscation of property, conscription, and most importantly of all, emancipation—all operated without serious legal challenge. Some of these issues did reach the Court after the war, but by then the personnel and the climate had changed. Other issues, like emancipation, were preempted by constitutional amendment. In the meantime, the Court would have found it difficult, if not impossible, to block the government in time of war. Taney, who seemed not to have learned from the *Dred Scott* experience, wanted to confront Lincoln. Fortunately for the Court, a majority of the justices recognized that such action would only exacerbate the crisis and seriously damage the prestige of the Court. As a result, numerous constitutional questions remained unresolved—such as the nature of the war itself—but this ambiguity worked to the benefit of the nation. For in the end, it did not matter whether one characterized the rebellion as war or as insurrection. As Lyman Trumbull of Illinois declared in the Senate, "We may treat them as traitors, and we may treat them as enemies."

The administration did just that, depending on circumstances. For example, the Treason Act of 1790 provided the only statutory definition of that crime at the outset of the war, but it would have been impossible to apply it to the several hundred thousand rebel soldiers levying war against the United States, much less to the several million citizens of the Confederate states who gave them aid or comfort. The United States treated captured troops not as traitors, but as prisoners of war, even though the denial of the Confederacy as a sovereign belligerent did not require this. Congress passed three measures— the Conspiracies Act of July 31, 1861, the First Confiscation Act of August 6, 1861 and the Second Confiscation Act, also known as the Treason Act, of July 17, 1862—to allow prosecution of those conspiring in the rebellion, as well as those in the United States who aided their cause. A number of grand jury indictments were subsequently handed down in the border states, but the government prosecuted only a handful. Even after the war, prosecution of Confederate leaders for treason remained selective, and Jefferson Davis, the president of the Confederacy, ultimately escaped punishment, although his case dragged through federal courts for more than three years.

In a similar manner, the Lincoln administration enforced a selective policy in confiscating enemy property. Congress passed two acts authorizing confiscation, the first directed only against property actually used in aid of the rebellion, and the second forfeiting all property of Confederate officials and persons supporting the rebellion. Lincoln doubted the constitutionality of the second bill, but after some modification by Congress, he signed it into law. In practice, he applied it only to property located in free states owned by rebels. The law did not provide for hearings to determine if the person had indeed been guilty of treason; instead, confiscation would be by *in rem* proceeding directly against the property of the enemy. The dual status of the conflict— war and rebellion—led to much confusion in the few cases arising from the statute, and while the Supreme Court upheld the law in *Miller v. United States* (1871), the several opinions did nothing to clarify the issue.

## The Growth of National Power

The war marked a major shift in governmental power away from the states and to the federal government, a process not unusual in wartime, but facilitated in 1861–65 by the Republican party's commitment to strong national programs. In the early months of the conflict, state officials in the United States, as in the Confederacy, took the lead in mobilizing for war. The states raised and outfitted militias and transported them where directed. But as the federal government began to play a larger role, friction inevitably developed between state and national authorities. In most instances, Lincoln was able to smooth out the differences, but while he could persuade state leaders to accept national direction, he had no constitutional authority to compel them to do so. As the war lengthened, however, state resources proved inadequate, and more and more functions came under direct federal control.

Banking and currency, for example, had been within the purview of the states since Jackson had killed the Second Bank of the United States, and although imperfect, the banking system had met the needs of a peacetime society. But local banks lacked the reserves and the flexibility to meet the demands of the war. Congress first addressed the problem by issuing $450 million in fiat money, called greenbacks, which, despite the absence of specie backing, were made legal tender for both public and private debt. In February 1863, Congress passed the National Banking Act, which, with amendments in 1864 and 1865, set up the framework for a national banking system. The nationally chartered banks were authorized to issue notes, based on their holdings of government bonds, which would be guaranteed by the federal government. The banks were required to pay for these bonds with gold, which strengthened the nation's finances both domestically and internationally. In addition, a 10 percent tax on state bank notes effectively drove them out of circulation, leaving a relatively uniform currency based on the nation's credit. Thus, despite the lack of a national bank, the Lincoln administration, under Secretary of the Treasury Chase, in effect created a national currency and a national banking system.

The need to move large numbers of men and vast amounts of materiel, as well as the secession of eleven Southern states (whose presence in Congress which had previously thwarted expenditures for internal improvements) led Congress to appropriate millions of dollars to build up the North's transportation network. In May 1862, Lincoln, acting under statute, took official possession of the railroads in order to guarantee that war transportation received the highest priority. Although the government rarely exercised more than nominal control, it secured the needed coordination and cooperation. Moreover, with the South absent, the long delayed plans for a transcontinental railroad finally moved forward. The Pacific Railroad Acts of 1862 and 1864 chartered two companies to connect the Pacific states to the terminus in Omaha, Nebraska, and provided them with extensive land grants and loans to finance the venture. Similarly, in 1862, Congress passed the Homestead Act and the Morrill Act, both of which Democrats had long opposed. The Homestead Act gave free land to settlers who successfully established farms in the West, while the Morrill Act provided for land grant colleges throughout the nation, to be funded by federal lands given to the states. Both programs, along with the various banking acts, illustrate how the war brought about a revolution in programs, policies, and constitutional theories, reversing those of Jefferson and Jackson, and in a sense reviving the nationalism of Hamilton and the Federalists.

One of the greatest expansions of federal power came in the form of compulsory military service. The Constitution unquestionably gives to Congress power "to raise and support Armies," and to call out, equip, and direct state militias when employed in federal service (Article I, Section 8). In 1861, the government maintained a small regular army, with limited combat experience gained from a few encounters with Indians in the 1850s. Lincoln augmented these troops by calling out state militias under a 1795 law, but volunteers constituted the bulk of Northern troops throughout the war. While no one doubted the government's authority to call for and accept volunteers, it became apparent that the army's needs, especially as the war stretched on, exceeded the supply of volunteers. Congress first responded in the Militia Act of July 1862, providing that all male citizens between 18 and 45 should be included in state militias. Lincoln then assigned quotas to the states and ordered state governors to draft men to fill unmet allocations. Whether Lincoln actually had the power to direct state-run conscription is debatable, but by mid-1862, draftees began appearing in U.S. Army uniforms.

State militias, varying so greatly in training, equipment, and organization, could not be expected to develop into a national army; nor did the states like to see their units assigned to separate theaters of war, under the command of national rather than state officers. So in March 1863, Congress passed a comprehensive draft law, making all male citizens between 20 and 45, as well as immigrants who had declared their intention to become citizens, liable for military service. The entire program, from registration to selection, training to assignment, came under federal control. The law, while necessary, aroused fierce resentment, especially in areas with strong pro-Southern sympathies, and the resistance occasionally turned violent. In New York, an antidraft riot raged for four days in July 1863. But for the most part, the system worked, if not perfectly, then at least well enough to provide men needed to fight the war.

No test case of the draft law ever reached the Supreme Court, but some critics, such as Governor Horatio Seymour of New York, called on Lincoln to suspend conscription because of its unconstitutionality. Lincoln believed the law was legitimate, however, and in a memorandum later found in his papers, he justified it with adequacy-of-the-Constitution logic.

> The Constitution provides that the Congress shall have the power to raise and support armies . . . but it does not provide the mode. . . . In such case Congress must prescribe the mode, or relinquish the power. There is no alternative. . . . The power is given fully, completely, unconditionally. It is not a power to raise armies if State authorities consent, nor if the men to compose the armies are entirely willing; but it is a power to raise and support armies given to Congress by the Constitution without an *if*.

Ironically, the government in Richmond resorted to conscription even before the United States, since state militias and resources proved totally inadequate to Confederate needs. The two constitutions had identical wording concerning the power to raise armies, and despite states' rights opposition in the South, a form of adequacy of the Constitution evidently prevailed there as well.

## The Emancipation Proclamation

The most radical extension of federal power was the emancipation of millions of Southern slaves. One might expect that the issue that had caused the war would evoke the most energetic response. Yet well into the conflict, most Northern leaders denied any intent to tamper with slavery. The reason for this was threefold.

First, Lincoln and most other Republicans believed that the national government had no constitutional power to tamper with slavery where it existed. Ultimately, the administration would discover the authority to end slavery in the Confederacy within the war powers of Congress and the president. But at the beginning of the war, few in Washington saw this power.

Second, when he first took office, Lincoln expected that the citizens of the seceding states would come to their senses and peacefully return to the Union. Any assault on slavery would undermine that.

Third, Lincoln had to balance an attack on slavery with the need to keep the four border slave states in the Union. At one point, Lincoln was told by a group of visiting clergymen that if he freed the slaves, he would have God on his side. Lincoln supposedly replied that "I would like to have God on my side, but I *need* Kentucky." Any precipitous attack on slavery might very well have pushed Kentucky and Missouri into the Confederacy.

Had the war ended quickly, a majority in the North would probably have welcomed the rebellious states back with their slaves and adhered to the 1860 Republican platform, which spoke only of prohibiting slavery in the territories. But as the conflict dragged on, abolitionist sentiment grew, and pressure increased on the administration to act—despite the doubts of most legal experts and political leaders that the government possessed the necessary constitutional authority. By 1862, a consensus began to emerge in the North that somehow or other the goals of the war included not only preservation of the Union but the ending of slavery as well. Congress acted hesitantly, first abolishing slavery in the District of Columbia in April 1862, with compensation to loyal owners. Three months later, it freed, without compensation, all slaves in the territories (a relatively small number). Then in July, Congress took a major step by passing the Second Confiscation Act, which declared that all slaves of persons engaged in the rebellion who escaped to Union lines, or had been freed by Union troops, would be "forever free of their servitude." The law had no immediate effect on slaves behind Confederate lines, nor did Lincoln ever push to implement it. For him, saving the Union remained the prime objective, and publicly he continued to declare that emancipation was not an end in itself, but as a tool for the greater good.

Lincoln had always hated slavery, but as a practical politician he had favored gradual, voluntary abolition of slavery, and as president he initially supported federal compensation to the owners. He vainly hoped that this approach would win over the reasonable leaders of the loyal slave states and in the Confederacy. In April 1862, at Lincoln's instigation, Congress passed a joint resolution promising to provide financial support to states taking this route. No rebellious state, and none of the loyal slave states, took up the offer, although Lincoln never abandoned his hopes for its success. Nevertheless, he also moved to the more drastic step of using emancipation a war policy.

Lincoln's route to emancipation illustrates his brilliant political skills as well as his respect for a constitutionally acceptable means of achieving his goal. In July 1862, he drafted what would become the Emancipation Proclamation. At the time, however, he showed it to no one, and still publicly supported voluntary and compensated emancipation. In August 1862, Horace Greely, the abolitionist editor of the *New York Tribune*, publicly called for emancipation. Lincoln responded with a careful letter that reaffirmed restoration of the Union as the central goal of his policies. In his letter, published in the *Tribune* on August 25, 1862, Lincoln wrote: "My paramount object in this struggle *is* to save the Union, and is *not* either to save or to destroy slavery. If I could save the Union without freeing *any* slave, I would do it; if I could save it by freeing *all* the slaves, I would do it; and if I could save it by freeing some and leaving others alone, I would also do that."

In fact, of course, by this time Lincoln had already decided to issue the Emancipation Proclamation, and was only waiting for a significant Union military victory to do so. On September 22, 1862, after the battle of Antietam, in which United States troops repelled an invasion of Maryland by General Robert E. Lee, Lincoln issued the preliminary Emancipation Proclamation. Relying on his authority as commander-in-chief, Lincoln warned that slavery would be abolished in any state in rebellion on January 1, 1863. On that New Year's day, with the war still raging, he issued the Emancipation Proclamation, designating those states or parts of states still in rebellion and freeing all persons held therein as slaves. The Proclamation did not apply to the border states, nor to those parts of the Confederacy occupied by Union troops.

Lincoln and his advisers had serious questions about the constitutionality of the proclamation, which the South as well as proslavery and antiblack elements in the North immediately attacked. The president himself confided that he hoped "measures otherwise unconstitutional" might be made lawful by becoming indispensable to the preservation of the Union. Even those who supported emancipation had grave doubts about the president's action. *The New York Times* expressed its relief that Lincoln had based the Proclamation on military necessity, and even then, it wondered whether the Supreme Court would allow him to repeal *state* laws on slavery.

Fears about what the Court would do troubled government officials throughout the war. "I am not willing to trust the court," declared Congressman W. McKee Dunn of Indiana, "because very much of the trouble in which we are now involved may be attributed to the fact that we had a proslavery judiciary." Ardent abolitionists, such as Wendell Phillips, denounced the Court and its chief justice as secessionist at heart: "God help the negro if he hangs on Roger B. Taney for his liberty." In fact, the Court never had to rule on the Emancipation Proclamation. It applied only to slaves in rebellious states and would not even be effective until those areas came under Union control. At that time, those who might complain of deprivation of their property would, as designated traitors, have difficulty seeking redress through federal courts.

The Proclamation only affected slaves still in rebel territory. Thus, Lincoln might be criticized only for freeing slaves where he had no power to implement his policy. But constitutionally, Lincoln had no power to free slaves within the United States; he could only free the slaves held by rebels, as a war measure. Practically, however, Lincoln had attacked the heart of slavery and offered the promise of liberty to the overwhelming majority of slaves in the South. Moreover, as the U.S. Army moved farther South, it became a vast agent of liberation. Sherman's famous march to the sea in 1864, for example, not only destroyed the war-making ability of Georgia and the Carolinas, but also brought liberty to a million or more slaves.

Lincoln further enhanced the substance of liberty by authorizing, for the first time, the enlistment of black soldiers. By the end of the war, more than 186,000 uniformed blacks would serve in the army and another 20,000 or so in the navy. This "sable arm" of the U.S. military effort set the stage for a revolution in citizenship rights. As the war progressed, it became increasingly clear that when the Confederacy was finally defeated, the black soldiers, and by extension all African-Americans, would have a strong claim to citizenship rights, including the ballot. Indeed, by the end of his life, Lincoln, who had once been unalterably opposed to political equality for blacks, endorsed black suffrage.

## The Thirteenth Amendment

Despite the practical reality of U.S. soldiers destroying slavery, many Republicans remained concerned about the legitimacy of the Proclamation. Moreover, they realized that even if the Proclamation stood, hundreds of thousands of blacks in Kentucky, Maryland, Missouri, and parts of Louisiana and Virginia would remain in slavery, since they were not under rebel control on January 1, 1863. These concerns led to the proposal and adoption of the Thirteenth Amendment, although supporters could not get the necessary two-thirds vote in the House of Representatives until January 1865. The amendment provided that "Neither slavery nor involuntary servitude, except as a punishment for crime whereof the party shall have been duly convicted, shall exist within the United States, or any place subject to their jurisdiction"; a second section gave Congress power to enforce the amendment.

With the war nearly over, the ratification process saw strenuous debate not only over the amendment's wisdom, but over its legality. Prior amendments had either explicated certain rights or corrected technical defects and had applied only to the federal government. The Thirteenth Amendment imposed a major reform on the nation, aimed directly at the internal affairs of the states. In addition, for the first time, an amendment, rather than limiting Congress, gave Congress explicit enforcement power. A revolution in constitutional theory and application was in the works. The constitutional abolition of slavery not only marked the end of decades of bitter debate, but also confirmed a major shift in power within the federal system from the states to the national government.

Despite criticism that the Constitution could not be changed to encompass so sweeping a reform, there is no doubt that, with the exception of the clause guaranteeing each state two Senate seats (and the prohibition on ending the slave trade before 1808), the amendment power is unlimited. The Framers not only created a mechanism for alteration, but explicitly provided that all amendments are "valid to all Intents and Purposes, as Part of this Constitution," a rule agreed to at the time of ratification. That an amendment may cause substantive as well as procedural change is obvious, as is the fact that the changes may be very broad and sweeping; but amendment is the device by which the people can keep the Constitution attuned to shifting needs and circumstances.

A more difficult question was how many states would be needed to ratify. By Lincoln's reckoning, the Confederate states had never left the Union because of the indissoluble nature of the constitutional pact; therefore 27 of the 36 states would have to ratify. Yet eleven states had seceded, and two border states that still had slavery, Kentucky and Delaware, rejected the proposal. At least four of the secessionist states, then, would have to ratify; in the end, eight of the provisional Reconstruction governments along with the remaining free states approved, and the Thirteenth Amendment went into effect on December 18, 1865. Within a short time, however, Congress refused to recognize these same provisional governments as valid, bringing into question the legitimacy of the ratification process. Congress, nonetheless, ignored this point, for it, like the nation, wanted an end to the problem that had plagued the country for so long.

# For Further Reading

Good overviews of the entire period are presented in James M. McPherson, *Battle Cry of Freedom* (1988); and the older, but still useful, James G. Randall and David Donald, *The Civil War and Reconstruction* (1969). For the secession period and competing constitutional arguments, see David M. Potter, *The South and the Sectional Conflict* (1968); William L. Barney, *The Road to Secession: A New Perspective on the Old South* (1972); Kenneth L. Stampp, *And the War Came: The North and the Secession Crisis, 1860–1861* (1950); Ralph A. Wooster, *The Secession Conventions of the South* (1962); and the essays in George H. Knoles, ed., *The Crisis of the Union, 1860–1861* (1965).

Harold M. Hyman and William M. Wiecek, *Equal Justice Under Law: Constitutional Development, 1835–1875* (1982), and Harold M. Hyman, *A More Perfect Union: The Impact of the Civil War and Reconstruction on the Constitution* (1973), offer persuasive arguments on the constitutionality of Lincoln's actions during the war. By looking at contemporary constitutional thought, the authors show how the Republicans developed the adequacy-of-the-Constitution doctrine. James G. Randall, *Constitutional Problems Under Lincoln* (1926; rev., 1951) is the classic, and outdated, statement of Lincoln exceeding the Constitution.

Confederate constitutional thought is examined in Charles R. Lee, *The Confederate Constitutions* (1963); Frank L. Owsley, *State Rights in the Confederacy* (1925); and Emory Thomas, *The Confederate Nation, 1861–1865* (1979). The use of political parties as a war tool is well explicated in Eric McKitrick's essay in Walter Dean Burnham and William Chambers, eds., *The American Party System: Stages of Political Development* (1967). Mark Neely, *Southern Rights: Political Prisoners and the Myth of Confederate Constitutionalism* (1999) explores the suppression of liberty and dissent in the Confederacy.

Lincoln's expansion of presidential power has been a source of continuing interest and controversy. See, among many others, Philip Paludan, *The Presidency of Abraham Lincoln* (1994) and *"A People's Contest": The Union and the Civil War, 1861–1865* (1988); James G. Randall, *Lincoln the President*, 4 vols. (1945–1955); Morgan Dowd, "Lincoln, the Rule of Law and Crisis Government: A Study of His Constitutional Law Theories," 39 *University of Detroit Law Journal* 633 (1962); David Donald, *Lincoln Reconsidered* (1961); and Robert M. Spector, "Lincoln and Taney: A Study in Constitutional Polarization," 15 *American Journal of Legal History* 199 (1971). Most of these studies, like Hyman's *A More Perfect Union*, regard Lincoln's policies as necessary and effective. Contrary views can be found in Gottfried Dietze, *America's Political Dilemma: From Limited to Unlimited Democracy* (1968), which criticizes Lincoln's expansion of presidential power; and Ludwell H. Johnson, "Jefferson Davis and Abraham Lincoln as War Presidents: Nothing Succeeds Like Success," 27 *Civil War History* 49 (1981), which alone claims Davis was the better chief executive.

For problems of internal security, see Harold M. Hyman, *Era of the Oath: Northern Loyalty*

*Tests During the Civil War and Reconstruction* (1954); Mark E. Neely, Jr., *The Fate of Liberty: Abraham Lincoln and Civil Liberties* (1991); and Paul Finkelman, "Civil Liberties and the Civil War: The Great Emancipator as Civil Libertarian," 91 *Michigan Law Review* 1353 (1993). On free speech issues and the *Vallandigham* case, see Michael Kent Curtis, *Free Speech, "The People's Darling Privilege": Struggles for Freedom of Expression in American History* (2001). For the Court during the war years, see the early chapters of Stanley I. Kutler, *Judicial Power and Reconstruction Politics* (1958); and David M. Silver, *Lincoln's Supreme Court* (1956). On amending the Constitution during the Civil War period (and all other periods of U.S. history), see David E. Kyvig, *Explicit and Authentic Acts: Amending the U.S. Constitution, 1776–1995* (1996).

Emancipation as a constitutional problem is well treated in John Hope Franklin, *The Emancipation Proclamation* (1963); La Wanda Cox, *Lincoln and Black Freedom: A Study in Presidential Leadership* (1981); and Herman Belz, *A New Birth of Freedom: The Republican Party and Freedmen's Rights, 1861–1866* (1976). On the importance of black troops to the Union cause and in changing the nature of constitutional thought, see Joseph T. Glatthaar, *Forged in Battle: The Civil War Alliance of Black Soldiers and White Officers* (1990); Dudley T. Cornish, *The Sable Arm: Negro Troops in the Union Army, 1861–1865* (1956); and James McPherson, *The Negro's Civil War* (1965).

# 20

# *The Union Unrestored*

*Problems of Military Occupation • Loyalty Oaths • Congress Takes a Hand • Expanding Federal Court Jurisdiction • Lincoln's 10 Percent Plan • The Wade–Davis Bill • Enter Andrew Johnson • Presidential Reconstruction • The Joint Committee on Reconstruction • Southern Intransigence • The Freedmen's Bureau Bills of 1866 • The Civil Rights Act • The Fourteenth Amendment • The Congressional Plan • Conclusion • For Further Reading*

Reconstruction of the Union began almost at the point at which it dissolved, for the Lincoln administration was determined, above all else, to preserve the Union. No one, however, expected that the Union would ever be the same as it had been before Fort Sumter. If prosecuting a civil war raised monumental constitutional issues, the rebuilding of a union that theoretically had never been destroyed posed even thornier questions. Who possessed the constitutional authority? How much, if any, power resided in the federal government to reconstruct the states? What was the status of the rebellious states and of the freed slaves? Under the best of circumstances, reconstruction would have been difficult, but the combination of Southern intransigence and political incompetence turned it into a disaster. All these issues came to the forefront when the Union forces made inroads into the South.

## Problems of Military Occupation

During the first year of the war, military events seemed to favor the rebellion, although from the beginning of the war, the geographical limits of the Confederacy contracted, while Union forces occupied more and more territory of the secessionist states. For the first time in a half century, armed troops, albeit American soldiers, occupied part of the United States; the defeated Southerners saw them as a conquering army, and did not know what to expect. To military officials, the situation proved no less confusing; nothing in the traditional rules of war governed a civil conflict of this magnitude. In

429

addition to the immediate needs of securing an area, the army had to deal with questions of governance, civil rights, and what to do with the slaves, or, after the Emancipation Proclamation, the freedmen. Decisions in these matters exceeded military policy alone and required political guidance from the president and Congress, as well as legal rulings from the courts.

Whatever personal feelings they may have harbored toward the "rebels," Lincoln and the Republican leadership wanted to restore normal conditions as quickly as possible. This did not mean, as many Democrats demanded, a return to the status quo ante. While this might have been possible in 1861, conditions in both the North and the South soon made it impossible to go back to the way it had been. The Emancipation Proclamation, issued on January 1, 1863, sealed the fate of slavery and led inevitably to a reconstruction of the South without bondage. If nothing else, the emancipation of millions of slaves and the destruction of the property value they represented guaranteed the demise of the Old South. But no New South stood waiting in the wings, so through trial and error, the army and its political overseers improvised, trying to adjust often vague guidelines to local conditions. None of this happened in secret; communications between soldiers and their home communities gave the Northern public extensive information about the problems of occupation and Reconstruction, and this in turn helped guide officials in Washington.

To the Southern communities, the presence of Union soldiers, however distasteful as a reminder of their defeat, affected daily affairs very little. Military officers had no desire to run local governments; as a result, they frequently left in place the governmental structure, with its elected and appointed civilian officials, such as sheriffs, mayors, and justices of the peace. Except for those matters governed by executive order or congressional statute, they also left state and local laws in place. In many instances, the destruction of war forced the army to take on functions such as feeding the population or providing fire and police protection. But as soon as possible, it returned these tasks to civilian hands.

To ascribe any coherent ideology to this phase of Reconstruction would be a mistake. Ideas ranged from the one extreme, advocated by many Democrats, of immediate restoration of full civilian control to the militant abolitionists' demand for a total restructuring of Southern society. For the most part, however, a rough working arrangement developed between those seeking guidance from constitutional provisions and the less extreme abolitionists, who were concerned over the freedmen's fate. Once again, the adequacy-of-the-Constitution theory provided the guidelines, and the document proved to be far more flexible than the static views expounded by Taney and the Democrats.

Within the army, especially early in the war, generals differed on what policies to adopt toward the slaves. General George B. McClellan, who would be the Democratic candidate for president in 1864, insisted on strict enforcement of the Fugitive Slave Act of 1850, even though this meant handing the runaways back to declared traitors. His subordinates often refused to enforce these directives, and Republican generals like Benjamin Butler and John C. Frémont completely ignored the 1850 act in the territories under their control. Eventually, the political leaders in Washington felt compelled to deal with the issue. Butler, a successful lawyer before the war, used his legal skills to discover a way to protect fugitive slaves without violating the 1850 act. When slaves ran to his encampment in Virginia, he refused to return them to their masters, claiming they were "contraband of war." However, since the U.S. government did not officially recognize slaves as property, Butler felt he had no choice but to free these "contrabands," as they were now called, and put them to work for the army. Thus, well before the official enlistment of blacks, thousands were serving the U.S. Army in noncombatant roles. Meanwhile, Congress took a few faltering steps in 1862, but not until 1864 would Congress actually repeal both the 1793 and 1850 Fugitive Slave Laws. The first and second confiscation acts in 1861 and 1862 allowed for the seizure of rebel property, including slaves. This process culminated in Lincoln's Emancipation Proclamation on January 1, 1863.

## Loyalty Oaths

Most soldiers, even if they brought racial prejudices with them, proved friendly to the blacks and found them trustworthy allies during the war. They remained far more suspicious of Southern whites, and local commanders often imposed some rough form of loyalty oath on civilians before allowing them to hold or resume public office. In August 1861, Congress required a loyalty oath of all federal civilian and military officers—a simple pledge of their intent to remain loyal to the Union. A year later, a tougher oath, including assurances of past as well as future loyalty, went into effect. Over the next three years, nearly everyone having business with the government, including contractors, applicants for pensions or passports, and even jurors and lawyers in federal courts, had to subscribe to it. The War Department used this "ironclad" oath for captured rebels who claimed to have served in the Confederate army under duress and who now wished to join the Union forces. Civilians in occupied territory wishing to hold office, do business with the Union forces, or even use the courts, also had to take the pledge.

The oath, made to the United States, emphasized the shift in authority away from the states to the federal government. Prior to the war, traditional theory had viewed the states as the repositories of civil rights and the national government as a potential enemy of liberty. The Bill of Rights had been designed to limit this danger, and the Founding Fathers had seen no need to impose similar restrictions on the states. The oaths now made enjoyment of many rights dependent on the federal government; one had to swear loyalty, not to one's state, but to the United States. Here again, there seemed to be a shift to viewing the Constitution less as a limiting document and more as a broad grant of power to the national government.

Administration of the oaths remained in military hands, and in order to secure uniform enforcement, the War Department developed guidelines and manuals, not only for the oaths, but eventually for most aspects of military occupation. Although Lincoln and other Republican leaders worried that too powerful an army posed a threat to democratic institutions, they recognized that in wartime the nation had to have a potent military force. Enforcing conscription, confiscating rebel property, and administering loyalty oaths, as well as fighting the war, made the army a strong force in the nation's affairs, a condition that could not be avoided. But in developing explicit policy directives, civilian officials could limit the military's discretion. Leading legal scholars joined the War Department to draft the manuals detailing military officers' legal duties and responsibilities. Judge Advocate General Joseph Holt published numerous circulars and opinions, and his office became a stringent regulator of occupation conduct. Law professor Francis Lieber of Columbia University drew up a concise compendium on martial law for use by occupational forces, and the abolitionist lawyer William Whiting wrote *War Powers Under the Constitution of the United States* for the government in 1863. By the spring of that year, nearly every field officer in the army carried a small but definitive library of War Department material detailing rules of war, martial law, and conduct in occupied areas.

## Congress Takes a Hand

With an ever increasing amount of occupied territory under Union control, Congress had to decide whether it wanted to play a part in determining policy, or whether it preferred to abdicate all responsibility to the army. As part of the restructuring and strengthening of the legislative branch, Congress had established the Joint Committee on the Conduct of the War in 1861; until then, joint committees had been practically unknown, except for ceremonial purposes. The committee consisted of the political leaders of both houses, men with sufficient political power to give the joint committee enormous influence. It held numerous hearings on all aspects of the war, subpoenaed witnesses—including Negroes—and used a staff to secure information on subjects under investigation. In a crude way, it foreshadowed the later and more extensive congressional committee system, with its close relation to the White House and use of the press to focus attention on its work. Perhaps its most important achievement was sharing responsibility with the president for keeping the military responsive to and under the control of elected civilian leaders. This goal had been largely achieved by mid-1863: close cooperation between Lincoln and the Congress forced the generals to accept that the political branches would determine military policy.

## Expanding Federal Court Jurisdiction

The work of the Joint Committee on the Conduct of the War led to legislation in March 1863 that confirmed the president's power to suspend habeas corpus, provided indemnification for civilians who could prove injury at the hands of military authorities, and authorized the removal of cases involving government officers from state to federal courts. The laws also provided guidelines for military conduct and remedies for their breach. The fact that in the midst of war, Congress and the administration should even consider expanding the power of the federal courts, allegedly manned by Southern sympathizers, is clear proof that the Republicans had far less fear that the judiciary would undermine the war effort than their rhetoric implied. They may have hated the politics of men like Roger Taney, but Lincoln and other Republicans never lost their faith in judicial institutions, and they now brought the courts in as partners in the control of the military.

Access to federal courts had been governed by the jurisdiction clauses of the Constitution and by Section 25 of the Judiciary Act of 1789. Aside from suits between citizens of different states that were tried in federal district courts, most litigation began and ended in state courts, which exercised concurrent jurisdiction over cases arising under the Constitution, treaties, and laws of the United States. If a federal question existed, or a litigant claimed that he had been deprived of some constitutional right, he or she had to wait until the state's highest court had disposed of the case before seeking review in the U.S. Supreme Court—the only federal court empowered to review state decisions. No federal court could intervene in a state court proceeding, nor could a federal judge order a defendant being held for state trial to be transferred to federal jurisdiction. Civilians with complaints against military or civil officers of the federal government preferred to pursue their claims in state courts, where local sympathies and prejudices worked to their advantage.

The various acts of 1863 shifted much of this litigation into the federal courts, although state procedural law would still be followed. Blacks could now testify against whites in federal courts, although a few Northern and all Southern states had denied them this right. Suits under these statutes did not have the diversity requirement or a dollar minimum. Conscription cases were also to be heard in federal courts, preventing hostile state judges from using writs of habeas corpus to free accused draft-evaders from military custody. The military benefited from the new standard procedures, which provided protection from biased local judges and juries, as well as reimbursement for defense costs against suits for acts they committed as agents of the government. In turn, however, the laws placed additional restraints on the military. Government officials had to report to federal judges all civilian arrests and the final disposition of prisoners. The nation benefited not only from assurances of fairer military procedure, but also from the imposition of uniform law on these subjects throughout the land. Litigants, especially blacks, who feared bias in local courts could now seek justice directly in the federal system.

## Lincoln's 10 Percent Plan

Occupying conquered territory was at best a temporary measure. No one wanted or expected military rule to be more than a step on the road to full restoration of the rebellious states to their proper place in the Union. Constitutionally, the question most discussed during the war concerned the status of the secessionist states during the rebellion. Republicans such as Thaddeus Stevens and Charles Sumner developed theories of "state suicide" or "conquered territories" to show that the rebellious governments no longer enjoyed the privileges of states. In the end, however, theory failed to provide an adequate rationale for what had to be done. Reconstruction treated the states as temporarily out of their proper orbit (without explicating their precise location), with the national government supervising the process by which a state would resume its normal place in the Union. Once that happened, all federal control over the state would end.

But what would that process be? And how extensive would federal control be in the interim? The early confiscation statutes and laws dealing with slaves, primarily punitive in intent, affected individuals and not states. Not until December 1863 did the administration put forward a plan to guide the conquered states back into the Union. Lincoln's 10 percent plan, as it came to be called, has entered historical legend as the thwarted effort of a great and compassionate president to bind up the nation's wounds. Had Lincoln lived, some have claimed, then the tragedy of Reconstruction would have been averted.

Lincoln's plan reflected his steadfast views of the indissolubility of the Union: the Southern states had never left, and their ordinances of secession had always been null and void. Getting the states back into their proper sphere within the Union necessitated crushing the military rebellion and installing loyal governments through election by loyal citizens; normal relations could then resume. The process would be overseen by the federal government, acting under Article IV, Section 4, which guaranteed to every state a republican form of government. In terms of federal action, Lincoln assumed that Reconstruction would be mainly a presidential function, deriving from his war powers and responsibility to see that the laws were faithfully executed. Unlike his successor, Andrew Johnson, Lincoln never denied Congress a role in the Reconstruction, but assumed that, as it had done during the war, it would follow his lead, offering advice and criticism when necessary.

The plan itself, announced through proclamation, offered a pardon to any rebel (with the exception of high-ranking Confederate civilian and military officers) who took an oath of future loyalty to the United States. Whenever the number of "loyal" persons who were eligible to vote equaled 10 percent of the qualified voters as of 1860, they would establish a state government that would operate under the protection of federal troops. Lincoln did not demand the abolition of slavery, although he strongly suggested it, and he made no mention of black suffrage. Under these terms, "loyal" governments were organized in Tennessee, Arkansas, and Louisiana in 1864 and 1865, and these states convened constitutional conventions that repealed the secession ordinances, abolished slavery, and created new state governments.

The scheme failed badly. The "loyal" governments had practically no popular support and survived only with the backing of the U.S. army. Although they abolished slavery, the all-white governments did nothing to grant blacks any form of equality or make them citizens. Congress, which had been willing to give Lincoln a chance at creating a Reconstruction policy, would have nothing to do with these regimes, and refused to seat the representatives they sent to the House and Senate. The president continued to believe his approach would be useful, but recognized that, as it operated in these states, it had many defects. The 10 percent plan should be viewed not as Lincoln's final proposal, indelibly etched in granite, but as his first suggestion, made in the midst of a war whose outcome remained in doubt. The president hoped to lure the rebels back into the Union with the offer of a lenient plan now, as against a potentially harsher one later. Had he lived, Lincoln's political acumen would no doubt have taken into account congressional antipathy in order to work out an acceptable compromise, the path he had followed throughout the war.

## The Wade–Davis Bill

In fact, the process of accommodation with Congress began before Lincoln's death. In early 1864, Republican leaders began exploring what role Congress should play in Reconstruction. The most apparent defect of the 10 percent plan was the problem of what to do with the former slaves. Congressional investigators went to the three states operating under Lincoln's plan. They reported that the harsh prewar slave and black codes basically remained on the statute books and that slavelike conditions endured in many areas. Congress was resolved to go much further than the president in restructuring society in the former slave states. Where Lincoln's plan left internal racial policies pretty much alone (with the exception of ending slavery as a legal institution), Congress, backed by abolitionist forces, read the "republican government" clause to mean protection and some measure of equality for all of a state's inhabitants, including the freedmen. Many, although not yet a majority, of Republicans, were also pushing for black suffrage. The fact that Lincoln's plan, in the form of a proclamation, relied on the presidential war powers, also struck many congressmen as constitutionally defective. The creation of states and their admission to the Union had always been a congressional function, as provided for in Article IV, Section 3, and the reconstitution of the rebel states would require some statutory authorization.

Congress took its first stab at a Reconstruction policy in July 1864. Although the Republicans had just nominated Lincoln to be their standard-bearer in the fall election, the Wade–Davis bill repudiated his Reconstruction program. The bill called on the president to nominate, with Senate approval, a provisional civilian governor for each conquered state to replace the military governors Lincoln had appointed without Senate confirmation. This governor would direct civil affairs in the state and oversee the creation of a new state government. Federal marshals would enroll all white male citizens, and once a majority (not 10 percent) swore future loyalty to the Union, the governor would oversee the election of delegates to a convention, which in turn would draft a new state constitution. The convention would conform all state laws to the federal Constitution in order to secure a republican government.

A republican government, according to the Wade–Davis bill, required all voters and elected officials either to have been civilians during the rebellion, or not to have held the rank of colonel or above in the Confederate army, or a position in the Confederate government beyond the clerical level. Slavery had to be abolished, and the Confederate debt repudiated. The new state constitution would be submitted to eligible voters, and upon majority approval, the governor would send it to the president. After he had obtained congressional assent, the president could then proclaim the state rejoined to the Union. Only after this had occurred could the governor order statewide elections for offices under the new constitution, including congressmen and presidential electors. Until the new government took over, the governor would enforce the prewar statutes—with the exception of the slave codes and black codes—and the federal courts had the power of habeas corpus to rescue any blacks who were still held in involuntary servitude.

Differing in many respects from Lincoln's plan, the Wade–Davis bill provided a more coherent policy than did the president's. Lincoln sought speed in returning the rebellious states to the Union and relied on the democratic process to reform internal policies. His own ambivalence at this time toward blacks led him to leave their future, after emancipation, under the control of whites. Congress wanted a more orderly procedure, based on statutory authority, that required substantive domestic changes before a state could return; Congress also wanted to ensure some protections for the freedmen. Republican leaders knew that Congress would be unable to secure these rights once a state returned to white control and had been readmitted to the Union, for they still believed that the Constitution did not give Congress power to interfere with the internal affairs of a state. Although it was not a perfect plan, the Wade–Davis bill provided far more guidelines than did the 10 percent plan and might have prevented the debacle under Andrew Johnson.

But for reasons that are still unclear, Lincoln killed the bill under the rarely used constitutional provision of a pocket veto (Article I, Section 7), in which bills sent within ten days of Congress's adjournment die if they do not receive the president's signature. Lincoln issued a rather vague statement on July 8, 1864, that he did not wish to be "inflexibly committed to any single plan of restoration," and he expressed doubt whether the president or Congress had the necessary constitutional power to require emancipation. Then, in a puzzling sentence, he expressed satisfaction with the bill and implied that Southern states could choose either his plan or that of Congress in returning to the Union.

Perhaps one can best explain Lincoln's action as a gesture of political compromise. Neither plan seemed perfect, so as the time approached for a more comprehensive Reconstruction program, Lincoln indicated his willingness to work with Congress in developing a plan that was satisfactory to both of them and that would meet constitutional standards. Evidence suggests that, by the spring of 1865, when the fighting ended, Lincoln had moved closer to the position of Republican congressional leaders, especially in the protection of black rights. On April 11, he indicated that he would soon announce a new Reconstruction scheme, one that contained greater assurances of civil rights. In his last public speech, Lincoln endorsed suffrage for black veterans of the U.S. Army as well as other classes of African Americans. A few days later he lay dead, the victim of an assassin's bullet.

## Enter Andrew Johnson

The administration of Andrew Johnson has been clouded with controversy for well over a century. His defenders claim that he attempted to carry out Lincoln's compassionate Reconstruction program against the wishes of vindictive Radical Republicans bent on unconstitutionally imposing their policies on a prostrate South. Critics respond that Johnson invited most of his troubles and, lacking both a political base and political sense, turned his would-be allies into implacable enemies. Certainly, Johnson's story is a tragic one, ending in impeachment and near conviction, yet it is not a simple one. A strong defender of states' rights, he arbitrarily exercised enormous executive authority over the states; his crudely racist defense of white supremacy stimulated a huge reaction in Congress and helped lead to the passage, over his vetoes, of numerous civil rights laws, as well as to the adoption of the Fourteenth Amendment, which wrote sweeping civil rights protections into the Constitution. A Southerner, Johnson brought down on the South a disaster that was in many ways more humiliating than military defeat.

Johnson was not the first vice president to assume office on the death of an incumbent, so no one questioned his succession to the powers as well as the title of chief executive. Like Vice President John Tyler, Johnson had few links to the party that had nominated him; a former Democrat, former slaveowner, and a thoroughgoing racist, he had been chosen to share the ticket because of his aggressive opposition to secession and his relentless pursuit of rebels while serving as military governor of Tennessee. Republicans nominated Johnson because they thought he would attract War Democrats to the party and help set the stage for wooing some Southern whites after the war. He had none of the political ties to the majority leaders in Congress that had enabled Lincoln to govern so effectively; but, of course, they had never expected him to become president.

Nonetheless, no real opposition faced Johnson when he took over. Many Republicans were shocked when he showed up intoxicated at his inaugural as vice president and then used crude language in haranguing the Senate in his first speech. His crude racism bothered many Republicans as well. But Radical Republicans were willing to overlook these flaws because they initially saw him as a likely ally. His tough policies in Tennessee made him popular among hard-line Republicans bent on remaking the South. When Johnson entered the White House, the abolitionist wing of the party had not yet coalesced into a power within the party. Ironically, Johnson's policies and ineptitude played a significant role in strengthening the party's emerging radicals. After a few months of Johnson's policies, these Republicans were able to convince increasing numbers of their more conservative colleagues to support stronger federal protections for black civil rights and white Southern unionists. But, in the spring of 1865, the various Republican organs, including newspapers that would later be his bitterest critics, wished Johnson well, recognizing the difficult problems that confronted him and the nation.

At first, Johnson seemed to share the emerging consensus that Reconstruction would have to be a joint venture of all the branches of government working within the general outlines of what Congress perceived as minimal for a republican government. He kept the army in the South, permitted local courts to reopen, and encouraged the revival of local governments. A few Northern leaders, such as Senator Charles Sumner of Massachusetts, had begun arguing for programs to guarantee the freedmen basic rights equivalent to those of white citizens, including the right to vote. But with the war barely over, most Republicans had not moved very far along that line of thought. A majority took a flexible and pragmatic attitude, willing to give Johnson relatively wide discretion in that post-Appomattox summer, and waiting to see what the former Confederate states would do. As for civil rights, something would have to be done for the freedom, but no one in the North knew exactly what this something should be, or how it should be attained.

## Presidential Reconstruction

Johnson began his tenure, as Lincoln had, with Congress adjourned, and like Lincoln, he preferred not to call a special session so that he could retain a free hand in developing Reconstruction policy. Since the war had expanded the powers of the government, he felt confident that he had the authority to handle affairs without additional statutory power; no decisions such as calling up the militia or spending unappropriated funds faced the new president. Congress would meet in December, and its leaders assumed that Johnson would not implement any irrevocable policies until then. They would watch what Johnson did; if it worked, he would receive their cooperation, and if not, they remained free to develop their own policies. No one anticipated the extraordinary steps Johnson would take within weeks of assuming office.

In an amazing display of unilateral executive authority, he issued a presidential proclamation based on the war power on May 9, 1865, which recognized the state governments that had been set up under Lincoln's 10 percent plan. On May 29, he proclaimed an amnesty for all rebels who would swear future loyalty to the Union, with the exception of certain high-ranking Confederate officials who could, however, petition for a presidential pardon. That same day, he issued a second proclamation establishing a Reconstruction procedure for North Carolina, which also served as a model for the other states. A provisional governor, backed by the army, would arrange for a constitutional convention that would renounce slavery and establish a new state government. Elections would take place for all local and state officials, and since the convention did not have to grant any rights to the freedmen, only whites would vote or run for office. The general amnesty, as well as free use of the pardon, ensured that the prewar elites—the leaders of the rebellion!—would play a key role in the new state administrations. Johnson wanted Reconstruction completed before the Thirty-ninth Congress convened in December.

Only in the Emancipation Proclamation and the blockade had Lincoln ever approached such an astounding exercise of executive power, and, unlike Johnson's Reconstruction plan, both of these policies had substantial support in the Republican party when Lincoln implemented them. Moreover, the Emancipation Proclamation extended policies that Congress had developed in the First and Second Confiscation Acts. Throughout his administration, Lincoln had gone out of his way to avoid clashes with Congress, preferring to gain its support through political negotiation and skillful use of patronage. In some of his more controversial measures, such as the enlistment of black soldiers, Lincoln carefully developed public support so that Congress could ratify his plan. The diligent attention Lincoln expended on Congress won him the freedom of action he needed, because Congress trusted him.

Had Andrew Johnson been able to show congressmen that his plan would secure the goals they wanted, he might have won them over, but in the crucial area of civil rights, the president had nothing to show. He had required the rebellious states to ratify the Thirteenth Amendment, but although he secretly importuned provisional governors to allow blacks to vote or hold office, he did not insist. As a result, the new state governments excluded blacks from political life, a policy no longer acceptable in the North. Had the Southern states made even a minimal good faith effort in this area, such as allowing token suffrage, congressional Republicans might have viewed presidential Reconstruction with more favor. Instead, they saw only Southern intransigence, backed by a president sympathetic to Southern attitudes, who insisted that the federal government had no power to force the states to adopt such policies.

To add insult to injury, the "reconstructed" state governments sent delegations to Congress in December that included the former vice president of the Confederacy, two generals, and a host of other high-ranking former Confederate officers and civilian officials. Johnson had privately warned that only delegates who could take the ironclad oath should be selected, but when the Southern states ignored this advice, he had not insisted. The Republican majorities in the House and Senate refused to admit the Southern delegations and referred the matter to committee. Johnson later condemned this as a trick by the "Radicals" in Congress to embarrass him, but no one else saw it that way. If Congress had admitted the Southern representatives, it would have meant that the former rebel states had been accepted back into the Union. Reconstruction, therefore, would have been over before Congress, representing the will of the people, had any chance to evaluate the situation or join in developing policy.

## The Joint Committee on Reconstruction

To construct its policy, Congress established the Joint Committee on Reconstruction, composed of nine representatives and six senators. Only three members were Democrats, and the Republicans included seven men who would later be identified as Radicals, including Thaddeus Stevens of Pennsylvania, Roscoe Conkling of New York, and George Boutwell of Massachusetts. At least initially, the committee expressed its desire to cooperate with the president. When Johnson proved obstinate, the committee eventually became a sort of congressional cabinet that, in many ways, virtually directed the government of the United States.

The committee immediately indicated its concern over the enforcement of two existing federal statutes, the ironclad test oath of 1862 and the Freedmen's Bureau Act of 1865. It also expressed its disapproval of the various Southern constitutional clauses and laws known as Black Codes, as well as the behavior of federal officials, the army, and local civilian officers toward the ex-slaves. This agenda should have alerted Johnson that Congress wanted to pursue a Reconstruction policy far different from his own, but the president could not or would not see this. In the ensuing months, he insisted that Congress had no power to meddle in local affairs and that he retained sole responsibility for Reconstruction. As Johnson grew more intransigent, so did Congress, which had expected that Johnson, like other chief executives, would engage in political negotiations in order to develop common policies with broad popular support. Instead, Johnson consistently derailed this process, creating a political and constitutional crisis of the first order.

The committee's great strength over the next few years derived from three basic elements. First, it included a number of powerful Republican leaders of the Congress and had the cooperation of the others. Second, it enjoyed much popular support, representing (as Johnson did not) the Northern bitterness toward the South for causing the war, as well as widespread concern over the fate of the freedmen. Third, and perhaps most important, Congress, had emerged from the war greatly strengthened. It had reorganized its committee structure, making it more efficient in designing and passing legislation. Before, the war committee assignments had been seen as onerous, but now congressmen sought appointment to key committees, and the chairmen formed powerful ad hoc steering groups in both houses. Congress's greatly expanded investigative function gave committees and their members increased visibility, a fuller understanding of the workings of the executive agencies, and closer ties to local interest groups and businessmen concerned about government operations. During the war, a strong president had successfully worked in close harmony with Congress, but now a poorly educated, unsophisticated, psychologically insecure, and personally offensive chief executive with no political base and abysmal political skills forced the legislators to carry the full load of policy making. Johnson acted arbitrarily, and the power of the presidency was immense; but he failed to understand the governmental process, and he lacked the institutional strengths Congress had developed.

The treatment of the former slaves became the crux of the dispute between the executive and legislative branches. Johnson opposed Northern demands for civil rights legislation. He argued that the Constitution did not grant Congress the power to interfere with a state's internal policies, and he vigorously fought every effort by Congress to alleviate the plight of the freedmen. His stubbornness led the South to ignore demands for more equitable treatment of ex-slaves, which finally drove many moderates into the emerging Radical camp.

## Southern Intransigence

The Thirteenth Amendment had been ratified by the time the Thirty-ninth Congress met, but the condition of blacks remained desperate. Hundreds of thousands of former slaves, their homes destroyed and their former owners no longer obligated to care for them, wandered as refugees across the Southern landscape. The Freedmen's Bureau, created in March 1865 to provide temporary relief, had inadequate resources for the task, although local officers did their best to provide legal aid and economic assistance. Johnson did not make their burden any easier, for he opposed the bureau's "illegitimate" interference in local matters. The bureau, for example, had been directed to divide the confiscated estates and distribute the land to former slaves, but the president ordered all confiscations and redistributions stopped.

In addition, every one of the Southern states enacted Black Codes, which greatly resembled the prewar slave codes. If blacks could no longer be bound to the soil as slaves, severe vagrancy and labor provisions created a peonage system that had the same effect. Criminal statutes prescribed harsher punishments for blacks than for whites convicted of the same crimes. Other laws criminalized acts when committed by blacks that were not criminal when committed by whites. Several states imposed racial segregation in schools and public facilities and ringed blacks with a variety of restraints on their conduct. Technically, no longer chattels, blacks were still not free. The national publication of various Southern Black Codes in the fall and winter of 1865–1866 aroused immense resentment in the North, which now accepted the proposition that the Civil War had been fought not just to save the Union, but to end slavery. Vicious attacks on blacks and their white allies, including Union veterans of both races, by former Confederate soldiers horrified the North. The deaths of hundreds of thousands would have been in vain if, after this bloody war, blacks enjoyed only a marginally better status than they had as slaves.

The rising tide of Northern indignation finally compelled a reluctant Johnson to send Carl Schurz, a former Union general, to investigate racial conditions in the South. Schurz confirmed that through the Black Codes and other devices, white Southerners were recreating a hierarchical structure that now treated blacks, formerly the slaves of single owners, as the slaves of society. The president disliked Schurz's report, so he ignored it. Congress would not sit idly by, however, especially as reports began filtering in of countless suits by white Southerners, abetted by local bar, bench, and police officials, seeking to apply sections of the Black Codes against army and Freedmen's Bureau personnel for interference with blacks had been coerced or tricked into signing labor contracts. The president, instead of using the legal arms of the federal government to protect its agents, as Lincoln had done, curtailed their operations, undermining the already low morale of those who were assigned to help the freedmen.

Despite Johnson's gutting of the Bureau of Military Justice, the army was determined to protect its own men, the many black veterans returning to the South, and the former slaves whose freedom they had purchased at so high a price. Secretary of War Edwin Stanton had already ordered the special Freedmen's Bureau courts to accept the testimony of black witnesses. On January 12, 1866, General Ulysses S. Grant issued General Order 3, requiring army commanders to protect federal personnel from prosecution in local courts for lawful acts performed in the course of their duties; it also ordered the protection of white Unionists from suits for actions during the war against rebel forces. But the most daring part of Order 3 was its call for protection of "colored persons from prosecution . . . [for] offenses for which white persons are not prosecuted or punished in the same manner or degree." Grant's Order 3 openly defied the president, reminding him that the army at least, and by implication the nation, still had responsibilities to the former slaves. Much as Johnson might have wanted to dismiss Grant, he could not do so; the greatest hero of the Civil War enjoyed enormous popularity throughout the North, and the publication of the order only increased his influence.

## The Freedmen's Bureau Bills of 1866

In 1866, the unfolding scenario pitted Congress and the army, both seeking a constitutional process by which to establish and protect civil rights for the freedmen, against the president and the former Confederate states, determined to resist any change in race relations. Congress took a major step on February 19, when it expanded the Freedmen's Bureau, extended its life indefinitely, and placed protection of black civil rights under direct control of the army. Persons in the former rebel states accused of depriving blacks of their rights could be tried by military tribunals or Freedmen's Bureau courts.

The bill, introduced by the moderate Republican Senator Lyman Trumbull of Illinois, triggered an extensive debate in Congress. Democrats and some Republicans attacked it as totally unconstitutional, claiming that control of civil rights resided with the states and that Congress had neither explicit nor implied powers in this area. Moreover, in their view the provision for military trial of civilians violated the procedural guarantees of the Fifth and Sixth amendments, which required a grand jury indictment and a jury trial for all criminal prosecutions, except in the armed forces, and thus excluded military trials of civilians in peacetime. In response, Trumbull pointed to the second section of the Thirteenth Amendment, which gave Congress the power to enforce the ban on involuntary servitude and thus the authority to enforce civil rights in the states. Indeed, this was the view that Charles Sumner had advocated during the debate on the amendment. As for the Fifth Amendment question, since the current troubles in the South derived from the recent war, military trials remained legitimate until full civilian authority could be restored.

Trumbull's argument that Congress had implied powers under the Thirteenth Amendment gained wide acceptance, for many Northerners had come to understand that freedom meant more than the technical abolition of slavery; it required the enjoyment and protection of fundamental rights without which liberty remained but a hollow shell. His justification of the military trials, however, required his colleagues to abandon the fiction that the rebellious states had never left the Union and to assume that either the states had been reduced to little more than conquered territories (a view gaining acceptance among the Radicals) or that the rebellion still existed (also accepted by the Radicals).

Johnson vetoed the bill, not only on the grounds that military trials violated the Fifth Amendment, but that Congress had no power to legislate for the eleven states excluded from the Union. In fact, he implied that, without the presence of nearly a third of the states, Congress had no right to pass any legislation! Congress sustained the veto by just a few votes, giving Johnson an apparent victory, but it would be his last. In July, Congress passed another Freedmen's Bureau bill, practically identical to the earlier version, and this time Congress easily overrode the president's veto. From then on, Reconstruction policy was firmly under congressional control.

## The Civil Rights Act

On March 13, 1866, after extensive debate, Congress passed the Civil Rights Act of 1866. Few measures of the Reconstruction period represented so dramatically the shift in constitutional perceptions as this bill and the Fourteenth Amendment, to which it gave rise. Until then, the protection of individual rights had been considered a function of the states; afterward, it was increasingly seen as a responsibility of the national government. Civil rights included the whole gamut of a person's legal responsibilities, rights, and remedies, such as the ability to sue or be sued, to engage in a lawful trade, own and convey property, and be secure in one's life and property. In general, civil rights touched on all the various activities in which free persons engaged; until 1866, the states, while not obliged to enact positive laws guaranteeing these rights, had been expected to avoid imposing restraints on them. When impediments to the free exercise of such rights arose, the injured parties could seek redress only in state courts, which interpreted the laws in the light of local majoritarian sentiment or the limitations of state constitutions. Since the decision in *Barron v. Baltimore* (1833), the Supreme Court had refused to apply the Bill of Rights to the states.

Equality of rights was not a fully developed concept at this time. All the states had some restrictions on particular groups that were seen at the time as being incompetent to participate in the political process. These included women, minors, the mentally impaired, and convicted felons. In addition, most states had various restrictions on adult males who were aliens or members of racial minorities. Blacks had equal political rights in most of New England, and some political rights in a few other northern states. On the other hand, Indiana, Illinois, and Oregon barred their settlement. They could not testify against whites in some Northern states. Prewar constitutional theory had held that no federal remedy existed to interfere with the way the states treated such groups. After the war, however, Northern sentiment demanded that some action be taken to protect the freedmen, since the former slave states could not be trusted to treat them fairly. This, in turn, required involving the national government in areas previously beyond its accepted scope of power. Questions of citizenship, legal rights, duties and remedies, and the role of federal agencies moved to the top of the nation's constitutional agenda.

Everyone, North and South, recognized that the end of slavery required a readjustment of the status of black persons; the debate centered on what this new status would be and who would enforce it. The failure of presidential Reconstruction, under both Lincoln and Johnson, to provide for civil rights, as well as the obstructionist tactics of the Southern states, led inevitably to Congress's assuming the task. Few members of Congress argued for perfect equality between the races; they sought instead legal protection to permit blacks to live freely and to enjoy the minimal rights that would give meaning to their newly achieved freedom.

Initially, many Northerners assumed that the Thirteenth Amendment would be sufficient, for they believed that no middle ground existed between slavery and freedom; one could not be half free. Take away the legal supports of slavery, abolish the power of one group to enslave another, and the blacks would automatically take on the legal rights and status of free persons. The experience of the year following Appomattox had shown the fallacy of this reasoning. Black Codes and the discriminatory use of state law enforcement had made freedom for blacks, as General Oliver O. Howard told Congress, "a mere abstraction recognized technically, but utterly inoperative to secure them the exercise of the cardinal right of a freeman or citizen." Where law failed to repress blacks, white terrorists, like the Ku Klux Klan, stepped in, often with the aid of law enforcement officers. During Reconstruction, more than 12,000 blacks, and a much smaller number of whites, would be murdered by white terrorists.

The 1866 Civil Rights Act attempted to establish national standards and protection for the freedmen. First, it made all persons ("excluding Indians not taxed") citizens of the United States, thus directly overruling the *Dred Scott* decision. All citizens, regardless of color, possessed certain rights, including the rights "to make and enforce contracts, to sue, be parties, and give evidence, to inherit, purchase, lease, sell, hold, and convey real and personal property," and to enjoy the "full and equal benefit of all laws and proceedings for the security of persons and property, as is enjoyed by white citizens."

Congress did not pass the bill without considerable doubts, for it ran counter to the long tradition of state supremacy in this area. President Johnson immediately vetoed the bill, on the identical grounds that he had employed in the Freedmen's Bureau bill, but this time Congress easily overrode him. Nonetheless, enough doubts persisted in the minds of many congressmen, even the Radical Republicans, that Congress decided to incorporate the gist of the Civil Rights Act into a new constitutional amendment that would make explicit the power of Congress to legislate on behalf of African Americans.

## The Fourteenth Amendment

The Joint Committee on Reconstruction had reached the conclusion fairly early on that the national government would have to assume the responsibility for protecting the rights of the freedmen. But what would happen after the secessionist states had been readmitted into the Union? The Thirteenth Amendment prohibited the reestablishment of slavery, but the Southern states had already shown their intention, through the Black Codes, of keeping their former slaves in a markedly inferior status. Would the national government be able to protect the freedmen? Since many of those who voted for the Civil Rights Act had misgivings regarding congressional authority, the obvious remedy was a constitutional amendment directly addressing this problem. Work had begun on drafting such an amendment even before the civil rights bill had passed; Johnson's veto and its subsequent repassage intensified the committee's determination to anchor the program in the Constitution itself.

To understand the Fourteenth Amendment, one must first recognize that many Northerners had initially believed its goals could be accomplished through the Thirteenth Amendment, since they assumed that the end of slavery would automatically create full citizenship for the freedmen; other Northerners expected that even if former slaves were denied political rights—such as the right to vote—they would nevertheless have most of the same civil rights as whites, and that the postwar governments would protect their life, liberty, and property; when these assumptions collapsed, Northerners sought a more specific constitutional remedy. Further, the Fourteenth Amendment provided Congress's most explicit statement of its Reconstruction policy. The amendment defined precise areas in which the former Confederate states would have to revise their legal structures so that the ex-slaves could participate fully in the economic, political, and legal aspects of life. The president—by refusing to demand any changes in the South and by insisting that the national government had no power to legislate for the states—had ignored the near universal Northern sentiment in favor of protecting the former slaves. He had, however, raised enough doubts about the constitutional powers of Congress to act through legislation that his opponents sought to embody the popular will in the Constitution. Finally, the Fourteenth Amendment not only epitomized the shift in authority from the states to the national government, but became the constitutional basis for much federal legislation and litigation in future years, providing the access through which Congress and the courts would affect the daily lives and activities of Americans in every state.

Section I of the amendment granted citizenship to all persons born or naturalized in the United States and made them not only citizens of the nation, but also of the states in which they resided. This provision remedied the lack of a citizenship clause in the original Constitution and finally wrote an end to the debate that had begun with the Missouri Compromise and been intensified by Taney in *Dred Scott*. Now there could be no half-free status; those freed by the Thirteenth Amendment explicitly became citizens under the amendment. Section I also granted them full rights in a lengthy sentence that has had profound constitutional implications ever since: "No State shall make or enforce any law which shall abridge the privileges or immunities of citizens of the United States; nor shall any State deprive any person of life, liberty, or property without due process of law; nor deny to any person within its jurisdiction the equal protection of the laws." This section, written by Representative John A. Bingham of

Ohio, spoke directly to the constitutionality of the Civil Rights Act. The "privileges and immunities" phrase came directly from Article IV, Section 2 of the Constitution, which deals with interstate comity and, according to Bingham and Jacob Howard of Michigan, who presented the amendment in the Senate, would apply the guarantees of the Bill of Rights to the states as well as to the federal government. Although the Supreme Court initially rejected this view in the *Slaughterhouse Cases* (1873), the doctrine of "incorporation," based on the Due Process Clause, finally gained the Court's acceptance in the twentieth century.

There is little doubt that Section I was intended to protect the ex-slaves, although some historians have claimed that the Radical Republicans, already in league with big business, had designed it to protect private property from state regulation. Roscoe Conkling of New York, while arguing on behalf of a corporate client, made this claim before the Supreme Court in 1882. Because Conkling had been a member of the joint committee, his argument has been given far more credence than it has deserved. The records of the joint committee evidence no interest in the affairs of business, just an overriding concern with the fate of the freedmen. Moreover, the entire question of due process and its application to economic issues did not become a major constitutional issue until a quarter-century later, because neither big business nor the states had yet become embroiled in matters of corporate regulation.

The wording of the Due Process Clause, lifted from the Fifth Amendment, supports the view that the committee meant to apply it to people, while Bingham chose the word "person" (later interpreted by the Supreme Court to include corporations) rather than "citizen" to ensure that it applied to aliens, immigrants, and even Native Americans not living in Indian communities. In Congressional debate, representatives from California and Oregon complained that the amendment would protect Chinese aliens and make their American-born children citizens of both the United States and California and Oregon. Supporters of the amendment, most of whom had never seen an Asian and had little interest in the fate of Chinese immigrants on the West Coast, nevertheless agreed this would be a result of the amendment, but they refused to limit the amendment to just whites and blacks. Some Republicans, such as Sumner and Stevens, doubtless saw the universality of the amendment as a vindication of abolitionist doctrines on the equality of all people.

Whether the Equal Protection Clause was intended to abolish all legal distinctions between the races is questionable. Only a few of the Radical Republicans espoused full equality at the time; the majority, though they wanted to extend legal rights to blacks and other minorities, still harbored racial prejudice and had no desire to embrace the freedmen as their social equals. The House specifically amended the Civil Rights Act to prohibit its application to state segregation statutes, because its sponsors believed Congress lacked constitutional authority. Whether its backers intended the Equal Protection Clause to remedy this lack is impossible to determine; that it could be applied in such a manner now seems obvious, but for many years, the clause carried little constitutional weight. Justice Oliver Wendell Holmes, Jr., who rarely showed any interest in racial equality, once derided it as the last refuge of a lawyer with no other arguments to make.

Section 2 of the Fourteenth Amendment attempted to force the South to adopt black suffrage, while at the same time avoiding a fight in the North over that issue.

Before the war, slaves had been counted for representation under the three-fifths ratio. Thus, one ironic result of emancipation was that after the war the South would have more representation in Congress than before the war, because all of the former slaves were now free and would be counted fully in allocating congressional seats. What made this result even more ironic was that blacks still could not vote in the South. Thus, the defeated rebels would have an even greater voice in the postwar Congress and blacks would remain unheard.

Section 2 attempted to deal with this problem by declaring that if a state did not enfranchise all adult male citizens, the state would lose seats in Congress "in proportion which the number of such male citizens shall bear to the whole number of male citizens twenty-one years of age in such States." There is no mention of a specific right to vote in Section 2, because Republicans assumed that the Southern states would not want to lose representation in the House. They also naively believed that the South would feel bound by Section 1 to permit all male citizens over twenty-one to vote. Even as late as the spring of 1866, Congress failed to gauge the depth of Southern resistance to change.

But, the white-controlled South refused to enfranchise former slaves. This led Congress to send yet one more amendment to the states, the fifteenth, prohibiting discrimination in voting on the basis of "race, color, or previous condition of servitude."

Unfortunately, neither the Fourteenth nor the Fifteenth Amendments created a positive right to vote. Thus, if states could think of ways to disfranchise blacks, without using race as the reason, they would be within constitutional bounds. After Reconstruction, the Southern states would accomplish black disfranchisement with literacy tests; poll taxes; confusing ballots; difficult registration procedures; the refusal of officials to even register blacks; and, when necessary, extralegal violence, including lynching, that was ignored by state and local officials. Unfortunately, although Congress still retained the power to reduce a state's representation proportionate to its disenfranchisement of any group, Congress never had the will to do this either during or after Reconstruction.

Section 3 prohibited any persons from holding state or federal office, elective or appointive, who had once held office and then supported the rebellion—unless he was pardoned by a two-thirds vote in each house of Congress. In some ways a severe sanction, it applied only to those who had held office before the rebellion and then had violated their oath to uphold the Constitution by joining the Confederacy. Congress retained the pardon power for itself to prevent Andrew Johnson from continuing his wholesale forgiveness of the rebels and also as a bargaining chip to ensure Southern compliance with the second section.

Section 4 to some extent confirmed the obvious—the legitimacy of the public debt the United States incurred in putting down the insurrection. But its second part, invalidating the Confederate debt as well as any claim for value lost through emancipation, clearly reflected the congressional Reconstruction policy that those who had financially supported the Confederacy should not be reimbursed for their treason. The issue of restitution for freed slaves had troubled Congress since the Emancipation Proclamation, for the Fifth Amendment held that no one shall "be deprived of . . . property, without due process of law." Lincoln's power to free the slaves had been justified by the "adequacy of the Constitution," but fears remained that even if he legitimately had the authority to act, the Fifth Amendment still required compensation; this reasoning applied to the Thirteenth Amendment as well.

Section 5, the last section, gave Congress the authority to enforce the previous four sections by appropriate legislation. Within the next few years, this section would be the justification for the sweeping measures that Congress adopted in its efforts to rebuild the South. The proposed amendment passed Congress on June 13, 1866, and immediately became the focus of congressional Reconstruction.

## The Congressional Plan

By this time, Congress had actually assembled a fairly comprehensive program, consisting of the Thirteenth and Fourteenth Amendments, the Freedmen's Bureau, and the Habeas Corpus and Civil Rights Acts. Together, they attempted to provide immediate material care for the ex-slaves: to fix their status as legally equivalent to that of white citizens and to define and protect the rights that they now possessed as citizens; and they also provided federal mechanisms to ensure that Southern states lived up to their obligations and indicated the route by which the secessionist states could rejoin the Union. In June 1866, few in the North considered this a harsh program. Other than invalidating the Confederate debt, precluding claims for the lost value of slave property, and imposing a ban on some Southerners from holding office, it imposed no penalties on the South.

In fact, the desire to restore the Union as quickly as possible is fully evident in the report of the Joint Committee on Reconstruction, issued in June 1866. The tone of the report, even while documenting Southern intransigence and oppression of the freedmen, is moderate. The committee had introduced a bill in April making ratification of the Fourteenth Amendment the condition for readmission, and although never formally adopted, it clearly indicated that the committee saw this as the basic test for the Southern states. As a matter of fact, as soon as Tennessee, which had always had a large Unionist faction, ratified, Congress promptly readmitted it to the Union in July 1866.

The report is also noteworthy for its partial repudiation of presidential Reconstruction and its extensive elaboration of the constitutional status of the former Confederate states. The theory of "forfeited rights" or "dead states" struck a halfway position between the conservative position, that the states had never left the Union and retained all their rights, and the radical view of "state suicide," that the states had ceased to exist as recognizable legal entities. The report stated instead, that through their treason, the Southern states had forfeited their basic political rights as members of the Union and could now enjoy only those rights granted to them by Congress. The legislature, not the executive, had the primary responsibility for restoring them to the Union, since the Constitution delegated the state-making power entirely to Congress. While denying that the president could fix the terms of settlement, the report did not explicitly repudiate the state governments that had been set up under presidential proclamation, and allowed them the opportunity of bringing their states back into the Union through ratification of the Fourteenth Amendment.

The inherent theoretical inconsistency of the program is obvious. The states had forfeited all political rights and existed as states only at the sufferance of Congress,

yet they retained the most important political power available under the Constitution—
the ability to amend the basic document of government, the Constitution itself. In fact,
they could only regain their regular status in the Union by exercising this power. Beyond that, in order to meet the three-fourths requirement, some of these "dead" states
would have to ratify the amendment. The committee members no doubt recognized
this dilemma, but saw it as part of the larger constitutional confusion that had been
created by the Civil War, in which some states had attempted to dissolve the indissoluble. If the Southern states would ratify the Fourteenth Amendment, the North would
ignore the theoretical difficulties for the sake of peace. Considering the terms that vic-
tors in other nineteenth-century wars imposed on the losers, the committee proposal
was generous indeed; had the South been agreeable, it could have spared itself the tor-
ment that it then brought down upon itself.

But the other secessionist states refused to follow Tennessee's example and ratify
the Fourteenth Amendment; they thus signaled their intention to deny their former
slaves the rights and status that Congress and the North deemed essential. Andrew
Johnson urged them not to ratify, and Southern leaders gambled that the congressional
Republicans would not be able to garner support for a radical restructuring of their society. They anticipated that in the fall elections, Johnson and the moderates would gain
control of the Congress and the Southern states would then be readmitted under the
president's far more lenient terms.

Johnson, as usual, had misread the political situation. The president hoped to rally
moderate Republicans and Democrats behind his policy, and in August, his friends
staged a National Union Convention in Philadelphia, where former enemies in blue
and gray marched arm in arm down the aisle, supposedly representing the reconciliation Johnson offered. The Radicals (by now the term did apply to the more militant
wing of the Republican party) mounted their own campaign, capitalizing on Northern
distrust of Southern intentions, a distrust that was reinforced by several racial riots in
the South that fall. Johnson responded with a "swing around the circle," a speaking
tour in which he vilified his opponents in harsh and shrill language. The plan failed
totally; in the 1866 election, the Republicans captured both houses of Congress by wide
margins, 42 to 11 in the Senate, and 143 to 49 in the House of Representatives. They
now had more than the two-thirds majority necessary to override any presidential veto.

## Conclusion

The early efforts to reconstruct the Union failed badly for several reasons. First, the
government had no previous experience on which it could base its policy. Congress—
and a large majority in the North—insisted that some reconstruction take place, since
otherwise the freeing of millions of slaves would mean nothing. But Congress did share
some of Andrew Johnson's concerns over its constitutional power to prescribe for states
not in the Union. Whereas Congress tried to work out a legitimate vehicle to accomplish its goals, the president appeared determined to prevent any meaningful reconstruction at all. Once Congress had decided on the Fourteenth Amendment as the basic—and minimal—criterion for readmitting a state to the Union, Johnson had several
options from which to choose. Unfortunately, as we shall see, he set upon a course that

brought ruin on himself, seriously weakened the presidency, and ensured another century of racial oppression by the white majority in the South.

# For Further Reading

General overviews of the Reconstruction period include John Hope Franklin, *Reconstruction After the Civil War* (1961); Kenneth M. Stampp, *The Era of Reconstruction* (1964); James P. McPherson, *Ordeal by Fire: The Civil War and Reconstruction* (1982); and Eric Foner, *Reconstruction: America's Unfinished Revolution* (1988). A good collection of essays on a variety of Reconstruction issues is Eric Anderson and Alfred A. Moss, eds., *The Facts of Reconstruction* (1991).

Overviews of the constitutional issues in this period are dealt with in Harold M. Hyman and William M. Wiecek, *Equal Justice Under Law* (1978); and James G. Randall, *Constitutional Problems Under Lincoln* (1951). More specialized books include Philip Paludan, *The Presidency of Abraham Lincoln* (1994); Harold M. Hyman, *A More Perfect Union;* and Heman Belz, *A New Birth of Freedom.* See also William Wiecek, *The Guarantee Clause of the U.S. Constitution* (1972), explicating this rather obscure Clause that became the basis for much of congressional policy. In this respect, see also, David Donald, *Charles Sumner and the Rights of Man* (1970), for an analysis of a leading Republican's thoughts on civil rights and Reconstruction. Harold Hyman, *The Era of the Oath: Northern Loyalty Tests During the Civil War and Reconstruction* (1954) deals with the important legal issues of loyalty oaths. Michael Kent Curtis, *"No State Shall Abridge"* (1986), is a useful examination of the origins and goals of the Fourteenth Amendment.

Federal policy toward the freedmen during the war is covered in Benjamin Quarles, *The Negro in the Civil War* (1953); and Louis Gerteis, *From Contraband to Freedman: Federal Policy Toward Southern Blacks, 1861–1865* (1973). The army's problems are examined in James E. Sefton, *The United States Army and Reconstruction, 1865–1877* (1967). Other studies on the initial stages of Reconstruction include Willie Lee Rose, *Rehearsal for Reconstruction* (1964); La Wanda Cox, *Lincoln and Black Freedom* (1981); and the early chapters of Leon F. Litwack, *Been in the Storm So Long* (1979).

Lincoln's proposals are examined in Paludan's *The Presidency of Abraham Lincoln.* Peyton McCrary, *Abraham Lincoln and Reconstruction* (1978), looks at how the Lincoln plan fared in Louisiana. Claude G. Bowers, *The Tragic Era* (1929), epitomizes the older sympathetic view of Johnson besieged by vicious Radicals; while Eric McKitrick, *Andrew Johnson and Reconstruction* (1960), details the president's gross political incompetence; a view that is shared by John H. Cox and La Wanda Cox, *Politics, Principle, and Prejudice* (1963); and William R. Brock, *An American Crisis* (1963). Johnson's constitutional views, often ignored in the debate, are given serious attention in Albert Castel, *The Presidency of Andrew Johnson* (1979); and James E. Sefton, *Andrew Johnson and the Uses of Constitutional Power* (1980).

Congressional policy is sympathetically analyzed in Hans L. Trefousse, *The Radical Republicans* (1969); Herman Belz, *Reconstructing the Union* (1969); and Michael L. Benedict, *A Compromise of Principle: Congressional Republicans and Reconstruction* (1974). For the Freedmen's Bureau, see George R. Bentley, *A History of the Freedmen's Bureau* (1955); and William S. McFeely, *Yankee Stepfather: O. O. Howard and the Freedmen* (1980). Southern white intransigence is examined in Michael Perman, *Reunion Without Compromise* (1973).

On the original meaning of the Fourteenth Amendment, see Richard L. Aynes, "On Misreading John Bingham and the Fourteenth Amendment," 103 *Yale Law Journal* 57 (1993); on the legal and Constitutional history of Reconstruction, see a series of essays in Paul Finkelman, ed., "Symposium on the Law of Freedom," 70 *Chicago-Kent Law Review* 325–800; 865–1387 (1994, 1995).

Civil rights is the subject of Donald G. Nieman, *To Set the Law in Motion: The Freedmen's Bureau and the Legal Rights of Blacks, 1865–1868* (1979). For the Fourteenth Amendment, see Jacobus Ten Broeck, *Equal Under Law: Anti-Slavery Origins of the Fourteenth Amendment* (1965); Belz, *A New Birth of Freedom*; and Joseph B. James, *The Framing of the Fourteenth Amendment* (1956). Alexander M. Bickel, "The Original Understanding and the Segregation Decision," 69 *Harvard Law Review* 1 (1955), and Raoul Berger, *Government by Judiciary* (1977), argue for a limited interpretation of the amendment.

# 21

# *Reconstruction*

T HE CIVIL WAR confirmed the indivisibility of the Union, but at its end the former
Confederate states remained out of their normal relationship. Although Andrew Johnson had attempted to restore them with minimal conditions, congressional Republicans,
backed by an overwhelming popular majority in the North, insisted that the Southern
states provide meaningful guarantees for the civil rights of freedmen. Had the South
made at least a good faith effort in this area, it might have escaped the traumas of congressional Reconstruction. The old view of Radical Republicans hell-bent on imposing a vindictive settlement has been discredited by historians, as have other myths of
the 1865-1877 period, but the issues raised continue to warrant our attention.

## Governmental Deadlock

By separating the executive and legislative authority, the Framers had sought to erect
checks and balances to prevent the federal government from developing into a tyranny.
They had assumed, however, that the two branches would work in harmony, resolving
their differences for the common welfare of the nation, and from 1789 to 1865 the plan
had worked well enough. The overwhelming repudiation of President Johnson's policy in the 1866 election left the nation in the unprecedented position of having its chief
executive totally bereft of public or congressional support. In a parliamentary system

of government, in which the prime minister heads the legislative majority, such a loss of support would have led to resignation and replacement by a new leader. In the United States, however, the president remains in office even if his party and policies are rejected at the midterm election. Andrew Johnson thus had two full years left in his term, and during that time, the normal political interaction between the legislative and executive branches became terribly distorted.

Neither Congress nor the president was powerless. Johnson retained control of the executive agencies and their patronage, and political savvy and a skillful use of executive authority—both of which he lacked—would have allowed him to exercise enormous influence in shaping governmental policy. The Republicans, with their overwhelming mandate from the people, had the power to direct Reconstruction through legislation and the necessary majority in each house to override easily any presidential veto. And, of course, as its ultimate weapon, Congress could remove a president by impeachment and conviction. But the potential for stalemate existed, and so long as the president and Congress remained locked in conflict, the normal processes of government could not fail to be adversely affected.

For almost a century, the label "Radical" has been affixed by historians and common usage to the Republican congressional leadership of this era, yet these men appeared radical only in comparison to Johnson and his Democratic allies, because of their desire to secure civil rights for the ex-slaves. Johnson himself was radical in his own hostility toward blacks. Before the Civil War, Johnson was a slaveholding Democratic senator from Tennessee. In the 1860 presidential election, he voted for John C. Breckinridge, the Southern Democrat in a four-way contest. Throughout his political career, he had always supported slavery, and in 1860, he had voted for the adoption of a slave code for the federal territories. He personally believed blacks were inferior to whites and better off as slaves, and kept this position as late as 1865. During Reconstruction, he denounced congressional support for blacks as laws "to protect niggers."

Recent scholarship shows that the Republicans were hardly vindictive in their Reconstruction policies, nor did they seek revenge or attempt to subjugate the South to the needs of expanding Northern capitalism. Instead, we can now place them firmly within the nineteenth-century reform tradition. Their main goals were to protect the civil rights of former slaves and Southern Unionists. They wanted to secure black suffrage; substantial equality for former slaves; physical and political protection for former slaves, Southern Unionists, and Northerners who had moved to the South in the wake of the war; and a remaking of the South that would exclude former Confederates from public office.

Senator Charles Sumner and Representative Thaddeus Stevens, pilloried as the masterminds of "a tragedy," had long fought for the rights of blacks. Stevens had refused to sign the 1838 Pennsylvania constitution because it disenfranchised the state's black citizens, while Sumner had successfully led a fight in the 1850s to integrate the Boston school system. Their efforts to secure civil rights enjoyed support not only from former abolitionists, but also from a broad spectrum of moderate and conservative Republicans who believed that eliminating slavery without guaranteeing blacks their full rights as citizens would be a hollow victory.

Since in the normal course of events the Congress elected in November 1866 would not meet until December 1867, the Thirty-ninth Congress had made a special provision, before its adjournment, that the Fortieth Congress would meet in March 1867. Republican leaders would not allow Andrew Johnson to enjoy again sole control of the government for an extended period, as he had done following Lincoln's assassination. Aware of both Northern impatience and of how continuing ambiguity over Southern status would affect the nation's governance, Republicans now took firm control of Reconstruction policy. They recognized that the longer they allowed Southerners to resist and delay, the harder it would be to secure adequate safeguards for the freedmen. The war had been over for nearly two years, and the American people wanted an end to the national trauma. Congress responded with the Military Reconstruction Acts.

## The Military Reconstruction Acts

The first Military Reconstruction Act, passed on March 2, 1867, declared that no legal governments existed in ten states and created five military districts, each to be commanded by a general appointed by the president. Military commanders would have the discretion to suspend outright the governments created by Johnson, and in any event, civilian governments would be subordinate to the military. To remove itself from military rule, a state could follow the procedures outlined in Section 5 of the act: The people would call a constitutional convention; blacks would vote, but whites who had participated in the rebellion would remain largely disenfranchised; the convention would draft a constitution, which, after ratification by the people, would go to Congress; if Congress approved, and if the state also ratified the Fourteenth Amendment, then it would be allowed representation in Congress; military occupation would end as soon as the Fourteenth Amendment became part of the Constitution. A second act, passed three weeks later, spelled out the procedures in more detail, but did not change the general plan of Section 5.

Even at this date, when the allegedly vindictive Radicals controlled Congress, the simplicity and generosity of the congressional plan was apparent. States had to provide in their constitutions for black rights and agree to the nationalization of these rights through the Fourteenth Amendment. The only vindictive aspect, if it can be called that, is the disenfranchisement of whites who had rebelled, and even Johnson had imposed a similar sanction in his plan. Drastic as military occupation of a state might appear, Congress plainly intended it to be a temporary expedient, one that the states themselves could abolish in a relatively short time. Once readmitted to the Union, the rebel states would suffer no further penalties, nor would the traditional relations between these states and the federal government be altered, save for the nationalization of certain rights in the Fourteenth Amendment. Congress clearly wanted a Reconstruction that was short in duration, but that would assure civil rights for the freedmen. With that achieved, the war and its traumas would be left behind. The Military Reconstruction acts, wrote Ulysses Grant, are "a fitting end to all controversy."

Predictably, Johnson vetoed both measures, but when Congress immediately overrode him, he complied by appointing military commanders to the five districts. The army now had an unambiguous mandate, spelled out in law, "to protect all persons in their rights of person and property, to suppress insurrection, disorder, and violence, and to punish, or cause to be punished, all disturbers of the public peace and criminals," either through existing civil agencies or through military commissions or tribunals. The army at once set about enrolling blacks on the voter lists, and the ex-slaves enthusiastically grasped this symbol of their new status. In five states, the registered black voters outnumbered whites; in the other five, the numbers were about equal. Within the next few months, new Reconstruction governments took office in the capitals of all the old Confederate states.

## The New State Governments

The state administrations established in the wake of the Military Reconstruction acts differed most markedly from the Southern state governments previously organized under Johnson's authority. Most notable was the absence of the old white, conservative elites. Northern migrants, insultingly called carpetbaggers, local whites willing to cooperate condemned by former Confederates as scalawags, and the newly enfranchised blacks, all combined, under Republican tutelage, in an effort to build a new political coalition. Military officers sympathetic to congressional aims refused to enroll many whites, and a third bill, the Military Reconstruction Act of July 19, 1867, expanded the army's control of voter registration, with the clear goal of eliminating the prewar elites from power. But the presence of blacks in Southern politics and state governments attracted the most attention then and later. Inexperienced politically and socially, they quickly became objects of scorn among most Southern whites and those Northerners who opposed congressional policy.

Opponents of Reconstruction complained of the ignorance of black officeholders, falsely asserting most were illiterate. In fact, where the information is available, 962 of 1,163 black officeholders in the South were literate. This includes more than 600 who had professional occupations such as teacher, minister, lawyer, and physician. Indeed, the new black legislators compared favorably with many of the inexperienced (and often illiterate) whites, who were organized by the Jacksonians in the 1830s and who held minor public offices in the South. While most black voters were illiterate, they seem to have fully understood which political party, or which candidates, were most likely to represent their interests. In this sense they were much like the millions of immigrants who were soon to be herded to the polls by political bosses in New York, Boston, and other northern cities. As one black delegate to the South Carolina convention of 1868 declared: "I believe, my friends and fellow citizens, we are not prepared for this suffrage. But we can learn. Give a man tools and let him commence to use them, and in time he will learn a trade. So it is with voting."

A surprising number of former slaves did measure up to the challenge. Despite the absurd behavior of some, caricatured later in films such as *Birth of a Nation*, the overwhelming majority of black Reconstruction politicians were literate and worked earnestly at learning their new trade. In only a few instances did blacks enjoy a majority in the constitutional conventions; most had only small delegations—10 percent in Texas, 11 percent in North Carolina. In the ensuing state governments, only one black, P. B. S. Pinchback of Louisiana, ever served as governor—and then only for forty-three days in 1872. Two men, Hiram Revels and Blanche K. Bruce, both from

Mississippi, served in the U.S. Senate, and fourteen blacks served in the House of Representatives. Only in South Carolina did blacks ever comprise a majority in both houses of the state legislature at the same time, and then only for two years. The balance of power always remained in white hands.

That there were excesses and corruption cannot be denied; yet, in perspective, the negative aspects of Reconstruction governments were no worse than those of many other legislatures of the time. Indeed, no Southern administration could compare with the corrupt governments of New York City during the era of "Boss" Tweed or the scandal-ridden Grant administration, neither of which could be blamed on the former slaves. One need not go so far as some revisionist historians—who have portrayed carpetbaggers as simple pioneers who went South instead of West and scalawags as merely "Old Line" Whig Unionists who had always opposed secession—to admit that neither group deserves the opprobrium later heaped upon them. Many were indeed good men seeking opportunity, but they had their share of scoundrels. But many were also former Abolitionists, dedicated to social reform and continuing the struggle for meaningful black freedom. On balance, the state constitutions they drafted and the governments they helped to run compare favorably with those in other states at this time.

Aside from providing for black suffrage and civil rights, the new state constitutions paralleled many Northern documents, and in fact, they often borrowed heavily from them. Universal adult male suffrage, legislative apportionment according to population, more state officers chosen by election, and the revision of outdated tax and finance provisions had been long overdue. North Carolina finally abolished political restrictions on Jews, the last state to do so. State legislative action and new constitutional provisions of the Reconstruction era that benefited all Southerners, white and black, included the establishment of public schools, orphan asylums, hospitals, provision for relief of the poor and handicapped, and the building and repair of roads and bridges.

## Southern Resistance

Congressional Reconstruction met strenuous opposition. Whites organized in every Southern state to prevent blacks from participating in politics and government. Conditioned by the rhetoric of slavery, most whites could barely conceive of their former slaves as equal human beings, much less as citizens. Opposition often turned violent. The worst of the terrorist gangs, the white-sheeted Ku Klux Klan, rode the countryside harassing, brutalizing, and often murdering blacks—as well as whites who cooperated with the Reconstruction regimes. Since the local militias proved unable to contain the Klan, Congress passed three Enforcement Acts in 1870 and 1871. The first penalized anyone who interfered with another person's right to vote; the second provided for the surveillance of congressional elections by federal marshals and supervisors. The third, the Ku Klux Klan Act, outlawed conspiracy, disguise, and intimidation—all characteristic Klan activities—and authorized the president to suspend habeas corpus where necessary to suppress "armed combinations." In October 1871, Ulysses S. Grant, by then the president, singled out nine counties in South Carolina as an example and suspended habeas corpus there, enabling federal attorneys to prosecute hundreds of arrested Klansmen. The federal program played a major role in breaking the

Klan, but its outrages had already begun to subside, as conservative Southerners found other means to circumvent Reconstruction.

For all its good intentions, congressional Reconstruction ultimately failed. Had the federal government adopted its tough stance in May 1865 instead of in March 1867, the chances of success would certainly have been better. Defeated and demoralized by the war, Southerners might have accepted the dictates of their conquerors, as the Germans and Japanese did in 1945. But by the time Congress acted, Andrew Johnson had already subverted the goal of securing a truly reconstructed South by demonstrating that influential citizens, including the president of the United States, had no desire to interfere with the internal racial affairs of the Southern states. Indeed, Johnson's policies and pronouncements encouraged racist and violent resistance to the changes brought about by the war. Although the Republicans won by a large majority in 1866, a significant bloc of Northern whites, mainly Democrats but including some Republicans, opposed the Radical plan, and urged the South not to cooperate.

Johnson and his attorney general, Henry Stanbery, did all they could to thwart congressional policy. In his vetoes and other statements, the president denounced military Reconstruction as unconstitutional and despotic, while Stanbery sent out official opinions advising local federal agents and army officers to ignore the disenfranchisement provisions. Both men saw to it that their views received extensive coverage in friendly newspapers, some of which openly counseled obstruction or even violence to oppose Reconstruction. The succession of Reconstruction statutes not only indicated a hardening of congressional attitudes, but also tried to undo the damage caused by the executive. To take but one example, when Stanbery ruled that minor rebel officers did not come within congressionally imposed disenfranchisement, Congress—which had intended the provisions to be fully inclusive—had to pass another act in July 1867 to counter the attorney general's directives.

Congressional leaders had hoped to avoid excessive involvement in local affairs; they did not want, as the black leader Frederick Douglass noted, "to station a federal officer at every crossroad." They believed that while they could justify this course under a conquered territories doctrine, such measures ran counter to American traditions of local authority; there was also federal reluctance to interfere with local matters. As a result, aside from the army, which lacked sufficient personnel or expertise, the government had few local agents committed to congressional policy. At a maximum, it had 15,000 soldiers and 900 Freedmen's Bureau agents in the South, and they were confined primarily to the state capitals and some of the major cities and county seats. Even after the Military Reconstruction acts, with the creation of new state governments and the disenfranchisement of many rebels, whites retained control of local governments.

Congress remained wedded to the idea of restoring democratic government. The congressional plan of admitting blacks to the suffrage in order to alter the political scene might have worked, given sufficient time and a willingness on the part of Southern leaders. Instead, Southern leaders took their cue from President Johnson who shared their racist sentiments. They refused to cooperate, assuming that if they stalled long enough, the North would tire of the emotional and political drain on its energies and leave them alone. In the end, that strategy worked, even though Republican leaders persevered for a long time and did their best to overcome the obstructionists. For example, worried over the failure of the Fourteenth Amendment to provide specifically for black suffrage and fearful that after Reconstruction, Southern states would amend their constitutions to disenfranchise their former slaves, Congress proposed what eventually became the Fifteenth Amendment, prohibiting the denial of the vote to any person on account of "race, color, or previous condition of servitude."

## Restricting the Executive

Aside from constitutional questions, Reconstruction involved crucial political decisions as well. Assuming that the victorious North had the authority to impose conditions on the defeated South, what should they be? Even Andrew Johnson's plan required some minimal concessions, although far fewer and much less severe than those enacted by Congress. The election of 1866 clearly manifested popular support in the North for congressional policy, and had the White House been occupied by someone less politically obtuse and less racist, compromises could have been reached to protect civil rights without imposing military rule. Since Johnson would neither cooperate with Congress nor resign, Congress had to choose either to abandon its own program (an option it rightly refused to entertain in light of the popular mandate it enjoyed), to attempt to bypass the chief executive legislatively (by taking away much of his discretion and authority in Reconstruction matters), or to remove the president by impeachment and conviction, a route fraught with constitutional and political danger.

Republican leaders initially chose the second alternative, and the Fortieth Congress was unique in its attempt not only to fashion a major national policy, but also to provide for its implementation outside the normal procedures of presidential execution. The successive Military Reconstruction acts shifted authority from the president to army officers. A rider to the Military Appropriations act of 1867 required the commanding general of the army to be stationed in Washington, and all orders from the president to the army had to be funneled through him. Although Johnson retained an independent constitutional power to grant pardons, Congress repealed an earlier statutory authorization that allowed him to issue pardons by proclamation. This was a bill of dubious constitutionality, but it was a sure indicator of dissatisfaction with presidential policy. To prevent Johnson from discharging government officers sympathetic to congressional Reconstruction, Congress then passed the Tenure of Office Act in 1867. Under its terms, a president could not discharge any officer whose appointment had been confirmed by the Senate without that chamber's approval. If Congress were in recess, the president could suspend—but not dismiss—an officer and then report and seek approval of the suspension after Congress reconvened.

No other Congress has ever tried—or been forced—to pursue such a policy, yet Republican leaders attempted to preserve normal constitutional government as much as they could. They did not limit presidential authority in any area outside Reconstruction, and even there they did not set up an alternative presidency. Johnson had to act through the general of the army, but he still retained authority as well as enormous discretion in enforcing the laws. Congress expected him to carry out his constitutional obligations to faithfully execute the laws—and took special care to try to make him understand the spirit and purpose of those laws.

Johnson grew increasingly militant in the latter months of 1867, however. With Congress in recess, he suspended Secretary of War Edwin Stanton in August and also removed military commanders Philip Sheridan, John Pope, and Daniel Sickles, as well as their key subordinates, all of whom were rigorously enforcing legislative directives. In their place, Johnson appointed Winfield Scott Hancock, George Meade, and John Schofield—all Democrats before and after the war—who favored the lenient presidential policy. Johnson defused some of the public outcry by naming as Stanton's temporary replacement Ulysses Grant, who also retained his post as commanding general of the army. But then, in his annual message to Congress in December 1867, Johnson cast racial aspersions on the freedmen, again characterized the Reconstruction laws as unconstitutional and despotic, and indicated that he had considered disobeying them, even by forceful resistance.

When Johnson finally reported Stanton's suspension in December 1867, the Senate Military Affairs Committee recommended against accepting it. Like many West Point–trained army officers, Grant had great respect for the congressional committees, so despite his earlier promises to Johnson, he relinquished the secretaryship back to Stanton. Although Johnson later claimed that he had intended to pursue a court challenge to the constitutionality of the Tenure of Office Act, he failed to take this opportunity to do so. Instead, he secretly sought an alliance with General Philip Sheridan, by which Sheridan would take command of an unauthorized army department near Washington, whose troops would be directly responsible to Sheridan and to Johnson and outside the regular army chain of command. Sheridan rejected the scheme, refusing to be the president's tool in a plan that could beget only discord and possibly even violence; he took himself off to the relatively more tranquil Indian frontier. On February 21, 1868, Johnson ordered Stanton's removal again, this time naming General Lorenzo Thomas as interim secretary. Thomas had been the adjutant general of the U.S. Army from 1861 to 1863, until he was replaced because of his poor performance.

Johnson could not have been unaware of the dangers of this move. Whatever one may believe about the wisdom of the Tenure of Office Act, it had been duly passed by Congress—and then repassed by the requisite majorities over the president's veto. Johnson later claimed the law was unconstitutional, but he had in fact complied with it until the Senate failed to approve his firing of Stanton. If he really believed the law was unconstitutional, he might have attempted to challenge it in the Supreme Court, whose decision Congress would have accepted. But, careful planning or a lawyerly attack on a law was not the style of the pugnacious, poorly educated, recalcitrant president. Perhaps Johnson believed his defiance of the law would rally anti-Reconstruction forces behind him and thus sink the entire congressional program. In essence, Johnson claimed powers that would later be described as imperial in nature: the right to decide unilaterally which laws were constitutional or not, and which he would enforce or ignore. In doing so, he threatened the entire system of checks and balances, just as he had already seriously damaged the political machinery of government.

## Impeachment

Impeachment did not suddenly spring up as a result of Johnson's second removal of Stanton. Although congressional leaders had tried to work around the president, the impeachment option had been openly discussed for over a year. In January 1867, representatives James Ashley of Ohio and Benjamin Loan of Missouri had called for an investigation of Johnson's conduct to determine if it warranted impeachment. The House Judiciary Committee worked for ten months, looking into all aspects of the president's conduct of Reconstruction, and in November, it reported by a 5 to 4 vote in favor of impeachment, on the general grounds that the president had failed to carry out the laws. After intense debate, the full House voted later in the month against impeachment, 108 to 75, primarily because of the imprecision in the Constitution concerning the grounds for impeachment, as well as its total silence on related and important issues.

The Constitution mentions impeachment several times. Article I, Section 2 gives the House of Representatives "the sole Power of Impeachment." Section 3 provides that "the Senate shall have the sole Power to try all Impeachments," requires a two-thirds majority of those present to convict, and stipulates that when the president of the United States is tried, the chief justice of the United States will preside. The crucial clause is Article II, Section 4: "The President, Vice President and all Civil Officers of the United States, shall be removed from Office on Impeachment for, and Conviction of, Treason, Bribery, or other high Crimes and Misdemeanors."

The Constitution defines treason quite specifically (Article III, Section 3), and bribery had long been well known in law, but what did "other high Crimes and Misdemeanors" mean? Did the acts have to be criminal in nature, ones for which a person could be indicted? Or could they be civil, such as misfeasance or nonfeasance of a duty? (These questions had been raised, but never satisfactorily resolved, at the earlier impeachment of Samuel Chase.) Did the president's obstruction of constitutionally enacted legislation fall into this category? Did the chief justice merely preside at the trial, or did he have power, through rulings on procedure and evidence, to affect its course and outcome? What status did the president enjoy during the proceedings? Did he continue to exercise all the rights, privileges, and duties of office, and if not, who would take his place?

All these questions received intense scrutiny in 1867, but little, if any, consensus emerged on answers. There had been earlier, though infrequent, impeachments, both in England and America, but no president had ever stood trial, and none of the earlier cases had defined "high Crimes and Misdemeanors." As for the necessity of an indictable offense (the position taken by Johnson and later by Richard Nixon), the weight of authority led to the conclusion that the Framers had meant something other than a normal crime. Indeed, it was possible to argue that a president could be removed without a criminal offense, but that some criminal offenses might not merit impeachment.

John Pomeroy, a contemporary legal scholar, for example, after surveying the works of leading constitutional writers since 1787, suggested that impeachment was meant to serve less as a control against outright criminal behavior than as a political check against a president's abuse of his discretionary authority. In effect, impeachment was a political process that was implemented through a careful, constitutionally mandated process. The fact that the only punishment for conviction was removal from office and the possibility of being prohibited from holding any future office suggests that impeachment was intended to be used to deal with a political problem, or with a betrayal of a constitutional duty, rather than with an actual crime.

---

### IMPEACHABLE OFFENSES: CRIMINAL OR NOT?

Could the president be impeached for something other than a crime? One standard for impeachment is failure to execute the law or uphold the oath to "protect and defend" the Constitution. One example might illustrate this. If Canada invaded Maine, and took the state over, and the president did nothing to defend the nation, it is likely the president would be impeached, even though he had committed no crime. Similarly, imagine a president who had failed to pay a number of parking tickets before his election. He would have violated the law, but would probably not be subject to impeachment. By these standards, had Johnson committed an impeachable offense?

---

As to whether a president could continue to function during the trial, no one could find a definitive answer. If a vice president had been available in 1867, one might have stretched Article II, Section 1 to mean that a president on trial is unable to discharge the powers and duties of his office, which would then devolve upon the vice president. But under the original terms of the Constitution (later changed in the Twenty-fifth Amendment), this would have been a permanent rather than a temporary measure—an irreversible one even if the president were acquitted. In the absence of a vice president, the Succession Act called for the president pro tempore of the Senate to assume the duties. This would have been Benjamin Wade, whose unorthodox fiscal views and aggressive personality troubled many of his colleagues. The thought of Wade as president undoubtedly helped derail impeachment in 1867; more important, congressional leaders believed that the various Reconstruction bills had tied Andrew Johnson's hands sufficiently to thwart his further subversion of their policy. Combined with a general reluctance to take such an extreme constitutional remedy, most observers considered impeachment a dead issue by the end of 1867. Then Andrew Johnson flogged it back to life.

On February 24, 1868, three days after Johnson's second removal of Stanton, the House of Representatives, by a party vote of 128 to 47, impeached him. A special committee then drafted the articles of impeachment, and their poor composition and legalistic wording indicated the trouble that the committee had in answering the major constitutional questions. Of the eleven articles, the first three charged Johnson with violating the Tenure of Office Act by removing Secretary of War Stanton, and the next five accused him of conspiring with General Lorenzo Thomas, Stanton's replacement, to violate the law. Conspiracy to violate a federal law constituted an indictable offense, so the drafters felt they had firm grounds, at least in this area. The ninth article charged the president with issuing orders directly to General William H. Emory instead of through the commanding general, as required by the Military Appropriations Act. Article 10 charged Johnson with attempting to bring Congress "into disgrace, ridicule, hatred, contempt and reproach" by his attacks on that body in the 1866 campaign. Finally, the real reason for impeachment was stated in article 11, the "catchall" provision that not only summed up the previous charges, but accused Andrew Johnson of "unlawfully devising and contriving" to violate the Reconstruction acts, contrary to his duty to execute the laws faithfully.

Despite the rapidity of the House's action, there can be no doubt that congressional leaders arrived at this distasteful and drastic action reluctantly. They had tried to work with the president; when that had failed, they attempted to work around him. If they had known the full extent of his obstructionist tactics—such as the proposal to set up an unlawful army outside the regular command—they could have made the indictment even stronger. It is a measure of their frustration that they undertook this path when Johnson had little more than a year remaining in his term; until the last moment, they had hoped they could maneuver around him for those twelve months. (While he could have been elected in his own right in 1868, no one thought he had much of a chance.) On March 3, 1868, the full House gave its assent to the eleven articles and named seven managers for the Senate trial, including party moderates John A. Bingham and James Wilson and radicals Benjamin F. Butler, John A. Logan, and Thaddeus Stevens. The following day, the seven men appeared before the Senate, which organized itself into a court, and on March 5, Chief Justice Salmon P. Chase took the chair to preside over the trial of Andrew Johnson.

## The Senate Trial

Four factors saved Johnson from conviction: the incompetence of the House managers, the skill of his defense attorneys, the reluctance of a group of Republican moderates to take such a drastic step unless absolutely convinced of its justice and necessity, and the politics of the upcoming presidential election. Tied to this last factor was the personality of Johnson's successor if the president was removed from office.

If the Senate convicted Johnson, he would be replaced by the president pro-tempore of the Senate, Benjamin F. Wade of Ohio. Wade was an uncompromising Radical; he opposed Johnson's Reconstruction program, while favoring black equality and a thorough remaking of the South. He was a powerful spokesman for the Radicals and even the mainstream of his party, but at the same time he offended many moderate and conservative Republicans, and even a few Radicals. Chief Justice Chase, also an Ohioan, who presided over the impeachment, personally despised Wade. While commanding the respect and loyalty of a majority of the Republicans in the Senate, Wade also had a number of opponents within his party, who for political and personal reasons would rather have Johnson continue in office for another year than see Wade move into the White House. From the beginning, Congressman Thaddeus Stevens, the most important supporter of impeachment, predicted that Wade's enemies within his own party would in the end vote against impeachment to avoid elevating the Ohio senator to the presidency.

The poorly drawn articles of impeachment, with their emphasis on the allegedly indictable offense of violating the Tenure Act, proved difficult to sustain. Although the deliberate flouting of a constitutional statute might be grounds for impeachment, the Constitution gave little guidance on the president's power to remove appointees; it had been debated even in Washington's time, and other presidents, notably Andrew Jackson, had dismissed Senate-confirmed officials. Johnson's attorneys argued that the law did not apply to Stanton, since he had been appointed under Lincoln, and the statute clearly specified that cabinet members served only during the term of the president appointing them. The prosecution then made the ludicrous claim that Johnson was serving only as an acting president, filling out Lincoln's term of office. That issue had been resolved nearly three decades earlier, when John Tyler had succeeded William Henry Harrison; no one had raised the issue when Millard Fillmore had entered the White House on the death of Zachary Taylor, or when Johnson himself had taken office three years before. The bombast and browbeating of witnesses by the House managers also contrasted sharply with the polite, professional demeanor of the defense.

Johnson's lawyers, headed by Henry Stanbery (who had resigned as attorney general to represent the president), chose a strategy first of delay and then of emphasizing fine legal points. Instead of the week or two that Thaddeus Stevens had anticipated, the trial stretched on for over two months. Due to the lack of precedent, a number of procedural issues had to be ironed out first, and these took an inordinate amount of time. What rules, for example, would the Senate follow? Would it act as a regular court, bound by the rules of evidence and able to convict only upon clear proof of guilt of a specific crime known either to federal or common law? Or would it also sit as a political body, hearing whatever evidence it wanted and capable of convicting Johnson on what might be essentially political grounds? What would be the role of the chief justice? Would he have the full powers of a judge, with the Senate being little more than a jury bound by his rulings, or would the senators sit as associate justices, sharing the judicial authority with him?

The prosecution wanted to limit Chase, whom they correctly suspected of harboring aspirations for the Democratic presidential nomination, to the restricted role of a presiding officer, allowing the Senate to determine its own course of action. The defense sought to make the trial a strictly judicial affair, recognizing that it would be difficult for the House managers to make out any indictable offense under regular evidentiary rules. It took nearly three weeks to resolve these questions; in the end, the defense won most of what it sought. By a vote of 31 to 19, the Senate authorized the chief justice to settle all questions of law, evidence, and procedure, unless the Senate as a body overruled him. Although individual senators remained free to vote as their political views dictated, the trial itself would at least follow the general rules of law, which would make it that much harder for the prosecution to prove that political differences between the executive and legislative branches warranted a president's removal.

The House managers began giving their evidence at the end of March, and, as the trial unfolded, it became obvious that the two sides differed considerably in their interpretation of what the Tenure of Office Act meant. Johnson's defense team argued that the act was unconstitutional; Johnson, as president, had as much right as Congress to evaluate a law's validity, and he had intended all along to secure a definitive ruling from the Supreme Court. Given the absence of specific constitutional provisions, Johnson's interpretation of the removal power had at least as much legitimacy as that of Congress. However, his strict adherence to the law from the time it was passed until he replaced Stanton, suggests that this defense may have been contrived and not sincere. The prosecution responded that the Tenure Act had been intended to clarify constitutional vagueness and to settle the question once and for all. In this exchange, the president clearly appeared to be the more moderate of the parties; he did not claim the sole power of constitutional interpretation—which the prosecution implied Congress had—but only an authority equal to that of the legislature in this area. He stood ready to submit the question to the recognized final arbiter of such issues, the Supreme Court; but to do that, he had to disobey in order to create a test case, since the Court did not issue advisory opinions.

Because both sides implicitly believed that conviction required proof of an indictable offense, the trial never focused on the crucial question that had led to impeachment—the president's subversion of congressional policy. The defense refused to deal with political issues, claiming that they had no place in a court of law; aside from that, the Constitution did not provide impeachment as a tool to settle political differences. The House, and a majority of the Senate, wanted Johnson's removal because he had, in fact, subverted congressional Reconstruction in such a manner as to throw the usual system of checks and balances out of kilter. The Founding Fathers had designed a program of government for rational, moderate persons willing to abide by the rules; Johnson, and later Richard Nixon, showed how fragile that system could be when confronted by a president who played outside the rules.

An unreal atmosphere enveloped Washington during the trial. Johnson remained in the White House, carrying out the duties of president, though he did abstain from further interference with Reconstruction policy. Congress carried on its regular business during trial recesses, and Chief Justice Chase worked at the Supreme Court when not presiding in the Senate. The public watched, alternately amused and amazed by the proceedings. Initially, few people gave Johnson any chance of acquittal; the Republicans controlled far more than the two-thirds of the Senate necessary for conviction. But the defense's insistence that only an indictable offense would suffice—a point that was historically, politically, and legally unsound—began to have its effect. The failure—or fear—of the prosecution to admit openly that impeachment had resulted from the president's ill-advised policies played into the hands of the defense, and some of the moderates began to question whether Johnson's actions, most of which they thoroughly disapproved, warranted his conviction.

Furthermore, the reality of presidential politics began to set in. By the time of his trial, Johnson had less than a year to go in his term. He was hamstrung by a veto-proof Republican majority, and was politically crippled throughout most of the nation. Though Johnson was hated, there might be no compelling reason to remove him. Furthermore, a number of Republicans wanted their party to nominate the nation's greatest hero, General Ulysses S. Grant, for the 1868 presidential campaign. If Johnson were removed from office, then Benjamin F. Wade, who many in his own party disliked, might keep the office. Thus politics, which had so devastated Johnson, also saved his presidency.

On May 16, 1868, the Senate finally began balloting on the articles of impeachment. On the leadership's instructions, Chase called for a vote on Article 11 first, the catchall that summed up the entire indictment. Thirty-five senators voted guilty, nineteen not guilty, one vote shy of the required two-thirds. Seven Republicans—William Fessendon (Maine), Joseph Fowler (Tennessee), James W. Grimes (Iowa), John B. Henderson (Missouri), Edmund G. Ross (Kansas), Lyman Trumbull (Illinois), and Peter G. Van Winkle (West Virginia)—risked their political careers to vote with the Democrats for acquittal. The close vote, however, is misleading. Most scholars recognize that three or four other Republicans, all supporters of Grant for the presidency, were ready to vote to acquit *if* their votes were necessary. On May 26, the Senate, again by a vote of 35 to 19, failed to convict Johnson on articles 2 and 3. With that, the leadership threw in the towel, and the Senate adjourned as a tribunal. The first trial of a president on impeachment came sputtering to an end, one vote short of conviction.

# The Meaning of Acquittal

In attempting to evaluate the long-term impact of the trial, scholars have differed on several issues. Some have argued that Johnson's acquittal saved the presidency from becoming an inferior branch of government, one in which chief executives would be subject to removal for daring to cross political swords with Congress. The trial did shift the weight of political influence to the legislature for several decades; there would be no strong president, one able to exercise leadership in the manner of a Jackson or Lincoln, until the twentieth century. But this argument overlooks the fact that Johnson did more than just differ from Congress; he attempted to undermine the entire congressional Reconstruction program, arrogating the power to decide, by himself, the measures he would enforce as constitutional and those he would ignore. He moved completely outside the regular political process, and in doing so, he brought the constitutional system as near to destruction as had the war itself. Indeed, many scholars of the period argue that Johnson not only deserved impeachment, but conviction as well.

A second issue is the viability of the impeachment procedure. The failure of the Senate to convict has led some commentators to suggest that an eighteenth-century device is useless. Yet, the process did serve to prevent Johnson from any further obstruction of Reconstruction policies. We can only wonder if, had Congress had acted sooner, Reconstruction would have been different. However cumbersome the process, in 1868, Johnson's impeachment failed not because of the constitutional machinery, but because of the incompetence of those seeking to use it and the political goals of those Republicans who voted to acquit.

So Johnson won his battle, but Congress won the campaign. Sobered by the experience, the president kept his hands off Reconstruction for the remaining ten months of his term. Stanton resigned shortly after the trial, and Johnson named General John M. Schofield to take his place. Although he was unenthusiastic about congressional policy, as commander of the Virginia military district, Schofield had carried out the laws in a quiet and efficient manner. Whatever chances Johnson might have had for the Democratic nomination evaporated, and he left office in March 1869, a bitter, angry man.

But in a larger sense, Johnson won the war. His lengthy trial and acquittal helped sap the energy of the North for prosecuting a vigorous Reconstruction; in fact, some scholars believe that the movement peaked with congressional passage of the Fourteenth Amendment. The trial had brought constitutional government near the point of collapse, and for many in the North, that proved too high a price to pay. In June 1868, Congress voted that seven Southern states—all save Mississippi, Texas, and Virginia—had met conditions for readmission to the Union. Congress rescinded Georgia's admission, however, when its legislature expelled twenty-eight black members (on the grounds that the state constitution did not allow their eligibility) and seated several former Confederate leaders in their place. The military commander of the Georgia district then forced the assembly to reseat the African Americans, and Congress required Georgia to ratify the Fifteenth Amendment before finally allowing the state back into the Union in July 1870. By then, the other three states had been readmitted, also under the requirement of ratifying the amendment. Military Reconstruction, however, continued in parts of the South for several more years.

## Reconstruction in the Courts

Unable to thwart Reconstruction in the Congress, Democrats appealed to the courts to preserve what they considered the correct view of state autonomy from federal interference, the same view advocated by Andrew Johnson. If Johnson could only keep subverting the congressional plan, if Southern resistance would wear down Northern energy, and if the Supreme Court would invalidate these measures, then eventually the Democrats could get the country back on the proper path, with their political strength in the North augmented by the return of their traditional Southern allies.

Fears that the Court might in fact strike down their Reconstruction policy haunted the Republicans through most of the Johnson years. Whatever theories the Republicans had developed to justify their actions, the fact remained that the Court had never spoken authoritatively on the constitutional relationship between the victor and the vanquished. Unsure of the constitutional ground on which they trod, Republicans sought some way to shield their measures from Court reversal. In January 1868, the House passed a bill requiring a two-thirds vote of the Supreme Court to declare a law unconstitutional, but it died in the upper chamber. The Democrats, who in the past had often scorned the Court, now rushed to its defense. The *New York World* termed the Republican bill the "most dangerous assault that by any possibility can be made on the Court." So certain were the Democrats that a majority of the Court would strike down Reconstruction legislation that during Johnson's trial, Representative George Woodward of Pennsylvania introduced a bill to test the constitutionality of questionable congressional acts. The bill provided that whenever Congress overrode a presidential veto, the president could bring a fictitious case to the Court to test the issue involved. Woodward's bill, obviously designed to secure judicial review of Reconstruction, never had a chance in the Republican-controlled Congress. Inevitably, however, the major questions of Reconstruction eventually came before the nation's highest tribunal.

## *Ex Parte Milligan*

The Court's initial decisions in Reconstruction cases seemed to confirm Democratic hopes and Republican fears. In *Ex parte Milligan* (1866), the Court ruled that military tribunals could not operate in areas where the regular civil courts remained open and functioning. Lambden P. Milligan, an antiwar militant, had been sentenced to death by an army court in Indianapolis in 1863 for disloyal activities. Lincoln delayed his execution, but after the assassination, Johnson approved the sentence. Milligan's attorney petitioned the circuit court in Indianapolis for his release under the terms of the 1863 Habeas Corpus Act. Justice Davis differed with the district judge as to whether local federal courts had jurisdiction of appeals from a military tribunal. Technically only a procedural issue, it gave the Supreme Court, if it wished, the opportunity to rule on the broader substantive questions of congressional power in Reconstruction.

All the justices agreed that the military court had failed to live up to the terms of the 1863 act. While the president certainly had a right and a duty to suspend habeas corpus where the civil courts were closed, he could not do so where they remained open. The Constitution, declared Justice Davis, "is a law for rulers and people, equally in war and peace, and covers with the shield of its protection all classes of men, at all times, and under all circumstances." The justices divided, however, over who had the power to decide when a crisis justified the expediency of imposing martial law. Justice Davis, in a totally unwarranted dictum, noted that a military commission did not meet the constitutional description of a court created by Congress, and he doubted that Congress had the power to create such tribunals. This led four justices to enter a partial dissent, in which they claimed Congress did have the power to determine when military justice should be established in areas remote from the actual theater of war.

*Milligan* has been hailed as a landmark in constitutional protection of civil rights, and its language certainly allows the courts to interpose themselves between the citizenry on the one hand, and the Congress, the president, and the army on the other. There is little doubt that the Lincoln administration occasionally overreacted to threats of potential disorder and pro-Confederate activity in the Northern states. The arbitrary use of executive authority—often without congressional approval—can only be justified by the unique conditions surrounding the war. Davis, with the benefit of hindsight after the war, could claim it had been unnecessary for the government to react so strongly to disloyalty in the North. Lincoln, having to act in the midst of crisis, knew that Southern sympathizers had already provoked violence in several areas and had no assurances that it would not happen again. If the imposition of military law later seemed too strong a step, Lincoln's policy did work and forestalled civil disorder. Moreover, as in other areas, Lincoln scrupulously avoided going too far; he utilized martial law sparingly and never attempted to impose a permanent military regime. *Milligan* has provided a useful limit on the use of the military in civilian areas. However, when it mattered most, during the internment of Japanese-Americans during World War II, *Milligan* proved to be unhelpful. In *Hirabayashi v. United States* (1943) and *Korematsu v. United States* (1944) the Court easily distinguished between the trial of civilians by the military in *Milligan* and civilian authorities using the military to guard civilians. Although the facts were quite different, the Court in the Japanese Internment cases might have used *Milligan* for the theory that incarceration by the military, even under congressional authority, is unnecessary, as long as the civil courts are open to try people who actually commit crimes or make plans to do so. However, in the Japanese Internment cases, the Court seemed to have amnesia when it came to remembering the principles set out in *Milligan*.

In its own time, *Milligan* seemed to call into question the more urgent issue of congressional power over the South. Justice Davis later voiced his dismay at this reaction, since the Court diligently avoided saying a word about Reconstruction. Yet Secretary of War Stanton told the president that in view of *Milligan*, his department could not "determine what cases, if any, . . . can be acted upon by the military authority." Even normally acute constitutional scholars like Francis Lieber accused the Court of undermining congressional policy.

Lieber's complaint gained more force when shortly afterward, in *Cummings v. Missouri* (1867), the Court, by the narrowest of margins, struck down a state-imposed loyalty oath for teachers, and in *Ex parte Garland* (1867), struck down a congressional statute requiring attorneys practicing in federal courts to take the ironclad oath. In both cases, Justice Stephen Field found that these requirements violated the prohibitions against bills of attainder and ex post facto laws. *Cummings* represents a major expansion of the Supreme Court's power of judicial review, for only once before, in *Dodge v. Woolsey* (1854), had the Court accepted jurisdiction of a claim that a state constitution violated the federal Constitution. Field's decision also presaged the Court's later use of federal guarantees to nullify states' use of their police powers. Liberty, he declared, included the protections of life, liberty, and property mentioned in the Declaration of Independence, as well as those listed in the Bill of Rights—the first time that the Court had applied these rights to limit state action. Both Garland and Cummings had property rights in their professions, and Field expressed a growing concern among conservatives that such rights required judicial protection against legislative restrictions, a concern that would occupy American courts for the next fifty years.

## Testing Congressional Reconstruction Powers

These three Supreme Court decisions thoroughly alarmed Republicans, who feared that the Court would rule that Congress had no powers over the defeated Southern states; yet in two important cases, the Court studiously avoided questioning congressional authority. Less than a month after Congress passed the first Reconstruction acts in March 1867, the provisional governments of Mississippi and Georgia (the so-called Johnson governments) requested the Court to enjoin the enforcement of allegedly unconstitutional legislation. Even Attorney General Henry Stanbery, who along with Johnson believed the measures illegal, urged the Court to deny the Mississippi request. Stanbery, who had consulted with the president, left no doubt that he considered the Reconstruction laws scandalous, but since Congress had passed the bills over Johnson's veto, and in *Mississippi v. Johnson* (1867), he argued to the Court that the president "had but one duty in his estimation . . . and that was faithfully to carry out and execute the laws." The Court should refuse the state's petition because it named the president as defendant and sought to restrain his proper obligation to execute the laws enacted by Congress. Although derided by some critics as a mere technicality (one never names the president in a suit, but directs it at a subordinate official), Stanbery's argument in fact addressed the substantive issue of the proper relationships among the branches of government. Chase, speaking for a unanimous Court in *Mississippi v. Johnson,* adopted the attorney general's position fully.

Chase narrowed the case to a single question: could the Court restrain the president from enforcing an allegedly unconstitutional act? Following *Marbury v. Madison,* Chase distinguished between ministerial and executive duties. The former involved no discretion, since the law directed the president to perform certain acts in a particular fashion, and they could be enjoined by the Court if it had the proper jurisdiction. But the Reconstruction acts did provide the president with discretionary authority, and he needed to employ political judgment in carrying out the laws; such executive duties could not be enjoined. Chase went on to point out the absurdity of Mississippi's request. Even if the Court issued the injunction, it had no power to enforce it should the chief executive refuse to obey. And if he heeded the Court, this would bring him into direct conflict with the Congress, possibly leading to impeachment. Would the Court then have to issue another injunction, preventing the Senate from trying the case? The absurdity of this position, Chase concluded, should be manifest to all.

The Georgia suit, also seeking enjoinment of the Reconstruction acts, named not the president but Secretary of War Stanton, General of the Army Grant, and General John Pope, commander of the Third Military District. (With the Court's permission, Mississippi amended its pleading to bring suit against Stanton, and the Court heard the Mississippi and Georgia cases together.) Georgia claimed that Congress had no right to annihilate a state and its government, thus depriving its citizens of their legal and political rights. Although Stanbery did not object to the Court's hearing the case, he argued that it involved political questions that, as the Court had ruled in *Luther v. Borden* (1849) should be properly determined by the legislative branch.

The Court, speaking through Samuel Nelson in *Georgia v. Stanton* (1867), again agreed with the attorney general. Issues submitted to the courts must be "appropriate for the exercise of judicial power; the rights in danger . . . must be rights of persons or property, not merely political rights, which do not belong to the jurisdiction of a court, either in law or equity." Georgia had called for the Court to protect its political existence, and the state's reference to the loss of its property only indicated a problem resulting from the loss of political power. The Court dismissed the suit for lack of jurisdiction, though Nelson hinted that if Georgia brought a new suit based solely on the property issue, the Court might then consider the substantive questions of the Reconstruction laws.

## *McCardle* and *Yerger*

Although Democrats attacked the Court for cowardice in refusing to rule on the constitutionality of Reconstruction because of a narrow, technical issue, the unanimity of the justices, including those opposed to congressional policy, indicated that the Court considered both suits ill founded. But the narrow majority in *Milligan*, and Nelson's suggestion that a rephrased suit on deprivation of property might be within the Court's jurisdiction, left Republicans fearful and Democrats hopeful that the Court would soon accept a case in which it would strike down Reconstruction. Against this background arose the most sensational of the Reconstruction cases, *Ex parte McCardle*.

William H. McCardle had been arrested in November 1867 by General E. O. C. Ord for a series of inflammatory editorials he had published in his *Vicksburg* (Miss.) *Times,* urging resistance to Reconstruction. McCardle appealed his arrest under the revised Habeas Corpus Act of 1867, claiming that he had been illegally detained and that under the *Milligan* doctrine the military commission had no jurisdiction over him. Ironically, the law McCardle invoked had been passed as part of congressional Reconstruction for the benefit of freedmen, allowing them direct appeal to federal courts as a safeguard against state action. Lyman Trumbull, the bill's sponsor in the Senate, appeared for the War Department (Attorney General Stanbery refused to defend the case) and urged the Court to dismiss McCardle's plea because the law expressly exempted persons in military custody for military crimes.

The Court heard arguments in early March 1868. By then, Congress had repealed certain sections of the 1867 act to make it clear that suits such as McCardle's did not come within the Court's appellate jurisdiction, but Johnson had not yet acted on the bill. Despite objections from justices Grier and Field, the Court decided to postpone its decision until the fate of the repeal bill had been determined. Johnson vetoed it, but Congress overrode the veto, so the Court announced that it would hear new arguments on the jurisdictional issue at the next term. In April 1869, Chief Justice Chase finally handed down the Court's opinion. He conceded Congress's right to define the Court's appellate power, and Congress had plainly made a "positive exception" in this area. "Without jurisdiction," he noted, "the Court cannot proceed at all in any cause." Moreover, citing his own opinion in *Insurance Co. v. Ritchie* (1867), Chase concluded that judgment could not be rendered in a suit after repeal of the statute under which it arose. This was in fact consistent with other antebellum cases.

The standard interpretation long held that *Ex parte McCardle* was indicative of both the weakness of the Court and the overbearing power of the Radicals. Fearful that the Court would strike down military Reconstruction, the argument went, the Republicans took away the Court's jurisdiction over Reconstruction questions and the justices supinely acquiesced. Jeremiah Black, one of McCardle's attorneys, complained that "the court stood still to be ravished and did not even hallo while the thing was being done." The Radicals, mourned ex-Justice Benjamin Curtis, "conquered one President, and subdued the Supreme Court."

Recent scholarship, however, has suggested a different view. Congress possesses authority under Article III, Section 2, to determine the appellate jurisdiction of the Court. Whatever their private emotions about the case or the repeal law, the justices properly recognized that once Congress withdrew jurisdiction, they no longer had the power to decide the case. More important, the repeal act restricted only a minute portion of the Court's jurisdiction. As Chase noted, it affected only certain appeals arising under the 1867 statute. It would be an error, declared the chief justice, to assume "that the whole appellate power of the court in cases in *habeas corpus* is denied."

Two months after the Court handed down its decision in *McCardle,* Edward M. Yerger stabbed to death Major Joseph Crane, an army officer who was assigned to act as mayor of Jackson, Mississippi. At Yerger's trial before a military commission, numerous witnesses testified not only to the unprovoked nature of the assault, but also to Yerger's long history of mental instability and irrational outbursts of violence. His lawyers objected to the jurisdiction of the military commission, claiming that as a civilian, Yerger should be tried by a civilian court under Mississippi law, and then only after indictment by a grand jury. They unsuccessfully sought a writ of habeas corpus from the circuit court, and then appealed to the Supreme Court.

Yerger's lawyers picked up on Chase's suggestion in *McCardle* and argued that the Supreme Court's appellate jurisdiction over habeas corpus derived not from the 1867 act, but from the Judiciary Act of 1789. The 1867 law merely amended and augmented the Court's power, and consequently, the 1868 repeal did no more than reduce the Court's authority to the 1789 limits. For a unanimous Court in *Ex parte Yerger,* Chase adopted this argument and affirmed the Court's power to issue the writ. The chief justice went on to propound a broad interpretation of the constitutional privilege of habeas corpus and the Court's role in protecting that right, along with a narrow reading of the 1867 act and its repeal a year later. The Constitution, as well as prior statutes and decisions, supported an expansive view of habeas corpus jurisdiction, the denial of which would "greatly weaken the efficacy of the writ, deprive the citizen in many cases of its benefits, and seriously hinder the establishment of that uniformity in deciding upon questions of personal rights which can only be attained through appropriate jurisdiction."

Chase's wording, especially compared with the restrained opinions in earlier cases, clearly indicated his desire to reassert the Court's independence and power and cannot be squared with characterizations of the Court as helpless during the Reconstruction era. Rather, the justices recognized that the tangled emotional and constitutional issues of the time required discretion on their part; the consequences of Roger Taney's rushing in to settle the slavery question in *Dred Scott* remained fresh in their memory. Yet even when compared with later activist courts, the Chase Court does not appear timid; it expanded the power of judicial review, striking down ten congressional statutes (compared with only two in the previous seventy-six years). But in its decisions, the justices, often unanimously, followed correct jurisprudential reasoning, much to the distress of those who wanted to enlist the judiciary in the struggle against Reconstruction. When a case with proper jurisdiction came before them, however, they did not hesitate to rule against congressional policy.

## Texas v. White

The Court spoke indirectly on general Reconstruction policy in *Texas v. White* (1869). The United States had issued bonds to Texas as part of its settlement of the Mexican boundary dispute. During the Civil War, the Confederate government of Texas had sold the bonds still in the state treasury to the public to help defray the cost of the war. The new Reconstruction government of Texas now sued the subsequent bondholders, seeking to recover the bonds, claiming that the original sale had been void. Since most of the holders were, like White, citizens of other states, the suit came directly to the Supreme Court under its original jurisdiction of Article III, Section 2. The Court had to consider two questions: the jurisdictional issue of whether Texas was a state and therefore entitled to bring the suit, and the substantive matter of who controlled the bonds.

Chase, speaking for a six-man majority, devoted three-fourths of his opinion to the jurisdictional question, and in doing so, he gave the Court's only extended pronouncement on the constitutional relationship of the states to the national government during the Civil War. The chief justice explored the nature of a state at length; he described it as basically a political community, occupying a defined geographic area, administered by a government created under a written constitution, and governed by the consent of the governed. The United States, contrary to prewar Southern writings, constituted more than a mere artificial construct. In Chase's most memorable phrase: "The Constitution, in all its provisions, looks to an indestructible Union, composed of indestructible States." The secession of Texas had been void from the start, and all the acts of the Confederate state government, including the sale of the bonds, were similarly void (this answered the substantive question). But although Texas had never left the Union, its relationship to it had obviously changed during the war. Since its citizens had refused to recognize their obligations, "the rights of the State as a member and of her people as citizens of the Union were suspended." The national government had the obligation and the power, under the Guaranty Clause, of restoring the disrupted relationship.

Although Chase noted that nothing in the case required the Court to pronounce judgment on the Reconstruction laws, he made it clear that just as the federal government had the power to suppress the rebellion, it also had the authority to reestablish the Union. Quoting Taney in *Luther v. Borden*, Chase affirmed that the means chosen to implement the Guaranty Clause constituted a question of political judgment, and therefore resided entirely in the legislature. He properly avoided mentioning particular Reconstruction laws, since they had not been challenged here, but his opinion definitely supported Republican claims that Congress had the power to create and enforce Reconstruction.

Some critics have charged that the Court allowed Reconstruction to stand by default; while it never expressly approved of congressional policy, neither did it ever disapprove. Others have claimed that a majority of the justices privately opposed Reconstruction but kept quiet out of fear of reprisal. Yet in *Milligan*, the Test Oath cases, and *Yerger*, they proved willing to go against Congress when they believed the facts and the law warranted doing so. The refusal to accept jurisdiction did not reflect cowardice so much as longstanding rules governing which cases a court can or cannot accept. That these rules often dovetailed with concerns of judicial security or restraint may be just fortuitous, or may be evidence of judicial statesmanship.

## Changing the Size of the Court

One of the more curious episodes of the time was an attempt to reduce the size of the Court. Like the Federalists who passed the Judiciary Act of 1801, the Republicans had mixed motives. One was political. They wanted to prevent Johnson from appointing anyone to the Court, to preserve their Reconstruction policy, and to assure that the Court would support the monetary scheme that had partially financed the Civil War. But, as in 1801, Court efficiency was also on the table.

The tale began in July 1866, when Congress reduced the number of justices on the Supreme Court from ten to seven. For many years, historians considered this as one of the opening salvos in the Radical campaign against Andrew Johnson, yet tension between the branches played only a minor role in the plan.

In 1863, the federal judiciary had been reorganized, the circuit lines redrawn, and a tenth circuit as well as a tenth member of the Supreme Court, was added. Almost immediately, Congress expressed dissatisfaction with this last feature, complaining that the Court had become too large and unwieldy and that an even number of justices offered greater potential for deadlock than an odd number. By reducing the seats, the Republicans not only blocked Johnson's recent appointment of Henry Stanbery to replace John Catron, who had died in 1865, but also deprived Johnson of the opportunity to name men to the next two vacancies on the bench. But Chief Justice Chase reportedly favored the reduction in order to make the Court more efficient, and the debate over the bill hardly even mentioned Johnson. When the vote came, the bill passed easily, but not on party lines; Republicans and Democrats could be found on both sides of the issue. Moreover, although he consistently vetoed nearly all Reconstruction bills, Johnson quickly signed this measure into law; he adhered to the old Jefferson-Jackson distrust of the judiciary and happily approved the elimination of several judges.

The bill did not appear to have been a slap at the Court. At the time, the Court had approved all the wartime policies that had come before it for review, and although it had announced in April how it would rule in *Ex parte Milligan,* the decision did not come down until the following December. Only then did Congress learn that five justices opposed the use of military courts in areas where civilian tribunals still functioned. If anything, Congress and the country held the Supreme Court in high respect in the summer of 1866, and one must take the reasons given for the reduction bill at face value: its proponents' belief that it would increase the efficiency of the Court.

As it turned out, the number never dropped to seven. The plan called for not filling the next two vacancies that occurred, but only one seat fell empty; James M. Wayne, who had been appointed by Jackson in 1835, died in 1867, and the Court again faced the problem of having an even number of justices, eight. In early 1869, Congress decided to raise the number of members back to nine, and also to provide nine additional circuit court judges. The bill reached Johnson's desk on the day before he left office; and he promptly vetoed it, partly out of spite, but mostly out of traditional Democratic antipathy to anything that would expand the personnel or power of the judiciary. The Forty-first Congress reenacted the measure when it convened in December 1869, and with the resignation of the ailing Robert Grier under pressure from his colleagues, the new president, Ulysses S. Grant, had two appointments to make to the Supreme Court.

Grant initially named Edwin M. Stanton and Attorney General Ebenezer R. Hoar, but Stanton died in December 1869, only four days after his confirmation, and the Senate refused to approve Hoar. On February 7, 1870, Grant nominated Joseph P. Bradley, a prominent Republican railroad lawyer, and William Strong, a former justice of the Pennsylvania Supreme Court, both of whom quickly gained Senate confirmation. That same day, the Supreme Court struck down the Legal Tender Act in *Hepburn v. Griswold* (1870).

## The Legal Tender Cases

To finance the enormous costs of the Civil War, the United States had relied on taxation and borrowing; when these had proved inadequate, it had issued paper notes backed only by the credit of the United States. Salmon Chase had been the secretary of the treasury at the time, and like other Republican leaders, he opposed paper money in principle, but accepted it in practice. There had been several state and lower federal court challenges to the paper currency, and the issue had come to the Supreme Court in 1863 on appeal from New York's highest court in the case of *Roosevelt v. Meyer.* In that case, the justices, with only one dissent, had dismissed the suit for lack of jurisdiction. Under Section 25 of the Judiciary Act of 1789, the Court clearly had the power to hear this case, but it chose not to, probably because of the fear of what results an adverse decision might have in the midst of war. In 1868, however, with the war over, the eight-man tribunal accepted jurisdiction and heard arguments over the validity of paper money.

In February 1870, Chief Justice Chase, speaking for a majority of four in *Hepburn v. Griswold* (Grier had resigned before the decision, which he favored) ruled the Legal Tender Act unconstitutional as it applied to debts contracted before its passage. The decision evaded the major question of whether Congress had the power to issue paper notes as legitimate money, by restricting itself to whether the government could force people to accept the notes in payment of debts that had been contracted under condition that payment be made in specie. Such a law, Chase declared, violated the Due Process Clause of the Fifth Amendment, as well as the constitutional prohibition against impairment of contract. Although that clause (Article I, Section 10) applied explicitly only to the states, Chase maintained that its spirit bound the federal government as well.

Justice Samuel Miller, joined by Noah Swayne and David Davis, dissented strongly. He noted the precarious condition of the Union at the time of the act, and argued that Congress had both the constitutional power to provide for the nation's currency and the discretion to determine what form that currency could take. To limit that power because of its indirect effects on some private contracts seemed "too abstract and intangible" an argument to overrule the judgment of Congress. The young Oliver Wendell Holmes, Jr., then editor of the *American Law Review,* also attacked the spuriousness of the majority opinion, and, typically, went right to the heart of the matter. Did Congress have the power to make the government's notes legal tender? If No, then the notes would be worthless for debts contracted *after* as well as *before* passage of the law. If Yes, then they ought to be good for all debts.

In none of the other cases at this time did the justices divide along party lines as they did here. All three Republicans voted in favor of the government's power to issue its notes as legal tender, while the four Democrats (Chase had by now returned to the party of his youth) opposed it. But with Grant's two new appointments, both Republicans, it seemed clear that the decision could be reversed; it would happen only a

---

## THE IRONY OF THE LEGAL TENDER CASES

Chase's opinion in the Legal Tender cases is ironic. As secretary of the treasury he had devised the very program he now struck down. Moreover, when Lincoln appointed Chase to the Court, he did so in the belief that Chase would be "right" on two issues: emancipation and paper money. Lincoln was only half right. Chase, a lifelong abolitionist, always supported emancipation; but he voted against paper money in *Hepburn.*

year later, in the *Second Legal Tender Cases* (*Knox v. Lee* and *Parker v. Davis*) (1871). William Strong and Joseph Bradley joined with the three earlier dissenters, and Strong, following Miller's dissenting opinion, approved Congress's power to control the currency. Critics charged that Grant had "packed" the Court to secure the reversal, but the sequence of events makes it clear that the decision to enlarge the Court, as well as the choice of the two new appointees, were made before either Congress or Grant learned of the *Hepburn* decision. No doubt Grant knew that his appointees favored the Legal Tender Act, but no president can afford to name a justice to the Supreme Court on the basis of one issue, nor is there evidence that Grant did so.

## The End of Reconstruction

With the selection of Grant in 1868, the electorate showed its continued faith in the Republican party, but politicians recognized that the American people wanted an end to the Reconstruction nightmare. The agrarian leader Ignatius Donnelly wrote: "Not a single issue of the many which agitated us in the past remains alive today—slavery—Reconstruction—rebellion—impartial suffrage—have all perished as issues. Let us bury them and . . . reconstruct from the bottom upward." But by 1870, when Donnelly scribbled this note, the national consensus seemed more intent on burying dead issues than on building a new society.

To some observers, at least, it seemed that enough had been done. The three Reconstruction amendments had banished slavery and given the freedmen basic rights, including the vote. Military Reconstruction measures had forced Southern states to ratify the amendments and had pushed blacks into the midst of state politics. To combat the Klan and other terrorist groups, Congress had enacted the three Force Acts, which Grant vigorously applied. Additional measures, such as the Civil Rights acts, had provided further evidence of the national government's desire to make the former slaves equal citizens in the eyes of the law. With blacks granted freedom, citizenship, equal rights, and the vote, surely further progress could be left to the natural workings of the political process.

Some worries remained, however, especially over what the states would do once the last traces of federal control were removed. In June 1868, with Johnson now quiescent, Congress required the six states not yet readmitted to incorporate into their state constitutions clauses to the effect that the constitutions could never be amended to deprive any citizens of their right to vote. But Republican party leaders recognized that once fully restored, the states would be relatively free to follow whatever course they chose. And because the Republicans remained committed to federalism and states' rights despite their Reconstruction program, they expected a diminished role for the national government after the end of Reconstruction.

After the acquittal of Andrew Johnson, congressional policy aimed at restoring the Southern states to the Union as rapidly as possible, while attempting to preserve previous gains. Civil warfare, however, broke out in several Southern states, notably Louisiana and Arkansas, where Republicans and local white conservatives set up rival governments, and President Grant had to send in federal troops to restore order. The conservatives had the overwhelming support of whites in all Southern states, and as normal conditions returned, they captured control of state and local governments from the racially integrated Republican alliances. By 1875, the conservatives controlled all but three of the former Confederate states, South Carolina, Florida, and Louisiana. The impeachment trial had upset many moderate Republicans, who feared that the strain of Reconstruction might permanently subvert constitutional government, and when the Democrats gained control of the House of Representatives in the 1874 elections, Republican leaders recognized how far disaffection with their policies had spread.

## The Election of 1876

The disputed election of 1876 marked the end of Reconstruction. Although Grant wanted to run for a third term, the scandals that had plagued his administration, as well as the Panic of 1873, led party leaders to insist on respect for the two-term tradition. Republicans thus nominated the three-term governor of Ohio, and former Union general, Rutherford B. Hayes. "A third rate nonentity," according to Henry Adams, Hayes was nevertheless honest, morally committed to clean government, and generally supportive of Reconstruction policies. The Democrats, sensing victory, quickly rallied behind Governor Samuel J. Tilden of New York, who had won national fame for exposing and overthrowing the corrupt Tweed Ring in New York City. In the campaign, both parties expressed support for civil service reform and the restoration of full home rule in the South. The Republicans, however, waved the bloody shirt, reminding the electorate of how they had saved the Union and warning about the return of "rebel rule" in the South.

The initial returns indicated a Democratic victory, but contested returns in four states left Tilden one vote shy of the 185 electoral votes he needed. Republicans claimed nineteen disputed votes from Florida, South Carolina, and Louisiana, the three Southern states they still controlled, while the Democrats counterclaimed votes in Oregon, where they had clearly lost. It is still uncertain who would have won if there had been an honest election instead of the most corrupt one ever to disgrace our political history. Massive violence by white terrorists in the Deep South kept tens of thousands of blacks away from the polls, while outright stealing of ballots, and even ballot boxes, took place as well. One wag suggested, the Democrats stole the election first, and then the Republicans stole it back.

The fact remained, however, that no candidate had an undisputed electoral majority, and the Constitution had no provision for such an event. The Twelfth Amendment addressed the situation in which, after all the votes had been tallied, no candidate had the necessary majority; it did not answer the question of what to do with disputed returns. The existence of rival governments in South Carolina and Louisiana complicated the matter, as did the fact that the Democrats controlled the House of Representatives, while the Republicans retained a majority in the Senate.

On January 29, 1877, the two houses agreed to set up a special Electoral Commission of fifteen members, five from each house and five from the Supreme Court, each party having seven seats, with Justice David Davis of Illinois (who had the reputation of being nonpartisan) as the neutral member. Most observers believed that the panel would recommend Tilden, but the Illinois Democrats, failing to recognize that

Davis leaned toward their national party's nominee, joined with the Greenbackers in the state legislature to name Davis to the U.S. Senate. Davis happily accepted, grateful to be rid of the commission responsibility. The selection of the Republican Joseph Bradley to replace Davis as the fifth justice tipped the scales in favor of Hayes. By a straight party vote of 8 to 7, the panel gave all the disputed votes to Hayes. On March 2, after a bitter debate and the threat of a Democratic filibuster, the House of Representatives accepted the report and declared Hayes the winner, by a margin of 185 to 184 electoral votes.

The House decision resulted from the defection of prominent Democrats, supposedly because of a bargain struck at the Wormley House hotel in Washington on February 26, 1877. The Republicans promised to withdraw the remaining federal troops from Louisiana and South Carolina, letting the Republican governments there collapse. In addition, Hayes's friends agreed to provide additional federal monies for levees along the Mississippi River and for a Southern transcontinental railroad, as well as to appoint a white Southerner as postmaster general, the cabinet office that controlled vast amounts of federal patronage. In return, the Democrats pledged good-faith obedience to the Reconstruction amendments and agreed not to oppose the election of James A. Garfield of Ohio as the new Speaker of the House. Whatever the truth is about the so-called corrupt bargain, Hayes withdrew the last federal troops from the South within a month after taking office.

Tilden's greatest service to his nation may be that he did not fight the commission's decision, nor did he attack the procedure in the courts. Had he done so, he might easily have created a situation that would have deprived the country of a president for weeks or even months. Although the Republican majority on the Supreme Court might have approved the establishment of the commission and the acceptance of its report, five of the justices had served on the panel and presumably would have had to disqualify themselves from hearing the case; with Davis gone, only three justices would have been available to judge the suit. The Electoral Commission device certainly lacked constitutional sanction, and the refusal to investigate the corruption surrounding the disputed returns did not lend it much credence in the popular mind. Aware of all this, Tilden nonetheless accepted the results, and Hayes took office on March 4, 1877.

## Conclusion: The Legacy of Reconstruction

Reconstruction left a mixed legacy. On the one hand, the Republican-controlled Congress had a noble goal, the securing of full civil rights for former slaves in order to make them equal citizens of the Republic. The three Reconstruction amendments failed to achieve this purpose in the short run. White terrorism in the South wore down Republican energies, while narrow interpretations of the Supreme Court, starting in 1873, undermined the new constitutional amendments. But the three amendments would be there in the next century to provide the constitutional basis for what historians have called Second Reconstruction of the 1950s and 1960s. At that time, black Americans finally began to gain the rights and privileges of which they had so long been deprived.

On the other hand, for nearly 100 years the strategy of Andrew Johnson and his Southern allies triumphed, preventing the reconstruction of a South in which the old racial animosities might have been buried. The nation paid a high price for the failure of Reconstruction—a legacy of hate, lynchings, and injustice would plague the country in general, and the South in particular, for decades to come.

After fifteen years of Civil War and Reconstruction, a careful observer would have noted that although slavery had been abolished, relations between the states and the federal government did not appear to be that much different in 1877 than in 1860. There had been a burst of national authority and an expansion of presidential power, but the former had been abandoned by the Republicans because of their innate commitment to states' rights and federalism, while Andrew Johnson's incompetence had destroyed the latter. Despite various amendments and legislation, control of racial relationships remained firmly in local hands. At the centennial of American independence, one could still read the Federalist Papers and find in them an accurate description of the nation's government. Yet the United States stood poised on the edge of a great constitutional revolution, in which Americans struggled to adapt the Constitution to the needs of modern industrial life.

# For Further Reading

For an overview of Constitutional history in this period, see Harold M. Hyman and William M. Wiecek, *Equal Justice Under Law: Constitutional Developments, 1835–1875* (1982). On Reconstruction in general, see many of the works cited in the previous chapter. For Reconstruction in the Southern states, John Hope Franklin, *Reconstruction After the Civil War* (1961), is the classic statement repudiating the older view of black incompetence and corruption. See also Eric Foner, *Reconstruction: America's Unfinished Revolution* (1988), for a much more extensive history of the period. Leon Litwack, *"Been in the Storm So Long"* (1979), offers a fine social history of blacks during Reconstruction. Alfred A. Moss and Eric Anderson, *The Facts of Reconstruction* (1991), provides a collection of essays on various aspects of Reconstruction, including the constitutional and legal issues. A useful overview of race relations and law, which has a fine chapter on Reconstruction, is Donald Nieman, *Promises to Keep* (1991). Donald Nieman, ed., *African American Life in the Post Emancipation South, 1861–1900,* 12 vols. (1994), contains most of the important scholarly articles on race and Reconstruction published before 1993. On the Constitutional history of Reconstruction, see the older, but still very important, Harold M. Hyman, *A More Perfect Union: The Impact of the Civil War and Reconstruction on the Constitution* (1975).

See also William Gillette, *Retreat from Reconstruction, 1869–1879* (1979); Jack B. Scroggs, "Carpetbagger Constitutional Reform in the South Atlantic States, 1867–1868," 27 *Journal of Southern History* 475 (1961); and Joel Williamson, *After Slavery* (1965). Allen W. Trelease, *White Terror* (1971), covers the Klan and other Southern vigilante groups. On the suppression of the Klan, see Lou Falkner Williams, *The Great South Carolina Ku Klux Klan Trials, 1871–1872* (1996).

Black officeholding is covered in numerous biographical studies of individual blacks. A fine composite study, Eric Foner, *Freedom's Lawmakers: A Directory of Black Officerholders During Reconstruction* (1996) provides valuable information on the skills and background of black officeholders.

A good introduction to Johnson is Eric McKitrick, *Andrew Johnson and Reconstruction* (1960). Impeachment in general is discussed in Emily Van Tassel and Paul Finkelman, *Impeachable Offenses: A Documentary History from 1789 to the Present* (1999), which provides discussion and articles of impeachment for all impeachment cases at the national level. See also Raoul Berger, *Impeachment: The Constitutional Problem* (1973), which argues that the Framers intended a broad definition of "high crimes and misdemeanors" to allow the legislature to punish political crimes that would be unreachable under common law. In contrast, Peter Charles Hoffer and N. E. H. Hull, *Impeachment in America, 1635–1805* (1984), argue that Americans rejected the broader English view, under which almost any cause could be grounds for impeachment, and adopted as narrow a scope for the process as possible. For the Johnson case, see Michael Les Benedict, *The Impeachment and Trial of Andrew Johnson* (1973), which acknowledges the difficulties between Congress and the executive, but suggests that the Stanton dismissal was the wrong issue; and Hans L. Trefousse, *Impeachment of a President: Andrew Johnson, the Blacks, and Reconstruction* (1975), which emphasizes Johnson's racism, but concedes the success of his strategy to defeat both his removal and congressional Reconstruction.

The Court's role is massively and painstakingly detailed in Charles Fairman, *Reconstruction and Reunion, 1864–1888: Part One* (1971), the sixth volume of the Holmes Devise. Fairman emphasizes the conservative nature of the Civil War amendments and does not believe their framers intended to do all that much about civil rights. Howard Jay Graham, *Everyman's Constitution: Historical Essays on the Fourteenth Amendment, the "Conspiracy Theory," and the Constitution* (1968), makes a persuasive case that the framers did intend to have the Fourteenth Amendment apply the Bill of Rights to the states in order to protect the freedmen's liberties. On the meaning of the Fourteenth Amendment, see Richard L. Aynes, "On Misreading John Bingham and the Fourteenth Amendment," 103 *Yale Law Journal* 57 (1993); and for an important critique of the work of Charles Fairman, see Richard L. Aynes, "Felix Frankfurter, Charles Fairman, and the Fourteenth Amendment," 70 *Chicago-Kent Law Review* 1197 (1995). On Chase's jurisprudence in this period, see Harold M. Hyman, *The Reconstruction Justice of Salmon P. Chase: In re Turner and Texas v. White* (1997). In the *Turner* case, Chase vigorously enforced and expanded the scope of the Thirteenth Amendment.

Stanley I. Kutler, *Judicial Power and Reconstruction Politics* (1968), shows that a strong, independent Court enlarged its power, and repudiates the older notion, popularized by Charles Warren, that the Court was a gutless victim of Radical Republicans. Robert J. Kaczorowski, *The Politics of Judicial Interpretation: Federal Courts, the Department of Justice, and Civil Rights, 1866–1876* (1985), also sees the Court and Congress allied in a surge of nationalism. For specific studies, see David M. Silver, *Lincoln's Supreme Court* (1956), and William Wiecek, "The Great Writ and Reconstruction: The Habeas Corpus Act of 1867," 36 *Journal of Southern History* 530 (1970).

On the process of amending the Constitution during Reconstruction, see David E. Kyvig, *Explicit and Authentic Acts: Amending the U.S. Constitution, 1776–1995* (1996), and essays by Richard Aynes and Donald Nieman, in David E. Kyvig, ed., *Unintended Consequences of Constitutional Amendment* (2000).

For the end of Reconstruction, see C. Vann Woodward's classic *Reunion and Reaction: The Compromise of 1877 and the End of Reconstruction* (1951), although some of its conclusions have been challenged in recent works, such as Keith Polakoff, *The Politics of Inertia: The Election of 1876 and the End of Reconstruction* (1973).

# 22

# The Court and Civil Rights

*The Abandonment of the Freedmen • The Civil Rights Cases •
Jim Crow Enthroned • The Treatment of Native Americans •
The Chinese Cases • The Insular Cases • The Incorporation
Theory • Women and the Law • The Court Draws Limits •
The Peonage Cases • A Few Small Steps • Conclusion • For
Further Reading*

FREEDOM HAD BEEN the driving force of American law in the first half of the nineteenth century, leading up to the fight to end slavery and the Civil War. However, the meaning of that freedom was often contested. For Southern whites, for example, "freedom" implied the right to own slaves; for African Americans and their white allies, freedom meant an end to bondage. After that great outpouring of energy and creativity to end slavery, the latter decades of the century marked a withdrawal, a time of consolidation rather than advance, and in some areas retreat. The Republican Congresses of the war and Reconstruction era had attempted to write some statutory as well as constitutional safeguards to protect the former slaves, but the Supreme Court nullified nearly all this work. The greatest impact of the Civil Rights Acts and the Fourteenth and Fifteenth Amendments would come nearly a century later in the civil rights struggles of the 1960s.

The Court also seemingly had little interest in expanding the protection of constitutional safeguards over other minorities as well, and in general acquiesced in congressional and presidential initiatives as well as state laws discriminating against Native Americans, Asians, and peoples living in the territories won in the Spanish-American War, as well as against Mormons. After some mid-century reforms, women found little that could be considered hopeful after the war. The suffrage drive had been shunted aside to focus all available energy on abolition and the drive for racial equality, and the effort to secure the vote would not be successfully revivified until the early twentieth century. Both at the state level and in the Supreme Court, judges interpreted the law to reflect the dominant social view that women had few rights and ought to be kept confined in their proper domestic sphere.

The few hopeful signs could be found only when bigotry pushed too far, but even then, the Court reacted slowly and cautiously. In terms of legal and constitutional agendas, the protection of minority rights did not place high on the list. The great drive to end slavery seemed to have consumed all the available energy in that area, and the nation wanted to move on to other things. The Court, which had always protected slavery before the war, helped lead the nation away from civil rights afterward.

## The Abandonment of the Freedmen

Most lawyers, teachers, and law writers of the latter nineteenth century gave little thought to rights other than property. They believed firmly in a federal system with state governments as the chief protectors of individual liberties. The Civil War and Reconstruction had given the national government enormous power vis-à-vis the states, but Republicans as well as Democrats saw that as a temporary aberration from the normal constitutional structure. While the Southern states would no longer be able to use the cry of "internal improvements" to block federal support of industrial expansion, for the most part the end of Reconstruction meant a return to the old relationship between states and national governments. This fit in perfectly with classic legal thought, but it carried a high price—the abandonment of the freed slaves to the prejudices of their former owners.

Prior to the Civil War, the inferior status of slaves and Southern free blacks had obviated the need for any formal laws segregating them from white people. Both races could work side by side, so long as the slave recognized that his or her place remained subordinate. In the cities, where most free blacks lived, rudimentary forms of segregation existed before the war, but no uniform pattern of separation; segregation rarely had the force of law, and enforcement varied. Moreover, every city had a demimonde in which the two races mixed freely. Free blacks in some parts of the North labored under harsher restrictions and often found a more formal and unyielding segregation than in the South. But, segregated facilities and opportunities were better than none at all. Thus, most Southern states prohibited blacks, free or slave, from attending schools, while in the North many towns and cities provided public education for blacks, but only in segregated schools.

One might have expected the Southern states to create immediately some system to segregate the races, but this did not happen. Instead, the confusion of Reconstruction led to a number of patterns, any one of which might have emerged as dominant in the end. In some states, the new Black Codes established fairly rigid separation in certain areas; Texas, for example, required that passenger trains carry one car in which all freedmen had to sit. Segregation in Southern schools seemed fairly widespread, although New Orleans had fully integrated public schools until 1877. In North Carolina, blacks sat on juries with little protest from whites, and shortly after the Civil War, the *Raleigh Standard* complained that "the two races now eat together, work together, visit and hold debating societies together." The Reconstruction Act of March 1867 encouraged freedmen in all parts of the South to protest, often successfully, against the incipient Jim Crow rules, and following the Civil Rights Act of 1875, blacks could be found riding railroad and steamer lines beside whites.

Inconsistent segregation practices dominated the North and South well into the 1880s. One white proponent of civil rights noted that in Virginia in 1885, blacks "may ride exactly as white people do and in the same cars." That same year, a black man took trains from Boston to South Carolina with the intent of discovering if any restrictions existed; although he was ready to find the worst, he admitted at the end of his journey that he had been treated far better in the South than in the North. Yet one must also note evidence of racial violence in the South, especially lynching, which reached an all-time high in the 1880s and early 1890s.

But if legally established and enforced segregation did not emerge immediately after the war, the evidence points to a widespread de facto separation of the races. There is a great deal of scholarly debate both over the extent of this de facto segregation, and also as to whether blacks as well as whites wanted separation. Howard Rabinowitz has suggested that the real option for blacks vis-à-vis public institutions such as schools and transportation in the 1870s and 1880s was not between segregation and integration (which occurred rarely), but between segregated facilities and total exclusion. Having a black school or a black railroad car would be preferable to having no school or no means of public transportation.

The proponents of overt segregation began to get the upper hand in the 1880s and early 1890s, when one Southern state after another adopted Jim Crow regulations that eventually reached into all aspects of life. Initially, segregation laws applied only to schools, passenger trains, steamboats, and other forms of transportation, though some states did not enact these restrictions until the turn of the century. By then, however, not only had Northern liberals abandoned Southern blacks, but the Supreme Court had given the segregation process a green light through its rulings in several civil rights cases.

## The Civil Rights Cases

In the last of the great Reconstruction statutes, the Civil Rights Act of 1875, the Republican majority in Congress tried to secure by law some semblance of racial equality that could be protected by the government and the courts. It is doubtful that the country as a whole endorsed this idea, for most white Americans, Northern and Southern, believed in white supremacy. Secretary of the Navy Gideon Welles captured the prevailing sentiment when he wrote: "Thank God slavery is abolished, but the Negro is not, and never can be the equal of the White. He is of an inferior race and must always remain so." No one, therefore, expected that civil rights legislation would change white attitudes or compensate for what many took as the natural inferiority of blacks; rather, the law aimed to protect the freedmen from deprivation of the minimal rights of citizenship.

A crucial feature of the law was a prohibition of racial discrimination in public places, what would later be called "public accommodations," which rested on Section 5 of the Fourteenth Amendment. Five cases testing the application of this section arose in both the North and the South, and the Court combined them for a single hearing in *The Civil Rights Cases* (1883). The government argued that the Thirteenth Amendment had not only abolished slavery, but had conferred all the rights of free citizens on the former slaves, while the Fourteenth Amendment had given Congress the power to legislate in order to protect those rights.

In his opinion for the Court, Justice Joseph Bradley denied both of the government's contentions and in doing so, robbed the amendments of much of their meaning. Bradley stood on fairly firm ground when he claimed that not every example of discrimination against blacks could be interpreted as a renewal of slavery, and therefore that the Thirteenth Amendment could not be invoked as a ban on all forms of racial prejudice.

Although the Fourteenth Amendment, on the other hand, had been drafted specifically to ensure freedmen's rights, Bradley decided to deny that Congress had any affirmative powers under the amendment. According to him, Congress could act only in a remedial manner; that is, if a state enacted a law that restricted black rights, Congress could act to correct the injustice. In the absence of positive state action, Congress could not initiate legislation in this area. Bradley also indicated that if a state failed to act itself, but by inaction tolerated private discrimination—such as exclusion from hotels, restaurants, and clubs—Congress could still not legislate. This essentially put so-called private discrimination beyond the reach of legislation. By this decision, the Court in one stroke severely restricted congressional power under the Fourteenth Amendment to protect the freedmen and left their fate to the states and the courts.

Justice John Marshall Harlan entered a lone dissent, pointing out correctly that the Court had deprived the Fourteenth Amendment of most of its meaning. He also noted the inherent bias in the Court's judgment, since before the war the Court had accorded Congress comparable powers in upholding the various fugitive slave laws. But although he wrote in dissent, Harlan sketched out a theory of "state action" that would become the basis of civil rights jurisprudence six decades later. He utilized the idea of "affected with a public interest," which the Court had expressed in *Munn v. Illinois* (1877), and argued that facilities such as railroads, hotels, restaurants, and theaters filled a public function, which is why they had long been regulated. If such businesses discriminated, then they did so with the consent of the state; this constituted state action, and could be reached under the Fourteenth Amendment, even using Bradley's limited view of Section 5 power.

The Civil Rights Cases effectively barred Congress both from taking affirmative steps against racial discrimination and legislating against private discrimination. But what if the states took positive steps to impose racial segregation? Theoretically, Congress still had the power to reach this type of state action; but if Congress did not choose to act, would the courts find a violation of the Fourteenth Amendment?

## Jim Crow Enthroned

In *Hall v. DeCuir* (1878), the Court ruled that states could not prohibit voluntary segregation by interstate common carriers, such as railroads, streetcars, or riverboats. A dozen years later, it approved a Mississippi statute requiring segregation on intrastate carriers in *Louisville, New Orleans & Texas Railway v. Mississippi* (1890); in doing so it acquiesced in the South's solution to the problems of race relations. Only Justices Harlan and Bradley dissented, on the grounds that such laws, even if confined to intrastate railway lines, interfered with interstate commerce.

In the best known of the early segregation cases, *Plessy v. Ferguson* (1896), Justice Henry Billings Brown asserted that distinctions based on race ran afoul of neither the Thirteenth nor Fourteenth amendments. Although the Fourteenth had been intended to establish an absolute equality of the races before the law, Brown noted that "in the nature of things it could not have been intended to abolish distinctions based upon color, or to enforce social, as distinguished from political, equality, or a commingling of the two races unsatisfactory to either." Although nowhere in the opinion can the phrase "separate but equal" be found, the Court's ruling approved legally enforced segregation, so long as the law did not make facilities for blacks inferior to those for whites.

In a famous and eloquent dissent, Justice Harlan protested that states could now impose criminal penalties on a citizen simply because he or she wished to use public highways and common carriers. Such legislation is "inconsistent not only with equality of rights which pertains to citizenship, National and State, but with the personal liberty enjoyed by everyone within the United States." As for the majority's disingenuous contention that segregation did not in itself constitute discrimination, the Kentucky-born justice condemned segregation statutes as "conceived in hostility to, and enacted for the purpose of humiliating citizens of the United States of a particular race." Such laws defeated the entire purpose of the Civil War amendments and made any real peace between the races impossible. "The destinies of the two races . . . are indissolubly linked together, and the interests of both require that the common government of all shall not permit the seeds of race hate to be planted under the sanction of law." Harlan's plea that the "Constitution is color-blind" fell on deaf ears, not only within the Court, but in the country as well. The surest sign of the changing temper of the nation was that where there had been a vociferous protest in the North over the Civil Rights Cases thirteen years earlier, the Plessy decision caused hardly a ripple.

The Court seemed only too willing to wash its hands of responsibility for minority protection and to leave the fate of minorities to state and local governments. The justices no doubt shared the general sentiment that enough had been done for blacks,

---

Why may [the State] not require all red-headed people to ride in a separate car? Why not require all colored people to walk on one side of the street and the whites on the other? Why may it not require every white man s house to be painted white and every colored man's black? Why may it not require every white man's vehicle to be of one color and compel the colored citizen to use one of a different color on the highway? Why not require every white business man to use a white sign and every colored man who solicits custom a black one? One side of the street may be just as good as the other and the dark horses, coaches, clothes and signs may be as good or better than the white ones. The question is not as to the *equality* of the privileges enjoyed, but *the right of the State to label one citizen as white and another as colored* in the common enjoyment of a public highway as this court has often decided a railway to be.

Brief of Albion Tourgée and James C. Walker, submitted to the Supreme Court in *Plessy v. Ferguson* (1896).

and the country ought to get on with its other business. If a regulation appeared to apply equally to all citizens, the Court would not look beneath the surface to see how it affected particular groups. It made this clear in upholding the conviction of a black man for murder in *Williams v. Mississippi* (1898). The case involved more than a federal court's unwillingness to interfere with the state criminal process, for Williams had claimed that his indictment by an all-white jury had been unconstitutional. Mississippi restricted jury duty to eligible voters; a literacy test and poll taxes effectively barred blacks from the franchise and thus from serving on juries.

A unanimous Court, speaking through the newly appointed Joseph McKenna of California, ignored the practical application and, in a marvel of formalistic logic, looked only at the letter of the law. Nothing in the Constitution prohibited either a literacy test or a poll tax, provided the law did not single out any specific group for discrimination. The fact that local officials *might* apply the law in a biased manner could not be used to attack the law's legitimacy.

Within a few decades after *Williams,* the Southern states had taken several steps to disenfranchise blacks. Poll taxes and literacy tests effectively deprived the vast majority of blacks of the right to vote, while loopholes such as grandfather clauses or good character vouchers allowed poor, illiterate whites to vote. And even if some black men learned to read and had the money to pay the poll tax, their vote had virtually no effect on an election. The primary, which Progressives hoped would curb the power of the urban machines, became in the South a useful tool of racism. Well before the turn of the century, all Southern states had become overwhelmingly Democratic. With the institution of the primary, whoever won the Democratic primary had for all practical purposes won the general election. When political parties became defined as private organizations in the 1920s, the states could exclude blacks from voting in the primary, the only election that really counted.

Between 1900 and 1920, Jim Crow—the legal and systematic segregation of the races—triumphed throughout the former slave states. Signs marked "Whites Only" and "Colored" showed up everywhere—in theaters, restaurants, railroad cars, boarding houses, and even water fountains. South Carolina prohibited blacks and whites from working together in the same room in textile plants, and from using the same entry ways, exits, or lavatories, as well. Mississippi statutes required segregation in hospitals, a practice soon adopted by other states. The state even forbade white nurses from attending black patients. Hundreds of Jim Crow laws existed on the books, but the laws by themselves did not provide an adequate gauge of the extent of segregation and its accompanying discrimination in Southern life at the turn of the century. The laws established minimal requirements; in practice, segregation normally went well beyond what the statutes required. Institutionalized segregation bred hatred and distrust among both whites and blacks, attitudes that would not be easily broken down even after the Supreme Court reversed itself and declared segregation unconstitutional in 1954.

But in sustaining racial segregation in the early 1900s, the Court certainly reflected popular opinion, not only in the South but in the North as well. When the Court in 1908, again over a strenuous objection from Justice Harlan, upheld a state statute requiring segregation in private schools (*Berea College v. Kentucky*), editorial opinion proved as favorable above the Mason–Dixon line as below it. President Theodore Roosevelt looked down on blacks "as a race and as a man . . . altogether inferior to the whites," despite making a few token black appointments and inviting educator Booker T. Washington to the White House. President Taft had no better opinion, and Wilson's was even worse. As the first Southerner elected president since the Civil War, Wilson and his lieutenants approved the segregation of all federal facilities. Indeed, racist thought permeated much of the Progressive movement.

## The Treatment of Native Americans

Given the nation's and the Court's acquiescence in the subjugation of the freedmen, it is little wonder that other minorities fared just as badly. Native Americans had been pushed constantly off their lands ever since European settlers had landed in Virginia in 1607. By the time of *Cherokee Nation v. Georgia* in 1831, the notion that the tribes could exercise any sovereignty comparable to that of the United States no longer made any sense. In that case, John Marshall redefined the status of Indian tribes from that of independent sovereigns to "domestic dependent nations." The chief justice described the Indians as "in a state of pupilage," with a relation to the federal government of "a ward to his guardian." For all practical purposes, the tribes and their members would henceforth be under the dominion of the United States.

Prior to the Civil War, federal policy had been to resettle most of the eastern tribes in the Great Plains, which most people thought unsuitable to cultivation. The years after Appomattox saw an enormous surge of white settlers to the West, and by the 1890s, official policy had destroyed tribal sovereignty among the Indians. Starting in 1871, Congress began weakening what little tribal authority remained by declaring that the government would no longer negotiate treaties (which implied some parity on both sides), but would instead enter into agreements. In the so-called *Cherokee Tobacco* case (1871), the Supreme Court handed down a new ruling regarding the relationship of Indians to the federal government: that general congressional acts would apply to the tribes unless Congress explicitly excluded them. In essence, congressional policy to disregard treaties with the tribes now received a judicial imprimatur.

In the next two decades, Congress exercised direct control over the tribes, and in the words of one scholar, it did so in a way "which, if asserted against State citizens, would not have survived constitutional challenge." In many ways, the legal status of Indians, members of "domestic dependent nations," resembled that of slaves before the war, in that they were neither citizens nor aliens, but simply subjects. The Fourteenth Amendment's definition of a citizen as anyone born within the United States did not apply to Native Americans born on reservations. The resulting breakdown in tribal society led to growing crime and disorder, and to demands for reform, which culminated in the Dawes Act of 1887.

To some extent, the Court made congressional action necessary after it ruled in *Ex parte Crow Dog* (1883) that the United States had no jurisdiction under existing law over crimes committed by Indians against each other, and in *Elk v. Wilkins* the following year that Indians who voluntarily left their tribes did not become citizens of the United States. Congress responded by establishing specific courts for Indian offenses, and in 1885, extended federal criminal jurisdiction over the reservations for major crimes such as murder, arson, and rape. Two years later, Congress passed the Dawes

Act, which supposedly looked toward assimilating the Indians into the larger society. It allotted tribal land within the reservations on an individual basis, although tribal law had never recognized the European notion of individual ownership of the land. By making individuals into property owners, Congress hoped to make Indian society more like that of the white man. To encourage assimilation, the act also subjected those Indians who accepted the allotments to the laws of the state or territory in which they resided. In addition, Indians who took the allotments or who voluntarily left their tribes became citizens of the United States; those who refused the allotment or stayed in the tribes remained excluded from citizenship.

In 1890, the government abrogated its last major treaty with the tribes by opening up the Oklahoma territory to white settlement, and resettled the so-called Five Civilized Tribes in what became known as the Indian Territory, comprising about twenty million acres within the current boundaries of the state. But good grazing land as well large mineral deposits proved too strong a lure, and the Curtis Act of 1898 unilaterally abrogated the treaties with the Five Tribes and gave over the land and its wealth to federal control. The government also continued the effort to make Indians into whites. In 1901, Congress conferred citizenship on tribal members living in the Indian territory. In 1919, all Indians who had served in the armed forces during World War I became citizens; in 1924, all other Indians finally became citizens of the United States. For all these efforts, the policy of assimilation proved a dismal failure. Most Native Americans fought against losing their cultural heritage. Those who left the reservations found themselves objects of racism, treated just as badly as other people of color. Life for those who stayed on the reservations proved just as dismal, subject on the one hand to poverty and sickness and on the other to the arbitrary and often corrupt rule of the Bureau of Indian Affairs. Not until the New Deal would the federal government finally abandon the policy of the Dawes Act and encourage Native Americans to reassert both tribal authority and traditional culture.

The Supreme Court gave its blessings to all of these measures. In *United States v. Kagama* (1886), the Court completely denied the existence of tribal sovereignty, and upheld the Major Crimes Act of the previous year. Four years later, in *Cherokee Nation v. Southern Kansas Railway Company*, the Court upheld a congressional grant of a right-of-way through acknowledged Indian lands without the consent of the tribes. Congress took this decision as a signal, and in the Omnibus Railroad Act of 1899, gave railroads, upon a simple application to the Interior Department, a general right-of-way to construct lines through reservations, across Indian lands, and even through individual allotments.

In *Ward v. Race Horse* (1896), the high court reversed a federal district court ruling that treaty rights granting Shoshone-Bannock certain hunting rights could not be

---

As with the American Indian, the only way to prevent his extermination is to civilize him, so the only way to preserve the remaining buffalo is to domesticate them.

—U.S. House of Representatives,
*Protection of American Bison and Other Animals* (1890)

overridden by Wyoming state laws. Speaking through Justice Edward D. White, a near unanimous Court ruled that for all practical purposes, treaties with the Indians no longer had any force, and any hunting rights provided for by treaty had to give way to the laws of the state. A few years later, the Court took the power of determining who is a member of a tribe out of the hands of tribal authorities and gave it over to a congressional commission charged with land allotments. (*Stephens v. Cherokee Nation* [1899]).

The rape of Indian lands and the judicial approval of it reached its apogee in *Cherokee Nation v. Hitchcock* in 1902 and *Lone Wolf v. Hitchcock* the following year. In the former case, the Court upheld the power of the secretary of the interior to grant mineral leases on Cherokee land with the approval of tribal elders, and in the latter it upheld the cession of tribal land to the United States, even though the transfer had been surrounded by fraud and had not complied with treaty requirements. According to Justice White, a treaty did not give rise to any property rights that fell under the protection of the Fifth Amendment. Whatever intent Congress may have had in assimilating Native Americans, the Court's decisions firmly established that Indians stood outside the constitutional community, even less protected than the former slaves.

## The Chinese Cases

The railroads that drove through western Indian lands often had been built by people of color, for tens of thousands of Chinese had been imported to the United States to work on the railroads. While for some Chinese life in the United States may have been better than what they had left behind, most found themselves subject to dangerous working condition, low pay, racial discrimination, and a law that offered little protection.

Chinese had begun coming to the United States in the middle of the nineteenth century, and were welcomed as a relief to the severe shortage of unskilled labor on the West Coast. Eventually, racial prejudice as well as fear that lower-paid Chinese would "steal" jobs from whites led to a demand for legislative action. In 1882, Congress suspended Chinese immigration for ten years, and in 1888, passed a law refusing readmission to Chinese workers who had left the United States even if they had identity cards entitling them to reenter the country. This second act directly contravened treaty provisions between China and the United States.

A Chinese national with an identity card, upon being denied readmission to the United States, sought a writ of habeas corpus, claiming the 1888 act not only violated exisiting treaty and statutory obligations, but also his vested right to return. The justices unanimously rejected this argument in *Chae Chan Ping v. United States,* commonly known as the *Chinese Exclusion Case* (1889). Just as the Court had found that Congress had the power to abrogate treaties with the Indian tribes, it now ruled that Congress could abrogate treaty provisions with foreign countries simply by passing legislation inconsistent with the treaty. Justice Stephen Field, who wrote for the Court, found sufficient justification for limiting Chinese immigration, and held that such an act based "on the experience of years," might well be essential not only to preserving the peace of communities on the West Coast, but also to the national civilization.

Congress tightened the restrictions in 1892 by requiring that Chinese laborers in the United States register and obtain certificates, and gave the administering officials in the Treasury Department broad and arbitrary discretion to determine who should receive the certificates. Those who could not get a certificate could be summarily deported by a federal judge. By a 5–3 vote in *Fong Yue Ting v. United States* (1893), the Court upheld the law, and ruled that aliens resided in the United States were under the absolute authority of Congress, which could expel them whenever it thought it appropriate. Justices Fuller, Brewer, and Field entered vigorous dissents, and argued that even aliens enjoyed some protection under the Constitution.

The *Chinese Exclusion* and *Fong Yue Ting* cases appeared to say that Asians, like Native Americans, stood outside the constitutional community. But other cases led to the opposite conclusion, that in some areas the Chinese did enjoy basic constitutional protection.

In *Yick Wo v. Hopkins* (1886), the Court struck down a San Francisco ordinance that required a permit to operate a laundry in a wooden building. On its face the ordinance seemed like a legitimate fire protection measure, but in practice it proved quite discriminatory. The city granted permits to all but one of the non-Chinese applicants and denied licenses to all 200 Chinese who applied, even though some of them had been operating laundries for more than twenty years. Anticipating the equal protection argument used by the Warren Court eight decades later, the Supreme Court concluded that the ordinance as applied discriminated against a particular group. The Chinese were not outsiders, Justice Matthews declared. "The Fourteenth Amendment . . . is not confined to the protection of citizens," but applies "to all persons within the territorial jurisdiction."

And what about the children of the Chinese workers, children born in the United States? Did they automatically become citizens under the Fourteenth Amendment, even though their parents could never be citizens? Undoubtedly anti-Chinese sentiment on the West Coast would have preferred to deny citizenship to the children, so that they too could be deported. But in *United States v. Wong Kim Ark* (1898), a majority of the Court ruled that all persons born in the United States of Chinese parents became citizens at birth under the Fourteenth Amendment, and no act of Congress could deny them this constitutional birthright. Chief Justice Fuller dissented, arguing that the Fourteenth Amendment did not apply when parents had been legitimately barred from citizenship, but although he apparently lobbied his colleagues for nearly two years, he could not get them to adopt his position.

Despite *Yick Wo* and *Wong Kim*, the Court for the most part deferred to the legislative branches in dealing with Asians. Congress had full control over immigration,

---

No euphemism can disguise the character of the act in this regard. It directs the performance of a judicial function in a particular way, and inflicts punishment without a judicial trial. It is, in effect, a legislative sentence of banishment, and, as such, absolutely void. Moreover, it contains within it the germs of the assertion of an unlimited and arbitrary power, in general, incompatible with the immutable principles of justice, inconsistent with the nature of our government, and in conflict with the written Constitution by which that government was created and those principles secured.

—Justice Fuller, dissenting in *Fong Yue Ting v. United States* (1893)

and if it wished to exclude certain groups, the Constitution posed no objections. But the times in general provided little tolerance for groups of color, be they from Africa, Asia, or the Americas, and the Court reflected these sentiments in its opinions.

## The Insular Cases

In the same era that the Court confirmed Jim Crow laws in the South and approved congressional dismemberment of the Indian treaties, it heard a number of cases, commonly called the Insular Cases, dealing with the reach of constitutional protection to the native inhabitants of America's newly acquired overseas territories—those gained in the settlement following the Spanish–American War of 1898.

Unlike previous acquisitions of territory, these new possessions did not strike contemporaries as likely to become future states. With the exception of the purchase of Alaska in 1867 (primarily to remove Russian colonial influence from the New World), lands acquired in the nineteenth century by purchase, annexation, or conquest had been contiguous to already existing states or territories, and it had been assumed that they would ultimately enter the Union as states. The march across the continent, even during the fever pitch of Manifest Destiny, had never been imperialistic; Americans sought new territory to permit growth, not to acquire subordinate colonies.

Puerto Rico, Guam, the Philippines, and Hawaii were already populated—and not by white races with "developed" cultures. If the United States retained them, it appeared that they would be nothing more than colonies, a proposal viewed with alarm by a highly vocal minority but with satisfaction by men like Theodore Roosevelt and Senator Henry Cabot Lodge. They believed that the time had come for the nation to join European countries in the race for empire and, in Rudyard Kipling's words, to "take up the white man's burden" of bringing Western civilization to Asia, Africa, Latin America, and the Pacific rim.

No one questioned the right of the nation to acquire new lands under its sovereign powers; that issue had been resolved years earlier in *American Insurance Co. v. Cantor* (1828). But if the new lands were to be colonies, then did the Constitution follow the flag, providing the residents of the new territories with the full range of constitutionally guaranteed rights? The imperialists claimed that the Constitution did not follow the flag and that Congress could govern colonies as it saw fit, its inhabitants enjoying only those rights that Congress specifically extended to them. The anti-imperialists argued that all persons under American jurisdiction had to be treated alike, the traditional policy of the Union toward residents of the continental territories.

The political branch resolved the question of whether or not the United States would keep these new possessions when the Senate ratified the Treaty of Paris with Spain in April 1899, and secured American possession of the former Spanish holdings. Defining the legal status of the new territories proved to be the chief business of the Supreme Court at the 1900 term. In the first of the Insular Cases, *Neely v. Henkel* (1901), the justices had little trouble agreeing that Cuba, although occupied by American forces, remained a foreign country, since at the outset of the war Congress had passed a resolution that Cuba could not be annexed to the United States. But the treaty also conveyed Puerto Rico and the Philippines as direct possessions, and their status had to be determined. In cases triggered by the tariff laws, a badly divided Court grad-ually worked out a doctrine to govern the future status of the new colonies.

In *DeLima v. Bidwell,* decided in May 1901, the Court had to decide whether, af-ter the cession by treaty of Puerto Rico, but before any specific congressional action, customs duties could be collected on goods imported into the United States from the island. The collector of the Port of New York had imposed duties on sugar, as if that product still came from a foreign country, and the purchaser then sued to recover, claiming that the Constitution prohibited taxes on goods exported from one part of the country to another. By a 5–4 vote, the Court held that as a consequence of the Treaty of Paris, Puerto Rico did not constitute a foreign country and that the tariffs had there-fore been unlawfully collected. Four justices—Joseph McKenna, Edward Douglass White, George Shiras, and Horace Gray—dissented strongly in separate opinions. McKenna claimed that Puerto Rico "occupied a relation to the United States between that of being a foreign country absolutely and of being domestic territory absolutely, and because of that relation its products were subject to the duties imposed by the Din-gley act." The majority claimed that this vague halfway status could not exist; Justice Henry Billings Brown, who delivered the majority opinion, argued that the island had to be one thing or the other, and to hold otherwise would place Puerto Rico in a dis-astrous position of "practical isolation."

## The Incorporation Theory

The most important of the Insular Cases proved to be *Downes v. Bidwell* (1901), which tested the constitutionality of the Foraker Act of 1900, which established a civil gov-ernment for Puerto Rico and established import duties from the island. Challengers claimed that the tariff provisions violated the constitutional requirement that duties be "uniform throughout the United States." A majority of five justices sustained the statute, but they could not agree on a common rationale. Justice Henry Billings Brown, speak-ing for the majority, reflected the imperialistic spirit of the day, and spoke of "alien races" and "Anglo-Saxon principles." While acknowledging that constitutional pro-tections of rights applied to some extent in the territories, he stopped just short of grant-ing Congress unfettered power over the nation's new possessions.

Justice White's concurring opinion in the *Downes* case proved to be the key in the Court's development of a viable constitutional doctrine, one he termed "incorporation." White emphasized the power of Congress to provide for new territories and its dis-cretion in defining their status. As for the application of the Constitution to these new lands, since mere acquisition did not bring them into the Union, neither did it entitle them to any of the rights and privileges guaranteed by the Constitution. So long as they remained in a subordinate condition, these territories would enjoy only those rights specifically granted by Congress; the full benefits of the Constitution would only ap-ply if and when Congress acted to incorporate the territory into the Union. In this case, the Constitution did not follow the flag.

White's theory did not gain immediate adherence from a majority of his brethren. Justice Harlan especially objected to the racist implications of White's argument, and he noted that the natives of these new lands did not enjoy any rights, but relied on the whims of the legislature, without any judicial review to protect them. In his *Downes* dissent, Harlan claimed that Congress could act only under the Constitution, and "the idea that this country may acquire territories anywhere upon the earth, by conquest or treaty, and hold them as mere colonies or provinces—the people inhabiting them to enjoy only such rights as Congress chooses to accord to them—is wholly inconsistent with the spirit and genius as well as with the words of the Constitution."

Over the next few years, White's incorporation theory moved from dicta in a concurrence to full acceptance as doctrine in *Dorr v. United States* (1904). Fred Dorr had been convicted for libel under an act passed, not by Congress, but by the Philippine Commission, and had been tried without a jury in Manila. Justice William R. Day, who had joined the Court in 1903, delivered the majority opinion. "Until Congress shall see fit to incorporate territory," he ruled, that territory "is to be governed under the power existing in Congress." In a patronizing dictum that fully reflected the racist views of the time, he denied that the Constitution followed the flag, since the natives of the new territories might be totally unfit to enjoy the advanced rights of Western civilization.

Finally, in *Dowdell v. United States* (1911), the entire Court, save Harlan, who consistently opposed the theory, joined in Justice Day's opinion that the Philippines had never been incorporated into the Union and thus that criminal trials there did not require a twelve-person jury. White's longevity on the bench assured him of success. By 1920, none of the original dissenters remained when he ruled in *Board of Public Utility Commissioners v. Ynchausti & Co.* that the Philippines had never been incorporated and that therefore constitutional limitations did not restrain Congress in its governance of the islands.

The Court, however, never imposed an absolute application of the doctrine that the Constitution did not follow the flag, which literally would have denied any rights except those granted by Congress. The early commercial cases had not involved personal rights, while the later criminal cases, although the procedures followed departed from nominal American standards, nonetheless still provided the basic requirements for a fair trial. But if local law imposed unacceptable results, the Court could find a way around it. In *Weems v. United States* (1910), for example, a Coast Guard officer had been convicted under an old Spanish law still in effect in the Philippines. He had falsified public documents, and for this he had been sentenced to fifteen years in prison at hard labor in chains and the perpetual loss of his civil liberties. Justice McKenna wrote that "such penalties for such offenses amaze those who have formed their concepts of [justice] . . . from the practice of the American commonwealths, and believe it is a precept of justice that punishment for crime should be graduated and proportioned to the offense." Although the question had not been raised in the lower court, McKenna cited the Eighth Amendment's ban on cruel and unusual punishment, of which a variant could be found in the Philippine law, and set aside both the conviction and sentence—the first time the Eighth Amendment had been invoked by the Supreme Court on behalf of a convicted defendant.

If a common thread ran from the *Civil Rights Cases* through the Insular decisions, it was the racism that permeated the nation—and Western Europe—in this age of imperialist expansion. Pseudolearned volumes appeared extolling the Anglo-Saxon or Teutonic "race" as superior to the colored peoples of the world. For evidence, commentators pointed to the allegedly primitive cultures of nonwhite groups and their inability to resist white expansion. Most Americans shared this view, and even if they believed that inferior peoples should not be enslaved, they did not consider brown and black people to be their equals. The Supreme Court merely reflected this sentiment; its decisions did not create a new prejudice so much as place an imprimatur of respectability on existing racism. But the Court did draw a line on how far this racism could go.

## Women and the Law

Although comprising half the population, and technically not a "minority," women had long been disfavored by the law. Earlier in the century, legislation had established judicial procedures for divorce and had given married women some control over their property, but women still had few real rights in the latter part of the nineteenth century. Despite the revolutionary era battle cry of "No taxation without representation!" women property owners had to pay taxes without the suffrage. The campaign for the vote begun at Seneca Falls, New York, in 1848 had stalled; women would not achieve success at the national level until 1920, with the passage of the Nineteenth Amendment.

After the Fourteenth and Fifteenth Amendments had been passed, however, one group of suffrage militants, known as the New Departure, attempted to use the Reconstruction provisions to secure the vote. In October 1869, a husband and wife team of Missouri suffragists, Francis and Virginia Minor, began offering an interpretation of the Constitution to prove that women already had the right to vote. They argued that popular sovereignty preceded and supported constitutional authority, and that the federal government had been created to protect individual rights. The Reconstruction amendments, they claimed, merely nationalized all rights, including the right to vote, and applied them to all persons, including the former slaves and women.

Virginia Minor attempted to vote, and when refused, she took her case to court, as had been her plan all along. Before the Supreme Court, she claimed the right to vote as one of the privileges and immunities enjoyed by all citizens under the Fourteenth Amendment. Chief Justice Morrison R. Waite, speaking for a unanimous court in *Minor v. Happersett* (1875), declared that women had always been citizens, but he denied that the right to vote constituted an essential privilege of citizenship. The power to award the suffrage belonged to the states, and the only restraint placed on that power had been that states could not use race to deny the vote. But all sorts of groups lacked the vote, Waite concluded, and if women were to get the ballot it would have to come through the states. The Constitution stood silent on the issue.

Some opportunities for women did open up in the latter part of the nineteenth century, as more colleges accepted women students, although formal training for the professions remained almost exclusively a male prerogative. A few women, however, began to study the law, since in those days, most lawyers prepared for the bar by reading in a law office rather than attending law school. At the same time that Virginia Minor was attempting to secure the franchise, Myra Bradwell tried to get the courts to permit her to practice law.

Bradwell had studied law, and then had petitioned the Illinois Bar for admission. Had she been a man, there is no question Bradwell would have been admitted, and the bar examiners made it quite clear that they had no intention of allowing a woman to practice. Bradwell brought the case up to the U.S. Supreme Court, where Matthew Carpenter, the Republican senator from Wisconsin represented her. Carpenter's argument for Bradwell's right to practice law ran parallel to Minor's claim for the vote, namely that the Fourteenth Amendment gave all citizens equal rights, and that a woman, as a citizen, could not be denied the right to be a lawyer.

Decided on the same day as the *Slaughterhouse* cases, *Bradwell v. Illinois* (1873) reinforced the judicial evisceration of the Fourteenth Amendment's key provisions aimed at regulating state conduct. Justice Miller, writing for the majority, denied any constitutional right to practice law, and declared that such privileges could be granted or withheld by the states. In a concurring opinion, Justice Bradley noted that "the natural and proper timidity and delicacy which belongs to the female sex" unfitted it for many of the occupations of civil life, including the practice of law. Women should stay at home, in "the domestic sphere . . . which properly belongs to the domain and functions of womanhood."

Despite these and other setbacks, women persevered. They gained the right to practice in some states and in the District of Columbia, and they also won the right to appear before the Supreme Court, thanks to the efforts of Belva Lockwood. Lockwood had studied at the National University Law School, where she suffered not only discrimination in classes but the authorities' refusal to grant her a diploma. Nonetheless, she applied to the D.C. bar, and after a long struggle won admission in 1873, shortly after the pioneering African American woman lawyer, Charlotte E. Ray, had also secured a license.

Lockwood established a busy practice, arguing cases in all the various divisions of the D.C. courts, as well as handling veteran pension claims. In 1874, Lockwood asked a Washington attorney, A.A. Hosmer, to sponsor her admission to the Claims Court bar, and given the *Bradwell* ruling the year before, it proved no surprise when the court turned her down, claiming that it had no power to authorize the admission of women into practice. Two years later, the Supreme Court also denied her request, and Lockwood then turned to Congress, where she lobbied successfully for a bill to remove such hindrances. A reluctant Congress in 1879 approved an "act to relieve certain legal disabilities of women," and ordered that any woman who met the qualifica-

---

[This court finds] no authority for the admission of females to the bar of any court of this state. . . . We cannot but think the common law wise in excluding women from the profession of the law. . . . The law of nature destines and qualifies the female sex for the bearing and nurture of the children of our race and for the custody of the homes of the world and their maintenance in love and honor. . . . [Admitting women as lawyers] would emasculate the constitution itself and include females in the constitutional right of male suffrage and male qualification. Such a rule would be one of judicial revolution, not of judicial construction.

—Chief Justice Edward G. Ryan, Motion to admit Lavinia Goodell to the bar
of the Wisconsin Supreme Court (1875)

tions of practice and good standing should be admitted to practice before the Supreme Court. A few weeks later, Belva Lockwood became the first woman admitted to the Supreme Court bar, and the year after she argued her first case before the high court, *Kaiser v. Stickney* (1880).

But the success of Lockwood and a few other women should not mask the fact that the law, even if it considered women citizens with certain rights, still treated them as second-class persons. If a man and wife mingled their monies, then courts considered it all as belonging to the husband. As the Industrial Revolution expanded, women began to work in large numbers outside the home, yet courts still held that a woman's labor belonged to her husband. Only if she could keep her work and wages completely separate from that of her husband could a woman make claim to her property under the recently passed "earnings" laws, an option not available to most working-class women. As her husband's property, a wife's earnings, even if not commingled, could be claimed for his debts. As the former Abolitionist, Rev. Thomas Wentworth Higginson aptly put it, the wife was only "half way out" of the "feudal shell," and courts seemed little interested in moving her any farther.

## The Court Draws Limits

Despite the Court's acquiescence in Jim Crow and its disregard for the claimed rights of other minorities, the era is not without some redemption. American occupation of the lands won from Spain eventually led to an administration that included nearly all the guaranties of the Constitution. Women began moving out of the confines of the domestic sphere, into college and, in limited ways, into the professions. Even the freedmen could look on this period with some hope and sense of accomplishment. In 1900, only half of all black adults could read; by 1913, the ratio had risen to seven out of ten. The number of blacks who owned businesses, houses, and farms rose steadily. Dedicated whites like Moorfield Storey joined black activists like W. E. B. Du Bois to organize the National Association for the Advancement of Colored People, which began the long, slow fight for justice. And much to everyone's surprise, during Edward Douglass White's tenure as chief justice, the Supreme Court began to interpret the Civil War amendments to reflect their original intent—to safeguard the rights of black persons.

The Louisiana-born White had been appointed to the Court by President Grover Cleveland in 1894, and for the next sixteen years, the former Confederate soldier voted with the majority in every case to uphold segregation or restrict blacks' rights. Yet after taking the center chair in 1910, he helped shape majorities for important civil rights decisions. Moreover, the White Court reached out to ensure racial justice in several cases in which it could easily have avoided the issue.

The first Jim Crow case to come before the White Court is *McCabe v. Atchinson, Topeka & Santa Fe Railway* (1914); the case marked the arrival on the Court of Charles Evans Hughes of New York, who took White's place as associate justice. Hughes refused to "wink" at the facts and applied the same legal logic to race cases as he did to other subjects coming before the Court. *McCabe* involved an Oklahoma law that required separate but equal railroad coaches but exempted luxury units, such as parlor, dining, and sleeping cars, which could be used by either race, but not jointly. Since few blacks had the funds for these services, railroads used the law to avoid providing separate black facilities. Black plaintiffs challenged the rule as discriminatory, although they did not attack the broader principle of segregation. In effect, they said they could accept "separate but equal," but objected to the inequality of "exclusive but not joint."

By a 5 to 4 vote, the Court sustained their argument. Hughes reiterated the *Plessy* rule and said that if railroads attached luxury cars for white passengers, equal facilities had to be available for blacks, regardless of the anticipated demand or lack of it. But after this refusal to accommodate to expediency, Hughes found a dodge to deny the petitioners relief—they had brought suit before the law went into effect and therefore lacked standing. The lower courts had erred in reaching the merits before determining if the question was ripe for adjudication. Hughes decided the merits anyway, in order to put Oklahoma and other states on notice that while the Court would accept racial segregation, it would insist that separate facilities be available and equal. But with the exception of one case, the Court would not deal with Jim Crow on the railroads again until 1941, when Hughes, then chief justice, had by this time begun to reverse the Court's position.

Residential segregation came before the Court in *Buchanan v. Warley* (1917), a case contrived by the NAACP to test segregation ordinances in Louisville, Kentucky. Warley, a black, arranged to buy a lot from Buchanan, a white who was friendly to the NAACP, and the contract was drawn to invite litigation. Warley refused to pay for the land, on grounds that residential segregation laws prevented him from building a house there, which the sales contract specifically identified as his reason for buying the property. Buchanan sued for payment, but the local court upheld the ordinance and declared it a full defense for Warley. Buchanan then appealed to the Supreme Court, where both parties had hoped to go anyway. Other Southern cities then considering similar ordinances all stopped to await the Court's decision. Moorfield Storey, a white lawyer from Boston, representing the NAACP, sought to distinguish residential segregation from other Jim Crow laws because it demeaned property rights, one of the bases of free government. Louisville's attorneys responded with the full rhetoric of racism: Law and Divine Writ demanded the full separation of the races.

The unanimous opinion Justice Day delivered masked internal disagreement in the Court over how far it should or should not go in such essentially local matters. The Fourteenth Amendment protected property, Day noted, but the state could certainly exercise some controls under its police powers to maintain health and safety. But could it regulate property solely on the basis of the skin color of the owner or would-be buyer? After an impassioned review of how the Civil War had been fought to protect civil rights, Day dismissed *Plessy* as controlling; in that case there had been no effort to deprive blacks of transportation, whereas in this case Louisville would neither allow blacks to buy certain property nor permit whites to sell it to them. He then held residential segregation laws unconstitutional—the first time the Supreme Court ever restricted the reach of Jim Crow.

# The Peonage Cases

The White Court also showed itself willing to defend black rights in the so-called *Peonage Cases, Bailey v. Alabama* (1911) and *United States v. Reynolds* (1914). Forced labor statutes had been passed in all Southern states, permitting arrests for vagrancy, breach of labor contract, and other crimes. Once convicted, the defendant could be bound to a term of labor on a chain gang to work off fines and court costs. Although some whites, especially new immigrants, became ensnared in the peonage system, for the most part it operated to control blacks; a number of reformers, including white Southerners, attacked peonage as a violation of the Thirteenth Amendment's ban on involuntary servitude. In fact, the two leading cases both came before the Court as a result of Southern reform efforts.

*Bailey v. Alabama* involved a state statute that made breach of a labor contract prima facie evidence of intent to injure or defraud the employer. As Booker T. Washington charged, this "simply means that any white man, who cares to charge that a Colored man has promised to work for him and has not done so, or who has gotten money from him and not paid it back, can have the Colored man set to the chain gang." Washington found a test case, one Alonzo Bailey, who had left his job without repaying a wage advance. Even before the state court had ruled, defense lawyers sought a direct appeal to the Supreme Court in 1908. Justice Oliver Wendell Holmes ruled that the case had come prematurely, since there had been no final decision from the lower court, and over objections from John Marshall Harlan, the Court sent the case back to Alabama for final adjudication.

After Bailey had been duly convicted in state court, his second appeal came before the White Court in 1911. He had been ordered to pay his employer $15 and assessed a fine of $30 and costs; since he had no money, the local court sentenced him to four and a half months at hard labor. Justice Hughes attacked the statute as a restriction of personal rights, and noted that the Alabama Supreme Court had previously struck down legislation abridging employees' contractual rights as a violation of the Fourteenth Amendment. The state was now trying to accomplish a similarly impermissible objective by criminal sanctions, and in doing so violated the Thirteenth Amendment. Hughes's decision relied on relatively narrow grounds and did not invalidate all forced labor statutes. Not until 1944, in *Pollock v. Williams,* did the Court finally strike a death blow to the peonage system.

*Bailey* dealt with peonage for the state. In *United States v. Reynolds* the following year, the Court dealt with another Alabama forced labor statute, one that assigned a person's labor to private parties. A person convicted of an offense could have his fine and costs paid by another person (a surety), who then executed a labor contract under which the defendant would work a set amount of time to pay off the debt. If the laborer defaulted, he could be convicted of breaching the contract and another surety would appear, pay off the debt and new fines, and bind the defendant to a still longer term of service. In May 1910, for example, Ed Rivers pleaded guilty to petit larceny in county court in Monroeville, Alabama. The judge fined him $15 and assessed $43.75 in costs. Since Rivers had no money, the judge sentenced him to ten days hard labor for the fine, and another forty-eight days to pay the court costs. One J. A. Reynolds paid the fine and costs, and Rivers agreed to work for him for ten months, at $6 a month, plus room, board, and clothing. After a month, Rivers left, but the police soon rearrested him and charged him with failing to perform his contractual duties. The same judge fined him only one penny, but assessed court costs of $87.05. A new surety came forward to pay, but now Rivers faced a contract for fourteen months, seven times what he would have had to work to pay his original sentence.

The Justice Department, under Attorney General Wickersham, had been looking for test cases to challenge the labor surety system, which it termed an "engine of oppression" against blacks. After fastening on the Rivers incident, it took the department more than two years to work out the details of how to proceed. Both the federal and state governments wanted a case that would go to the Supreme Court, so as to resolve the issue, since planters and others who stood the surety needed to know if the system would continue. The government promised that if the Court found against the sureties, it would ask for a minimal fine, since it did not want to punish individuals, but test the system.

In the end, a unanimous Court, speaking through Justice Day, struck down the surety contract, but it did so in a formalistic and defensive manner—as if the justices knew that it was wrong to permit blacks to be so mistreated, but could not quite figure out why. Day, like Hughes in *Bailey*, did not want to point out the racial nature of the system. Most prisoners condemned to the chain gang for breach of contract, or bound to a surety, were black; peonage constituted one of the South's means of controlling blacks in a way that assured a reliable labor force. Holmes, who dissented in *Bailey*, grudgingly concurred in *Reynolds*, and his brief opinion bespoke volumes about the innate racism that afflicted many Northern Progressives. But, even if for the wrong reason, the Court at least put an end to one of the worst aspects of Southern racism.

## A Few Small Steps

The White Court also took hesitant steps to address the widespread disenfranchisement of blacks by Southern states. It will be recalled that in *Williams v. Mississippi* (1898), the Court had indirectly given its approval to restrictions such as the poll tax and literacy test. Five years later, in *Giles v. Harris* (1903), Holmes admitted that the Court did not have the capacity to remedy discrimination in voter registration. The question of the grandfather clauses, however, came before the bench in a strange case. Oklahoma, where blacks comprised less than 10 percent of the population, and which, unlike other Southern states, had a vigorous two-party political system, had adopted a grandfather clause shortly after it became a state. As the head of the Oklahoma Republican party complained, the clause had been adopted to stop blacks from voting not because of their race, but because they voted Republican.

In *Guinn v. United States* (1915), the Justice Department attacked the Oklahoma grandfather clause as violating the Fifteenth Amendment. At the same time, the Court heard a challenge to a similar Maryland statute in *Myers v. Anderson*. The clauses waived the literacy test for voting for anyone entitled to vote under any form of government, for those living in a foreign country as of January 1, 1866, and for their lineal descendants. Since neither clause specified race, both states denied any constitutional violation; both also claimed that voting requirements remained primarily a matter of state and local jurisdiction. Chief Justice White disagreed. Although neither law mentioned race, their application worked specifically to keep blacks from voting, while allowing whites to bypass the literacy test and poll tax. In a companion case, *United States v. Mosely*, the Court upheld the conviction of Oklahoma officials for depriving blacks of their right to vote, in violation of Section 19 of the Ku Klux Klan Enforcement Act of 1870.

# Conclusion

The promise of freedom made during the Civil War era remained unfulfilled for many Americans at the turn of the century. African Americans may not have been formally enslaved as they had been before the war, but they lived and worked in a demeaning system of apartheid that clearly marked them as second-class citizens. Native Americans, Asians, and people living in the nation's new colonies also failed to share in the promise of equality made in the Fourteenth Amendment, while women remained disfavored by the law. There were some bright spots, and a few glimmerings in the Court that racism embedded in law could go only so far. But the bright spots were few, and the glimmerings would take more than six decades before they would flower into the Warren Court's attack on segregation.

# For Further Reading

A good general work looking at the South after the Civil War is Edward L. Ayers, *The Promise of the New South: Life After Reconstruction* (1992). In terms of segregation, the key work is C. Vann Woodward's classic, *The Strange Career of Jim Crow* (3rd ed., 1989), which argues that segregation need not have become the dominant pattern in Southern racial relations. A case study testing and supporting this thesis is Joseph H. Cartwright, *The Triumph of Jim Crow: Tennessee Race Relations in the 1880s* (1976). A variation on the Woodward thesis is Howard Rabinowitz, *Race Relations in the Urban South, 1865–1890* (1978), while questions of black interest in separation as well as the timing of segregation laws are explored in two books by Joel Williamson, *After Slavery: The Negro in South Carolina during Reconstruction, 1861–1877* (1965) and *The Crucible of Race: Black-White Relations in the American South since Emancipation* (1984). Specifics on various states are found in Pauli Murray, *State Laws on Race and Color* (1952), which documents the adoption of Jim Crow laws. Other works dealing with the treatment of blacks after the Civil War include William Gillette, *Retreat from Reconstruction, 1869–1879* (1979), and Daniel A. Novak, *The Wheel of Servitude: Black Forced Labor After Slavery* (1978). Also important is William Cohen, *At Freedom's Edge: Black Mobility and the Southern White Quest for Racial Control, 1861–1915* (1991).

Some specialized studies include J. David Hoeveler, Jr., "Reconstruction and the Federal Courts: The Civil Rights Act of 1875," 31 *History* 604 (1969); John A. Scott, "Justice Bradley's Evolving Concept of the Fourteenth Amendment from the Slaughterhouse Cases to the Civil Rights Cases," 25 *Rutgers Law Review* 552 (1971); and Roger L. Rice, "Residential Segregation by Law, 1910–1917," 34 *Journal of Southern History* 179 (1968). The standard work on *Plessy* is Charles A. Lofgren, *The Plessy Case: A Legal-Historical Interpretation* (1987). The worsening position of blacks in Southern agriculture is detailed in William Cohen, "Negro Involuntary Servitude in the South, 1865–1940: A Preliminary Inventory," 42 *Journal of Southern History* 31 (1976), and Harold D. Woodman, "Post-War Southern Agriculture and the Law," 53 *Agricultural History* 319 (1979). For peonage, see Peter Daniel, *The Shadow of Slavery: Peonage in the South, 1901–1969* (1972), and David E. Bernstein, *Only On Place of Redress: African-Americans, Labor Regulations and the Courts from Reconstruction to the New Deal* (2001). For the Insular cases, see José A. Cabranes, *Citizenship and the American Empire* (1979), and Julius W. Pratt, *America's Colonial Experiment* (1950). On blacks and the legal profession in this period, see J. Clay Smith, *Emancipation: The Making of the Black Lawyer, 1844–1944* (1993).

For Indian policy, the basic collection of documents is Francis P. Prucha, *The Great Father: The United States Government and the American Indian* 2 vols. (1984), while a good overview of federal policy during this period is Frederick E. Hoxie, *A Final Promise: The Campaign to Assimilate the Indians, 1880–1920* (1984). For the Court's role, see David E. Wilkins, *American Indian Sovereignty and the U.S. Supreme Court* (1997). For materials on specific cases, see Blue Clark, *Lone Wolf v. Hitchcock: Treaty Rights and Indian Law at the End of the Nineteenth Century* (1994); Brian Czech, "*Ward v. Race Horse*—Supreme Court as Obviator?" 35 *Journal of the West* 61 (July 1996); and Robert K. Heimann, "The Cherokee Tobacco Case," 41 *Chronicles of Oklahoma* 299 (1967).

For the Chinese cases, see Hyung-Chan Kim, *A Legal History of Asian Americans, 1790–1990* (1994); Stuart Creighton Miller, *The Unwelcome Immigrant: The American Image of the Chinese, 1785–1882* (1969); Lucy E. Salyer, *Laws Harsh as Tigers: Chinese Immigrants and the Shaping of Modern Immigration Law* (1995); and chapter 10 of Owen M. Fiss, *Troubled Beginnings of the Modern State, 1888–1910* (1993). For the Insular Cases, see James Edward Kerr, *The Insular Cases: The Role of the Judiciary in American Expansionism* (1982). The development of the incorporation doctrine is explicated in Robert B. Highsaw, *Edward Douglass White: Defender of the Conservative Faith* (1981).

The literature on women and the law is growing rapidly, but for this era, see Sandra F. Van-Burkleo, *"Belonging to the World": Women's Rights and American Constitutional Culture* (2001); Joan Hoff, *Law, Gender and Injustice: A Legal History of U.S. Women* (1991); Virginia G. Drachman, *Women Lawyers and the Origins of Professional Identity in America* (1993); and *Sisters in Law: Women Lawyers in Modern American History* (1998). The issue of taxation without representation is discussed in chapter 3 of Linda K. Kerber, *No Constitutional Right to Be Ladies: Women and the Obligations of Citizenship* (1998). Legal burdens faced by average women after the Civil War is detailed in Amy Dru Stanley, *From Bondage to Contract: Wage Labor, Marriage, and the Market in the Age of Slave Emancipation* (1998). For two unusual women lawyers, see Jane M. Friedman, *America's First Woman Lawyer: The Biography of Myra Bradwell* (1993); and Jill Norgren, "Before It Was Merely Difficult: Belva Lockwood's Life in Law and Politics," 1999 *Journal of Supreme Court History* 16 (April 1999), the first installment of a forthcoming biography.

# APPENDIXES

# *The Declaration of Independence*

W HEN IN THE course of human events, it becomes necessary for one people to dissolve the political bands which have connected them with another, and to assume that Powers of the earth, the separate and equal station to which the Laws of Nature and of Nature's God entitle them, a decent respect to the opinions of mankind requires that they should declare the causes which impel them to the separation.

We hold these truths to be self-evident, that all men are created equal, that they are endowed to their Creator with certain unalienable rights, that among these are Life, Liberty, and the pursuit of Happiness. That to secure these rights, Governments are instituted among Men, deriving their just powers from the consent of the governed. That whenever any Form of Government becomes destructive of these ends, it is the Right of the People to alter or to abolish it, and to institute new Government, laying its foundation on such principles and organizing its powers in such form, as to them shall seem most likely to effect their Safety and Happiness. Prudence, indeed, will dictate that Governments long established should not be changed for light and transient causes; and accordingly all experience hath shown, that mankind are more disposed to suffer, while evils are sufferable, than to right themselves by abolishing the forms to which they are accustomed. But when a long train of abuses and usurpations, pursuing invariably the same Object evinces a design to reduce them under absolute Despotism, it is their right, it is their duty, to throw off such Government, and to provide new Guards for their future security.—Such has been the patient sufferance of these Colonies; and such is now the necessity which constrains them to alter their former Systems of Government. The history of the present King of Great Britain is a history of repeated injuries and usurpations, all having in direct object the establishment of an absolute Tyranny over these States. To prove this, let Facts be submitted to a candid world.

He has refused his Assent to Laws, the most wholesome and necessary for the public good.

He has forbidden his Governors to pass Laws of immediate and pressing importance, unless suspended in their operation till his Assent should be obtained; and when so suspended, he has utterly neglected to attend to them.

He has refused to pass other Laws for the accommodation of large districts of people, unless those people would relinquish the right of Representation in the Legislature, a right inestimable to them and formidable to tyrants only.

He has called together legislative bodies at places unusual, uncomfortable, and distant from the depository of their public Records, for the sole purpose of fatiguing them into compliance with his measures.

He has dissolved Representative Houses repeatedly, for opposing with manly firmness his invasions on the rights of the people.

He has refused for a long time, after such dissolutions, to cause others to be elected; whereby the Legislative powers, incapable of Annihilation, have returned to the People at large for their exercise; the State remaining in the mean time exposed to all dangers of invasion from without, and convulsions within.

He has endeavoured to prevent the population of these States; for that purpose obstructing the Laws of Naturalization of Foreigners; refusing to pass others to encourage their migrations hither, and raising the conditions of new Appropriations of Lands.

He has obstructed the Administration of Justice, by refusing his Assent to Laws for establishing Judiciary powers.

He has made Judges dependent on his Will alone, for the tenure of their offices, and the amount and payment of their salaries.

He has erected a multitude of New Offices, and sent hither swarms of Officers to harass our People, and eat out their substance.

He has kept among us, in times of peace, Standing Armies without the Consent of our legislature.

He has affected to render the Military independent of and superior to the Civil Power.

He has combined with others to subject us to a jurisdiction foreign to our constitution, and unacknowledged by our laws; giving his Assent to their Acts of pretended Legislation:

For quartering large bodies of armed troops among us:

For protecting them, by a mock Trial, from Punishment for any Murders which they should commit on the Inhabitants of these States:

For cutting off our Trade with all parts of the world:

For imposing taxes on us without our Consent:

For depriving us of many cases, of the benefits of Trial by jury:

For transporting us beyond Seas to be tried for pretended offences:

For abolishing the free System of English Laws in a neighbouring Province, establishing therein an Arbitrary government, and enlarging its Boundaries so as to render it at once an example and fit instrument for introducing the same absolute rule into these Colonies:

For taking away our Charters, abolishing our most valuable Laws, and altering fundamentally the Forms of our Governments:

For suspending our own Legislatures, and declaring themselves invested with Power to legislate for us in all cases whatsoever.

He has abdicated Government here, by declaring us out of his Protection and waging War against us.

He has plundered our seas, ravaged our Coasts, burnt our towns, and destroyed the lives of our people.

He is at this time transporting large armies of foreign mercenaries to compleat the works of death, desolation, and tyranny, already begun with circumstances of Cruelty & perfidy scarcely parralleled in the most barbarous ages, and totally unworthy the Head of a civilized nation.

He has constrained our fellow Citizens taken Captive on the high Seas to bear Arms against their Country, to become the executioners of their friends and Brethren, or to fall themselves by their Hands.

He has excited domestic insurrections amongst us, and has endeavoured to bring on the inhabitants of our frontiers, the merciless Indian savages, whose known rule of warfare, is an undistinguished destruction of all ages, sexes, and conditions.

In every stage of these Oppressions We have Petitioned for Redress in the most humble terms: Our repeated Petitions have been answered only by repeated injury. A Prince, whose character is thus marked by every act which may define a Tyrant, is unfit to be the ruler of a free people.

Nor have We been wanting in attention to our British brethren. We have warned them from time to time of attempts by their legislature to extend an unwarrantable jurisdiction over us. We have reminded them of the circumstances of our emigration and settlement here. We have appealed to their native justice and magnanimity, and we have conjured them by the ties of our common kindred to disavow these usurpations, which, would inevitably interrupt our connections and correspondence. They too must have been deaf to the voice of justice and of consanguinity. We must, therefore, acquiesce in the necessity, which denounces our Separation, and hold them, as we hold the rest of mankind, Enemies in War, in Peace Friends.

We, therefore, the Representatives of the United States of America, in General Congress, Assembled, appealing to the Supreme Judge of the world for the rectitude of our intentions, do, in the Name, and by Authority of the good People of these Colonies, solemnly publish and declare, That these United Colonies are, and of Right ought to be FREE AND INDEPENDENT STATES; that they are Absolved from all Allegiance to the British Crown, and that all political connection between them and the State of Great Britain, is and ought to be totally dissolved; and that as Free and Independent States, they have full Power to levy War, conclude Peace, contract Alliances, establish Commerce, and to do all other Acts and Things which Independent states may of right do. And for the support of this Declaration, with a firm reliance on the Protection of Divine Providence, we mutually pledge to each other our Lives, our Fortunes, and our sacred Honor.

The foregoing Declaration was, by order of Congress, engrossed, and signed by the following members:

*John Hancock*

**New Hampshire**
*Josiah Bartlett*
*William Whipple*
*Matthew Thornton*

**Massachusetts Bay**
*Samuel Adams*
*John Adams*
*Robert Treat Paine*
*Elbridge Gery*

**Rhode Island**
*Stephen Hopkins*
*William Ellery*

**Connecticut**
*Roger Sherman*
*Samuel Huntington*
*William Williams*
*Oliver Wolcott*

**New York**
*William Floyd*
*Philip Livingston*
*Francis Lewis*
*Lewis Morris*

**New Jersey**
*Richard Stockton*
*John Witherspoon*
*Francis Hopkinson*
*John Hart*
*Abraham Clark*

**Pennsylvania**
*Robert Morris*
*Benjamin Rush*
*Benjamin Franklin*
*John Morton*
*George Clymer*
*James Smith*
*George Taylor*
*James Wilson*
*George Ross*

**Delaware**
*Caesar Rodney*
*George Read*
*Thomas M'Kean*

**Maryland**
*Samuel Chase*
*William Paca*
*Thomas Stone*
*Charles Carroll,*
*of Carrollton*

**Virginia**
*George Wythe*
*Richard Henry Lee*
*Thomas Jefferson*
*Benjamin Harrison*
*Thomas Nelson, Jr.*
*Francis Lightfoot Lee*
*Carter Braxton*

**North Carolina**
*William Hooper*
*Joseph Hewes*
*John Penn*

**South Carolina**
*Edward Rutledge*
*Thomas Heyward, Jr.*
*Thomas Lynch, Jr.*
*Arthur Middleton*

**Georgia**
*Button Gwinnett*
*Lyman Hall*
*George Walton*

*Resolved,* That copies of the Declaration be sent to the several assemblies, conventions, and committees, or councils of safety, and to the several commanding officers of the continental troops; that it be proclaimed in each of the United States, at the head of the army.

# Articles of Confederation

To ALL TO whom these Presents shall come, we the undersigned Delegates of the States affixed to our names send greeting.

Whereas the Delegates of the United States of America in Congress assembled did on the fifteenth day of November in the Year of our Lord One Thousand Seven Hundred and Seventy-seven, and in the Second Year of the Independence of America agree to certain articles of Confederation and perpetual Union between the States of Newhampshire, Massachusetts-bay, Rhodeisland, and Providence Plantations, Connecticut, New York, New Jersey, Pennsylvania, Delaware, Maryland, Virginia, North-Carolina, South-Carolina and Georgia in the Words following, viz.

"Articles of Confederation and perpetual Union between the States of Newhampshire, Massachusetts-bay, Rhodeisland and Providence Plantations, Connecticut, New-York, New-Jersey, Pennsylvania, Delaware, Maryland, Virginia, North-Carolina, South-Carolina and Georgia.

ARTICLE I. The stile of this confederacy shall be "The United States of America."

ARTICLE II. Each State retains its sovereignty, freedom and independence, and every power, jurisdiction and right, which is not by this confederation expressly delegated to the United States, in Congress assembled.

ARTICLE III. The said States hereby severally enter into a firm league of friendship with each other, for their common defense, the security of their liberties, and their mutual and general welfare, binding themselves to assist each other, against all force offered to, or attacks made upon them, or any of them, on account of religion, sovereignty, trade or any other pretence whatever.

ARTICLE IV. The better to secure and perpetuate mutual friendship and intercourse among the people of the different States in this Union, the free inhabitants of each of these States, paupers, vagabonds and fugitives from justice excepted, shall be entitled to all privileges and immunities of free citizens in the several States; and the people of each State shall have free ingress and regress to and from any other State, and shall enjoy therein all the privileges of trade and commerce, subject to the same duties, impositions and restrictions as the inhabitants thereof respectively, provided that such restrictions shall not extend so far as to prevent the removal of property imported into any State, to any other State of which the owner is an inhabitant; provided also that no imposition, duties or restriction shall be laid by any State, on the property of the United States, or either of them.

If any person guilty of, or charged with treason, felony, or other high misdemeanor in any State, shall flee from justice, and be found in any of the United States, he shall upon demand of the Governor or Executive power, of the State from which he fled, be delivered up and removed to the State having jurisdiction of his offence.

Full faith and credit shall be given in each of these States to the records, acts and judicial proceedings of the courts and magistrates of every other State.

ARTICLE V. For the more convenient management of the general interests of the United States, delegates shall be annually appointed in such manner as the legislature of each State shall direct, to meet in Congress on the first Monday in November, in every year, with a power reserved to each State, to recall its delegates, or any of them, at any time within the year, and to send others in their stead, for the remainder of the year.

No State shall be represented in Congress by less than two, nor by more than seven members; and no person shall be capable of being a delegate for more than three years in any term of six years; nor shall any person, being a delegate, be capable of holding any office under the United States, for which he, or another for his benefit receives any salary, fees or emolument of any kind.

Each State shall maintain its own delegates in a meeting of the States, and while they act as members of the committee of the States.

In determining questions in the United States, in Congress assembled, each State shall have one vote.

Freedom of speech and debate in Congress shall not be impeached or questioned in any court, or place out of Congress, and the members of Congress shall be protected in their persons from arrests and imprisonments, during the time of their going to and from, and attendance on Congress, except for treason, felony, or breach of the peace.

ARTICLE VI. No State without the consent of the United States in Congress assembled, shall send any embassy to, or receive any embassy from, or enter into any conference, agreement, alliance or treaty with any king, prince or state; nor shall any person holding any office of profit or trust under the United States, or any of them, accept of any present, emolument, office or title of any kind whatever from any king, prince or foreign state; nor shall the United States in Congress assembled, or any of them, grant any title of nobility.

No two or more States shall enter into any treaty, confederation or alliance whatever between them, without the consent of the United States in Congress assembled, specifying accurately the purposes for which the same is to be entered into, and how long it shall continue.

No State shall lay any imposts or duties, which may interfere with any stipulations in treaties, entered into by the United States in Congress assembled, with any king, prince or state, in pursuance of any treaties already proposed by Congress, to the courts of France and Spain.

No vessels of war shall be kept up in time of peace by any State, except such number only, as shall be deemed necessary by the United States in Congress assembled, for the defence of such State, or its trade; nor shall any body of forces be kept up by any State, in time of peace, except such number only, as in the judgment of the United States, in Congress assembled, shall be deemed requisite to garrison the forts necessary for the defense of such State; but every State shall always keep up a well regulated and disciplined militia, sufficiently armed and accoutred, and shall provide and constantly have ready for use, in public stores, a due number of field pieces and tents, and a proper quantity of arms, ammunition and camp equipage.

No State shall engage in any war without the consent of the United States in Congress assembled, unless such State be actually invaded by enemies, or shall have received certain advice of a resolution being formed by some nation of Indians to invade such State, and the danger is so imminent as not to admit of a delay, till the United States in Congress assembled can be consulted: nor shall any State grant commissions to any ships or vessels of war, nor letters of marque or reprisal, except it be after a declaration of war by the United States in Congress assembled, and then only against the kingdom or state and the subjects thereof, against which war has been so declared, and under such regulations as shall be established by the United States in Congress assembled, unless such State be infested by pirates, in which case vessels of war may be fitted out for that occasion, and kept so long as the danger shall continue, or until the United States in Congress assembled shall determine otherwise.

ARTICLE VII. When land-forces are raised by any State of the common defence, all officers of or under the rank of colonel, shall be appointed by the Legislature of each State respectively by whom such forces shall be raised, or in such manner as such State shall direct, and all vacancies shall be filled up by the State which first made the appointment.

ARTICLE VIII. All charges of war, and all other expenses that shall be incurred for the common defense or general welfare, and allowed by the United States in Congress assembled, shall be defrayed out of a common treasury, which shall be supplied by the several States, in proportion to the value of all land within each State, granted to or surveyed for any person, as such land and the buildings and improvements thereon shall be estimated according to such mode as the United States in Congress assembled, shall from time to time direct and appoint.

The taxes for paying that proportion shall be laid and levied by the authority and direction of the Legislatures of the several States within the time agreed upon by the United States in Congress assembled.

ARTICLE IX. The United States in Congress assembled, shall have the sole and exclusive right and power of determining on peace and war, except in the cases mentioned in the sixth article—of sending and receiving ambassadors—entering into treaties and alliances, provided that no treaty of commerce shall be made whereby the legislative power of the respective States shall be restrained from imposing such imposts and duties on foreigners, as their own people are subjected to, or from prohibiting the exportation or importation of and species of goods or commodities whatsoever—of establishing rules for deciding in all cases, what captures on land or water shall be legal, and in what manner prizes taken by land or naval forces in the service of the United

States shall be divided or appropriated—of granting letters of marque and reprisal in times of peace—appointing courts for the trial of piracies and felonies committed on the high seas and establishing courts for receiving and determining finally appeals in all cases of captures, provided that no member of Congress shall be appointed a judge of any of the said courts.

The United States in Congress assembled shall also be the last resort on appeal in all disputes and differences now subsisting or that hereafter may arise between two or more States concerning boundary, jurisdiction or any other cause whatever; which authority shall always be exercised in the manner following. Whenever the legislative or executive authority or lawful agent of any State in controversy with another shall present a petition to Congress, stating the matter in question and praying for a hearing, notice thereof shall be given by order of Congress to the legislative or executive authority of the other State in controversy, and a day assigned for the appearance of the parties by their lawful agents, who shall then be directed to appoint by joint consent, commissioners or judges to constitute a court for hearing and determining the matter in question: but if they cannot agree, Congress shall name three persons out of each of the United States, and from the list of such persons each party shall alternately strike out one, the petitioners beginning, until the number shall be reduced to thirteen; and from that number not less than seven, nor more than nine names as Congress shall direct, shall in the presence of Congress be drawn out by lot, and the persons whose names shall be so drawn or any five of them, shall be commissioners or judges, to hear and finally determine the controversy, so always as a major part of the judges who shall hear the cause shall agree in the determination: and if either party shall neglect to attend at the day appointed, without reasons, which Congress shall judge sufficient, or being present shall refuse to strike, the Congress shall proceed to nominate three persons out of each State, and the Secretary of Congress shall strike in behalf of such party absent or refusing; and the judgment and sentence of the court to be appointed, in the manner before prescribed, shall be final and conclusive; and if any of the parties shall refuse to submit to the authority of such court, or to appear or defend their claim or cause, the court shall nevertheless proceed to pronounce sentence, or judgment, which shall in like manner be final and decisive, the judgment or sentence and other proceedings being in either case transmitted to Congress, and lodged among the acts of Congress for the security of the parties concerned: provided that every commissioner, before he sits in judgment, shall take an oath to be administered by one of the judges of the supreme or superior court of the State where the cause shall be tried, "well and truly to hear and determine the matter in question, according to the best of his judgment, without favour, affection or hope of reward:" provided also that no State shall be deprived of territory for the benefit of the United States.

All controversies concerning the private right of soil claimed under different grants of two or more States, whose jurisdiction as they may respect such lands, and the states which passed such grants are adjusted, the said grants or either of them being at the same time claimed to have originated antecedent to such settlement of jurisdiction, shall on the petition of either party to the Congress of the United States, be finally determined as near as may be in the same manner as is before prescribed for deciding disputes respecting territorial jurisdiction between different States.

The United States in Congress assembled shall also have the sole and exclusive right and power of regulating the alloy and value of coin struck by their own authority, or by that of the respective States—fixing the standard of weights and measures throughout the United States—regulating the trade and managing all affairs with the Indians, not members of any of the States, provided that the legislative right of any state within its own limits be not infringed or violated—establishing and regulating post-offices from one State to another, throughout all of the United States, and exacting such postage on the papers passing thro' the same as may be requisite to defray the expenses of the said office—appointing all officers of the land forces, in the service of the United States, excepting regimental officers—appointing all the officers of the naval forces, and commissioning all officers whatever in the service of the United States—making rules for the government and regulation of the said land and naval forces, and directing their operations.

The United States in Congress assembled shall have authority to appoint a committee, to sit in the recess of Congress, to be denominated "a Committee of the States," and to consist of one delegate from each State; and to appoint such other committees and civil officers as may be necessary for managing the general affairs of the United States under their direction—to appoint one of their number to preside, provided that no person be allowed to serve in the office of president more than one year in any term of three years; to ascertain the necessary sums of money to be raised for the service of the United States, and to appropriate and apply the same for defraying the public expenses—to borrow money, or emit bills on the credit of the United States, transmitting every half year to the respective States an account of the sums of money so borrowed or emitted,—to build and equip a navy—to agree upon the number of land forces, and to make requisitions from such State for its quote, in proportion to the number of white inhabitants in such State; which requisition shall be binding, and thereupon the Legislature of each State shall appoint the regimental officers, raise the men and cloath, arm and equip them in a soldier like manner, at the expense of the United States; and the officers and men so cloathed, armed and equipped shall march to the place appointed, and within the time agreed on by the United States in Congress assembled; but if the United States in Congress assembled shall, on consideration of circumstances judge proper that any State should not raise men, or should raise a smaller number of men than the quota thereof, such extra number shall be raised, officered, cloathed, armed and equipped in the same manner as the quota of such State, unless the legislature of such State shall judge that such extra number cannot be safely spared out of the same, in which case they shall raise officer, cloath, arm and equip as many of such extra number as they judge can be safely spared. And the officers and men so cloathed, armed and equipped, shall march to the place appointed, and within the time agreed on by the United States in Congress assembled.

The United States in Congress assembled shall never engage in a war, nor grant letters of marque and reprisal in time of peace, nor enter into any treaties or alliances, nor coin money, nor regulate the value thereof, nor ascertain the sums and expenses necessary for the defence and welfare of the United States, or any of them, nor emit bills, nor borrow money on the credit of the United States, nor appropriate money, nor agree upon the number of vessels to be built or purchased, or the number of land or sea forces to be raised, nor appoint a commander in chief of the army or navy, unless nine States assent to the same: nor shall a question on any other point, except for adjourning from day to day be determined, unless by the votes of a majority of the United States in Congress assembled.

The Congress of the United States shall have power to adjourn to any time within the year, and to any place within the United States, so that no period of adjournment be for a longer duration than the space of six months, and shall publish the journal of their proceedings monthly, except such parts thereof relating to treaties, alliances or military operations, as in their judgment require secrecy; and the yeas and nays of the delegates of each State on any question shall be entered on the Journal, when it is desired by any delegate; and the delegates of a State, or any of them, at his or their request shall be furnished with a transcript of the said journal, except such parts as are above excepted, to lay before the Legislatures of the several States.

ARTICLE X. The committee of the States, or any nine of them, shall be authorized to execute, in the recess of Congress, such of the powers of Congress as the United States in Congress assembled, by the consent of nine States, shall from time to time think expedient to vest them with; provided that no power be delegated to the said committee, for the exercise of which, by the articles of confederation, the voice of nine States in the Congress of the United States assembled is requisite.

ARTICLE XI. Canada acceding to this confederation, and joining in the measures of the United States, shall be admitted into, and entitled to all the advantages of this Union: but no other colony shall be admitted into the same, unless such admission be agreed to by nine States.

ARTICLE XII. All bills of credit emitted, monies borrowed and debts contracted by, or under the authority of Congress, before the assembling of the United States, in pursuance of the present confederation, shall be deemed and considered as a charge against the United States, for payment and satisfaction whereof the said United States, and the public faith are hereby solemnly pledged.

ARTICLE XIII. Every State shall abide by the determinations of the United States in Congress assembled, on all questions which by this confederation are submitted to them. And the articles of this confederation shall be inviolably observed by every State, and the Union shall be perpetual; nor shall any alteration at any time hereafter be made in any of them; unless such alteration be agreed to in a Congress of the United States, and be afterwards confirmed by the Legislatures of every State.

And whereas it has pleased the Great Governor of the world to incline the hearts of the Legislatures we respectively represent in Congress, to approve of, and to authorize us to ratify the said articles of confederation and perpetual union. Know ye that we the undersigned delegates, by virtue of the power and authority to us given for that purpose, do by these presents, in the name and in behalf of our respective constituents, fully and entirely ratify and confirm each and every of the said articles of confederation and perpetual union, and all and singular the matters and things therein contained: and we do further solemnly plight and engage the faith of our respective constituents, that they shall abide by the determinations of the United States in Congress assembled, on all questions, which by the said confederation are submitted to them. And that the articles thereof shall be inviolably observed by the State we respectively represent, and that the Union shall be perpetual.

In witness thereof we have hereunto set our hands in Congress. Done at Philadelphia in the State of Pennsylvania the ninth day of July in the year of our Lord one thousand seven hundred and seventy-eight, and in the third year of the independence of America.

# Constitution of the United States

W E THE PEOPLE of the United States, in Order to form a more perfect Union, establish Justice, insure domestic Tranquility, provide for the common defence, promote the general Welfare, and secure the Blessings of Liberty to ourselves and our Posterity, do ordain and establish this Constitution for the United States of America.

## Article I

*Section 1.* All legislative Powers herein granted shall be vested in a Congress of the United States, which shall consist of a Senate and House of Representatives

*Section 2.* The House of Representatives shall be composed of Members chosen every second Year by the People of the several States, and the Electors in each State shall have the Qualifications requisite for Electors of the most numerous Branch of the State Legislature.

No Person shall be a Representative who shall not have attained to the Age of twenty five Years, and been seven Years a Citizen of the United States, and who shall not, when elected, be an Inhabitant of that State in which he shall be chosen.

Representatives and direct Taxes shall be apportioned among the several States which may be included within this Union, according to their respective Numbers, which shall be determined by adding to the whole Number of free Persons, including those bound to Service for a Term of Years, and excluding Indians not taxed, three fifths of all other Persons. The actual Enumeration shall be made within three Years after the first Meeting of the Congress of the United States, and within every subsequent Term of ten Years, in such Manner as they shall by Law direct. The Number of Representatives shall not exceed one for every thirty Thousand, but each State shall have at Least one Representative; and until such enumeration shall be made, the State of New Hampshire shall be entitled to chuse three, Massachusetts eight, Rhode Island and Providence Plantations one, Connecticut five, New-York six, New Jersey four, Pennsylvania eight, Delaware one, Maryland six, Virginia ten, North Carolina five, South Carolina five, and Georgia three.

When vacancies happen in the Representation from any State, the Executive Authority thereof shall issue Writs of Election to fill such Vacancies. The House of Representatives shall chuse their Speaker and other Officers; and shall have the sole Power of Impeachment.

*Section 3.* The Senate of the United States shall be composed of two Senators from each State, chosen by the Legislature thereof, for six Years; and each Senator shall have one vote.

Immediately after they shall be assembled in Consequence of the first Election, they shall be divided as equally as may be into three Classes. The Seats of the Senators of the first Class shall be vacated at the Expiration of the second Year, of the second Class at the Expiration of the fourth Year, and of the third Class at the Expiration of the sixth Year, so that one third may be chosen every second Year; and if Vacancies happen by Resignation, or otherwise, during the Recess of the Legislature of any State, the Executive thereof may make temporary Appointments until the next Meeting of the Legislature, which shall then fill such Vacancies.

No Person shall be a Senator who shall not have attained to the Age of thirty Years, and been nine Years a Citizen of the United States, and who shall not, when elected, be an Inhabitant of that State for which he shall be chosen.

The Vice President of the United States shall be President of the Senate, but shall have no Vote, unless they be equally divided. The Senate shall chuse their other Officers, and also a President pro tempore, in the Absence of the Vice President, or when he shall exercise the Office of President of the United States.

The Senate shall have the sole Power to try all Impeachments. When sitting for that Purpose, they shall be on Oath or Affirmation. When the President of the United States is tried the Chief Justice shall preside: And no Person shall be convicted without the Concurrence of two thirds of the Members present.

Judgment in Cases of Impeachment shall not extend further than to removal from Office, and disqualification to hold and enjoy any Office of honor, Trust or Profit under the United States: but the Party convicted shall nevertheless be liable and subject to Indictment, Trial, Judgment and Punishment, according to Law.

*Section 4.* The Times, Places and Manner of holding Elections for Senators and Representatives, shall be prescribed in each State by the Legislature thereof; but the Congress may at any time by Law make or alter such Regulations, except as to the Places of chusing Senators.

The Congress shall assemble at least once in every Year, and such Meeting shall be on the first Monday in December, unless they shall by Law appoint a different Day.

*Section 5.* Each House shall be the Judge of the Elections, Returns and Qualifications of its own Members, and a Majority of each shall constitute a Quorum to do Business; but a smaller Number may adjourn from day to day, and may be authorized to compel the Attendance of absent Members, in such Manner, and under such Penalties as each House may provide.

Each House may determine the Rules of its Proceedings, punish its Members for disorderly Behavior, and, with the Concurrence of two thirds, expel a Member.

Each House shall keep a Journal of its Proceedings, and from time to time publish the same, excepting such Parts as may in their Judgment require Secrecy; and the Yeas and Nays of the Members of either House on any question shall, at the Desire of one fifth of those Present, be entered on the Journal. Neither House, during the Session of Congress, shall, without the Consent of the other, adjourn for more than three days, nor to any other Place than that in which the two Houses shall be sitting.

*Section 6.* The Senators and Representatives shall receive a Compensation for their Services, to be ascertained by law, and paid out of the Treasury of the United States. They shall in all Cases, except Treason, Felony and Breach of the Peace, be privileged from Arrest during their Attendance at the Session of their respective Houses, and in going to and returning from the same; and for any Speech or Debate in either House, they shall not be questioned in any other Place.

No Senator or Representative shall, during the Time for which he was elected, be appointed to any civil Office under the Authority of the United States, which shall have been created, or the Emoluments whereof shall have been increased during such time; and no Person holding any Office under the United States, shall be a Member of either House during his Continuance in Office.

*Section 7.* All Bills for raising Revenue shall originate in the House of Representatives; but the Senate may propose or concur with amendments as on other Bills.

Every Bill which shall have passed the House of Representatives and the Senate, shall, before it become a Law, be presented to the President of the United States; If he approve he shall sign it:, but if not he shall return it with his Objections to that House in which it shall have originated, who shall enter the Objections at large on their Journal, and proceed to reconsider it. If after such Reconsideration two thirds of that House shall agree to pass the Bill, it shall be sent, together with the Objections, to the other House, by which it shall likewise be reconsidered, and if approved by two thirds of that House, it shall become a Law. But in all such Cases the Votes of both Houses shall be determined by Yeas and Nays, and the Names of the Persons voting for and against the Bill shall be entered on the Journal of each House respectively. If any Bill shall not be returned by the President within ten Days (Sunday excepted) after it shall have been presented to him, the Same shall be a Law, in like Manner as if he had signed it, unless the Congress by their Adjournment prevent its Return, in which Case it shall not be a Law.

Every Order, Resolution, or Vote to which the Concurrence of the Senate and House of Representatives may be necessary (except on a question of Adjournment) shall be presented to the President of the United States; and before the Same shall take Effect, shall be approved by him, or being disapproved by him, shall be repassed by two thirds of the Senate and House of Representatives, according t:o the Rules and Limitations prescribed in the Case of a Bill.

*Section 8.* The Congress shall have Power To lay and collect Taxes, Duties, Imposts and Excises, to pay the Debts and provide for the common Defence and general Welfare of the United States; but all Duties, Imposts and Excises shall be uniform throughout the United States;

To borrow Money on the credit of the United States;

To regulate Commerce with foreign Nations, and among the several States, and with the Indian Tribes;

To establish an uniform Rule of Naturalization, and uniform Laws on the subject of Bankruptcies throughout the United States;

To coin Money, regulate the Value thereof, and of foreign Coin, and fix the Standard of Weights and Measures;

To provide for the Punishment of counterfeiting the Securities and current Coin of the United States;

To establish Post Offices and post Roads;

To promote the Progress of Science and useful Arts, by securing for limited Times to Authors and Inventors the exclusive Right to their respective Writings and Discoveries;

To constitute Tribunals inferior to the supreme Court;

To define and punish Piracies and Felonies committed on the high Seas, and Offences against the Law of Nations;

To declare War, grant Letters of Marque and Reprisal, and make Rules concerning Captures on Land and Water;

To raise and support Armies, but no Appropriation of Money to that Use shall be for a longer Term than two Years;

To provide and maintain a Navy;

To make Rules for the Government and Regulation of the land and naval Forces;

To provide for calling forth the Militia to execute the Laws of the Union, suppress Insurrections and repel Invasions;

To provide for organizing, arming, and disciplining, the Militia, and for governing such Part of them as may be employed in the Service of the United States, reserving to the States respectively, the Appointment of the Officers, and the Authority of training the Militia according to the discipline prescribed by Congress;

To exercise exclusive Legislation in all Cases whatsoever, over such District (not exceeding ten Miles square) as may, by Cession of particular States, and the Acceptance of Congress, become the Seat of the Government of the United States, and to exercise like Authority over all Places purchased by the Consent of the Legislature of the State in which the Same shall be, for the Erection of Forts, Magazines, Arsenals, dockYards, and other needful Buildings;—And

To make all Laws which shall be necessary and proper for carrying into Execution the foregoing Powers, and all other Powers vested by this Constitution in the Government of the United States, or in any Department or Officer thereof.

*Section 9.* The Migration or Importation of such Persons as any of the States now existing shall think proper to admit, shall not be prohibited by the Congress prior to the Year one thousand eight hundred and eight, but a Tax or duty may be imposed on such Importation, not exceeding ten dollars for each Person.

The Privilege of the Writ of Habeas Corpus shall not be suspended, unless when in Cases of Rebellion or Invasion the public Safety may require it.

No Bill of Attainder or ex post facto Law shall be passed.

No Capitation, or other direct, Tax shall be laid, unless in Proportion to the Census or Enumeration herein before directed to be taken.

No Tax or Duty shall be laid on Articles exported from any State.

No Preference shall be given by any Regulation of Commerce or Revenue to the

Ports of one State over those of another; nor shall Vessels bound to, or from, one State, be obliged to enter, clear or pay Duties in another.

No Money shall be drawn from the Treasury, but in Consequence of appropriations made by Law; and a regular Statement and Account of the receipts and Expenditures of all public Money shall be published from time to time.

No Title of Nobility shall be granted by the United States: And no Person holding any Office of Profit or Trust under them, shall, without the Consent of the Congress, accept of any present, Emolument, Office, or Title, of any kind whatever, from any King, Prince or foreign State.

*Section 10.* No State shall enter into any Treaty, Alliance, or Confederation; grant Letters of Marque and Reprisal, coin Money; emit Bills of Credit, make any Thing but gold and silver Coin a Tender in Payment of Debts; pass any Bill of Attainder, ex post facto Law, or Law impairing the Obligation for Contracts, or grant any Title of Nobility.

No State shall, without the Consent of the Congress, lay any Imposts or Duties on Imports or Exports, except what may be absolutely necessary for executing its inspection Laws: and the net Produce of all Duties and Imposts, laid by any State on Imports or Exports, shall be for the Use of the Treasury of the United States; and all such Laws shall be subject to the Revision and Controul of the Congress.

No State shall, without the Consent of Congress, lay any Duty of Tonnage, keep Troops, or Ships of War in time of Peace, enter into any Agreement or Compact with another State, or with a foreign Power, or engage in War, unless actually invaded, or in such imminent Danger as will not admit of delay.

# Article II

*Section 1.* The executive Power shall be vested in a President of the United States of America. He shall hold his Office during the Term of four Years, and, together with the Vice President, chosen for the same Term, be elected, as follows

Each State shall appoint, In such Manner as the Legislature thereof may direct, a Number of Electors, equal to the whole Number of Senators and Representatives to which the State may be entitled in the Congress: but no Senator or Representative, or Person holding an Office of Trust or Profit under the United States, shall be appointed an Elector.

The Electors shall meet in their respective States, and vote by Ballot for two Persons, of whom one at least shall not be an Inhabitant of the same State with themselves, And they shall make a List of all the Persons voted for, and of the number of Votes for each; which List they shall sign and certify, and transmit sealed to the Seat of the Government of the United States, directed to the President of the Senate. The President of the Senate shall, in the Presence of the Senate and House of Representatives, open all the Certificates, and the Votes shall then be counted. The Person having the greatest number of Votes shall be the President, if such Number be a Majority of the whole Number of Electors appointed; and if there be more than one who have such Majority, and have an equal Number of Votes, then the House of Representatives shall immediately chuse by Ballot one of them for President; and if no Person have a Majority, then from the five highest on the List the said House shall in like Manner chuse the President. But in chusing the President, the Votes shall be taken by States, the Representation from each State having one Vote; a quorum for this Purpose shall consist of a Member or Members from two thirds of the States, and a Majority of all the States shall be necessary to a Choice. In every Case, after the Choice of the President, the Person having the greatest Number of Votes of the Electors shall be the Vice President. But if there should remain two or more who have equal Votes, the Senate shall chuse from them by Ballot the Vice President.

The Congress may determine the Time of chusing the Electors, and the Day on which they shall give their Votes; which Day shall be the same throughout the United States.

No Person except a natural born Citizen, or a Citizen of the United States, at the time of the Adoption of this Constitution, shall be eligible to the Office of President; neither shall any Person be eligible to that Office who shall not have attained to the Age of thirty five Years, and been fourteen Years a Resident within the United States.

In Case of the Removal of the President from Office, or of his Death, Resignation, or Inability to discharge the Powers and Duties of the said Office, the Same shall devolve on the Vice President, and the Congress may by Law provide for the Case of Removal, Death, Resignation or Inability, both of the President and Vice President, declaring what Officer shall then act as President, and such Officer shall act accordingly, until the Disability be removed, or a President shall be elected.

The President shall, at stated Times, receive for his Services, a Compensation, which shall neither be increased nor diminished during the Period for which he shall have been elected, and he shall not receive within that Period any other emolument from the United States, or any of them.

Before he enter on the Execution of his Office, he shall take the following Oath or Affirmation:-"I do solemnly swear (or affirm) that I will faithfully execute the Office of President of the United States, and will to the best of my Ability, preserve, protect and defend the Constitution of the United States.

*Section 2.* The President shall be Commander in Chief of the Army and Navy of the United States, and of the Militia of the several States, when called into the actual Service of the United States; he may require the Opinion, in writing, of the principal Officer in each of the executive Departments, upon any Subject relating to the Duties of their respective Offices, and he shall have Power to grant Reprieves and Pardons for Offences against the United States, except in Cases of Impeachment.

He shall have Power, by and with the Advice and Consent of the Senate, to make Treaties, provided two thirds of the Senators present concur; and he shall nominate, and by and with the Advice and Consent of the Senate,shall appoint Ambassadors, other public Ministers and Consuls, Judges of the supreme Court, and all other Officers of the United States, whose Appointments are not herein otherwise provided for, and which shall be established by Law: but the Congress may by Law vest the Appointment of such inferior Officers, as they think proper, in the President alone, in the Courts of Law, or in the Heads of Departments.

The President shall have Power to fill up all Vacancies that may happen during the Recess of the Senate, by granting Commissions which shall expire at the End of their next Session

*Section 3.* He shall from time to time give to the Congress Information of the State of the Union, and recommend to their Consideration such Measures as he shall judge necessary and expedient; he may, on extraordinary Occasions, convene both Houses, or either of them, and in Case of Disagreements between them, with Respect to the Time of Adjournment, he may adjourn them to such Time as he shall think proper; he shall receive Ambassadors and other public Ministers; he shall take Care that the Laws be faithfully executed, and shall Commission all the Officers of the United States.

*Section 4.* The President, Vice President and all Civil Officers of the United States, shall be removed from Office on Impeachment for, and Conviction of, Treason, Bribery, or other high Crimes and Misdemeanors.

# Article III

*Section 1.* The judicial Power of the United States, shall be vested in one supreme Court, and in such inferior Courts as the Congress may from time to time ordain and establish. The Judges, both of the supreme and inferior Courts, shall hold their Offices during good Behaviour, and shall, at stated Times, receive for their Services, a Compensation, which shall not be diminished during their Continuance in Office.

*Section 2.* The judicial Power shall extend to all Cases, in Law and Equity, arising under this Constitution, the Laws of the United States, and Treaties made, or which shall be made, under their Authority;-to all Cases affecting Ambassadors, other public Ministers and Consuls; to all Cases of admiralty and maritime Jurisdiction; to Controversies to which the United States shall be a Party; to Controversies between two or more States; between a State and Citizens of another State; between Citizens of different States; between Citizens of the same State claiming Lands under Grants of different States, and between a State, or the Citizens thereof, and foreign States, Citizens or Subjects.

In all Cases affecting Ambassadors, other public Ministers and Consuls, and those in which a State shall be Party, the supreme Court shall have original Jurisdiction. In all the other Cases before mentioned, the supreme Court shall have appellate Jurisdiction, both as to Law and Fact, with such Exceptions, and under such Regulations as the Congress shall make.

The Trial of all Crimes, except in Cases of Impeachment, shall be by Jury; and such Trial shall be held in the State where the said Crimes shall have been committed; but when not committed within any State, the Trial shall be at such Place or Places as the Congress may by Law have directed.

*Section 3.* Treason against the United States, shall consist only in levying War against them, or in adhering to their Enemies, giving them Aid and Comfort. No Person shall be convicted of Treason unless on the Testimony of two Witnesses to the same overt Act, or on Confession in open Court.

The Congress shall have Power to declare the Punishment of Treason, but no Attainder of Treason shall work Corruption of Blood, or Forfeiture except during the Life of the Person attainted.

# Article IV

*Section 1*. Full Faith and Credit shall be given in each State to the public Acts, Records, and judicial Proceedings of every other State. And the Congress may by general Laws prescribe the Manner in which such Acts, Records and Proceedings shall be proved, and the Effect thereof.

*Section 2*. The Citizens of each State shall be entitled to all Privileges and Immunities of Citizens in the several States.

A Person charged in any State with Treason, Felony, or other Crime, who shall flee from Justice, and be found in another State, shall on Demand of the executive Authority of the State from which he fled, be delivered up, to be removed to the State having Jurisdiction of the Crime.

No Person held to Service or Labour in one State, under the Laws thereof, escaping into another, shall, in Consequence of any Law or Regulation therein, be discharged from such Service or Labour, but shall be delivered UP on Claim of the Party to whom such Service or Labour may be due.

*Section 3*. New States may be admitted by the Congress into this Union; but no new State shall be formed or erected within the Jurisdiction of any other State; nor any State be formed by the Junction of two or more States, or Parts of States, without the Consent of the Legislatures of the States concerned as well as of the Congress.

The Congress shall have Power to dispose of and make all needful Rules and Regulations respecting the Territory or other Property belonging to the United States; and nothing in this Constitution shall be so construed as to Prejudice any Claims of the United States, or of any particular State.

*Section 4*. The United States shall guarantee to every State in this Union a Republican Form of Government, and shall protect each of them against Invasion; and on Application of the Legislature, or of the Executive (when the Legislature cannot be convened) against domestic Violence.

# Article V

The Congress, whenever two thirds of both Houses shall deem it necessary, shall propose Amendments to this Constitution, or, on the Application of the Legislatures of two thirds of the several States, shall call a Convention for proposing Amendments, which, in either Case, shall be valid to all Intents and Purposes, as Part of this Constitution, when ratified by the Legislatures of three fourths of the several States, or by Conventions in three fourths thereof, as the one or the other Mode of Ratification may be proposed by the Congress; provided that no Amendment which may be made prior to the Year One thousand eight hundred and eight shall in any Manner affect the first and fourth Clauses in the Ninth Section of the first Article; and that no State, without its Consent, shall be deprived of its equal Suffrage in the Senate.

## Article VI

All Debts contracted and Engagements entered into, before the Adoption of this Constitution, shall be as valid against the United States under this Constitution, as under the Confederation.

This Constitution, and the Laws of the United States which shall be made in Pursuance thereof; and all Treaties made, or which shall be made, under the Authority of the United States, shall be the supreme Law of the Land; and the Judges in every State shall be bound thereby, any Thing in the Constitution or Laws of any State to the Contrary notwithstanding.

The Senators and Representatives before mentioned, and the Members of the several State Legislatures, and all executive and judicial Officers, both of the United States and of the several States, shall be bound by Oath or affirmation, to support this Constitution; but no religious Test shall ever be required as a Qualification to any Office or public Trust under the United States.

## Article VII

The Ratification of the Conventions of nine States, shall be sufficient for the Establishment of this Constitution between the States so ratifying the Same.

Done in Convention by the Unanimous Consent of the States present the Seventeenth Day of September in the Year of our Lord one thousand seven hundred and Eighty seven and of the Independence of the United States of America the Twelfth. In witness thereof We have hereunto subscribed our Names.

*G$^o$. WASHINGTON-Presid$^t$*
*and Deputy from Virginia*

# ARTICLES IN ADDITION TO, AND AMENDMENTS OF, THE CONSTITUTION OF THE UNITED STATES OF AMERICA, PROPOSED BY CONGRESS, AND RATIFIED BY THE SEVERAL STATES, PURSUANT TO THE FIFTH ARTICLE OF THE ORIGINAL CONSTITUTION.

## Amendment I

Congress shall make no law respecting an establishment of religion, or prohibiting the free exercise thereof; or abridging the freedom of speech, or of the press; or the right of the people peaceably to assemble, and to petition the Government for a redress of grievances.

## Amendment II

A well regulated Militia, being necessary to the security of a free State, the right of the people to keep and bear Arms, shall not be infringed.

## Amendment III

No Soldier shall, in time of peace be quartered in any house, without the consent of the Owner, nor in time of war, but in a manner to be prescribed by law.

## Amendment IV

The right of the people to be secure in their persons, houses, papers, and effects, against unreasonable searches and seizures, shall not be violated, and no Warrants shall issue, but upon probable cause, supported by Oath or affirmation, and particularly describing the place to be searched, and the persons or things to be seized.

## Amendment V

No person shall be held to answer for a capital, or otherwise infamous crime, unless on a presentment or indictment of a Grand Jury, except in cases arising in the land or naval forces, or in the Militia, when in actual service in time of War or public danger; nor shall any person be subject for the same offence to be twice put in jeopardy of life or limb; nor shall be compelled in any criminal case to be a witness against himself, nor be deprived of life, liberty, or property, without: due process of law; nor shall private property be taken for public use, without just compensation.

## Amendment VI

In all criminal prosecutions, the accused shall enjoy the right to a speedy and public trial by an impartial jury of the State and district wherein the crime shall have been committed, which district shall have been previously ascertained by law, and to be informed of the nature and cause of the accusation; to be confronted with the witness against him; to have compulsory process for obtaining Witnesses in his favor, and to have the Assistance of Counsel for his defense.

## Amendment VII

In Suits at common law, where the value in controversy shall exceed twenty dollars, the right of trial by jury shall be preserved, and no fact tried by a jury, shall be otherwise re-examined in any Court of the United States, than according to the rules of the common law.

# Amendment VIII

Excessive bail shall not be required, nor excessive fines imposed, nor cruel and unusual punishments inflicted.

# Amendment IX

The enumeration in the Constitution, of certain rights, shall not be construed to deny
or disparage others retained by the people.

# Amendment X

The powers not delegated to the United States by the Constitution, nor prohibited by
it to the States, are reserved to the States respectively, or to the people. [*The first ten
amendments were ratified Dec. 15, 1791.*]

# Amendment XI

The Judicial power of the United States shall not be construed to extend to any suit
in law or equity, commenced or prosecuted against one of the United States by Citizens of another State, or by Citizens or Subjects of any Foreign State. [*Ratified Jan.
8, 1798*]

# Amendment XII

The Electors shall meet in their respective states and vote by ballot for President
and Vice-President, one of whom, at least, shall not be an inhabitant of the same
state with themselves; they shall name in their ballots the person voted for as President, and in distinct ballots the person voted for as Vice-President, and they shall
make distinct lists of all persons voted for as President, and of all persons voted for
as Vice-President, and of the number of votes for each, which lists they shall sign
and certify, and transmit sealed to the seat of the government of the United States,
directed to the President of the Senate; The President of the Senate shall, in the
presence of the Senate and House of Representatives, open all the certificates and
the votes shall then be counted; The person having the greatest number of votes for
President, shall be the President, if such number be a majority of the whole number of Electors appointed; and if no person have such majority, then from the persons having the highest numbers not exceeding three on the list of those voted for
as President, the House of Representatives shall choose immediately, by ballot, the
President. But in choosing the President, the votes shall be taken by states, the representation from each state having one vote; a quorum for this purpose shall consist of a member or members from two-thirds of the states, and a majority of all the

states shall be necessary to a choice. And if the House of Representatives shall not choose a President whenever the right of choice shall devolve upon them, before the fourth day of March next following, then the Vice-President shall act as President, as in the case of the death or other constitutional disability of the President— The person having the greatest number of votes as Vice-President, shall be the Vice-President, if such number be a majority of the whole number of Electors appointed, and if no person have a majority, then from the two highest numbers on the list, the Senate shall choose the Vice-President; a quorum for the purpose shall consist of two-thirds of the whole number of Senators, and a majority of the whole number shall be necessary to a choice. But no person constitutionally ineligible to the office of President shall be eligible to that of Vice-President of the United States. [*Ratified Sept. 25, 1804*]

# Amendment XIII

*Section 1*. Neither slavery nor involuntary servitude, except as a punishment for crime whereof the party shall have been duly convicted, shall exist within the United States, or any place subject to their jurisdiction.

*Section 2*. Congress shall have power to enforce this article by appropriate legislation. [*Ratified Dec. 18, 1865*]

# Amendment XIV

*Section 1*. All persons born or naturalized in the United States and subject to the jurisdiction thereof, are citizens of the United States and of the State wherein they reside. No State shall make or enforce any law which shall bridge the privileges or immunities of citizens of the United States; nor shall any State deprive any person of life, liberty, or property, without due process of law; nor deny any person within its jurisdiction the equal protection of the laws.

*Section 2*. Representatives shall be apportioned among the several States according to their respective numbers, counting the whole number of persons in each State, excluding Indians not taxed. But when the right to vote at any election for the choice of electors for President and Vice President of the United States, Representatives in Congress, the Executive and Judicial officers of a State, or the members of the Legislature thereof, is denied to any of the male inhabitants of such State, being twenty-one years of age, and citizens of the United States, or in any way abridged, except for participation in rebellion, or other crime, the basis of representation therein shall be reduced in the proportion which the number of such male citizens shall bear to the whole number of male citizens twenty-one years of age in such State.

*Section 3*. No person shall be a Senator or Representative in Congress, or elector of President and Vice President, or hold any office, civil or military, under the United States, or under any State, who, having previously taken an oath, as a member of Congress, or as an officer of the United States, or as a member of any State legislature, or as an executive or judicial officer of any State, to support the Constitution of the United States, shall have engaged in insurrection or rebellion against the same, or given aid or comfort to the enemies thereof. But Congress may by a vote of two-thirds of each House, remove such disability.

*Section 4*. The validity of the public debt of the United States, authorized by law, including debts incurred for payment of pensions and bounties for services in suppressing insurrection or rebellion, shall not be questioned. But neither the United States nor any State shall assume or pay any debt or obligation incurred in aid of insurrection or rebellion against the United States, or any claim for the loss or emancipation of any slave; but all such debts, obligations and claims shall be held illegal and void.

*Section 5*. The Congress shall have power to enforce by appropriate legislation, the provisions of this article. [*Ratified July 28, 1868*]

# Amendment XV

*Section 1*. The right of citizens of the United States to vote shall not be denied or abridged by the United States or by any State on account of race, color, or previous condition of servitude.

*Section 2*. The Congress shall have power to enforce this article by appropriate legislation. [*Ratified March 30, 1870*]

# Amendment XVI

The Congress shall have power to lay and collect taxes on incomes, from whatever source derived, without apportionment among the several States, and without regard to any census or enumeration. [*Ratified Feb. 25, 1913*]

# Amendment XVII

The Senate of the United States shall be composed of two Senators from each State, elected by the people thereof, for six years; and each Senator shall have one vote. The electors in each State shall have the qualifications requisite for electors of the most numerous branch of the State legislatures.

When vacancies happen in the representation of any State in the Senate, the executive authority of such State shall issue writs of election to fill such vacancies: Provided, That the legislature of any State may empower the executive thereof to make temporary appointments until the people fill the vacancies by election as the legislature may direct.

This amendment shall not be so construed as to affect the election or term of any Senator chosen before it becomes valid as part of the Constitution. [*Ratified May 31, 1913*]

# Amendment XVIII

*Section 1.* After one year from the ratification of this article the manufacture, sale, or transportation of intoxicating liquors within, the importation thereof into, or the exportation thereof from the United States and all territory subject to the jurisdiction thereof for beverage purposes is hereby prohibited.

*Section 2.* The Congress and the several States shall have concurrent power to enforce this article by appropriate legislation.

*Section 3.* This article shall be inoperative unless it shall have been ratified as an amendment to the Constitution by the legislatures of the several States, as provided in the Constitution, within seven years from the date of the submission hereof to the States by the Congress. [*Ratified Jan. 29, 1919*]

# Amendment XIX

The right of citizens of the United States to vote shall not be denied or abridged by the United States or by any State on account of sex.

Congress shall have power to enforce this article by appropriate legislation. [*Ratified Aug. 26, 1920*]

# Amendment XX

*Section 1.* The terms of the President and Vice President shall end at noon on the 20th day of January, and the terms of Senators and Representatives at noon on the 3rd day of January, of the years in which such terms would have ended if this article had not been ratified; and the terms of their successors shall then begin.

*Section 2.* The Congress shall assemble at least once in every year, and such meeting shall begin at noon on the 3rd day of January, unless they shall by law appoint a different day.

*Section 3.* If, at the time fixed for the beginning of the term of the President, the President elect shall have died, the Vice President elect shall become President. If a President shall not have been chosen before the time fixed for the beginning of his term, or if the President elect shall have failed to qualify, then the Vice President elect shall act as President until a President shall have qualified; and the Congress may by law provide for the case wherein neither a President elect nor a Vice President elect shall have qualified, declaring who shall then act as President, or the manner in which one who is to act shall be selected, and such person shall act accordingly until a President or Vice President shall have qualified.

*Section 4.* The Congress may by law provide for the case of the death of any of the persons for whom the House of Representatives may choose a President whenever the right of choice shall have devolved upon them, and for the case of the death of any of the persons from whom the Senate may choose a Vice President whenever the right of choice shall have devolved upon them.

*Section 5.* Sections 1 and 2 shall take effect on the 15th day of October following the ratification of this article.

*Section 6.* This article shall be inoperative unless it shall have been ratified as an amendment to the Constitution by the legislatures of three-fourths of the several States within seven years from the date of its submission. [*Ratified Feb. 6, 1933*]

# Amendment XXI

*Section 1.* The eighteenth article of amendment to the Constitution of the United States is hereby repealed.

*Section 2.* The transportation or importation into any State, Territory, or possession of the United States for delivery or use therein of intoxicating liquors, in violation of the laws thereof, is hereby prohibited.

*Section 3.* This article shall be inoperative unless it shall have been ratified as an amendment to the Constitution by conventions in the several States, as provided in the Constitution, within seven years from the date of the submission thereof to the States by the Congress. [*Ratified Dec. 5, 1933*]

# Amendment XXII

*Section 1.* No person shall be elected to the office of the President more than twice, and no person who has held the office of President, or acted as President, for more than two years of a term to which some other person was elected President shall be elected to the office of the President more than once. But this Article shall not apply to any person holding the office of President when this Article was proposed by the Congress, and shall not prevent any person who may be holding the office of President, or acting as President, during the term within which this Article becomes operative from holding the office of President or acting as President during the remainder of such term.

*Section 2.* This article shall be inoperative unless it shall have been ratified as an amendment to the Constitution by the legislatures of three-fourths of the several States within seven years from the date of its submission to the States by the Congress. [*Ratified Feb. 27, 1951*]

# Amendment XXIII

*Section 1.* The District constituting the seat of Government of the United States shall appoint in such manner as the Congress may direct:

A number of electors of President and Vice President equal to the whole number of Senators and Representatives in Congress to which the District would be entitled if it were a State, but in no event more than the least populous State; they shall be in addition to those appointed by the States, but they shall be considered, for the purposes of the election of President and Vice President, to be electors appointed by a State; and they shall meet in the District and perform such duties as provided by the twelfth article of amendment.

*Section 2*. The Congress shall have power to enforce this article by appropriate legislation. [*Ratified Mar. 29, 1961*]

# Amendment XXIV

*Section 1*. The right of citizens of the United States to vote in any primary or other election for President or Vice President, for electors for President or Vice President, or for Senator or Representative in Congress, shall not be denied or abridged by the United States or any State by reason of failure to pay any poll tax or other tax.

*Section 2*. The Congress shall have power to enforce this article by appropriate legislation. [*Ratified Jan. 23, 1964*]

# Amendment XXV

*Section 1*. In case of the removal of the President from office or of his death or resignation, the Vice President shall become President.

*Section 2*. Whenever there is a vacancy in the office of the Vice President, The President shall nominate a Vice President who shall take office upon confirmation by a majority vote of both Houses of Congress.

*Section 3*. Whenever the President transmits to the President pro tempore of the Senate and the Speaker of the House of Representatives his written declaration that he is unable to discharge the powers and duties of his office, and until he transmits to them a written declaration to the contrary, such powers and duties shall be discharged by the Vice President as Acting President.

*Section 4*. Whenever the Vice President and a majority of either the principal officers of the executive departments or of such other body as Congress may by law provide, transmit to the President pro tempore of the Senate and the Speaker of the House of Representatives their written declaration that the President is unable to discharge the powers and duties of his office, the Vice President shall immediately assume the powers and duties of the office as Acting President.

Thereafter, when the President transmits to the President pro tempore of the Senate and the Speaker of the House of Representatives his written declaration that no inability exists, he shall resume the powers and duties of his office unless The Vice President and a majority of either the principal officers of the executive department or of such other body as Congress may by law provide, transmit within four days to the President pro tempore of the Senate and the Speaker of the House of Representatives their written declaration that the President is unable to discharge the powers and duties of his office. Thereupon Congress shall decide the issue, assembling within forty-eight hours for that purpose if not in session. If the Congress, within twenty-one days after receipt of the latter written declaration, or, if Congress is not in session, within twenty-one days after Congress is required to assemble, determines by two-thirds vote of both Houses that the President is unable to discharge the powers and duties of his office, the Vice President shall continue to discharge the same as Acting President; otherwise, the President shall resume the powers and duties of his office. [*Ratified Feb. 10, 1967*]

# Amendment XXVI

*Section 1.* The right of citizens of the United States, who are eighteen years of age or older, to vote shall not be denied or abridged by the United States or by any State on account of age.

*Section 2.* The Congress shall have power to enforce this article by appropriate legislation. [*Ratified June 30, 1971*]

# Amendment XXVII

No law varying the compensation for the Services of the Senators and Representatives shall take effect, until an election of Representatives shall have intervened. [*Ratified May 14, 1992*]

# Justices of the U.S. Supreme Court

THE NUMBER (1) indicates the Chief Justice; the other numbers show the order in which the original members of the Court were appointed, and then the order of succession. For example, if we follow the number (4) we see that James Wilson was succeeded first by Bushrod Washington, then by Henry Baldwin, and so on.

Many of those who have served on the nation's highest court have either not been well served by biographers or have been outright ignored. There are good sources for biographical and analytical essays on these, and in fact on all the justices. The most recent scholarship is contained in the essays in Melvin I. Urofsky, ed., *The Supreme Court Justices: A Biographical Dictionary* (1994). Leon Friedman and Fred L. Israel, eds., *The Justices of the United States Supreme Court, 1789–1978: Their Lives and Major Opinions* 5 vols. (1969–1980) is still useful, and also has some of the more important opinions.

## Appointed by George Washington

(1) *John Jay* (1745–1829); Federalist from New York; served 1789–1795; resigned.

(2) *John Rutledge* (1739–1800); Federalist from South Carolina; appointed 1789; resigned 1791 without ever sitting.

(3) *William Cushing* (1732–1810); Federalist from Massachusetts; served 1789–1810; died.

(4) *James Wilson* (1742–1798); Federalist from Pennsylvania; served 1789–1798; died.

(5) *John Blair, Jr.* (1732–1800); Federalist from Virginia; served 1789–1796; resigned.

(6) *James Iredell* (1751–1799); Federalist from North Carolina; served 1790–1799; died.

(2) *Thomas Johnson* (1732–1819); Federalist from Maryland; served 1791–1793; resigned.

(2) *William Paterson* (1745–1806); Federalist from New Jersey; served 1793–1806; died.

(1) *John Rutledge* (1739–1800); Federalist from South Carolina; unconfirmed recess appointment in 1795.

(5) *Samuel Chase* (1741–1811); Federalist from Maryland; served 1796–1811; died.

(1) *Oliver Ellsworth* (1745–1807); Federalist from Connecticut; served 1796–1800; resigned.

## Appointed by John Adams

(4) *Bushrod Washington* (1762–1829); Federalist from Pennsylvania and Virginia; served 1798–1829; died.

(6) *Alfred Moore* (1755–1810); Federalist from North Carolina; served 1799–1804; resigned.

(1) *John Marshall* (1755–1835); Federalist from Virginia; served 1801–1835; died.

## Appointed by Thomas Jefferson

(6) *William Johnson* (1771–1834); Republican from South Carolina; served 1804–1834; died.

(2) *Henry Brockholst Livingston* (1757–1823); Republican from New York; served 1806–1823; died.

(7) *Thomas Todd* (1765–1826); Republican from Kentucky; served 1807–1826; died.

## Appointed by James Madison

(5) *Gabriel Duvall* (1752–1844); Republican from Maryland; served 1811–1835; resigned.

(3) *Joseph Story* (1799–1845); Republican from Massachusetts; served 1811–1845; died.

## Appointed by James Monroe

(2) *Smith Thompson* (1768–1843); Republican from New York; served 1823–1843; died.

## Appointed by John Quincy Adams

(7) *Robert Trimble* (1776–1828); Republican from Kentucky; served 1826–1828; died.

## Appointed by Andrew Jackson

(7) *John McLean* (1785–1861); Democrat (later Republican) from Ohio; served 1829–1861; died.

(4) *Henry Baldwin* (1780–1844); Democrat from Pennsylvania; served 1830–1844; died.

(6) *James Moore Wayne* (1790–1867); Democrat from Georgia; served 1835–1867; died.

(1) *Roger Brooke Taney* (1777–1864); Democrat from Maryland; served 1835–1864; died.

(5) *Philip Pendleton Barbour* (1783–1841); Democrat from Virginia; served 1836–1841; died.

## Appointed by Martin Van Buren

(8) *John Catron* (1786–1865); Democrat from Tennessee; served 1837–1865; died.

(9) *John McKinley* (1780–1852); Democrat from Kentucky; served 1837–1852; died.

(5) *Peter Vivian Daniel* (1784–1860); Democrat from Virginia; served 1841–1860; died.

## Appointed by John Tyler

(2) *Samuel Nelson* (1792–1873); Democrat from New York; served 1845–1872; resigned.

## Appointed by James K. Polk

(3) *Levi Woodbury* (1789–1851); Democrat from New Hampshire; served 1845–1851; died.

(4) *Robert Cooper Grier* (1794–1870); Democrat from Pennsylvania; served 1846–1870; resigned.

# Appointed by Millard Fillmore

(3) *Benjamin Robbins Curtis* (1809–1874); Whig from Massachusetts; served 1851–1857; resigned.

# Appointed by Franklin Pierce

(9) *John Archibald Campbell* (1811–1889); Democrat from Alabama; served 1853–1861; resigned.

# Appointed by James Buchanan

(3) *Nathaniel Clifford* (1803–1881); Democrat from Maine; served 1858–1881; died.

# Appointed by Abraham Lincoln

(7) *Noah Haynes Swayne* (1804–1884); Republican from Ohio; served 1862–1881; resigned.

(5) *Samuel Freeman Miller* (1816–1890); Republican from Iowa; served 1862–1890; died.

(9) *David Davis* (1815–1886); Republican (later Democrat) from Illinois; served 1862–1877; resigned.

(10) *Stephen Johnson Field* (1816–1899); Democrat from California; served 1863–1897; resigned.

# Appointed by Ulysses S. Grant

(4) *William Strong* (1808–1895); Republican from Pennsylvania; served 1870–1880; resigned.

(6) *Joseph Philo Bradley* (1803–1892); Republican from New Jersey; served 1870–1892; died.

(2) *Ward Hunt* (1810–1886); Republican from New York; served 1873–1882; resigned.

(1) *Morrison Remick Waite* (1816–1888); Republican from Ohio; served 1874–1888; died.

## Appointed by Rutherford B. Hayes

(9) *John Marshall Harlan*; Republican from Kentucky; served 1877–1911; died.

(4) *William Burnham Woods* (1824–1887); Republican from Georgia; served 1880–1887; died.

## Appointed by James A. Garfield

(7) *Stanley Matthews* (1824–1889); Republican from Ohio; served 1881–1889; died.

## Appointed by Chester Arthur

(3) *Horace Gray* (1828–1902); Republican from Massachusetts; served 1881–1902; died.

(2) *Samuel M. Blatchford* (1820–1893); Republican from New York; served 1882–1893; died.

## Appointed by Grover Cleveland (First Term)

(4) *Lucius Quintus Cincinnatus Lamar* (1825–1893); Democrat from Mississsippi; served 1888–1893; died.

(1) *Melville Weston Fuller* (1833–1910); Democrat from Illinois; served 1888–1910; died.

## Appointed by Benjamin Harrison

(7) *David Josiah Brewer* (1838–1910); Republican from Kansas; served 1889–1910; died.

(5) *Henry Billings Brown* (1836–1913); Republican from Michigan; served 1891–1905; resigned.

(6) *George Shiras, Jr.* (1832–1924); Republican from Pennsylvania; served 1892–1903; resigned.

(4) *Howell Edmunds Jackson* (1832–1895); Democrat from Tennessee; served 1893–1895; died.

## Appointed by Grover Cleveland (Second Term)

(2) *Edward Douglass White* (1845–1921); Democrat from Louisiana; served 1894–1911; promoted to chief justice.

(4) *Rufus Wheeler Peckham* (1838–1909); Democrat from New York; served 1895–1909; died.

## Appointed by William McKinley

(10, now 8) *Joseph McKenna* (1843–1926); Republican from California; served 1898–1925; resigned.

## Appointed by Theodore Roosevelt

(3) *Oliver Wendell Holmes, Jr.* (1841–1935); Republican from Massachusetts; served 1902–1932; resigned.

(6) *William Rufus Day* (1849–1923); Republican from Ohio; served 1903–1922; resigned.

(5) *William Henry Moody* (1853–1917); Republican from Massachusetts; served 1906–1910; resigned.

## Appointed by William Howard Taft

(4) *Horace Harmon Lurton* (1844–1914); Democrat from Tennessee; served 1909–1914; died.

(7) *Charles Evans Hughes* (1862–1948); Republican from New York; served 1910–1916; resigned.

(1) *Edward Douglass White* (1845–1921); promoted from associate justice; served 1910–1921; died.

(2) *Willis Van Devanter* (1859–1941); Republican from Wyoming; served 1910–1937; resigned.

(5) *Joseph Rucker Lamar* (1857–1916); Democrat from Georgia; served 1911–1916; died.

(9) *Mahlon Pitney* (1858–1924); Republican from New Jersey; served 1912–1922; retired.

## Appointed by Woodrow Wilson

(4) *James Clark McReynolds* (1826–1946); Democrat from Tennessee; served 1914–1941; retired.

(5) *Louis Dembitz Brandeis* (1856–1941); Democrat from Massachusetts; served 1916–1939; retired.

(7) *John Hessin Clarke* (1857–1945); Democrat from Ohio; served 1916–1922; resigned.

## Appointed by Warren G. Harding

(1) *William Howard Taft* (1857–1930); Republican from Ohio; served 1921–1930; resigned.

(7) *George Sutherland* (1862–1942); Republican from Utah; served 1922–1938; retired.

(6) *Pierce Butler* (1866–1939); Democrat from Minnesota; served 1922–1939; retired.

(9) *Edward Terry Sanford* (1865–1930); Republican from Tennessee; served 1923–1930; died.

## Appointed by Calvin Coolidge

(8) *Harlan Fiske Stone* (1872–1946); Republican from New York; served 1925–1941; promoted to chief justice.

## Appointed by Herbert Hoover

(1) *Charles Evans Hughes* (1862–1948); Republican from New York; served 1930–1941; retired.

(9) *Owen Josephus Roberts* (1875–1955); Republican from Pennsylvania; served 1930–1945; resigned.

(3) *Benjamin Nathan Cardozo* (1870–1938); Democrat from New York; served 1932–1938; died.

## Appointed by Franklin D. Roosevelt

(2) *Hugo Lafayette Black* (1886–1971); Democrat from Alabama; served 1938–1971; retired.

(7) *Stanley Forman Reed* (1884–1980); Democrat from Kentucky; served 1938–1957; retired.

(3) *Felix Frankfurter* (1882–1965); Independent from Massachusetts; served 1939–1962; retired.

(5) *William Orville Douglas* (1898–1980); Democrat from Connecticut; served 1939–1975; retired.

(6) *Frank Murphy* (1843–1949); Democrat from Michigan; served 1940–1949; died.

(4) *James Francis Byrnes* (1879–1972); Democrat from South Carolina; served 1941–1942; resigned.

(1) *Harlan Fiske Stone* (1872–1946); promoted from associate justice; served 1941–1946; died.

(8) *Robert Houghwout Jackson* (1892–1954); Democrat from New York; served 1941–1954; died.

(4) *Wiley Blount Rutledge* (1894–1949); Democrat from Iowa; served 1943–1949; died.

## Appointed by Harry S. Truman

(9) *Harold Hitz Burton* (1888–1964); Republican from Ohio; served 1945–1958; retired.

(1) *Frederick Moore Vinson* (1890–1953); Democrat from Kentucky; served 1946–1953; died.

(6) *Tom C. Clark* (1899–1977); Democrat from Texas; served 1949–1967; retired.

(4) *Sherman Minton* (1890–1965); Democrat from Indiana; served 1949–1956; retired.

## Appointed by Dwight D. Eisenhower

(1) *Earl Warren* (1891–1974); Republican from California; served 1953–1969; retired.

(8) *John Marshall Harlan* (1899–1971); Republican from New York; served 1955–1971; retired.

(4) *William Joseph Brennan, Jr.* (1906–1997); Democrat from New Jersey; served 1956–1990; retired.

(7) *Charles Evans Whittaker* (1901–1973); Republican from Missouri; served 1957–1962; retired.

(9) *Potter Stewart* (1915–1985); Republican from Ohio; served 1958–1981; retired.

## Appointed by John F. Kennedy

(7) *Byron Raymond White* (1917– ); Democrat from Colorado; served 1962–1993; retired.

(3) *Arthur Joseph Goldberg* (1908–1990); Democrat from Illinois; served 1962–1965; resigned.

## Appointed by Lyndon B. Johnson

(3) *Abe Fortas* (1910–1982); Democrat from Tennessee; served 1965–1969; resigned.

(6) *Thurgood Marshall* (1908–1993); Democrat from New York; served 1967–1991); retired.

## Appointed by Richard M. Nixon

(1) *Warren Earl Burger* (1907–1995); Republican from Minnesota; served 1969–1986; retired.

(3) *Harry Andrew Blackmun* (1908–1999); Republican from Minnesota; served 1970–1994; retired.

(2) *Lewis Franklin Powell, Jr.* (1907–1998); Democrat from Virginia; served 1972–1987; retired.

(8) *William Hubbs Rehnquist* (1924– ); Republican from Arizona; served 1972–1986; promoted to chief justice.

## Appointed by Gerald Ford

(5) *John Paul Stevens* (1920– ); Republican from Illinois; served 1975– .

## Appointed by Ronald Reagan

(9) *Sandra Day O'Connor* (1930– ); Republican from Arizona; served 1981– .

(1) *William Hubbs Rehnquist* (1924– ); promoted from associate justice; served 1986– .

(8) *Antonin Scalia* (1936– ); Republican from Ohio and Virginia; served 1986– .

(2) *Anthony M. Kennedy* (1936– ); Republican from California; served 1988– .

## Appointed by George Bush

(4) *David Hackett Souter* (1939– ); Republican from New Hampshire; served 1990– .

(6) *Clarence Thomas* (1948– ); Republican from Georgia; served 1991– .

## Appointed by William Clinton

(7) *Ruth Joan Bader Ginsburg* (1933– ); Democrat from New York; served 1993– .

(3) *Stephen G. Breyer* (1938– ); Democrat from Massachusetts; served 1994– .

# Case Index

# Subject Index